CHRISTIAN
MARRIAGE

CHRISTIAN MARRIAGE

A Historical Study

Edited by Glenn W. Olsen

SPONSORED BY THE WETHERSFIELD INSTITUTE

A Herder & Herder Book
The Crossroad Publishing Company
New York

The Crossroad Publishing Company
481 Eighth Avenue, New York, NY 10001

Printed in the United States of America

Library of Congress Cataloging-in-Publication Data

Christian marriage : a historical study / Francis Martin ... [et al.] ;
edited by Glenn Olsen.
    p. cm.
"A Herder and Herder Book."
"Sponsored by The Wethersfield Institute."
ISBN 0-8245-1886-1 (alk. paper)
   1. Marriage – Religious aspects – Christianity – History of doctrines.
2. Marriage – Biblical teaching.   I. Martin, Francis, 1930-
II. Olsen, Glenn.
BT706 .C47 2000
261.8′3581′09 – dc21
                                   00-011412

1 2 3 4 5 6 7 8 9 10   06 05 04 03 02 01 00

CONTENTS

EDITOR'S PREFACE

In 1993 the Wethersfield Institute of the Homeland Foundation of New York City asked me to organize a conference on the History of Christian Marriage, which was held in New York in late 1994. The goal of the conference was twofold. First, period by period, specialists were to present a statement of what is currently known about the history of marriage in a manner accessible to an educated general audience. Second, in doing this the findings of a long-established tradition of study of the theology of Christian marriage were to be joined to recent discoveries by social historians about change over time in the practice of marriage. Each participant in the project was to trace the "idea of marriage" during the period of his or her specialization, setting this within the context of the actual practice and place of marriage within society. To the end of achieving a diversity of approach, I asked specialists from different disciplines, theology, history, and literature, to participate in the project.

The conference was a great success, and the Wethersfield Institute asked me to prepare a book from the papers originating in it. Some of these as now found in the present book have been only lightly revised, but some have been substantially changed, sometimes substantially lengthened. What had been one conference paper on the biblical period became the two substantial chapters which begin the book. One conference paper has not been included in the book. Universality and completeness have been beyond the constraints of a single volume, and other histories of Christian marriage could have been written. The book has a Western and European center. Its story originates in the Near East, goes through the ancient Mediterranean and medieval European worlds, and for the most part ends in twentieth-century North America. Much has, regretfully, been omitted. Further, each author was encouraged to approach the materials from the viewpoint and with the methods of his or her discipline. Thus some chapters are particularly strong in the range of literary works considered, others concentrate on social setting, and others pay particular attention to the development of the law, theology, and liturgy of marriage.

Many debts have been incurred in preparing this book, above all to Msgr. Eugene V. Clark, the president of the Wethersfield Institute, whose idea the conference and book were. Msgr. Clark has been from the first the gracious host and good shepherd of the project. He was aided at the Wethersfield Institute by first Mrs. Patricia Puccetti Donahoe, and now Miss Mary Schwarz. Both have with good cheer and great energy given aid at every step. All the authors have also been helped by the principal editor used for this book by Crossroad Publishing Company, Mrs. Ellen Wilson Fielding, who has given much sage advice. Finally, special thanks are due to the Wethersfield Institute itself for its financial support.

The reader will find that one of the most central and persistent symbolisms of marriage, inherited from pre-Christian practices and continuing to the present, has been that of the joining of right hands by those marrying. In the first flush of the new social history more than a generation ago, much was said which did not take such symbolism seriously. Sometimes marriage before the modern period was portrayed as cold and loveless. This book hopes to correct such misperceptions and to give a more just view of that most central of human institutions.

GLENN W. OLSEN

CONTRIBUTORS

JOHN M. HAAS is the president of the National Catholic Bioethics Center and former John Cardinal Krol Professor of Moral Theology at St. Charles Borromeo Seminary in the Archdiocese of Philadelphia. He has his Ph.D. from the Catholic University of America and his S.T.L. from the University of Fribourg in Switzerland. He is married to Martha Gannoe, and they are the parents of nine children.

PROFESSOR JAMES HITCHCOCK is professor of history at St. Louis University and author of half a dozen books on the contemporary religious scene.

REV. FRANCIS MARTIN, a priest of the Archdiocese of Washington, D.C., is professor of biblical studies at the John Paul II Institute for Studies on Marriage and Family, also in Washington. He is the author of several books and articles in the fields of Scripture and theology. His most recent books are *The Feminist Question, The Life Changer,* and *Narrative Parallels to the New Testament.*

GLENN W. OLSEN is professor of medieval history at the University of Utah, Salt Lake City. He is widely published in ancient and medieval intellectual and ecclesiastical history, as well as in modern philosophy, theology, and political thought.

TERESA OLSEN PIERRE received her licentiate in mediaeval studies from the Pontifical Institute of Mediaeval Studies in Toronto. The subject of her thesis was Hugh of St. Victor's theology of marriage. Her Ph.D., on William of St. Thierry's views of the human body, was conferred by the University of Toronto. She is an independent scholar living with her husband and children in Toronto.

PROFESSOR R. V. YOUNG is a professor of English at North Carolina State University. His most recent book is *Doctrine and Devotion in Seventeenth-Century Poetry.*

ABBREVIATIONS

ACW	Ancient Christian Writers
ADB	*Anchor Dictionary of the Bible*
ANET	*Ancient Near Eastern Texts Relating to the Old Testament*
CHR	*Catholic Historical Review*
CSEL	Corpus Scriptorum Ecclesiasticorum Latinorum
DS	Denziger-Schönmetzer, *Enchiridion symbolorum definitionum et declarationum de rebus fidei et morum*
FOC	Fathers of the Church
Fontes	*Codicis Iuris Canonici Fontes*
JECS	*Journal of Early Christian Studies*
JEH	*Journal of Ecclesiastical History*
NPNF	Nicene and Post-Nicene Fathers
PL	Patrologia latina
TDOT	*Theological Dictionary of the Old Testament*

Chapter One

MARRIAGE IN THE OLD TESTAMENT AND INTERTESTAMENTAL PERIODS

Francis Martin

A study of marriage in the biblical period should proceed in two sections corresponding to the classical division of biblical history into the periods of the two covenants. The first covers the period from approximately 1700 B.C. to the end of the first century A.D., and is itself divided into two subsections. They correspond to the period of Israelite history before and during the exile (1700–520 B.C.), and the post-exilic, or second temple period (520 B.C.–70 A.D.). The second part covers the New Testament period, roughly up to the year A.D. 100.

I accent two aspects of marriage that, together, may be called "matrimony." They are the process of becoming married, and the state of being married. In connection with the latter, a brief mention will be made of "family life," which includes all the other aspects of marriage not directly considered in relation to the spouses themselves: the extended family, children, servants and slaves, and so forth.

Marriage in the Pre-Exilic Period

The Patriarchal Narratives

It is generally agreed that the marriage customs described in Genesis reflect a world very similar to that of Hurrian culture, found in the area known as Haran (Gen. 11:31; 12:5) and known to us from the Nuzi tablets.[1] This is all the more remarkable given that many of the actions attributed to the patriarchs are contrary to later Israelite legislation.[2] While this indicates the tenacity of historical memory against the pressure of a current practice, it does not completely solve for us the exact significance of the history we are reading. As John Bright observes, however, it does tend to locate the patriarchal narratives within the genre of heroic tales about real ancestors who have become the vehicle both of creating a context for Israel's past and interpreting its future.[3]

The matrimonial process was basically the same throughout the Near East. It is described in all its stages in the narrative of the marriage of Isaac and Rebekah, recounted in Genesis 24.[4] The father of the groom proposes to the father of the prospective bride that a marriage might be concluded. While this reflects the interests of both families in the legal and financial consequences of the union, it also reflects the practical reality that the prospective spouses were usually not yet fifteen years old, and hence too young to take a leading role in such decisions. In the case of Isaac and Rebekah, Abraham's servant represents the groom's father and makes his proposal to the girl's brother and mother, presumably because her father, Bethuel, is dead. The important role of Laban, Rebekah's brother, corresponds to what is prescribed in the Nuzi tablets: he acts in some ways as the father of the bride.

When agreement was reached, the groom, as part of the agreement, provided the bride's father (brother) with gifts. This is frequently and inaccurately referred to as the "bride price." Actually, the function of this gift is threefold: it guarantees the seriousness of the proposal;[5] it establishes the ability of the groom to provide for his future wife and family; and it may form part of the dowry by which, in turn, the father of the bride provides for his daughter in the event of her husband's death or her divorce.[6]

Part of the dowry, at least among the wealthy, consisted of a slave or slaves given to the bride. This was undoubtedly intended as an amenity, but as we will discuss, it could also serve a particular purpose if the bride were unable to have children. Examples of such dowry gifts are the slaves and "nurse" who accompanied Rebekah (Gen. 24:59–61); the slaves given to each of his daughters by Laban when they married Jacob (Gen. 29:23–24, 28–29); Hagar, Sarah's Egyptian slave (Gen. 16:1); and the five slaves whom Abigail brought with her when she married David (1 Sam. 25:42).

A peculiarity of the betrothal of Rebekah is that she is asked if she is willing to accompany Abraham's servant, and thus to become Isaac's wife. Her answer, "I will go," is her consent to the marriage, something, according to the Nuzi tablets, that must be obtained from the bride in the event that her father is dead (Gen. 24:59). Another striking dimension of the Rebekah story is the large role played by prayer which, while it serves to indicate the special care exercised by God in this marriage, is but a reflection of a widespread conviction in Israel: "Home and possessions are an inheritance from parents, but a prudent wife is from the Lord" (Prov. 19:14). Finally, the newlyweds are blessed by the families (Gen. 24:60), who invoke upon them (especially the woman) the gift of fertility.[7]

The next and definitive step in the matrimonial process occurs when the spouse conducts his bride into his home or tent: "And Isaac brought her into his tent, and he took Rebecca, and she became a wife to him" (Gen. 24:67).[8]

Marriage among the ancients was the means by which the reality of the clan — its name, its possessions, its existence — was made tangible and perpetuated.[9] In fact, the wife's ability to bear children (especially sons) and the man's desire to have a large family explain most of the complex family relationships in the patriarchal and subsequent periods.

When Sarah was unable to have children, she gave her slave Hagar to Abraham as a surrogate wife (not exactly a "concubine" as we use the term today) so that Sarah might be "built up," a common Hebrew expression which plays on the resemblance between the word for "build" and that for "son" (Gen. 16:1–16). In so doing, Sarah was following the customs of the time, as outlined both in the Code of Hammurabi and in a text from Nuzi, thereby most probably making it impossible for Abraham to take a second wife.[10] Sarah's complaints about Hagar's subsequent insubordination may also have a legal basis, as some of the terminology attributed to her is legal. This whole sorry tale hints at the fact that Sarah's action and Abraham's acquiescence, while legal, were caused by a lack of faith in the promise reiterated to Abraham in the preceding chapter.[11]

Many of the same customs can be seen in the narrative about Jacob, his relation to his uncle Laban, and his marrying of the sisters Rachel and Leah (Gen. 29–35). In place of the *mohar,*[12] or marriage gift, Jacob gives Laban what he asks for, namely, fourteen years of work, just as David brought Saul the foreskins of one hundred Philistines (1 Sam. 18:25–27) and Othniel won Caleb's daughter by taking Kiriath-seper (Jos. 15:16=Judg. 1:12).[13] When Rachel saw that she was childless, she gave her maid Bilhah to Jacob so that she could be "built up/son-ed" by her (Gen. 30:2). The expression "bear on my knees" used by Rachel refers to a gesture by which the father or mother (the effects would be quite different) confers a legal relation to the child. Leah, seeing that she herself had stopped bearing, followed suit (Gen. 30:8). While the complexity of Jacob's situation could well be due to the work of a redactor dealing with many traditions in recounting the progeny of the patriarch, the fact that two sister wives and two "concubines" were assigned to Jacob would not have caused surprise in the patriarchal world.

In the event that the woman was not able to bear children, three courses of action were legally acceptable: she could be divorced, she could continue as her husband's wife even while he took a second wife, and/or she could bear children through one of her servants who acted as her surrogate by becoming her husband's "concubine" (*pilegesh*). However, in the patriarchal narratives as they have come down to us, this last expedient, while generally considered acceptable, is judged to demonstrate a lack of faith by the patriarchs and their wives in God's promise or his willingness to answer their prayers. Furthermore, every biblical example we see of multiple women in the household of one man is a disaster.[14] This theological preference for monogamy, by far the most common arrangement in Israel, is manifest in nearly every aspect of the Old Testament tradition.

Matrimony and Marriage in the Pre-Exilic Legal Texts

Israelite law had much in common with the law of its neighbors with regard to its prescriptions. It is unique, however, in viewing its theater of activity as the whole life of a people, both in relation to God and in relation to each other. This was the result of a covenant initiated by God and based on his choice of this people in the person of their ancestors. He manifested his fidelity to this choice by saving them from Egypt.[15]

This concept would have been more easily understood by ancient peoples than by us. The so-called "codes" of law in force at that time were an expression of the "justice" and "truth" embodied in the collective wisdom of the people and expressed by the king. The codes were considered a useful collection of guiding insights rather than a body of norms which strictly obligated the judge (who was him/herself not a magistrate but an elder respected for divine gifts of wisdom and probity).[16] Even at their most stringent, they were a source of reference rather than a binding set of legislative decrees.

The closest modern parallel is the attitude of English law, with its search for precedent, rather than the Latin view that law expresses normative principles. The attitude toward law in ancient Israel is made clearer when we realize that the term *torah* means "instruction," not "law" in our sense of the term. Then too, there is the unique Israelite habit of joining motivation to law: explaining the reasoning behind the legislation (Deut. 22:24; Exod. 23:8), relating the enactment directly to God (Exod. 20:5; Lev. 18:5, 6, 30 etc.), appealing to Israel's memory of how God has treated them (Exod. 23:9; Lev. 19:36; Deut. 5:15; 24:18 etc.), or, finally, adjoining a threat or a curse to a law (Lev. 20:19–21).

For these reasons, the study by Anthony Phillips, "Some Aspects of Family Law in Pre-Exilic Israel,"[17] while helpful, should be read with an awareness that our modern Western divisions of criminal and civil law and the classifications of "cultic" and "family" law would not be understood as separate categories by an Israelite "judge," especially in the pre-exilic period.

Despite the difficulty in assigning dates to the various legal codes, it will be useful, however, to list what are generally considered the five codes or collections as they are currently found in the Pentateuch (the only place containing such material):

1. *The Decalogue, or "Ten Words," of Yhwh* (Exod. 24:28; Deut. 4:13; 10:4) are now found in Exodus 20:2–17 and Deuteronomy 5:6–21. This brief collection is now generally acknowledged to be a unit which is anterior

to, and independent of, the classical "sources" invoked in Old Testament research, and is perhaps similar in form to other examples in the Old Testament.[18]

2. *The Code of the Covenant* (Exod. 20:22–23:33) is a composite document whose earliest levels are probably quite ancient. It is intended as a commentary and application of the Decalogue.

3. *The Deuteronomic Code* (Deut. 12–26) was probably originally composed from disparate material in the Northern Kingdom before its fall (721 B.C.). Roland de Vaux says of it:

> This code seems designed to replace the old code [the Code of the Covenant] by taking account of a whole social and religious evolution; it also reveals a change of spirit by its appeals to the heart and by the tone of exhortation in which its prescriptions are often couched. Fundamentally, it is certainly the "law" discovered in the temple in the time of Josias (2 Kings 22:8f.).[19]

4. *The Law of Holiness* (Lev. 17–26) was also composed of disparate material, probably toward the end of the period of the monarchy (587 B.C.). Its interest in ritual and priesthood and its insistence, sometimes in the form of a refrain, on the holiness of Yhwh and of his people indicate a different milieu from the Deuteronomic code. It bears clear marks of a post-exilic reworking.

5. *The Priestly Code* is represented in the first sixteen chapters of Leviticus, usually divided into laws about sacrifices (Lev. 1–7), the installation of priests (Lev. 8–10), and the law of purity (Lev. 11–16). It also includes various enactments found scattered throughout Exodus and Numbers.[20]

While the customs governing the matrimonial process are not directly promulgated in the legal material, they are presupposed. Thus, a man who seduces a virgin is obliged to give to her father the marriage gift (*mohar*) provided for by custom, even if the father does not give her in marriage to him (Exod. 22:15–16). The so-called levirate custom by which a man takes his brother's widow in marriage in order to preserve his brother's name and property underlies the narratives in Genesis 38 and Ruth 4. It is never explicitly found in a legal text as such, but the custom is presupposed in the law (Deut. 25:5) which provides for a public humiliation of the man who refuses this obligation.[21]

Two steps in the matrimonial process, the commitment through the marriage gift and the conducting of the bride into her husband's dwelling, are operative principles in many laws. In Deuteronomy 22:23–29 a distinction is made between a forced sexual union between a man and a betrothed virgin and that between a man and a virgin not betrothed. A betrothed man is excused from battle: "lest he die in battle and another take her to wife" (thus leaving a "married" man childless; Deut. 20:7; see also Deut. 24:5). Other practices from ancient times, particularly those in regard to adultery and divorce, are also reflected in pre-exilic legislation and will be covered later in this discussion.

Marriage in the Pre-Exilic Wisdom Tradition

The wisdom tradition is broader than the wisdom literature. The teaching of the wisdom literature contains three major marriage themes: (1) the relation between the spouses; (2) fidelity to one's spouse; and (3) the formation of children. Since there was not much change in these themes over time, both pre- and post-exilic texts can be used in discussing them.

The Relation between the Spouses

The wisdom literature tends to look at marriage from a man's perspective. The woman is not ignored — it is she who makes the home — but no texts speak of the joy of finding a good husband as do those which speak of finding a good wife. Nevertheless, it is obvious that the sages knew of the joy of mutuality and affection between spouses: "With three things I am delighted, for they are pleasing to the Lord and to men: harmony among brethren, friendship among neighbors, and the mutual love of husband and wife" (Sir. 25:1).[22] This text, and indeed nearly all the wisdom texts which speak of marriage, presume a mutually monogamous relationship.

In addition to the passage cited above, many others assert that a good wife is a very special blessing from the Lord: "He who finds a wife finds happiness; it is a favor he receives from the Lord" (Prov. 18:22; see 12:4 and especially 31:10–31; also Sir. 26:1–3, 13–18). It is the woman who gives to the man his place in society: "A wife is her husband's richest treasure, a helpmate, a steadying column. A vineyard with no hedge will be overrun; a man with no wife becomes a homeless wanderer" (Sir. 36:25). This accent on character is implied in the advice not to overestimate physical beauty, which, nonetheless is to be esteemed (Sir. 26:13; 36:22): "Like the sun rising in the Lord's heavens, the beauty of a virtuous wife is the radiance of her home" (Sir. 26:16).

Passages that speak of the relation between spouses are numerous. Many of them, faithful to the earlier strata of the wisdom material, are found in later books such as Sirach. This is part of the advance of Israelite thought as a whole toward a greater appreciation of the individual.

> All the higher, therefore, is the value set upon raising a family, and the duty of building it up. One result of this is that the woman is now valued as an independent personality, a development which holds in check other views of an opposite tendency. . . . And by attaching more

importance to her piety than to her outward attractions, and thus basing marriage on agreement in the highest matter of all, he accords her the worth of a personality in the fullest sense of the term.[23]

The "opposite tendency" referred to by Walther Eichrodt is often described as the "misogyny" of the wisdom authors. A closer look at these texts, however, reveals that most of them are really attempting to describe the impact of a woman on her home and her husband.[24]

The wisdom reflection on marriage presupposes monogamy. This requires a degree of interpersonal commitment that would be hard to imagine in a polygamous household.

Fidelity to One's Spouse

The theme of fidelity is closely allied to that of mutuality. It should be born in mind that adultery in this culture was considered primarily, but not exclusively, an offense against the husband of the adulteress. Thus, while the exhortations to marital fidelity are addressed to the young man, the description of the adulteress is a vivid reminder of what ruin she brings to her household as well as to her lover.

A long and vigorous warning against adultery is given in Proverbs 5:1–23 (also Prov. 7:4–27), stressing the shame and corrupted relationships that result. The same type of warning is found in Sirach 23:18–27, with the significant remark that the man's infidelity not only offends against the rights of his partner's husband, but also "dishonors *his* marriage bed" (Sir. 23:19). The obligations to divorce an adulterous woman and to kill the adulterer were probably presumed in this literature. As the death penalty was first extended to the woman (Deut. 22:22) and then attenuated for both, these legal situations were also presumed.[25] For the rest, the question of divorce does not come up in the wisdom texts, except for the remark in Sirach 25:25–26. The manner in which the covenant seems always to lie somewhere just beneath the surface of these texts is a remarkable aspect of the polemic against adultery and licentiousness in general. But then, as we have already seen, Israel's legal texts are undergirded by the nation's covenant relationship with Yhwh.

The Formation of Children

Children, especially sons, were the most obvious sign of God's blessing on a marriage (Ps. 128).[26] Three aspects of this dimension of family life are accented in the wisdom literature. The first is the mutual obligation of education and respect between parents and children. From this flows the second aspect, namely, the need to discipline children, and the third aspect, the recognition that the behavior of children brings honor or shame to the parents.

Unique in its time, Israel put an accent on the fact that both father and mother are educators of their children: "Hear, my son, your father's instruction, and reject not your mother's teaching" (Prov. 1:8).[27] Such respect was undoubtedly included in the commandment, "Honor your father *and* your mother" (Exod. 20:12; Lev. 19:3; Deut. 5:16). The one matter that was insisted upon was the duty of the father to pass on to his children, especially his sons, the sacred tradition of Israel. This was the way to wisdom, and it was especially this that was envisaged when the educational activity of the parents was referred to as "training/discipline," "instruction," and the like. Love and respect for one's parents is urged in terms of genuine tenderness: "The Lord set a father in honor over his children; a mother's authority he confirms over her sons....He who fears the Lord honors his father, and serves his parents as rulers....My son, take care of your father when he is old; grieve him not as long as he lives. Even if his mind fail, be considerate with him; revile him not in the fullness of your strength" (Sir. 3:2–13). God himself was given as the model for parents: they were to discipline out of love. "The discipline of Yhwh do not despise my child, do not resent his reproof; for Yhwh reproves those he loves as a father those whom he loves" (Prov. 3:11–12).

Marriage in the Pre-Exilic Prophetic Tradition

The pre-exilic prophetic tradition is deeply dependent upon the covenant and the legal and narrative traditions that articulated the practical demands of the covenant.[28] Another aspect of the prophetic view that is extremely important in the whole biblical understanding of marriage is the use of terminology referring to marital infidelity when speaking about covenant infidelity. Ultimately, because of the overlap of language that has been stressed before, these two types of predication were interwoven to form the basis for the prophetic symbolic speech concerning the covenant/marriage between Yhwh and his people.[29] Not only did this deepen an understanding of covenant, it revealed unsuspected depths to the reality of marriage itself. An example of this overlap of language can be seen in the manner in which the technical term for adultery, "the great sin," was applied in the Israelite tradition to the people's worship of the golden calf in the desert (Exod. 32:21, 30, 31) and to the golden calves set up by Jeroboam (2 Kings 17:21). The linking of these two incidents by a common terminology is probably the work of a later redactor. There is, however, other vocabulary usage that is quite ancient, particularly that connected with the root *znh,* which we usually translate as "prostitution," though the semantic field of this word is broader. "The verb *znh* designates primarily a sexual relationship outside of a formal union."[30] The semantic potential of the root *znh* was exploited by Hosea (c. 760–722 B.C.), who used it sixteen times, only one of which referred literally to prostitution.[31] In the account of Hosea's marriage, which is probably the stylized narration of an actual event,[32] Hosea is commanded by Yhwh: "Go, take a wife of whoredom [*zenunim*] and children of whoredom, for the land goes off a-whoring away from Yhwh" (Hos. 1:2). This probably means that Hosea should marry an "average" Israelite woman, thus a member of a "whoring" people. It may also allude to the fact that she had participated in pagan temple prostitution in order to insure her fertility in marriage — a not uncommon practice in eighth-century Israel.[33]

Hosea's marriage is thus meant to be a symbolic prophetic gesture, and the names of his children symbolic warnings of what is to come (compare Isa. 7:3). Hosea's third child is called "Not-My-People," "for you are not my people and I am no more to you a God" (Hos. 1:8). The name is modeled on the formula used in divorce when the offended husband took his wife to the door and said to her: "Not my wife" (Hos. 2:4). Yhwh has severed the covenant with his people; he will restore it when he says to Not-My-People, "You are my people," and they respond, "My God!" (Hos. 2:25).

The genius of Hosea lay in the fact that he took a metaphor with an established link between the legal dimension of marriage and that of a covenant and amplified that metaphor by adding the notes of interpersonal relationship and love. Based on his own experience of his marriage to his wife, Gomer, Hosea was able to understand that Israel's infidelity to Yhwh offended not only against an agreed upon relationship, but more profoundly against the love that was meant to animate that relationship. Yhwh loves Israel (Hos. 3:1, 11:1, 4), yet when Hosea applies the word "love" to Israel, as he does twelve times, it refers, with only one exception (Hos. 10:11), to Israel's love for anything but Yhwh. This lack of covenant fidelity is a lack of love, a lack of that obedience and trust that marks the very nature of the relationship expected in a covenant.[34] The overlap in terminology between marriage and covenant and the fact that Hosea's advance of the metaphor was so easily taken up by subsequent prophets has led some scholars, on the basis of Malachi 2:10–16, to investigate the possibility that marriage itself was considered to be a covenant in Israel. We will return to this in our discussion of post-exilic prophecy.

Some representatives of the prophetic tradition after Hosea appear to be affected by his development of the analogy between human marriage and the covenant with Yhwh. Isaiah calls Jerusalem a harlot (Isa. 1:21) and designates wanton commercial activity as "harlotry" (Isa. 23:17), but these seem to reflect the usage of *znh* prior to Hosea. Jeremiah, on the other hand, is clearly dependent upon Hosea's imagery and thought world, as can be seen from his graphic descriptions of Israel's infidelity in chapters 2, 3, 30, and

31 of his work. The same can be said of Ezekiel, particularly in chapters 16 and 23, though he is probably dependent upon both of these predecessors. A remarkable feature of the marriage as covenant metaphor in the pre-exilic period is that it is used principally to portray Israel as unfaithful to the covenant with Yhwh.[35]

Marriage in the Post-Exilic Period

The edict of Cyrus in 539 allowed the Jews to return to their ancestral homeland. After having striven for two generations in Babylon to retain their identity, they returned with a conviction that, from then on, the lessons learned in captivity would have to be put into practice. This meant an insistence on the institutions of their religious culture in a way that had not characterized their life prior to the exile. After a period of intense struggle, this movement of reform began to prevail, with the result that the fifth century B.C. is often referred to as the golden age of Israel's religious literature.[36] All of this had a profound effect upon how marriage was lived and thought about.

The previous section considered the narratives about the patriarchs. While these narratives were, of course, edited into their final place in the Pentateuch in the era following the exile, their basic message continued to be expressed even in a new literary context.

Matrimony and Marriage in the Post-Exilic Legal Texts

In Israel, the legal system was considered not only a codification of custom, but part of the covenant relation with Yhwh. The extant material leaves many gaps in information of central interest to a study such as ours. In some cases, it is legitimate to fill these gaps by arguing from the prevailing jurisprudence in contiguous cultures.

Two Ways of "Taking a Woman" That Were Not Marriage

In the Near East in general and in ancient Israel in particular, marriage was a very specific legal reality and differed radically from other forms of sexual relations between men and women. Failure to appreciate this fact gave rise to the Marxist notion that monogamous and permanent marriage arrangements are but a facet of the capitalist system of private ownership.[37] This view is still found in some modern, particularly feminist, studies of marriage in Israel,[38] and has been effectively challenged by Angelo Tosato. Tosato, whose work has influenced this part of the present study,[39] bases his argument on the frequent use of the verb "to take" (*lqh*). He distinguishes three different relationships: "to take a woman" as a prisoner or slave; "to take a woman" as a prostitute; and "to take a woman" as a wife.

In regard to the first usage, taking a woman as a prisoner or slave, the owner of a foreigner could sell the slave to anyone, for whatever price he could get, as with the case of any other property. This was never true of a husband with his wife, even if she had been a slave (Deut. 21:10–14), or a father with his daughter,[40] or an owner of an Israelite slave, who could be sold but not to a stranger (Exod. 21:2–11). The second usage, taking a woman as a prostitute, would include not only prostitution in our sense of the term, but also cultic prostitution and fornication, in brief, any sexual relation with a woman outside a marriage bond or the bond of slavery. Such a taking implied no legal relationship or responsibility for either the woman or a child born of such a union. These children were considered fatherless and were called "children of prostitution."

This does not mean, however, that the law was indifferent to such liaisons. Cultic prostitution was identified with the worship of a foreign god (see also Deut. 23:18–19). Fornication with a young woman still living in her father's house obliged the man to marry the woman, paying a *mohar* of fifty silver shekels, and to forfeit the ability to divorce her (Exod. 22:16; Deut. 22:28). Forcing a daughter to become a prostitute corrupts the whole land (Lev. 19:29), while a priest may not marry "a woman who has been a prostitute, or has lost her honor, nor a woman who has been divorced by her husband" (Lev. 21:7).

Taking a Woman as a Wife: The Fundamental Terminology

One of the most striking aspects of the languages of the ancient Near East is that terms which seem to us colorless actually possessed effective force within their social context. We ourselves are familiar with such contexts and the force of language within them. Think of such phrases as: "I christen you the Ship *Midway*," or "I take you to be my husband," or even "I want you to have this." Theoreticians of language describe such utterances, made within specific contexts, as "performative" statements; that is, they have a social effect.[41]

A characteristic of Hebrew culture is that the social situations that conferred an effective power upon language regarding such covenant-like statements as "my wife," "my husband," "not my wife," "my people," "my God," etc., also affected analogous phrases which were often accompanied by a symbolic gesture.[42] The whole procedure by which a man became a husband and a woman became a wife, conferring upon both a new social (and in this culture "legal") status, was described in terms that also governed other social states.[43] It is important to bear this in mind as we consider the basic terms used in the matrimonial process and the ways in which the marriage relation was described.

The matrimonial process consisted of two steps — a "constitutive" step and a "completing" step. This first, constitutive step can be broken down into four moments, corresponding to the transactions and commitments entered into by the negotiating families (or individuals). These moments were expressed by the terms: (1) to "ask" or "request" someone as wife; (2) to "give" the woman as wife; (3) to "take" the woman as wife; and (4) "to become" or "to be" a wife.[44]

Movement through these four moments created a marriage which was as yet incomplete, until the performance of the second, formative step, itself made up of three moments: (1) the actual marriage ceremony, (2) the blessing of the bride by the father, and (3) the conducting of the bride into her husband's house.

The State of Marriage Itself

The four most important legal aspects of the married state are (1) the primary reason for marriage and the biological thinking that undergirded the legal prescriptions governing marriage; (2) the rights and duties of husband and wife, with particular attention to the use of the root *baal* [lord or possessor] in connection with marriage; (3) the treatment of adultery in Israel; and (4) the rights of daughters and widows. Later we will consider the related aspects of polygyny, polygamy, and divorce.

1. *The primary reason for the institution of marriage.* In the legal thinking of the ancient Near East, the primary reason for the institution of marriage (as opposed to other forms of male and female sexual relations) was to insure for the man a legitimate heir to continue the family line and possess the family property. The whole logic of the legal system governing marriage derived from this premise.

It is difficult for us to understand the importance of this motive without understanding that people in this culture achieved immortality in their "seed." The values of honor and shame were primary and were interwoven with those of family and its perpetuity. The need for a legally ascertainable male heir who was, with certainty, descended from this particular man was the single greatest preoccupation of life. This preoccupation makes sense of such texts as Judges 9:56, which attributed the humiliating death of Abimelech to God paying him back "for the evil he had done to *his father* in killing his [Abimelech's] seventy brothers [all the male heirs]."[45] In accenting this legal motivation one must not forget all that the patriarchal narratives and particularly the wisdom tradition have to say about marriage as the place of friendship, companionship, stability, and the acquiring of a true humanity.

The view that only the male played an active biological role in perpetuating the family was common throughout most of the world until quite recently. This view was the successor, in most cultures, to an earlier view that attributed conception to the activity of the gods or family spirits and that saw little connection between sexual intercourse and the conception of a child.[46] One notion was that the seed of the male was deposited in the female where it grew and congealed in a totally mysterious manner.[47] This notion contributed to the formation of a social role for the father and to the permanent bonding of husband and wife. It also had the effect of relegating the woman to an inferior position in this most important affair of life.[48]

2. *The rights and duties of the husband and wife.* The two factors we have just discussed, the need for a male heir to continue the family identity, and the view that the woman made no active contribution to the conception of a child, explain the assignment of rights and duties within marriage.

As the discussion of terminology above showed, being a wife constituted a very specific legal status which differed radically from that of a slave or a *zonah*.[49] The legal duties of a husband toward his wife prescribe undertaking with her a common life and included care for her physical needs for food, clothing, and shelter; performing the marital debt; and treating her with respect, that is, not abusing her as though she were a slave or a *zonah* or failing to honor the rights of her children, even if the husband took another woman as wife or as inferior wife.[50] In addition, the husband was to respect his wife's rights to the money of her dowry and of the *mohar* and render these to her in the case of divorce. The primary duty of the wife was to give her husband the unilaterally exclusive right to have intercourse with her. The reason for this was to provide absolute security regarding the identity of the (male) children who were born to her.

The woman's obligation to reserve herself exclusively for her husband not only helped guarantee the husband's paternity of male heirs, but also contributed to her well-being. Not only was she protected under penalty of death from the predatory appetites of unruly males, but she was honored as the vessel of transmission and source of education through whom the family existence was preserved. (Other obligations, such as raising the children, caring for the home, etc., had the force of custom, not law, although failure to meet them might result in divorce.)

In this matter of reciprocal rights and duties it is often alleged that the wife was really little more than the property of her husband and that it is misleading to speak of reciprocity. Such critics point to the frequent use of words relating to the root *baal* in regard to marriage. The basic meaning of this root seems to be "lord" or "possessor."[51] The semantic range of *baal* is much greater than that of comparable words in Western languages: archers are "possessors of arrows" (Gen. 49:23), a bird is a "possessor of wings" (Prov. 1:17), an angry man is a "possessor of anger" (Neh. 1:2). "In another sense *baal* can indicate that a person participates in a community."[52] It can also signify a partner to a covenant (Gen. 14:13). Thus the verb "to become the *baal* of" or to be "lorded" as applied to marriage did not signify "to become the owner of" or "to be owned." It implied the exclusive conjugal rights of the husband to the body of his wife and the fact that the woman has accepted these rights. A husband could not sell his wife into slavery; neither could he concede his rights to her body to another.[53] He is not her "possessor."

It is sometimes also argued that the tenth commandment presumes a husband's ownership of his wife. The two wordings of the commandment are as follow:

> You shall not crave the house of your neighbor; you shall not crave the wife of your neighbor, and his male slave, and his female slave, and his ox and his ass and all that belongs to your neighbor. (Exod. 20:17)

> You shall not crave the wife of your neighbor; you shall not covet for yourself the house of your neighbor, his field, and his male slave, and his female slave and his ox and his ass and all that belongs to your neighbor. (Deut. 5:21).

The text in Exodus 20:17 appears to be older. The Deuteronomic text gives greater prominence to the wife, and neither that text nor the Exodus redaction treats her as property. As William Moran, comparing these texts with some Ugaritic parallels, says:

> For, if Dt 5,21b [the section which begins with the mention of house] is a typical list of common possessions subject to sale, exchange or inheritance, then there is no place in it for a man's wife, for no more in Israel than at Ugarit was she a property from a legal viewpoint in the same sense as other possessions; she was not, for example, subject to sale. And consequently there is nothing more archaic about the list in Ex 20,17 which cannot be understood in the sense that a man's wife was just a common chattel.[54]

Sometimes the disparity between the legal freedom of the husband to have sexual relations with other women and the woman's obligation to keep herself exclusively for her husband is portrayed in such terms that one thinks the male was free to do as he pleased, while his wife was kept in a position little better than slavery. This is a caricature of the actual situation. The very fact that virginity before marriage and exclusivity after marriage were so highly regarded meant that the Israelite male, whether married or unmarried, was circumscribed by a whole battery of legal restrictions, with a range of serious penalties, up to and including death, imposed for transgression.[55] Included in these restrictions were severe laws regarding incest.[56]

In sum, the Israelite nation, as a people bound by covenant to Yhwh, was strongly biased against profligacy and held marital fidelity on the part of the husband in great esteem.[57] This is but one more indication that we cannot understand the biblical view of marriage by concentrating exclusively on the legal texts.

3. *The manner in which adultery was treated.* In both accounts of the Decalogue, or "ten words" (the nuclear expression of the covenant requirements), we read, "You shall not commit adultery" (Exod. 20:14=Deut. 5:18). Adultery was considered a transgression against the husband's right to exclusive access to his wife; it was a sin against God, a violation of the covenant; and, according at least to some sapiential and prophetic texts, a violation of a covenant of marriage as well.[58] The legal dimensions of adultery were concerned with establishing the conditions under which it was determined to have occurred and the penalties to be meted out for it.

The usual punishment was death. After the betrothal had occurred and the woman was committed, but before the second step in the matrimonial process had taken place, intercourse with anyone but her prospective spouse was considered adultery. In this case, both parties were punished with death if the act took place in the city, since the woman (presumably still in her father's care) could have cried out and been saved; otherwise only the man was put to death (Deut. 22:23–24). When, however, the woman was a slave who had been "assigned" (*neherepet*, a term unique to this text) to a man (other than her owner), intercourse was not considered adultery, but the man was obliged to make a sin offering of a ram (Lev. 19:20).[59]

It seems best, then, to consider the penalty for adultery as death, though early legislation envisaged only the death of the man, while the woman may have been stripped in order to indicate that her husband no longer had care of her and as a humiliation (Hos. 2:3; perhaps also Jer. 13:22, 26). Later enactments, particularly those in the Deuteronomic code, treated the woman as a responsible agent and assigned the death penalty to her as well: "If a man is caught lying with the wife of another man, both of them shall die, the man who lay with the woman as well as the woman. So you shall purge the evil from Israel" (Deut. 22:22; also Lev. 20:10).[60] (It was not until later in the post-exilic period that the death penalty ceased to be applied to adultery and was restricted only to murder, with adultery punished by exclusion from the community [see Prov. 5:9–14].)[61]

4. *The rights of daughters and the rights of widows.* The Bible speaks of the "legal provision for daughters" in Exodus 21:9, and in Deuteronomy 10:18 and 27:19 it speaks of the "legal provision for widows." In the legal tradition of the ancient Near East and especially in Israel, a young woman who was a daughter, either by birth or by adoption, had the right not to be reduced to slavery, not to be treated as a *zonah*, and not to become the sex partner of her near relatives.[62] In brief, she had the right to be a *wife*.

A woman whose husband died was to be treated according to the legal provision for widows. Failure to appreciate this important point has led to the opinion that, since the wife was the "property" of her husband, she and her goods reverted to her husband's family upon his death. Quite the contrary. A widow — that is, a woman who had lost her husband and was not provided for by a male kin[63] — was not only entitled to her own goods (her dowry and the *mohar*) but was also entrusted with the goods of her husband.[64] The widow, along with the orphan and the "sojourner" (someone from another land who had no family or clan ties), were considered vulnerable and in need of special protection because they did not have the normal societal means of protecting their rights. In all the ancient Near East, kings and other rulers were ideally to ensure protection for these persons.[65] Many Near Eastern laws and customs also provide for these three classes.[66]

Three options were open to the widow: she could remarry (but she could not marry the high priest: Lev. 21:13–15) and arrange her own marriage; she could undertake a profession or craft; or she could return to her father's house.[67] The first option implies that, like a daughter, she had the right to be a wife and to not be reduced to slavery or treated as a *zonah* (see Exod. 22:21–22). Further, a special provision was made for the widow of a man who died without a male heir. This provision is usually referred to as the levirate marriage, from the Latin term *levir*, meaning brother-in-law (Hebrew *yabam*). While there is reference to this custom in Genesis 38 and in the Book of Ruth, the only legal expression of this practice is found in Deuteronomy 25:5–10.

Given the value placed on establishing legitimate heirs for a man in order to continue his name and that of the family, it is probably correct to accept the motivation for the levirate marriage as presented in the Deuteronomic text, that is, "that his name not be blotted out." Another powerful motivation for the use of the levirate marriage was undoubtedly that of maintaining the dead man's estate within the family. However, it must be borne in mind that the levirate arrangement was a much more onerous method of achieving this goal than would be the simple absorption of the brother's goods into one's own.

We can see that the law had in mind the care of the widow as well as concern for the deceased's family line. The widow was definitely no mere chattel who became part of the estate of the deceased. In fact, one provision of the law protected her against relatives who might otherwise be freed from the obligation of caring for her, thereby forcing her to live on her dowry and the *mohar* while trying to find another husband for herself.[68]

5. *Polygyny, polygamy, divorce and remarriage.* The three issues of polygyny, polygamy, and divorce touch upon some of the most significant differences between the rights of the husband and those of the wife. Israelite

males were inhibited by various legal enactments and social pressures from promiscuity in sexual relations. Within the parameters of these constraints, however, a married Israelite male still had the opportunity for, and the right to, a multiplicity of relationships with the opposite sex which were not correspondingly available to a married woman. The husband could have sexual relationships with other women (polygyny), whereas the wife was obliged to relate exclusively to her husband; the husband could marry another woman (polygamy); and the husband could sever the relationship with his wife (divorce).[69]

Polygyny and polygamy are, by definition, closely related practices. However, polygyny, as just defined, was not an accepted or common occurrence in Israel. The question of polygamy, however, has many facets. It seems to have occurred infrequently among commoners, but to have been accepted, for certain specific reasons connected to their official responsibilities, among Israelite leaders. In addition, different strictures applied to polygamy, depending on whether it involved relations with women of the same, or different, social classes. It may be said of polygamy in Israel that it existed, that it was rare, that it was presumed but never legislated for in any positive sense, and that it was discouraged and perhaps actually legislated against. Monogamy was considered to be the norm and the ideal, not only in the sapiential and prophetic literature, but in the legal texts as well.

Gordon Paul Hugenberger's summary of the situation in regard to polygyny and polygamy in the cultures contiguous to Israel is just as aptly applied to Israel itself:

> Nevertheless the legal texts leave little doubt that unjustified polygyny, that is, polygyny unmotivated by infertility or illness, was officially and widely discountenanced. Accordingly, the majority of cuneiform texts which allude to marriage, whether in the legal corpora or wisdom literature etc., presuppose monogamy as the normal, if not also the ideal, form of marriage in Mesopotamia.[70]

Royal polygamy was a special case. The marriage alliances of a king, chieftain, or other ruler were first and foremost political arrangements, and as such were generally governed in the ancient Near East by *public* law.[71] In Israel two legal provisions were made in this regard. The first, as we have seen, was that the ruler's women (wives and concubines) passed to his successor: this fact adds a specific dimension to Absalom's act of publicly lying with his father's concubines after driving David from Jerusalem (2 Sam. 16:20–22). The second legal provision regarding royal polygamy is found in the "Law for Kings" in Deuteronomy 17:14–20. With an obvious allusion to Solomon, the Deuteronomist says that the reason why the king should not "multiply wives for himself" is so that his heart will not become "estranged" (Deut. 17:17).

Polygamy in the broader sense, what Angelo Tosato calls a "differentiated polygamy,"[72] occurred when the women involved were of unequal social or legal status. This could occur in two ways: if one of the women was a concubine (*pilegesh*), a term which could apply to a slave of an infertile wife given to the husband as a surrogate, as in the case of Hagar, or to several other classes of women;[73] or if one of the women was a slave, either by purchase or as a prisoner in war.[74] (This second situation differs from that described in Deuteronomy 21:10–14, which addresses a woman prisoner who is made a *wife,* and who thus can never be enslaved again.)

Divorce and remarriage are yet another facet of polygamy which must be considered. Our study will be limited to the relation between *husband and wife,* as these terms have been defined up to now. We will first consider the capacity of the husband to institute a divorce, taking in turn cases where he could divorce, could not divorce, and was required to divorce; and second, the woman's capacity to terminate the marriage. It is a commonly accepted opinion that divorce was an arbitrary, unilateral, and private act, and consisted of expelling the wife from the house of her husband.[75] This is not the case. If the woman was legally recognized as a *wife,* then this understanding of divorce needs serious revision, even in regard to the extra-biblical cultures of the day.[76] In Israel itself, as in contiguous cultures, divorce was neither arbitrary (that is, dependent only upon the preferences of the husband), nor particularly easy. Perhaps most important, it was not unilaterally invocable by the husband; the wife could also break the juridical bond under certain circumstances.

In the ancient Near East, laws allowing a man to divorce ran a considerable gamut. Generally, however, the codes tended to enumerate situations in which a man *might* divorce his wife. These included, first, instances where there was some fault on the part of the woman: desire to leave the house; lying about her husband's conduct in order to free herself from her obligation to him; and, in some codes, adultery. It is possible that infertility or illness may also have been a basis for dissolving the marriage bond. Most divorce legislation, however, seemed to have been designed to protect the woman from neglect, especially in the case of illness or infertility.[77]

This attitude seems to have governed prevailing practice not only in Israel but throughout the Near East regarding divorce because of some defect in the woman.

Instances are found where there was no fault on the part of the woman but the man, after going through the matrimonial process, decided not to take the woman as wife. In this case, the Code of Hammurabi stipulated that the father of the prospective bride "shall keep whatever was brought to him."[78] As noted, the Code of Eshnunna provided for the case of a woman divorced by her husband through no fault of her own after having borne him children. In Israel, if a woman were divorced with no fault on her part, her husband was obliged to render to her the *mohar* he paid when the marriage was agreed upon. (In normal cases this amounted to fifty silver shekels [Deut. 22:29].) In addition, the husband was obliged to return the woman's dowry[79] and provide her with a bill of divorce in order to establish the fact that she was free to remarry (Deut. 24:1–4).[80]

The requirement to return the *mohar* and her dowry to the wife could present a substantial financial burden to the husband who wanted a divorce, and thereby served both to protect the financial interests of the woman and to discourage divorce. Husbands sometimes went to great lengths to avoid repaying these moneys. This was done either by claiming the woman was not a virgin at the time of the marriage, or that she had engaged in conduct that rendered her liable to the suspicion of adultery. In the first case, if the husband brought "shameful charges" against the wife and they proved false, the husband had to pay a hundred silver shekels (a considerable sum, double the usual value of the *mohar* whose repayment he had sought to avoid) to his father-in-law, and could never divorce the woman. On the other hand, if the husband's charges proved true, the woman was to be stoned to death at the door of her father's house (Deut. 22:13–21). In the case of suspected adultery, the woman was submitted to an "ordeal," the exact nature of which is not totally clear from the extant text (Num. 5:11–31).

In both Israel and the ancient Near East in general, the law stipulated certain cases in which divorce was not allowed. Nearly all of these are sanctions against the man designed to protect a woman who has been wronged. A man who forced a virgin to have intercourse was required to marry her and could not divorce her (Deut. 22:28–29). The Middle Assyrian Laws went even further and stipulated that the father of the wronged girl must take the wife of the offender and not return her.[81] As noted above, a false accusation regarding non-virginity at marriage also prohibited the man from ever divorcing his wife (Deut. 22:19). Further, the Code of Hammurabi forbade a man to divorce his sick wife, while allowing him to marry another woman. If the sick woman preferred to return to her father's house, she took her dowry with her.[82]

Finally, there are cases in which a man was required to divorce his wife. The Code of Hammurabi prescribed that the prospective groom must break off the commitment to his prospective bride if she had intercourse with his father and must pay her a considerable sum of money and return her dowry and marriage gift. Other codes prescribed that if a man wished to divorce his principal wife, he must divorce the secondary wives as well; this was to protect the interests of the principal wife. Still other laws regulated who must relinquish a woman after the husband, detained by war or other calamity, finally returned.[83]

Under non-Israelite law, there does not seem to have been an obligation to divorce in the case of adultery. In Israel, as we have seen, divorce was always required in such cases, and, until late in Israelite history, the imposition of the death penalty was necessary as well. Laws forbidding incest obviously rendered marriage within certain degrees of relationship invalid. (See, for example, Deut. 27:20, 22, 23; Lev. 18:6–17; 20:11–20). In addition, in post-exilic Israel, marriages with non-Israelites had to be broken off, seemingly under threat of loss of citizenship and goods (Ezra 10:7–8; also Ezra 9:10; Neh. 10:30–31).

Contrary to the prevailing view, the wife's choice to continue participation in the marriage was not irrevocable. In fact, the wife could initiate divorce in four different cases in the cultures contiguous to Israel. Some of these were also found within the law codes of Israel itself; and some, while not found in the writings available to us, may be inferred. The four grounds for divorce on the part of the wife were: (1) failure to consummate the marriage;[84] (2) failure to support the woman, whether because the husband is held captive, has failed to return, has fled the city, or for some other reason.[85] (This same logic is found in Exodus 21:7–11 where failure to support a slave-bride allows her to terminate the relation without any cost to her. It may be presumed that if such is the case with a slave-bride, it is much more the case with a wife.); (3) lack of respect;[86] and (4) annulment of the matrimonial agreement before consummation (with payment of a fine).[87]

To sum up, post-exilic Israel had developed a restrictive set of legal enactments governing divorce. Monogamy was both the norm and the ideal; divorce was tolerated, but not favored in any way, and much of the divorce legislation dealt with its regulation and limitation. Divorce tended to be restricted to the terminating of an illicit marriage bond or to grave fault on the part of either spouse.

Marriage as a Covenant and Considerations of Divorce

As seen in the post-exilic prophets, there was a widespread view, reflected as well in the intertestamental period, that divorce was not in keeping with the covenant. This is evidenced in legal and other vocabulary used for divorce. Marriage and infractions of marital obligations were no longer considered merely private affairs, but were the subject of legislation in the covenantal code; most significant, marriage itself was considered a covenant between a man and a woman, reflecting the covenant between Yhwh and his people. Indications that marriage was considered a covenant may be classified under four headings: (1) vocabulary; (2) the view of the biblical world and to a degree the extra-biblical world that marital infidelity was a sin against God (the gods); (3) the invocation of God as a witness and executor of justice in the event of infidelity; and (4) the prohibition against marriage with pagans, because the marriage ceremony itself involved swearing to God in a covenant context.[88]

Marriage in the Post-Exilic Wisdom Tradition

Enough has been said above about the humanity of the sapiential under-standing of marriage and fidelity, friendship in marriage, the duties of parents and children. The post-exilic tradition followed in this tradition. There is, however, one aspect of wisdom tradition thinking that deserves very special attention. It is the effort of the sages of Israel to understand the mystery of the origins of the universe and specifically of the human race. It is to that tradition, as it is found in the early chapters of Genesis, that we will now briefly turn our attention.[89] For the sake of brevity, I will restrict the discussion largely to the second and third chapters of Genesis, since these treat more directly of the actual situation of marriage in our world of diminished existence.[90]

In regard to the two traditions found in chapters 1, 2, and 3, respectively, of Genesis, Gerhard von Rad once remarked:

> The two presentations are alike in that they have as their chief end, though doing it in different ways, the creation of man, that is, mankind as male and female — with the result that the rest of the world is ordered round them as the chief work of Jahweh in Creation.... The world and its fullness do not find their unity and inner coherence in a cosmological first principle such as the Ionian natural philosophers tried to discover, but in the completely personal will of Jahweh their creator.[91]

The authorities are divided in their opinions as to whether the material found in Genesis 2 and 3 is the product of one author or is derived from multiple sources. The Yahwistic epic, so called because God is referred to as Yhwh, begins with an account of origins; continues through an account of universal history, mostly a history of sin and forgiveness; finds its turning point in the call of Abraham; proceeds with a series of episodes in the life of the patriarchs; and finally tells of the exodus, the desert wandering, and the sending of spies into the Promised Land. The Yahwistic account is in all probability an earlier, pre-exilic narrative incorporated by the editing activity of the author or editor of the first chapter of Genesis.

Genesis 2 and 3 and Israel's Wisdom Tradition

The second and third chapters of Genesis should be considered as belonging to that class of literature we call "sapiential." The wise men of Israel were, to coin a phrase, "inspired philosophers." The questions that loom in the minds of anyone who reflects on human existence were precious and important to them. These wise men of Israel pondered these questions and the responses given by generations of their counterparts throughout the Middle East (who also undertook such searching in the context of religion). The answers of these inspired philosophers came, however, from their faith in Yhwh and the light he gave them.[92]

Someone — I will call him the Yahwist for the sake of simplicity — took up fragments of the symbol system constituted by the thought world that surrounded Israel and made of it a narrative that began at the beginning. Then, in a process of narrowing attention, the story begins to center on Israel as a nation constituted by relating to God. In the chapters that concern us, this narrative first deals with God's direct activity in forming man and providing for him in a place of intimacy. It then tells of a covenant injunction, of man's superiority over the animals, of his incomplete state without community, of the gift Yhwh made to man and woman by giving them to each other, and the depth of their friendship. The narrative goes on to deal with the intrusion of a third element (a dark and rational force that leads the man and the woman into disobedience to God) and to the tragic consequences of their disobedience that scar human existence for us all, though even this is not left without a glimmer of hope.

It was in the light of the movement of thought toward historical causes that the wise men pondered the mystery of the disorder, sin, and suffering in human life. The prophetic tradition had considered various segments of Israel's history and had found some clarification of the mystery of such sin and suffering by rising in thought to one antecedent moment in the history of God's people when a sin set loose its evil into the world. For this prophetic tradition the rhythm was: God's initiative, covenant, rebellion, punishment, and a diminished form of continued existence which, however, contained a promise of restoration.

The Creation of Man and Woman

1. *The meaning of adam in Genesis 2 and 3.* It is important for our discussion to clarify what *adam* means in these chapters.[93] According to a popular but doubtful etymology, *adam* is linked to *adamah*, "earth," and both are linked to the root *adam*, which means "red." This popular etymology surely underlies Genesis 2:7, where it is said that Yhwh God formed *adam* "dust from the *adamah*," and in the sad realization of the implications of this in Genesis 3:19: "till you return to the *adamah* for from it you were taken."[94] The word has a more generic ring than the term *ish*, which means "man" and not "woman," and *zakar*, "male," as opposed to *neqebah*, "female."

The word *adam* comes forty-six times in the story of universal origins in Genesis 1–11, but only once in the rest of the book.

The first mention of *adam* in the Yahwist account intimates something of his place and role in the world. Genesis 2:4b, employing the formula "there was not yet," describes a waste and barren place "because Yhwh God had not sent rain upon the earth and there was no man to cultivate the earth." We then have the famous description of God fashioning the man like a potter: "And Yhwh God fashioned the man, (with) dust from the earth, and breathed into his nostrils the breath of life and the man became a living soul."

This description contains three important elements. First is the earthly composition of man, a commonplace in stories of origins. Second is the direct and personal action of Yhwh God, who forms the man with his fingers and then breathes into him "the breath of life." The word "breath" (*neshama*) in this latter phrase is often used in parallel with the broader term *ruah,* which can be translated according to context as "spirit," "breath," or "wind." The accent in our text is that life is directly transmitted from God to *adam* and because of that he is a "living soul." The third element is being a *nepesh hayyah,* "a soul alive." Note that this is not what distinguishes *adam* from the rest of creation; the same is said in Genesis 2:19 of all the animals named by the man and is used in Genesis 9:9, 1:20, 21, 24 of various living things. What makes man unique is that he has been given life-breath directly by God; there is something of God in him.[95]

2. *The garden and Yhwh's words of commandment to the man.* The notion that Yhwh God took the man from the arid place and put him in the garden carries allusions to the exodus and ultimately to the temple. But the text refers most basically to God's direct and loving care for the man, who was created not to alleviate the work-load of discontented lower gods — there is only Yhwh God — but to find his delight in cultivating and keeping God's gift to him.

It is important to advert to all the words of the commandment given by Yhwh God to the man: "And Yhwh God gave a commandment to the man saying: 'From all the trees of the garden you may eat; but from the tree of the knowledge of good and evil, you shall not eat of it; for on the day you eat of it, you must die'" (Gen. 2:16).[96] In speaking of God as giving a command we are already in the atmosphere of a covenant relation.

There are three parts in the words of the "command." First, there is the largess of God, giving the man permission to eat of all the trees of the garden as he wishes. Second, there is the prohibition, expressed in the language of what is called the "apodictic imperative," "Thou shalt not" laws as in some of the ten commandments and elsewhere.[97] Third, there is the description of the consequences of disobedience expressed, as we have seen, more in the language of divine or royal threat than in strictly legal terms and providing a "motive clause."[98]

The Near East generally regarded trees as being mysteriously endowed with a life-force, and the Garden of Eden is described as being amply provided with trees. But aside from this, there does not seem to be any particular motive for selecting the tree as the metaphorical expression of the means for gaining knowledge of good and evil. The prohibition is clear: "You shall not eat of it."[99] In less symbolic language, the commandment reads: "Enjoy, experience, draw life from and have authority over all that I have given you in this garden, but you shall not stretch out your hand to be as wise as God and to determine for yourself what is good and what is evil."

The command is directly and personally given, thus providing the opportunity for an obedience based on trust. It is couched by the Yahwist in covenant terms because he makes this narrative an anticipatory recapitulation of Israel's history. Sin is not merely the perversion of good order; it is a transgression of a personal command offered as the basis for a deeper relation founded on covenant trust. The consequence of disobedience is death. "In the Old Testament life therefore means: to have relationship. Above all: to have a relationship with God . . . the whole life of man passes into death at the precise moment when the praise of God falls silent."[100] While the pain and the fright of a death inflicted by the community or by God is a terrible punishment, the heart of the punishment is being cut off from a shared life. Physical death is but the extreme expression of an alienation that begins with sin: a personal denial of the basis of communion.

3. *The creation of woman and her relationship with the man.* It is remarkable that after the sevenfold reiteration, in chapter 1 of Genesis, that God's creation was "good," God's first deliberative words to himself in chapter 2 express the fact that the man's being alone is "not good."[101] The words follow immediately upon the threat of death, thus emphasizing in a new way that the man is not yet complete (*tob,* "good," means much more than does our English term) until he can share life with someone.

The phrase, "Let me make for him a helper matching him," now echoes the "Let us make" of chapter 1. More than that, however, it defines the nature of what is needed to make the human situation "good." For human life to be good there must be communication, there must be a reciprocal sharing of life. In Hebrew, neither the noun "helper" nor the adjective phrase qualifying it gives any hint as yet that the companion is to be feminine. Actually the term *ezer,* "helper," far from meaning "servant," connotes someone who helps another realize what cannot be realized alone and is most often applied to God, who saves and protects in situations of peril.[102] The qualification of the helper as *kenegdo,* literally "facing him," or as Gordon Wenham well translates, "matching him," means that the helper must be what *adam* is so there can be the kind of help that can only come from a "mate."

Why is the companion described as a "help" at all? Or to phrase the question another way, what is it that *adam* needs to do but cannot do alone? There has been no mention of procreation, and at this point there has been no use of a feminine word to designate the helper. Therefore, while it is true that the man cannot procreate without the woman, this is not what is envisaged here. The blessing of fecundity follows upon something more profound, both in this text and in Genesis 1:27–28. If we understand the task of *adam* to be that of "cultivating and keeping" the place of meeting God, then the implication is that this cannot be done without human community. Continuing in this line of thought, the fact that the man's being alone is denied the appellation "good" means that there is something lacking to the man as he is without someone to share life. He needs "help" in order to be human.[103]

The verses that follow (Gen. 2:19–20) establish three things. First the man and the animals have the same origin. Of the animals too it is said that Yhwh God formed them from the earth, and they are called *nepesh hayya*. Second, the man is their superior: though he cannot create them, he names them. Third, none of the animals qualifies as a helper who matches man.

"Then Yhwh God caused a deep sleep to fall upon the man, and he slept." We moderns might first think of some "divine anesthetic" being applied, but the author would not mention this here unless something more were intended. The term translated here "deep sleep" (*tardema*) occurs seven times in the Old Testament. It is often the result of a divine action and may be the occasion for "visions in the night" (Job 4:13). Here it is the occasion for a sacred action as in the other occurrence in Genesis, that of the covenant made with Abram in Genesis 15:12. The fact that God takes a rib from the man may allude to a theme known to us from a word play in Sumerian,[104] but its use in the narrative is to establish the theme of union and provide a basis for the poem to follow. God is said to "build" the rib "into a woman" and then bring her, as the midrash expresses it, like "the friend of the bridegroom," to the man.[105]

The very first words of *adam* in the biblical text are a short poem expressing, in terms of delight and wonder, a faith vision of the relation between man and woman:

> This one, at last
> is bone from my bone and flesh from my flesh;
> this one shall be called woman,
> for from man was
> this one taken.

The helper is someone who matches *adam* but is not a replica. She is woman (*ishah*) because she is taken from, but differs from, man (*ish*). Communion is between likes who are yet unlike. In naming her, *adam* himself assumes a new name: her presence "matching him" is a revelation of who both of them are in relationship. With all the wonderment of genuine philosophy and with the insight of a mind enlightened by God, the author of this poem puts into the mouth of *adam* the fundamental appreciation of God's intention to have a human being reach fulfillment in the communion of complementarity.[106] The likeness of woman to man is expressed in the opening line of the poem: she is "bone from my bone and flesh from my flesh."

The marriage relationship as a symbol for the covenant relationship with Yhwh. The result of a man leaving his father and mother and cleaving to his wife is that they "become one flesh." This expression indicates much more than a bodily union or even a shared domestic life. In the words of Maurice Gilbert, the phrase refers to "the unity of two corporal beings in all the dimensions which the attachment of man and woman to each other can assume."[107] By way of confirmation Gilbert points to four texts, later than Genesis 2, where there are echoes of Genesis 2:24.

The first of these is Genesis 1:26–27. The second, Tobit 8:7, is quite doubtful. The most illustrative text is the difficult Malachi 2:10–16, which is a strong protest against divorce and in defense of monogamous fidelity. The next remark of the Yahwist is one of considerable depth: "And the two of them were naked, the *adam* and his wife, and they felt no shame with each other." We may first note the lexical choice made, probably by the author or at least by the Massoretic tradition, in spelling the word "naked" in such a way (*arummim*) that it is echoed in the very next line which describes the serpent as "astute" (*arum*). By stating that the man and the woman were naked and felt no shame with each other, the author is pointing to the universal human experience of shame as a boundary experience. The very presence of shame evokes reflection on the possibility of an existence without shame.[108] In making this statement, the Yahwist is asserting a mode of existence for the *adam* and his wife that is beyond our experience. In linking this statement to the notion of nakedness he is claiming a form of integrity for them, an unprotected, unveiled communication between them.

Not only did the sexual drives with their symbolic impact on the personality lack their present vulnerability to egocentricity, disorder, and violence, but the whole of the personality was unburdened, free of the memory of sin, both individual and collective, and thus able to live without the effort to defend an autonomy that bears the seeds of its own lie within it. The discovery of nakedness after the act of disobedience is highlighted by the Yahwist: "the eyes of the two of them were opened and they came to know that they were naked. . . . I hid because I was naked . . . who made known to you that you were naked?" (Gen. 3:7–10). An uncovered body, which in itself is a neutral thing, is in the present state of things, particularly in sophisticated cultures, a symbolic experience of vulnerability and humiliation. Freedom from shame is an eschatological promise in the Old Testament linked to freedom from sin and the experience of God's saving power: "Israel is saved by Yhwh with an everlasting salvation; you shall not be ashamed or confounded to all eternity" (Isa. 45:17; see 29:22); "On that day you shall not be ashamed because of all the deeds by which you rebelled against me" (Zeph. 3:11).[109]

The Sin of the Man and the Woman

In positing a before and an after and in linking the transition to the experience of shame, the Yahwist is asserting that a change too place in humanity. Changes take place in time, thus in history. In stating that the man and his wife were naked but not ashamed with each other, the author is appealing to the other side of the boundary and declaring that such a situation actually existed. While we cannot tax him with our modern conception of "history," neither can we attribute this statement to a mythic motif. The innocence ascribed to the couple here is purposely linked to a lack of shame in relating to each other and to God.

The effect of *adam*'s sin is very real, a part of human experience, and the author is teaching that this effect is a real change from a previous state in which there was no shame because the source of shame was absent.

The moments in the episode designated as "rebellion — diminished existence" are found in the present chapter 3. The first word of Genesis 3:1 is "the serpent." "And the serpent was *arum* more than any of the wild beasts that Yhwh Elohim made." We lack the historical information necessary to know what image the serpent would have evoked in that time. All that can be said is that the juxtaposition of "serpent" and "astute/shrewd" is calculated to alert the reader to the advent of something sinister which, however, is not outside of God's control: the serpent has been made by God. The serpent approaches the woman. Never in all the text is there any direct contact between the *adam* and the serpent. Both here, in the initial dialogue, and later in the curse of the serpent, the direct relation is always between the woman and the serpent. We will return to consider this later. The ensuing dialogue is the most masterful presentation in all literature of the process by which human beings yield to the solicitation of evil.

Then, in the following scene, all the other actors are absent. Yhwh God has not been mentioned though he has been discussed (as "God"); the serpent has retired. The two are alone. Convinced of the utterly unwarranted and unverifiable hypothesis that God is jealous and is holding something back, the woman now sees the tree with new eyes and reaches out to take its fruit in a covetous desire to gain that knowledge that will ensure success. "And she took from the tree and she ate and she even gave it to her husband beside her and he ate."

The Effects of Sin and the Diminished Existence of Man and Woman

1. *The knowledge of good and evil, and shame.* And now, all the deception of the serpent is apparent. The eyes of the man and the woman are opened and they see not their wisdom but their nakedness. Shame, not control over their existence, is now their first knowledge of good and evil. And this new knowledge leads them to cover themselves. The community between them is now guarded. Then, in an ironic twist on the covenant terms "hear" and "fear," the man and his wife hide themselves when they hear the sound/voice of Yhwh Elohim. This is the second way they have come to the knowledge of good and evil: they are afraid of God, they do not reverence him.

In the first six verses of chapter 3 of Genesis "the woman" is the subject of a verb four times. "Her husband" is mentioned once, in the act of eating of the tree. In the next two verses, which describe the consequences of the sin, the couple are linked together, "the two of them," "the man and his wife," and the verbs are in the plural. In verse 9, as the equilibrium is restored in the form of a legal action consequent upon breaking the commandment/covenant, Yhwh God calls out only to "the man," and upon hearing of his nakedness and fear, asks him: "Can it be that of the tree which I commanded you [sing.] not to eat, you have eaten?"

The man answers by describing the former object of his song of gratitude as "the woman whom you gave [to be] beside me," and in that one phrase distances himself from her and accuses God.[110] The communion established by God has become antagonism. Next, Yhwh Elohim questions the woman: "What is this you have done?"

2. *The woman is adjudicated by God.* After the juridical investigation comes the sentencing which proceeds in inverse order. This is the only place in the Old Testament where God himself directly declares and administers the punishment.[111] The serpent is cursed: *arum* becomes *arur.* The first part of the curse is a symbolic transmutation: the unclean and humiliated serpent, writhing and eating dust, embodies the state of God's enemy.[112] The second part relates the woman and the serpent in a mysterious struggle. First, there is a perpetual enmity between them. Second, there is an enmity between the seed of the serpent and the seed of the woman which actualizes the hostility between the woman and the serpent. This seed, or posterity, will trample on the head of the serpent who will snap at his heel.

This seems to be the best way to interpret the wordplay based on the roots *shwp* and *sh'p.*[113] While on one level an endless struggle is depicted, a victory must be implied for the woman and her seed. Otherwise it is hardly a curse for the serpent. Jewish tradition later interpreted this text messianically.[114] It is hard to determine whether the interest that the Yahwist has in the Davidic kingship and its continuance in his seed has had any influence on the wording of this text.[115]

It is remarkable that the enmity is established between the serpent and the woman in a text that is accounting for a permanent state of affairs and that contains a prophetic hint of victory. It is even more remarkable that the posterity is described as being that of the woman and that it is called her seed. The Hebrew word *zera* covers much of the same semantic field as the English word "seed," though, except for biblically influenced language, we do not speak of a person's posterity as being their seed. This is one of six texts in the Old Testament which attribute *zera* to a woman.[116] The expression is not common because it stretches the biological foundation of the attribution in a culture where women, as we have seen, were considered to have no active part in reproduction and certainly had no seed.

We have, then, a prominence attributed to the woman in both the sin and the ultimate victory. In both cases she is placed in relation to the serpent, not the man. It is difficult to articulate in discursive language the significance of this fact in a text so full of symbolic teaching. This much seems clear, however: neither the defeat and the ensuing struggle nor the overcoming of the serpent can be understood without an understanding of the causality of the woman. Most modern commentators are intent to disclaim any validity to the early Christian notion that Genesis 3:15 contains a Protoevangelium, yet they rarely consider the importance of the woman in relation to the serpent and they do not take into account the curious use of the term "seed" in relation to her.

The teaching in this text attributes a particular power to woman, both for good and ill, related to the solicitation of evil and its ultimate overcoming. An understanding of Mary's motherhood of Jesus as being more than merely biological shows us that she concretizes in a surprising way the intuition of the Yahwistic author.

Neither the woman nor the man are cursed. Rather, the form of diminished existence we now know is explicitly seen as the consequence of the rebellion of the *adam* and his wife. Two aspects of the woman's existence are highlighted: her painful labor in bringing forth children and her connivance in the domination by her husband. The first part of the text should be translated: "I will greatly multiply the distress of your childbearing, in distress you will bring forth children." Thus, that which is the very glory and unique prerogative of the woman is also the source of pain and distress. The second part of the sentence reads literally: "And towards your husband (will be) your urge, and he will dominate you." Both principal terms in this passage, "urge" and "dominate," are repeated in Yhwh's warning to Cain in the very next chapter: "for you is its (sin's) urge and you must/can dominate it" (Gen. 4:7).[117]

This purposeful repetition is not meant to equate woman with sin. It serves rather to accent the fact that many actually existing cultural and psychological dimensions of woman-man relationships are not the will of God, but are characteristic of the diminished existence brought into the world by sin. The two sides of this warped relationship, dependence and domination, illustrate the depth of what has gone wrong in human life. Just as the ideal manner of relating described above as "complementarity" is typified in the man-woman relationship, so too is the twisted dimension of any human relating, with its connivance in the same twofold degradation of dignity, also found there in a typological form.

Though the text is directly concerned with the existence of the woman, this cannot be described without considering the sin of the man. Once again, as with the notion of shame, our very awareness of something deeply wrong stimulates us to search for something on the other side of the boundary. The patristic notion was that the healing grace of Christ can bring us back to paradise — that without the obedience and asceticism of learning from God how to rectify their relationships, humans will continue to force into existence utopias born of their own woundedness and thus bearing the marks of that which has to be healed.

3. *The man is adjudicated by God.* The adjudication of the man's situation is exactly three times as long as that of the woman's. The first statement explicitly mentions the disobedience: "Because you listened to the voice of your wife and ate of the tree about which I commanded you saying, 'You shall not eat of it.'" The tree is described in terms which are almost exactly the same as in verse 11, while the broken command is expressed in the same legal terms as Genesis 2:17. The new dimension here is that *adam* did this because, as the Hebrew expression "listen to the voice" connotes, he yielded to the wishes of his wife: he obeyed her rather than God.[118] It seems that this remark is intended once again to point to the power of the woman. The heart of the transgression, however, is that *adam* went directly against the covenant command.

The earth (*adamah*) is cursed because of *adam*, as though the curse went right through him to strike the foundation of his existence.[119] From now on he will eat of it in distress and it will yield only grudgingly, more often than not betraying his exertions. Finally, he will return to the earth from which he was taken: he returns to dust because he is dust. Humankind's *techne*, the effort to bend the universe to serve our existence, is tainted by the shadow of a struggle whose outcome is inevitable. Death means being cut off from shared life. Formed from dust and endowed with the breath of God, *adam* no longer has the enduring possession of a life shared with God and with others.

4. *The existence of man and woman remains a blessing, although a diminished one.* The new mode of existence and the corresponding knowledge of death are not, however, the last word. The concluding lines of this episode speak of life and compassion as much as of expulsion and alienation. Once again the man names the woman. This time she is called *hawwah* "because she was the mother of all the living." Why such a title and why at this point? The name *hawwah* may have admitted of many interpretations, but at some point "mother of all the living" was appended, explaining after the fact ("she was") the significance of the name given to her. The blessing of life, the transmission of human life, is still meaningful and woman's part in that is more encompassing than man's. Thus, though we may wonder at the source and possible interpretations of the phrase, it suggests that though human existence has been diminished, even warped, it is still an inestimable blessing and bears a possibility and a promise of even greater blessing. For the original audience of this text that blessing included life in a covenant with God on the land promised by him and made a sacrament of his presence.

The next part of the narrative uses the verb "make" to describe Yhwh Elohim's intimate care of the man and his wife. Up to now this word has described the creative activity of God. Now it describes the act by which he "makes" tunics of skin and clothes them. This text is undoubtedly linked to humankind's inheritance of shame and the efforts of the man and the woman to protect themselves from what was once a completely open communication. In this action, Yhwh Elohim is portrayed as easing the pain of the present state in a way that shows he is able to work even within the disrupted existence we now know. We are reminded of later moments in Israelite history when God continues his plan in a lesser key after a primal sin: the son born to Abraham by Hagar, the fruit of his lack of faith in the promise, is promised a future.[120]

Marriage in the Post-Exilic Prophetic Tradition

The most striking characteristics of the later, post-exilic, prophetic tradition are its use of the marriage image to describe Yhwh's relationship with his people and its opposition to divorce expressed in the text of Malachi 2:10–16. In the pre-exilic period the image of husband and wife had been employed to portray Israel's infidelity to Yhwh. In the post-exilic period this image came to be used in promises of restoration. This use, which was foreshadowed in the writings of Hosea (Hos. 2:16–3:5),[121] seems to have been more fully developed during the exile itself. It can be seen in Isaiah 54, where the basic image of the renewed relation between Yhwh and the people is that of a renewed marriage as in Hosea: "The Lord calls you back like a

wife forsaken and grieved in spirit; a wife married in youth and then cast
off, says your God. For a brief moment I abandoned you, but with great
tenderness I will take you back" (Isa. 54:6–7). The same theme is found
later in the same book (Isa. 62:1–5), along with the promise of a renewed
fruitfulness (Isa. 66:7–16).

The Song of Songs, although not part of the prophetic tradition as such,
is another work which promises restoration using the imagery of spousal
love.[122] This remarkable poem or drama transposes human sexual love, and
even transposes the poems which celebrate that love, to the level of the
passionate love which God has for Israel and the response it evokes. In so
doing, the Song of Songs builds upon the prophetic and wisdom literature's
ability to transpose the human reality of marriage to the level of the relation
between God and his people.

The kind of literary borrowing in which the original meaning of a literary
work has been completely transposed can be dramatically illustrated by a
poem of St. John of the Cross entitled, "The Shepherd Boy." This work
was once a popular love poem, and was transposed by John of the Cross
according to a popular practice of his time called *a lo divino*. The poem
is about a shepherd boy whose love was rejected and who climbed upon a
tree, spread his arms, and died; it has been read for centuries, and correctly,
as an expression of a mystic's understanding of the passionate love of Christ
for each person and for his Church. So completely did the context transpose
the poem that no one ever adverted to its original matrix.[123]

This is an example of the power of a symbol to effect an analogy between
human love and divine love; it opens our eyes to a fuller understanding of
the symbolic aspect of the relation between man and woman. In the same
way, the Song of Songs takes love poems or songs and, by a deft use of
language and structuring, opens up their deep power to express who God is
and how he loves us. Sexual love is a great and precious reality in its own
right, but it has, in God's eternal plan, the further capacity to intimate to us
something of God himself. Thus the Song of Songs uses human sexual love
and marriage to embody God's restorative purpose for his people, and it is
thus that the Song has always been understood in the scriptural tradition of
interpretation.[124]

The post-exilic tradition's opposition to divorce is highlighted in the Book
of Malachi. This work was probably composed in the fifth century B.C.,
perhaps before the reforms of Ezra and Nehemiah. Its message was one of
assurance to the returned exiles that, despite the sufferings they endured,
Yhwh still loved them, and required of them a return of honor, obedience
to the covenant, and trust in his plan.[125] The most difficult passage in the
book, Malachi 2:10–16, is precisely the one which addresses the question
of divorce. It merits close study not only because it witnesses to a stream

of thought in Israel after the exile, but also because its line of thought, deriving from the teaching of chapters 1 and 2 of Genesis, is a forerunner of the argument given by Jesus on the issue of divorce.

Malachi 2:10–16 proceeds in the form of a dispute in which Malachi, representing Yhwh, accuses the people of their infidelity and answers their objections. Verse 10 begins by contrasting the faithlessness of the Israelites with the fidelity of God, the Creator, who is the "one father of us all." The result of this conduct is that the people are "profaning the covenant of our fathers." Then, after indicting Judah in general and those who marry foreign wives in particular, Malachi goes on to state that "Yhwh will not turn toward the offering anymore or receive it with favor from your hand" (Mal. 2:11–13). To the people's imagined challenge, "Why?" Malachi answers:

> Because Yhwh has witnessed between you and the wife of your youth with whom you have been faithless. Yet she is your companion and the wife of your covenant. Did he not make one being with flesh and spirit to it? And what does this One seek? Godly offspring. So guard yourself in your spirit, and do not be faithless to the wife of your youth. For I hate divorce, says Yhwh, the God of Israel, and covering one's garment with violence, says Yhwh Sabaoth. So guard yourself in your spirit and do not be faithless. (Mal. 2:14–16)

The key concepts here are represented by the terms: "wife of your youth," "faithless," "covenant," "one being with flesh and spirit,"[126] "Godly offspring," and "hate divorce." The phrase "wife of your youth" refers to the woman a man marries as his original wife (Prov. 5:18). The crime, then, consists in divorcing this wife and taking another. This is called "faithlessness," a term which evokes the notion of covenant, and which is applied here explicitly to marriage.[127] The most significant phrase, of course, is "I hate divorce," where divorce is metaphorically likened to immersing oneself in violence. The basic argument seems to be drawn from Genesis 2:7, which the author of Malachi alludes to with the phrase "one being with flesh and spirit." This argument is then extended by the allusion to Genesis 2:24, which states that this *adam,* so made by God, is "one flesh" with his wife. Thus, God made "one being" in marriage, consisting of two human beings of flesh and spirit. His purpose is that there be "godly offspring" — lawful children of a lawful marriage — to perpetuate the family through generations and thus continue God's plan in history.[128]

The text of Malachi coalesces all those presuppositions of Israelite sapiential, prophetic, and legal thinking which looked upon marriage as a monogamous union. No other text, with the possible exception of Leviticus 18:18, is so clearly opposed to divorce. Most texts, even those which speak of divorce, treat it as a fact of life but not as a stipulation of the covenant law which governed Israel.[129] We will proceed now to a discussion of marriage in the intertestamental period.

Some Aspects of Marriage in the Intertestamental Literature

The "intertestamental" period, for our purposes, extends from the two centuries before the Christian era through the first century A.D. For this period we will consider those works which are not in the canonical collection of the Scriptures (including the Septuagint). Two factors render study of this literature difficult. First is the problem of dating the material. This is particularly the case with the rabbinic tradition as it is now found in the Mishnah and the Talmud, whose multiple layers of redaction and conflicting attributions of sayings to different rabbis make it extremely difficult to be certain whether an opinion or a view expressed was actually known during the intertestamental period.[130] Something similar can be said of the commentaries on Scripture, or Midrashim, and the translations of the Scriptures into Aramaic knows as Targums.[131] The second difficulty has to do with the fact that the literature yields strongly contrasting views regarding marriage, the position of women, and the extent of divorce. Despite these difficulties, it is extremely important that we understand the environment in which the Gospel was first preached by Jesus and then continued by the authors of the New Testament.

An account that studies only the theoretical and legal thinking about marriage tends to ignore its simple human component: how was marriage actually lived out day by day in Palestine and the Diaspora? What literature can witness to the relation between husband and wife and parents and children, thus corresponding to the excerpts we have seen from the wisdom tradition concerning friendship, care for children, and the like? Information on these questions can be gleaned from anecdotes told in the Talmud and other literature, as well as from some of the discoveries about daily life uncovered by archeology.[132]

The Qumran Covenanters and Marriage

Earlier, we considered how the Priestly redactor used the term *adam* to express the unity of man and woman that he saw set forth in the Yahwistic text. In the period immediately preceding the Christian era and continuing well into the final stages of the redaction of the Talmuds (fifth/eighth centuries), these same texts were often used to illustrate the anthropological basis for marriage, particularly for monogamy both simultaneous (only one wife) and successive (no divorce). We will see this verified in one writing from Qumran and then other rabbinic speculation.

The Damascus Document, composed at least as early as 100 B.C., expressed the view of the Qumran group that Israel as a whole was living in infidelity to God.[133] In column 4 the text speaks of the "three nets of Belial by which they are being captured." The first of these is sexual "irregularity" (*zenut*), which is described in this way:

> They are caught twice in *zenut:* [first] by taking [marrying] two women in their lifetime even though the principle of creation is "Male and female he created them"; and those that went into the ark "two by two they went into the ark" (Gen. 7:9); and about the prince it is written, "let him not multiply wives for himself" (Deut. 17:17).[134]

Bigamy and divorce, which are called *zenut,* are thus both included in the term *zenut,* and the argument against them is based on four texts. There is first an allusion to Leviticus 18:18: "And a woman [in addition] to her sister you shall not take as a rival to her [=another wife in addition to the first], to uncover her nakedness in her [the first wife's] lifetime." Even in its original context, this could be seen as a prohibition against bigamy, understanding the term "sister" to refer to any fellow Israelite woman.

The second text is Genesis 1:27, repeated in 5:2. Here a formulaic use of the text "male and female he created them," refers to that whole line of thought described above which includes the texts of chapter 2 of Genesis regarding the rib from Adam, the covenant use of "flesh of my flesh," etc., and the expression "one flesh": the union of man and woman realizes the unity of male and female ordained by God at the beginning. The third argument, that from the Genesis description of the animals in Noah's ark, seems to be confirmatory, though later rabbis were careful to point out that the ideal of "one flesh" can only be realized between humans. The final text invoked a prescription in the code for the king (Deut. 17:14–20) about not multiplying wives for himself. It is extended to apply to commoners as well, according to a principle enunciated in another passage in the Damascus Document and frequently elsewhere.[135]

The second way the Israelites practice sexual irregularity or *zenut* is by disobeying the laws against incest in Leviticus 18:13 through marrying their nieces (Damascus Document 5,8–9). Another Qumran text, also in the Temple Scroll (11 Q19 57, 17–19), also alludes to Leviticus 18:18 and Deuteronomy 17:17 in a passage prescribing conduct for the king that clearly prohibits both bigamy and divorce:

> And he shall not take a wife from all the daughters of the nations, but from his father's house he shall take unto himself a wife, from the family of his father. And he shall not take upon (in addition to) her another wife, for she alone shall be with him all the days of her life. But should she die, he may take unto himself another (wife) from the house of his father, from his family.[136]

The passages from the Damascus Document and the Temple Scroll establish the fact that, at Qumran at least, there was a strong opposition to divorce as well as hesitancy at least regarding marriage after the death of a spouse.[137] This current of thought was thus neither isolated nor unknown in first-century Palestine.

Rabbinic Speculation on Marriage

A question that must be addressed here is what role the "natural law" played in the thinking of the Rabbis. They recognized, of course, that the history of Israel does not begin until chapter 12 of the Book of Genesis, and they thus considered that the first eleven chapters contained principles meant to govern all of the human race. They referred to the commandments given to Adam or to Noah and in this way elaborated an understanding of a natural moral law.[138] This understanding is usually summed up in seven precepts.

> The children of Noah were enjoined concerning seven things: Idolatry, incest, murder, cursing the Divine Name, civil law (providing laws to protect the other six), and a limb torn from a living animal (Midrash Genesis Rabbah 34, 8; Soncino edition, 272).[139]

Other authorities set these out in different ways, but the overall content is nearly the same. The precept that touches most closely on concepts in the New Testament is the ban on incest. The Rabbis debated what degree of consanguinity applied to the children of Noah, but they agreed that if a man and his wife were related within certain degrees he must divorce her if he becomes a Jew. Most of the rabbinic speculations were occasioned by their understanding of Genesis 2:24: "For this reason a man shall leave his father and mother and cleave to his wife."

> It was taught: If a man became a [Jewish] proselyte, and he was [previously] married to his paternal sister, he must, in Rabbi Meir's opinion, divorce her. (Midrash Genesis Rabbah 18, 5; Soncino edition, 143)

There was much discussion as to whether or not the Gentiles were allowed to divorce, since there is no mention of this in the first eleven chapters of Genesis. It was often concluded that they were not. Thus, Rabbi Hanina ben Papa (fourth century) is credited with the argument from Malachi:

> Throughout the Book of Malachi the phrase "The Lord of Hosts" is used, whereas here [in reference to divorce] we have "The God of Israel" (Mal. 2:16). It is as though one might say, his name has no bearing on divorce except in the case of Israel alone (Midrash Genesis Rabbah 18, 5; Soncino edition, 144).

While these texts are quite late, they do indicate a certain orientation of thought that has bearing on the practice of matrimony among Jewish Christians and, by extension, among Gentiles who, as we will see, were obliged by the "Council of Jerusalem" to abide by the Noahide laws concerning "meat sacrificed to idols, blood, meats of strangled animals, and irregular sexual unions (*porneia*)" (Acts 15:29; compare 15:20).

The Role of Women in Judaism and the Question of Divorce

The question of women's status in first-century Judaism is intensely debated at present. The older view was that women were considered inferior, had few rights, and could be married and divorced by men almost at will. The work of Ben Witherington III contains an impressive list of the laws governing the legal status of women, drawn mostly from the Talmuds.[140] He concludes:

> It is fair to say that a low view of women was common, perhaps even predominant before, during and after Jesus' era. Since many of the positive statements about women to which we have referred come from later Tannaitic and Amoraic times [different generations of Rabbis], it is conceivable that a woman's lot in Judaism improved in some ways after the destruction of the Temple made impossible full observance of various precepts of the Law.... There was no monolithic entity, rabbinic Judaism, in Tannaitic times [first century A.D.] and ... various opinions were held about women and their roles, though it appears that by the first century of the Christian era a negative assessment was predominant among the rabbis.[141]

In contrast to this moderate assessment of the literature is the evidence of archeology, which indicates that many wealthy Jewesses were considered to be benefactors of synagogues and that, at times, titles were applied to them that were generally reserved for male synagogue officials.[142] It may be that these titles were honorific, in recognition of the women's generosity. The fact remains, however, that these inscriptions indicate the existence of a class of wealthy women, perhaps some widowed, who had their property at their own disposal.

In addition, there are other indications that suggest the legal enactments of the Rabbis may have been considered more academic than relevant to actual life situations. Certainly there are many indications that the Rabbis themselves promoted great respect for women and wives, and that affection and trust were the attitudes they most enjoined in the marital relationship.

In regard to marriage and divorce, we have the famous text describing the debate between the two great masters of rabbinic Judaism, Hillel and Shammai, coupled with a remark of Rabbi Akiba. They are all interpreting

Deuteronomy 24:1, a text which, we have seen, does not legislate for divorce but only provides guidelines regarding remarriage of a divorced wife.

> The School of Shammai says: A man may not divorce his wife unless he has found unchastity [*debar erwah*, literally, "something indecent"] in her, for it is written: 'Because he has found something indecent in her [stressing indecent].' And the School of Hillel says: [He may divorce her] even if she spoiled a dish for him, for it is written: 'Because he has found something indecent in her [stressing something].' Rabbi Akiba says: Even if he found another fairer than she, for it is written, 'And it shall be that if she find no favor in his eyes' (Mishnah, Gittin 9, 5).[143]

Again, it is difficult to know if we are dealing here with an academic debate. There are other texts which speak of the dishonor that a man brings on his family through divorce (Mishnah Nedarim 9, 9); or which cite Rabbis who invoke Malachi 2:16, to the effect that God hates divorce, and who maintain that the altar sheds tears over one who divorces his first wife (Babylonian Talmud, Gittin 90b). Then too, while divorce was a legal act belonging to the man, provided he could pay his wife her *ketubah*,[144] a woman was able to precipitate a divorce by returning home or by proving that her husband did not consummate the marriage, was impotent, had leprosy, or worked in an unpleasant occupation (Mishnah Nedarim 11, 12; Ketuboth 5, 5; 7, 2–5; 9–10).[145]

We may conclude this final section of our consideration of marriage in the Old Testament by simply stating that the period into which Jesus was born was characterized by great variety in culture and religious practice. Most marriages were monogamous, fidelity and affection were esteemed, and children were cared for. Nevertheless, the position of women was generally inferior to that of men, and the availability of divorce, at least in some quarters, made life uncertain for them. At the same time, groups connected with the Qumran covenanters engaged in a relativizing of marriage in the light of their eschatological demands.[146] These groups, relying upon Genesis 1–3 and texts such as Malachi 2:14–16, nevertheless insisted that divorce was not permitted by God. These same two positions will be among those which, as we will see, characterize Jesus.

Notes

1. The most complete discussion of this dimension of Genesis is found in Ephraim A. Speiser, *Genesis,* Anchor Bible 1 (New York, 1962) in his commentary on the relevant passages. For a discussion of the tablets themselves, see Martha A. Morrison, "Nuzi," *Anchor Dictionary of the Bible,* ed. David Noel Freedman (New York, 1992), 1156–62 (hereafter *ADB*).

2. Thus, Jacob married two sisters (Gen. 29:21–30), contrary to the injunction in Lev. 18:18; Judah and Simeon married Canaanites, and Joseph an Egyptian, despite the strong opposition to this in later laws such as Exod. 34:16 and Deut. 7:3. For a more detailed discussion of this discrepancy between the recorded actions of the patriarchs and the law in force at the time of the redaction of these stories, see Gordon Wenham, *Genesis 16–50*, ed. John D. W. Watts, Word Biblical Commentary 2 (Dallas, 1994), xxv.

3. John Bright, *A History of Israel* (Philadelphia, 1981), 77–103.

4. See Pietro Dacquino, *Storia del matrimonio cristiano alla luce della Bibbia: Inseparabilità e monogamia* (Torino, 1988), 1:9–13; Speiser, *Genesis*, 174–85.

5. In the Code of Hammurabi 159–61, it is prescribed that if the prospective groom does not actually marry the woman, her father keeps the betrothal gift and the marriage price, whereas if the bride's father refuses to give her in marriage, he must pay back double "the full amount that was brought to him." James Pritchard, ed., *Ancient Near Eastern Texts Relating to the Old Testament*, 3d ed. (Princeton, N.J., 1969), 173 (hereafter *ANET*).

6. Wenham, *Genesis 16–50*, 149–50, is correct is describing the gifts in this way (though he uses the term "bride-money"). The most ample treatment of the *mohar* and the *shilluhim* (spousal gift and dowry) is that of Angelo Tosato, *Il matrimonio israelitico*, Analecta Biblica 100 (Rome, 1982), 95–96, 100–106. See also Roland de Vaux, *Ancient Israel* (New York, 1965), 1:26–29. Regarding the dowry, Johs. Pedersen says: "From her family the wife generally received a present to serve as a tie between her and her father's house. It gives her a support and a certain independence in regard to her husband." Johs. Pedersen, *Israel: Its Life and Culture I–II* (London and Copenhagen, 1926/1959), 69.

7. In this case, of course, only the family of the bride is present. The wording of the blessing most probably reflects the era in which the tradition was consigned to writing. For another example of a blessing, see Ruth 4:11.

8. Dacquino, *Storia*, vol. 1, chap. 4, considers the two moments of the matrimony (*sponsali e nozze*). For a discussion of the significance of the verb "take" (*lqh*) in describing matrimony, see Tosato, *Il matrimonio israelitico*, 73–76.

9. For a masterful presentation of the mentality governing the whole marriage relationship, see Pedersen, *Israel I–II*, 46–81.

10. Hammurabi 144–46, *ANET*, 172. For the Nuzi material, see Speiser, *Genesis*, 120. Genesis 25:1 mentions that Abraham took Keturah to wife after the death of Sarah. This would preserve his "monogamous" state in that he had only one *wife*. It may be to accent that fact that in 1 Chron. 1:32 Keturah is called his "concubine" (*pilegesh*).

11. It is probably not a coincidence that Abraham is described as "listening to the voice of his wife" (Gen. 16:2), an act attributed in identical terms to Adam (Gen. 3:17). See Wenham, *Genesis 16–50*, 7–8.

12. In the interest of simplification, the usual diacritical marks are omitted in transliterating Hebrew and Greek words in this and the following chapter.

13. In the ensuing verses in Judg. 1:14–16, Caleb's daughter asks for and obtains additional "blessing," that is, two pools of water adjacent to the land in the Negeb he had already given to her as a dowry.

14. See the helpful remarks by Wenham in *Genesis 16–50*, 243–50.

15. This section is indebted to the treatment of Israelite law and justice to be found in de Vaux, *Ancient Israel*, vol. 1, *Social Institutions*, 143–63.

16. For an instance of a woman who judged Israel, see the description of Deborah in Judges 4:4–5. Regarding the shift from informally recognized judges to profes-

sional magistrates (see Deut. 16:18; 2 Chron. 19:5), one may consult the remarks in the article by Anthony Phillips, "Another Look at Adultery," *Journal for the Study of the Old Testament* 20 (1981): 3–25.

17. *Vetus Testamentum* 23 (1973): 349–61.

18. See the brief but excellent discussion in John I. Durham, *Exodus,* ed. John D. W. Watts, Word Biblical Commentary 3 (Waco, Tex., 1987), 280–81.

19. de Vaux, *Ancient Israel,* 1:144.

20. This division of the material in the Book of Leviticus into two blocks (17– 26 and the rest) is sufficient for our purposes. For a more nuanced presentation, see John E. Hartley, *Leviticus,* ed. John D. W. Watts, Word Biblical Commentary 4 (Dallas, 1992), 247–60.

21. For a study of this single mention of the levirate in the legal texts of Israel, see Raymond Westbrooke, *Property and the Family in Biblical Law,* Journal for the Study of the Old Testament Supplemental Series 113, ed. David J. A. Clines and Philip R. Davies (Sheffield, 1991).

22. Most often in numerical sayings, the enumeration proceeds to a climax with the last. We can catch a glimpse into what home life was for the Israelite family by considering the relation between Elkanah and Hannah (1 Sam. 1:4–8, 22–23), between the woman of Shunem and her husband (2 Kings 4:8–24), and between the parents of Tobiah and those of Sarah in the Book of Tobit.

23. Walther Eichrodt, *Theology of the Old Testament,* ed. G. Ernest Wright, John Bright, James Barr, and Peter Ackroyd, trans. J. A. Baker, Old Testament Library (London, 1961), 2:339.

24. This question, which would require looking closely at the "hard texts," has been competently treated by Maurice Gilbert in "Ben Sira et la femme," *Revue Théologique de Louvain* 7 (1976): 426–42.

25. See Patrick W. Skehan and Alexander A. Di Lella, *The Wisdom of Ben Sira,* Anchor Bible 39 (New York, 1987), 324–25 (on Sir. 23:18).

26. For a complete treatment of how children were regarded in Israel, see de Vaux, *Ancient Israel,* vol. 1, chap. 4.

27. Other examples are Prov. 6:20; 23:22; 31:26; Sir. 3:1–16. For this portion of my study I am indebted to John W. Miller, *Biblical Faith and Fathering: Why We Call God Father* (New York, 1989), esp. chap. 6, "New Modes of Human Fathering."

28. An impressive list of the covenant blessings and curses found in the Pentateuch (esp. the Book of Deuteronomy) that figure in the prophetic preaching is presented by Douglas Stuart, *Hosea-Jonah,* ed. John D. W. Watts, Word Biblical Commentary 31 (Waco, Tex., 1987), xxxiii–xliii.

29. Though the discussion here will be restricted to the biblical texts, it is important to note that similar terminology can be found in the extra-biblical milieu of the first millennium. See D. R. Hillers, *Treaty-Curses and the Old Testament Prophets,* Biblica et Orientalia 16 (Rome, 1964), esp. 58–60.

30. S. Erlandsson, *"znh,"* *Theological Dictionary of the Old Testament,* ed. G. Johannes Botterweck and Helmer Ringgren, trans. David Green (Grand Rapids, Mich., 1980), 4:99–104, citation at p. 100 (hereafter *TDOT*).

31. Stuart, *Hosea-Jonah,* 16.

32. Hans Walter Wolff, *Hosea: A Commentary on the Book of the Prophet Hosea,* trans. Gary Stansell (Philadelphia, 1974), 10–11. See Andre Jolles, *Einfache Formen* (Tübingen, 1958), 200–217.

33. See Wolff, *Hosea,* 12–15. This same double allusion to covenant infidelity in and through the practice of Canaanite sexual rituals can be seen, for instance, in the manner in which the priests are said to possess a "spirit of whoredom" (Hos. 4:12).

34. For a development of this latter point, see William L. Moran, "The Ancient Near Eastern Background of the Love of God in Deuteronomy," *Catholic Biblical Quarterly* 25 (1963): 77–87.

35. For a more developed treatment of the marriage of Hosea and its relevance for a theology of marriage see Francis Martin, "Israel as the Bride of Yhwh," *Anthropotes* 9 (2000): forthcoming.

36. For a good account of this period, see Bright, *A History of Israel*, chaps. 9 and 10.

37. In the family the man is the bourgeois; the woman represents the proletariat. Friedrich Engels, *The Origin of the Family, Private Property, and the State, in Light of the Researches of Lewis H. Morgan* (New York, 1972), chap. 2, "The Family," esp. 128–46, "The Monogamous Family."

38. Carol Myers rightly faults Rosemary Radford Ruether's conception of "slavery" within the Hebrew family in "Feminist Interpretation: A Method of Correlation," *Feminist Interpretation of the Bible*, ed. Letty M. Russell (Philadelphia, 1985), 119. See Carol Myers, "Women and the Domestic Economy of Early Israel," in *Women's Earliest Records from Ancient Egypt and Western Asia*, ed. Barbara S. Lesko, Brown Judaic Studies 166 (Atlanta, 1989), 265–81; citation at 266, n. 4.

39. Tosato, *Il matrimonio israelitico*, chaps. 3 and 4.

40. Ibid., 134–35. Tosato correctly interprets Exodus 21:7–11 as the selling of a daughter as a *servant*, not a slave. This explains the detailed account of her rights. See the longer discussion which follows later in this study.

41. For a discussion of performative and self-involving language, see J. L. Austen, ed., *How to Do Things with Words* (Oxford, 1962).

42. de Vaux, *Ancient Israel*, 1:168–69, mentions the transaction between Abraham and Ephron in Genesis 23 and speaks of the role of the sandal and the foot in the transfer of land.

43. For a discussion of these terms, see Tosato, *Il matrimonio israelitico*, chap. 5.

44. Though it might be possible to find these four dimensions in the marriage of Abigail to David (1 Sam. 25:40–42), for instance, they are not as clearly marked because this is a marriage between two adults who are free to dispose of themselves as they wish. It is not clear whether a poor widow would have the same mobility.

45. See also 2 Sam. 14:7; Jer. 16:1–4; and Num. 16:31–33.

46. For a discussion of this point, see Miller, *Biblical Faith and Fathering*, chaps. 1 and 2. The notion just described was not the only one in antiquity. For a discussion of how Aristotle and Thomas Aquinas viewed woman in relation to man vis-à-vis reproduction, see Michael Nolan, *Defective Tales: The Story of Three Myths* (Dublin, n.d.).

47. Qoh. 11:5; 2 Macc. 7:22.

48. Even in antiquity, the predominant view that the woman contributed nothing actively to conception was challenged. See Emma Thérèse Healy, *Woman according to Saint Bonaventure* (Erie, Pa., 1956); Gillian Clark, *Women in Late Antiquity: Pagan and Christian Life-Styles* (Oxford, 1993), 70–73.

49. The *zonah* is any unmarried woman who has sexual relations with a man. In a culture like Israel, she is usually a prostitute. The outraged brothers of Dinah declare that Shechem had treated their sister "like a *zonah*" by raping her (Gen. 34:31).

50. Three of these duties are specifically prescribed as being incumbent upon a man who has elevated a Hebrew slave to be his wife and then marries another woman: "If he does not grant her [the ex-slave] these three things [food, clothing, conjugal rights], she shall be given her freedom absolutely, without cost to her"

(Exod. 21:10; compare Isa. 4:1). The notion of "respect" is not treated explicitly in our legal documents, but it is a theme in the codes of other Near Eastern cultures whose laws closely resemble those of Israel. See Tosato, *Il matrimonio israelitico*, 194–95. Regarding the rights of the woman's children, see the case legislated for in Deut. 21:15–17 regarding the first born son, even if he happens to be the son of the woman who is "disliked" (literally, "hated").

51. See M. J. Mulder, *"baal," TDOT*, trans. John T. Willis (Grand Rapids, Mich., 1977), 2:181–200.

52. Ibid., 182. See Judg. 9:2, 3, 6; 20:5. This expressions seems to evoke the sense of the (free?) sharers in the reality of Shechem, Gibeah, etc.

53. This latter action would be an offense against the family honor and right to legitimate heirs. The former action, if we may argue from parallel laws and customs, was permitted when the whole family sold itself into servitude to requite a debt. For a discussion of this matter, see Tosato, *Il matrimonio israelitico*, 140–42.

54. William L. Moran, "The Conclusion of the Decalogue (Exod. 20, 17=Deut. 5, 21)," *Catholic Biblical Quarterly* 29 (1967): 543–54; citation at 552.

55. For a treatment of this issue, see Gordon Paul Hugenberger, *Marriage as a Covenant: : A Study of Biblical Law and Ethics Governing Marriage, Developed from the Perspective of Malachi* (New York, 1994), 313–37.

56. For a study of one block of these laws in Leviticus 18:6–18, see Susan Rattray, "Marriage Rules, Kinship Terms and Family Structure in the Bible," *Society for Biblical Literature Seminar Papers* 26, ed. K. H. Richards (Atlanta, 1987), 537–43.

57. In Job 31:1, Job, taking an oath of innocence, mentions a covenant with his eyes "not to linger on any virgin." Compare Sirach 9:5; 36:21–27; Proverbs 5:15–23.

58. In regard to adultery being a sin against God, note such texts as Genesis 20:6 in which God tells Abimelech that in preventing him from having relations with Sarah, "I kept you from sinning against me." David's sin with Bathsheba and the murder of her husband is characterized as being "evil in the eyes of Yhwh," while David himself acknowledges, "I have sinned against Yhwh" (2 Sam. 11:27; 12:13). The proscription of adultery in the covenant text itself makes it clear that adultery is considered an offense against the covenant.

59. For an extensive discussion of this text, see Hugenberger, *Marriage as a Covenant*, 282–88.

60. Both of these texts appear to be comprised of previously existing material which was redacted and expanded at the time of insertion into their present context. See Anthony Phillips, "Another Look at Adultery," 6.

61. This point is developed by Anthony Phillips, *Ancient Israel's Criminal Law: A New Approach to the Decalogue* (Oxford and New York, 1970), 28ff. For a treatment of how the Deuteronomic code evinces a developed sense of individual dignity, see Louis Stulman, "Sex and Familial Crimes in the D Code: A Witness to Mores in Transition," *Journal for the Study of the Old Testament* 53 (1992): 47–63.

62. For a brief treatment of the laws of incest, see de Vaux, *Ancient Israel*, 1:31–32; Rattray, "Marriage Rules," 537–44.

63. Tosato, *Il matrimonio israelitico*, 147, n. 40, maintains against the opinion of several others that the term "widow" means simply, and without qualification, a woman whose husband has died.

64. "Widows who had no grown sons were entrusted with the property of their deceased husbands. If a widow had a young son, as soon as he was of age he took over his father's property and the responsibility of caring for his mother." Harry A. Hoffner, *"almanah," TDOT*, 1:287–92; citation at 290.

65. For a brief treatment of the ideal of kingship in Israel, see Marvin E. Tate, *Psalms 51–100*, Word Biblical Commentary 20 (Dallas, 1990), 219–26 (on Ps. 72).

66. For examples of legal texts and prophetic indictments regarding the rights of these groups, see Exod. 21:21–23; Isa. 1:17, 23; 10:1; Jer. 7:6; Zech. 7:9; Ps. 68:6, 94:6, and 146:9; Prov. 15:25. For examples of legal texts that provide for these three classes, and the poor in general, see Deut. 24:21–23; Exod. 23:10–11; Lev. 19:9–10.

67. An exception seems to be made in the case of the wives of a king. Since they were considered to be part of the network of political alliances of the king, they were to remain in the palace as wives or concubines of the king's successor, with the mother of the successor occupying a particular place of honor. See Tosato, *Il matrimonio israelitico*, 150–52.

68. For a more complete discussion of levirate marriage, see Tosato, *Il matrimonio israelitico*, 147–59; Hugenberger, *Marriage as a Covenant*, 114–15, et passim; Westbrooke, *Property and the Family in Biblical Law*, chap. 4.

69. It must be noted that, unlike polygyny and polygamy, the right to divorce was not exclusive to the male. In some cases the wife as well had the right to sever the marital relationship

70. Hugenberger, *Marriage as a Covenant*, 110. Hugenberger uses the term "polygyny" in a broader sense to include what I am calling "polygamy."

71. This does not exclude the possibility that rulers also provided themselves with large harems in order to demonstrate their wealth and power.

72. Tosato, *Il matrimonio israelitico*, 185–91.

73. See J. P. Brown, "Literary Contexts of the Common Hebrew-Greek Vocabulary," *Journal of Semitic Studies* 13 (1968): 163–91, esp. 166–69; and Chaim Rabin, "The Origin of the Hebrew Word *Pileges*," *Journal of Jewish Studies* 25 (1974): 353–64. See also the discussion regarding the fluidity of the term in Hugenberger, *Marriage as a Covenant*, 108, n. 96.

74. Tosato, *Il matrimonio israelitico*, devotes the third chapter of his book to this situation. It is interesting to observe that the Code of Hammurabi, 170–71, *ANET*, 173, makes provision for the children of the slave-wife who were adopted by their father and thus have an equal share in the estate.

75. See for instance Z. W. Falk, *Hebrew Law in Biblical Times: An Introduction* (Jerusalem, 1964), 154. For another opinion regarding divorce, see A. Kornfeld, "Mariage, I. Dans l'Ancien Testament," in *Dictionnaire de la Bible Supplement* (Paris, 1957), 905–26.

76. See Tosato, *Il matrimonio israelitico*, 198–204.

77. For a complete treatment of the topic of divorce, see Tosato, *Il matrimonio israelitico*, 192–211. See also the Code of Hammurabi, 141–43, *ANET*, 172.

78. Code of Hammurabi, 159, *ANET*, 173. Among the goods brought to the father would be the *biblum* (gift) and the *terhatum* (specifically marriage gift, what in Hebrew is called the *mohar*).

79. The Elephantine papyri add to the sum just mentioned the rather insignificant amount of seven and a half shekels. A. E. Cowley, ed., *Aramaic Papyri of the Fifth Century B.C.* (Oxford, 1923), 15. This rather lax custom, perhaps influenced by the divorce practices in Egypt, contrasts with the nearly contemporaneous prohibition of divorce in Malachi 2:10–16.

80. As will be pointed out later, the purpose of this law is to prevent the wife from returning to her first husband after the death of her second husband or after being divorced. While this law provided for the consequences resulting from the event of divorce, it did not sanction or approve of divorce itself.

81. Middle Assyrian Laws, Tablet A, 55, *ANET,* 185.

82. Code of Hammurabi, 148–49, *ANET,* 173.

83. For the first instance, see the Code of Hammurabi, *ANET,* 172; for the second and third, see Tosato, *Il matrimonio israelitico,* 204.

84. A marriage contract from Ugarit describes the penalty attaching to a certain Buriyanu if he does not consummate his marriage to Eliyawe in three days. *ANET,* 546. See also the Code of Hammurabi, 159, *ANET,* 173.

85. For examples of these cases, see the Code of Hammurabi, 133–36, *ANET,* 171; Middle Assyrian Laws, Tablet A, 36, *ANET,* 183.

86. Examples of this lack of respect would be: "If a woman so hated her husband that she has declared, 'You may not have me,' her record shall be investigated at her city council, and if she was careful [=not adulterous] and was not at fault, even though her husband has been going out and disparaging her greatly, that woman, without incurring any blame at all, may take her dowry and go off to her father's house" (Code of Hammurabi, 142, *ANET,* 172). The term "hate" in this text may indicate a desire for divorce. The divorce price, to be paid by either husband or wife, depending upon who initiates the proceedings, is described by the Elephantine papyri as "hate money." For a discussion of the vocabulary of divorce, see Reuven Yaron, "On Divorce in Old Testament Times," *Revue International des Droits de L'Antiquité,* Ser. 3, 4 (1957): 117–28. "If that woman [a sick woman whose husband has taken another wife] has refused to live in her husband's house, he shall make good her dowry to her which she brought from her father's house and then she may leave" (Code of Hammurabi, 149, *ANET,* 172).

87. Code of Hammurabi, 160, *ANET,* 173. The Code of Hammurabi has often been invoked here because it sums up the legislation of the previous millennium. Bright, *A History of Israel,* 59.

88. For a discussion of these points, see Hugenberger, *Marriage as a Covenant,* chap. 8.

89. Some of this material has appeared in another form in my article "Male and Female He Created Them: A Summary of the Teaching of Genesis Chapter One," *Communio* 20 (1993): 240–65. It is used here with the kind permission of the editor.

90. For a more complete analysis of the teaching on *adam* in the first chapter of Genesis see Francis Martin, "The New Feminism: A New Humanism?" forthcoming in *Josephinum* (2000).

91. Gerhard von Rad, *Old Testament Theology,* trans. D. M. G. Stalker, vol. 1, *The Theology of Israel's Historical Traditions* (New York, 1962), 141.

92. For a good appreciation of the wisdom tradition in Israel one may consult Gerhard von Rad, *Wisdom in Israel,* trans. James D. Martin (London, 1972); Roland Murphy, "Introduction to Wisdom Literature," in *The New Jerome Biblical Commentary,* ed. Raymond E. Brown, Joseph A. Fitzmyer, Roland E. Murphy (Englewood Cliffs, N.J., 1990), 447–52. Neither of these scholars, however, considers the author of Genesis 2–3 in their discussion of wisdom literature.

93. See Fritz Maass, *"adam,"* TDOT, 1:75–87, and Claus Westermann, *Genesis 1–11: A Commentary,* trans. John J. Scullion (Minneapolis, 1984), 201–3, and the literature given there. Also, F. Vattioni, "La sapienza e la formazione del corpo humano (Gn 1:26)," *Augustinianum* 6 (1966): 317–23.

94. The wisdom overtones of this and the other many plays on words have been studied by Jean De Fraine, "Jeux des mots dans le recit de la chute," *Melanges bibliques redigés en honneur d'André Robert,* Travaux de L'Institut Catholique de Paris 4 (Tournai, 1957), 47–59.

95. There are places in the Book of Job that reflect the same notion of being formed from earth and possessing the spirit/breath of God. Thus Elihu says to Job: "For the spirit [*ruah*] of God has made me, the breath of the Almighty [*nismat Shadday*] gives me life. . . . Behold I am like yourself with respect to God, I, too, have been pinched from clay" (Job 33:4, 6; see also 34:14–15). In the same vein, the Book of Wisdom describes the miserable lot of the potter who makes clay gods: "His heart is ashes, his hope meaner than dirt, and his life more ignoble than clay, because he knew not the one who fashioned him and infused him with an active soul and breathed into him a vital spirit" (Wisd. 15:10–11). The translation is taken from David Winston, *The Wisdom of Solomon,* Anchor Bible 43 (New York, 1979), 285.

96. It is difficult in a Western language to mediate the subtlety of the balance between "you may eat" and "you must die." Both are constructed with a future verb and an absolute infinitive. The first implies permission, the second obligation. See Paul Joüon, *Grammaire de l'Hébreux Biblique,* 2d ed. (Rome, 1947), §113, l.m.

97. See J. Van der Ploeg, "Studies in Hebrew Law," *Catholic Biblical Quarterly* 12 (1950): 248–59, 416–27; 13 (1951): 28–43, 164–71, 296–307.

98. See Wenham, *Genesis,* 67, and the literature given there.

99. The root *akal* is found more than twenty times in these two chapters: seven times in the dialogue between Eve and the serpent, and seven times in the sentencing by God.

100. Hans Walter Wolff, *Anthropology of the Old Testament,* trans. Margaret Kohl (Philadelphia, 1974), 106–7, 111. Consult the following texts: Ps. 115:17, 88:10–12; Isa. 38:18ff; Job 7:21.

101. It is impossible to decide whether these words were found in just this way before the integration of chapter 1 with what follows. In any event, the redactor could not have missed the force of the expression in its present context.

102. Nineteen of the twenty-one instances of the noun refer to divine help. See Jena-Louis Ska, " 'Je vais lui faire un allié qui soit son homologue' (Gn 2, 18): A propos du terme 'ezer-aide,' " *Biblica* 65 (1984): 233–38. Marie de Merode, " 'Une aide qui lui corresponde': L'exégèse de Gen 2, 18–24 dans les récits de l'Ancien Testament, du judaïsme et du Nouveau Testament," *Revue Théologique de Louvain* 8 (1977): 329–52.

103. There is an interesting comment on this notion in Eccles. 4:7–12, which reads in part: "Woe to the solitary man! For, if he should fall, he has no one to lift him up." There are as well two texts in Sirach that reflect upon the statement in Gen. 2:18. The best reconstructed text of Sir. 36:29 would read literally: "He who acquires a wife, [makes] the best of all acquisitions; [she is] a helper like his bone [or 'a helper and a fortified city'], a column of support." In Sir. 13:15–16 we read (again literally): "All flesh loves its own kind, and every *adam* what is like him; all flesh [belongs] next to its own kind, and *adam* seeks fellowship with his own kind."

104. Westermann, *Genesis,* 230, quotes James B. Pritchard to the effect that "in Sumerian there is established through a play on words, a definite connection between the rib and 'the lady who makes live.' "

105. Rabbi Abin said: "Happy the citizen for whom the king is the 'best man' [or bridegroom's friend]." *Genesis Rabbah,* 18, 4.

106. There are acknowledged weaknesses to this term. I am not sure, however, that these weaknesses should persuade us to do away with the best word we have to express in technical language what this inspired poem says better in its way.

107. Maurice Gilbert, " 'Une seule chair' (Gen 2, 24)," *Nouvelle Revue Théologique* 100 (1978): 78.

108. "In modern phenomenology, a boundary experience is one that does not actually carry us over to direct contact with what lies on the other side of that from which we have come, but it does indirectly point to it and bring us closer to it." Kenneth Schmitz, *At the Center of the Human Drama: The Philosophical Anthropology of Karol Wojtyla/Pope John Paul II* (Washington, D.C., 1993), 143. The finest phenomenological analysis of shame easily available is that by Karol Wojtyla, "The Metaphysics of Shame," in *Love and Responsibility,* trans. H. T. Willets (New York, 1981), 174–93.

109. The Zephaniah text goes on to forge an intimate link between deception and guilt, a link also established in Ps. 32:1–5. This link is operative in the biblical notion of shame.

110. See Job 40:8: "Would you condemn me that you may be justified?"

111. Westermann, *Genesis,* 193.

112. The unclean state of writhing animals is declared in Lev. 11:42. For the notion of enemies eating dust, see Isa. 65:25, 49:23; Ps. 72:9; Mic. 7:17.

113. See Westermann, *Genesis,* 259–60; Wenham, *Genesis,* 80; Umberto Cassuto, *A Commentary on the Book of Genesis* (Jerusalem, 1961–64), 161 (who translates the second verb as "crave").

114. The presence of the masculine pronoun, not necessary in Hebrew, refers back to "seed," a masculine noun: "it/he will crush your head." The Septuagint exploits this by using the masculine pronoun "he" (*autos*) where it should have used a neuter pronoun, thus hinting at a singular individual through whom the curse will be implemented. The general sense of the various targums at this point is that when the sons of the woman (the Israelites) are faithful to the law, they will smite the serpent on the head and kill him. However, when they are unfaithful, the serpent will wound them on the heel. One day, however, there will be a victory for the sons of the woman, "in the days of King Messiah." For a study of these texts, see M. McNamara, *The New Testament and the Palestinian Targum to the Pentateuch,* Analecta Biblica 27 (Rome, 1966), 217–22.

115. For a brief presentation of the arguments, see W. Wifall, "Gen 3:15 — A Protoevangelium?" *Catholic Biblical Quarterly* 36 (1974): 361–65.

116. Gen. 3:15, 4:25, 16:10, 24:60; Lev. 22:13; Isa. 54:3. Additional texts which merit attention are Num. 5:28; 1 Sam. 2:20; Ruth 4:12; Gen. 19:32, 34, 38:9.

117. The only other instance in the Old Testament of the word translated here as "urge" is found in Song 7:11, where it seems to accentuate more the aspect of "yearning" in a romantic sense.

118. The notion of "listening to the voice" implies some sort of obedience, an acceding to the wishes of someone; see Gen. 16:2; 2 Kings 10:6; etc.

119. See Gerhard von Rad, *Genesis,* Old Testament Library, trans. John H. Marks (Philadelphia, 1961), 91.

120. Other such moments include that the covenant is still made at Sinai after the initial idolatry, that David's heir is the son of the woman whose husband he murdered to cover his adultery, and that the prophets promise restoration to the Northern Kingdom even after their rebellion from Solomon and their idolatry.

121. There seem also to be espousal overtones in the pre-exilic Zephaniah 3:14–18.

122. For a brief discussion of the history of the interpretation of the Song of Songs and a bibliography, see Roland Murphy, "Song of Songs, Book of," *ADB* 6:150–55. However, Murphy, along with many modern commentators, does not appreciate the dynamics of what will be called here "transposition."

123. For a discussion of this poem as an example of transposition, see Luis Alonso-Schökel, *The Inspired Word: Scripture in the Light of Literature and Language,* trans. Francis Martin (New York, 1965), 200–202.

124. For an extended analysis of how the language of the Song of Songs is able to speak of both realities at one and the same time, see Raymond Jacques Tournay, *Word of God, Song of Love: A Commentary on the Song of Songs,* trans. J. Edward Crowley (New York, 1988). The greatest Christian commentary is that by Origen. It might be noted that context can have the same transposing power even in regard to the plastic arts. The figure of a man drawing someone out of the underworld may be that of Hercules so drawing Cerberus, but in the Christian Middle Ages the same statute portrays Christ drawing Adam out of hell. See Edwin Panofsky, *Studies in Iconology* (New York, 1962), 16.

125. For a discussion of these issues and for an elenchus of the various opinions concerning Malachi 2:10–16, see Ralph L. Smith, *Micah–Malachi,* Word Biblical Commentary 32 (Waco, Tex., 1984), 318–25.

126. The translation of this phrase is difficult, as is the passage as a whole, though most modern commentators are of the opinion that the text is speaking about divorce.

127. The thesis of Hugenberger, *Marriage as a Covenant,* is that this text fully develops what is latent in Israelite thinking about marriage, namely, that it is a covenant. This may be true; Hugenberger's arguments are strong. But it may also be, given the Semitic capacity for establishing analogous relations between realities, that this covenant terminology is one more instance of such thinking rather than direct predication. For other examples, some stronger than others, where marriage is treated as a covenant, see Hos. 2:18–22; Prov. 2:17; Ezek. 16:8, 59, 60, 62; Gen. 31:50; Jer. 31:32; 1 Sam. 18–20 (ibid., chap. 8).

128. It is clear that the J tradition has both Abraham and David in mind while telling us of the generations of *adam.* See Walter Brueggemann, "Yahwist," *The Interpreter's Dictionary of the Bible, Supplementary Volume* (Nashville, 1976), 971–75.

129. This is the case, for instance, with Sirach 25:26 which, in common with, but in a manner very different from, Malachi, alludes to the theme of "one flesh" from Genesis 2:24: "Allow water no outlet, and be not indulgent to an erring wife. If she walks not by your side, cut her away from your flesh with a bill of divorce" (translation from Skehan and Di Lella, *The Wisdom of Ben Sira,* 343–44). On the other hand, the allusion to Genesis in the Book of Tobit (8:6) seems to share the monogamous presuppositions of Genesis.

130. The Mishnah is a collection of originally oral rabbinic statements in regard to various interpretations of the Torah as a norm of action. It was compiled by Rabbi Judah the Prince about the year 200 A.D. The Talmud, or rather the two Talmuds, that of Babylon and that of Palestine (sometimes called "of Jerusalem"), contain basically the commentary upon the Mishnah made by the various generations of scholars and finally was considered as closed by the middle of the fifth (Palestinian Talmud) and eighth (Babylonian Talmud) centuries. A partially parallel supplement to the Mishnah exists; it is called the Tosephta. Whenever any of these works are cited here a full reference will be made. For more information, see H. L. Strack and G. Stemberger, *Introduction to the Talmud and Midrash,* trans. Markus Bockmuehl (Edinburgh, 1991). An exhaustive study can be found in Shmuel Safrai, ed., *The Literature of the Sages, First Part: Oral Torah, Halakha, Mishnah, Tosephta, External Tractates,* Compendia Rerum Judaicarum ad Novum Testamentum, section 2: The

Literature of the Jewish People in the Period of the Second Temple and the Talmud (Assen, 1987).

131. For the Midrashim, see Strack and Stemberger, and Roger Le Déaut, "A propos d'une définition du midrash," *Biblica* 50 (1969): 395–413. For the Targums, see idem, *Introduction à la littérature targumique* (Rome, 1966). For a complete account of this literature, see Michael E. Stone, ed., *Jewish Writings of the Second Temple Period: Apocrypha, Pseudepigrapha, Qumran Sectarian Writings, Philo, Josephus,* Compendia Rerum Judaicarum ad Novum Testamentum, section 2: The Literature of the Jewish People in the Period of the Second Temple and the Talmud (Assen, 1984).

132. For an insightful reconstruction of family life on a daily basis, which, despite its strong reliance on the Talmudic evidence, has much to say about our period, see *The Jewish People in the First Century: Historical Geography, Political History, Social, Cultural and Religious Life and Institutions,* ed. Shmuel Safrai and Michael E. Stone, Compendia Rerum Judaicarum ad Novum Testamentum, section 1 (Philadelphia, 1976), vol. 2, esp. chap. 14, by Shmuel Safrai, "Home and Family." One may also consult Joachim Jeremias, *Jerusalem in the Time of Jesus,* trans. F. H. Cave and C. H. Cave (Philadelphia, 1969).

133. For an account of this document and the Qumran documents in general, see Devorah Dimant, "Qumran Sectarian Literature," in *Jewish Writings of the Second Temple Period,* 483–550.

134. Damascus Document 4, 20–5, 2.

135. Damascus Document 7, 16, while commenting on Amos 9:11, says of the "king" in that verse, "The king is the congregation."

136. Translation by Yigael Yadin, ed., *The Temple Scroll* (Jerusalem, 1983), 2:258. For an extended study of this text, see Johann Maier, *The Temple Scroll: An Introduction, Translation and Commentary,* trans. Richard T. White, Journal for the Study of the Old Testament Supplement Series 34 (Sheffield, 1985).

137. This latter depends upon how the phrase "in their (masculine or feminine?) lifetime" is read in the Damascus Document quotation given above. For a discussion of this, one may consult, in addition to Yadin and Maier, John Kampen, "A Fresh Look at the Masculine Plural Suffix in CD iv 2," *Revue de Qumran* 16 (1993): 91–97.

138. The most complete study of this point is that by David Novak, *The Image of the Non-Jew in Judaism: An Historical and Constructive Study of the Noahide Laws,* Toronto Studies in Religion 14 (New York, 1983). See also S. Krauss, "Les préceptes des Noachides," *Revue des Etudes Juives* 47 (1903): 32–40.

139. The text which in the tradition is the basis for these precepts is Genesis 2:16: "And Yhwh God gave *adam* a command saying, 'Eat as you will of every tree in the garden.'" See Midrash Genesis Rabbah 16, 6 (Soncino edition, 131).

140. Ben Witherington III, *Women in the Ministry of Jesus: A Study of Jesus' Attitudes to Women and Their Roles as Reflected in his Earthly Life,* SNTS Monograph Series 51 (Cambridge, 1984). See also Jeremias, *Jerusalem at the Time of Jesus.*

141. Witherington, *Women in the Ministry of Jesus,* 10.

142. This evidence has been collected by Bernadette J. Brooten, *Women Leaders in the Ancient Synagogue: Inscriptional Evidence and Background Issues,* Brown Judaic Studies 36 (Chico, Calif., 1982).

143. For the translation, see Herbert Danby, *The Mishnah* (Oxford, 1938), 321.

144. In this instance, the word *ketubah* refers to "a marriage settlement or sum of money payable by the husband or his estate to his wife on the dissolution of the marriage." Michael Satlow, "Reconsidering the Rabbinic *ketubah* Payment,"

The Jewish Family in Antiquity, ed. Shaye J. D. Cohen, Brown Judaic Studies 289 (Atlanta, 1993), 133–54, citation at 133.

145. It is quite likely that Jewish women in the Diaspora sometimes exercised the rights available to them in the civil law of the place where they lived. We have seen this already in the divorce formulae in the Elephantine papyri dating from the fifth century B.C. See Tosato, *Il matrimonio israelitico,* 197.

146. See A. Marx, "Les racines du célibat essénien," *Revue de Qumran* 7 (1969– 72): 323–42.

Chapter Two

MARRIAGE IN THE NEW TESTAMENT PERIOD

Francis Martin

We are considering the history of *Christian* marriage. This means we are
meditating upon that mysterious interaction of divine grace and human activity by which the Holy Spirit moves the Church through the centuries
toward the complete recapitulation of all things in Christ so beautifully asserted in the Letter to the Ephesians and initially developed by the genius
of St. Irenaeus.[1] I would like here to point to some specific challenges that
confront us when we undertake to ask the New Testament, and particularly
the Gospels, about marriage.

The basic challenge is that the New Testament text was never designed to
answer our question. Hence we must keep in mind the overall vision of the
New Testament itself and not become trapped in the sort of "tunnel vision"
that, instead of simply bracketing out what is not our immediate concern,
eliminates it altogether.

This study has two parts: first, a consideration of the Gospels' record
of the teaching of Jesus on marriage, and then a reflection on the New
Testament, especially the Pauline corpus, as it presents the reality of marriage in the light of the full revelation of humanity's destiny in the risen
Christ. Here, as elsewhere, the statement of *Gaudium et Spes* is eminently
applicable:

> In reality it is only in the mystery of the Word made flesh that the
> mystery of man truly becomes clear. For Adam, the first man, was
> a type of him who was to come, Christ the Lord. Christ the new
> Adam, in the very revelation of the mystery of the Father and of his
> love, fully reveals man to himself and brings to light his most high
> calling. (§22)[2]

The Teaching of Jesus in the Gospels

This part of the study is divided into four sections:

1. Jesus' teaching, by word and example, regarding marriage. This includes a study of the key texts regarding the stability of marriage and the impossibility of divorce.

2. Reflections on Jesus' relationship to his own family.

3. Jesus' portrayal of marriage and family in the Kingdom of God, in light of the demands of discipleship.

4. Jesus' description of marriage and family in light of the *consequences* of discipleship.

Before applying historical methods to the Gospel text, it is helpful to recall Form Criticism's insight that the Spirit-endowed teachers and leaders of the early Christian communities transmitted the tradition about Jesus orally and in writing before confiding it to the written text of the Gospels. In this period before the written Gospels, the deeds and sayings of Jesus received a certain set form which itself contributed to their interpretation. This interpreting narrative activity was taken up and modified by the Gospel writers, who thereby continued the process.[3] Three levels in the transmission process can be distinguished: "the life and teaching of Jesus; the oral tradition; the written Gospels."[4] This understanding guides the study of the Gospel material which follows.

The Teaching of Jesus on Marriage Itself

Many Gospel texts suggest Jesus' regard for marriage. He counters the Pharisaic use of *qarban* (the removal of an object from secular use), in regard to the financial support of one's parents, with the solemn injunction from the Decalogue, "Honor your father and your mother" (Exod. 20:12; Deut. 5:16), and adds the words from Exodus 21:17 and Leviticus 20:9 threatening with death anyone who speaks evil of father or mother (Matt. 15:14–16; Mark 7:9–13).[5] In his reply to the young man asking about attaining life, Jesus repeats again this same command from the Decalogue and prefaces it by the command: "You shall not commit adultery" (see Matt. 19:16–22; Mark 10:17–22; Luke 18:18–23). In addition, on several occasions Jesus performs a miracle to heal a child and relieve the suffering of a grieving parent: the Synagogue Official with a Sick Daughter (Matt. 9:18–26; Mark 5:21–43; Luke 8:40–56); the Royal Official With a Sick Son (John 4:46–53; Matt. 8:5–15; Luke 7:1–10); the Syrophoenician Woman with a Sick/Possessed Daughter (Matt. 15:21–28; Mark 7:24–30); the Widow at Nain (Luke 7:11–17); and the Father of an Epileptically Possessed Boy (Matt.

17:14–20; Mark 9:14–28; Luke 9:37–42). There are also examples of Jesus'
relation to children: he uses a child as a model for those who, willing to start
life over again, are apt for the Kingdom and goes on to identify himself with
a child received in his name (Matt. 18:1–5; Mark 9:36–37; Luke 9:48).
He rebukes his disciples when they try to prevent children from approaching him (Matt. 19:13–15; Mark 10:13–16; Luke 18:15–17). Finally, in his
parables and teaching, Jesus often shows his awareness of the inner work-
ings of family life.[6] It is, however, in his teaching on divorce that Jesus shows
most clearly his view of the holiness of marriage.

The Gospel tradition solidly attests that Jesus forbade divorce and thus
placed himself squarely in the line of thought represented by the text of
Malachi 2:10–16 and the intertestamental literature. His teaching clarifies
this position, grounds it clearly in the teaching of Genesis 1–2, and endows
it with his own authority. We will first consider the basic teaching found
in the Gospels, especially Matthew and Mark, and then look at the famous
"exception clause" found in Matthew 5:31–32 and 19:9.

The teaching of Jesus on divorce is referred to in a mysteriously un-
attached saying in Luke 16:18,[7] is appealed to as the Lord's "charge" in
1 Corinthians 7:10, and seems to influence the thinking in the Deutero-
Pauline literature limiting Church leaders and widows to only one spouse
(1 Tim. 3:2, 12; 5:9; Titus 1:6). It is presented in a developed form in Matthew 19:3–9 and Mark 10:2–12 and is also found in Matthew 5:31–32,
in a form similar to Luke 16:18. The Matthean and Markan texts are typical in their Synoptic convergence and divergence. It is neither desirable nor
necessary to presume that one text was composed earlier than the other and
on that basis explain the differences as due to conscious theological editing
of the earlier version by the later writer. In this, as in all Synoptic study, we
must adhere to the principle of "responsibility," which states that an author
is responsible for his text no matter how it is derived; the author must not
be relegated to a mere theological modifier of a previous text.[8]

Both the Matthean and Markan texts exhibit two clearly differentiated
sections. The first is the debate between Jesus and the Pharisees (Matt. 19:3–
8; Mark 10:2–9). This is followed by a saying of Jesus regarding the status
of a divorced or divorcing spouse (Matt. 19:9; Mark 10:10–12), which in
the Markan text is distinguished from the prior section by a literary notice
typical of the second Gospel, namely, that Jesus was now "in the house."
In Matthew it is introduced by "I say to you." This second section is also
echoed in the Matthean text in the Sermon on the Mount (Matt. 5:31–32)
and in the free-floating Lukan text (Luke 16:18) already referred to. The debate itself has three components: (1) the approach of the Pharisees "testing
him" with a question about divorce; (2) Jesus' reply based on Genesis 1:27
and 2:24 and concluding; with a statement of his own: "That then, which

God joined together let not man divide"; and (3) the further issue of previous Mosaic legislation, primarily Deuteronomy 24:1–4. These components are ordered differently in the two Gospels, but the teaching is the same. It concerns the supplanting of Deuteronomy 24:1–4 and the return to God's original intention for the whole of the human race, as set forth in Genesis, repeated in texts such as Malachi 2:10–16, and witnessed to in other Old Testament and intertestamental texts which we have considered.

The reason for the Mosaic legislation is given as *sklerokardia* — hardness of heart — a typical Septuagintal term translating various Hebrew expressions whose common field of meaning is that of disobedience and lack of a faith response to God.[9] Not only does this reply indicate that such legislation was a divine accommodation (something that earlier Jewish tradition had suspected), but by declaring the time of hardness of heart to be over, Jesus indirectly says something about himself and the Kingdom. Marriage itself is being transposed to a new plane. This will become more evident when we look at the demands of discipleship and their relation to marriage and family.

A more fundamental dimension of Jesus' teaching has to do with the very nature of marriage itself. By returning to the teaching of the early chapters of Genesis, Jesus reinstates them as the definitive expression of the will of God for marriage. The first of the texts invoked, "male and female he made them" (Gen. 1:27), reminds us that it is only as male and female that *adam* is the image of God. This mystery of the relating of the sexes in marriage is inscribed by the Creator into the very fabric of humanity. To trivialize this, to make sexual activity and procreation serve other ends such as power, pleasure, and family alliances, and to restrict a consideration of family to these worldly expectations is to short-circuit the true destiny of humankind. The second text (Gen. 2:24) reflects the same thinking, this time as expressed in the "J" tradition. There are covenant overtones to the expressions "leave" and "cling to," and "one flesh" is a term evoking a common bond in human physical existence made deeper by the covenant relation. By using this text here, the whole notion of marriage as a covenant within the covenant between God and his people is sounded; this will be picked up again by Ephesians 5:31.

Next comes a saying attached variously to the preceding section, as we have seen. This saying appears in a slightly different wording in Matthew 5:31–32 and Luke 16:18 and was probably not indigenous to the context we are considering but was inserted here in the Gospel transmission process because it draws out the consequences of what has already been asserted in the first section. That is, by placing the statement on remarriage next to the teaching on the indissolubility of marriage, indissolubility is further explained and clarified. We will consider all four versions of the saying together, reserving for the moment a discussion of Matthew's "exception clauses."

The form in Matthew 19:9 is the simplest: "I say to you: whoever sends away his wife — not on the ground of *porneia* — and marries another commits adultery." This is a revolutionary notion. A man who sends away his wife and marries another commits adultery *against his first wife*. For the reasons already discussed in chapter 1, this concept of adultery has never before been encountered in Judaism, where it is understood as an offense against a man's right to be sure that his children are truly his. The mutuality of personal rights implied in this statement will be developed in 1 Corinthians 7:2–4, but its radical nature is often not appreciated. Mark's text (Mark 10:10–12) clarifies this by adding that the adultery is "against her" and goes on to speak of a woman sending away her husband, a rarity in Judaism but common enough in the world of Roman society where the second Gospel probably took its origin. The other forms of this saying, at Luke 16:18 and Matthew 5:31–32, make the same point. This time the Lukan text is simpler, clearly indicating that the adultery is against the offended wife and adding that "one marrying a woman sent away commits adultery." Matthew's text reflects a more Jewish viewpoint by insisting that "anyone sending away his wife — except for a matter of *porneia* — makes her commit adultery [when she marries again]," and then proceeds more or less as in Luke. Thus, in Matthew there are two forms of this saying, one containing the revolutionary notion that it is possible to commit adultery against one's wife, and the other reflecting a more Jewish viewpoint. Such variations are not uncommon in the Matthean doublets and are part of Matthew's theological technique, which often sets texts derived from the previous tradition in contrast, enhancing their full theological impact through a sort of mental counterpoint.[10]

We now come to the famous "exception clauses," which, because of their importance in the whole ensuing history of Christian marriage, deserve more than cursory treatment. The clauses are found in the material we have just considered, namely, the second section of the debate with the Pharisees concerning divorce (Matt. 19:9). They form a corollary to the teaching about adultery in the Sermon on the Mount (Matt. 5:31–32). While the wording is not exactly the same and the phrase in Matthew 5:32 is more Semitic in character, in keeping with the more Semitic flavor of the whole passage, the basic notion is the same: "Anyone sending away his wife — except for a matter of *porneia* [*parektos logou porneias*] — makes her commit adultery." "I say to you: whoever sends away his wife — not on the ground of *porneia* [*me epi porneia*] and marries another commits adultery." Clearly an exception is being made, and it has to do with *porneia*. The two forms of the saying indicate that this is not merely a Matthean pastoral adaptation of the teaching of Jesus; it is part of the tradition to which he has access, not a contradiction of the words of the Master so insistently repeated in the tradition. To understand this requires a sense of how *porneia* is used in this context. I will briefly mention two important ancient understandings (still maintained by excellent scholars), and then set forth the two most likely understandings and mention some others.[11]

A significant patristic understanding of this phrase is well summarized by Raymond Collins, "To divorce except for *porneia* is adulterous and to divorce and remarry is adulterous."[12] That is, the term "divorce" (*apoluein*) must be understood here, in a uniquely Christian sense, to mean separation from bed and board. The principal difficulty with this understanding is that, given first-century social conditions, such a course of action is impossible: to send a wife away always implied that she was free to remarry. The second important interpretation, which relies on the translation of *porneia* itself, is that it refers to adultery and constitutes a genuine exception to the teaching of Jesus: there is no divorce except in the case of adultery. Some who maintain this position point to the fact that the "just" Joseph, upon discovering that Mary was pregnant, decided to "divorce" (*apoluein*) her quietly (Matt. 1:19). However, this venerable understanding of the exception clauses labors under two difficulties. First, if Matthew wanted to say that adultery constituted a genuine exception, he would have used *moicheia*, the technical term for adultery, since he uses the verb frequently in this same context. Second, we cannot be sure that Joseph had reached his decision to divorce Mary under the misunderstanding that she had committed adultery.[13] Joseph may have been suffering from a different misunderstanding. The case of a woman who is discovered not to have been a virgin at her marriage (a situation covered by Deuteronomy 22:13–21) would indeed call for divorce. But Deuteronomy 22:23–27 records the applicable law for Mary and Joseph's situation. This treats of a betrothed woman who is violated in a country place where she could not call for help. In certain more rigorous circles it was nevertheless required that the prospective husband divorce her.[14] We thus need to understand more clearly the possible signification of *porneia* in this context.

Porneia is used to refer to prostitution, unchastity, fornication, and indeed every kind of unlawful sexual intercourse.[15] In this latter sense it can also mean adultery, although, as we have seen, *moicheia* is the special term for adultery, and *porneia* and *moicheia* often stand next to each other in vice lists, as separate items. In the Greek-speaking Jewish world, *porneia* can refer to marriage within bounds forbidden by the Law or by Rabbinic decree, thus representing the term *zenut*. This is clearly the case in 1 Corinthians 5:2 and Acts 15:20, 29, and 21:25, and in these latter texts we have an instance of the Noahide laws being applied to converts from paganism.[16] One of the first to propose that the divorce exception for *porneia* referred to forbidden limits of consanguinity was Joseph Bonsirven. He pointed out that, as referred to in Acts 15, an important problem facing the early Church was what to do about pagan believers who were married under conditions that Jewish and sometimes even secular jurisprudence would consider incestuous.[17] This interpretation of *porneia* is strongly supported by the Qumran material, considered in chapter 1, where incest is clearly labeled as *zenut* and thus *porneia*.[18] Matthew and the tradition he incorporated were making pastoral provision for those married converts who, because of consanguinity, were not in true marriages.

Another understanding of *porneia*, equally sensitive to the importance of Jewish thought on the Christian understanding of marriage, is presented by Tarcisio Stramare, who maintains that the term refers to mixed marriages, that is, between Christians and pagans.[19] Based on the analogy of mixed marriages between Jews and pagans, these Christian marriages could be considered sexually irregular and thus *porneia*. In such cases, particularly when the non-believing spouse is making life difficult for the Christian, the marriage is considered to be non-existent. We would thus have not an exception, but a pastoral application of Jesus' teaching that is not far from Paul's position in 1 Corinthians 7:12–16. The principal objection to Stramare's solution is that it places an untoward weight on the term *porneia* and leaves itself open to the charge that the word itself cannot mean only those mixed marriages that are in conflict over the Christian faith. Then too, mixed marriages, particularly between Christian women and pagan men, were one of the most effective means of evangelization in the early Church.

We have considered two proposals, drawn from the historical milieu of the day, which attempt to explain the meaning of *porneia* in the Matthean exception clauses. The advantage of these two interpretations is that they respect the strong influence of Jewish moral thinking on Christian life, particularly marriage. Of these two, the first understanding, which equates *porneia* with unions made irregular because of consanguinity, seems the more likely.

The Relation of Jesus to His Own Family and the Messianic Family

In the preceding section we met with Jesus' prophetic understanding of the Torah in the light of the Kingdom. Jesus prophetically initiated an understanding of human life, marriage included, that was fulfilled by the new life he offered after his death and resurrection. Marriage has been sublated by being taken up into the field of energy of the cross and resurrection. I take here the definition of sublation given by Bernard Lonergan; its relevance to our topic will become apparent as this study proceeds:

What sublates goes beyond what is sublated, introduces something new and distinct, yet so far from interfering with the sublated or destroying it, on the contrary needs it, includes it, preserves all its proper features and properties, and carries them forward to a fuller realization within a richer context.[20]

In order to appreciate the sublating power of Jesus' teaching, it is necessary to consider both his relation to his own family and the contours of the Messianic family he describes.

Jesus and His Own Family

John explains the ignorant insistence of Jesus' relatives that he go up to Jerusalem and make himself known by the laconic statement, reflective of an earlier tradition: "For even his brothers did not believe in him" (John 7:5). It seems as though the demands of the Kingdom and the potential for division in families were first experienced by Jesus himself. However, in order to appreciate the apparently derogatory remarks in the Synoptic tradition and to grasp the meaning of Jesus' teaching on family, we must first have some understanding of what is meant by "the brothers/sisters of Jesus." This question has been with us for almost two millennia.[21]

Who are Jesus' relatives and, more precisely, who are "the brothers of the Lord"? It should first be pointed out that the reference is to prominent members of the early community who were very much believers in Jesus. These are mentioned by Paul as being worthy of imitation: "Do we not have the right to be accompanied by a sister woman, as the other apostles and the brothers of the Lord and Cephas?" (1 Cor. 9:5). In fact, the phrase "the mother and brothers of Jesus" seems to be a formula referring to these relatives of Jesus who were recognized as important in the community (Matt. 12:46; Mark 3:31; Luke 8:19; John 2:12; Acts 1:14; *Gospel of the Nazarenes,* 2). They figure prominently in two Synoptic texts, namely, the rejection at Nazareth and the discussion regarding the true family of Jesus. In the first of these texts the brothers are named and their presence at Nazareth contributes to the scandal caused by Jesus' presuming to teach and do wonders:

And coming to his own country he taught them in their synagogue, so that they were astonished, and said, "Where did this man get this wisdom and these mighty works? Is not this the carpenter's son? Is not his mother called Mary? And are not his brothers James and Joseph and Simon and Judas? And are not all his sisters with us? Where then did this man get all this?" And they took offense at him (Matt. 13:53–57).

The Markan form of this text is basically the same, except that Jesus himself is called a "carpenter" (*tekton*), and the names of the four brothers are given as James, Joses, Judas, and Simon. Luke's account of Jesus' visit to Nazareth (Luke 4:16–30) is quite different. The name of James appears first, both because he was probably the oldest and also because he was the most prominent of the group.[22] It is not clear from the text whether or not, at this point, these brothers and sisters are understood by Matthew and Mark as forming part of the "opposition party." Most likely they are being named simply because of their ordinary circumstances and their proximity to Jesus' townsfolk.[23]

A word must be said about the relationship of the brothers of the Lord to Jesus. First, they are never called "brothers of Jesus," but always "brothers of the Lord" or something similar (Acts 1:14 is a special case), thus indicating that, while they have a human relation to Jesus, they relate to him now as "Lord." The exact nature of that human relation has been a matter of debate since the fourth century. Briefly, there are three opinions, each of which, over the centuries, has known variation and each of which has its modern proponents. The first opinion, the Helvidian (Helvidius, fourth century), maintains that the brothers and sisters of Jesus are the children of Joseph and Mary. This opinion flatly contradicts the theological and historical tradition still maintained by the Roman Catholic and Orthodox churches, among many others.

The second view, called the Hieronymian (Jerome 342–420, who opposed Helvidius), considers the brothers and sisters of Jesus to be in fact cousins, the use of the term *adelphos* not being a major obstacle to this. That this terminology is used according to how people perceived Jesus, rather than according to a precise biological definition, is reflected in Joseph being called Jesus' "father" even by authors who explicitly mention the virgin birth (e.g., Luke 2:48). In Jerome's reconstruction, James and Joses of Mark 6:3 are the same as James the Little and Joses of Mark 15:40, whose mother is named Mary, and who could be the "Mary of Clopas" of John 19:25 — a sister of Mary, the mother of Jesus. The third view, the Epiphanian (Epiphanius, 315–403), considers these brothers and sisters of Jesus to be the children of Joseph by a previous marriage, who probably lived with Jesus in Nazareth. An interesting study by Richard Bauckham challenges John Meier's overly facile dismissal of the Epiphanian view in favor of the Helvidian and reinstates this understanding as the more probable, based on the fewer difficulties attached to it.[24]

The Messianic Family

Two incidents recorded in the Gospels are especially helpful in understanding the manner in which Jesus establishes what is often called the "Messianic

Family," into which the family as it was then understood was subsumed.[25] These two incidents are Jesus' reply when told that his mother and brothers were outside in the crowd looking for him and his promise of a hundredfold family to those who left everything for him.

If we apply the three-tiered Gospel transmission process to Matthew 12:46–50 and its parallels (Mark 3:20–22, 31–35; Luke 8:19–21), we may proceed from the historical reconstruction of the incident to an investigation of the interpretive narrative of each Gospel.[26] It seems that sometime early in his ministry members of Jesus' family were concerned about him and approached him. Jesus replied that his brothers, mother, and sisters were those who embraced the will of God as it was being manifested in and through him. He thus established a Messianic family, making it the integrating factor for all other relationships, including those of marriage and family.

The Markan account of this incident makes it the third of three reactions to Jesus and his preaching. In the first part of the Markan account (Mark 3:20–21), "those near him" felt that he was "out of his mind." It seems that Mark is reporting here the thinking of some of Jesus' friends and relatives, but it is not clear that he intends to attribute this opinion to Jesus' "mother and brothers." More likely, in my opinion, Mark 3:31–35 is not a continuation of the account begun in Mark 3:20–21 (though this is a stylistic procedure common in Mark), but rather the third in a series of reactions to Jesus. (Compare, for instance, the three reactions to Jesus in Mark 14:1–11.) Thus Mark makes of the mother and brothers of Jesus, prominent and well-known members of the early community, examples of a failure to understand the true dimensions of the Kingdom. This probably reflects the actual occurrence. We know that both Mary and those who were later known as "brothers of the Lord" had to grow in their faith understanding of the true significance of Jesus.[27] Thus, Mark uses these leaders as he does the Twelve, to stir his audience to strive for a deeper understanding of Jesus and of his teaching on the Messianic family.[28]

Matthew's account is not part of a serial presentation of reactions to Jesus, but rather forms part of a section in which conflict stories lead up to the chapter on parables. The teaching is basically the same as Mark (provided Mark 3:20–21 is not considered an interrupted part of the story). Luke's shorter version retains the same basic orientation: Those constituting the new family of Jesus are those who "hear the word of God and do it" (Luke 8:20). This same outlook is repeated in Luke 11:27–28, where Jesus replies to the woman who blessed the woman who bore and nursed him. Thus, Jesus lays the foundation for a new understanding of human existence, in which it is no longer the biological family from which a person derives identity and security, but the relation to Jesus and to fellow disciples.

The second text which treats of the Messianic family concerns Peter's question about those who have "left everything" for Jesus. In Matthew (19:27–30) and Mark (10:28–31), and slightly less so in Luke (18:28–30), the context is clearly that of teaching on family: Jesus has just been discussing divorce (Matt. 19:3–9; Mark 10:2–12); celibacy (Matt. 19:10–12); children (Matt. 19:13–15; Mark 10:13–16; Luke 18:15–17); possessions and discipleship (Matt. 19:16–22; Mark 10:17–22; Luke 18:18–23); the danger of possessions (Matt. 19:23–26; Mark 10:23–27; Luke 18:24–27); and finally, our passage. The Markan form of Jesus' response is as follows:

> Jesus said, "Truly, I say to you, there is no one who has left house or brothers or sisters or mother or father or children or lands, for my sake and for the Gospel, who will not receive a hundredfold now in this time, houses and brothers and sisters and mothers and children and lands, with persecutions and in the age to come eternal life" (Mark 10:29–30).

The wording of Matthew and Luke is similar, though both omit mention of the Gospel and persecutions, and Luke adds "wife" to the list of family members "left" by the disciple. The accent in the text is on the Gospel hundredfold that the disciples receive, that is, on the whole world of committed relationships that characterize the Christian community. Clearly this is a description of the Messianic family, with its bonds of love and trust, mutual sharing and secure commitment. This new family provides, in a sublated form, the identity and security which were so highly prized in the ancient world and which the Jews were so justly proud of providing through their family relationships. But there is more. The disciple who, for the sake of Jesus and the Gospel (Mark), steps out of the world of family and social ties and renounces the use of possessions that characterizes such a world is promised not only a whole other world offering meaning, identity, and human ties, but also "eternal life." The Messianic family is another way of describing the Kingdom of God.

Difficulties arise when we try to understand what is meant by "leaving" (*aphienai*) the former world of relationships. "Leaving" the persons and goods mentioned variously in the three Synoptic texts is part of what characterizes the disciples. All the texts add: "we have followed you." Some light will be shed on how the Gospels themselves understand this "leaving" when we consider other texts in the next section. It suffices to note that we are dealing here with what may be called "paradigmatic thinking." What all disciples are required to do in one form or another is fully and literally carried out by some of them, who in so doing become a clear model for the others. These others thus share in this activity, even if they do not live it as literally or radically as their "paradigms." This kind of expression, called a "focal instance," is characteristic of Jesus' ethical teaching, in which he gives his disciples concrete, striking, even exaggerated, examples portraying what must be in their hearts if they are to live out the life of the Kingdom.[29]

We thus read in Acts 2:44–45 that "all the believers were together and had all things in common; they would sell their property and possessions and divide them among all according to each one's need." In Acts 4:32–35, which again describes the whole "community of believers," we read that none held anything privately and that those who owned property sold it and brought the proceeds to the apostles. Nevertheless, when Peter confronts Ananias with his duplicity, he states: "While it remained unsold, did it not remain yours? And when it was sold, was it not still in your control?" (Acts 5:4). Obviously, what Luke ascribes to all was really done along a scale. Some, like Barnabas (who is expressly singled out because he sold a piece of property he owned and "brought the money and put it at the feet of the apostles" [Acts 4:36]), were the paradigms in whose generosity all the others participated, each according to his or her ability.[30]

In inaugurating the Kingdom of God, Jesus established a Messianic family whose life, demands, and eternal consequences far exceeded anything hitherto expected. Family life itself was uprooted from worldly expectations and placed in a new soil. Something new was introduced, something exacting demands on all the disciples, married or single. Even so, it is incorrect to conclude that the early Church was faced with an unresolved pluralism of forms of life, each invoking a part of Jesus' teaching.[31] Jesus effected a genuine transposition or sublation of family life, which, as aptly stated by Bernard Lonergan, does not destroy family life, but "on the contrary needs it, includes it, preserves all its proper features and properties, and carries them forward to a fuller realization within a richer context." All believers are challenged to "leave" their present context and "follow Jesus." Some do so in a radical and exact copying of Jesus' own life, entailing many of the same difficulties he experienced. Others, like the women who accompanied Jesus and ministered to him and the apostles from their own resources (Luke 8:1–3), heed the call in their own less radical and literal yet still authentic ways. A look at Jesus' demands upon the disciples confirms this.

The Demands of Discipleship

In both Matthew (16:24–28) and Mark (8:34–9:1), the first prediction of the passion and resurrection is followed by Peter's remonstrating with Jesus, Jesus' rebuke of Peter, and his teaching on discipleship. This same rhythm, of passion prediction, disciples' failure to understand, and teaching on discipleship is clearly repeated twice more in Mark's Gospel (Mark 9:30–37; 10:32–45). A close reading of this passage helps us understand the call to discipleship and its explicit relation to marriage. The text is composed of six sayings, most probably juxtaposed in a pre-Gospel level of the tradition, and repeated, with one significant difference, by Matthew and Mark (see also Luke 9:23–27). According to Mark they are addressed to "the multitude with his disciples"; Luke simply says they are addressed to "all." These sayings are listed below, numbered from Matthew 16:24–28, who gives the audience as "his disciples":

1. "If any man would come after me, let him deny himself and take up his cross and follow me."

2. "For whoever would save his life will lose it, and whoever loses his life for my sake will find it."

3. "For what will it profit a man, if he gains the whole world and forfeits his life?"

4. "Or what shall a man give in return for his life?"

5. "For the Son of Man is to come with his angels in the glory of his Father, and then he will repay every man for what he has done." (Mark: "For whoever is ashamed of me and of my words in this adulterous and sinful generation, of him will the Son of Man also be ashamed, when he comes in the glory of his Father with the holy angels.")

6. "Truly, I say to you, there are some standing here who will not taste death before they see the Son of Man coming in his kingdom."

The sayings numbered 1, 2, 5, and 6 frame sayings 3 and 4. The first two sayings are clearly on discipleship, while the last two have a strong eschatological tone. The last saying, as understood in the Gospel tradition, probably refers to the anticipation of the Son of Man coming in glory that was realized at the resurrection (see Matt. 26:64; Mark 14:62; Luke 22:69). Taken by themselves, sayings 3 and 4 are wisdom sayings contrasting the certainty of death with the uncertainty of wealth and the inability of money to buy one's life. However, in this context sayings 3 and 4 are clearly discipleship sayings because the four sayings framed together achieve a new context: conduct in regard to money is now viewed within the field of energy set up by the cross. A transposition has been effected.

Now consider the following sayings, which closely resemble saying number 1 above, and note how here family life is placed within the context of the cross:

Matthew 10:37–38: "He who loves father or mother more than me is not worthy of me; and he who loves son or daughter more than me is not worthy of me; and he who does not take his cross and follow me is not worthy of me."

Luke 14:26–27: "If any one comes to me and does not hate his own father and mother and wife and children and brothers and sisters, yes, and even his own life [i.e., himself], he cannot be my disciple. Whoever does not bear his own cross and come after me cannot be my disciple."[32]

The respective context of each is significant. In Matthew, the general context is what is called the "Missionary Discourse" (Matt. 10:1–42). This saying is the second of three which form a block within the discourse. The first will be dealt with in the next section; the third closely resembles saying number 2, above.[33] Luke, on the other hand, places the saying within the teaching on discipleship, which picks up and comments on the widespread invitation described in the immediately preceding parable of the great feast (Luke 14:15–24). Thus, as Joseph Fitzmyer notes, the discipleship saying and the two comparisons which follow — to a man building a tower or a king going out to battle — fulfill the same function as the mysterious guest without a wedding garment mentioned at the end of the Matthean version of the wedding feast parable (Matt. 22:1–14): All spell out the demands of discipleship on those who are invited.[34] It is important to notice once again how family relations are placed within the context of the call to embrace the cross.[35] Discipleship is costly, regardless of whether marriage and family is totally renounced or is uprooted, sublated, and subsumed within the framework of the Kingdom. What was said about "paradigms" applies here as well, of course. In this twofold form of saying, discipleship is linked with putting Jesus ahead of other ties. Once again the human reality of family is placed within the field of energy (grace) created by the cross and resurrection. This forms both an inter- and intra-Gospel commentary on the notion of "leaving" discussed in the previous section.

Two other Gospel passages testify to the demands of discipleship and family life. The first of these is the call to the rich young man, with its subsequent discussion of the danger of riches, followed by Peter's concluding question and Jesus' response concerning the hundredfold which we have already considered. In all three Synoptics, as we noted earlier, the incident is placed within a general treatment of family affairs. Jesus' response is given as follows:

Matthew 19:21–22: "Jesus said to him, 'If you would be perfect, go, sell what you possess and give to the poor, and you will have treasure in heaven; and come, follow me.' When the young man heard this he went away sorrowful; for he had great possessions."

Mark 10:21–22: "And Jesus looking upon him loved him, and said to him, 'You lack one thing; go, sell what you have, and give to the poor, and you will have treasure in heaven; and come, follow me.' At that saying his countenance fell, and he went away sorrowful; for he had great possessions."

Luke 18:22–23: "And when Jesus heard it, he said to him, 'One thing you still lack. Sell all that you have and distribute to the poor, and you will have treasure in heaven; and come, follow me.' But when he heard this he became sad, for he was very rich."

The advice of Jesus and the account of the man's reaction are almost identical in the three accounts. The man "lacks one thing" (Mark, Luke), or requires one more thing to be "perfect," which in Matthean terms means to be wholeheartedly committed to God's plan of salvation. The call is to the "paradigmatic" existence as a disciple, one described by Peter in Matthew 19:27 and parallels, and in the summary statements we have just considered in Acts. Jesus invites the rich young man to renounce material possessions to give him the freedom to preach the Gospel as an itinerant; but the whole community will be able to share in his paradigmatic act. While this text does not address marriage directly, it is obvious that we are dealing with a call similar to that found in Peter's question and Jesus' reply. Again it is a question not only of renunciation, but of following Jesus and of the solemn promise of having "treasure in heaven" (see Matt. 6:19–21; Luke 12:33).

The last text which considers the demands of discipleship is made up of a series of three (Luke 9:57–62) or two (Matt. 8:19–22) apothegmata that put the following of Jesus ahead of security, filial duty, and family affection. We meet here various people who want to follow Jesus and who hear various responses concerning the "birds of the air and the foxes," the "dead burying their dead," and the man "who puts his hand to the plow and then looks back."

Matthew names the first interlocutor as a "scribe" and the second as "another of the disciples." By leaving the designations vague, Luke concentrates on the sayings and their implication for discipleship and presumes they are addressed to all believers. The first saying is an invitation to find security only in following Jesus. This, in a literal imitation of Jesus, means renouncing the family ties so dear to Judaism, from which so many derived both identity and security. While the Graeco-Roman world also valued family ties, their realization was seldom as intense or as exclusive. Here again is an invitation to a paradigmatic way of life.

The second saying seems to imply that those who do not follow Jesus are spiritually dead and thus fit to bury the physically dead. The accent is on the urgency of preaching the Kingdom of God. Even the most sacred (for Jews) of family obligations is not to be compared with this solemn responsibility. The third saying derives its imagery from the call of Elisha by Elijah (1 Kings

19:19–21), and alludes to the fact that Elisha, who was plowing when he was called, asked Elijah: "Let me kiss my mother and father and then I will follow you." Elijah's enigmatic response, "Go back again, for what have I done to you?" apparently allows Elisha to return and contrasts with the reply given by Jesus. Entering discipleship in the Kingdom being inaugurated by Jesus is too serious to allow any second thoughts.

The Consequences of Discipleship

There is a series of Synoptic texts, all of which echo or cite Micah 7:6, that speak of the conflicts that will take place in families. As we shall see, these conflicts are part of the Messianic woes of the last times. The New Testament considers the last times to have begun with the coming, and especially the resurrection, of Jesus (see 1 Cor. 10:11; Heb. 1:2, etc.). The most explicit reference to Micah 7:6 is found in a passage very similar in Matthew and Luke, but placed in very different contexts. In Luke's Gospel the saying forms part of Jesus' commentary on his own ministry. This is very probably its original context in the first stage of the tradition (Jesus' life). Matthew, on the other hand, uses the text as a description of the ministry of the disciples. He places it within the Missionary Discourse, as the introduction to the block containing other family texts which we have already considered. Earlier in the same discourse, in a block which speaks of the persecution of the missionaries, he sounds the same theme. The texts which follow are the Lukan use of Micah 7:6, its closest parallel in the Matthean text, and then the allusion to Micah 7:6 earlier in the Missionary Discourse:

> Luke 12:51–59: "Do you think that I have come to give peace on earth? No, I tell you, but rather division; for henceforth in one house there will be five divided, three against two and two against three; they will be divided, father against son and son against father, mother against daughter and daughter against her mother, mother-in-law against her daughter-in-law and daughter-in-law against her mother-in-law."

> Matthew 10:34–36: "Do not think that I have come to bring peace on earth; I have not come to bring peace, but a sword. For I have come to set a man against his father, and a daughter against her mother, and a daughter-in-law against her mother-in-law; and a man's foes will be those of his own household."

> Matthew 10:21–22: "Brother will deliver up brother to death, and the father his child, and children will rise against parents and have them

put to death; and you will be hated by all for my name's sake. But he who endures to the end will be saved."

The actual text of Micah is found in a lament which comprises the first six (or seven) verses of chapter 7. The prophet is decrying the evils of his time (about 700 B.C.), and sees the social and familial chaos all around him as being at once the source and the symbolic expression of the spiritual devastation wrought by Israel's infidelity. The last two verses of the lament read:

Micah 7:5–6: "Put no trust in a neighbor, have no confidence in a friend; guard the doors of your mouth from her who lies in your bosom; for the son treats the father with contempt, the daughter rises up against her mother, the daughter-in-law against her mother-in-law; a man's enemies are the men of his own house."

The final two allusions to the Micah text are found in the Eschatological Discourse. Significantly, Matthew alludes to the theme of persecution in the last days, but avoids any allusion to Micah, thus reserving his text's application to the actual participation in the last days being experienced now by the Church. The Markan and Lukan texts are as follows:

Mark 13:12–13: "And brother will deliver up brother to death, and the father his child, and children will rise against parents and have them put to death; and you will be hated by all for my name's sake. But he who endures to the end will be saved."

Luke 21:16–17: "You will be delivered up even by parents and brothers and kinsmen and friends, and some of you they will put to death; you will be hated by all for my name's sake."

Almost certainly Jesus introduced the theme evoked by Micah 7:6 to describe his own activity. In so doing, he showed himself to be a child of the Jewish tradition of his time, which had already begun to envisage the "last days," the "days of the Messiah," as a time of great turmoil and suffering. One indication of this is the manner in which Micah 7:6 appears in second-century Jewish literature, leading to the conclusion that it figured much earlier in thinking on this topic.[36] The theme of social and generational conflict is sounded in the second century B.C. work known as the *Book of Jubilees*. Though the wording reflects the conflicts of Maccabean times, the theme is cast in the tone of the evils of the last generation and may well reflect the influence of Micah 7:6:

And in this generation children will reproach their parents and their elders on account of sin, and on account of injustice, and on account of the words of their mouth.... Some of these will strive with others, youths with old men and old men with youths, the poor with the rich, the lowly with the great. (*Jubilees* 23:16, 19).[37]

This evidence leads Pierre Grelot to the conclusion: "It is plausible that the Micah text provided the Jewish milieu with the content of a literary 'common place' that existed already in the time of Jesus, though the text itself does not surface until the middle of the second century."[38] Why did Jesus use this text and why did the tradition retain it? The answer is twofold: First, the theme evoked by the Micah text in Jesus' time was that of the last and decisive days of the Messianic age. In alluding to this theme Jesus was saying something about himself and his role in God's establishment of the Kingdom of the last days. In saying that he came to cause division or to bring the sword (Matt. 10:34; Luke 12:51), Jesus is not saying that his purpose is to divide families (though this was a consequence of his activity) any more than his citation of Isaiah 6:9–10 (Matt. 13:14–15; Mark 4:12; Luke 8:18) means that he used parables to harden the hearts of his listeners. The second reason Jesus used the text was, therefore, to indicate that the time of God's definitive activity had begun.

The early community used the text for the same reasons. Matthew directly applies it to the missionaries who went out to preach the Good News, and the Markan and Lukan accounts use it in their account of the Eschatological Discourse. Division and betrayal were sad facts in time of persecution; the Christian community clung to this text less as a theology of family than as a sign that what they were suffering was under the prophetic aegis of the Son of God. This has been pointed out in some recent studies which use the Gospel of Mark as a means to understand the milieu of Neronic persecution, with its inevitable consequence of heroic fidelity and tragic betrayal. John R. Donahue notes that the story of Peter's betrayal of Christ allows other Christians, who now have to face their own failure, to take courage from his later martyrdom in Rome itself. Similarly, the experience of family division and betrayal loses some of its terrible impact when seen in light of Jesus' use of Micah 7:6, which places the events in the lives of the early Christians in the context of the definitive epoch of the Messianic days.[39] Further, for Mark and the other Evangelists, "family" no longer primarily means the blood family, but the Messianic family, which also experienced the divisions prophesied by Jesus.[40]

One other aspect of Old Testament teaching must be introduced here. The concluding verses of the last book in the prophetic section of the Old Testament (Mal. 4:4–6) promise that, at the moment of God's definitive act, there will be reconciliation in families. This is probably a theological addition by the inspired editor, who wanted the prophetic word — stretching from Joshua to Malachi — to culminate on a positive note.[41] We read that the returning Elijah "will turn the heart of the fathers to the sons, and the heart of sons to the fathers" (Mal. 4:6). These words are also applied to John the Baptist in Luke 1:17, thus preserving in that Gospel the theological counterpoint effected by the editor of Malachi.

We must acknowledge, however, that Jesus knew from his own experience the tragedy of rejection and clearly taught that discipleship may be very costly. Suffering is a consequence of uprooting family ties, even to plant them in the richer but more demanding context of discipleship. This kind of division, characteristic of the eschatological moment of the Church's actual history and the ultimate moment of the end of history, is a solemn reminder that the healing power of grace does not reinforce or restore what we consider "normal," but instead works to change and sublate our present situation.

Conclusion

The most useful philosophical category for understanding Jesus' teaching on marriage is that of "sublation." Jesus returns to the original intention of God as it is found in chapters 2 and 3 of Genesis, insisting on marriage as a permanent union between a man and woman. This permanent union results in a covenant reality of "one flesh" that, as we saw when we analyzed the word "flesh" in chapter 1, includes the family arising from this union. But the family, the most sacred human reality given to God's people, is not the ultimate context in which human beings find meaning, identity, and security. The ultimate context is the Kingdom of God, the Messianic Family inaugurated by Jesus. This notion gave even his own family and close acquaintances difficulty, and some of them refused to believe in Jesus as an authoritative teacher sent by God. Even those who did respond, and later made up the group known as "the mother and brothers of the Lord," had to grow in their understanding of the depth and newness of the teaching of Jesus. Modern perspective allows us to understand Jesus' vision of each person as a physical and spiritual reality, whose identity and security is derived not from what is conferred by family or society, but from a personal and eternal relation to the Father. In this light, the family ceases to be the ultimate reference point for human life and becomes but one aspect of a new life within the profound and embracing dimension of the Kingdom.

Discipleship thus both promises and demands much. This is seen in the descriptions of the costs of discipleship given and lived by Jesus. It is also demonstrated by those who enter into marriage as a paradigmatic existence which takes up the partners into the field of energy set up by the cross and resurrection of Jesus. Finally, in these, the last days, we may see the division and chaos among members of a blood family or the Messianic family that the prophets already described for our times. Jesus has already spoken about this: "I have told you this so that you may not fall away. . . . I have told you this so that when their hour comes you may remember that I told you" (John 16:1–4).

Having thus abstracted all that the Gospels have passed on to us concerning Jesus' teaching on marriage, we are faced with the further task of integrating what we have learned back into the total context of the Gospel message lest it become subservient to another, more limited context. The second part of this study will focus on how Christian marriage, as a sublation of a precious human reality, created a genuine development of doctrine whose main lines are still apparent in the New Testament.

Marriage in the Rest of the New Testament

Jesus included marriage in the Kingdom and delineated many of its features in his teaching on discipleship. We can detect similarities between this call to discipleship and the examples of the subordination of family found in both the biblical and extra-biblical literature, such as the call to Abraham to "go from your land, and your clan and your father's house to a land I will show you" (Gen. 12:1).[42] But a fundamental difference lies in how Jesus' call affects and includes the whole family and not only the individual, who may or may not be called to be an effective role model in the community. This teaching on the family is embodied in and extended by the teaching of the rest of the New Testament, particularly those parts that, unlike the Gospels, are not narrative but discourse, and more specifically the letters of direction written by Paul, as well as other material mostly within the Pauline tradition.[43]

This part of our discussion will proceed in three steps: the world into which the Gospel message first came; Pauline teaching in those Letters that are commonly agreed upon as authentic (that is, having Paul as their author); and the teaching in those Letters almost certainly not authentic (primarily the Domestic Codes, as principally found in Ephesians 5:21–6:9). Wherever there is material similar or parallel to the Pauline material in this wider sense, it will be included in the proper place.

The World That Received the Gospel Message

From the point of view of the preaching of the Gospel message, the first-century Mediterranean basin may be imagined as three concentric circles. The outer circle (the governmental and social context) was created by the Roman world; the next inner circle (that of culture, education, and philosophy) was the product of the Greek world; and the most immediate circle (that of religion, namely, monotheism and a history of divine activity and

promises and the ethical thought related to that religion) was provided by
the Jewish matrix.[44] These were not hermetically sealed compartments; they
interacted with and mutually affected one another. This is the world that
the early Christians encountered, changed, and healed.

The Roman World: The Impact of Its Government and Culture on Early Christianity

No matter where one lived in the first-century Mediterranean world, one was
affected by the power of Rome — through its governors, procurators and
other administrators, its military presence, its administrative procedures,
its financial interests, its citizens and subject peoples, and its laws. While
Rome allowed a great deal of freedom to the various parts of its empire,
Roman attitudes and practices exerted a powerful influence on every aspect of life within that empire. Thus, studies of marriage and family in the
Roman empire must recognize Roman practice, while allowing for local
differences.[45]

Marriage in the ancient world, particularly ancient Roman marriage, has
been the object of extended study in recent times.[46] For men especially, there
was a clear distinction between the marriage relationship and sexual relationships. An apt summary of this is provided by the famous statement of
Pseudo-Demosthenes (mid-fourth century B.C.):

> We have wives to bear us children, concubines [*pallakas*] for the daily
> care of our persons, mistresses [*hetairas*] we keep for the sake of
> pleasure (*Against Neara* 1, 22).[47]

The purpose of marriage was twofold: It was the matrix within which
children were brought up to be citizens of the empire, and it was the means
of providing for the transmission of family property. This latter function of
marriage — to provide a mechanism for the transmission of property — was
greatly complicated by the manner in which children were legitimized. Birth
within the household was not the sole determinant of a child's legitimacy
for inheritance purposes. Legitimate children of the family were as likely to
be adopted by the head of the house as to have been generated by him and
his wife. Thus, the natural-born and adopted children of a household were
often in competition for the inheritance. The hatred of sons for their father,
as they chafed under his authority (all their lives) and awaited his death,
was proverbial throughout the empire.

We have detailed information about only upper-class families. Those
classed as "poor" in Roman culture, or who so classed themselves, were in
reality the "second-class" rich. They lived in badly built, fire-prone, three-
or four-story apartment houses and clustered small houses called *insulae*
(islands). About them we have but little information. As for impoverished

serfs and others who lived outside the cities, either farming for themselves or, more often, providing labor for the estates of the city-dwelling rich, we have practically no data at all. While marriage laws and customs applied to the poor as well, it must have been difficult to enforce them. In any event, it was not until the laws passed by Augustus (19/18 B.C.) that marriage itself became an affair of the state; prior to that, Rome concerned itself only with family matters involving patrimony.

Most marriages, at least in the Mediterranean basin, followed a two-stage process similar to that of marriages in Israel:

> Greek law required that marriage be preceded by a betrothal agreement. A father's pledge of his daughter to a prospective bridegroom was formal, with witnesses on both sides and her dowry was agreed upon. In Rome by the end of the Republic this betrothal became a looser system — an informal business arrangement in writing before witnesses which was easily renounced by either party and did not necessarily lead to marriage. The dowry was considered the daughter's share of the parental estate.[48]

Early Rome had known three different types of marriage, all resulting in the woman coming under the authority of her husband. By the time of the empire, however, nearly all marriages were the result of mutual consent between the bride and bridegroom. Following her marriage, the woman remained legally part of her father's household. This allowed her to retain more of her father's patrimony. As a result, many upper-class women became independently wealthy through divorce. Thus, while society continued to consider the wife the ward of her husband — more like a daughter than an equal — in practice, Roman women could be quite independent, and even unfaithful to their husbands, without incurring much blame.[49]

Girls were often betrothed and married even before puberty, to further the good of the family. The pain and shock of being thus introduced to sexual life before physical development was a common fact of married life. The resentment and even hatred this produced is often alluded to in the literature.[50] Another phenomenon of the time was the lending of wives to other men, most often for the sake of producing offspring. (Low fertility was a problem during the empire: many girls were exposed at birth, many women died in childbirth, and probably at least as many died during abortions, and abortions also rendered many other women sterile.)[51]

> It [the political interpretation of frequent divorce and remarriage] takes even less account of a fact that Plutarch (*Parallel between Lycurgus and Numa* 3) noted in his role as an ethnographer: Romans would often lend out their wives if one of their number did not have enough

children. Unlike the Spartans, who took into their home the fellow
citizen whose strong healthy sons they wanted, Roman men passed
their wives around. . . . Seneca, talking about services by friends to each
other, mentions this inordinate loaning of wives (*De beneficiis* 1.9.3).[52]

Many men did not want to bother getting married. Relating to a wife
was considered onerous and it could lead to financial entanglements. Things
became so bad that the Emperor Augustus, alarmed by the low birth-rate
among Roman citizens, enacted legislation that limited the inheritances allowed to bachelors, provided special benefits to fathers and mothers of
three or more children, and attempted (largely unsuccessfully) to punish
adultery. It is difficult to assess the actual effect of these laws. However,
when combined with the "family values" thinking promoted by the popular
philosophy of the day, it is clear that another view of marriage was thus
introduced into Roman life.

All of this indicates the limits of toleration in the Roman empire. It is
perfectly legitimate to presume that there were families, not only among the
upper classes, but also among the less financially and socially fortunate as
well, who remembered and practiced a family morality more reminiscent of
Rome's earlier days. Indeed, much recent scholarship suggests that divorce
became less frequent as one descended the social scale, although this may
have been due to a correspondingly greater inability to afford it.

Three other aspects of family life in the empire affect our understanding of the New Testament texts, and thus need a brief description: the
household, children, and slaves. Literary and archeological research has increased our understanding of the ancient household. Our focus will be on
the upper classes, about whom we have the most information, with a few
words concerning the less privileged who lived in the *insulae.*

The average household was made up of husband and wife, natural and
adopted children, and slaves. (Only the very poor had no slaves.) Wealthy
households also included clients, "friends,"[53] and freed slaves who came at
all times to pay their respects. When the head of the house — usually a man
but sometimes a wealthy widow or divorced woman — was a Christian, the
house served as the meeting place for the Christians. Their meetings must
have resembled large dinner parties, with the more important guests and the
presider reclining in the *triclinium,* while the rest found a place on chairs in
the peristyle.[54]

The poorer folk, living in their cramped *insulae,* lacked both privacy and
space. Even their cooking was often done outside. For them it was easier to
buy food at the ancient equivalent of a fast food shop. As Carolyn Osiek,
borrowing a phrase from Caroline Dexter, expresses it: "The rich ate in,
the poor ate out."[55] Christians of this class either attended meetings in the

households of the wealthy or, often with their patrons, were likely to gather in shops or rented halls.

The status of legitimacy was conferred on a child only upon its formal acceptance by the male head of the house *(paterfamilias)*. When a child was born, it was placed on the ground before the head of the house. If he picked it up *(tollere infantem)*, he thereby recognized it as his. The *paterfamilias* could also choose to recognize as his own children those not born of him or his wife.[56] Should the head of the house choose not to accept a child, he could command that it be exposed. This was likely to happen if the child was a girl, or defective, or if there was concern about the extent of the inheritance. It would also often occur if the mother was not his wife, but a slave or other woman whose child would likely be deemed unworthy of adoption. Children ordered to be exposed either died or were picked up by others to be made slaves or prostitutes.

While genuine affection existed between fathers and children (more likely fathers and daughters), enmity between father and sons and even patricide were not unusual happenings. This occurred because of the ever-present possibility of disinheritance in favor of someone adopted and because a Roman man could not be considered a *paterfamilias*, with all the legal and civic implications of this term, until the death of his father.[57] This state of affairs adds meaning to the injunction in Colossians 3:21: "Fathers, do not provoke your children, or they may lose heart."

The limits of this study do not permit a consideration of the education and upbringing of Roman children. We must also pass over the institution of slavery, noting only that impersonalization of the slave was directly challenged by the introduction of the Christian understanding of the word "person" and the notion of a dignity inherent in all human beings, constituted by their relationship to God and to others. As important as these topics are for a full understanding of the revolution introduced into the Roman empire by Christianity, the reader must be referred to other studies.[58]

The World of Greek Thought: Its Impact on and Reflection in the Roman Empire

We will consider only those aspects of Greek thought current in the world contiguous to the New Testament and concerned with marriage, family, and households. Most of this thinking reached the authors of the New Testament, either directly or through the Jewish-Hellenistic environment which first came in contact with the Gospel, as part of a common heritage propagated by popular philosophical preachers. These philosophers, while often asserting allegiance to one particular school of thought (usually Stoicism), had already effected a synthesis and produced a certain "common" popular philosophy.

With the exception of the Jews, the ancients did not consider religion the source of or motivation for ethical teaching and practice. The role of religion was to ensure correct relations within the society and with the "divine" powers (conceived anthropomorphically by the masses and in a demythologized manner by the educated). Religion had to do with a proper sense of order and one's place within that order, as expressed in a series of domestic or public rites. (For example, an ancient Roman watching the national anthem sung before a sporting event in the United States would probably consider this a "religious" act.) Philosophy, on the other hand, addressed itself to the question, "How shall we live?" During the first century of the Roman empire, there were many popular philosophers, whose teaching touched on cosmic issues and discussed the nature of the gods, but was primarily ethical.[59]

Discussion of marriage and household in the first century was tributary to three different streams of philosophical thought:

- the discussion of *oikonomia* (household management) associated with the Platonic and Aristotelian treatises and continued in their successors;

- the discussion of *kathekon* (what is fitting or appropriate), which characterized the Stoic understanding of a person's duties, particularly after the practical turn given to Stoicism by Panaetius (185–109 B.C.);

- and finally the neo-Pythagorean (first century B.C.–first century A.D.) moralizing, which tended to adapt the Stoic teaching to the Aristotelian tradition.[60]

The basic Aristotelian text is found in Book I of the *Politics:*

Household management [*oikonomia*] falls into departments corresponding to the parts of which the household [*oikia*] in its turn is composed; and the household in its perfect form [*teleios*] consists of slaves and freemen. The investigation of everything should begin with its smallest parts, and the primary and smallest parts of the household are master and slave, husband and wife, father and children; we ought therefore to examine the proper constitution of each of these three relationships.[61]

The androcentrism of the text is obvious, and Aristotle goes on to distinguish the different types of authority exercised by the head of the household in regard to each of the three categories of relationship:

Hence there are by nature various classes of rulers and ruled. For the free rules the slave, the male the female, and the man [*aner*] the child in a different way. And all possess the various parts of the soul, but possess them in different ways; for the slave has not got the deliberative part at all, and the female has it, but without full authority [*akyron*], while the child has it but in an undeveloped form.[62]

The two most salient features, repeated in a series of successive texts, are the three pairs (master-slave, husband-wife, and parent-child), and the attribution to the male head of the house, sometimes in a more nuanced form, of the right to exercise authority.[63] Aristotle's thought, probably based on previous philosophers, including Plato, was reflected by a whole series of thinkers and was summed up, with some Stoic shadings, by the syncretic Stoic philosopher Arius Didymus (a friend and consultant to the Emperor Augustus).[64] Another highly modified example of this line of thought is that of the Middle Platonist Plutarch (approx. A.D. 50–120), whose *Advice to Bride and Groom* reflects the humanism introduced into this topic by the Stoics.[65]

The Stoic material is based on a notion of what is "fitting." It is more varied and has not been as well preserved.[66] What is "fitting" is determined by what is in keeping with nature, as perceived and transmitted by the "unwritten law" accepted among the Greeks. The usual perspective of such considerations is that of "duty"; it treats the individual as the center of attention and then considers his relations to others. Thus, Hierocles (early first century) divided his work *Elements of Ethics* into sections such as "How to Conduct Oneself towards the Gods," "How to Conduct Oneself towards the Fatherland," "How to Conduct Oneself towards Parents," etc.[67] Partial remains of the work of Musonius Rufus (A.D. 30–101), another famous Stoic philosopher and the teacher of Epictetus, have come down to us. Among the titles of his *Discourses* we find such topics as: "That Women Should Also Philosophize," "Should Girls and Boys Be Given the Same Education?" "Concerning Sexual Pleasures," and "The Principal Goal of Marriage."[68] Among the more famous statements of Musonius are:

> Those who do not live a life of moral softness and are not given over to vice should consider that the only sexual pleasures permitted are those in marriage and which have as their goal the procreation of children, for these are in conformity with the law.[69]

> To live together and to cooperate in the procreation of children, this is the principal goal of marriage. The husband and wife, he [Musonius] used to say should come together both to have a life in common and to bring forth children, to consider that all is in common between them, and that there is personally possessed not even their bodies.[70]

Due to the thinking of Musonius and others like him, the first century saw a rise of a popular philosophical concentration on "family values" and common acceptance of the notion of "the couple." It is difficult to know how much this thinking affected actual marital practice, though it must have had some impact. There exist touching statues from this period of "the couple" — a man and wife holding hands — some of which are found on sarcophagi, accompanied by sentimental inscriptions often expressed in formulaic terms similar to those found in our modern greeting cards; we cannot know whether they were any more deeply felt. An ideal expressed is not necessarily reflective of a standard lived by.[71]

While overlap between *persona* and "obligation" (*kathekon*) is a characteristic of other thinkers of this time, it is most striking in the works of Seneca (55 B.C.–41 A.D.) and Epictetus (A.D. 55–135). This overlap provides a basis for understanding the extent of the sublation effected by New Testament thought in its discussion of household living. Seneca, for instance, in his Ninety-fourth Letter, discusses philosophers who give practical advice: "How a husband should conduct himself towards his wife, or how a father should bring up his children, or how a master should rule his slaves."[72] Here we see the Aristotelian characteristics of androcentric perspective and implied, albeit softened, inferiority of the wife.

Epictetus, however, is a classic Stoic. Unlike his teacher Musonius, he left no explicit treatise on the nature of marriage, but his thinking can be applied to this topic. His basic principle is "Our duties [*kathekonta*] are in general measured by our relationships."[73] Thus we read: "You have been given such a body, such parents, such brothers, such a country, such a position in it; and then do you come to me and say, 'Change the task for me'?"[74] Another example of this type of relational thinking surprisingly includes the status of "wife" as indicative of duties deriving from "both the natural and the acquired relationships . . . those namely of son, brother, citizen, wife, neighbor, fellow-traveler, ruler and subject."[75]

Neo-Pythagorean thought is also, unfortunately, poor in written remains.[76] What can be gleaned from extant writings shows neo-Pythagorean dependency on the Aristotelian notion that household management is a subset of political theory and that it is to be viewed through its constituent (paired) components — husband-wife; father/parents-children, and master/mistress-slave. Their treatment of this theme, however, also contains an eclectic blend of Platonic and Stoic elements. For example, Callicratidas combines the Stoic notion of marriage as a "communion" with an Aristotelian-style analysis of the authority exercised by a husband and places them in the context of practical and moral thinking:

> Hence also wedlock is established with a view of the communion of life. Those husbands that govern their wives despotically are hated by them, but those that govern with a guardian authority are despised by

them. For they appear to be, as it were, appendages and flatterers of their wives. But those that govern them politically are both admired and beloved.[77]

The variety and eclecticism of this material does not lend weight to the existence of a rigid *topos* (with attendant philosophy) taken up by the New Testament authors in their discussion of marriage and family.

The Jewish World: The Diaspora and Its Influence on Early Christianity

The third and innermost circle, one thoroughly influenced by the other two, and in turn very influential in the early tenor and spread of the Christian message, is that of the Jewish world, especially the Diaspora. This vast subject exceeds the few pages dedicated to it here. Certain key points must be noted for our understanding of the New Testament teaching on marriage, particularly in the Domestic Order Texts.

First, biblical thought has never been closed to its surroundings. Literary and archeological remains show that neither Palestinian nor Diaspora (Hellenistic) Judaism remained closed to its environment.[78] When the Gospel was preached outside of Palestine, it found its most receptive audience in the varied Jewish communities of the Roman empire, among some of the Jews and especially among the proselytes (non-Jews who adhered closely to Jewish worship and practice) and "God-fearers" (sympathetic non-Jews who accepted the Jewish understanding of ethical monotheism, kept the basic Jewish moral tenets, and worshiped one God).[79] Hence the New Testament not only cites the Old Testament, but often builds its position through subtle allusions and Jewish methods of Scripture use. The sexual morality presupposed in the New Testament is based on Jewish thought and practice. This is evident both from the state of sexual morality in the Roman empire in general, and from the overt attacks on Jewish marriage and sexual practice by some pagan authors in particular. Tacitus, for instance, in his famous polemic against the Jews, mentions that, among their aberrant customs, "they regard it as a crime to kill any child among the *agnati* [those born after the father's will naming the children for whom he would provide had been made]."[80]

The audience to which Jewish moral teaching was addressed and the content of that teaching are two other aspects of Jewish Diaspora life that particularly touch upon our topic. The audience for this teaching was twofold: proselytes and God-fearers.[81] (The latter was a large group; very often the success or failure of Christian preaching in a given area was directly related to their acceptance or rejection of that preaching.) While little direct information exists about the content of Jewish teaching directed to this

audience, the Jewish moral teaching in the Torah set forth the basic tenets
which were considered applicable to all people. These were often listed as
the seven injunctions given to Noah: against blaspheming the one true God,
idolatry, incest, murder, robbery, and eating meat torn from a living ani-
mal; and the obligation to establish a civil law that embodied these.[82] Many
of these injunctions are also found in Leviticus 17–19 (the first part of the
"Holiness Code"); these are specifically directed to the *ger,* or resident alien
(rendered as *proselytos* in the Septuagint).[83]

This teaching, a sort of Jewish exposition of the "natural law," was
buttressed by the prevailing popular philosophical preaching, from which
the teachers selected variously and eclectically. Evidence of the influence of
the three streams of philosophical thought (usually a combination of Aristotelian and Stoic) is found in the work of Philo and Josephus[84] and is
reflected in the work of Pseudo-Phocylides. This latter was most likely a
first-century Jew, who set forth Jewish teaching under the name and in the
style of the sixth-century B.C. Greek poet, to strengthen Jews in their faith
and God-fearers in their adherence and to win Gentile respect and support.
The concluding lines of his poem teach about marriage and family:

> Do not let a woman destroy the unborn babe in her belly,
> nor after its birth throw it before the dogs and the vultures as a
>   prey. . . .
> Love your wife, for what is sweeter and better
> than whenever a wife is kindly disposed toward (her) husband and a
>   husband toward (his) wife.
> Do not be harsh with your children, but be gentle.
> And if a child offends against you, let the mother cut her son down to
>   size
> or else the elders of the family or the chiefs of the people.[85]

This combination of Jewish moral teaching and Stoic idealization of the
couple is characteristic of the eclecticism of first-century Jewish thought. It
indicates how freely the Jewish authors — and after them the New Testament writers — found in the philosophical teaching of the day themes and
doctrines that could be incorporated into their own teaching, thereby recon-
textualizing it to serve a new vision. This leads us to our final consideration,
namely, whether or not this teaching actually constituted a *topos.*

Was There a Marriage and Family Topos in the Popular Philosophy of the Roman Empire That Was Taken Up by Judaism and Christianity?

In much of the discussion of New Testament teaching on marriage, references can be found to the notion of *topos.* The term is not really defined,
but a description can be gleaned from the way the various commentators

use it. The Domestic Code *topos* is a literary form common to ancient pagan authors whenever they discussed life in a household. Most often structured according to the Aristotelian threefold pair model, it embodies the basic presuppositions of antiquity regarding the locus of authority in the male head of the house. The New Testament Domestic Codes are just one instance of the ancient *topos;* they share with the world around them the same literary conventions and presuppositions as the other treatises on household living.

This account of *topos* presents three problems. First, the term *topos* is misapplied. It is confusing at best and misleading at worst.[86] For Aristotle and his contemporaries, "the *topoi* were devices enabling the speaker to find those arguments that would be most persuasive in a given situation."[87] Though this understanding may have been expanded somewhat by ancient writers, there was never a *topos* in regard to Domestic Codes, certainly not in the sense of a literary form with a specific vocabulary and structure that imposed itself whenever the topic was discussed.[88] Second, the varied nature of the extant texts, reflected in the early Christian literature and the New Testament itself, belies such an identification.[89] Most texts in this latter category do not even possess the threefold pair structure considered by David Balch and others to be a hallmark of *topoi.*

The third problem with this approach is its assumption that every discussion of household life employing these categories must also share the philosophical presuppositions of its predecessors. This would mean that the appearance in the New Testament literature of households represents "loss of nerve," a capitulation from an initial egalitarianism to the patriarchalism of the pagan world around it.[90] It is alleged that the early Christians began to speak this way for one of two reasons: either to avoid persecution, since groups allowing too much freedom to women (by not accepting the traditional household) were often considered subversive by the Roman officials, or as a reaction against those fellow Christians who ignored the intrinsic patriarchal bias of traditional society by taking too seriously Paul's dictum that there is "not male and female" (Gal. 3:28).

The countervailing argument, that the New Testament texts have not been subjected to a Domestic Code *topos,* is persuasive. First, New Testament authors were free to discuss the topic and to avail themselves of relevant material in the popular philosophy without accepting either the literary form or the philosophical presuppositions of some its proponents. Second, the attribution of a fall from pristine egalitarianism to pagan patriarchalism requires certain key New Testament texts, which argue for a very different model of Christian origins, to be ignored.[91] Third, and most important, such a structure falsely presupposes that subsequent discussions are dependent upon, and must adopt the worldview of, the earlier ones. Those insights of the popular philosophers which were valid and helpful could be taken up into a Christian discussion of household living, as aids in presenting a Christian understanding of marriage. In modern theological terms, these authors recognized that grace sustains nature and that the presence of healing grace in the community enabled people to bring to a new and hitherto unrealized level, to fulfill, the best of human aspirations.

The Pauline Articulation of a New Testament Understanding of Body

The power of the reality of the resurrection of Christ and the future resurrection of believers is an aspect of the vast subject of New Testament anthropology central to our discussion: "For if we believe that Jesus died and rose, so too will God, through Jesus, bring with him those who have fallen asleep" (1 Thess. 4:14). It is impossible to overestimate how profoundly the understanding of this reality affected the New Testament thinking about sexuality and marriage. All that the best in Jewish thought had prepared for reached its goal in the Christian discovery that the true vocation of human beings is to live eternally with God, in their full totality as bodily persons joined to Christ.[92]

While not every text concerning sexual morality explicitly invokes this vision, it is nevertheless implicitly present, animating an understanding of what is sound and right in the Jewish and pagan statements about this aspect of human life. We read, for instance, in Hebrews 13:4: "Let marriage be held in honor among all [defending marriage against an exaggerated asceticism or a pagan unwillingness to undertake its obligations], and let the marriage bed be undefiled, for God will judge the immoral and the adulterous." And of course, terms such as "sexual immorality," "fornication," and "adultery" figure in nearly every New Testament catalogue of vices to be avoided.[93] There is, however, one text that explicitly invokes the promise of a future life on the basis of the present chaste state of the believer's body. This is worth considering here.

The Pauline Understanding of Sexuality

In 1 Corinthians 6:12–20, Paul undertakes to combat an understanding of sexuality which would trivialize it and bring it under the "liberty" claimed by certain of the Corinthian community for their eating habits (which Paul discusses in chapter 8) and their sexual activity. While the slogan "all things are lawful for me" could have a positive interpretation, it is used by some at Corinth to legitimate indiscriminate sexual activity, whether because physical reality is already completely sanctified or (more likely) that it is not worthy of being taken into account by those who have become "spiritual." To understand Paul's rejoinder, one must appreciate his understanding of *soma* (body). Our modern Cartesian schemata posits the body as an alienated mechanistic system which somehow relates to the interior self, but Paul understood "body" as the whole person considered under the aspect of his or her physical dimension. Body is the way we are present to and make history; it is thus that the Church is the Body of Christ. Since the whole person is called to eternal life, that call lays hold even now of the physicality of the person. Even in the midst of the ambiguity of our historical existence, the body is the residing place and the symbolic manifestation of the grace of God.

That is why Paul attacks the Corinthian parallel between food-stomach and sex-body. The stomach as an organ has a specific function in our present mode of existence, but the *whole body* (not merely the genitals) is involved in sexual activity; it is the activity of the *person*. God will "put an end" to both food and stomach, but as regards the body: "the body is for the Lord and [remarkably] the Lord is for the body. God raised the Lord and he will raise us too by his power" (1 Cor. 6:13–14).[94] The physical existence of the believer is even now in union with Christ; he or she is a member of Christ, and therefore sexual union with a prostitute is a deviation of the whole person; it means taking "the members of Christ and making them the members of a prostitute." The share in the divine life effected by the death and resurrection of Christ has already begun to have its effect on the believer's bodily existence: "If the Spirit of the one who raised Jesus from the dead dwells in you, the one who raised Christ from the dead will give life [a logical as well as chronological future] to your mortal bodies also, through his Spirit who dwells in you" (Rom. 8:11). This is why Paul can ask the libertines among the Corinthians, "Do you not know that *your body* is the temple of the Holy Spirit within you, whom you have from God, and that you do not belong to yourselves?" (1 Cor. 6:19). This principle underlies all the New Testament teaching on marriage, and it must be borne in mind when discussing what, on some levels, seems to be merely ethical exhortation.

Advice on Sexual Abstinence to Various Classes of People

It is significant that most of the teaching on sexuality in the Pauline corpus is to be found in the First Letter to the Corinthians, addressed to a group that seems to have been largely made up of former pagans rather than "God-fearers" and therefore largely untouched by the Jewish teaching on sexual morality.[95] In chapter 7 of this Letter Paul answers a series of questions posed to him by the Corinthians regarding abstinence from sexual activity. As a result, we do not have a treatise on sexuality but a pastoral response to people wounded in their culture and very often in their own lives as well. They needed a response to help them steer a course between the extremes of fear of sexuality and undue concern over those who embrace a call to celibacy.[96] We will touch on only some of the significant statements in this passage.

To understand the first five verses of this chapter, addressed to married people who wish to abstain from sexual intercourse, it is important to understand the opening statement not as a general principle, but as an expression of this desire: "It is good for a [married] man not to touch a woman [that is, his wife]." After laying down the counter-cultural principle that each spouse has rights in regard to the other's body (understood in the sense given above), Paul concludes with simple advice to any couple wishing to abstain:

> Do not deprive each other unless perhaps by some agreement for a fitting time that you may be freer for prayer, and then come together again; so that Satan does not tempt you through your abstinence [not "lack of self control"] (1 Cor. 7:5).

To older singles, Paul gives the advice that it is better to remain single, but not if such a course of action will result in being continually distracted by sexual passion (1 Cor. 7:6–9). He then addresses those concrete situations in the community in which some husbands and wives have sought to be separated permanently from their spouses for the sake of living a celibate life. After appealing to the tradition which transmits Jesus' teaching on divorce (Matt. 19:3–9 and par.), Paul considers the case of an unbeliever who wishes to live with his or her newly converted spouse (1 Cor. 7:1–11, 12–16). Finally, in a manner common in his letters, Paul leaves the immediate consideration to appeal to a more general principle.[97] This principle is the call of the Lord: each one should remain, not in the state in which he or she was called (slaves should take the opportunity to be free if it presents itself), but in creative fidelity to the *personal call* of the Lord (1 Cor. 7:17, 20, 24).

The last sixteen verses of this chapter are directed to various concrete questions posed to Paul regarding engaged couples who are considering — often to the great consternation of their families — whether to remain celibate or not.[98] In a time when there was no real provision for this way of life, perhaps the only way those — especially women — called to celibacy could so live was to remain engaged to another celibate. (The disruption introduced into the society by the freedom these women exercised is difficult to estimate.)[99] Basically, Paul says that those who marry do well and those who remain single do better.

This difficult chapter does not yield much direct teaching on marriage and family, but is valuable in showing the depth of the struggle experienced by some of those coming directly from paganism into Christianity. It also provides an insight into Paul's pastoral — and still timely — qualities of humanity, wisdom, and balance as he applies the light of Christ to human sexuality.

The Domestic Codes in the New Testament

Those passages explicitly concerned with marriage among Christians, namely, the Domestic Codes, were briefly discussed and enumerated in the preceding section.[100] We will now look at the principal New Testament passages on marriage to understand their specific theological outlook and teaching and the use they make of the abundant material available to them in the popular philosophy of the day. We will begin with Colossians 3:18–4:1, the text generally considered to be the first of these exhortations, then look at the material in 1 Peter 2:13–3:12 and the Pastoral Letters (1 Tim. 2:8–15; 6:1–2; Titus 2:1–10, 11–15), and conclude with Ephesians 5:21–6:9, the most mature of these Codes.

The text of Colossians 3:18–4:1 is given here for the convenience of the reader:

> Wives, subordinate yourselves to your husbands as is fitting in the Lord. Husbands love your wives and do not be embittered with them.
>
> Children, obey your parents in everything, for this is pleasing in the Lord. Fathers, do not provoke your children lest they become discouraged.
>
> Slaves obey in everything those who are masters according to the flesh, not with eye-service as man pleasers but in simplicity of heart, fearing the Lord. Whatever you do, carry it out from your inner being [*psyches*] as for the Lord and not for men, knowing that you will receive from the Lord the reward of the inheritance.
>
> Serve the Lord Christ. The one who acts unjustly will be requited for what he has done wrong. Masters, show justice and equity to your slaves, knowing that you too have a Lord in heaven.

This passage, and the comparable passage in the Letter to the Ephesians, contains the clearest articulation of the three-pair schema of many philosophical texts. Its correspondence to those texts is simply because this subject matter has, since Aristotle, frequently been considered in this three-pair scheme. A close look at the vocabulary reveals that some of the popular thinking about marriage is pressed into service to show how the human reality, as viewed in its ideal light, has been sublated by Christ: we are witnessing an instance of philosophy used as an aid to theology.

Some of the significant vocabulary indicators should be noted. Wives are not told to be "subject" or "submissive" to their husbands; they are exhorted to "subordinate themselves," using a term which, with two exceptions, is never used in the extant pagan or Jewish literature to describe the wife's relation to her husband.[101] Further, with the exception of the allusion to Sarah in 1 Peter 3:6, the terms "obey" and "obedience" are never used in the New Testament to describe this relation. We have here a Christian adaptation of an existing, specific vocabulary to describe a new reality. The term *hypotassesthai* is in the middle voice, addressing the woman as a free person exhorted to conform freely to the will of God in relation to her husband. Thus, while the term indicates a willingness to "give way" to another, the avoidance of the usual obedience vocabulary in regard to the wife (though it is used of children and slaves) shows that something new is being suggested within a culture that could not envisage actual reciprocity between man and wife. It is difficult to understand what kind of relation the New Testament is describing by using this vocabulary, but, from the fact that Ephesians urges mutual subordination, we see that an advance has been made in a biblical understanding of anthropology: it is a question of love.

> The remaining use of *hypotássomai* in NT exhortation suggests that the general rule demands readiness to renounce one's own will for the sake of others, i.e. *agápe,* and to give precedence to others. . . . The findings as a whole suggest that the term *hypotássomai* played a general cathechetical-type role in primitive Christian exhortation.[102]

In regard to other vocabulary, the wife's free act of self-subordination is described as "fitting in the Lord." The term fitting (*aneken*) is a Stoic term which measures fittingness according to the norms of nature. By adding "in the Lord," the whole basic context is changed or sublated. Now it is not nature, but the Kingdom or life in the Body of Christ, that sets the standard for fittingness. It is for this reason that the term "Lord" is used six more times in this short passage. In the exhortation to the husbands, they are told to "love" their wives, something that is linked with consideration in all the exhortations (Eph. 5:22; 1 Pet. 3:7; Titus 2:6), and which, of course, evokes the very core of Christian ethical thinking, one that reinforces the best of popular philosophy and brings it to another level. Given the real conditions of married life, this exhortation is again countercultural, describing an actuality to be lived based on the new life in Christ, not an ideal to be discussed.

This is not an abstract treatise on life in a household: all parties are addressed directly. This is a Christian exhortation on how the life of love is to be lived out in the home. This type of exhortation is unique to the principal New Testament codes; it is not found in extra-biblical Domestic Codes.[103] Children are thus exhorted, using Old Testament terms, to obey their *parents,* both mother and father, a motif found in several Old Testament texts. Fathers are warned against discouraging their children, a notion which evokes their legal power in the family, including the right to disown and adopt. The exhortation to slaves addresses them as endowed with free will and capable of a deep and sincere interior life directed to the Lord. This last is a particularly striking example of how far the Christian Domestic Codes actually are from the philosophical and ethical thinking of the surrounding environment, including the Jewish environment. Before examining the Ephesians text, where the differences are forcefully brought home, let us first look at texts of a slightly different orientation, namely, the First Letter of Peter and the Pastoral Letters.

Addressed to Christians living in the cities of Asia Minor in the last quarter of the first century, the First Letter of Peter may well be based on Peter's preaching, as well as motifs from the baptismal preaching of Rome.

> Their [the Christians'] situation in society is like that of Israel in Egypt. The parenesis instructs them in their existence as foreigners and leads them to questions about suffering in society. Suffering is the counterpoint of existence in society. Accordingly the letter develops a thematic focus: the existence of Christians in a non-Christian society and overcoming that society by being prepared to bear oppression, i.e. to "suffer."[104]

By the close of the first century A.D., the total number of Christians in the whole of the Roman empire probably did not exceed eight thousand out of a total population of sixty million. Their refusal to take part in what seemed to their neighbors to be the very essence of good citizenship — namely, the practice of "religion," including emperor worship — provoked bitter hostility and sporadic mob persecution, mostly unofficially organized.[105] Christians were early suspected of great crimes against humanity; Christian women and slaves in non-believing households were a highly disruptive force because they did not participate in the religious acts of the family.[106] Hence, the suffering envisaged in the First Letter of Peter is, as Leonard Goppelt describes it, a form of "oppression." Christians are urged to continue loving and to convince others of the authenticity of the hope that is in them by their lives. There is no suggestion that the Christians suffered a "loss of nerve" or were urged by their leaders to conform to a more "patriarchal" mode of household living to avoid being lumped together with other "subversive" sects, such as the Isis cult, that promoted the freedom of women. Rather, through their radical call to live a life of love, this tiny minority — many of whom had been a part of the prevailing culture — stirred that culture to enmity, persecution, and at times civil action against them.[107]

Having considered the sociological matrix of 1 Peter, we will next consider the theological aspects of its address to slaves, wives, and husbands (the threefold pair structure is noticeably lacking). The exhortations are found in the second and central part of the Letter (1 Pet. 2:11–4:11), which, as Goppelt points out, draws from the first part "the apparently paradoxical deduction that being a foreigner in relation to society is to be confirmed precisely through responsible investment of oneself in the institutions of society."[108] This investment constitutes a witness of faith, obvious from the opening exhortation (2:11–13), which urges Christians to be good citizens and then addresses slaves, who, in suffering injustice, are given the example of Jesus (2:14–25). The next section, addressed to wives (3:1–6), begins with the word "likewise." The women are urged to subordinate themselves even when they are married to unbelievers, since this can "win them over" (a term of evangelization). They are given the example of Sarah. The exhortation to Christian husbands also begins as does the address to the wives, and urges the men, in the nuanced translation of the Revised English Bible:

> In the same way, you husbands must show understanding in your married life: treat your wives with respect, not only because they are physically weaker, but also because God's gift of life is something you share together. Then your prayers will not be impeded. (1 Pet. 3:7)

This last section, with its perspective of "the couple," again shows the theological understanding of marriage as shared life, both human and divine. When both parties are believers, living such an understanding is possible. It depends on the love of the wife who, though completely equal in her graced humanity, willingly subordinates herself to the order of marriage, and the love of the husband, who learns to be considerate and respectful of his wife as "coheir of the grace of life."

The Pastoral Letters form a group with many common aspects. They stand midway between the Letters recognized as Pauline and the early Christian texts found in the letters of Ignatius, the First Letter of Clement of Rome, and similar documents. The difficult questions concerning possible layers of redaction building upon original Pauline letters aside, this material, particularly in its ethical sections, bears the marks of greater contact with the literary world of Hellenism than do most New Testament documents: the style is most akin to Luke-Acts, but the vocabulary has a flavor of its own.[109]

There are two principal passages to be considered: 1 Timothy 2:8–15; 6:1–2; and Titus 2:1–10, 11–15. Both of these are in the form of direct address, giving the recipient of the Letter instruction for good order in the community. Neither has any resemblance to a Domestic Code "form," but each has directives for married people and slaves (not children) embedded in a much broader spectrum of advice to the community leader regarding various classes of people in the group. The tone of these directives is less hortatory than the texts in Colossians and 1 Peter, and the vocabulary is more reflective of the popular philosophical reflection of the day.

The text in Titus 2:1–10 resembles a list of duties in the Stoic mode and includes advice concerning older and younger men, and older and younger women, as well as slaves. The whole of this advice is taken up into a

Christian context, not as powerfully as in Colossians and Ephesians, but nevertheless effectively, by the concluding line of the section, which speaks of the grace of God that trains us for a godly life as lived in this age (see Titus 2:11–15). The discussion of men and women in 1 Timothy (2:1–3:13) occurs in a section regarding conduct at worship. First we hear of what to pray for (2:1–7), then how men should conduct themselves at worship (2:7), and finally how women should conduct themselves and why (2:8–15). The remarks about slaves (6:1–2) are in a very different context, placed the last in a series of directives concerning the conduct of members of the community.

Despite the fact that so many continue to call this a Domestic Code, little in 1 Timothy 2:8–15 has to do with marriage. The outlook of the text shows Jewish influence, particularly the remark about Eve's responsibility for the first sin. Elsewhere I have written about the behavior that seems to have elicited these remarks:

> The most plausible scenario underlying this text is as follows. Some women were acting in a way which was "seductive" in many senses of the term. Their conduct and mode of dress was immodest and they were teaching false doctrines, which probably had to do with "myths and genealogies" (1 Tim. 1:3–5), the forbidding of marriage and the need for an ascetic diet (1 Tim. 4:3), and, in general, things that did not agree with "the sound words of Our Lord Jesus Christ" (1 Tim. 6:3–5).... The ministry of teaching was being abused and treated as though it were the office of teaching. The teaching, moreover, was probably of a gnostic character.[110]

The allusion to Adam's having been formed first reflects the same teaching in 1 Corinthians 11:8–9 and probably depends upon it and the doctrine behind it. The remark that Eve was deceived, reflecting as it does one strand of Jewish thinking obliquely referred to by Paul only once (2 Cor. 11:3),[111] is probably invoked here to accent the notion that the women in question have been deceived, a theme present elsewhere. The statement that women will be saved through childbearing is a rebuttal of the doctrine that forbade marriage and envisages not only the conception and birth of children but the whole Christian activity of raising children referred to in 1 Timothy 5:10.

The Advice to Households in the Letter to the Ephesians

The Letter to the Ephesians is in many ways the most profound expression of Pauline thought in the New Testament, though the exact nature of Paul's authorship of the Letter is difficult to determine.[112] The exhortation to members of households is found in a section extending from 5:15 to 6:9. Though its overall relation to the Letter is variously understood, it may be called "exhortation to wise and Spirit-filled living in worship and in household relationships."[113] The advantage of this designation is that it takes into account the close bond between verses 21 and 22. A characteristic of Ephesians is that it employs, often in a deepened sense, vocabulary and phrases from earlier Pauline writings. A Jewish coloration is found in some of the vocabulary, in the use of the Old Testament, and in ethical judgments, particularly as to pagan sexual morality (4:17–24).

The exhortation regarding household living shows dependence upon the text in Colossians we have considered. Here again we see the threefold pairs and the explicit sublation of marriage and family into the life of Christ. We also find new insights and a new vocabulary. In fact, with the exception of the terms "wives-husbands," "children-parents," and "slaves-masters," none of the significant words in this passage is found in the extant pagan household texts: vocabulary taken over from pagan thought is thoroughly transformed. We consider now indications that this teaching is a development of thought within the New Testament itself and is the most mature expression of New Testament teaching on marriage and family.

The exhortations to children and parents, slaves and masters, make little advance over the teaching in Colossians. Once again children are exhorted to obey their *parents;* this Old Testament theme is further strengthened by the citation of Exodus 20:12/Deuteronomy 5:16. Fathers are exhorted not to anger their children. The advice is much the same as in texts such as Ps-Phocylides discussed earlier: "Do not be harsh with your children, but be gentle." The further notions of the "training [*paideia*] and admonition of the Lord" take up Greek ideals, already present in Judaism, and put them in a Christian context. As in Colossians, the address to slaves is long and appeals to them as endowed with free will and the grace of Christ. The Colossians and Ephesians texts are very similar, but subtle adaptations, such as the omission of "in everything" after the imperative "obey," can be noted.[114]

The exhortation to wives and husbands extends through 12 verses: Ephesians 5:22–24 is addressed to wives, and 5:25–33 is addressed to husbands, except for the last remark in 5:33, which again addresses wives. Thus, the exhortation to husbands is approximately three times as long as that to the wives, and is the longest single section in the passage. The section is introduced by the last of five participial expressions having imperative force:[115] "being subordinate to each other in the fear of Christ," and is immediately followed, with no repetition of the verb, by the first of the exhortations to those in households: "Wives to your own husbands as to the Lord because a husband is head of the wife as Christ is also head of the Church: he is the savior of the Body. But just as the Church subordinates itself to Christ, so too wives to their husbands in everything" (5:22–24).

The injunction to mutual subordination is general: all Christians should relate to each other in this way. This is a new formulation of a familiar exhortation to mutual love and respect for one another, an example of which is found in Philippians 2:2–4:

> Be of the same mind, having the same love, being in full accord and of one mind. Do nothing from selfish ambition or conceit, but in humility regard others as better than yourselves. Let each of you look not to your own interests but to the interests of others.

The introductory participial imperative undoubtedly uses *hypotassesthai* in order to bring the notion of love even further into the orbit of Christian thought. The motive is the "fear of Christ," which transfers to Christ all the Old Testament teaching on the "fear of Yhwh" — awe at his presence and works of power, respect for his majesty, wonder at his love, awareness of his justice — and adds as well the expectation of Christ's ultimate triumph.[116]

As has been observed, the exhortation opens without any verb. In this way the notion of self-subordination, while it is applied to the wives, is also preserved in its overtones of mutuality. The three notions that are new in the address to wives are those of "head," "Body," and "Savior." These are key to our understanding of the sublimation effected by the author; unfortunately they are all difficult to define, though their meaning here becomes clearer in the consideration of the whole text. The notion of "head," borrowed from 1 Corinthians 11:3, where it carries overtones of authority,[117] is modified here by its placement in the context of Christ's headship, which is founded on his saving activity. The discussion is about husbands and wives, not men and women; thus there is no reversion to the notion that whatever role is attributed to the husband derives from his superiority.[118] An understanding of what is being said must come from an analysis of the term of the comparison: "*just as* Christ is Head of the Church: he is the savior of the Body."

In Ephesians there are two notions of Christ's headship: his authority (Eph. 1:22–23) and his reality as "source" (*ex ou*) of the growth of the Body (Eph. 4:15–16). Thus, the divinely intended union between Christ and the Church is founded upon God's gift of Christ to the Church (Eph. 1:22) and upon the self-sacrificing act of Christ as savior which is perpetually at work in the Church. The result is that the relation of the wife to the husband is now seen to be a participation in, and a symbolic expression of, the way the Church, as the new Eve, relates to Christ as the new Adam.[119] The development of this insight is found in the address to the husbands which takes up the rest of the passage:

> Husbands, love your wives just as Christ loved the Church and gave himself over for her that he might make her holy, purifying her in the

washing of water, with a word, that he might present to himself the
Church resplendent, not having spot or wrinkle of anything of the sort,
but that she might be holy and without fault. (Eph. 5:25–27)

The main thrust of these lines is to describe the action of Christ and to
hold this up not only as a model for imitation but as a reality from which the
husband can draw life and empowerment.[120] The rhythm "love–gave himself over" purposely evokes the same combination of terms as in Ephesians
5:2, which is itself a taking over of Galatians 2:20: all of these connect the
death of Christ with his personal love. New here is the twofold expression
of purpose (*ina*): "that he might make her holy," "that he might present
to himself." The first expression describes the act by which the Church is
prepared to be the bride of Christ, namely, the life-giving death and resurrection of Christ imparted to the Church through baptism. The second
expression depicts Christ now presenting the Church to himself (compare
2 Cor. 11:2) as a bride. Just as Yhwh God brought Eve to Adam, so here
Christ presents the new Eve to himself as a bride without any blemish (the
terminology alludes to Ezek. 16:10–14 and Song of Songs 4:7). These two
actions of Christ are permanent and abiding: baptism perpetuates the constitutive saving act by which the Church is formed and Christ's continuous
action in the Church (see Eph. 4:16). The love of the husband for his wife
and his willingness to lay down his life for her makes the action of Christ
present to her, just as her response to him makes their marriage a realization
of the Church.

"Even so husbands are obliged to love their own wives as their own
bodies. He who loves his own wife loves himself. No one ever hated his own
flesh; rather he provides and cares for it, just as Christ [does] for the Church,
because we are members of his Body" (Eph. 5:28–30). It is amazing that
loving one's wife as his own body is described as an *obligation* (*opheilousin*).
This line of thought is based in the "one flesh" terminology, as this was
understood in Genesis 2:24.[121] However, the text goes on to say that Christ
himself cares for the Church in the same way: once again he is Adam and
the Church is Eve; his care for the Church is that of a husband for his own
"flesh" or as "members of his Body." This prepares us for the following
revelation of the deeper meaning of the Genesis text:

For this reason a man will leave his father and mother and be attached
to his wife and the two will become one flesh. This Mystery is great,
but I am speaking about Christ and about the Church. (Eph. 5:31–32)

It is here, after long and careful preparation, that the understanding of
Christ and the Church as the new Adam and new Eve finally emerges. The
Church is the Body of Christ, and he is its Head precisely because, as the

new Adam, God has set Christ in his exalted position "for the Church which is his Body" (Eph. 1:22). The saving act of love by which Christ created his bride is also the act by which he sustains her and builds her up. This is more than a striking analogy. Not only does marriage provide an analogy for this relation, it is itself a realization on another level of this mystery of love. It is an actualization of that act by which Christ "ascended far above all the heavens that he might fill all things" and, giving gifts to men, "equips the holy ones for the work of ministry for the building up of the Body of Christ...to the perfect Man [Adam/Christ] to the measure of the stature of the full measure of Christ" (Eph. 4:10–13).

Husband and wife, as mutually subordinate, have received their gifts from Christ. They exercise them as sharing in the mystery of the new Adam and Eve. They too form one flesh in a way previously unavailable and unthinkable, for now they are not only one human unity, one source of a family, they are one in Christ, and by the exercise of their roles as "head" and "self-subordinate," they build up the Body of Christ. It may be wondered why the term *hypostassesthai* is never applied to the husband as it is to the wife, though discreetly (the word "wife" is never the explicit subject of the verb). We may also ask why the verb "love" is not used for the wife's activity. It may be that the terminology, though now "water made wine," still bears the marks of its origins. Or it may be that within the exercise of mutual self-subordination the mystery of this relationship still contains aspects that are hidden from our highly individualistic and rights-oriented thinking. This latter explanation is more likely. In any event, living out this relationship produces a new reality in human life:

> To have fulfilled one's role and carried out one's duties under the guidelines of mutual submission, and as a wife to have subordinated oneself voluntarily to a husband who cherishes one with a self-sacrificial love, would have been to experience a very different reality than that suggested by traditional discussions of household management.[122]

The final words of this section evoke two other Old Testament texts and return to the one with which it opened: "But still, let each of you individually love his wife as himself; as for the wife, let her fear her husband" (Eph. 5:33). The application of Leviticus 19:8 to marriage is found elsewhere in Jewish literature postdating our texts, but it may have been a commonplace at this time.[123] In the same chapter of Leviticus, we read, "Let a man fear his mother and father" (Lev. 19:3). Our text ends with themes from the Holiness Code which, now realized in Christ, tell the husband to fulfill the law of love and the wife to hold this relationship in awe as being, through her activity, the actualization of the union between Christ and the Church.

This last text is undoubtedly the most profound and explicit articulation of how the life of Christ, now shared by believers, has taken hold of human existence and raised it to a completion beyond human resources. The Genesis text sets forth Adam and Eve as the embodiment of God's plan for marriage. Our author not only appreciates this but builds on the Adam typology already found scattered in the New Testament and reveals that the marriage imagery applied to Yhwh and Israel has now taken on a human form in Christ and the Church. Just as the most profound of the Christological texts of the New Testament provides us with the context for understanding the other Christological texts, so this text on marriage brings together and raises to a new level the teaching on the relation between husband and wife. Building on the same key texts from Genesis as did Jesus, the author has opened up the full implications of the wedding between the Word and humanity. The remainder of the history of Christian marriage reveals how the continued leavening of the New Testament teaching works within the recalcitrant lump of humanity that we are, to raise us, little by little, to the "full stature of Christ."

Notes

1. For an account of the thought of Irenaeus, see Hans Urs von Balthasar, *The Glory of the Lord: A Theological Aesthetics,* trans. A. Louth, J. Saward, M. Simon, R. Williams, Studies in Theological Style: Lay Styles 3 (San Francisco, 1986), 31–94.

2. Translation in Austin Flannery, ed., *Vatican Council II: The Conciliar and Post Conciliar Documents* (Northport, N.Y., 1975), 922 (mispunctuation corrected).

3. I have discussed some of the theological consequences of this insight elsewhere. See *Narrative Parallels to the New Testament,* SBL Resources for Biblical Study 22 (Atlanta, 1988); "Literary Theory, Philosophy of History and Exegesis," *The Thomist* 52 (1988): 575–604.

4. See *Catechism of the Catholic Church* §126, which itself is drawing on *Dei Verbum* §19.

5. While some of this text may reflect later Christian-Jewish debate, its core derives from the first level of the tradition as described earlier. For a discussion of the passage, see Robert A. Guelich, *Mark 1–8:26,* Word Biblical Commentary 34A (Dallas, 1989), 358–71.

6. Some examples would be: the Prodigal Son (Luke 15:11–32); the Two Sons (Matt. 21:28–31); the Woman Searching for a Lost Coin (Luke 15:8–10); Fathers Who Know What to Give Their Children (Matt. 7:7–11; Luke 11:11–13); the Friends of the Bridegroom (Matt. 9:15–16; Mark 2:19–20; Luke 5:34–35; Gosp. Thom. §104); and the "Best Man" (John 3:29–30). The dynamics of a household are seen in such examples as: The Unmerciful Servant (Matt. 18:23–35); Slaves When Their Master Is Away (Matt. 24:45–51; Luke 12:41–46); and Slaves Entrusted with a Sum of Money (Matt. 25:14–30; Luke 19:11–27).

7. See, however, the attempt to contextualize this verse in John J. Kilgallen, "The Purpose of Luke's Divorce Text (16,18)," *Biblica* 76 (1995): 229–38.

8. In saying this, I am conscious of going against a common current in Synoptic interpretation which, usually on the basis of Markan priority, attempts to explain the Matthean text as a development of the Markan material. One must, how-

ever, distinguish the important *literary* question of Synoptic interrelationship from the *theological* question of an author's teaching, and not make this latter question depend upon a necessarily hypothetical reconstruction of the former.

9. In this context, the expression indicates "the persistent unreceptivity of a man to the declaration of God's saving will, which must be accepted by the heart of man as the center of his personal life." Johannes Behm, *"sklerokardia,"* in *Theological Dictionary of the New Testament,* ed. Gerhard Kittel and Gerhard Friedrich (Grand Rapids, Mich., 1965), 3:613–14, at 614. See also the article in Horst Balz and Gerhard Schneider, eds., *Exegetical Dictionary of the New Testament* (Grand Rapids, Mich., 1993), 3:254.

10. For a discussion of doublets in Matthew, see W. Davies and Dale C. Allison, *The Gospel according to Saint Matthew,* International Critical Commentary 1 (Edinburgh, 1988), 91–92.

11. A convenient beginning can be made by consulting Raymond Collins, *Divorce in the New Testament* (Collegeville, Minn., 1992). This work has a suitable bibliography and many summaries of opinions, but some of its conclusions are, in my opinion, inadequate. The classic in this field is still Heinrich Baltensweiler, *Die Ehe im Neuen Testament: Exegetische Untersuchungen über Ehe, Ehelosigkeit und Ehescheidung* (Zürich and Stuttgart, 1967).

12. Collins, *Divorce,* 200.

13. For the significance of this in the interim or "engagement" period, see chap. 1.

14. For a complete discussion of this question, along with a bibliography and an example of a contemporary "quiet" divorce, see Salvador Muñoz Iglesias, *Los Evangelios de la Infancia,* Nacimiento e Infancia de Jesús en San Mateo 4 (Madrid, 1990), 160–66.

15. See Balz and Schneider, eds., *Exegetical Dictionary of the New Testament,* 137–40. For more complete studies, consult Friedrich Hauck and Siegfried Schulz, *"porne, pornos, porneia,* etc." in Kittel and Friedrich, eds., *Theological Dictionary of the New Testament,* 6:579–95; Joseph Jensen, "Does *Porneia* Mean Fornication? A Critique of Bruce Malina," *Novum Testamentum* 20 (1978): 161–84; and Bruce Malina, "Does *Porneia* Mean Fornication?" *Novum Testamentum* 14 (1972): 10–17.

16. See the discussion of these laws in chap. 1 and the study by David Novak, *The Image of the Non-Jew in Judaism: An Historical and Constructive Study of the Noahide Laws,* Toronto Studies in Religion 14 (New York, 1983).

17. Joseph Bonsirven, *Le divorce dans le Nouveau Testament* (Paris, 1948).

18. For a good summary of this material, see Joseph A. Fitzmyer, "The Matthean Divorce Texts and Some New Palestinian Evidence," *Theological Studies* 37 (1976): 197–226.

19. Tarcisio Stramare, *Matteo divorzista? Studio su Mt 5, 32–19, 9,* Studi Biblici 76 (Brescia, 1986). See also M. Dumais, "Sermon sur la Montagne," in *Supplément au Dictionnaire de la Bible,* ed. Jacques Briend and Éduoard Cothenet (Paris, 1994), cols. 843–51.

20. Bernard Lonergan, *Method in Theology* (New York, 1972), 241.

21. The most complete and balanced study of this problem, to which the present treatment is indebted, is that by Richard Bauckham, *Jude and the Relatives of Jesus in the Early Church* (Edinburgh, 1990).

22. For a discussion of this James, his differentiation from "James the Little" of Mark 15:40, and the complicated problem of Mary, who was the mother of a James and a Joses, as well as the traditional names of Jesus' sisters, the reader is referred to Bauckham, *Jude,* 5–19.

23. For this reason, I find Stephen C. Barton excessively negative. See *Disciple-ship and Family Ties in Mark and Matthew,* Society for New Testament Studies Monograph Series 80, ed. Margaret E. Thrall (Cambridge, 1994), 86–96.

24. See Richard Bauckham, "The Brothers and Sisters of Jesus: An Epipha-nian Response to John P. Meier," *Catholic Biblical Quarterly* 56 (1994): 686–700, responding to the works by John Meier, "The Brothers and Sisters of Jesus in Ecu-menical Perspective," *Catholic Biblical Quarterly* 54 (1992): 1–28, and *A Marginal Jew: Rethinking the Historical Jesus* (New York, 1991), 1:316–32.

25. For a complete treatment of this theme in the Gospel of Mark, and a basis for further study, see Xabier Pikaza, "Familia messiánica y matrimonio en Marcos: Introducción exegética," *Estudios Trinitarios* (Salamanca) 28 (1994): 321–421.

26. For a successful application of this approach, refer to René Latourelle, *The Miracles of Jesus and the Theology of Miracles,* trans. Matthew J. O'Connell (New York, 1988).

27. This is surely illustrated in the story of the finding of Jesus in the temple (Luke 2:41–52). Ponder as well the excellent lines in the papal encyclical *Mother of the Redeemer* (§§12–19), or the reflections in Adrienne von Speyer, *Handmaid of the Lord,* trans. E. A. Nelson (San Francisco, 1985).

28. "Their failure is so great that it is sometimes suggested that Mark is launch-ing a deliberate attack on the Twelve, who perhaps represent a group in his own community. It is more likely, however, that Mark's emphasis on the inability of the Twelve to comprehend the truth about Jesus is due to his insistence that this truth is revealed through the cross and resurrection. The disciples thus act as a foil to Mark's own readers, who are able to recognize the good news for what it is." Morna D. Hooker, *The Gospel according to Saint Mark,* Black's New Testament Commentary (Peabody, Mass., 1991), 20–21.

29. For a study of this point, see Jacques Dupont, "Le langage symbolique des directives éthiques de Jésus dans le Sermon sur la Montagne," in *Études sur les Évangiles Synoptiques,* ed. Franz Neirynck (Leuven, 1985), 2:763–78; and Robert C. Tannehill, "The 'Focal Instance' as a Form of New Testament Speech: A Study of Matthew 5:39b–42," *Journal of Religion* 50 (1970): 372–85.

30. I have discussed this type of thinking at more length in: "Monastic Com-munity and the Summary Statements in Acts," in *Contemplative Community: An Interdisciplinary Symposium,* ed. Basil Pennington, Cistercian Studies 21 (Washing-ton, D.C., 1972), 13–46.

31. I thus differ in this point from Carolyn Osiek, "The Family in Early Chris-tianity: 'Family Values' Revisited," *Catholic Biblical Quarterly* 58 (1996): 1–24, whose article does contain much that is valuable.

32. There is a similar form of this saying, dependent upon the Synoptic tradition, in the *Gospel of Thomas, 55.* The variants offered by the *Gospel of Thomas* are neither significant nor reliable enough as evidence for an alternate early form of the sayings to be useful for our purposes.

33. See Matthew 10:39 and John 12:25, in addition to the Lukan form of this saying in Luke 14:26.

34. Joseph A. Fitzmyer, *The Gospel according to Luke I–IX,* Anchor Bible 28 (New York, 1981), 1060–61.

35. Luke concludes this passage with the saying: "So therefore whoever of you does not say farewell to all that he has cannot be my disciple" (Luke 14:33).

36. In the brief remarks which follow, I am indebted to the fine study by Pierre Grelot, "Michée 7, 6 dans les évangiles et dans la littérature rabbinique," *Biblica* 67 (1986): 363–77.

37. Translation by O. S. Wintermute in *The Old Testament Pseudepigrapha*, ed. James H. Charlesworth (New York, 1985), 2:101.

38. Grelot, "Michée 7, 6," 375.

39. See John R. Donahue, "Windows and Mirrors: The Setting of Mark's Gospel," *Catholic Biblical Quarterly* 57 (1995): 1–26.

40. For this aspect, see Bas M. F. Van Iersel, "Failed Followers in Mark: Mark 13:12 as a Key for the Identification of the Intended Readers," *Catholic Biblical Quarterly* 58 (1996): 244–63, esp. 257.

41. See the analysis by Ralph L. Smith, *Micah–Malachi*, Word Biblical Commentary 32, ed. David A. Hubbard and Glenn W. Barker (Waco, Tex., 1984), 340–42.

42. Examples are collected in Barton, *Discipleship and Family Ties*, chap. 2.

43. Some interesting insights into the interaction between Graeco-Roman culture and the message of the Gospels can be gained from the narrative in the Book of Acts: someone becoming a believer, along with "his whole household" (Acts 18:8; also 10:2; 11:14; 16:15, 31); the four daughters of Philip, "virgins [celibate?] who had the gift of prophecy" (Acts 21:9); and the independent businesswoman, a dealer in purple from Thyatira, who owned a home in Philippi (Acts 16:14, 40).

44. I owe this image to the excellent study of Everett Ferguson, *Backgrounds of Early Christianity* (Grand Rapids, Mich., 1987).

45. For a good, short overview of the variety of social roles and ranks of women in the Roman empire, see Ben Witherington III, *Women in the Earliest Churches*, ed. G. N. Stanton, Society for New Testament Studies Monograph Series 59 (Cambridge, Mass., 1988).

46. In addition to the already classic work by Susan Treggiari, *Roman Marriage: Iusti Coniuges from the Time of Cicero to the Time of Ulpian* (Oxford, 1991), Judith Evans Grubbs provides a list of studies in " 'Pagan' and 'Christian' Marriage: The State of the Question," *Journal of Early Christian Studies* 2 (1994): 361–412. See also André Burguière, Christiane Klapisch-Zuber, et al., eds., *A History of the Family*, vol. 1 of *Distant Worlds, Ancient Worlds* (Cambridge, Mass., 1996); esp. the studies therein by Yan Thomas, "Fathers as Citizens of Rome, Rome as a City of Fathers (Second Century BC–Second Century AD)," 228–69; and Aline Rouselle, "The Family under the Roman Empire: Signs and Gestures," 270–310.

47. Pseudo-Demosthenes, *Private Orations,* vol. 3, trans. A. Murray, Loeb Classical Library (Cambridge, Mass., 1939), 445–46.

48. Ferguson, *Backgrounds,* 54.

49. For a penetrating, if depressing, account of Roman married life, see Paul Veyne, "The Roman Empire," in *From Pagan Rome to Byzantium*, ed. Paul Veyne, vol. 1 of *A History of Private Life* (Cambridge, Mass., 1987), 5–234, esp. 33–49.

50. "These very early marriages were consummated: according to Suetonius, Nero while celebrating his homosexual marriage, 'imitated the shouts and screams of virgins being deflowered.' " Rouselle, "The Family under the Roman Empire," 281.

51. For a detailed description of this aspect of Roman life, see Rodney Stark, *The Rise of Christianity* (Princeton, N.J., 1996), chap. 5.

52. Thomas, "Fathers as Citizens of Rome," 256–58. Thomas goes on to point to the various legal entanglements which resulted from these practices, problems which were by no means restricted to the highest echelons of the population.

53. I put the word "friend" in quotation marks because the term *amicus* often evokes that type of superficial affection and loyalty common in our present business or political culture.

54. For an excellent study of these aspects of early Church life, see Bradley Blue, "Acts and the House Church," *The Graeco-Roman Setting*, ed. David W. J. Gill and Conrad Gempf, vol. 2 of *The Book of Acts in Its First Century Setting* (Grand Rapids, Mich., 1994), 119–222; also the article by Osiek, "The Family in Early Christianity."

55. Osiek, "The Family in Early Christianity," 12.

56. According to Veyne, "The frequency of adoption is yet another proof that nature played little part in the Roman conception of the family." "The Roman Empire," 17.

57. For a discussion of this point, see ibid., 25–29.

58. For more on the formation of children, see Rouselle, "The Family under the Roman Empire," and Peter Brown, *The Body and Society: Men, Women and Sexual Renunciation in Early Christianity* (New York, 1988); see also Henri I. Marrou, *A History of Education in Antiquity*, trans. George Lamb (New York, 1956), esp. chap. 3, "Pederasty in Classical Antiquity." On the matter of slavery, see Stanislaus Lyonnet and Léopold Sabourin, *Sin, Redemption, and Sacrifice: A Biblical and Patristic Study*, Analecta Biblica 6 (Rome, 1970), esp. part 2, chaps. 2 and 3; Veyne, "The Roman Empire," 51–69; and, for a development of the difference between persona and person, Martin, *The Feminist Question*, chap. 10.

59. For a discussion of the ancient understanding of *theos*, see Karl Rahner, "Theos in the New Testament," *Theological Investigations I* (Baltimore, 1961), 79–148.

60. Interest in the "Domestic Codes" or "Household Order Texts" in the New Testament has amassed a vast amount of scholarly material. For an account of recent research, see David Balch, *Let Wives Be Submissive: The Domestic Code in 1 Peter*, ed. James Crenshaw, Society of Biblical Literature Monograph Series 26 (Chico, Calif., 1981); idem, "Neopythagorean Moralists and the New Testament Household Codes," in *Aufstieg und Niedergang der römischen Welt*. 2/26, ed. H. Temporini and W. Haase (Berlin and New York, 1982–88), 380–411; idem, "Household Codes," in *Greco-Roman Literature and the New Testament: Selected Forms and Genres*, ed. David E. Aune (Atlanta, 1988), 25–50; James E. Crouch, *The Origin and Intention of the Colossian Haustafel*, ed. Ernst Käsemann and Ernst Würthwein, *Forschungen zur Religion und Literatur des Alten und Neuen Testaments* 109 (Göttingen, 1972); J. Paul Sampley, *"And The Two Shall Become One Flesh": A Study of Traditions in Ephesians 5:21–33*, ed. Matthew Black, Society for New Testament Studies Monograph Series 16 (Cambridge, 1971).

61. Aristotle, *Politics I*, ii, 1–9 (1253b, 1–9), trans. H. Rachman, Loeb Classical Library 21 (Cambridge, Mass., 1972), 12.

62. Ibid., 1260a, 9–14.

63. See, for instance, Aristotle, *Nicomachean Ethics VII*, x, 4 (1160b, 23–1161a, 10), Loeb Classical Library (Cambridge, Mass., 1982), 428–29.

64. For the text of Arius Didymus, preserved by the fourth-century compiler Stobaeus, see Balch, "Household Codes," 41–44; and for a good collection of texts reflecting the cumulative influence of Aristotle, see Balch, *Let Wives Be Submissive*.

65. For a study of this treatise and a comparison with the New Testament, see Kathleen O'Brien Wicker, "First Century Marriage Ethics: A Comparative Study of the Household Codes and the Conjugal Precepts," in *No Famine in the Land: Studies in Honor of John L. McKenzie*, ed. James W. Flanagan and Anita Weisbrod Robinson (Missoula, Mont., 1975), 141–53.

66. In addition to Balch, see Crouch, *The Origin and Intention*.

67. The works of Hierocles are not extant except in what has been preserved by Stobaeus, the fourth-century compiler mentioned earlier.

68. The most convenient edition of the extant works of Musonius is *Entretiens et fragments: Introduction, traduction et commentaire,* ed. Yvon Belaval and Gerhard Funke, trans. Amand Jagu, Studien und Materialen zur Geschichte der Philosophie 5 (Hildesheim and New York, 1979).

69. Ibid., *Discourse* 12, "On Sexual Pleasures," 62. These sentiments are echoed in Clement of Alexandria, *The Pedagogue II,* 10, 92, 2, Sources Chrétiennes, 108, 178; and Seneca, *Letters,* 88, trans. Richard Gummere, Loeb Classical Library (Cambridge, Mass., 1953), 29.

70. Musonius, *Discourse* 13, "On the Principal Goal of Marriage," Jagu, *Entretiens et Fragments,* 65. Jagu cites a similar teaching of Hierocles, and one must bear in mind the Pauline teaching on the fact that husband and wife have mutual authority over each other's bodies (1 Cor. 7:4), though the term *soma* has a different connotation in Paul than it does among the Stoics.

71. Failure to make the distinction between ideal and actuality in the pagan world of this time seriously flaws the article by Grubbs, " 'Pagan' and 'Christian' Marriage."

72. Seneca, *Letter XCIV,* vol. 3 of *Ad Lucilium Epistlae Morales,* trans. Richard M. Grummere, Loeb Classical Library (Cambridge, Mass., 1953), 11.

73. Epictetus, *Encheiridion,* 30, vol. 2 of *The Discourses as Reported by Arrian, the Manual and Fragments,* trans. W. A. Oldfather, Loeb Classical Library (Cambridge, Mass., 1959), 511.

74. Epictetus, *Discourse 1,* xxix, 39, vol. 1 of *The Discourses,* Loeb Classical Library (Cambridge, Mass., 1959), 197.

75. Epictetus, *Discourse 2,* xiv, 18, vol. 1 of *The Discourses,* 309. For a more complete list of Stoic statements on daily and household life, see Crouch, *The Origin and Intention.*

76. The best study of this material and its relation to New Testament teaching on marriage is that by Balch, "Neopythagorean Moralists." See also the summary of this in Balch, *Let Wives Be Submissive,* 56–58.

77. Callicratidas, *On the Happiness of Households,* 106, 1–10, trans. Thomas Taylor, *Political Fragments of Archytas and Other Ancient Pythagoreans Preserved by Stobaeus and Also Ethical Fragments of Hierocles* (London, 1822). Cited by Balch, *Let Wives Be Submissive,* 57.

78. For Palestine, the classic work is that by Martin Hengel, *Judaism and Hellenism: Studies in Their Encounter in Palestine during the Early Hellenistic Period,* trans. John Bowden, 2 vols. (London, 1974). Two new studies in relation to Diaspora Judaism, very important for an understanding of our topic, are Irina Levinskaya, *Diaspora Setting,* ed. Bruce W. Winter, vol. 5 of *The Book of Acts in Its First Century Setting* (Grand Rapids, Mich., 1996), and Peder Borgen, *Early Christianity and Hellenistic Judaism* (Edinburgh, 1996), esp. chap. 8, "Catalogues of Vices, the Apostolic Decree and the Jerusalem Meeting," 233–52.

79. For a good sociological analysis of this process, see Stark, *The Rise of Christianity,* esp. chap. 3, "The Mission to the Jews: Why It Probably Succeeded."

80. Tacitus, *The Histories V,* v, vol. 2 of *The Histories,* Loeb Classical Library (Cambridge, Mass., 1946), 183. For further examples of this type of attack on Jews and their sexual morality, see Menahem Stern, "The Jews in Greek and Latin Literature," in *The Jewish People in the First Century: Historical Geography, Political History, Social, Cultural and Religious Life and Institutions,* ed. Shmuel Safrai and Michael E. Stone, vol. 2, sect. 1 of *Compendia Rerum Judaicarum ad Novum Testamentum* (Philadelphia, 1976), 1101–59.

81. The best treatment of this topic is to be found in the study of Levinskaya, *Diaspora Setting*. See also Martin Goodman, "Jewish Proselytizing in the First Century," in *The Jews among Pagans and Christians: In the Roman Empire*, ed. Judith Lieu, John North, and Tessa Rajak (London and New York, 1992), 53–78.

82. For a treatment of the Noahide laws, see Novak, *Image of the Non-Jew in Judaism;* for their application to the New Testament, see Borgen, "Catalogues of Vices."

83. For a discussion of this latter point, see Crouch, *The Origin and Intention*, 92ff.

84. An ample selection is given by both Balch and Crouch.

85. Pseudo-Phocylides, lines 184–209, trans. P. W. Van Der Horst, in vol. 2 of *Old Testament Pseudepigrapha*, ed. Charlesworth, 562–63.

86. For a discussion of the ineptitude of the term, see John C. Brunt, "More on the Topos as a Literary Form," *Journal of Biblical Literature* 104 (1985): 495–500. For a complete criticism of the deficiencies of the mode of argument used by modern proponents of the view I have just described, see L. Hartman, "Some Unorthodox Thoughts on the 'Household-Code Form,' " in *The Social World of Formative Christianity and Judaism: Essays in Tribute to Howard Clark Kee*, ed. Jacob Neusner, Peder Borgen, et al. (Philadelphia, 1988), 219–32.

87. Edward P. J. Corbett, "The Topoi Revisited," in *Rhetoric and Praxis*, ed. Jean Dietz Moss (Washington, D.C., 1986), 43–57, at 45.

88. I say this despite the apparent use of the term to denote a discussion of household living in the Stoic author Bryson. See Balch, *Let Wives Be Submissive*, 56.

89. James D. G. Dunn gives a schematic presentation of the threefold pair structure as it is present in those early Christian texts usually designated as Household Order Texts (3:18–4:1; Eph. 5:21–6:9; 1 Pet. 2:18–3:7; 1 Tim. 2:8–15; 6:1–2; Titus 2:1–10; *Didache* 4:9–11; *1 Clement* 21:6–9; *Barnabas* 19:5–7; Polycarp, *To the Philippians* 4:2–3; and Ignatius, *To Polycarp* 4:1–5:2). James D. G. Dunn, "The Household Rules in the New Testament," *The Family in Theological Perspective*, ed. Stephen Barton (Edinburgh, 1996), 44–46.

90. Dunn's response to this view is expressed by the remark: "The emergence of a structured teaching regarding the threefold relationships of a typical household should therefore occasion no surprise or require any special or unexpected stimulus; it was simply bound to happen." Dunn, "Household Rules," 56.

91. I have discussed this more at length in *The Feminist Question*, chap. 3, "Christian Origins and the Roles of Women."

92. For a more adequate discussion of this topic, one may consult Martin, *The Feminist Question*, chaps. 11 and 12; Olivier Clément, *Corps de mort et de gloire* (Paris, 1995); Eduard Schweizer and Friedrich Baumgärtel, *"soma,"* in vol. 7 of *Theological Dictionary of the New Testament*, ed. Kittel and Friedrich, 1024–94.

93. For a brief treatment of these catalogues, see H. Conzelmann, *1 Corinthians,* trans. James W. Leitch, *Hermeneia* (Philadelphia, 1975), 100–101.

94. For a different translation, one, however, that does not affect our argument here, see Norbert Baumert, *Woman and Man in Paul: Overcoming a Misunderstanding,* trans. Patrick Madigan and Linda M. Maloney (Collegeville, Minn., 1996), 132.

95. For a discussion of the population of Corinth at this time, see H. D. Saffrey, "Aphrodite à Corinthe: Réflexions sur une idée reçue," *Revue Biblique* 92 (1985): 359–74.

96. In what comes next, I will follow for the most part the work of Norbert Baumert, *Ehelosigkeit und Ehe im Herrn: Eine Neuinterpretation von 1 Kor 7,*

ed. Rudolf Schnackenburg and Josef Schreiner, Forschung zur Bibel 47 (Würzburg, 1984). Though there are aspects of Baumert's interpretation with which I do not agree, the merit of his study is that it provides a clear and concise perspective on a very difficult passage. A summary of Baumert's position is found in *Woman and Man in Paul,* 25–129. For a different approach, see Will Deming, *Paul on Marriage and Celibacy: The Hellenistic Background of 1 Corinthians 7,* ed. Margaret E. Thrall, Society for New Testament Studies Monograph Series 83 (Cambridge, 1995).

97. This "ABA" structure can be seen in many places. One example is the teaching on the charismatic gifts in 1 Corinthians 12 and 14, which is governed by the discourse on love in chap. 13.

98. This situation is most likely the one envisaged in 1 Thessalonians 4:3–8. The term "vessel" should be taken to apply to one's fiancée or wife. See Daniel Harrington, "Wisdom at Qumran," in *The Community of the Renewed Covenant: The Notre Dame Symposium on the Dead Sea Scrolls,* ed. Eugene Ulrich and James Vanderkam, Christianity and Judaism in Antiquity Series 10 (Notre Dame, Ind., 1994), 146, referring to 4Q416, frg.7 ii 21 in which the sage is warned against dishonoring "the vessel *(kili)* of your bosom." See also Jouette M. Bassler, "Skeuos": A Modest Proposal for Illuminating Paul's Use of Metaphor in 1 Thessalonians 4:4," in *The Social World of the First Christians: Essays in Honor of Wayne A. Meeks,* ed. L. Michael White and O. Larry Yarbrough (Minneapolis, 1995), 53–66.

99. For a study of this impact, see Brown, *The Body and Society.* This must be read, however, in the light of the critiques of Robin Darling Young, "Recent Interpretations of Early Christian Asceticism," *The Thomist* 54 (1990): 123–40; and Charles Kannengiesser, "Early Christian Bodies: Some Afterthoughts on Peter Brown's *The Body and Society,*" *Religious Studies Review* 19 (1993): 126–29.

100. There are other texts which treat of the roles of women in early Christianity. For a brief treatment of these, and for further literature, see Martin, *The Feminist Question,* chap. 11.

101. For a complete study of *hypotasso,* see Gerhard Delling, "*tasso,* etc.," in vol. 7 of *Theological Dictionary of the New Testament,* ed. Kittel and Friedrich, 27–49. The two exceptions mentioned above are to be found in Plutarch, *Advice to Bride and Groom, 33* (142e), in *Moralia,* Loeb Classical Library, 2 (Cambridge, Mass., 1956), 323, and Ps-Callisthenes Hist. Alex Magnii, I.22.4.

102. Delling, *"tasso,"* 45.

103. Balch, in "Household Codes," 36–37, attempts to adduce some examples of "direct address" from the pagan literature, but these are rather an ethical use of a rhetorical device, not an address to a concrete audience.

104. Leonhard Goppelt, *A Commentary on 1 Peter,* ed. Ferdinand Hahn, trans. John E. Alsup (Grand Rapids, Mich., 1993), 19.

105. For a presentation of the numerical information about early Christianity and a description of what the Christians faced, see Stark, *The Rise of Christianity,* 7 and chap. 6.

106. Tertullian, a hundred or so years later, was still warning Christian women of the inconveniences, at best, of marrying pagan men, though the practice continued and was a principal means of evangelization. See Tertullian, *To His Wife* ii, 8, 1–5.

107. For a very balanced assessment of this aspect of early Christian life, see Stark, *The Rise of Christianity.* I realize that in taking this position I am going against the opinion of those who, basing themselves on a "deterioration" model of early Church history, see in the Domestic Codes a proof of their thesis. See Balch, *Let Wives Be Submissive;* Elisabeth Schüssler Fiorenza, *In Memory of Her: A Feminist Theological Reconstruction of Christian Origins* (New York, 1987), etc.

108. *A Commentary on 1 Peter,* 20.

109. For a balanced discussion of these points, see Jerome Quinn, "Timothy and Titus, Epistles to," *ADB,* 560–71.

110. Martin, *The Feminist Question.* See also, Simone Pétrement, "The Signs of Gnosticizing Heresies at Ephesus," part 1, chap. 4 of *A Separate God: The Christian Origins of Gnosticism,* trans. Carol Harrison (San Francisco, 1990).

111. For examples from early Jewish literature which accent Eve's responsibility and those which place the blame on Adam, see Susanne Heine, *Women and Early Christianity: A Reappraisal,* trans. John Bowden (Minneapolis, 1988), 14–19.

112. For an assessment of the question of authorship, one may consult any modern commentary. One commentary that argues for Pauline authenticity is that by Markus S. Barth, *Ephesians 1–3,* ed. William Foxwell Albright and David Noel Freedman, Anchor Bible 34 (New York, 1974). A recent study which also argues in this direction is that of Albert Vanhoye, "Personnalité de Paul et exégèse paulienne," *L'Apôtre Paul: Personalité, style et conception du ministère,* ed. Albert Vanhoye, Bibliotheca Ephemeridum Theologicarum Lovaniensium 73 (Leuven, 1986), 3–15.

113. The expression is from Andrew T. Lincoln, *Ephesians,* ed. David Hubbard, Word Biblical Commentary 42 (Dallas, 1990), xliii. See also Baumert, *Woman and Man,* 213–27.

114. For a treatment of this text, see Lincoln, *Ephesians,* 412–15.

115. See the discussion by David Daube, appended note to Edward Gordon Selwyn, "The First Epistle of Peter," *Thornapple Commentaries,* 2d ed. (rpt., Grand Rapids, Mich., 1981), 467–88.

116. The most adequate treatment of the meaning of *phobos* in this context is found in Markus Barth, *Ephesians 4–6, Anchor Bible 34A* (New York, 1974), 608, 648–50, 662–68.

117. For a discussion of this controverted term, see Joseph Fitzmyer, "Another Look at KEPHALE in 1 Corinthians 11.3," *New Testament Studies* 35 (1989): 503–11. For a balanced treatment of the whole passage, consult Joël Delobel, "1 Cor 11, 2–16: Towards a Coherent Interpretation," in *L'Apôtre Paul,* ed. Vanhoye, 369–89.

118. It may be for this reason that the term "own" (*idios*) is used in connection with the spouse so often in this text.

119. For a development of this theme, see Stephen F. Miletic, *"One Flesh": Eph. 5.22–24, 5.31: Marriage and the New Creation,* Analecta Biblica 115 (Rome, 1988).

120. For a development of the relation between imitation of Christ and participation in Christ, see Francis Martin, "Critique historique et enseignement du Nouveau Testament sur l'imitation du Christ," *Revue Thomiste* 93 (1993): 234–62.

121. The notion that a wife is the "flesh" of her husband is found in the first-century *Life of Adam and Eve,* 3. In response to Eve's plea that Adam kill her in order to placate God, Adam says, "How is it possible that I should let loose my hand against my flesh?" Charlesworth, *The Old Testament Pseudepigrapha,* 2:258.

122. Lincoln, *Ephesians,* 391.

123. "Our rabbis taught: Concerning a man who loves his wife as himself, who honours her more than himself . . . Scripture says, 'And thou shalt know that thy tent is in peace.'" Babylonian Talmud, Yebamoth 62b; cited by Crouch, *The Origin and Intention,* 113.

Chapter Three

PROGENY, FAITHFULNESS, SACRED BOND
Marriage in the Age of Augustine
Glenn W. Olsen

A text studied in the last chapter, the question of the Gospel of Matthew's rich young man — "What good must I do to win eternal life?" (19:16) — reverberates through the first Christian centuries. When the young man further stated that he had kept the commandments since his youth, Jesus responded, "If thou hast a mind to be perfect, go home and sell that belongs to thee; give it to the poor...then come back and follow me" (19:21). This presumably foreclosed the possibility of marriage. Quest for perfection seemed grounded in the abandonment of marriage and property: this was the opinion of a tradition of Christian asceticism which coalesced into the institution of monasticism about 300. The last chapter argued that the invitation to perfection found in Matthew was not an invitation to a higher form of discipleship, but to a more radical form of the vocation of every disciple. St. Basil of Caesarea (c. 330–79) presumably would have agreed with such a reading; he desired that all become "complete Christians," vowed to celibacy but remaining within their local churches rather than fleeing to the desert. But there was a distinct tendency in post-biblical writers, growing over time, to rank "states of life" according to their perfection, with the married state at the bottom of almost everyone's list.[1]

Celibacy and Marriage

Luke 20:34–35 and similar texts explicitly associated the celibate life with a foreshadowing of the resurrection of the just: "Jesus told them, The children of this world marry and are given in marriage; but those who are found worthy to attain that other world, and resurrection from the dead, take neither wife nor husband; mortal no longer, they will be as the angels in heaven are, children of God, now that the resurrection has given them birth." Those who pondered this and similar sayings of Jesus continued the relativizing of marriage and family already found in the Qumran covenanters and noted in chapter 1. By setting marriage and family within the perspectives of Kingdom and Messianic family described in the last chapter such sayings (without denying the holiness of marriage) placed marriage in a larger framework. Relation to Jesus, the Kingdom, and the Messianic family is more basic to human identity than marriage and family. A rather spectacular instance of fidelity to this insight was the early third-century North African martyr Perpetua, a mother who rejected all her father's pleas on behalf of familial and maternal duties and sensibilities, insisting, as she prepared to die for her faith, that the only proper name for herself was "Christian." Martyrdom, not motherhood, defined what she was.[2] The Church Fathers commonly said that virginity looks forward to the future kingdom. Marriage is earthbound, part of the present age which is passing away, and a reminder of the Fall. If perfection was associated with celibacy, one might well conclude that the married reveal a certain lack of single-mindedness. Paul said as much when he described the "distress" (1 Cor. 7:28) marriage carries with it and presented marriage as, among other things, a remedy for concupiscence (1 Cor. 7:9: "better to marry than to feel the heat of passion").[3]

Thus also Jesus' discussion earlier in the same chapter (19:10–12) in which addressed the rich young man. Glossators beginning at least as early as Clement of Alexandria (c. 150–c. 215) virtually all agreed that the "eunuchs, who . . . have made themselves so for love of the kingdom of heaven," referred to those who had voluntarily embraced celibacy. According to Eusebius's (c. 265–c. 339/40) report, Origen (d. c. 254) literally castrated himself.[4] Some have traced syneisactism, the practice of two unmarried ascetics of the opposite sex celibately living together, to the earliest beginnings of Christianity. Though such *virgines subintroductae,* as they were later called, faced uniform hostility throughout ancient Christianity, their existence was one more expression of the high value placed on celibacy. The last chapter noted that at a time when there was no provision for women who wished to follow the call to celibacy, one way of doing this may have been betrothal to another celibate. Another practice was spiritual marriage (permanent abstention from sexual relations either from the beginning or from some point within marriage). In addition to Paul's own expressed preference in 1 Corinthians 7:8 that the single remain single, at 7:29 he asked "those who have wives to behave as though they had none." This plea could be read in various ways. The most obvious was that Paul was asking married couples to separate from their spouses to devote themselves completely to the Lord's service. Another reading was that Paul was recommending that the married abandon sexual relations, but continue to live together. Such spiritual marriage was presumably never very common but like syneisactism naturally open to notoriety: Ignatius of Antioch's *Letter to Polycarp* 5.2, discussed below, both praised married celibacy and asked its practitioners to keep its practice secret.[5]

Though he never advanced this as an obligation, Christ had presented celibacy for the Kingdom — a gift of the Spirit for those who receive it — as an alternative to marriage. The twelfth-century Byzantine writer Theophylaktos, archbishop of Ohrid, in his *Defense of Eunuchs,* thus could look back to the Hebrew view that fertility reflected one's moral worth and point out that this system of values was now at odds with the Church. Roman law, which (as noted in the last chapter) had begun to shape marriage from the time of Augustus, punished those who would not marry, and such legislation had been included in Justinian's (527–65) *Code* (529). But Theophylaktos noted that the whole Christian esteem for celibacy had made such attitudes anachronistic. The champion of those "eunuchs" whose goal is a holy life of celibacy, Theophylaktos did not deny that the Christian emperors had encouraged reproduction; however, such legislation ignored Christianity's eschatological end, expressed in the celibate life. Against this backdrop, Christian marriage from the first was presented as a relative good — not as exalted as celibacy, but nevertheless a good of this world.[6]

Orthodox opinion, even if it vindicated the married state as good and used the word *caritas* for both the chaste friendship of celibates and marital love, was bound to acknowledge a certain inferiority in marriage. Pseudo-Cyprian, in *On the Celibacy of the Clergy,* declared, "What a great miracle, that the love between virgins makes them as the married, and the love between the married makes them as the virgins!"[7] But Gregory Nazianzen (c. 330–90) expressed common fourth-century opinion, "Marriage is a legitimate and honorable condition; but still it belongs to the Flesh: Liberty from the flesh is a better condition by far."[8] John Chrysostom (c. 349–407), with Augustine the first to set forth a detailed ethics of the married life, did not deny this ranking, but wished marriage and virginity to be praised together: "Whoever denigrates marriage also diminishes the glory of virginity. Whoever praises it makes virginity more admirable and resplendent. What appears good only in comparison with evil would not be truly good. The most excellent good is something even better than what is admitted to be good."[9]

Because of his authorship of three works on marriage, Tertullian (c. 155–c. 220) is our earliest extended entrance into post-biblical thinking. He was only one early writer who spoke of orders of "widows" and "the monogamous."[10] Though he passed over a period of years from Catholicism to the prophetic movement Montanism, he agreed with Catholic opinion that the married, by their attachment to the world and active sexuality, are, though good, at the bottom of the pyramid of perfection. Various dualist movements such as Manicheanism went further and disparaged marriage and reproduction, associating both with diabolical matter. Some interpreted Luke 20:34–36 to mean that only those who abstained from sexual relations would participate in the resurrection; the Encratites, prominent in Syrian Christianity, were one such group. Conversely, to remain continent was to anticipate the resurrection. The serious Christian was to abandon marriage and procreation altogether, and renunciation of sexual activity was a precondition for baptism. Those already married at the time of conversion were to abstain from further sexual activity and to raise their already existing children as virgins.[11]

Christian reflection on marriage by writers such as Tertullian and Clement of Alexandria often was an attempt to differentiate a proper Christian view from the denigration of marriage in such movements.[12] In Spain from the 370s, for instance, contemporaries understood the strict asceticism of Priscillianism as a condemnation of marriage.[13] The Gnostics like many others associated the female element with the material order and the male with the spiritual: the restoration of cosmic order involved the destruction of the female, and hence Valentinian Gnostics practiced a form of marriage in which the woman "became male," or spiritual. In general, for Gnostics the sexual differences which had divided Eve from Adam were to be undone and merged to obtain the goal of an asexual state of spirit. Gnostic Christians allowed unaccustomed familiarity between the sexes. Not surprisingly, though many orthodox writers thought that an original androgyny or unsexed and sinless creation would be recovered in the return of the world to its Creator, Catholics portrayed Gnostic Christians as promiscuous.[14]

The continuing tension between marriage, viewed as legitimate, and celibacy, viewed as more perfect, is nicely illustrated by the place of the widow in ancient Christianity. In both the ancient and medieval Mediterranean worlds — indeed into modern times — there was often a considerable difference in age between husband and wife, especially in the upper classes. Patterns varied by region and social class. In northern Europe with the coming of the Germanic peoples, non-aristocratic partners tended to be of approximately the same age, women married later than in the south, and choice in such matters increased as one descended the social scale.[15] In the ancient world the disparity in age of the spouses resulted in an abundance of young widows, with the attendant threat of a life of poverty. In addition to the concern for widows shown in the Book of Acts, the early second-century Christian authors Polycarp and Hermas wrote of the obligations of priests and bishops to be financial patrons of widows. Paul and the authors of the pastoral Epistles had responded in various ways to the question of remarriage of widows. From one side came counsel against second marriages and from the other counsel that, as a hedge against sin, young widows should remarry. This disagreement was connected to the radical monogamy and indissolubility of marriage Christ had preached. Some thought widows were to be exemplars of chastity for the whole community. They should not remarry. Polycarp saw them as pure offerings to God.[16] So important was chastity in a widow that an early fourth-century canon (72) of the oldest surviving local church council, Elvira in Spain, punished a widow who slept with one man but married another with perpetual excommunication, a harsher punishment than that meted out to a virgin doing the same.[17] The rigorist Tertullian was apparently the first post-biblical writer to advance the idea of an exceptionless indissolubility. By the early third century, perhaps in conjunction with his Montanist eschatology, he had also joined those prohibiting all second marriages. This rendered widowhood by definition a celibate state. Against this not uncommon view of Christian marriage's radically monogamous character, Church Fathers such as Ambrose (c. 339–97) and Augustine (354–430), while preferring that widows not remarry, argued against prohibiting them to do so. Still, Jerome (c. 347–419) pleaded that widows not repeat the mistake of marriage. They should rather take advantage of their husband's death to devote themselves wholly to the Lord.[18] In Late Antiquity feminine virtue was being redefined, and a new idealized Christian heroine appeared, who refused the marriage bed. By Jerome's day such devotion expressed itself in entrance into a convent, where a woman could become the "mother of many" spiritually. Indeed, an influential article by Edwin A. Judge argues that when monasticism appears about the beginning of the fourth century, it "represents the point at which the men at last followed the pattern long set for virgins and widows, and set up houses of their own in town, in which the life of personal renunciation and service in the church would be practiced."[19] Thus widowhood was historically a halfway house on the road from the married to the monastic state.

The taking of a nuptial veil by a virgin or a widow to show that she was becoming a spouse of Christ appropriated a central symbolism of marriage for a more perfect form of union than that of the flesh. As Jerome put it in his Letter 107.12, instructing Laeta on how her daughter Paula should study the Scriptures, Paula is to understand that the Song of Songs is a marriage song of spiritual betrothal. Jerome and others applied a language of virility — praising a woman for "manly" or "soldierly" qualities — to those they were urging either to the virgin life or to remain widows, in an argument that they were thus equal to men. The monastic life could be seen as either a hedge against sexual temptation or a path to perfection fortuitously opened. In *On Widows* Ambrose, in a formula with a great future before it, championed both a hierarchy ordered by celibacy and a variety of life in which marriage received due praise:

There are three forms of the virtue of chastity: the first is that of spouses, the second that of widows, and the third that of virgins. We do not praise any one of them to the exclusion of the others.... This is what makes for the richness of the discipline of the Church.[20]

From the first, some Christian clergy were also caught between marriage and celibacy, for they came to the clerical state already married. Debate continues as to whether in the first centuries there was a requirement of priestly celibacy, that is, that already married men agree to relinquish sexual intercourse from the time of ordination. The letters of Cyprian, bishop of Carthage from 249 to his martyrdom in 258, provide a window on this world and illustrate the problems of assessing it. Cyprian tells us that his predecessor as bishop of Carthage had been married with children and that two of Cyprian's clergy were married. However, he does not tell us whether these priests had adopted celibacy at ordination, though we know Cyprian himself encouraged a celibate priesthood.[21] So it remained into the fourth century, when provincial councils and individual bishops increasingly explicitly asked celibacy of the clergy. A canon (33) included with those of the Council of Elvira but possibly written later in the fourth century ordered married bishops and clergy, including deacons, to give up sexual relations. Canons of other councils deposed clerics who married after ordination, and as the fourth century progressed, various churches expected sexual activity to cease after ordination.[22] The requirement of continence was an expression of a liturgical tradition which linked celibacy and continence with the higher clergy's intercessory eucharistic role.

Toward the end of the fourth century, Augustine, too, inherited married clergy when he assumed his bishopric. Of these he asked continence, but the life in community he gave to his cathedral clergy ruled out any form of priestly married life.[23] In the middle of the next century, Pope Leo the Great (440–61) noted the existence of married priests and bishops in his letters, but judged that all who minister at the altar must be celibate. Anyone already married who wished to enter sacred orders had to live a spiritual marriage, relinquishing sexual relations. Despite increasing attack through the Middle Ages, a married and not always celibate clergy never disappeared from Latin Christendom and is found into the modern world in the Orthodox East and in Protestantism.[24]

The Distinctiveness of Christian Marriage

The first Christian non-biblical reference to marriage occurs at the beginning of the second century. Ignatius of Antioch writes in his *Letter to Polycarp*, 5.2, that husbands are to love their wives as Christ loves the Church and that marriage is to be made in the Lord, not for the sake of passion. Here Ignatius used the nuptial imagery of Ephesians 5 (as Clement of Alexandria would later) to stress marriage's dignity, ordered around mutual and self-sacrificing love, and to diminish the perceived distance between virginity and marriage as degrees of perfection. Tertullian's idea of companionate marriage, in which the Christian couple share every aspect of their lives, is directly descended from this "marriage in the Lord," as is the repeated exhortation to mutual love found in writers such as John Chrysostom.

Ignatius advised that spiritual marriages, in which married couples lived without sexual relations, be revealed only to one's bishop. Presumably he wanted to avoid the curiosity that spiritual marriage could attract and hoped that all would see marriage as more than an acceptable way to express sexual passion. In effect he argued that the practical concerns addressed in 1 Corinthians 7 should be ordered to the theology of Ephesians 5. Those intending to marry should receive the approval of the bishop to ensure that the marriage was the Lord's will. Though early practices seem to have varied widely and we cannot presume the presence of clergy at any stage of Christian marriage in the first centuries, by the end of the fourth century, certain regions at least expected a marriage to be blessed by a priest.[25]

Against the background of Roman and Germanic practices, Christianity set itself apart in two important ways. First, following the mutuality of rights taught in Matthew 19:9 and 1 Corinthians 7:2–4, Christian writers tended to treat the spouses as moral equals in such matters as adultery (in the later empire, mutual spousal consent was needed to separate before leaving the married for the monastic state). Clergy, often against lay resistance, tried to impose the same standards of fidelity on both sexes. As pointed out in chapter 1, Judaism understood adultery as an offense against men — that is, against a man's right to know with certainty that his children are truly his. Later several Gospel texts revolutionized this understanding by recognizing adultery against women also. By contrast, Roman society upheld double standards. The law allowed men, single or married, to sleep with slaves and women of low status while demanding virginity of single women and marital fidelity of respectable women. For a man to sleep with a slave or a woman of low status did not count as adultery: This label was reserved for sexual relations with married women of respectable status. In this context, the Christian formulation of a single standard for all, if not quite unprecedented (some pagan thinkers also condemned the double standard) was distinctive. This is not to say that the double standard was overcome in practice, including pastoral practice, though Christians were stricter in holding both sexes to the same standards than Jews and pagans had been. However, in Late Antiquity a double standard remained in many Christian aristocratic households; and church councils continued the cultural assumption that adultery is a female crime — and their sanctions generally fell very unequally on women. Just beyond the period covered in the present chapter, Caesarius of Arles (c. 470–543) preached against a double standard in regard to adultery and concubinage and stated, "whatever is not lawful for women is equally unlawful for men." But he declared (*Sermons* 42.5; 43.2–5) that the number of men who have concubines before marriage is so large they could not all be excommunicated.[26]

Christianity also set itself apart in its emphasis on indissolubility, following Jesus' ban on divorce. In a sense Christianity continued the story Judaism had been developing. While stressing indissolubility, early Christians sometimes divorced for adultery and allowed the "Pauline privilege," based on 1 Corinthians 7:15, whereby a marriage could be dissolved by a pagan because of the conversion, after marriage, of his or her spouse to Christianity.[27] Long-established patterns persisted, and there is some evidence from the first centuries of Christians divorcing and remarrying for other reasons. Origen, who thought this contrary to Jesus' teaching, noted that, to avoid fornication, some bishops sanctioned remarriage while a divorced spouse lived. In the West, with Tertullian and North African Christianity leading the way, the Church tended to insist by about 400 on the invalidity of remarriage following divorce. The story in the East was more complicated and in the end represented less of a break from former practices. From the time of Constantine unilateral divorce came under an imperial attack, which varied from reign to reign. In 542 Justinian prohibited divorce by mutual consent, but Justin overturned this decree in 566. Although scholars have repeatedly affirmed Christian influence on post-Constantinian legal development, it is difficult to show that this legislation imposed anything beyond the traditional "Augustan" concern for upper-class morality, reinforced by Constantine's concern for a return to a stratified social order. The post-Constantinian East stressed indissolubility but treated remarriage under penitential discipline as adultery: after a remarried couple had undergone penance as adulterers, they could be readmitted to the sacraments and remain together. This remains the practice of the Orthodox churches. The principal legal concern regarding remarriage was the property rights of children thus affected. Because marriage remained part of the civil law, the Church's first interest was pastoral and penitential: to declare the indissolubility of marriage and to prescribe the appropriate penance for those recognized by the State as divorced and remarried. As in the history of Israel, the insistence on indissolubility put the Church on the side of protecting women, and some historians have argued that Christian families experienced less dislocation because of divorce than pagan families.[28]

We must remember that, especially in the Roman world, marriage was based on continuing accord between the spouses. When such accord disappeared, divorce was allowed, either by mutual consent or through repudiation. As we saw in the last chapter, passion was often separated from marriage, being channeled into prostitution, pederasty, adultery, and concubinage — the last fed by Roman prohibition of marriage between classes. Roman men did not necessarily expect their sexual desires to center on their wives and did not necessarily expect marriage to satisfy sexual passion. According to Michel Rouche, we find already in the Roman upper classes' long-standing inability to replace themselves a kind of "plague of the rich" resulting from a dissociation of sexuality from fecundity.[29]

Though love and affection between spouses was common and the procreation of children was a central expectation of Roman marriage, the fidelity expected of spouses was asymmetrical because of different standards for husbands and wives.[30] The matter is complicated. Ovid, for example, advocated an anti- or extramatrimonial love that expresses this double standard and, if one were to believe writers such as C. S. Lewis, filled the ancient world. Yet he has so much to say about faithful love that one author has written an entire chapter on "Ovid's Endorsement of Married Love."[31] Nevertheless, no one can doubt the assymmetry present in the sometimes draconian punishment for adultery (death or exile) which we find from the third century (though it was not regularly imposed) directed in traditional fashion against adulterous women.

In the face of those who took such a double standard for granted, Jesus, Paul, and Augustine centered sexual expression on the marital relationship. Whether satisfied or thwarted, passion was to remain within the marital bond. Paul was so absorbed by this question in 1 Corinthians 7 that he presented marriage more as a licit expression of passion within a spiritual and moral partnership than as the sphere of propagation. Similarly, when the Manichees played off a pro-reproductive Old Testament against an ascetical New Testament, theologians like Augustine (once a Manichee himself) knew their views could not be summarily dismissed. They may not have gotten it right, but such groups showed great moral seriousness in wondering whether carnality ties down, deflects, or destroys all that is highest in humankind.[32]

The Good of Marriage

A mingled attitude of suspicion of and fascination with Eros in its many meanings runs through the ancient world. Among the Romans, Seneca condemned all (selfish) sexual desire directed toward one's spouse. Like his first-century Stoic contemporary Musonius Rufus, he held that only the desire for children justifies intercourse.[33] An appetitive desire or acquisitive love might be condemned, but some spoke of another kind of marital love — a fixed intellectual commitment, a firmness of will, a steady regard for the

good of another.[34] Such views formed the background of Christian thought
about both marriage and celibacy. They fed the idea (common though not
universal throughout ancient and medieval Christianity) that sexual pleasure should not be sought for its own sake, should not be the justification
for sexual relations.[35] Even so, throughout the history of Christianity, we
must distinguish the views of Christian intellectuals (often inclined to some
form of asceticism or some Christian parallel to Stoicism) from those of the
"average" Christian. Judith Evans Grubbs argues a high degree of continuity between pagan and Christian values and practice, especially in the first
three centuries of Christian history; she warns against false impressions of
discontinuity fostered by the study of polemical literature written to further
the cause of celibacy in Augustine's day. For certain parts of the East from
the third to the sixth centuries, sufficient epigraphic evidence survives to estimate Christian family size, and there we find averages of six children (four of
whom lived to at least five years of age) per couple.[36] The Romans normally
understood the procreation of children as the raison d'être of marriage. The
tabulae nuptiales, a part of the marriage contract that often concluded a betrothal, stated this. A second-century Christian writer such as Justin Martyr
(d. c. 165) agreed, writing in his *First Apology*, 29, that Christians marry
only to bring up children.

In a world of brief life expectancy, most Roman fathers were preoccupied
with the need to provide for their children's future before they themselves
died. As in earlier cultures, one way of doing this was through wedding gifts
and dowry. The warning given in the first chapter above about seeing the
wedding gift and dowry as no more than financial transactions also applies
to our understanding of the Romans. Certainly family and financial considerations were important. Few adult men had living fathers, and all had to
assume that this would be their sons' fate also. The common pattern of late
marriage for men only aggravated the likelihood that a new bride would
end a widow. Roman fathers also faced the possibility of a daughter either
divorcing her husband or losing him early; hence the common practice of
a father granting only sufficient dowry to his daughter to maintain her. A
married daughter remained legally a part of her father's household, and it
was wise for a father to keep back the bulk of his patrimony for later inheritance should her husband die or divorce occur. Aside from such financial
and juridical concerns, the Romans expected love and affection to be shown
toward both children and wife, as the last chapter showed. By the late Republic they had formed a "sentimental ideal...focused on a standard of
companionate (but not necessarily equal) marriage and a delight in children
as individuals and as symbols of the home comforts."[37] This sentimental
ideal, which must frequently have been superficial, seems to have existed at
every social level. Evidence survives of both freemen and slaves imitating

upper-class marriage in appropriating the languages of law and love to describe their own permanent relationships. A freedwoman "bound by love" might call her husband "dearest" (*coniunx carissimus*). Romans were less suspicious of such sentiments than were some of their philosophers. Pliny the Younger (c. A.D. 61–113) began a letter to his wife: "You cannot believe how much I miss you." This of course does not mean that Roman marriage was built on the self-giving love which was the goal of the Christian Scriptures. Roman ideals and practices were far from uniform. Before the early third century, brother-sister and other forms of close-kin marriage and bigamy were found in Egypt and the Near East. After A.D. 212, when citizenship and thus the Roman law was extended to all free inhabitants, the Romans continued to tolerate a wide variety of practices in the provinces. Nevertheless, Roman marriage customs expressed ideals of discipline and fidelity, even of love, with which Christians could identify. Pliny's contemporary Plutarch defined marriage as copartnership. Writing *Advice to the Bride and Groom* for newlyweds, he says:

> It is a lovely thing for the wife to sympathize with her husband's concerns and the husband with the wife's, so that, as ropes, by being intertwined, then get strength from each other, thus, by the due contribution of goodwill in corresponding measure by each member, the copartnership may be preserved by the joint action of both. (*Moralia*, trans. Loeb, vol. 3, 313)

Two centuries later, the convert Lactantius speaks of the equal right (*ius*) of man and wife in marriage. He draws an analogy between how birds and humans "marry," live in concord of mind and affection, and love their offspring. Such a melding of pagan and Christian ideals should warn us of the danger in too sharp a contrast between a debauched pagan Rome and high Christian sexual mores. The charge is sometimes made of general Roman laxity in sexual matters before the time of Constantine, after which we find a harsh and moralizing legislation epitomized by the Theodosian Code later in the fourth century. The situation was never so simple. The increasing severity of much late Roman legislation was in place by Diocletian's day (284–305), before the victory of Christianity, and this should warn us against simplistic notions of a general Roman moral laxness. Many Christians, like many Jews before them, made various moralizing comparisons to their fellow citizens, but to the degree that the surviving records allow assessment, adultery, abortion, and divorce seem to have been uncommon in all centuries of the Roman world. The same cannot be said of the abandonment and exposure of infants, which Lactantius like other Christians roundly condemns.[38]

Getting Married

An older form of Roman marriage, *cum manu,* resembled a matrimonial process existing throughout the ancient Near East. In this, the father of the prospective groom proposed marriage to the father of the prospective bride on the basis of family interests: Roman law required both the couple and their fathers or paternal grandfathers to consent. As noted above, Roman marriage was initially a private and family transaction, but from the time of Augustus increasingly became a public concern. The last chapter ascribed a two-stage process — betrothal and marriage — to Greek and Roman marriage. Some scholars, however, differentiate betrothal from the negotiations which preceded it, thus marking three stages: *petitio* (negotiations), *desponsatio* or *sponsalia* (betrothal), and *nuptae* (wedding).

In marriage *cum manu,* the wife joined her husband's *familia* and thus was under his authority, with her property in his power. As Jewish wisdom literature also shows, the affection and love of husband and wife, though mutual, did not create an equal relationship. Marriage *sine manu* — in which the wife was seen as an adult in her own right and not simply under the tutelage of her husband or transferred to his family — was the predominant practice by the time of Christ and virtually the only practice by the third century. Though it encouraged a sense that marriage was a partnership between adults, most spouses must have taken for granted a certain social/legal, perhaps ontological, inequality between husband and wife. Spouses were to be comparable socially, but that did not require them to be equal in other ways. Widespread cultural assumptions associated male sexuality with activity and domination, and female sexuality with passivity and reception. This of itself involved a form of subordination which — for those few who knew their Roman authors — fell short of the Ciceronian idea of friendship between equals ("Friendship is agreement on both human and divine affairs, combined with good will and mutual esteem"). Marital love between near-equal partners was the ideal.[39]

The biblical writers had given Christians distinctive ideas about the meaning and practice of marriage, but no specific procedure or liturgy for marrying. The development of these was the work of centuries. Like everyone else, Christians contracted marriage according to Roman law. A word for the Roman marriage contract, *foedus,* had as one meaning "covenant" and allowed Christians into the Middle Ages to attach to the Roman act biblical understandings of the marriage covenant. Christians agreed with the Roman law that "consent makes a marriage" and thus like the Romans tended to see *sponsalia,* betrothal, as the decisive stage in forming a marriage. It ratified the transfer of dowry or property, and those seeking to break the betrothal suffered penalties. The spouses commonly lacked the wherewithal to set up a home. Thus some transfer of property at the point of marriage, such as the dowry (*dos*), usually given by the father of the bride was usually critical. (Despite many permutations, this would remain true into the early modern world.) A dowry was not necessary for contracting a marriage, but was in the woman's interest, not least because the Roman law used it to differentiate between concubinage and marriage. In the later empire dowry was frequently paired with a substantial pre-nuptial gift (*donatio*) from *sponsus* to *sponsa* (pre-nuptial gifts, presents, might be given by either spouse), until Justinian declared that *dos* and *donatio* should be equal. The *donatio* could also be viewed as compensation for loss of virginity, as was the case among the Germans. In the eastern Mediterranean and among Semitic peoples, this gift, like the dowry, remained in the husband's control as long as he lived, but was returned to the wife or her father in the case of death or divorce without good reason and was intended to help support her in such contingencies.[40]

Sponsalia was often marked by an elaborate party. Some form of document, possibly mentioning the dowry the bride had brought to the marriage or the property of each at the time of marriage, was usually drawn up, and often other family rites led up to or composed *nuptae*. Between *sponsalia* and the wedding could come an exchange of gifts, and the *sponsus* would send a ring as pledge of his fidelity to the *sponsa*. The pagan writer Aulus Gellius, writing in the second half of the second century A.D., tells us in *Attic Nights* X.10 that both Greeks and Romans wore a ring on the fourth finger of the left hand because a fine nerve connected that finger to the heart, the supreme human organ. No specific act or ceremony was necessary to conclude the betrothal, although one common rite was the *dextrarum iunctio* — the joining of the bride and groom's right hands. Such a sign of marital concord was very old. In the Glypothek in Munich there is an Attic woman's grave monument from about 375 B.C. showing the gesture, which could signify that in death a couple remain united in spirit. In Rome the joining of right hands, a sign of political agreement among men, also came to symbolize marital concord. A double sarcophagus from about A.D. 240 (also in the Glypothek) shows a man and wife with a little Hymen (the spirit of marriage) standing below their joined right hands. Such ceremonies simply fulfilled a contract already formed. Thus there was a lack of precision about what act constituted marriage, and little uniformity in the matter of *nuptae*, marriage's third stage. This may stand behind the apparently weak link in early Christian practice between betrothal and any subsequent wedding ceremony or nuptial mass.[41]

This lack of specificity about the point at which two people were married may help explain Christian acceptance of the Roman idea that the spouses married each other, rather than being married by some third party. Roman

practices inclined Christians to see consent as what makes a marriage; they
then added to this an ecclesiastical blessing as token of the Church's witness.
As early as Tertullian's *On the Veiling of Virgins* 11.9 (before 207), veiling, a
kiss, and a joining of right hands constituted the stages of Christian *desponsatio,* a term which, while used in various ways, often signified betrothal.
Tertullian notes that in Carthage men choose their own wives, and physical
attractiveness plays a part in this choice. It is unusual for a Christian of the
early centuries to say this. A century later Tertullian's fellow North African
Lactantius goes further (anticipating the mature views of that third North
African, Augustine) by saying that sexual desire is natural and acceptable.
Lactantius approved marital sexual relations when procreation was impossible, including (alone among known early Christians) during pregnancy.
Here his reasoning was derived from Paul and anticipated Augustine: the
desire itself is natural, and immorality is prevented by centering it on one's
spouse. Both procreation and the licit expression of desire justify sexual
relations.[42]

Debate continues as to Roman law's understanding of consummation (in
addition to consent) as essential to the existence of a marriage. By the later
fourth century, the sufficiency of consent became involved in theological controversy. (By Roman standards, Mary and Joseph had had a true marriage,
even absent consummation.) Tertullian, in his second treatise, *To His Wife,*
2.8, written sometime between 202 and 206, witnesses to the importance of
consent, telling us that "children do not rightly and lawfully wed without
their fathers' consent." That is, Tertullian (as a good Roman) understood
the marital consent on which marriage to include that of the fathers.[43]

Especially in an age when marriage involved the very young, "consent"
must rarely have involved actual choice of the partner. No one knew the use
of marriage to advance family interests better than Augustine himself. In his
native North Africa, the great landowners understood that even the religious
divide between Catholic and Donatist could be surmounted in pursuit of a
profitable marriage. At the bidding of his mother, who wanted him to better
his place in society, Augustine reluctantly abandoned a fourteen-year liaison
to become engaged to a ten–year-old girl "of good family." *Concubinatus,*
the state which Augustine thus abandoned, had since Augustus's time been
promoted as an alternative union between parties who, perhaps because of
social inequality, could not enter *iustum matrimonium,* a legal marriage.
Similarly, in the Middle Ages a young noble might take a concubine who
would be replaced when he married a woman of his own social class to
produce legitimate children.[44]

The question of whether a Christian marriage rite existed in the patristic
period is disputed.[45] If we mean by this a universal or even fairly common
rite, the answer is that it did not. But clearly various rites were celebrated. In

the *Letter to Polycarp,* 5.2, referred to above, Ignatius wished the bishop to examine a couple's Christian understanding of what they were doing before they entered marriage. A century later, Tertullian provides evidence of an incipient Christian marriage ceremony. We have noted his implicit adoption of the Roman notion that betrothal and marriage take place by stages, and his citing of various ceremonies: the veil, the kiss, the joining of right hands. He also portrays the bishop visiting the newlywed couple's house to say prayers, and by 400 the priest's blessing on a marriage, perhaps at betrothal, seems common. In lines immediately preceding those quoted above about parental consent, Tertullian speaks of "that marriage which the church unites, the offering strengthens, the blessing seals, the angels proclaim, and the Father declares valid" (*To His Wife,* 2.8). Many regard this as evidence for a specifically Christian marriage ceremony by about 200, involving a nuptial mass — Tertullian's "offering." Of course we have only references to or descriptions of such a rite, not the rite itself. However, this supports Chiara Frugoni's theory that the most common objects from the third to the fifth century portraying Christian marriage — gold glass cups — are memento nuptial communion cups. Tertullian's probable reference to a nuptial mass and clear reference to the witness of angels and God stresses that, whatever the similarities between Christian and pagan marriage, Christian marriage was entered into "before God."[46]

The development of this Christian idea of marriage "before God" received iconographical expression in the late empire by occasional representations of marriage on the gilded glasses (found in large numbers in the catacombs at Rome), which Frugoni takes to be nuptial communion cups. Here Christ holds marriage crowns over the couple's heads.[47] Only from the end of the fourth and the early fifth century do we find actual texts of a nuptial veiling (*velatio*) and blessing (*benedictio*), two paired acts which subsequently occur with great frequency. Thus the Leonine sacramentary, composed from the end of the fourth through the sixth century, contains prayers for a *velatio nuptialis,* literally the veiling of a bride (presumably in the sense of a nuptial mass), and for the blessing of a marriage. John Chrysostom seems to describe an evening Christian blessing preceding a wedding ceremony the next day. The epithalamium of Paulinus of Nola from about 405 A.D., quoted at the close of the present chapter, assumes that Christian weddings — with veiled spouses and a bishop's blessing — are celebrated in church. We may be misled here, however, for Paulinus was a married priest, and in his day priests were increasingly required to marry in church: this suggests that many laymen did not do so. It is unclear how much we should rely on the earliest surviving liturgical texts of the Roman nuptial blessing for evidence of the patristic period. In any case, Paulinus seems to witness to a specifically Christian marriage ceremony existing by

Augustine's day. But only well into the medieval period do we find a required church ceremony, in either the East or the West. As a footnote we might add that Ambrose (c. 339–97) and Augustine, knowing that Roman wedding festivities were occasions for possible scandal, were reluctant to have priests present at them.[48]

Being Married

The Romans spoke of marriage as a communion of life, but generally meant this in the straightforward sense that the couple shared their lives, or lived together. They expected a vague *affectio maritalis* of marriage. As a legal term this originally meant little more than consent to have another as spouse. This developed as a way of distinguishing concubinage from contubernium. (Legally, concubinage was a state in which at least one of the partners did not intend marriage; any children from such a union would be illegitimate but acknowledged.) *Contubernium*, which originally signifies "living together," a stable relation with a slave, could produce legal children. Both pagans and Christians sometimes also spoke of companionship in marriage. A famous text of Tertullian in *To His Wife*, already partially cited above, shows this idea flowering very early in Christian circles. Speaking against marriage outside the Christian community, that is, between Christian women and men who remain pagans, Tertullian describes the Christian couple thus:

> What a bond is this: two believers who share one hope, one desire, one discipline, the same service! The two are brother and sister, fellow servants. There is no distinction of spirit or flesh, but truly they are *two in one flesh* (Gen. 2:24; Mark 10:8). . . . Together they pray, together they prostrate themselves, together they fast, teaching each other, exhorting each other, supporting each other.
>
> Side by side in the church of God and at the banquet of God, side by side in difficulties, in times of persecution, and in times of consolation. Neither hides anything from the other, neither shuns the other, neither is a burden to the other. They freely visit the sick and sustain the needy. . . . They do not have to hide the sign of the cross, or be afraid of greeting their fellow Christians, or give blessings in silence. They sing psalms and hymns to one another and strive to outdo each other in chanting to their Lord.

Here we go far beyond the legal idea of *affectio* to what might be termed Christian companionate marriage, in which the spouses see their shared life as a communion in all things, "teaching each other" and urging each other to grow in the faith.[49] 1 Corinthians 7:14, in which Paul had suggested that an unbelieving spouse might be sanctified by the prayers of a believer, seems to lie behind Tertullian's ideas. In marriage each spouse should seek the salvation and sanctification of the other. Many (perhaps most) Christians saw spiritual progress in marriage as a work of the spouses separately rather than of the couple jointly. But the early Tertullian saw the Christian couple as made to "think and pray together," engaging in life's activities as a couple, though he could also present the death of a spouse as a release from the enslaving bonds of matrimony. Tertullian's Christian couple is almost a "domestic church," and indeed about this time Clement of Alexandria applied Matthew 18:20, with its statement that Christ is present where two or three are gathered together, to the family.[50]

By the late empire, under Christian influence, the legal idea of *affectio* developed in the direction of our "affection," receiving an emotional coloration that could designate something like respect or esteem. Christians such as Methodius of Olympus (d. 311) went much further, presenting marital union as a continuation of creation and the pleasures of procreation as an enchantment in love in which everything is forgotten in desire for children, two becoming one.[51] John Chrysostom also spoke of the "union of love between wife and husband" and of marriage as ordered around "love and desire." In a well-known homily he suggests that the young husband should say to his wife:

> I have taken you in my arms, and I love you, and I prefer you to my life itself. For the present life is nothing, and my most ardent dream is to spend it with you in the life reserved for us. . . . I place your love above all things, and nothing would be more bitter or painful to me than to be of a different mind than you.[52]

Here we have something very different from Seneca's suspicion of desire directed toward one's spouse, though the *eros* of which Chrysostom speaks is not appetitive. His language is of tenderness and unending life together, recalling what the eighteenth-century poet James Thomson would call "esteem enlivened by desire."[53] Jean H. Hagstrum has attempted to trace the origins of the modern concept of companionate marriage, built on the union of sexual desire with marital friendship. Unfortunately, Hagstrum's treatment of the Church Fathers is inadequate and most selective.[54] He never mentions Methodius, who clearly appreciates marital sexual ecstasy. If Chrysostom's reference to the husband taking his wife in his arms is tender rather than passionate, clearly his expectation was of mutual esteem. What Cicero had associated with friendship between males has been transferred to married couples.[55] Though he does not specifically envision the marital relationship as ripening friendship, Chrysostom presents a companionate marriage joining mutual esteem and sexual desire. As with Tertullian, he holds up a specifically Christian, self-sacrificing love, a love which seeks the good of the other. Chrysostom does not seem very different from his contemporary, Augustine, who in his mature thought saw desire as natural to humans even in prelapsarian Eden. Augustine argued that the "pledge of affection of the soul," not physical relations, was the center of marriage. The holiest examples of marriage were not individualistic quests for the salvation of the spouses in isolation, but a shared mental intercourse or companionship.[56]

Peter Brown and others have argued that Christians absorbed many of their most basic attitudes toward marriage and procreation from the world around them. Romans who had imbibed certain Stoic attitudes were particularly likely to see sexual intercourse as undignified and animal-like. It was necessary to propagate the family, but when indulged in for pleasure, was a kind of suspension of reason, of the desired control of mind over passion. In Augustine's description of sexual intercourse, "so intense is the pleasure that when it reaches its climax there is an almost total extinction of mental alertness; the intellectual sentries, as it were, are overwhelmed."[57] In part this was a question of dignity. Jerome (c. 347–419), following Sextus the Pythagorean, would famously say, "The too ardent lover of his own wife is an adulterer."[58] For a man to approach his wife dominated by the goal of seeking pleasure was to treat her as a mere object of passion. Augustine taught his congregation the distinction between raw desire or lust, and a conjugal love which need not be expressed physically at all. Marriage might exist without sexual intercourse or procreation per se, but could not come into existence without agreement between spouses to live a shared life: "intercourse of the mind . . . is more intimate than that of the body." A marriage, Augustine held, does not dissolve because of complete continence. Old people are no less married for the absence of carnal relations. The greatest of the three goods of marriage, its sacrament or bond, that which makes it indissoluble, remains in infirmity and old age, whether sexual intercourse is possible or not.[59] Marital intercourse in the larger Roman view was one of life's duties, appropriate to the early years of marriage when one was forming a family. Hence the close association of intercourse with propagation: it was not just the philosophers who thought that only the desire to conceive a child sanctioned an act of intercourse. Such thinking led Jerome and many after him to consider sexual relations during pregnancy most shameful.[60]

Almost certainly (we say "almost" because there is some debate about the effectiveness of ancient methods of artificial contraception) such views were socially reinforced by the absence of reliable methods of artificial contraception. Spouses were advised to calculate very carefully the responsibilities they might incur for a few minutes of sexual pleasure. Wisdom was on the side of strict control of sexual appetite, of having intercourse only when a child was desired. The idea found first in Justin Martyr (c. 110–c. 165) — that no act of intercourse was without sin unless engaged in for the purpose of conceiving a child — was widely accepted among theologians. Between 220 and 230, Hippolytus of Rome apparently authored an attack on his rival Pope Callixtus in which he denounced Callixtus for allowing contraception.[61] The facts are uncertain, and Hippolytus's logic rather tortured: He accused the ex-slave Callixtus of permitting marriages between free women and slaves. Because propertied women would want to avoid the dissipation of their property through the children of such unions, Hippolytus accused Callixtus of encouraging contraception and abortion, both understood as murder. (The *Didache,* the oldest source of Christian law, dating from about the late first or first half of the second century, declared, "You shall not kill the embryo by abortion and shall not cause the newborn to perish."[62]) In sum, aside from the condemnation of abortion and infanticide, the Christian idea of spiritual marriage, which in the ancient period usually involved continence from some time later in the marriage, differed primarily only in its spiritual rationale from one pattern of marital practice found among the Roman upper classes. Either for a time, or permanently after their family was completed, the couple mutually agreed to forgo sexual intercourse.

Some of the background for this call for Christian couples to practice periods of sexual abstinence was not specifically Christian. It was widely believed that during certain periods, such as pregnancy and lactation, abstinence was in order. In addition, certain Jewish ideas of ritual impurity carried over into Christianity and reexpressed themselves in the ideas that a couple should abstain from sexual relations before taking communion, or until the wife had been "churched" after childbirth, or during certain penitential periods of the liturgical calendar. The suggestion of 1 Corinthians 7:5 that one might wish to abstain from sexual relations for a time for prayer assumed that a pleasure-seeking attitude interferes with prayer and self-examination. As Origen (heavily influenced by Plato) observed before the middle of the third century, marriage is a state caught between flesh and spirit. Placed between body and soul, marriage partakes of both and must be disciplined if the attractions of the flesh are not to obstruct movement toward the Spirit.[63] Even in writers who tried to give the daily activities of an active life their due, such as Augustine, we find a powerful logic of purity and superiority at work, against which sexual expression itself — indeed every worldly activity — is a potential distraction from prayer. In *Sermon* 205, Augustine says that Lent should be a period of sexual abstinence. Time previously occupied in paying the conjugal debt should be spent in supplication, and the body which has been dissolved in carnal desire should reach out in pure prayers. The hand formerly entwined in embraces should be extended in address to God — as though the body is a zone of carnality from which one must extract one's hand to pray. Ascetical and impurity themes reinforce one another to render the idea that there is a time and season for everything. The relative importance of "purity" vis-à-vis ascetical themes varied from author to author. Clement and Augustine, for example, consciously attempted to reduce or eliminate those taboos of the purity codes for which they could not find a spiritual rationale. Thus Clement attacked the need to purify oneself by washing after intercourse.[64]

Debate on the Dignity of Marriage during the Age of Augustine

Some authors pursued the logic of perfection outside boundaries acceptable to the *Katholikon* and concluded not just that marriage was inferior to celibacy, but that it was intrinsically impure or evil. In the late 380s and 390s Augustine took issue not only with the Manichaean attack on all things material, but also with overzealous orthodox writers such as Jerome. On the other hand, he also opposed spirits such as Jovinian, who in the 390s had insisted that the married state was in no way inferior to virginity and that there was no ascetical rank of merit.[65] Modern scholars have traced Augustine's ambivalence to his attempt to mediate between two opposing views: the attack on marriage found in certain ascetical movements, both orthodox and heretical, and the unstinting praise of marriage and sexuality by the Pelagians.[66]

With the birth of monasticism in Syria-Palestine and Egypt around 290, marriage had increasingly been placed on the defensive. The promoters of monasticism, which spread into the West about 350, often advanced their cause by attacking the married state or labeling it inferior. Giving a Christian form to a tradition of attack on women and marriage going back to Hesiod, works such as Jerome's *Against Helvidius Concerning Mary's Perpetual Virginity* enumerated marriage's disadvantages.[67] With its unrelenting circle of daily tasks, marriage leaves little time for prayer or peace, and thus, the complaint goes, is distinctly inferior to virginity. Until the twelfth century, when the monks themselves finally reassess their attitudes and present marriage and women in a more favorable light, monastic propaganda worked to marriage's disadvantage.[68] Great monk-popes warned that marriage contained more tears than laughter.[69]

But the proponents of radical asceticism often found it hard going in the larger Christian community. Fathers and mothers were reluctant to see their sons and daughters disappoint family expectations and adopt a radical mode of Christian life. Upper-class families were especially concerned with perpetuating their family lines, and this obligation lay particularly heavily on women.[70] Constant reiteration of the inferiority of the married state also drew a more theological reaction, with here and there voices insisting that the married state was in no way inferior. In the later fourth and early fifth centuries, a great debate engaged some of the most prominent figures on both sides. Vigilantius, Jovinian, Helvidius, and especially the formidable Pelagian Julian of Eclanum tended to reject all long-standing schemas of perfection that presented virginity as a particularly meritorious state. To some extent these writers merely maintained earlier views of the naturalness of sexual desire and procreation in a time of increasing propaganda for asceticism. On the other side Jerome, Ambrose, and Augustine defended traditional ideas of the superiority of virginity in one form or another, but also developed new distinctions under the impact of controversy.[71]

For Augustine (interpreting Paul in 1 Cor. 7), there was a real difference in the degree to which the various states of life could single-mindedly serve the Church, but also a difference in the gifts given to people. Virginity was superior to marriage, as he argued in *Holy Virginity* (c. 401), but this point could be made without deprecating the lesser state of life. Further, one had to distinguish between the degree of perfection found in each state of life in general and the love embodied in any particular life: by the quality of their love some laymen stand higher than some priests and monks. Others might simply place the virgins in the top rank, but Augustine advanced a "mixed" notion of perfection in which the most perfect Christian was the one who united the highest state of perfection, virginity, with office in the Church. Those who united the virgin state with priesthood were to be placed highest, followed by the continent and the chaste married, the latter those who lived faithfully within the laws of marriage.[72]

The Good(s) of Marriage according to Augustine

In *The Good of Marriage* (401), Augustine lists the three goods of marriage as progeny (*proles*), faithfulness, specifically sexual fidelity (*fides*), and sacred bond or indissolubility (*sacramentum*). The title of this work speaks of the *good* of marriage in the singular, and this is the procreation of children, but the work itself speaks of *goods* in the plural, as does all his subsequent writing on the subject.[73] With him is aligned a whole tradition, extending down to and beyond Vatican II, that attempts to find the proper relation between the individual marital goods so that the goodness of the institution as a whole may be grasped. This is no easy task. Augustine's thought roves between the physical and spiritual sides of marriage, between a procreation dependent on physical intercourse and a marital companionship spiritual in nature. For him consent, not consummation, makes marriage, and, though children are its specific good, love is its end. This end, as Augustine writes in *Good of Marriage*, 18, 21, is no less than the unity of the heavenly city signified in the union of man and woman in marriage.[74] The inner reality of marriage parallels that of the Church: the goal is a full joining of spirits in a forgiving love which patiently bears with the other and heals pride and self-ishness in mutual service (6, 6). Chap. 3 of *Good of Marriage* speaks of the bond between Christian spouses as an "order of love." While the perfection of unity will only be found after this life, in Christian times the polygamy of the Old Testament has been reduced to monogamy in sign of this unity.[75] As to the first of his three goods, procreation, Augustine reversed the stance of the Manichaeans. They were pro-contraceptive and anti-reproductive; he was the opposite.[76]

All three goods enunciate the preeminently social view of marriage Augustine had by this time come to take. In the dialogues written before his ordination as bishop of Hippo in 395, Augustine understood the themes of the Kingdom of God in Matthew's Gospel as defining paradise and heaven, man's original and final states. Sexual relations were excluded from both, and the highest forms of human life centered on the contemplative relation of the individual to God, not blood relations. Augustine continued to reserve an exalted place for all forms of spiritual relationships — married, clerical, and monastic. But in *Good of Marriage* Augustine's emphasis was on the nobility of the customary forms of human association. God created all men from one man so that they would be held together by common membership in the human race. Human nature is social and possesses the great natural good of the capacity for friendship. Augustine agreed with Ambrose, who a little more than a decade earlier in *On the Duties of Ecclesiastics,* 1.69, had spoken of *amicitia,* friendship or benevolence, as "placed by God in man and woman to make them one in spirit as well as body."[77]

The first expression of this friendship for Augustine — the first natural tie — is between man and wife. This is so strong, he later writes in the midst of the Pelagian controversy, in Book 14 of *The City of God* (418–19), that it accounts for Adam's cooperation in the first sin. While Eve, the weaker member of the first couple, was deceived by Lucifer, Adam was not. Yet, following a line of thought which chapter 1 above found in the Genesis story itself, Augustine holds that Adam was faithful to a social instinct and refused to separate from his "only companion." In all the twists and turns of controversy, Augustine never abandoned this view that marriage is centered on something not simply sexual, but on the social tie of husband and wife, their friendship. Though as members of the human race all share one blood, marriage is not to be "consanguineous" — that is, turned in on one's kin in an egoism focussed on building up family property. Later, the medieval Church would attack all forms of endogamy (marriage within the clan or group).[78] Augustine's idea that marriages contracted outside the blood family are a means of diffusing God's love may have played a part in the medieval Church's attitude. Meanwhile, ideas such as Augustine's that the first human relation was between man and wife continued to weaken the old assumption that full friendship can exist only between men. Indeed, a recent historian, thinking of spiritual friendships such as those between Jerome and Paula or Chrysostom and Olympias, has described this as a time when Christian "male-female friendships became possible in ways hard to imagine in pagan society."[79]

Good of Marriage maintains that marriage exists even when a couple is childless, past the age of child-bearing, or mutually consents to abstain from sexual relations. Indeed, Augustine contends the bond between spouses in "spiritual marriage" is stronger because it must be sustained by voluntary affection rather than carnal desire. Adam and Eve were not joined as strangers, but one was made from the other, Eve from Adam's rib. In sign of this side-by-side joining, they walk through life together "and observe together where they are walking." Even had there not been sexual intercourse, man and wife would have been joined in "a kind of friendly and genuine union of the one ruling and the other obeying."[80] Augustine takes women to be physically weaker than men, but what he has in mind here is that Eve was from the beginning not just different from Adam; she was "weaker" in a way that made her prey to Lucifer's deception, weaker in her power of reasoning so that she was naturally suited to Adam's direction. Female weakness is not so marked as to prevent marriage from being a "friendly union" providing intellectual and spiritual companionship — and Augustine describes wives as confidants and counselors — but there is a natural hierarchy between male and female, the image of the hierarchy "Christ-Church."[81]

Famously, about 410 in Book 9 of *The Literal Meaning of Genesis* (401/414), Augustine remarked that for everything but procreation, a male companion was preferable.[82] This did not mean that women were incapable of intellectual companionship, but that they were less capable of it than men.[83] Yet it has been remarked that the reserved and prudent stance that Augustine took in his relations with women after the death of his mother, Monica, did not extend to his correspondence with them. Here, to quote Gerald Bonner, "Augustine, in his letters to women, treated his correspondents as intellectual equals and never shrank from theological exposition on the highest level because of the sex of his correspondent."[84] Augustine at once affirmed inequality and equality, refining Jerome's idea that women are "equal in soul, unequal in body." So far as marriage is concerned, Augustine's view was that in certain respects the spouses are naturally different, that is, unequal but complementary, and in certain respects they are equals. Woman is subject to man because of her difference and is man's equal because she is a moral being created for a shared communion.

Augustine does not develop very far the idea of a spiritual equality from which marital companionship and friendship may develop as part of a shared spiritual pilgrimage.[85] He never applied very directly to mar-

ried couples as couples the view advanced in the *Confessions* of himself as
an ever-changing and developing individual.[86] He could see in himself an
ongoing "history of the soul," but did not think clearly of marriage as a
shared history of two who had become one. His remark that two males
make for better companionship suggests that the inveterate letter writer was
quite oblivious to, perhaps inexperienced in, the quality of feminine companionate conversation.[87] Still, he was especially careful not to rewrite the
story of the first couple in Eden as a Roman story of male domination —
the forcing of another to one's will. "Government" or "ruling" need not
equal "domination," which was sinful. The views of the *City of God* must
be kept in mind. Lust for domination characterizes the City of Man, humans after the Fall, while serving the other in love characterizes the City
of God, and is what the Christian is called to. This kind of "government"
is allowed the husband in Christian marriage. Natural governance was per-
verted at the Fall, when it became aggressive and domineering, but from
the beginning marriage entailed complementarity and friendship. Patriarchy
is the original, natural, or defining state of the race for Augustine, but a
patriarchy of love, service, and cooperation, not of aggression, power, and
envy.[88] Peter Brown has written powerfully of an inversion forming here,
in which Christian ideas about poverty, love, and humility came to form a
Christian language of power which competed with and undermined the control of traditional elites in late Roman cities.[89] Kari Børresen has suggested
that the term "equivalence" best describes his idea of the "identical value
of the sexes," "the identical value of man and woman as human persons,"
affirmed "without saying that they [do not] differ."[90]

With other Church Fathers, Augustine affirms:[91]

> ... every one knows that the duty of a wife is to obey her husband.
> But in reference to the body, we are told by the apostle [in 1 Cor. 7:3–
> 4] that the wife has power over her husband's body, as he has over
> hers; so that, while in all other social matters the wife ought to obey
> her husband, in this one matter of their bodily connection as man and
> wife their power over one another is mutual.

James Brundage has summarized this view as holding "equality of the sexes
in marriage meant equality in the marriage bed, not outside of it," but this
fails to bring out the manner in which Augustine sees both spouses as everywhere equal moral persons.[92] Thus, whereas both Roman and German law
allowed cuckolds to rectify their grievance even to the point of homicide,
Augustine says that bigamy is preferable to killing one's adulterous spouse
and urged women to hold their husbands to their own standards of fidelity.
The role of wife is neither more nor less important than that of husband: it

is simply different. Husband and wife not only are held to the same moral standards, but aim at the same virtue.

Such views were not Augustine's alone. About 390 Paulinus of Nola and his wife, Therasia, renounced their conjugal rights. Probably between 400 and 405, Paulinus wrote an epithalamium for Julian of Eclanum, Augustine's opponent to be, and his wife, Titia, who seem also at some point to have pledged abstinence. In Poem 25, redolent with the praise of spiritual marriage and holy love, Paulinus wrote that Eve was formed from Adam's rib, thus establishing the pairing and partnership of humans. The two abiding in one flesh refers to indivisible love. Eve was Adam's twin, his other self. Titia is told to strive for equality with her husband by humbly welcoming Christ's presence in him. Since she is also told that her husband is to be her head as Christ is his, presumably this equality is again an equality of virtue or soul. But Titia is also told that "in such a marriage as this Eve's subservience came to an end, and Sara became the free equal of her holy husband." Thus spiritual marriage might undo any form of submission of wife to husband, but Paulinus probably meant that, freed from sexual intercourse, the woman stands as a free equal. Thus, although Paulinus has been portrayed as having a sunnier view of marriage than that of Augustine, and possibly a view more subversive of patriarchy, his views do not seem very dissimilar. Both stressed the union of agreement, rather than sexual intercourse, as the heart of marriage.[93]

By the time he wrote *Good of Marriage,* 25, 17, Augustine held that Adam and Eve were created sexually differentiated for procreation, and that from the original union of Adam and Eve, the first parents, marriage in the Church "bears a kind of sacred bond [*sacramentum*]," which may be dissolved only in death.[94] The shifting meanings of *sacramentum* in Augustine's thought have generated a large scholarly literature. One function of this word was to translate the Greek *mysterion,* an obvious meaning of which in English is "mystery." The word *sacramentum* only regularly acquired its modern meaning as a vehicle of grace in the eleventh and twelfth centuries. For Augustine it most commonly designated a sacred sign, something which somehow pointed to or was connected with or expressed a divine reality: thus marriage was "a sign of the union between Christ and the Church."[95] Generally for patristic and early medieval writers, signs and symbols participated in and made concrete some higher reality. Thus we find the Leonine *sacramentum et exemplum,* a liturgical formula based on Augustine's contrast between the "sacrament of the interior man," the source of grace, and the "example of the exterior man," the model of Christian life.[96] We note how tentative Augustine's language was in the phrase from *Good of Marriage,* 25, 17, just quoted: marriage "bears a kind of sacred bond."

Good of Marriage only cautiously explored the nature of the *sacramen-tum* of marriage. When he wrote *On Marriage and Concupiscence* almost two decades later, Augustine insisted on the specific Christian significance of all marriage's goods. He compared the two becoming one to the union of Christ and Church, and of individual Christian and Church; said the good of progeny makes possible the peopling of the Kingdom; and wrote that sexual fidelity is a reminder of one's heavenly reward for chastity in this life. Ephesians 5:32 describes the *sacramentum magnum,* the Great Mystery, between Christ and Church of which the sacramental bond of marriage is the *sacramentum minimum,* the little mystery. One recalls the parallelism of John Chrysostom's description of the home and family as the domestic church.[97]

Writers such as Dyan Elliott and John Boswell have seen a depreciation of human marriage in the comparison of the marital relation of man and wife to that of Christ and Church. Boswell wrote: "By applying marital imagery to relationships and institutions more important than matrimony in their eyes Christians devalued the latter in favor of the former." This seems particularly wrong-headed. Biblical and patristic imagery of family and marriage seem commonly to have been chosen to develop an analogy between human and divine love. The Greek Fathers especially saw the Incarnation as a marriage of Christ's two natures, that is, of God with humankind. *Conubium,* marriage between God and man, is the basic form of the cosmos, expressing itself primordially in the marriage of divine and human in Christ's hypostatic union, then in the marriage of Christ and Church. For the Fathers to say that all marriages somehow reflect the primordial marriage is to hold that human marriage manifests, is connected to or an expression of, the central mystery of the universe. Social historians such as Dyan Elliott — insisting on carnal union as "real" marriage — take any language of a cosmic *conubium* which would make a virgin a *sponsa Christi* to be a derogation of "actual" marriage. This seems a refusal to take theological categories seriously. Nuptial symbolism carried positive connotations and was chosen because it was a human reality participating in and suitable to imaging the highest realities. As chapter 1 pointed out in discussing the Song of Songs, sexual love between man and woman intimates something of God's love. The Scriptures end in a wedding feast (Rev. 19:7, 9).[98]

The Novelty of Augustine's Thought

Peter Brown has noted the novelty of Augustine's views, both compared to earlier Christian writers or to Augustine's Greek Christian contemporaries. Many besides Origen had characterized conjugal relations as an expression of man's fallen, corporeal state. For them, intercourse was a product of the

Fall. It passed on man's first sin. Until Augustine's day common theological opinion held that sexuality was something added or secondary to the human person. Humans were originally asexual or angelic and contemplative. Adam, man before the Fall, was passionless, in a state of *apatheia*. Some affirmed that Adam and Eve's bodies were purely spiritual, a view that especially influenced Augustine's early thought.[99] In their treatment of the creation story, Christians in the ascetic tradition commonly argued either that originally there was only one sex or (in the spirit of Philo Judaeus) that there was one human type or incorporeal idea, neither male nor female. The division into two sexes and the onset of intercourse were results of the Fall, and celibacy was a path back to the restoration of unity and a partial anticipation of man's final state. It made possible clarity of soul. Clement of Alexandria wrote that neither in paradise nor in heaven was there division of the sexes or desire: these exist only in the interim of history between our first and last state. There were variations. Gregory of Nyssa (335/40–after 394) initially held the view that the human being was originally androgynous, although his later writings witness a shift taking place in the second half of the fourth century. While still hoping for release from carnality through celibacy, Gregory now abandoned the view of an original androgyny. Basil of Ancyra (d. after 363) saw in virgins a realized eschatology in which there was neither male, female, nor passion.[100] Marriage and family ties would be dissolved in the resurrection.

Still in flight from the physical sexuality that had bound him personally for so many years, and with an eye to Manichean criticism of the anthropomorphisms of the Old Testament, Augustine continued the spiritualization or allegorization of the Fall practiced by his contemporaries in his first exegetical work on the creation story, *On Genesis against the Manichees* (388–89). He interpreted the command to reproduce found in chapter 1 of Genesis as a command for spiritual union, maintaining that physical union took place only after the Fall.[101] Even in the later *Against Faustus the Manichee* (397/98), Augustine insisted that the patriarchs had been motivated in their polygamy not by lust but solely by the desire to "be fruitful and multiply."[102] Presumably this meant that after the Fall some had kept complete reign over their sexual desires; the patriarchs had exercised their sexuality without concupiscence or disordered desire, as if there had been no Fall. We should take into account the widespread belief of his contemporaries that the only proper sexual act was one motivated solely by desire for children, a belief presumably founded on a psychology which thought such a single-minded and pure intention possible. Still, it is hard to believe that Augustine, now in his forties and in so many matters so psychologically acute, meant to rule out some role for lust in all postlapsarian life. True, when he writes of the seduction of Lot by his daughters, Augustine stresses how strong the desire to preserve the race must have been, "for they supposed that there were no other men to be found, thinking that the whole world had been consumed in that conflagration [of Sodom and Gomorrah]."[103] Still, to write of the patriarchs as moved only by desire for progeny suggests the grip of the inherited views of paradise on Augustine even in the late 390s. The patriarchs apparently were exempt from what became his settled position, that after the Fall at least venial sin was present in even licit sexual acts. In this latter view, the discipline of faithfulness between spouses and procreation were remedies for the lust that had become a part of sexual relations with the Fall. Two decades later Julian of Eclanum, relishing his role as champion of marital desire, suggested that Augustine still harbored views he had long publicly repudiated and really preferred to believe that there had been sexless reproduction in Eden. This perhaps carried just enough truth to hit its mark. Anyone who could have thought the story of the seduction of Lot was simply about an intense desire to propagate the race had left himself open to such an attack.

These early views of man's first state found in the writings of Augustine's contemporaries are for Brown so different from anything in fallen historical experience as to leave one at a loss as to what exactly was being claimed.[104] Genesis itself had presented the shame of Adam and Eve as a boundary experience, a wondering about the possibility of existence without shame, of completely open human communication. Brown intriguingly suggests that the unbidden sexual fantasies and feelings of *concupiscentia,* not sinful in themselves, are for Augustine flashbacks to or lingering symptoms of the primal sin.[105] Augustine came to see that if the Church was to be the guardian of marriage, marriage and procreation (or the capacity for procreation, since he came to rest in the view that Adam and Eve sinned before they were able sexually to unite) needed to be acknowledged as originally intended by God. Man and woman are made for each other. They were not originally isolated contemplative beings but sexual beings made for society. While *concupiscentia,* disordered desire, did not exist in paradise, one of Augustine's innovations was that he eventually allowed the hypothesis that sexual desire itself could have existed in paradise. The effect of the first sin, he asserted in his anti-Pelagian writings following 412, was concupiscence, the corruption of the sex act. Disorderly sexual appetite became a law unto itself, manifesting itself, for instance, in unwanted erections, the raising of the flag of bodily revolt.[106]

The message of the anti-Pelagian *On Marriage and Concupiscence* (419/21) was that such concupiscence was to be distinguished from the intrinsic goodness of marriage. Presumably this view was related to the more basic, if finally inconclusive, development in his thought in Book XIV of *The City of God* (chap. 4). In certain other works Augustine also departed increasingly from the Platonic tradition and insisted that soul and body compose one human living being. However, he far from abandoned the master of his earlier years. His rejection around 417/18 of the Plotinian view of man as fallen soul seems to have been temporary rather than decisive, and such a view competes with a Christian incarnationalism until the end. Augustine hesitates to affirm that the only difference between intercourse before and after the Fall lay in ordered and disordered desire. He suggests that in prelapsarian sexual congress Adam's seed would have entered Eve without destroying her virginity, by a process rather the reverse of the flow of menstrual blood. This line of thought probably resulted from his realization of the implications of allowing an unqualified human intercourse into Eden. If the first state of man was marital rather than virginal (and marriage that is *sacramentum*), it is hard to explain how virginity can define the paradisal state. Augustine perhaps sensed a contradiction in allowing the possibility of sexual intercourse in paradise while refusing it to heaven — which after all is a restoration and enhancement of the prelapsarian state. He fell back on his "thought-experiment" of a prelapsarian "virginal intercourse" as a way of retaining a celibate heaven, with no marriage.[107] His definition of marriage as consent, not consummation, eased his position here, but could not resolve the complexities of envisioning man's first state as in any bodily sense marital. In any case, Augustine's Eve would have remained a virgin in the prelapsarian sex act just described. In *Marriage and Concupiscence*, 1.11.12, Augustine argued that a spiritual marriage (as compared to a sexually active marriage) creates a stronger bond because the couple is held together not by voluptuous desire but by voluntary affection. This was not an attack on carnal desire, but an argument for a higher form of desire, which he called desire of the soul. Looked at from this perspective, Augustine was suggesting that the lower forms of marital love are those in which one is swept away in satisfying sensual desire, and the higher forms are those that are voluntary and spiritual.[108]

A number of scholars have argued that Augustine's views increasingly projected the temporal order of his day back into paradise, and this chapter has spoken of his increasing naturalism (understood as making Eden relatively more like our fallen world) in portraying the social and sexual aspects of Eden. While such approaches help us understand the relationship between context and idea, Caroline Bynum has observed that they are tautological, "finding that ideas reflect the context against which one chooses to locate them."[109] Bynum apparently exempts Elaine Pagels from this particular criticism, though it is unclear why. Pagels notes that Augustine's sexual naturalism and more literal reading of Genesis continued to develop in *The Literal Meaning of Genesis* and concludes that he constructed an Eden increasingly like the Roman world, with its sexual differentiation and submission of female to male.[110] Pagels's first interests are not theological but social and feminist. She and other scholars like her see Augustine recasting his earlier views to create an Eden that would sanction Roman Christian marriage and existing gender roles. Dyan Elliott similarly argues that Augustine constructed his ideas about the subjection of wife to husband to counter the tendency of spiritual marriage to liberate wives. Freed from the obligation of sexual intercourse, and thus inclined in other ways to autonomy, such women needed to be told they were still subject to their husbands.[111] Here, the limitations of social history appear most sharply. Over the course of his five works on Genesis, Augustine presumably thought that his understanding of the text slowly improved under the impact of factors as diverse as growth in his exegetical abilities and the stimulus of current controversy. But if we are to believe certain social historians, he was doing little more than plundering the text to keep women in their place. It would be surprising if social considerations played no role in Augustine's thought, but he undermined Roman hierarchies as much as he shored them up, and it is unclear why historians should assign this one factor as the predominant explanation of his position. Elliott's claims are merely suggestive half-truths.

Elliott espies in Augustine a "nostalgia for Edenesque purity."[112] This is one of those statements that is true as far as it goes. Because she apparently overlooks the larger theological picture, Elliott does not fully appreciate that, in an age filled with nostalgia, Augustine is the least nostalgic of writers and retains the least attachment to any *illud tempus,* any "once upon a time." His thought is directed toward the future, toward "reform to the better."[113] He seeks to build on the past rather than recover it. The portrayal of prelapsarian sexual discipline is an ideal model for an analogous discipline in contemporary marriages. Augustine knows paradise cannot be recovered: he wishes, rather, to hold up revelation of what man intrinsically is before the present. In a world full of misshapen lives and mistaken ideas, Eden is his "pure case," and despite his growing naturalism, he always allows for Eden's *différence.* This is rather the opposite of writing present social structures into paradise: Instead, Augustine is trying to reform the present in the light of Eden. The Genesis story has caused him to reflect on such things as what a human life without shame and with unveiled communication might look like.

Many scholars realize that Augustine's move from viewing Adam and Eve before the Fall as possessing spiritual bodies to seeing them as having fully corporeal bodies was occasioned by his controversies with the Pelagians. But social historians underestimate the extent to which such insights have their own life. They don't just develop in a social context, but within a theological tradition.[114] In one way or another, such ideas may be shaped by social context, but they are also linked to the history of theology and ultimately, in this case, to the developing doctrine of the Incarnation. For Elliott, Augustine's insistence on the prelapsarian subordination of woman to man expresses his anxiety about good order in society, as he writes late Roman social needs into the Garden of Eden. Though this is reasonable as a suggestion, it does not address Augustine's theological interest in such questions as the complementarity between the sexes. Had he been told that his developing views of Eden were various forms of coming to terms with social problems of his own day, he might well have agreed, but only to a point. His larger view, after all, was the human mind has been darkened in the Fall and that no one can "remember" Eden. Therefore the only knowledge we have of the first state of the race is from God, as preserved in Genesis.

Augustine claims that revelation has given Christians a view of the original condition of the race and the original relation between the sexes. Although presumably his mind moved back and forth from Eden to the present, at heart his views were not projections from the present back to Eden, but meditations on what God has revealed about his intentions for creation. If Augustine meant simply to sanction the institutions of his own day, even his mature views about the first state of the race must be admitted to retain rather a large amount of, to use Elliott's term, "fantasy," of undigested supernaturalism.[115] Elliott's "fantasy" is actually that part of Augustine's thought that resists social-historical analysis, i.e., whose source is not in fourth- and fifth-century social institutions but in the Genesis account. "Fantasy" is Elliott's name for what is specifically theological. In a brilliant critique which applies equally well to Elliott, Verna Harrison points out that Kari Børresen and Rosemary Radford Ruether "presuppose that all concepts of God mirror and confirm human cultural constructs." Harrison suggests that this inverts the perspective of the subjects they write about: "This assertion rejects traditional Jewish and Christian affirmations of divine self-revelation and effectively turns the concept of divine image upside down, making God a reflection of the human." Harrison notes that if we seek dialogue between past and present, such an approach not only presents past thinkers in a form they would certainly reject, but cuts off the possibility of dialogue at the first step.[116] In addition, would it ever be incorrect to link concern with marriage with concern with social stability? Georges Duby has noted the parallel attempts of Hincmar of Rheims and Hugh of St. Victor in the ninth and twelfth centuries to make marriage sacred as the framework of society.[117]

In Augustine's mature view, male and female were from the creation made both to desire one another and to live in friendship and physical intimacy, although there could be exceptional cases in which valid marriages existed without progeny, or even sexual intercourse. Theological considerations, specifically the attempt to eliminate a Manichean residue of depreciation of the flesh from his thought, might well have been more important in the evolution of Augustine's ideas about marriage than anxiety about society's ills.

Conclusion

In the fifth-century epithalamium quoted above, Paulinus of Nola banished the pagan goddesses of love and urged his friends Julian of Eclanum and Titia to a spiritual marriage like his own, or, if they were incapable of that, to raise children who themselves would remain virgins. Though hardly a typical writer, Paulinus communicates the ambiguous attitude toward earthly marriage at the end of the patristic age. Following Augustine, Paulinus insists that marriage is a part of God's primordial plan, and he also agrees that consent is more central to marriage's definition than carnal union. Though virginity is preferable, holiness may be found in marriage also:

> Harmonious souls are being united in chaste love, . . .
> Christ our God, lead to your reins these well-matched doves, and
> Govern them under your easy yoke.
> . . . the harmonious bond of marriage shares at once in the
> Love of piety, the dignity of love, and the peace of God.
> With his own lips God made this union holy,
> By the divine hand he established the human couple.
> He made the two abide in one flesh,
> In order to create a love more indivisible.[118]

In Paulinus's view love and consent are central to marriage, but all things carnal remain as problematic as the idea of two becoming one flesh without becoming one flesh. This was the view of serious, learned Christians at the end of the Age of Augustine.

Notes

1. Paul Fedwick, *The Church and the Charisma of Leadership in Basil of Caesarea* (Toronto, 1979), esp. 12–32, 97–100, and Philip Rousseau, *Basil of Caesarea* (Berkeley, Calif., 1994), index under "asceticism" and chap. 6. For early Christian asceticism, see Pier Franco Beatrice, "Continenza e matrimonio nel cristianesimo primitivo (secc. I–II)," *Etica sessuale e matrimonio nel cristianesimo delle origini,* ed. Raniero Cantalamessa (Milan, 1976), 3–68. Jeremy Cohen, *"Be Fertile and Increase, Fill the Earth and Master It": The Ancient and Medieval Career of a Biblical Text* (Ithaca, N.Y., 1989), by presenting the larger Jewish background, gives an introduction to the many tensions Jesus and the ascetical dimension of Christianity formed in regard to Jewish orientation toward terrestrial life. All biblical quotations are from the Knox version of the Holy Bible (London, 1963), a translation of the Vulgate.

2. On both Perpetua and the development of "spiritual motherhood" see Clarissa W. Atkinson, *The Oldest Vocation: Christian Motherhood in the Middle Ages* (Ithaca, N.Y., 1991), with the review of Mary Martin McLaughlin in *Catholic Historical Review* 81 (1995): 607–10.

3. Philip L. Reynolds, *Marriage in the Western Church: The Christianization of Marriage during the Patristic and Early Medieval Periods* (New York, 1994), while not abreast of study of the Roman family, is fundamental and traces, especially for Augustine, thought about marriage as a remedy for concupiscence. In his review of this book, David G. Hunter, *Theological Studies* 56 (1995): 779–81, rightly criticizes Reynolds's treatment of Augustine as in places unduly harsh, and occasionally simply wrong. In a review in *Speculum* 71 (1996): 200–202, Jean A. Truax also points out some important flaws in this seminal work.

4. For the early history of interpretation of Matthew 19:12, see Kathryn M. Ringrose, "Living in the Shadows: Eunuchs and Gender in Byzantium," in *Third Sex, Third Gender: Beyond Dimorphism in Culture and History,* ed. Gilbert Herdt (New York, 1994), 85–109, 507–18 (notes), at 99–101, 517–18. J. P. Broudéhoux, *Mariage et famille chez Clément d'Alexandrie,* Théologique historique 2 (Paris, 1970), is basic for Clement.

5. Peter Brown, *The Body and Society: Men, Women, and Sexual Renunciation in Early Christianity* (New York, 1988), 79, 135, 149–50, 378, with Dyan Elliott, *Spiritual Marriage: Sexual Abstinence in Medieval Wedlock* (Princeton, N.J., 1993), 40–41, who summarizes the history of scholarship on syneisactism (2–13) and Paul's views (19–24). In regard to the understanding of Gal. 3:28, Elliott accepts the idea, criticized in the last chapter above, of a fall in early Christianity from egalitarianism to patriarchalism. For other flaws in her book, see my review in *Speculum* 70 (1995): 363–64, and that of Elizabeth Makowski in *Catholic Historical Review* 80 (1994): 328–30, in addition to my "Marriage, Feminism, Theology, and the New Social History: Dyan Elliott's *Spiritual Marriage*," *Communio* 22 (1995): 343–56. See also Elizabeth Clark, "John Chrysostom and the *Subintroductae*," *Church History* 46 (1977): 171–85. Both Jo Ann Kay McNamara, *Sisters in Arms: Catholic Nuns through Two Millennia* (Cambridge, Mass., 1996) and its review by Fiona MacCarthy, "The Power of Chastity," *New York Review of Books* 43, no. 20 (December 19, 1996): 31–33, are unevenly informed and sometimes theologically confused. McNamara emphasizes that syneisactism was radical in holding for the equal spiritual capacity of men and women, but the last chapter above showed that this was simply New Testament teaching. Kiernan Scott and Michael Warren, eds., *Perspectives on Marriage: A Reader* (Oxford, 1993), 9–68, sketches marriage from the Bible to the present. Jean Gaudemet, *Le Mariage en Occident* (Paris, 1987), is a fine survey, and Theodore Mackin, *The Marital Sacrament* (Mahwah, N.J., 1989), if not always reliable, is useful.

6. Ringrose, "Living in the Shadows," in Herdt, ed., *Third Sex,* 102–8, at 104–5, on Theophylaktos. The story was more complicated than Theophylaktos indicates: Constantine had, for instance, repealed the Augustan penalties on celibacy. See Judith Evans Grubbs, " 'Pagan' and 'Christian' Marriage: The State of the Question," *Journal of Early Christian Studies* 2 (1994): 361–412 at 393–94, and *Law and Family in Late Antiquity: The Emperor Constantine's Marriage Legislation* (New York, 1995), 103–39. In addition to works listed in the last chapter, see David I. Kertzer and Richard P. Saller, eds., *The Family in Italy from Antiquity to the Present* (New Haven, Conn., 1991) and Keith R. Bradley, *Discovering the Roman Family: Studies in Roman Social History* (New York, 1991).

7. Pseudo-Cyprian, *De singularitate clericorum*, 32, Corpus Scriptorum Ecclesi-asticorum Latinorum (hereafter CSEL) 3.3, 207, is of uncertain authorship and date: see Eligius Dekkers, *Clavis Patrum Latinorum*, 3d ed., ed. Aemilius Gaar (Steenbrugis, 1995), 18. John Boswell, *Same-Sex Unions in Premodern Europe* (New York, 1994), 121–22, considers Christian fraternal language. Boswell's is a most uneven book: 111–19 are embarrassingly confused. Brent D. Shaw, "A Groom of One's Own?" *New Republic* (July 18 and 25, 1994): 33–41, is a devastating rejoinder to Boswell's overall argument for the existence of ancient and medieval gay Christian marriage ceremonies. Bernadette J. Brooten, *Love between Women: Early Christian Responses to Female Homoeroticism* (Chicago, 1996), 51–53, 64–66, 126–28, 138–39, 320–37 studies "marriages" between women.

8. The translation of Nazianzen is from Elliott, *Spiritual Marriage*, 16, and see 20, 39.

9. The translation of Chrysostom is from the treatment of matrimony in *Catechism of the Catholic Church* (Vatican City, 1994), 405. See more generally the selections in *St. John Chrysostom on Marriage and Family Life*, trans. Catherine P. Roth and David Anderson (New York, 1986), but the Introduction to this book is unreliable.

10. *To His Wife*, 1. c. 7, a work of his Catholic period, trans. with all three works by William P. Le Saint in *Tertullian: Treatises on Marriage and Remarriage* Ancient Christian Writers (hereafter ACW) 13 (Westminster, Md., 1956), 20; and *Monogamy*, c. 12, trans. Le Saint, 98–100, a work of his Montanist period; with Georges Duby, *The Three Orders: Feudal Society Imagined*, trans. Arthur Goldhammer, with a foreword by Thomas N. Bisson (Chicago, 1980), 68, 74, 76. Duby habitually cites the Church Fathers in dated editions with crabbed references. Tertullian's three works, each different from the last, are summarized in Johannes Quasten, *Patrology*, 4 vols. (Utrecht-Antwerp, Westminster, 1966–86), 2:302–6. F. Forrester Church, "Sex and Salvation in Tertullian," *Harvard Theological Review* 68 (1975): 83–101; Paul Mattei, "Du divorce, de Tertullien, et de quelques autres sujets.... Perspectives nouvelles et idées reçues," *Revue des Etudes Augustiniennes* 39 (1993): 23–35; and Caroline W. Bynum, "Images of the Resurrection Body in the Theology of Late Antiquity," *Catholic Historical Review* 80 (1994): 215–37 at 224–25, are important correctives to widespread misunderstandings of Tertullian's views on women and marriage.

11. On this and the following paragraph, see Ton C. Van Eijk, "Marriage and Virginity, Death and Immortality," in *Epektasis: Mélanges patristiques offerts au Cardinal Jean Daniélou*, ed. Jacques Fontaine and Charles Kannengiesser (Paris, 1972), 209–35 at 215, described by Elliott, *Spiritual Marriage*, 18 (confusing Lukan texts), and see 25–31, 39.

12. Evans Grubbs, " 'Pagan' and 'Christian' Marriage," 387–94, summarizes pre-Nicene thinking. Daniel H. Hoffman, *The Status of Women and Gnosticism in Irenaeus and Tertullian* (Lewiston, N.Y., 1995), is an important book centering on critique of the work of Elaine Pagels (see below n. 14) and correcting many widespread mistaken ideas about the views of writers such as Tertullian.

13. M. Simonetti, "Priscillian — Priscillianism," *Encyclopedia of the Early Church*, ed. Angelo Di Berardino, trans. Adrian Walford, with a foreword and bibliographic amendments by W. H. C. Frend, 2 vols. (New York, 1992), 2:711–12, surveys the changing scholarship on Priscillianism. See also Virginia Burrus, *The Making of a Heretic: Gender, Authority, and the Priscillianist Controversy* (Berkeley, Calif., 1995).

14. A good tonic against the great amount of nonsense that has been written about Gnosticism, especially about the role it gave to women, by scholars like Elaine Pagels is M. J. Edwards, "New Discoveries and Gnosticism: Some Precautions," *Orientalia Christiana Periodica* 55 (1989): 257–72, and see above n. 12. For John the Scot and androgyny in the ninth century, see in addition to the comments on androgyny in the exegesis of the Genesis text in chap. 1 above, the discussion following Robert Fossier, "La femme dans les sociétés occidentales," *Cahiers de Civilisation Médiévale Xe–XIIe Siècles* 20 (1977): 93–104 at 103.

15. For early Christianity see Evans Grubbs, " 'Pagan' and 'Christian' Marriage," 392–93, and for the Middle Ages see Carolyne Larrington, *Women and Writing in Medieval Europe: A Sourcebook* (London, 1995), 7–8. Tim G. Parkin, *Demography and Roman Society* (Baltimore, 1992), is comprehensive.

16. Harry O. Maier, "Purity and Danger in Polycarp's Epistle to the Philippians: The Sin of Valens in Social Perspective," *Journal of Early Christian Studies* 1 (1993): 229–47 at 237 and 244, discusses Polycarp and Hermas. Widows are among the subjects studied by Susanna Elm, *"Virgins of God": The Making of Asceticism in Late Antiquity* (New York, 1994), esp. chap. 5.

17. Evans Grubbs, " 'Pagan' and 'Christian' Marriage," 399–402, with *Law and Family,* 14–16, on dating.

18. Glenda McLeod, *Virtue and Venom: Catalogs of Women from Antiquity to the Renaissance* (Ann Arbor, Mich., 1991), chap. 2, describes Jerome's hierarchy of feminine worth and the existence of antithetical views of femineity (McLeod's word) into the Middle Ages.

19. "The Earliest Use of Monachos for 'Monk' (P. Coll. Youtie 77) and the Origins of Monasticism," *Jahrbuch für Antike und Christentum* 20 (1977): 72–89 at 80, with James E. Goehring, "The Encroaching Desert: Literary Production and Ascetic Space in Early Christian Egypt," *Journal of Early Christian Studies* 1 (1993): 281–96 at 286 and 293. For the new ideals of womanhood, see Kate Cooper, *The Virgin and the Bride: Idealized Womanhood in Late Antiquity* (Cambridge, Mass., 1996).

20. The translation of Ambrose is from *Catechism of the Catholic Church,* 564. See also Charlotte Methuen, "Widows, Bishops and the Struggle for Authority in the *Didascalia Apostolorum*," *Journal of Ecclesiastical History* 46 (1995): 197–213.

21. Because unaware of the bibliography listed below in n. 24, the consideration of Cyprian's *Letters* 40, 52, and 67.6.3, in Richard Seagraves, *Pascentes cum disciplina: A Lexical Study of the Clergy in the Cyprianic Correspondence* (Fribourg, 1993), 131–32, cannot be trusted. Evans Grubbs, *Law and Family,* 132–336, is not always as precise as she could be on theological matters.

22. Evans Grubbs, " 'Pagan' and 'Christian' Marriage," 399–403, and *Law and Family,* 223–24, on adultery and remarriage of priests' wives, 315.

23. Peter Brown, *Augustine of Hippo: A Biography* (Berkeley, Calif., 1967), 197–98, and *Body and Society,* index under "married clergy."

24. For Leo see *Letters,* trans. Edmund Hunt, Fathers of the Church (hereafter FOC) 34 (New York, 1957), index under "marriage of clerics," esp. 167, p. 292: Leo interpreted Paul's prescription that the bishop should be the husband of one wife to mean not only that bishops must be married no more than once, but that they could not marry widows, for that would make their wives twice-married. Christian Cochini, *The Apostolic Origins of Priestly Celibacy,* preface by Alfons M. Stickler, trans. Nelly Marans (San Francisco, 1990), argues for the apostolic origin of the requirement of continence of married clergy and is followed by Roman Cholij, *Clerical*

Celibacy in East and West, foreword by Alfons Stickler, preface by Michael Napier (Leominster, Herfordshire, 1989). Cholij agrees with Cochini that Orthodox practice rests upon a mistaken interpretation of texts of the Council of Carthage (A.D. 390) by the Quinisext Council (in Trullo, 691–92). Against widespread opinion, Cholij argues that the Latin discipline of prohibiting sexual relations to all priests is the older tradition, and the Orthodox practice of allowing sexual relations to the secular clergy a canonical innovation at Trullo against earlier tradition. We return to this in the next chapter.

25. Evans Grubbs, " 'Pagan' and 'Christian' Marriage," 389–90. Clement of Alexandria's *Stromateis,* Book 3, has been translated as "On Marriage" by John E. L. Oulton and Henry Chadwick in *Alexandrian Christianity* (London, 1954), 40–92 (see also the General Introduction, 21–39).

26. Trans. Mary Magdeleine Mueller, *Saint Caesarius of Arles: Sermons,* vol. 1, FOC 31 (New York, 1956), 212–17 at 215, not particularly accurately described in Gillian Clark, *Women in Late Antiquity: Pagan and Christian Lifestyles* (New York, 1993), 38. See also Evans Grubbs, " 'Pagan' and 'Christian' Marriage," 382, and *Law and Family,* 242–54, espying a greater tendency in urban than in rural areas to uphold a single moral standard.

27. John T. Noonan Jr., "Development in Moral Doctrine," *Theological Studies* 54 (1993): 662–77 at 663, with this author's *Power to Dissolve* (Cambridge, Mass., 1972), 343.

28. Reynolds, *Marriage in the Western Church,* is fundamental. See also Evans Grubbs, " 'Pagan' and 'Christian' Marriage," 374–75, 378ff., 386–87, 390–92, 397, 404–5, on this and both the last and the following paragraphs, and *Law and Family,* 28, 38–40, 49–51, 123–321, specifically 242–53, on ideal and reality in the matter of divorce; Antti Arjava, *Women and Law in Late Antiquity* (Oxford, 1996), which covers a range of topics similar to those covered by Evans Grubbs, and with a similar perspective, that the Christianization of Roman society was in many respects superficial (4–6, 257–61); and Roger S. Bagnall, "Church, State and Divorce in Late Roman Egypt," *Florilegium Columbianum: Essays in Honor of Paul Oskar Kristeller,* ed. Karl-Ludwig Selig and Robert Somerville (New York, 1987), 41–61, giving an excellent overview. The standard history of divorce, Henri Crouzel, *L'Église primitive face au divorce: Du premier au cinquième siècle,* Théologie Historique 13 (Paris, 1971), is defended by Crouzel, *Mariage et divorce, célibat et caractère sacerdotaux dans l'église ancienne* (Turin, 1982), and updated by Evans Grubbs. See also Mattei, "Du divorce," 26–30.

29. Michel Rouche summarized his views in an article written with Paul-Marie Couteaux, "Clovis, Chef Franc," *Le Figaro Magazine* 16114 (June 8, 1996): 124–25. See also the following notes. Diana E. E. Kleiner and Susan B. Matheson, ed., *I, Claudia: Women in Ancient Rome* (New Haven, Conn., 1996), is a treasure trove of the artistic evidence: see esp. 116–80.

30. Susan Treggiari, *Roman Marriage: "Iusti Coniuges" from the Time of Cicero to the Time of Ulpian* (Oxford, 1991), is a work of great scholarship on the late Republic and Principate: see Part 2 on the place of choice, love, and affection, in Roman marriage, and Part 3 on the relationship of husband and wife. Suzanne Dixon, *The Roman Family* (Baltimore, 1992), chap. 3, is more accessible to the general reader. See also Michel Foucault, *The History of Sexuality,* vol. 3: *The Care of the Self,* trans. Robert Hurley (New York, 1986), 145–85.

31. Henry Ansgar Kelly, *Love and Marriage in the Age of Chaucer* (Ithaca, N.Y., 1975), 71–100, which throughout attacks or seriously qualifies various theses advanced in Lewis's *The Allegory of Love* (London, 1936). Kelly begins part 1 of his

book, 29, with a quotation from Ovid, *Metamorphoses* 4.757–62, on the compatibility of love and marriage. Catherine Osborne, *Eros Unveiled: Plato and the God of Love* (Oxford, 1994), 6, 8, 51, notes the historical and theological inadequacies of Lewis's "four loves." See also M. L. Stapleton, *Harmful Eloquence: Ovid's Amores from Antiquity to Shakespeare* (Ann Arbor, Mich., 1996). David Konstan, *Sexual Symmetry: Love in the Ancient Novel and Related Genres* (Princeton, N.J., 1994), shows that the sexual symmetry founded on *eros* of the Greek novel was reconfigured asymmetrically in its Latin descendant.

32. Elizabeth Clark, " 'Adam's Only Companion': Augustine and the Early Christian Debate on Marriage," in *The Olde Daunce: Love, Friendship, Sex, and Marriage in the Medieval World*, ed. Robert R. Edwards and Stephen Spector (Albany, N.Y., 1991), 15–31, 240–54 (notes) at 245 n. 61, gathers passages from Augustine rejecting the Manichean playing of Old against New Testament. The standard study is Samuel N. C. Lieu, *Manichaeism in the Later Roman Empire and Medieval China*, 2d ed. (Tübingen, 1992).

33. Evans Grubbs, " 'Pagan' and 'Christian' Marriage," 372–73, conveniently summarizes Musonius and his student Hierocles, who in his defense of the idea that philosophy can be pursued within marriage, i.e., that the life of reason is not incompatible with marital desire, challenges common views. Martha C. Nussbaum, *The Therapy of Desire: Theory and Practice in Hellenistic Ethics* (Princeton, N.J., 1994), as at 149–50 on *eros*, and 316–401 on Stoicism, while quirky, gives an idea of the range of opinion.

34. I am rewriting Foucault, *Care of the Self*, 145–85, who does not seem to notice how "unstoical" some of his Stoics are. The Stoics disagreed among themselves, some seeing all emotion as suspect, others distinguishing between good and bad emotions.

35. James A. Brundage, *Law, Sex, and Christian Society in Medieval Europe* (Chicago, 1987), as at 282, 449, 508, considers various medieval texts on the question of pleasure during coitus.

36. " 'Pagan' and 'Christian' Marriage," at 361–62, 410–12, an argument worked out in detail in *Law and Family*. Evans Grubbs specifically counsels in regard to Brown, *Body and Society*. On this and the following see Elliott, *Spiritual Marriage*, 40, 42, 44, 47, 57, 61, 229–30, and Larrington, *Women*, 10.

37. Suzanne Dixon, "The Sentimental Ideal of the Roman Family," in *Marriage, Divorce, and Children in Ancient Rome*, ed. Beryl Rawson (New York, 1991), 99–113 at 111 (this article argues the existence of a widespread sentimental ideal centered on a nuclear family, but also the common divergence of reality from this ideal; its frontispiece portrays the *dextrarum iunctio* considered below in n. 41), with Evans Grubbs, " 'Pagan' and 'Christian' Marriage," 363, but see the entire article. See also Susan Treggiari, "Women in Roman Society," in Kleiner and Matheson, ed., *I Claudia*, 116–25 at 115, 121. On marriage as weaving see John Scheid and Jesper Svenbro, *The Craft of Zeus: Myths of Weaving and Fabric*, trans. Carol Volk (Cambridge, Mass., 1996). See also Beryl Rawson and Paul Weaver, *The Roman Family in Italy: Status, Sentiment, Space* (New York, 1996), and Thomas Wiedemann, *Adults and Children in the Roman Empire* (New Haven, Conn., 1989). For the history of marriage, see Treggiari, *Roman Marriage*, esp. 100–103, on love in marriage, and Richard P. Saller, *Patriarchy, Property and Death in the Roman Family* (New York, 1994), on the position of the *paterfamilias*, demography and family structure, marriage patterns, love of wife and children, analysis of the Roman life-cycle, and dowry, with the intelligent criticisms in the review by Keith Bradley, *American Historical Review* 100 (1995): 1231–32. See also Dixon, *Roman Family*; Bradley, *Discovering the*

Roman Family, at 125–30, on love in marriage; Roger S. Bagnall, *Egypt in Late An-tiquity* (Princeton, N.J., 1993), 92–99, 130–33, on women and property, chap. 5 on demography, sex, marriage, and divorce, and 202, on love of children.

38. Evans Grubbs, " 'Pagan' and 'Christian' Marriage," 365–75, 382–85, 394–98, 406–11, discussing Pliny and making distinctions by social class, century, and region; noting the persistence of bigamy among Jews in the Near East, but not in the Diaspora; quoting Plutarch, whose "companionate" ideal in the lines quoted centers on mutual support, a community of life, but elsewhere includes passionate love, which Evans Grubbs compares to love in the Greek romantic novel (see above n. 31) and in Paul; analyzing Lactantius; and studying the epigraphic evidence. Evans Grubbs, *Law and Family*, 50–51, 102–12, 203–5, 283–94, considers the growing harshness of the law, and see index under "Lactantius," and 238 and 259, on the in-frequency of divorce. Saller, *Patriarchy*, as at 2, is properly cautious about claims for and against high divorce rates. For contraception see John M. Riddle, *Contraception and Abortion from the Ancient World to the Renaissance* (Cambridge, Mass., 1992) and below n. 61.

39. In addition to the preceding and following notes and n. 55 below, see Evans Grubbs, " 'Pagan' and 'Christian' Marriage," 365–66, 378ff., and *Law and Family*, 140–202, on the formation of pagan and Christian marriage bonds. Arjava, *Women*, 28–41, details getting married, and 123–33, 155–56, its forms.

40. In addition to the following note and n. 96 below (on *sacramentum*), for law, theology, the independence of liturgical developments and the Christianization of marriage, see Reynolds, *Marriage*. For the development of marriage rites see Kor-binian Ritzer, *Formen, Riten und religiöses Brauchtum der Eheschliessung in den christlichen Kirchen des ersten Jahrtausends*, ed. Ulrich Hermann and Willibrord Heckenbach, 2d ed. (Münster, 1981). For a wider compass, see Angeliki E. Laiou, ed., *Consent and Coercion to Sex and Marriage in Ancient and Medieval Societies* (Washington, D.C., 1993). Evans Grubbs, *Law and Family*, 156–71, treats betrothal and nuptial gifts, and 172–83, betrothal: cf. Arjava, *Women*, 52–62.

41. In addition to the preceding and following notes, see Evans Grubbs, " 'Pagan' and 'Christian' Marriage," 364–65, 371, 409, on Concordia or Juno Pronuba standing between the couple on sarcophagi and coins from the late second cen-tury following, and 376–77, on the pre-nuptial gift. The Attic grave monument and Roman sarcophagus, the latter of which was reused in a Christian church, are de-scribed and pictured in Dieter Ohly, *The Munich Glypothek: Greek and Roman Sculpture*, 2d rev. English ed. (Munich, 1992), 41, 44–47, 104, 133–34. Cf. a grave marker with a woman sitting, dating about 385–80, in the Boston Museum of Fine Arts: John H. Herrmann Jr., *In the Shadow of the Acropolis: Popular and Private Art in Fourth Century Athens* (Boston, 1984), 18–19. Rings portraying the *dex-trarum iunctio* survive, as do rings portraying busts of the bride and bridegroom. Two examples from the fourth or fifth century of the former are found in the British Museum, M & LA 197–1, 8–2, 4–5, and for examples of the latter from the same period see in the same collection M & LA AF 304–5. In the Metropolitan Museum in New York City, see also an early Christian, fourth or fifth century, gold glass mar-riage scene with right hands joined, probably from Rome, with the inscription "Live in God" (Rogers Fund, 1926. 26.258); and a gold and hematite necklace found in Rome, composed of a second-century amulet joined with an early fifth-century gold marriage medallion with the facing heads of a couple above each of which a crown is held (Rogers Fund, 1957. 58.12). See on these materials Kleiner and Matheson, ed., *I Claudia*, esp. 150–52, and also Jutta-Annette Bruhn, *Coins and Costume in Late Antiquity* (Washington, D.C., 1993), on marriage rings and *encolpia*.

42. Evans Grubbs, " 'Pagan' and 'Christian' Marriage," 388, 397–98. On Tertullian see above nn. 10 and 12 and below nn. 43, 46, and 48.

43. Clark, " 'Adam's Only Companion,' " 16, 29–30, presents the Roman law of marriage as more ambiguous about consent than does Elliott (see above n. 36), and, 22–28, 30–31, treats Mary and Joseph. See nn. 10, 12, and 42 above, and nn. 46 and 48 below on Tertullian.

44. Clark, " 'Adam's Only Companion,' " 16, 29–30, considers Augustine's views on consent: see also 17, on Augustine's own "marital" history; and 29, on age at marriage. See also Peter Brown, *Augustine and Sexuality* (Berkeley, Calif., 1983), 2–3 (Augustine had another liaison during the two-year betrothal before his fiancée achieved the legal age of marriage), *Body and Society,* chap. 19, and *Augustine,* 226–27, for religiously mixed marriages in Augustine's world, which the anti-Donatist legislation after 393 targeted; Bagnall, *Egypt,* 199–201, on family life-cycles; Kertzer and Saller, eds., *Family in Italy;* and Evans Grubbs, *Law and Family,* 155, 294–300.

45. William Basil Zion, *Eros and Transformation: Sexuality and Marriage: An Eastern Orthodox Perspective* (Lanham, Md., 1992), as at 108–9, is more confused than helpful.

46. Chiara Frugoni, "L'iconografia del matrimonio e della coppia nel medioevo," *Il matrimonio nella società altomedievale,* Settimane di Studio del Centro Italiano di Studi sull'Alto Medioevao 24, 2 vols. (Spoleto, 1977), 2:901–66, at 926. See above nn. 37 and 40 on the liturgy, and nn. 10, 12, 42, and 43 above and 48 below, on Tertullian. The theme of marriage "before God" found expression on such objects as marriage-rings: Clark, *Women in Late Antiquity,* Illustration 1, is of a late sixth-century marriage-ring with a group composed of Christ and Mary standing between the couple, under which is "(h)omonoia," the ancient hope for "concord." Evans Grubbs, *Law and Family,* 179–80, gives an example of blessing at betrothal.

47. In addition to n. 46 above, see Ernst Kitzinger, *Early Medieval Art,* 2d ed. (Bloomington, Ind., 1983), 13–14 and plate 1, for both the cups and the Projecta Casket.

48. See n. 46 above. For the quotations from Tertullian which follow in the next two paragraphs, Paulinus, and the nuptial liturgy, see David G. Hunter, trans. and ed., *Marriage in the Early Church* (Minneapolis, 1992), 25–28, who gathers texts on marriage from the New Testament through the sixth century. Boswell, *Same-Sex Unions,* 132–33, gives a misguided translation of Tertullian strikingly different from that of Hunter (see on the issues of translation Le Saint, *Tertullian: Treatises on Marriage and Remarriage,* 35 with notes); and 163–65 (and 198, 203–4) states, without sufficient argument, that the prayers Tertullian refers to are simply a blessing of the bride. See Kenneth Stevenson, *Nuptial Blessing: A Study of Christian Marriage Rites* (New York, 1983), 31, on priests marrying in church (21–26, 97–121, of this unevenly informed and sometimes incautious book are on the Eastern rites neglected in the present book). See also Evans Grubbs, *Law and Family,* 149–50, and Jean Gaudemet, "Le lien matrimonial: Les incertitudes du haut Moyen Âge," in *Le lien matrimonial,* ed. René Metz and Jean Schlick (Strasbourg, 1970), 81–105, at 91.

49. On this and the next paragraph, see John T. Noonan, "Marital Affection in the Canonists," *Studia Gratiana* 12 (1967): 482–89, developed by Michael M. Sheehan, "*Maritalis affectio* Revisited," in *Olde Daunce,* ed. Edwards and Spector, 32–43, 254–60 (notes), here at 35–36, and also in the same book Clark, " 'Adam's Only Companion,' " 29–31. Treggiari, *Roman Marriage,* 51–52 and index under "concubinae," "concubinatus," treats concubinage.

50. *Stromata* 3.10.68, trans. Oulton and Chadwick, *Alexandrian Christianity,* 79–80, with Elliott, *Spiritual Marriage,* 42.

51. *Symposium,* Logos 2.1–2, trans. ACW 27, 48–50.

52. The translation is from the *Catechism of the Catholic Church,* 568, and see Boswell, *Same-Sex Unions,* 104, and 153 and 175.

53. Osborne, *Eros Unveiled,* shows that Anders Nygren's contrast between *eros* and *agape* has little to commend itself as an explication of ancient usage, and that *eros* was used by both pagan and Christian writers to describe both appetitive and non-appetitive loves. See esp. chaps. 3 and 7.

54. *Esteem Enlivened by Desire: The Couple from Homer to Shakespeare* (Chicago, 1992), at 175–78, for Chrysostom (there is no mention of Tertullian), with Edwards and Spector, eds., Introduction to *The Olde Daunce,* 1–13, 237–39 (notes) at 1.

55. Reginald Hyatte, *The Arts of Friendship: The Idealization of Friendship in Medieval and Early Renaissance Literature* (Leiden, 1994), opens with a chapter on classical theories of friendship.

56. Elliott, *Spiritual Marriage,* 42 (with Clark, " 'Adam's Only Companion,' " in *Olde Daunce,* ed. Edwards and Spector, 25, for the quotation from Augustine's *De nuptiis* 1.12[11]; the general argument of Clark's article, followed by Elliott, seems to me somewhat myopic), 191. While it is quite true that Augustine in his late anti-Pelagian writings was so preoccupied with defending the sexual and reproductive aspects of marriage that he failed to develop further the companionate side which had earlier interested him, as I note below, following Émile Schmitt, *Le Mariage chrétien dans l'oeuvre de saint Augustin: Une théologie baptismale de la vie conjugale* (Paris, 1983), he had already developed this side further than Clark indicates. It is simply a mistake, Clark, 31, to suggest that controversy with Manicheans and Pelagians prevented the volitional factors in marriage from emerging as central in Augustine's thought: they are central from beginning to end.

57. *The City of God,* 14.16, trans. Henry Bettenson, intro. David Knowles (Harmondsworth, 1972), 577.

58. Jerome, *Commentariorum in Hiezechielem* 6, Corpus Christianorum, Series Latina 75.235–36, quoted and trans. Pierre J. Payer, *The Bridling of Desire: Views of Sex in the Later Middle Ages* (Toronto, 1993), 107, with 231 n. 127, and see Kelly, *Love,* chap. 10.

59. Clark, " 'Adam's Only Companion,' " in *Olde Daunce,* ed. Edwards and Spector, 22–31, at 23–24 for the quotation from *Contra Faustum* 23,8, trans. A Select Library of the Nicene and Post-Nicene Fathers of the Christian Church (hereafter NPNF), ed. Philip Schaff, vol. 4: *St. Augustin: The Writings against the Manichaeans and the Donatists* (rpt. Grand Rapids, Mich., 1989), 315.

60. Brundage, *Law,* 91.

61. John T. Noonan Jr., *Contraception: A History of Its Treatment by the Catholic Theologians and Canonists,* enlarged ed. (Cambridge, Mass., 1986), 122–23, considers Hippolytus, with the question of authorship, with Evans Grubbs, *Law and Family,* 260–316, on mixed-status unions, at 309–10, 312–13. Cf. Angus McLaren, *A History of Contraception: From Antiquity to the Present* (Oxford, 1990). Boswell, *Same-Sex Unions,* 114–15, makes useful comment on the social psychology of the lack of reliable artificial contraceptives. On this and the following, see also Elliott, *Spiritual Marriage,* 38, 41, 48–49 (the criticisms of Augustine do not seem to me consistently well thought out), 135–36 (Jerome and Peter Lombard on intercourse as seeking conception).

62. The translation of the *Didache* is from *Catechism of the Catholic Church*, 547. Bibliography on Christian opinion about when the soul is present in the embryo, on abortion in theology and canon law, is given in the next chapter.

63. The classic study is by Henri Crouzel, *Virginité et mariage selon Origène*, Museum Lessianum, section théologique, 58 (Paris, 1962).

64. Clement, *Stromata* 3.82–83, trans. Oulton and Chadwick, *Alexandrian Christianity*, p. 79. Clark, " 'Adam's Only Companion,' " 26, describes Augustine's view of the Christian marital life cycle in *Contra Julianum* 3.43(21). Cohen, *"Be Fertile,"* esp. 231ff., traces the early Christian procreative attitudes. For the development of periods of abstinence related to the liturgical cycle, see Noonan, *Contraception*, 70.

65. One may obtain entrance both to Jerome's thought and to its later influence in Philippe Delhaye, "Le dossier anti-matrimonial de l'*Adversus Jovinianum* et son influence sur quelques écrits latins du XIIe s.," *Mediaeval Studies* 13 (1951): 65–86, and see McLeod, *Virtue*, chap. 2. On his unjustified misogynist reputation and on divorce for adultery, see Evans Grubbs, *Law and Family*, 248–50, 255. Schmitt, *Mariage chrétien*, 19–41, develops in detail the relations between the Manichean controversy (387–400) and Augustine's doctrine of marriage.

66. Clark, " 'Adam's Only Companion,' " in *Olde Daunce*, ed. Edwards and Spector, 15 and 18–19, and see David G. Hunter, "Helvidius, Jovinian, and the Virginity of Mary in Late Fourth-Century Rome," *Journal of Early Christian Studies* 1 (1993): 47–71, and the introduction by Theodore de Bruyn to his translation, *Pelagius' Commentary on St. Paul's Epistle to the Romans* (Oxford, 1993). Cf. R. A. Markus, *Sacred and Secular: Studies on Augustine and Latin Christianity* (Brookfield, Vt., 1994), and Gerald Bonner, *Church and Faith in the Patristic Tradition: Augustine, Pelagianism, and Early Christian Northumbria* (Brookfield, Vt., 1996), esp. III, 355, 357, distinguishing between the views of Pelagius and later Pelagianism, V–VII.

67. Katharina M. Wilson and Elizabeth M. Makowski, *Wykked Wyves and the Woes of Marriage: Misogamous Literature from Juvenal to Chaucer* (Albany, N.Y., 1990), and see Elliott, *Spiritual Marriage*, as at 36. More generally see Georges Duby and Michelle Perrot, gen. eds., *A History of Women in the West*, vol. 1: *From Ancient Goddesses to Christian Saints*, ed. Pauline Schmitt Pantel, trans. Arthur Goldhammer (Cambridge, Mass., 1992), and Clark, *Women in Late Antiquity*, esp. chap. 5.

68. For this development see below chaps. 4–5.

69. Gregory the Great, *Dial.* 4.13, Sources Chrétiennes 165, 3:56.

70. Brown, *The Body and Society*, 99.

71. Elliott, *Spiritual Marriage*, 43–45, with Brown, *Body and Society*, 387–95. See also Evans Grubbs, " 'Pagan' and 'Christian' Marriage," 412, and David G. Hunter, "Resistance to the Virginal Ideal in Late-Fourth-Century Rome: The Case of Jovinian," *Theological Studies* 48 (1987): 45–64. Elizabeth A. Clark, *The Origenist Controversy: The Cultural Construction of an Early Christian Debate* (Princeton, N.J., 1992), chap. 3, considers other defenders of marriage and reproduction, Epiphanius of Salamis and Theophilus. The unknown author of the somewhat later (possibly fifth or sixth century) apocryphal *Cave of Treasures* or *Book of Adam and Eve*, which survives only in an Ethiopic version, had a celebratory view of marriage: Valerie I. J. Flint, *The Rise of Magic in Early Medieval Europe* (Princeton, N.J., 1991), 373–74.

72. Gerhart B. Ladner, *The Idea of Reform: Its Impact on Christian Thought in the Age of the Fathers*, rev. ed. (New York, 1967), is a particularly careful exposition of Augustine's ideas about perfection.

73. Charles Wilcox, introduction to *The Good of Marriage* in *Treatises on Marriage and Other Subjects*, ed. Roy Deferrari, FOC 27 (New York, 1955), introduces the vast bibliography on this subject. John M. Rist, *Augustine: Ancient Thought Baptized* (New York, 1994), 196–98, 212, 246–52, 321, at 246, remarks that Augustine's teaching of "marriage is concerned more essentially with the intended *birth* of children than with their conception." In addition see Clark, " 'Adam's Only Companion,' " 18–19, 243–44 (listing further bibliography on the possible influence of Jovinian), François-Joseph Thonard, "La morale conjugale selon saint Augustin," *Revue des Études Augustiniennes* 15 (1969): 113–31, and Emanuele Samek Lodovici, "Sessualità, matrimonio e concupiscenza in Sant'Agostino," in *Etica sessuale*, ed. Cantalamessa, 212–72. I follow the suggestions for translation here of Elliott, *Spiritual Marriage*, 46–47, which is also used in what follows.

74. Bonner, "Augustine's Attitude to Women," in *Homo spiritalis: Festgabe für Luc Verheijen zu seinem 70. Geburtstag*, ed. Cornelius Mayer and Karl Heinz Chelius (Würzburg, 1987), 272–73; Rist, *Augustine*, 246–47; and Pier Cesare Bori, *Chiesa primitiva: L'immagine della comunità delle origini — Atti 2,42–47; 4,32–37 — nella storia della chiesa antica* (Brescia, 1974), chaps. 4–5 and 260–79.

75. *De bono coniugali*, CSEL 18.21, p. 214, trans. Wilcox, 35. J. Patout Burns, "Response," in Brown, *Augustine and Sexuality*, 15, develops the parallel between marriage and ecclesiology. Robert J. O'Connell's more radical and philosophical "Response," 22–25, not engaged by Brown, while realizing that Augustine is not completely consistent on such matters, wonders whether Augustine's eudaemonism is not so controlling as to make impossible any principled friendship or intercourse built on outgoing love.

76. Noonan, *Contraception*, 151–75, with Clark, " 'Adam's Only Companion,' " 20.

77. Erik Kooper, "Loving the Unequal Equal: Medieval Theologians and Marital Affection," in *Olde Daunce*, ed. Edwards and Spector, 262 n. 20, and see William Joseph Dooley, *Marriage according to St. Ambrose* (Washington, D.C., 1948). As the "Responses" in Brown, *Augustine and Sexuality*, of Burns, Xavier Harris (17), and Margaret Miles (19–20) suggest, we find significant crumbling of the ascetic paradigm of sexuality in Augustine's thought well before 412, but also its presence until the end: rather than the social paradigm of sexuality simply replacing the ascetic paradigm, the two competed in Augustine's mature thought. Burns's "Response," 14, notes the shift in Augustine's thought to reflection on blood and social relations. In *De bono coniugali* 1.1, CSEL 41, 187–88, trans. Wilcox, 9, Augustine called Adam and Eve "friends": see the following notes.

78. See Martin Aurell, *Les noces du comte: Mariage et pouvoir en Catalogne (785–1213)* (Paris, 1995), 67–68.

79. Averil Cameron, *The Later Roman Empire* (Cambridge, Mass., 1993), 148–49, and see Clark, " 'Adam's Only Companion,' " 15–16. Augustine's developed position is found in *The City of God*, XIV.

80. *De bono coniugali* 1, CSEL 41, sect. 5, pt. 3, p. 188, trans. Wilcox, 9, for the quoted phrases. On the "rib-topos," which runs through medieval thought, see D. L. D'Avray and M. L. Tausche, "Marriage Sermons in *Ad status* Collections of the Central Middle Ages," *Archives d'Histoire Doctrinale et Littéraire du Moyen Âge* 47 (1980): 71–119, esp. 106, with Kooper, "Loving the Unequal Equal, 44–56, 260–65 (notes) at 45–46. On friendship, marital and otherwise, see Bonner, "Augustine's Attitude to Women," in *Homo Spiritalis*, ed. Mayer and Chelius; John Rist, "Saint Augustine: Virginity and Marriage — 2," *Canadian Catholic Review* 5 (1987): 57–

64, who stresses Augustine's comments about the pleasures of married friendship; Brown, *Body and Society,* 387–425; and Carolinne White, *Christian Friendship in the Fourth Century* (Cambridge, 1992), on which see Gerald Bonner, "Friendship in Christ: A Fourth-Century Change of Perspective," *Catholic Historical Review* 80 (1994): 97–101. For the perhaps overly scholastic distinction between the purpose and essence of marriage, see Elliott, *Spiritual Marriage,* 47.

81. Schmitt, *Mariage chrétien,* 273, 280–87, 290.

82. In addition to Elliott, *Spiritual Marriage,* 49, see Bonner, "Augustine's Attitude to Women," in *Homo spiritalis,* ed. Mayer and Chelius, 260–63, which I would recast to observe that as "homo," that is, a human being, woman is for Augustine man's equal, but as "femina," that is a woman, she is unequal or different. O'Connell, "Response" to Brown, *Augustine and Sexuality,* 22, takes the *De Genesi ad Litteram* to be an exploratory work, highly tentative in its conclusions.

83. Thus Brundage, *Law,* 85, is doubly wrong in saying "Augustine… considered women frankly inferior to men, both physically and morally," and "As for the notion that women were destined to be man's companion, Augustine would have none of it."

84. "Augustine's Attitude to Women," in *Homo spiritalis,* ed. Mayer and Chelius, 260.

85. Elliott, *Spiritual Marriage,* 49, with the editors' introduction to *Olde Daunce,* 1. In this volume the article of interest here is Clark, " 'Adam's Only Companion,' " unclearly described by Elliott.

86. Glenn W. Olsen, "St. Augustine and the Problem of the Medieval Discovery of the Individual," *Word and Spirit: A Monastic Review* 9 (1987): 129–56.

87. Bonner, "Augustine's Attitude to Women," in *Homo spiritalis,* ed. Mayer and Chelius, 263–64, remarks that Augustine's attitude toward female companionship is that of a civilization.

88. For all questions regarding Augustine's views on the relations between the sexes, see Kari E. Børresen, *Subordination and Equivalence: The Nature and Role of Woman in Augustine and Thomas,* trans. from the revised French edition by Charles H. Talbot (Washington, D.C., 1981). A review (below n. 116) of a book which Børresen later edited, *Image of God and Gender Models in Judaeo-Christian Tradition* (Oslo, 1991), points out inconsistencies in her analysis.

89. Brown has pursued the analysis of *Body and Society* in *Power and Persuasion in Late Antiquity: Towards a Christian Empire* (Madison, Wisc., 1992), esp. the chapter "Poverty and Power." The social historians tell us that Christianity had from the first largely been a religion of the "upwardly mobile," of the lower middle and middle classes, especially from about 300 spreading into all classes: Grubbs, *Law and Family,* 8–17.

90. *Subordination,* XVI, for the phrases quoted, and 315, problematically (because raising the question of what "government" then could mean) stating that for Augustine man and wife possess identical rational souls. Erik Kooper prefers the terminology "equal in inequality": "Loving the Unequal Equal," *Olde Daunce,* ed. Edwards and Spector, with 4 of the editors' Introduction.

91. *Against Faustus the Manichee,* XXII, 31, trans. NPNF 4.284.

92. *Law,* 93.

93. Trans. P. G. Walsh, *The Poems of St. Paulinus of Nola,* ACW 40 (New York, 1975), 245–53, at 250, for the phrase quoted, with the discussion of Elliott, *Spiritual Marriage,* 51–53, which I am in part correcting.

94. CSEL 41.209, trans. Wilcox, 31.

95. Dimitri Michaélidès, *Sacramentum chez Tertullien* (Paris, 1970), part 3, treats *sacramentum* and *mysterion* with the Gnostics and St. Paul. Schmitt, *Mariage chrétien*, 215–33, is basic. See for context Johan Chydenius, *The Theory of Medieval Symbolism*, Commentationes Humanarum Litterarum 27, 2 (Helsingfors, 1960).

96. Basile Studer, " 'Sacramentum et exemplum' chez saint Augustin," *Recherches Augustiniennes* 10 (1975): 87–141.

97. Above n. 9 and Clark, " 'Adam's Only Companion,' " 25. Schmitt, *Mariage chrétien*, parts 3 and 4, in developing the relation between marriage and baptism, 224–25, discusses the parallel great/little sacrament. See also Reynolds, *Marriage in the Western Church*, 280–311. Paulinus of Nola, Poem 25, line 167, ACW 40.250, writes of the "great mystery" of the wedding of Church to Christ.

98. Boswell, *Same-Sex Unions*, 115, follows Elliott. Hans Urs von Balthasar, *Explorations in Theology*, vol. 1: *The Word Made Flesh*, trans. A. V. Littledale with Alexander Dru (San Francisco, 1989), 202, and vol. 2: *Spouse of the Word* (San Francisco, 1991), 158, 163, 181, remarks on the marriage of God with humankind.

99. In addition to the following notes, see Elliott, *Spiritual Marriage*, 38, for each of these points, and Brown, *Augustine and Sexuality*, 5–10, on this and the following. On Origen see Crouzel, *Virginité*, 18, 26, 44–58, 82, 39. Caroline Bynum, *The Resurrection of the Body in Western Christianity* (New York, 1995), argues that in general historians have exaggerated the importance of the soul/body dichotomy in Christianity and that most Christians understood the body as essential to the definition of the human. The specific subject of Bynum's book perhaps leads her to underestimate a Platonic tendency in many patristic writers to think of man as his soul. Rist, *Augustine*, 92–147, examines Augustine's ideas about the relation of body and soul in Eden, after the Fall, and in the next life.

100. In addition to Brown, *Body and Society*, see Elliott, *Spiritual Marriage*, 30–31, 36, 39, 45. For Philo and Gregory of Nyssa, see Marie-Thérèse d'Alverny, "Comment les théologiens et les philosophes voient la femme," *Pensée médiévale en Occident: Théologie, magie et autres textes des XIIe–XIIIe siècles*, ed. Charles Burnett (Aldershot, Hampshire, 1995), XI, 106, the reprint of an influential article which, though centered on the twelfth century, surveys earlier materials. See also Édouard Jeauneau, "La division des sexes chez Grégoire de Nysse et chez Jean Scot Érigène," in *Études Érigéniennes* (Paris, 1987), 343–64.

101. Clark, " 'Adam's Only Companion,' " 17–18, noting the presence of this view still in book 13 of the *Confessions* (398). Augustine's five works on the beginning of Genesis are sorted out by Roland J. Teske in his introduction to *Saint Augustine on Genesis: Two Books on Genesis against the Manichees and On the Literal Interpretation of Genesis: An Unfinished Book*, FOC 84 (Washington, D.C., 1991). Payer, *Bridling of Desire*, chap. 1, gives a summary of Augustine's teaching.

102. Clark, " 'Adam's Only Companion,' " 20, 245 n. 61. Rist, *Augustine*, 249–50, does not note the problems caused by the patriarch's postlapsarian status.

103. *Against Faustus*, XXII, 43, NPNF 4.288. Clark, " 'Adam's Only Companion,' " 27–28, describes Julian's attack on Augustine. For all these matters, again see the chapters on Augustine in Reynolds, *Marriage in the Western Church*, and Rist, *Augustine*, 321–27.

104. *Body and Society*, esp. 399ff.

105. I am recasting Brown, *Augustine and Sexuality*, p. 10.

106. It is Augustine who has the wicked sense of humor: *The City of God*, 14.15–19. Clark, " 'Adam's Only Companion,' " 21, delineates the relation between original sin and sex as we now experience it. Schmitt, *Mariage chrétien*, by organizing Augustine's thought chronologically, shows the development of his views on a number

of issues which have commonly been presented in modern scholarship as fixed. See especially on the development of his understanding of *concupiscentia* and *libido,* 49–62, 83–105, 183–212. In addition, see Bonner, *Church and Faith,* VII, 33, 40–41. The idea that there could have been a sinless intercourse in Eden lies in the background of those twelfth-century thinkers such as of the school of Abelard, who envision married intercourse after the Fall as essentially without sin: see chap. 5 below and Seamus Heaney, *The Sacramentality of Marriage: From Anselm of Laon to Thomas Aquinas* (Washington, D.C., 1963), 86–88. Kelly, *Marriage in the Age of Chaucer,* index under "sexual intercourse," at 252–53, notes that from the end of the twelfth century certain canonists came to defend the idea that intercourse could be sinless.

107. Margaret R. Miles, "Response" to Brown, *Augustine and Sexuality,* 21. O'Connell's "Response" in the same work rejects any reading of Augustine which sees him as having definitively abandoned Plotinus on the soul (22), and questions, inconclusively in my opinion, Brown's understanding of the "social" in Augustine (23). Schmitt, *Mariage chrétien,* 107–36, studies the relations between neo-Platonic pessimism about the body and Augustine. With the tradition Augustine held there will be no marriage in heaven, though at the very end of his life he insisted that in the resurrection sexual distinction between men and women would remain, not for child-bearing but to proclaim the diversity of God's works: see Bonner, "Augustine's Attitude to Women," in *Homo Spiritalis,* ed. Mayer and Chelius, 274, on *City of God,* 22, 17. On later medieval division of opinion as to whether there would be sexual differentiation after the resurrection, see Philippe Buc, *L'ambiguïté du livre: Prince, pouvoir, et peuple dans les commentaires de la Bible au Moyen Âge* (Paris, 1994), 131–32, esp. n. 21, and see the following note.

108. Elliott, *Spiritual Marriage,* 45–48, and Clark, " 'Adam's Only Companion,' " 21.

109. Bynum, "Images of the Resurrection Body," 218, which should be read with Bynum's *Resurrection of the Body,* 26 (esp. n. 13), 109–13, a very sensible discussion.

110. *Adam, Eve, and the Serpent* (New York, 1988), chap. 5. This book is full of anachronisms and false perspectives. See above nn. 12 and 14.

111. *Spiritual Marriage,* 30, 63. Presumably the poem of Paulinus discussed above, n. 94, would be an example of this.

112. *Spiritual Marriage,* 46.

113. This is the principal argument of Ladner, *Idea of Reform.*

114. This development in Augustine's thought is summarized in Elliott, *Spiritual Marriage,* 45 n. 121, and worked out in Schmitt, *Mariage chrétien,* 91–94.

115. *Spiritual Marriage,* 46.

116. Review, *Journal of Early Christian Studies* 1 (1993): 319–21 at 320.

117. *Three Orders,* 370 n. 11.

118. Analysis and trans. in Hunter, *Marriage,* 25, 128–40 at 128–29.

Chapter Four

MARRIAGE IN BARBARIAN KINGDOM AND CHRISTIAN COURT
Fifth through Eleventh Centuries

Glenn W. Olsen

Virginity and Marriage, Perfection and Imperfection, Purity and Impurity

During the more than six centuries considered in the present chapter, monks, though commonly retaining many ties to their own families, continued to affirm the biblical idea that the new and true family is the spiritual family of those who do the will of God. Ancient Christian ideals of perfection spread in all the regions in which barbarian successor kingdoms replaced the Roman empire. Especially women embraced the idea that by giving up marriage they could pursue a higher form of motherhood, spiritual motherhood, in which they became the nurturers of more than any actual mother nursed. In spite of the best efforts of conscientious priests to impart a Christian appreciation of marriage, absorption with the virgin ideal continued to deflect attention from consideration of marriage's special situation and needs. In late Anglo-Saxon England, toward the end of the period studied in the present chapter, the Old English lives of St. Margaret of Antioch took the nuptial imagery of the *sponsa Christi* ([a woman or nun] "betrothed of Christ") to make a common contrast between the false love shown by Margaret's human suitor and true intimacy and love, for God.[1]

Though from about the time of Pope Gregory I, the Great (590–604), pious married people were more likely by mutual consent simply to abandon marriage and join monasteries than to stay together in a spiritual marriage, spiritual marriage continued to exist in various forms. It called the goodness of carnal union in question.[2] In the Iberian northwest a halfway house between marriage and monasticism appeared. In this patronal monasticism developed around the work of St. Fructuosus of Braga (c. 600/610–c. 665), parents with children were allowed to join monasteries.[3] The attraction monastic life had for already existing marriages presented sufficient problems that an interpolation of the Rule of St. Isidore of Seville (c. 560–636) raised once again the question of what was to be done when a married man wished to enter the monastic life while his spouse still lived.[4] A century and a half later Einhard, the biographer of Charlemagne (768–814), retired from court life with his wife, Emma, to Seligenstadt. There they jointly presided as an apparently celibate lay couple over the monastic community they had founded, somewhat in the fashion of such notable fifth-century figures as Paulinus of Nola. The monastic author of the oldest *Life* of Ida of Boulogne (c. 1040–1113), writing between 1130 and 1135, presented a kind of trope on spiritual marriage in which he praised Ida for her wifely devotion in submitting to intercourse in a chaste way. He says Ida underwent rather than enjoyed sexual relations. That is, active sexuality was present in her marriage, but Ida's mind and body were distanced from the sexual act. Our monastic author, clearly preferring virginity above marriage, praised Ida for being in effect a virginal mother.[5]

The assumption was that a good married life was simply a diluted imitation of monastic perfection.[6] Much in the New Testament was beyond the comprehension of the barbarians, with the coming of whom prehistory had burst into history. The nobility of the gift-giving societies of the North showed great facility in accepting the gift of Christianity, eternal life, in exchange for support of the Church, while retaining a pre-Christian style of life. When the future nun and saint Radegund of Poitiers (c. 520–87) married Clothar I (511–61) in 540, nine years after Clothar had won her as a war prize, she apparently became his fifth wife (he also had concubines).[7] For such a man what was needed pastorally was law and discipline to form basic Christian habits. Clergy turned to the Old Covenant for guidance.[8] Especially in Celtic lands from the sixth century, many Levitical sexual precepts obtained new life. Women were viewed as unclean after childbirth until churched. Men were given severe penances for nocturnal emissions. Intercourse itself was commonly viewed as polluting. Irish missionaries in turn spread such views on the continent.[9] Everywhere these notions overlapped ideas more directly related to New Testament teaching, such as the desirability of abstention from sexual relations before prayers or eucharistic communion or in Lent. Since antiquity Lent was a period during which one could not be betrothed or marry.[10] All through our period ascetical ideas and notions of pollution reinforced the very severe penitential discipline in place in some Roman regions by the fifth century.[11] As in the age of the Fathers, there was much wavering between the demanding norms of bishops such as Caesarius of Arles (c. 470–543) and acceptance of the inevitability of much sub-Christian practice. "Christianization," spreading often very superficially in the late Roman world from urban episcopal elites to rural peripheries, was a negotiation between clerical demands and lay vested interests and habits.[12] As cities declined in the early Middle Ages, the difficulty of penetrating the countryside with any uniform message or practice only increased.

One expression of admiration for virginity over marriage was the expansion of the periods of abstinence from intercourse penitentials (guidebooks for priests to use for confession) requested of the married.[13] Demands in this regard varied greatly over time and place. Even those who understood what difference there was between an ascetic practice and what is now called a taboo, between abstinence for reasons of self-discipline or prayer and abstinence for reasons of avoiding impurity or pollution, must often have been unsure about what was asked of them. There is in this regard a tendency in a great deal of modern scholarship to see sex as no more than a battleground over which various forces contended for "power." The last chapter took notice of such views, which Michel Foucault and many feminists have embraced. Such a way of looking at things can be very revealing, but a warning advanced by John T. Noonan bears remembering. Reviewing a fine book, *The Language of Sex,* dealing with the twelfth century, Noonan took exception to its idea that the requirement of annual confession by the Fourth Lateran Council of 1215 established "the mechanism to supervise the sexual lives of lay men and women throughout Latin Christendom." Noonan observed that the Council understood the sacrament of confession to be medicinal, part of the "cure of souls," and that the modern scholar obscures this by transforming it into simply an instrument of control.[14] The battle in the Middle Ages was first a battle for souls, not simply to control but to teach, to help people assume new points of view for themselves.

The ideas of Eutropius of Valencia typified much learned and monastic thought. At the end of the sixth century he contrasted the *sanctus,* or monk, who followed a life of renunciation and sought perfection, with the *profanus,* or secular man.[15] However, just as the last chapter had to insist that monastic ideas of perfection were but one strand of Christian reality in the age of the Fathers, this chapter must insist that in the early Middle Ages there existed more than simply world-fleeing spirituality. This was a time of great brutality, of plunder in battle, rape, and abduction marriage (*Raubehe*). Women were sometimes called to lives of heroic worldly involvement. A Christian wife was often the instrument of her husband's conversion, as in the case of Queen Clotilde, wife of Clovis (481–511).[16] The Pauline obligation to pray for the salvation of an unbelieving spouse achieved a classical missionary expression in a letter of Pope Boniface V (619–25), included in Bede's (c. 672–735) *Ecclesiastical History.* Just a generation after the initial missionary trip of St. Augustine of Canterbury to convert the Anglo-Saxons, Boniface instructed an early convert, Queen Æthelburh, on the strategy of persuasion to conversion to be used with her husband. Boniface portrayed Æthelburh as the instrument chosen by God to effect the salvation of husband and people, the enkindling of love for God. Recalling the two becoming one flesh of Genesis 2:24, Boniface said that while King Edwin remained attached to idolatry, a part of Æthelburh's body remained alienated from acknowledgment of the Trinity. Those tied in carnal affection (*copulatio carnalis affectus*) are in a manner one body and should by unity of faith be kept in unending fellowship after death. Presuming that Boniface understood this fellowship (*in perpetua societate conservet*) to begin in this life, we can describe him as viewing marriage as a shared fellowship which was imperfect unless built on a shared faith.[17]

There was great variety of attitudes in regard to the world and its renunciation. For instance, there was a shift, not permanent but for a time, in some saints lives written about Merovingian women of the sixth and seventh centuries. This shift, evident too in what Pope Boniface asked of Æthelburh, was from the ancient self-disciplined world-fleeing saint, presented as an ideal to be read about by educated aristocrats, to a more world-entering saint who performs great deeds and is presented in the relatively more popular format of the saint's festival sermon. The women of these saints lives speak with confidence and authority and are known for their virtue, largesse, and political skills, that is, for public rather than ascetic or domestic virtues. A number of them are married but eventually convert to the monastic life. The lives treat the married stage of their subjects' careers from differing perspectives. The *Life* of Waletrude suppressed the fact that she had children and gave no portrayal of any love or happiness she might have had for them or for family life. On the contrary, her *Life* states that she abhorred sexual relations, though she loved her husband in a spiritual way even after he had preceded her in entering the monastic life. Rictrude, on the other hand, was shown to have had a model marriage embodying the teaching of the Carolingian reform clergy, who continued the expectation of Merovingian society that aristocratic mothers should give religious and moral instruction to their children.[18] Rictrude's husband married her "not through lack of self-control but in order to have beloved offspring," their marriage was characterized by unanimity, and their children were brought up in the fear of the Lord. When she became a nun after he was murdered, she betrothed her three daughters to Christ and taught them by her example, mourning at the premature death of one of them. Her hagiographer saw no incompatibility between her motherly and religious obligations and no reason to suppress recounting the former.[19]

The variety of circumstance and theme in such stories stands as a warning against attempts to generalize about a "status of women" which can be measured over time.[20] In the case of individual questions such as women's rights in property or their right to consent to their own marriages, some rough measurement is possible. However, assessing a "status" typically involves evaluating a large number of not necessarily commensurate and always changing factors simultaneously. The status of an individual, let alone of some large category as "women," depends on a host of factors. These range from age and class through economic circumstances to the possession of various forms of personal freedom. Even if specified in the medieval sources, these have inevitably to be ranked by some scale of values, either our own or a composite coming from the period under study. In the present instance, it is hard to know what weight to give to legal advantages these Merovingian women shared with many early medieval women against the various trials found in their lives, including their vulnerability to violation. On the one hand, they benefited from the greater number of rights in regard to property and inheritance accorded them by German, in comparison to Roman, law; on the other hand, they often knew little of, or did not even have expectations for, the joys of married life.[21]

From a certain perspective, Charlemagne (768–814) continued the activism displayed by many of the women in Merovingian saints' lives. His goal, as long as he did not have to keep all the rules himself, was building the City of God in Frankland. Under his successor Louis the Pious (814–40), Jonas, bishop of Orléans from 818 to 843, about 830 wrote *The Education of the Laity,* one of the "mirrors" or manuals of instruction popular in Carolingian pastoral care. In this manual Jonas pursued the regulation of marital life and gave instruction on conjugal morality, the sanctification of marriage, and the obligation for heads of families to give religious instruction. His goal was a positive presentation of marriage as a means of salvation and of building up a Christian society. For him the married couple formed a society of equals.[22] In every subsequent century similar attempts to give a positive evaluation of marriage, and to see in it more than simply the procreation of children, stood beside more negative judgments. When in the tenth century King Henry I, the Fowler, and his wife, Matilda (ca. 895–968), were praised for marital chastity, this elaborated an ideal of Christian married life lived in the world going back to Jonas. This ideal spread from Saxony throughout the eleventh-century Ottonian empire. It laid one foundation for the increased appreciation of marriage and "incarnational" modes of existence present from the time of the Gregorian Reform associated with Pope Gregory VII (1073–85). The marital chastity attributed to Henry and Matilda was not renunciation of sexual relations, but marital purity, living within the laws of the Church and being a good example to others.[23]

World-fleeing tendencies did remain very powerful. In the years around 1000 some doubted that lay life could win salvation. Though marriage could be something prized, ascetic writers continued to describe it as no more than remedy for concupiscence. A little before 1000 Abbot Abbo of Fleury declared, "As concerns the married state, it is permitted only for motives of leniency, in order to avoid man's falling into an even worse state at an age at which temptations due to the frailty of the flesh are powerful."[24] Though marriage was good, carnal union for such writers was an embarrassment to be entered into reluctantly. A half century after Abbo, Peter Damian spoke of the elephant which "impelled to the act of propagation, turns its head away, showing thereby that it is acting under compulsion from nature, against its will, and that it is ashamed and disgusted at what it is doing."[25] However, the pastoral obligations of the clergy inclined them to more encouraging views. Bishop Marbod of Rennes, also in the eleventh century, declared "of all the things which are seen to have been bestowed through God's gift to the advantage of humanity, we consider nothing to be more beautiful or better than a good woman."[26] Still, it was hard for the learned to forget the attacks of writers such as Jerome on both women and the married state. Before Albert the Great and Thomas Aquinas in the thirteenth century, most theologians thought intercourse at least a venial sin.[27]

The lives early medieval hagiographers thought worth writing about for the edification of society remained largely those of virgins. The virgin life was so praised that, as in the ancient Church, more than one advocate who had succeeded in persuading women to the religious life found himself the subject of attack. This could take the coloration of the categories of magic and sorcery which filled the lives of early medieval people. Thus St. Lonoghyl, having persuaded St. Agnofleda to reject an offer of marriage in favor of the religious life, had to defend himself before the king against the accusation of the disappointed suitor that he had practiced magic on Agnofleda.[28] Chroniclers, often building on the legends of Roman saints such as Thecla and Alexius, who respectively on their wedding days had persuaded their spouses to continence, liked to recount stories of married women who by their wiles avoided consummation of their marriages. These ultimately might achieve the status of virgin-widow, a stock figure of the early Middle Ages. Another stock figure was the king or warrior who in old age entered a monastery, that is, renounced the lay life to embrace perfection. In such literature the assumption was that holy people would not be married. The best of the married would be those who had renounced sexual relations. Though by 1100 such ideas were losing ground, in 1130 a Flemish hagiographer declared, "To observe celibacy once children have been born is a great thing."[29]

Though, as we will see, clergy such as Archbishop Hincmar of Rheims (845–82) viewed carnal union as holy, during the early Middle Ages there does not seem to have been much integration of the sensual aspects of marriage into some larger theological framework. We may be deceived on such matters by the sources, which overwhelmingly describe life through a rel-

atively learned, male monastic or clerical eye. Had we the views of the
unlettered, things might present themselves very differently. There are sufficient materials for post-Reformation England to know how women then
understood churching after childbirth. These show churching to have been
an occasion for female socializing, far removed from the impurity categories
beloved of scholarly interpretation.[30] If we had similar evidence for the early
Middle Ages, we might also have to adjust our views and generalizations
about it. The sources we have are full of distrust of the flesh. They exhibit
a traditional tendency to see soul and intellect, associated with the male, as
ontologically higher than the physical and sensual, associated with the female. Customs varied, but it was common to ask the "nights of Tobias" of
the newly married couple, three or some other number of nights of abstention from consummation after marriage in order to pray. This was based on
Tobias 6:18, the request of the angel Raphael to Tobias to remain continent
for three days after his marriage to Sarah. At least in Caesarius of Arles's
sixth-century Gaul, the newly married couple were not to enter a church for
thirty days.[31]

Just as Greeks, Jews, and Romans had their impurity categories, all the
territories from which Europe formed in the early Middle Ages had theirs.
Christianity's own ideas about impurity were only worked out through attention to questions of the kind we meet in the missionary Augustine of
Canterbury's queries to Gregory I. These are found in Book I, 27, of Bede's
Ecclesiastical History. The early Middle Ages was caught between two traditions. One centered on ancestral magic and taboos, on menstrual blood and
spilled semen. It was typified by St. Jerome's statement that a menstruating
woman pollutes all she touches. The other tradition, while not denying some
efficacy to, or at least being willing to compromise with, impurity categories,
tended to retain or dismiss these according to whether they could be given
a spiritual meaning and be set to spiritual purposes. This second tradition
was typified by Gregory the Great's declaration that a menstruating woman
could take communion and is found in Gregory's responses to Augustine
as recorded by Bede. There, though Gregory affirmed that carnal union is
for procreation only, not pleasure, he (I, 27, 8) did not assume that every
act of intercourse rendered one unsuitable to take the Eucharist. He left this
judgment to those who have had intercourse and best know their state of
mind.[32]

The fear of pollution is no better illustrated than by the idea that if an
erotic dream ends in ejaculation, one must not take communion. Such a
view was expressed by prominent writers such as Caesarius of Arles and
Isidore of Seville (d. 636), though again Gregory opposed it (Bede, I, 27, 9).
There always had been disagreement about this matter, and there had been
considerable discussion of whether daytime thoughts reexpress themselves

in dreams in a manner entailing responsibility. While such ideas may not be completely absent from Caesarius's and Isidore's thinking, their notion seems primarily that emission itself pollutes. In contrast to the thought of earlier writers like Sts. Basil and Augustine, Caesarius and Isidore viewed seminal pollution as a dark force which might seize one "from the outside." This should be seen against the background of widespread belief in Dusii, particularly dangerous demons who spend their time tempting humans to carnal sin, riding them as incubi and succubi.[33] Jonas of Orléans was one of the most effective exponents of the "Gregorian" tradition of finding spiritual meaning in impurity proscriptions, though he was willing to compromise with those who felt they needed to practice these to the letter:

> Although the faithful people, through the grace of Christ, is immune from the weight of the law with which the Jewish people is still laden because of its incredulity, and although it understands and judges the law spiritually, yet there are certain things which Christian habit, despite the mystical understanding of it, to this day keeps according to the law because of the honour and cleanliness of the body. Thus it is with those women who, because they are giving birth, stay away from the doors of the church, or similarly because they suffer their menstrual flow of blood, although in most provinces they are not at all forbidden [entrance to] the buildings of the basilica because of the uncleanness of their flesh. And although these things, as the blessed pope Gregory teaches, have to be understood spiritually, it is yet not unbefitting, nor dishonourable, nor contrary to spiritual understanding, if these things are observed to the letter according to the former Christians [i.e., the Jews] beyond what is permitted.[34]

This very neatly capsulizes a writer committed to advancing spiritual understanding without disorienting those more literal-minded than himself. As the voice of a growing interiorization of Christianity found in a number of Carolingian authors, Jonas warned husbands that they should not prefer their wives' external beauty and taking carnal delight in them to chaste love of what they were interiorly. He adopted Augustine's distinction between use and enjoyment to present marriage as something providential, which can be an impediment to spiritual growth, but was made to be its aid.[35]

We know that Christian missionaries and pastors found much in pagan belief strange. Some of the Church's teachings appeared equally strange or unreasonable to people who, although having their own taboos, had thought little about their sexual practices. Jonas of Orléans tells us that many married men "impudently object" to having to abstain from sexual relations with their wives for any reason: " 'Our wives,' they say, 'are linked to us in law; we do not sin if we use them for our pleasure when and however we want.' "[36] Frequently the Christian missionary and pastor bringing even the message that the Ten Commandments were to be kept must have appeared as the bearers of an unwanted message. In the seventh century the Irish missionary Kilian was martyred at Würzburg by his recent convert, Duke Gozbert, for trying to impose the canons of marriage on him.[37] The teachings of the penitentials and the canon law were written in a language only a small elite could read. In a largely oral society, the communication of such teaching depended almost solely on the clergy. These were far from uniformly well informed themselves, and sometimes embraced ostensibly Christian practices which seem confused by earlier or later standards. What are we to make of the minor motif in the lives of some early Irish saints involving a miracle in which the saint blesses the womb of a pregnant woman to cause the pregnancy to disappear? In a period in which there was disagreement about when "ensoulment" took place (canon law came to number this at the fortieth day), it is difficult to know exactly what was intended here. The goal seems to have been either what we call miscarriage or abortion, but even in the high Middle Ages theologians thought a woman pregnant only when the fetus had formed. Drugs were taken (sinfully, because at least intending contraception) before this point to "prevent pregnancy." Obviously, in those lives where the woman was a nun who knew herself pregnant, blessing to make a pregnancy disappear was a way of dealing with embarrassment. Such blessings seem to reveal a world in which it is not always easy to distinguish between Christian and traditional magical practices (perhaps the text of Numbers 5:11–31 lay behind this usage).[38]

Many clergy remained caught between marriage and celibacy. By the late fourth century the higher clergy (deacon, priest, and bishop: the status of the subdiaconate remained a matter of controversy) had been bound to celibacy. In subsequent centuries, some continued to marry but obeyed the mandate of celibacy from the time of ordination. It has been both argued and denied that the Byzantine Council in Trullo (691–92) mistakenly interpreted an earlier Council of Carthage to allow the requirement of clerical continence to lapse in the Orthodox world.[39] In any case sexually active clerical marriages became common in both East and West. In the long run the Western Church seems to have been more resolute, and therefore more intrusive in the life of the individual, in trying to refashion all things sexual by its understanding of Christianity. The Eastern Church was more accommodating to the world in which it found itself. Peter Brown has said of Byzantine civilization that it left "large areas of the human body" outside "the fixed order of the church," and any reader of Eve Levin's study of sex in Orthodox Slavic society must be struck by the many eventual differences between East and West.[40] The last chapter compared the Western drive for an exceptionless indissolubility to Eastern permission of second marriages after penance for adultery.

One of the more sure-footed recent comparative historians has remarked, "In Justinian's laws the Christian concept that marriage was indissoluble is almost completely lacking.... However disapproved of and seen as a way to explore sexual opportunities in remarriage, divorce remained a matter of secular law, into which canonical enactments only slowly and irregularly spilled over."[41] To informed Westerners the Eastern stance on this and many other sexual questions have seemed obvious accommodations to inherited social customs, allowing large areas of the body to be insufficiently reformed by Christianity. To Easterners, the Western tradition has lacked pastoral compassion.

In the short run, there were many similarities between East and West. All through the Latin early Middle Ages, especially the rural clergy, who were often former serfs, married or had common law wives. In the first centuries after the barbarian invasions, and then again in the Carolingian period, these clerical wives were given distinctive clothes and were asked to vow celibacy. Unsurprisingly, many felt this to be something coerced and ignored the law. Married clergy came to form one of the chief propertied classes.[42] In the West marriages after ordination to major orders, though against Church law, were considered valid once formed. With the Council of Bourges of 1031 the tide began to change in the Latin world. Since the fifth century and the pontificate of Leo I, priests had been forbidden to abandon their wives: Bourges asked priests to send their wives away. A generation later, the Gregorian reformers insisted that all marriages of those in major orders were invalid.[43]

A story may convey how complicated the situation had become by the eleventh century. In January 1025, Gerard of Cambrai, bishop of Cambrai-Arras, preached a sermon in the cathedral of Arras before a small number of heretics he had come to judge.[44] An antisacramental sect had formed in Artois, which promised salvation through a life of *justicia*. Having heard of this sect, Gerard had conducted an investigation and had those few members he could find seized. Their "master" eluded him. In the consistory called to judge the heretics, they responded to Gerard's questions by saying that they had received their doctrine from an Italian who had preached to them, relying only on the New Testament. Their sect seems to have been one of the first of the radical reform movements increasingly traveling the routes from town to city as the eleventh century and the revival of urban life and commerce progressed. Among other teachings, the sectarians of Artois regarded all sacraments as useless and condemned marriage. We may presume that they would never have, as had their contemporary William of Volpiano, compared a newly reconstructed church to a bride adorned for her wedding.[45] In the discussion which followed, Gerard pointed out that everything they condemned was found in the New Testament. The sectarians persevered in their intention to stifle carnal desire. Next, Gerard preached his sermon or "brief."[46] Latin was translated into the vernacular for the simple folk, and the official record says the heretics recanted.[47]

In his treatment of marriage, Gerard had to argue on more than one front. The sectarians wished marriage to be generally proscribed. There were many of an opposite mind who wished marriage to be allowed even to the clergy. In England in the late tenth and early eleventh century, reformers such as Aelfric of Eynsham and Wulfstan II, archbishop of York, had tried to draw a line between the lives of laity and clergy by holding priests to celibacy.[48] Gerard like Ademar of Chabannes agreed and similarly defended clerical celibacy.[49] Laymen who sympathized with such a point of view easily became critics of non-celibate clergy. In 1010 Bishop Burchard of Worms, finding himself caught in the middle, responded to such criticism by giving punishments to laymen who refused to attend the services of married priests or priests with common-law wives. Sixty-five years later Gregory VII took the opposite view and asked especially rulers and knights to take measures, even by force, against concubinate priests.[50] With Gerard we are a generation before this extended attack on nicolaitism, clerical marriage, which formed about mid-century in the writings of men such as Humbert of Silva Candida (d. 1061). The defenders of clerical marriage in Gerard's day argued that men are not angels and that continence is a gift of grace. This was a kind of antiperfectionist rendition of the Pauline admission that it is better to marry than to burn. Gerard responded that certain men are indeed partly angels: "a part of mankind reigns already, sharing the company of the angels; another portion still wanders on earth amidst the sound of sighs — aspiring [to rise also]."[51] Priests follow a rule of life which separates them from the people. Marriage is polluting and those who indulge in sex have "impure hands."[52]

Determined to stop clerical marriage once and for all, Pope Leo IX's First Lateran Council of 1049 declared both wife and child of a priest to be serfs of the Church. Since canon law forbade serfs from becoming priests, the intent was to stop the descent of priestly office and lands from priestly father to priestly son. The pious Henry III (1039–56) of Germany accepted these decisions, while Henry I (1031–56) of France rejected them. In any case married men continued to be ordained. The resistance to the prohibition of priestly marriage was intense, especially among the lesser clergy. In a synod in 1075, 3600 (sic!) clergy of the diocese of Constance rejected the Gregorian prohibition. A long generation later, about 1110, Aelred of Rievaulx was born in the north of England to a line of married priests, albeit a line feeling the pressure of the new Gregorian ways sufficiently that Aelred's father eventually entered a cathedral monastery. The married priesthood, though much diminished in numbers from the late eleventh century, continued to be an unending source of pastoral problems involving pastors themselves.[53]

From about the middle of the eleventh century groups like the Pataria in Milan boycotted the services of married priests and increasingly attempted to limit all contact between priests and women, going so far as to invade priests' houses to drive out their "whores." An irony of their attack was its provocation of responses which defended clerical marriage by underlining the holiness of marriage itself and holding that, as something holy, marriage should be open to all. The cardinal archdeacon Guibert, the spokesman for the Milanese married clergy, declared "learn that sin pertains to the individual, not to sex. For sex is holy." Further, "all laity and clergy, whoever are sons of the Church, are priests."[54] Thus Guibert used the biblical and patristic doctrine of the universal priesthood of all believers to overturn traditional hierarchical schemas of perfection and to forge solidarity between priests and laity, who being of equal estate should all have access to marriage.

The lay-clerical dichotomy which Guibert tried to overcome runs through these centuries. Carolingian society was composed of a hierarchy of "orders" and various ways of schematizing the relations of these to each other. The *Apologeticus* of 993 of Abbo of Fleury affirmed "that in the holy . . . Church there are three orders [virgins, abstainers, couples], three ranks, for the faithful of both sexes."[55] Abbo left no doubt that the monks rank highest, and married couples, slowed in spiritual advance by indulgence in the sexual act, lowest. Even the architecture of churches reflected these ideas of perfection. At Cluny an enclosure surrounded the "zone of perfection" inhabited by the monks. Only on a few days were the laity admitted through the cloister wall to observe the monks in the hope that they would develop a taste for perfection, a desire for "conversion" or "second baptism," and would enter the monastic life themselves.[56] Earlier in the century, about 920, the message of Odo of Cluny's *Life of Gerald of Aurillac* was that a layman could live a holy life and be a model warrior. Odo showed Gerald to have taken no booty or ransom, to have released prisoners, and to have avoided bloodshed. However, like Abbo, Odo understood indulgence in the marital act to be an impediment to holiness. He asked his readers to avoid the sins occasioned by lovemaking, and showed that Gerald had renounced the use of marriage. Thus Odo sanctioned fighting in a just cause, but left marriage doubtful. Gerald, like many earlier laymen deemed holy, was in effect a monk in disguise.[57]

Some years after Odo and Abbo, in the early eleventh century, Dudo, a canon of Saint-Quentin at Rouen, repeated Abbo's schema. Dudo, however, was a canon and as a priest set Abbo's schema to a more pastoral end. In treating Christian perfection Dudo distinguished between the theoretical and practical paths, the former the road of the monks, the latter that of the clergy and laity. He insisted that all proceeded toward heaven at the same pace. In the early eleventh century, Burchard of Worms, too, insisted that all three states traveled the same road to salvation.[58] Although Dudo's optimistic belief that all Christians proceed toward heaven at the same pace seems linked to the fact that he was a priest giving pastoral encouragement, many insisted on the essential goodness of marriage. As Aelred of Rievaulx reiterated in the twelfth century, virginity is higher than widowhood, which is higher than conjugal chastity, but all are states of virtue.[59]

The Place of Consent and Consummation in the Formation of Marriage

The assertion of the primacy of consent in the formation of marriage had a labored history in the early Middle Ages. Two questions were involved: (1) whether the existence of a marriage was to be defined by consent, consummation, or some combination of the two, and (2) whether the consent which was to be given was of the couple themselves, their parents, or some combination of the two. The first question arose because of the clash between Roman views, which saw consent as constituting marriage, and German views, which though seeing legal marriage (*Muntehe*) as formed by stages, thought of intercourse as essential to its existence.[60] The second question had an old history, and the last chapter noted that whereas Tertullian believed that the consent given to marriage was that of both couple and fathers, Augustine centered marriage on the consent of the couple themselves. In the early Middle Ages, the idea that families, not individuals, should control marriage was ever present in the manipulation of marriage especially by the top ranks of society. In Visigothic Spain in 683, two years after Ervig had been recognized as king, the Thirteenth Council of Toledo found it necessary to legislate that after his death, Ervig's queen could not be remarried, forced into concubinage, killed, mutilated, dispossessed, exiled, or forced to become a nun. Almost two centuries later, the pseudonymous Benedictus Levita listed the consent of those who exercise *dominatio* over a woman, her close relatives, as one of the things which must be present for legitimate marriage.[61]

The history of this question of who consents has long been presented as a progression from the early Middle Ages, during which the role of families in giving consent dominated, to the twelfth century, when the couple came into view. Though there is considerable truth in such a schema, especially if we attend to the development of ideas among canon lawyers and theologians, increased study of regional history and social structure has tended to qualify such generalizations. Régine Le Jan has drawn the picture of an initially undifferentiated and cognatic (descended from a common ancestor) Frankish society, which increasingly in Carolingian times became centered on the conjugal family. The long-term development was from households (collections of people under one roof), to families, though households, extended families, and nuclear families coexisted in all centuries. Tenth-century development subsequently gave the French aristocracy a more bilateral form of descent, in which power passed through the paternal line and nobility or rank passed matrilinearly. In certain respects this strengthened the conjugal family, and aristocratic wives collaborated even more with their husbands within the family than they had in Carolingian times. But in other respects, as we will see below, the spread of primogeniture, inheritance by the eldest son, emphasized male prerogatives and lessened women's property rights. Robert Jacob's study of the north of France has suggested that non-aristocratic families at the end of our period remained nuclear and dominated by the couple themselves, but that family interests often restricted the options open to aristocratic couples. All this counsels that we must beware of affirming any simple progress by which the conjugal couple came to define families. Patterns always varied by social class and geography. Jacob's further examination of the north of France in the thirteenth and fourteenth centuries, when the power of the commune tended to replace that of feudal lords, has suggested that at least among bourgeois and peasant families, blood ties and kin reasserted themselves at the expense of the conjugal couple.[62]

At the beginning, consent in any form was closed to many women, for various kinds of abduction to marry were common in the late Roman world and among the northern peoples. The practice of plunder included the capture of women for wives, and in the case of the higher ranks of society, the quest for concubines. Germanic insistence that a marriage did not exist until sexual relations had taken place likely expressed an idea common in societies which think of marriage as a process by which a man obtains a woman, whether by abduction, rape, or some other method of acquisition. One "marks" one's woman by having sexual relations with her.[63] Closely related is the idea of brideprice for sexual services and of *Morgengabe,* "morning gift," for the bride's having surrendered her virginity on her wedding night. Her retention of her purity to that point is guarantee to her husband that offspring of the union will be his. "Marking," the taking of a woman's virginity, simultaneously spoils her for others and takes possession for one's self. *Raptus* could designate rape in our sense, against one's will, but medieval writers extended the term to various forms of marriage formation in which the bride had some say. In societies in which a wide range of marriage practices from the consensual to the non-consensual existed, the Church's hope was to penalize violation of women and set in clearer relief the idea that marriage was a union between consenting moral equals.[64]

Though it has been said that the Germanic legal codes were not much concerned with protecting women from violent assault, they did allow women to press charges for rape. Depending on time and place, punishment ranged

from fines to death. As with many other ecclesiastical initiatives in this period, the Church's campaign to penalize rape had only limited success. To
take Spain as an example, a secular law of Jaca from 1063 dealing with
violation survives. "Violation" had a range of meanings running from rape
against one's will to consensual premarital sex. The law of Jaca not un-
typically required a man who had violated a woman either to marry her
or, if she was married, to make financial restitution to her husband. There
may have been ancient continuities here. A canon traditionally passing with
those of the oldest surviving local church council, of Elvira, also in Spain,
seems to have held that a young man should marry an unmarried woman
with whom he has slept. Like some of the Israelite practice described above
in chapter 1, the requirement that a man marry a woman he has violated
strikes us as more a punishment of him than a protection of the woman.
However, in a society of continuing violence, provision for a violated or
"spoiled" woman by insisting that her violator marry her likely was aimed
at reducing her exposure to further ill fortune, and akin to long-standing
legal attempts to protect repudiated women and widows. Throughout the
Middle Ages and beyond, canon lawyers struggled with the question of possible marriage between the victim of a violation and her aggressor.[65] Old
habits perhaps took on a new form in a good deal of vernacular literature
appearing just at the end of our period. The *pastourelle* of twelfth-century
Provence presented itself as about dalliance and flirting, but Kathryn Grav-
dal suggests it is not simply about playful sex but about rape.[66] Churchmen
tended to deep suspicion of such literature.

In the early Middle Ages the doctrine of consent was faced on all sides
by family pressures and the idea in German law that cohabitation created
the marriage bond. In 753 a Frankish capitulary declared that if any woman
protested that her husband had never paid the conjugal debt they were to go
to a cross and if the claim was true they could separate and she do what she
willed (the *iudicium crucis*, a quest for judgment by placing a controversy
at the foot of a cross, was common at this time). If consummation had not
taken place, no marriage existed.[67] In the short run the emphasis on human
intentionality which had expanded in Augustine's thought generally, receded
in the early Middle Ages in the face of Germanic culture's emphasis on act
rather than intent, on what one had done rather than on why one had done
it. Christian missionary strategies too could obscure categories of consent.
The calculated decision to marry a Christian woman to a non-Christian
ruler to obtain his conversion, or to obtain peace between conqueror and
conquered, easily obscured the consensual nature of marriage.[68]

Pope Leo I (440–61) continued the Roman view that consent formed
marriage. According to him, what was necessary for marriage was free-
born status, dowry, and public celebration. Throughout the early Middle

Ages, insistence on public celebration characterized the Church's attempt to give marriage both a sacred and public dimension. Leo's views passed into canon law, but often enough had little impact on customary ways of marrying. Within a century of his death, the Council of Orléans of 541, c. 22, reasserted the rights of parents by excommunicating couples who contracted marriage without the consent of the bride's parents. Another century later, the *Hispana,* a collection of the *acta* of 73 church councils, Spanish and otherwise, as well as of 103 papal decretals, in turn attacked the notion that without consummation no marriage existed. The *Hispana* asserted that after receiving the betrothal blessing by a priest, a marriage was indissoluble. The influence of the *Hispana* spread well beyond Spain, but everywhere encountered resistance from German insistence on the necessity of consummation. Both Pope Nicholas I (858–67) and Hincmar of Rheims linked the returning interest in interiority sometimes found in their day with questions of consent. Having given a list of the acts which constitute marriage similar but not identical to that of Benedictus Levita, Nicholas, a champion of consent, stated that it was not sinful if some of them were absent. Nicholas was more interested in situating marriage in a context of morality and conscience than simply in a legal context preoccupied with questions of validity. About the same time Hincmar reached toward a notion of annulment by saying that, even if all the forms of marriage had been observed, if a sincere consent had not been given there was no marriage in God's eyes. One's interior state was decisive. In describing the stages of becoming married, Hincmar made it clear that his idea of consent included that of parents. The guardians of the bride were to be approached to secure their acceptance of the marriage. Approval by the parents was to be followed by betrothal and betrothal blessing, *dotatio* (dowry), *traditio* (the handing over of the bride), and a sealing nuptial mass. In regard to quest for parental approval, Hincmar tells a story in which while a father had had his way (for what it is worth, Hincmar says this is rare) in arranging his daughter's marriage, his disapproving wife proceeded through a charm to render the groom impotent so that consummation was impossible. Clearly consent was contended territory.[69]

Hincmar was the most important Carolingian thinker to bridge the distance between Roman and German emphases. He simply added consummation to Leo I's earlier list of the conditions necessary for a valid marriage to exist. Hincmar held both that marriage was indissoluble from the moment of consummation and that it did not exist without consent. He wished to strengthen marriage, which he took to be the basic institution of lay society, by communicating a specifically Christian idea of it.[70] To this end he thoroughly Christianized the understanding of consummation, and did not shy from calling conjugal union "nuptial mystery" and "in itself the sacrament of Christ and Church."[71] The Gregorian Sacramentary (the *Hadrianum*), which in its oldest form dates from the eighth century, had introduced Ephesians 5 to declare: "O God, you have consecrated the bond of marriage with such an excellent mystery as to prefigure in the covenant of marriage the sacrament of Christ and his Church."[72] For Hincmar it was carnal union itself that was a sacrament, and this in Augustine's sense, as a sign of something sacred.[73]

When describing the social expectations of his society, Hincmar like Jonas of Orléans spoke of marriage as "between equals" and listed five conditions as legally and socially necessary for marriage: liberty and equality of condition (he said nothing of marriages between non-free), consent (of the father of the bride), dowry, a public wedding, and consummation.[74] Hincmar's position pointed the way to later compromise between Roman emphasis on consent and German emphasis on consummation, but by the end of our period his opinion was viewed by some reformers as a capitulation to Germanic custom. Thus Peter Damian's (1007–72) Letter 172 attacked the notion that consummation has any place in the definition of marriage. Damian followed Augustine in seeing the marriage of Mary and Joseph, in which only consent was involved, as a model. As we will see in the next chapter, though discussion continued, about 1140 Gratian essentially accepted Hincmar's compromise and argued that normally both consent and consummation were necessary for a marriage to exist.[75]

Two Views of Marriage

The struggle between consent and consummation was only one expression of a larger clash of worldviews between Christian teaching and all that had gone before. Some background is necessary. The strong tendency of both Roman society and Christian monogamy had been toward a nuclear family. However in determining who could marry whom, degrees of relationship had been counted differently according to time and place. Christianity followed Roman law in computing degrees of relationship by counting from an individual who wished to marry, ascending to a common ancestor, and then descending from that ancestor to the intended spouse. German practice simply counted the generations from the intended couple to a possible common ancestor. The seventh grade by Germanic computation became the thirteenth or fourteenth by Roman computation, the number of degrees found in any relationship being virtually doubled. Put more concretely, German practice allowed a much closer degree of relationship in marriage, and many Germanic marriages seemed incestuous by Latin Christian standards. What counted as incest for early Christians initially had been unclear and had varied from region to region. One place might consider the successive marriage of a woman to two brothers to be incest; another place marriage to a stepdaughter. A law attributed to the late fourth-century emperor Theodosius described all marriage within the seventh degree of kinship as incest, and this was the opinion held in the eighth century by the missionary to the Germans, St. Boniface. The view that the degrees should be numbered at four also had its partisans, not least at Rome. In the early Middle Ages the determination of prohibited degrees of marriage was more the work of local councils than of the papacy, and not surprisingly, given the variety of inherited practices, even after the papacy took up the question in a sustained way in the eighth century, many remained unclear as to what constituted incest. At the end of our period the Irish, for instance, continued to receive much criticism in the matter. The advance of views coming from Rome is evident in the inclusion by the first Carolingian ruler, Pepin the Younger (751–68), of the canonical definition of consanguinity in his own law. In the following century Benedictus Levita wished the priest, as a part of the nuptial ceremony, to inquire before the congregation whether anyone knew of such impediments to the marriage as too close relationship, bigamy, or adultery.[76]

There is debate about the degree to which the Germanic nobility practiced polygamy, understood as one man having two or more legal wives. It seems to have been common in Merovingian times but to have been disappearing by about 600. After that date the practice was polygynous, with one man having sexual relations with or attachment to two or more women, rather than specifically two or more simultaneous legal wives. A youth might take one or more women as concubines, whom he might or might not dismiss at the point of marriage to a woman of his own class. He might also practice "serial monogamy," marriage and dismissal of several wives, again possibly with concubines on the side. Another alternative was "serial polygyny," a sequence of wives and interspersed concubines. The important point is that by 600 in Germanic societies generally one woman was recognized as having the status of chief wife. German concubinage was quite distinct from the Roman law's definition of concubinage as a marital union between people of different social classes. The last chapter noted that the early Christians had accepted concubinage as thus defined. The First Council of Toledo (c. 397–400), 17, similarly allowed men with either a wife or concubine (but not both) to receive communion. At the same time the legal status of concubinage in Roman law improved. Various gifts were allowed to concubines (in lieu of dowry), and the children of concubinage could now receive small inheritances. By the time of Justinian, concubinage was accorded virtually the same status as marriage. Such concubinage, which was a name for monogamous marriage between people of different social classes, should always be distinguished from polygamous and polygynous concubinage.[77]

While realizing the difficulty in eliminating concubinage as a non- or extra-marital practice, the late Roman Church expressed its disapproval and early medieval Christians often were appalled by many Germanic practices. The chronicler Fredegarius declared he did not have the space to name all the concubines of King Dagobert (629–39), who also had three wives, and labeled his son Clovis II (639–57) "fornicator and exploiter of women." A little earlier St. Columbanus (585–615) was exiled for refusing to accept the practice, still followed by Charlemagne two centuries later, of protecting the royal succession by encouraging grandsons to concubinage. This custom protected the dynasty from liaisons unsuitable to dynastic succession. While a laxist tendency can be found in earlier French councils, in 744 the Council of Soissons condemned remarriage to those whose former spouse still lived. This hardly touched Charlemagne himself, who in 774 repudiated his spouse and remarried. Eventually he had five successive marriages (some while his divorced wives still lived), and six concubines. Fearing the political alliances they might form, he insisted that his daughters not marry and tolerated the dalliances they pursued instead. Charlemagne was in these respects through most of his life far different from the pious picture painted of him three centuries later in the *Song of Roland.* Only in his sixties did a heightened seriousness about Christianity lead him to exclaim: "We need to consider whether we are really Christians — hence to inspect the lives and conduct of our people."[78]

The scale of the struggle between old and new in the early Middle Ages was epic. Christianity won over as much as it did in part through what Valerie Flint has called "Christian magic." Christian leaders paid careful attention to the patterns and needs of pagan life and then engaged in "re-invention." Again and again a pattern repeated itself in which missionary or priest rejected this or that pagan practice, only to refashion it for incorporation into Christian life. Sacred trees, groves, and places of worship were cut down or deconsecrated, only to be replaced by Christian shrines and churches.[79] When we have allowed for all the ways in which old habits were kept alive and took on Christian dress, it is remarkable how much pastoral determination was able to change in even the most intimate details of the lives of thousands. In 800 the Carolingian royal house still practiced polygyny. Undeterred, clerics such as Theodulf, bishop of Orléans, instructed their laity through diocesan legislation in the most intimate aspects of their lives: among the things Theodulf listed as impious were masturbation and coitus interruptus. What he hoped of the laity was a penitential life formed by confession. We will never know precisely what impact such teaching had, but there is clear evidence of new habits in formation. Cyrille Vogel has observed that whereas Greek and Roman law allowed a husband to execute an adulterous spouse, and many Germanic peoples also de facto tolerated this practice, the hostility to it of the penitential tradition and other ecclesiastical sources ultimately affected social perceptions of what was acceptable.[80]

Louis the Pious, the first Carolingian ruler who willingly embraced a Christian understanding of marriage, packed off Charlemagne's daughters to a convent. Though Frankland was far from prepared to follow Louis's personal marital example, he persisted and, in reaction to Charlemagne's profligacy in the matter of illegitimate children, by a decree of 817 excluded bastards from all rights of succession. Such legislation continued the narrowing of the fluid boundaries of the traditional Germanic household. Eventually the royal house settled down to an acceptance of monogamy in principle, of course not without the customary philandering.[81] By the end of the ninth century, the Church had made significant inroads against all forms of polygyny. Church law had restricted licit separation ("annulment" was still an idea in formation: see the second section below) to the grounds of incest or impotence of the husband. Subsequently there was some tendency to extend the degrees within which marriage was prohibited, but this was never uniform across Europe: in the 1060s Peter Damian considered any marriage within the sixth degree (fifth cousins) consanguineous. The Fourth Lateran Council of 1215 mandated seven degrees, only to have the high medieval Church retreat from such computation because of the number of annulments it generated.[82]

Georges Duby understood the medieval aristocracy to have been the main force in maintaining old pagan habits and concerns centered on blood, power, and property. He saw in the early Middle Ages and beyond a clash between two views of marriage. One originated in warrior traditions and was aristocratic and carried by secular law. The other was ecclesiastical and carried by canon or Church law. The struggle between the two views only increased toward the end of our period, as the Church's impact on society increased. "The bitterest political conflicts in eleventh-century France were fought for the control of marriage."[83] We need only think of the many disputes into the modern period between kings and popes over royal marriages, adulteries, and divorces to realize that the struggle to teach a Christian view of marriage "from the top down" was long drawn out. In the later ninth century, pope faced down king to insist that no one who claimed to be Christian was exempt from Christ's marital teaching. Church councils in the tenth and eleventh centuries condemned royal and noble bigamy and incest. In the time of Philip I (1060–1108) of France, the issues had changed little. Philip, with his first wife alive, incurred the charges of bigamy and incest by marrying his cousin. To stand up to one's king was an act for which few bishops had the backbone. Of all the bishops in France only Ivo of Chartres had the courage publicly to criticize Philip.[84] Rare though they might be, such acts of defiance continued the teaching role of the Church in the face of profoundly resistant habit.[85]

There is much to be said on behalf of Duby's ideas, though they concentrate too much on the Church's struggle against the aristocracy rather than against society as a whole. Duby's occasional labeling of the two views as lay (rather than specifically aristocratic) and ecclesiastical seems better to reflect the situation. After the various Germanic successor kingdoms replaced Roman government in the West, there was no one to uphold a single set of legal institutions. Law and custom varied endlessly, though Roman and canon law gave some degree of commonality and penetrated even those Celtic areas which earlier generations of scholars saw as idiosyncratic.[86] Still, especially in the early medieval centuries, there usually was a great gap between the views of canon and secular law and a temptation to use the latter to avoid the teaching of the former. In the ninth century Jonas of Orléans, writing against all non-marital sex, declared: "Let nobody flatter himself with secular law: every sexual extravagance is adultery."[87] Kings sometimes helped the Church enforce sexual discipline or spread its views by reiterating its laws in their own laws. Thus a law of Cnut (1016–35) accepted the Church's view of free consent: "neither widow nor maiden is to be forced to marry a man whom she herself dislikes, nor to be given for money, unless he chooses to give anything of his own free will."[88] However, secular law tended to emphasize the rights of fathers, parents, and families. Duby saw this emphasis as central to the aristocratic view of marriage. Canon law and pastoral practice emphasized the rights and equality of the spouses. Duby saw this as the preoccupation of the ecclesiastical view of marriage. In the face of widespread premarital sexual activity, for instance, Jonas of Orléans warned that only the marriages of virgins could be blessed in church. Caesarius of Arles had said the same.[89]

In *Medieval Marriage* and other books, Duby argued that a profound transformation of medieval French society occurred around the year 1000.[90] One aspect of this was the reorganization of marriage patterns. Duby spoke of this process as a sacralization of marriage. By this he meant that well into the Middle Ages, the primary model of marriage was private and familial, a contract arranged between families. Its ceremonies were secular, part of the practices of, and watched over by, the authorities of lay society. Only slowly, in a world in which many marriages remained illicit, irregular, furtive, or clandestine, did a second, sacramental model sponsored by the Church spread, especially from Carolingian times. Ultimately aspects of both merged into a marriage practice at once familial and sacramental.[91] "Christianization," a word sometimes used by Duby, would perhaps be a better word than "sacralization" to describe this process, since, as in traditional societies generally, marriage had always been viewed in pre-Christian Europe within a sacral framework. The eventual outcome, still working itself out at the end of our period, was that control over marriage increasingly passed from heads of households to the administrative and judicial supervision of the Church, from domestic to public space.[92]

Scholars such as Dominique Barthélemy have subjected Duby's views about the nature of the changes in society which accompanied changes in the practice of marriage to searching critique and have suggested various refinements of or alternatives to them. In some ways controversy has been not so much about the nature of the great changes which French — and not only French — society clearly underwent, but about their dating. Barthélemy sees the changes Duby centered on 1000 as more characteristic of the early twelfth century. Only then, Barthélemy argues, did the slow change of earlier centuries achieve a kind of "modernization." The details of Duby's views still haunt subsequent study and merit cautious attention. What follows is a synthesis following the general outlines of Duby's argument, but introducing significant contributions by others.[93]

First, a number of studies, especially by Karl Schmid, suggested that in the early Middle Ages descent could be calculated both through male and female lines. In the unsettled tenth and early eleventh centuries, aristocratic family structure changed. Previously, the fate of many important families had been tied to horizontal patronage relationships. These involved personal attendance on, or favors received from, kings. From around 1000 aristocratic families were "territorialized" or settled on hereditary estates dominated by castles. Now these families' interest was in assuring retention of these newly attained holdings intact within the family. For this the best means seemed descent through the male line or securing one's place in a vertical family tree. Thus primogeniture tended to replace the "equal" partibility of traditional Germanic society, in which all sons, and some daughters, had inherited.[94] This development seems to have worked to the disadvantage of women by reducing their rights in property and inheritance, and many students of especially the Mediterranean late Middle Ages and Renaissance have remarked on women's diminished property rights. By the end of the eleventh century, a male dominated, agnatic, lineage in which eldest son succeeded father had been put firmly in place, replacing the more cognatic early Carolingian lineage. We find this into the twelfth century in Germany as well as France. Commonly marriage itself was the occasion for a young man coming into his inheritance, or a share in the patrimony. Marriage could also be the occasion for receiving an office from the family into which one was marrying.[95]

Everything political was first familial, nothing more so than the planning of marriage alliances. At the top of society, one goal of this planning was to make sure that only one of the king's or territorial prince's sons be married. This insured that the power and lands of the king or prince would be inherited entire by a single male. In this system brides were valued for the property they could bring to a marriage and viewed as responsible for the production of a male heir. Younger sons of kings and princes were not to marry, or were to remain unmarried for considerable time. Those younger, unpropertied, sons who did not become clergy or monks commonly formed a disruptive group. They engaged in much illicit sexual and military activity and were a source of bastards and unrest. Duby saw the development of courtly love in the twelfth century against this background, as ritualized challenge of one's lord. Within the nobility the lord, or *maître du château,* was the "father" of a group of warriors whose marriages he planned. These warriors' advice was to be sought before the lord's own son or daughter was promised in marriage.[96] Earlier scholars tended to assume, because aristocratic marriage had so much about it of a property arrangement, that within the aristocracy equals married equals. Some recent study suggests that it was common for men to marry into families higher than their own.[97]

Martin Aurell has with particular care studied developments in Catalonia from 785 to 1213.[98] His chronology of the pace of development there is closer to that of Barthélemy for France than to Duby. Aurell sees three stages in the matrimonial politics of the comital houses of Catalonia. In the first, the especially unsettled years from 870 to 930, the heads of lines did not look far from home for wives, and the result was marriage between relatives, often cousins. The declaration of the Visigothic Code in favor of exogamy (marriage outside the clan) was ignored and, though primogeniture was appearing, early medieval endogamy (marriage within the clan) and definition of the family according to matrilinearity and cognate relations continued. By 1100 primogeniture had won out among the aristocracy but was just beginning to make inroads among the peasantry, who only slowly relinquished equal inheritance among sons. The majority of ninth-century comital marriages were at about the third degree of relationship as counted in canon law. As the aristocracy understood it, a principal goal of marriage was to make a pact between families, each spouse receiving new "parents" against whom violence was prohibited. By an exchange of a woman, standing grievances between two families were composed. This made the position of noble wives precarious, for with a shift in power the wife who had sealed last year's truce might be repudiated. So might a sterile woman, though in this age of continuing polygyny, succession might be provided through the offspring of a concubine.

From 930 to 1080 horizons and ambitions expanded and we find increasing instances of marriage outside the family, generally to a non-Catalonian woman or to a viscount or châtelain. By the middle of the eleventh century, the average marriage stood at about the fifth degree. Occasionally daughters of the Christian aristocracy were sent into Islamic harems, and Islamic women were received as the concubines of Christian kings. The Prophet had preached that women were a part of plunder and had approved the practice of the Islamic conqueror making the wife or daughter of the vanquished his wife or concubine. The Moslems made wives, concubines, and slaves of the Christian women they conquered. Conversely, in the 1090s the widow of the Islamic Emir of Seville became the concubine of Alfonso VI, king of Castile (1065–1109), to bear him his only son. As in England or the north of France, primogeniture encouraged hypergamic marriages (with someone of equal or superior status) among those younger sons who married and who had to acquire lands through knightly service or marriage. A wealthy widow became a great prize to be fought over, and a common form of *raptus*, a kind of rite of initiation, was seizing her as one's wife, as did Guislabert II (1074–1102), Count of Rousillon. The story is as old as that of Penelope's suitors.

Finally, from about 1080 to about 1210, we have "conquering marriage." This marriage policy was an instrument of the territorial expansion of Catalonia then taking place. Once and for all the Catalonians under papal reprimand began to abandon the endogamous practices of the early Middle Ages. They now married between the fourth and seventh degrees. Though throughout the whole period studied by Aurell the Church's teaching was often ignored and there was much compromise and accommodation, the Church had had significant successes in according marriage a greater dignity. If Radulf, bishop of Urgell from 914 to 941 and the father of two sons, could live publicly in concubinage and treat his episcopal office as family property, applying to it strategies very much like those used by his secular counterparts, by 1100 monogamy had largely won the battle with polygyny. Incestuous marriage as defined by the Church had receded; the obligation of indissolubility was better understood; wives and children had been given some protection against the practices of the age; and a sense of the need for free choice of one's spouse was growing.

Becoming Married

Europe in the early Middle Ages was a kaleidoscope of practices, but we can continue to view marriage as having three stages: negotiations, betrothal, and wedding. The lists of the acts, liturgical and otherwise, which constitute marriage advanced by various early medieval ecclesiastical writers were far from uniform, though they did communicate the idea, central to the Eastern rites, that one married by stages. The sacramentaries or liturgical books varied significantly.[99] For instance, a betrothal rite was found in the Visigothic liturgy but not in the Roman sacramentaries (Leonine [Veronense], Gregorian, and Gelasian), of the early sixth century and following.[100] However, books such as the Gelasian sacramentary, of the seventh or eighth century, placed *nuptae,* a marriage ceremony, within a church and nuptial mass.[101] Secular works such as the Visigothic *Liber judiciorum,* used throughout the Iberian peninsula into the high Middle Ages, took particular interest in prenuptial questions. Prenuptial law considered who might marry, and by insisting that the spouses in a fully proper marriage be of equal class and lineage, continued long-standing social prejudices. Abduction, bride theft, or elopement were alternatives open to those of unequal status who wished to marry or those lacking the property to conclude a proper marriage. Elopement was an assertion of the desire of the couple to play a decisive role in their own union. Law on this act evolved over time but came to allow subsequent regularization. Such exceptions aside, the role of fathers or male relatives in prenuptial negotiations remained large. They were the ones who consented to the marriage, participated in negotiations about dowry and gifts, and gave daughter or niece away.[102]

In Frankland as elsewhere marriage was a bond of kinship or tie between comrades. The Church early seized on *Muntehe* as the Germanic form of marriage closest to Christian ideas and promoted and reshaped it to the detriment of other German modes of marriage. As a part of its promotion of marriage's consensual aspects, the Church viewed *Muntehe* as including a formal contract. This requirement was inherited from the late Roman attack on clandestine marriage, marriage of which there was no public witness such as exchange of gifts. From the late empire the *tabulae matrimoniales* were often written out by a priest.[103] Legal marriage included a *dos,* or bride gift, from husband to wife. Some scholars have contrasted a Roman practice, in which the parents of the bride gave a marriage gift or dowry, with a Germanic practice, in which a dower was given by the groom to his bride. This misleadingly simplifies. Where the matter has been studied carefully, as for Catalonia around the year 1000, dowry (in this region commonly a tenth of one's property) and other forms of marriage gifts and dower coexisted, as they had in Rome. Dower was given especially by husbands to wives. Some gifts from parents to daughters were given only after a year of shared life.[104] Already in the Merovingian period Germanic peoples had seen a marriage portion, given by the groom as a hedge against widowhood, as essential to marriage. In part this was because this documented that a marriage had taken place. Still in the twelfth century the canonist Gratian declared that without a dowry there was no marriage.[105] Practices varied widely. In thirteenth-century England a *maritagium* or bride gift given by the father of the bride to his daughter remained in the husband's control during the marriage to pass to the wife's lineal heir at her death.[106]

In the early Middle Ages traditional Germanic bride purchase declined in favor of bride gift. The presence of the latter distinguished legal marriage from the lesser union *Friedelehe,* a form of polygamy in which two noble family lines united or formed peace through a man of one family setting up a freely consenting woman of the other as mistress of her own house. *Friedelehe* lacked dowry or a betrothal agreement, and its offspring could not inherit. The Church saw in it no more than concubinage and worked for its elimination. Germanic perception was that in a legal marriage a woman should receive property at marriage over which she retained rights, should share in property acquired after marriage, and should be able to inherit.[107] From the sixth century the Church's repeated legislation on consanguinity helped develop Leo the Great's notion of publicity. To avoid incest, marriages were to be preceded by the announcing of banns and formed with the knowledge of kin, priest, and neighbors. In spite of disagreement over how incest was to be defined, the Church's understanding of publicity complemented German practices, which also took public betrothal to be important. Merovingian law penalized a man who broke an engagement.[108]

All during the period studied in the present chapter, domestic or private marriage rites competed with or were found in combination with church or public rites. In 866 Pope Nicholas I described Western marital practices as he would have liked them to be in a letter to the Bulgarians, who had inquired about communion with Rome. Without specifying where this was to take place, Nicholas wrote that there was to be a betrothal ceremony in which the couple covenant (*foedera*) to be married in the future and a ring and gift are exchanged. This precedes by some time a marriage ceremony in church, where a priest blesses and veils the couple. After, outside the church, the couple is given marriage crowns. Nicholas was of course addressing people used to an Eastern rite, but "crowning," the placing of nuptial crowns on the couple, had also been found in the West. This symbolism had a long and varied history. Crowns were already being blessed for Christian marriage in the fourth century, apparently initially as part of the betrothal ceremony. We often find the crown later symbolizing the virginity of the couple about to marry, or at least of the bride. In the fourth and fifth century in the East, crowning was combined iconographically with the joining of right hands, and a form of this continued in Western iconography. Here most commonly Christ, having replaced the pagan *Concordia* as *pronubus,* the promoter of the marriage, was portrayed as placing the crowns on the couple's heads. Isidore of Seville, who specified that the marriage blessing should take place in church, mentions that the garland is white and purple, symbolizing purity and the blood of the generations to follow.[109]

In fact, marrying in church seems to have been uncommon in Nicholas's day. The ninth- or tenth-century *Durham Collectar,* with roots in both the Gregorian Sacramentary and a domestic marriage rite involving blessing of bedchamber, ring, and bed, gives us a rite with both domestic and public el-

ements. The eleventh-century Spanish *Liber ordinum,* too, seems composed
of a domestic rite to which has been added a nuptial mass in church. A certain number of couples may simply have gone to church to have the bride
or the couple blessed, but some sacramentary prayers explicitly occur in
a mass-setting. Thus the tenth-century *Sacramentary of Fulda,* as Gelasian
sacramentaries generally, has a mass or "Nuptial Action" in which marriage
prayers mentioning the "union of flesh and agreeableness" (*unitatem carnis
atque dulcedinis*), the "conjugal union of those who are covenanting" (*qui
coniugali copulandi sunt foedere:* there also are further references to *foedus coniugale*), and the "bond of love" (*uinculo dilectionis:* there also is
a reference to *fructificent caritate* and to *mutuam coniugalis gratiae cari-
tatem*), are offered during a mass followed by a marriage ceremony. In this
latter the couple approach the priest and the parents of the bride hand her
over (*tradent*) to him. The priest then veils her and prays for peaceableness,
equality of soul, and mutual charity between the spouses (*det eis sensus paci-
ficos, pares animos, mores mutua caritate deuinctos*). Then he hands over
the bride to the groom, admonishing both because of the holy communion
they have just taken to abstain that night from intercourse (*ut pro sancta
communione ea nocte se abstineant a pollutione*). Though this *Sacramentary*
does not use the word *sacramentum,* here clearly the Church was pressing
its views, for instance inserting the priest in the *traditio,* or handing-over,
by which the bride was conveyed from her parents to the groom. Though
intercourse itself was seen as polluting, the language of marrying speaks of
love, equality, and covenant.[110]

The Council of Trent declared in the sixteenth century that all valid marriages had to occur *in facie ecclesiae,* at the church's facade or entrance.
Before then the struggle was to bring marriage to the church door, *ad jan-
uas ecclesiae,* that is, to take it from the private or semi-private spheres of
home, domestic rite, or unwitnessed promise and to bring it into the public
space of a church. Public witness did not necessarily mean a rite celebrated
inside a church. Some scholars have compared the manner in which medieval
village life was organized "from below" by the community to African land
shrines. Village life was more regulated by custom than by village lord or
any written body of ecclesiastical discipline. At the center of community life
was the parish church, sanctuary, and churchyard. It was to these that the
marrying couple came for a "church wedding."[111] It has been suggested that
the addition or expansion of porches on eleventh-century churches reflects
one of their primary functions, to provide a setting for marriage ceremonies
"at the church door."[112]

In 1100 many continued to marry in some combination of domestic and
public rites. One might begin with domestic rites in the home, perhaps the
blessing of bed or ring, and then proceed to the church to marry. One might

betroth at home and proceed to the church to receive a blessing. Only in the twelfth century did earlier separate rites tend to come together into one ceremony of betrothal and marriage, as we find in the English Sarum Rite of 1085. This rite specified that betrothal, "before the door of the church, or in the face of the church," would be public so that it could be established that no impediment existed. First the banns were to be asked, and then announcement made that the couple was to be joined "that they may earn together eternal life." Inquiry about the dower of the woman and about whether the spouses would love one another and be faithful was followed by father or friend handing over the woman, joining of right hands, exchange of vows, and giving of a ring by the man to the woman. The party then entered the church and the couple kneeled before the step of the altar where the priest gave further blessings. Bride and groom then moved to a position between choir and altar for the preliminary part of the mass. After the Sanctus they prostrated themselves at the foot of the altar and a pall or veil was placed over them, after which the mass was finished. The next night the priest blessed the bed-chamber with the couple in their bed.[113] Where ecclesiastical norms had been accepted, twelfth-century French ceremony began "at the church door" and was similar to that specified in the Sarum Rite. In England a little later Bracton understood that if a named dowry had been given by a groom to his bride "at the church door," her property rights were secure.[114] Still in the fifteenth century, Joan of Arc's first ecclesiastical trial concerned whether her vow of virginity could stand in the light of the fact she had earlier contracted — but in what sense? — marriage.[115]

In the early Middle Ages, before church weddings were common, consent seems naturally enough to have been especially associated with betrothal, marriage's second stage. By the high Middle Ages this was evidenced at the popular level in the expectation, found for instance in the twelfth-century frontier towns of Léon and Castile, that a betrothed couple could consummate their marriage. Such an expectation was quite opposed to the marriage procedure outlined in the Spanish liturgy. Generally in Spain at the end of our period, the liturgical expectation was that domestic rites would occur first, then marriage rites in church, and then the nights of Tobias. In northern France by comparison, church marriage was followed by marriage feast and domestic rites, ending with the blessing of the couple in bed: i.e., presumably by consummation. Study of fourteenth- and fifteenth-century Normandy reveals customs which seem to run deep into the Middle Ages and were again at odds with the liturgy and canon law. In Normandy sexual activity had a commonly accepted role in courtship, whether preceding or following a promise to marry, and whether leading to stable cohabitation or more formal solemnization. Marriage seems to have been viewed as much a process as an event, and the laity seem not infrequently to have regarded a certain degree of unregulated sexual activity as part of the process of which a "church wedding" might be the solemnization.[116]

At the center of artistic representation of marrying was the portrayal of the *dextrarum junctio* or of a variation in which both hands of both spouses joined.[117] These signs of the concord or harmony expected of marriage, which continued to be invoked on Byzantine wedding rings, persisted throughout the Middle Ages as marriage's most common iconographic representation. They were often associated with presentation of the Betrothal and Marriage of the Virgin Mary or of the Marriage Supper of the Lamb (Rev. 19:9).[118] We find representations in a range of materials beginning with the late fifth-century portrayal of the marriages of Moses and Sephora and Jacob and Rachel in the mosaics of Santa Maria Maggiore in Rome. Here the iconography of the marriage of Sarah and Tobias described in Tobit 7:15 interpreted the traditional Roman joining of right hands. Tobit described the father of Sarah, Raguel, as placing her right hand in that of Tobias. The gesture of joined hands continued on a wide range of objects, from a sixth- or seventh-century Byzantine marriage belt in the Dumbarton Oaks collection on which Christ joins the hands of the couple; to the portrayals of the Wedding of the Virgin in two manuscripts from Reichenau, the Gospels of Otto III, of about 1000, and the Bernulfus Gospels of the eleventh century; to, in the late Middle Ages, manuscript illustration of the marriage of David and Bathsheba. In the wake of the inclusion of marriage among the seven sacraments at the Fourth Lateran Council of 1215, an iconography of the Seven Sacraments developed, in which marriage had its part.[119] Late medieval manuscripts give additional information: a fourteenth-century Flemish manuscript now in the Bodleian Library at Oxford shows a bride with her male kin and entourage approaching a church door at which a priest stands with the bridegroom and his kin.[120]

From the late fourth century the wedding of Cana came to be associated with the marital relation between Christ and Church in the liturgy of Epiphany, January 6. The Magi had originally held center stage in this feast. Then, especially in northern Italy and Gaul, another event thought to have taken place on the same day, the miracle of Cana, came to share the feast. Neither the miracle of changing water into wine nor the banquet of the Marriage at Cana illustrated some essential part of marriage, but these were presented in art, sculpture, and theology with some frequency. Tenth-century Fulda sacramentaries have the two stories, of Magi and Cana, composing one tableau.[121] Cana also could be considered by itself. Thus the preamble of the Roman *Marriage Document of Empress Theophano* of 972, known through an illuminated manuscript now in Wolfenbüttel and prepared for the marriage of Otto II of Germany and the Byzantine princess Theophano, described marriage as sanctified by the miracle at Cana.[122] The Matilda Gospels, an Italian Gospel Book of the late eleventh century in the J. Pierpont Morgan Library, also portrayed the Marriage at Cana, in which the couple is joined at their wedding feast by Mary, Christ, disciples, and guests.[123] This too was the case in a Romanesque tympanum at Charlieu. On one side of an early twelfth-century historiated capital in the East Gallery of the cloister of Moissac, Christ changes water into wine, and on the other the wedding feast takes place. The bride is one of those seated at the banquet table.[124] Such representations, like those of the exchange of rings, crowning, and the joining of right hands, stood in their various iconographic traditions and give us little definite information about contemporary marriage practices.

The portrayal of contemporary marriage seems to have become more common from the later twelfth century, and portrayals of Cana in Gothic art show the participants in medieval rather than ancient dress.[125] Cana aside, pictures of medieval marriages into the thirteenth century continued to present fathers as the principal players in the making of marriages.[126] A miniature from the *Libro de Feudos* of Alfonso II of Aragón, written between 1162 and 1196 but picturing a marriage which took place in 1110, portrays Viscount Bernat Ató of Béziers standing between his daughter and her husband-to-be. In a variation of the *dextrarum junctio,* the viscount grasps the right wrist of each. Presumably Alfonso's miniature pictures the act of *traditio,* the handing over of daughter by father, within a betrothal ceremony. The viscount's wife looks on and makes a gesture of blessing, but no clerics are present. In other manuscripts fathers invoked the blessing of God on the couple. In much Spanish portrayal of married couples of the same social status, ranging from Adam and Eve to Castillian royal couples, man and wife, though differentiated in dress and role, are portrayed equally prominently side by side. In our miniature Bernat, more in the foreground and larger, is the central figure.[127]

Indissolubility, Divorce, and Annulment

Consent was a double-edged sword, and as we saw in the last chapter, under the Christian emperors the Roman law continued to allow divorce, at least in the form of mutual withdrawal of consent. This was to remain the practice in Christian Byzantium. Nevertheless, it was increasingly difficult for either spouse to remarry. Only with Justinian, in 548, were the penalties for initiating unjustified divorce actions equalized between the sexes.[128] In the Western early Middle Ages, we find unending diversity. The traditional practice of repudiation took varied forms according to people and place. In Anglo-Saxon England unilateral repudiation was open to both sexes, and a repudiated wife could have custody of her children as well as half the couple's joint property. Opinion is divided as to whether unilateral repudiation was also open to both sexes in Frankish regions, or whether repudiation was a male prerogative. Probably the Franks allowed repudiation and remarriage to both spouses. According to the *Burgundian Laws,* which allowed repudiation to both husband and wife, a man might obtain a divorce for adultery, witchcraft, or violation of graves. To the latter two grounds a woman could add homicide. The clergy, especially in the sixth and seventh centuries, either tolerated or could do little about repudiation. Much uncertainty existed, and the tack taken often did not go beyond the pragmatic and pastoral. Thus the Council of Epaonne (A.D. 517) prescribed "separation" for incest in the case of couples whose marriage had not been consummated, but refused to dissolve already existing incestuous unions. The term *separare* covered almost any separation of spouses, including the existential equivalent of divorce and remarriage. After the conversion of the Visigoths from Arian to Catholic Christianity, in 650 Chindaswinth restricted the traditional right to repudiation to one ground only, a wife's adultery.[129] In Iceland, to judge by later evidence, either husband or wife had simply to declare divorce.

Augustine had interpreted the *separare* of Matt. 19:6 ("what God...has joined, let not man put asunder") to mean that a secular divorce left the marriage bond intact, as did dismissal of a spouse because of adultery. In the early Middle Ages, the use of *separare* was equivocal, and various reasons for "separating" spouses entered the law. Often these had to do with what was perceived as a defect in how the marriage had begun and so were related to the Roman idea of nullity, declaration that a marriage had never existed. This was the case with marriage within the prohibited degrees of relationship. But the vocabulary of nullity had disappeared and separation, divorce, and annulment as they later were understood were not clearly distinguished. Thus if it was discovered that a married couple were spiritually related (were god-parent and god-child), Nicholas I allowed separation, meaning a declaration that a valid marriage had never existed. Individual writers said that if discord reigned in a marriage, the couple could be separated by mutual agreement, and that a man could remarry after his wife had committed adultery. The secular law could take a Germanic point of view and authorize remarriage after an unconsummated marriage. In the Merovingian period it is not clear that the papacy itself was sure what canon law should teach, but from the beginning of Carolingian times both pope and council spoke increasingly in defense of indissolubility.[130]

There is no easy correlation between later understandings of annulment, divorce, and indissolubility and the categories of early medieval thought. To begin with, the argument has been made that the Romanization of the Germanic societies actually spread the practice of divorce. That is, the argument goes, in traditional Germanic society clan and family so controlled marriage that it was a very stable institution, not much subject to the wishes

of individuals. Only with the introduction of the relatively more individu-
alized or consent- and couple-centered practices of the Romans did Roman
conceptions of divorce spread.[131] However this may be, the practices of
polygyny, endogamy, frequency of concubinage, possibility of repudiation
of one's spouse, and divorce by mutual consent which existed among the
Germanic and other northern peoples entailed very different notions of the
firmness of the marriage bond from those found in canon law. Among the
reasons that might be given for divorce according to the secular law of
Christianized peoples were such things as impotence and obesity to a degree
which made sexual relations impossible. This suggests the absence of any
clear idea of annulment. Though it is always difficult to know how much
law reflected practice, the many opportunities open in secular law to men for
divorce seems to indicate a situation prejudicial to women. A wife might be
divorced for as light a reason as neglecting her household tasks. In traditional
Germanic society the first year of marriage had commonly been viewed as a
trial period which could be terminated unless pregnancy occurred. Almost
from the first, as in Visigothic Spain, the resources of Roman law were used
to try to outlaw such ideas.[132]

Church councils advanced shifting and inconsistent grounds for divorce
until the Council of Friuli of 796–97 finally listed adultery as the only
ground. Charlemagne took this teaching into a capitulary of 802, though
he himself continued to marry while his previous wives lived. The Council
of Friuli also "according to indulgence rather than law" allowed something
like later annulment, calling it separation. Friuli allowed remarriage to a
spouse who, even though inquiry had been made, had unknowingly in good
faith entered an incestuous marriage. While the Irish penitentials of the sixth
and seventh centuries customarily were rigorous in such matters, the Anglo-
Saxon penitentials of the late seventh and early eighth centuries tended to
a relaxed stance on remarriage, a stance more relaxed than that of English councils of the period. Thus the so-called *Penitential of Theodore* not
only allowed a husband to remarry whose wife had committed adultery,
but allowed the wife herself to remarry after two years of penance. This
penitential's double standard prohibited a wife repudiating a husband for
any reason.[133] One of the central aims of the Carolingian reform of pastoral practice was the upholding of indissolubility. Thus, influenced by the
thought of Jonas of Orléans, the council of Paris of 829 forbade the remarriage of a cuckolded husband if the wife was still living — which the
penitential of Theodore had allowed.[134]

In the face of the demands of the ruling classes that marriage be flex-
ible enough to allow manipulation for reasons of politics and inheritance,
the ninth-century monk Christian of Corbie explained the obligations of
Christian monogamy in the following words:

[Be she] gluttonous, quarrelsome or sickly, a wife must be kept until the day of her death. . . . Therefore, before he accepts a wife, a man must get to know her well, both with regard to her character and health. He should not do anything rash that may cause him sorrow for a long time. If all decisions are to be made with advice, this one even more so; in matrimony a man surrenders himself. Most men, when they choose a wife, look for seven [*sic*] qualities: nobility, wealth, looks, health, intelligence, and character. Two of these, intelligence and character, are more important than the rest. If these two are missing, the others might be lost.[135]

From Carolingian times popes and bishops increasingly faced off against kings who wished to end their marriages. Nicholas I famously confronted Lothair II (855–69). Before his marriage for political reasons to Theutberga, Lothair had been passionately attached to a concubine, Waldrada, herself of the lower nobility, by whom he had two or more children. When the political advantages of his marriage to Theutberga had passed, Lothair wished a divorce to marry Waldrada. Controversy over the matter dragged on for more than a decade, with Lothair accusing Theutberga of a wide range of offenses, from incest to abortion. At his death, the case was still unresolved. We are particularly well informed of this matter because of two writings of Hincmar of Rheims, one of which used the word "divorce" (*divortio*) in its title. Though in the event less firm than Nicholas, Hincmar was, almost without reserve, a defender of indissolubility. Once a marriage had been contracted, Hincmar allowed separation only on the biblical grounds of unchastity. While trying to separate Lothair from his mistress, Hincmar treated her gently and specifically rejected the idea that in these matters men might be treated more lightly than women. Indeed, he concluded from the fact that women are weaker than men that men were therefore to be punished more seriously for their sins. He thought love must reign between spouses. As long as a marriage was not within the prohibited degrees, "incestuous," nor irremediable impotence subsequently discovered, it was indissoluble. Against many of his predecessors and contemporaries, he disallowed second marriage after adultery.[136]

Regino of Prüm's early tenth-century canonical collection, *De synodalibus causis*, witnesses continuing indecision on many marital questions. In the matter of indissolubility, Regino first (II, 101–6) listed six ancient and medieval texts which prohibited a second marriage after dismissal of a spouse. Then (II, 118–19, 124) he reproduced three texts from one of the most liberal of the eighth century French synods, which had permitted remarriage in such specified situations as after repudiation of a wife who had plotted against her husband. Regino did not attempt to reconcile these texts, or give any indication of whether somehow in his mind he saw them as compatible. Rather, he in turn passed unreconciled materials to his canonistic successors, to Burchard of Worms and Ivo of Chartres, in the early and late eleventh century respectively. Continuing resort to divorce by the great of society, notorious in the cases of Louis V and Robert II late in the tenth century, lay behind the opinion of Thietmar of Merseburg, writing in the time of Henry II of Germany (1002–24), that so much pastoral effort expended over so much time had hardly made a difference. In his *Chronicon*, VIII, 3, Thietmar lamented current moral decline, especially within marriage.[137]

In sum, during the more than six centuries between Augustine and Ivo of Chartres, but especially from Carolingian times, indissolubility always had its advocates. The collision of this ideal with cultures in which it had had no part commonly caused great conflict, as well as considerable doubt and vagueness of position in champions of the Church themselves. Often it was a question of courage. In 1069 no courtier dared oppose the plan of Henry IV of Germany (1056–1106) to divorce his wife, until Peter Damian successfully intervened. Henry's contemporary Philip I (1060–1108) of France, who repudiated his wife in 1092 and settled in what the Church deemed concubinage with Countess Bertrada of Montfort, remained in office and continued to invest bishops to the end. A series of ineffective ecclesiastical censures of Philip culminating in anathematization by the Council of Clermont in 1095 was followed by de facto papal tolerance.[138] Though by 1100 the Church had far from won the day on this issue, it seems that the general result of insistence on indissolubility was a greater stabilization of marriage generally working to the advantage of women. As Jean Chélini has observed of the Carolingian period, the Christian veneration of an idea of the family centered on the condemnation of adultery, divorce, and infanticide strengthened the woman's place in the family, although many social inequities remained.[139]

Being Married

In the early Middle Ages, virtually all thought was hierarchical, but no one view of male authority or of women's legal or moral rights prevailed.[140] If in the order of domestic governance women were subject to the "head of the house," ecclesiastical writers stressed that this governance could only take certain forms. The stream in patristic thought which had seen all as originally equal and domination as entering only with the Fall, and the equally Augustinian stream which had held that even in Eden there had been government, both continued to flow in Carolingian times. The world after the Fall was perceived as one of hierarchy, but also one in which men and women were equals or near equals in dignity. Some scholars have noted that Carolingian terminology is rich in words with double connotations, at once hierarchical and egalitarian. *Familiaritas* simultaneously evoked patriarchal authority and companionship.[141] Jonas of Orléans put himself in the wife's place when he wrote that the lack of sexual moderation evident in a lord having sexual relations with a servant "dissolves the tenderness of . . . [his own] marriage."[142] The marriage union was to be an egalitarian *societas,* and the wife to be described as *socia,* friend or companion, rather than *ancilla,* servant. This was the message repeatedly insisted on by the Carolingian bishops, whose hope was to redefine societal expectations via their "mirrors" so that marriage could be seen as a *pactum inter aequales,* a covenant between equals. Both parents were to participate in the education of their children. Continuously the Carolingian clergy preached *fides,* faithfulness, as defining marriage. A freely undertaken marriage alliance was the foundation of both mutual fidelity between spouses and the submission of wife to husband. The clergy's hope was to reach noble couples, who, in their treatment of each other, would become models for the rest of society.[143]

There was in fact considerable variety of relationship between husband and wife. Commonly, if not in law, the wife was "in the hand" of her husband and the son in the hand of his father. As in the ancient Roman world, the husband's position in the family must often in the higher social ranks have been reinforced by difference in age between man and wife.[144] This said, the tendency of recent scholars such as Le Jan to place the conjugal couple at the center of early medieval society, especially from Carolingian times, has involved highlighting certain facts. Aristocratic wives, viewed by Le Jan as collaborators with their husbands, participated in the administration of conjugal property, exercised authority in the absence or after the death of their husbands, and managed their own properties. Widows enjoyed considerable social independence.[145] In some regions, the range of marital arrangements legally open to women allowed them considerable independence. The Irish called a woman who had formed a "union on mutual contribution," that is, had made an equal contribution to her marriage-property, a "woman of condominium" or "a woman who is co-ruler with him," to indicate her independent status.[146]

As we noted earlier, the development of primogeniture tended to reduce the sphere of noble wives' activities outside the *familia,* to "domesticate" them. Sometimes in the name of family interests women were deprived of powers formerly possessed. Already endowed daughters might be disinherited because of some new marital arrangement desired by their family. Widows might lose their guardianship over their children. At the same time wives' collaboration with their husbands within the family increased. By 1000 in some regions a lord could not alienate the family patrimony without the consent of both wife and sons. Through the following centuries we continue to find women exercising various forms of political power, administering family property, and playing a large role in the life of the Church, especially as patrons. Prescriptive documents asked from husbands, in return for the authority they wielded, support, protection, and the promotion of the spiritual well-being of all family members. A life of good deeds would produce divine favor, and the father, by word and deed, was to be an example to his household. Jonas of Orléans insisted that neither spouse could send the other away because of illness: each was to take care of the other. The household was to be a place of justice. Children were to be loved, instructed, whipped if necessary, and taught as did Job, "whose efforts to educate his children were such that he did not only make them perfect externally in work and speech, but also cleansed their hearts." Children were to honor their parents and take care of them in their old age.[147]

A subtle study of Old Norse society, based largely on thirteenth-century materials but describing the entire conversion of Iceland and its effect on marriage, again illustrates the difficulty of assessing changes over time in the status of women. As elsewhere in Germanic-Nordic society, pagan marriage in Iceland had been polygynous, with a clear distinction between a man's legal wife and his concubines and mistresses. With the coming of Christianity a traditional Norse view of women as passive victims tended to be replaced with a view of them as the agents of sexual misconduct. Gain or loss? As so often had been the case, the Church's insistence that women give consent to their marriages and that men be faithful was often ineffective. This again suggests that, no more than in Ireland, had there been in Iceland a previous pagan Golden Age for women which was undone by the introduction of Christian patriarchalism. If under Christian influence women had such difficulty in winning the right to consent to their own marriages, their autonomy must have already been strictly limited in such matters in pagan culture. Though the evidence is ambiguous, it seems to reveal coolness and distance between mother and children in the pagan period, and growing affection between mother and child, modeled on Mary and Jesus, after the conversion of Iceland.[148]

Though fascination with the Holy Family was mostly a late medieval and early modern development, from Carolingian times it played a modest role in developing theological understanding of the family. The Bible had given little biographical information about Mary, Joseph, or the childhood of Jesus, but interest in such matters was apparent by the second centuries. It appeared in the treatment of Anne and Joachim, Mary's parents, in the *Protoevangelium of James*. However, in the early Middle Ages typically the Virgin and Child, not the Holy Family, was the subject of iconographic portrayal. The message was likely of incarnation rather than childhood or family life. Texts considering Mary in some aspect or another increased in the eighth and ninth century. The *Book concerning the Birth of Blessed Mary and the Childhood of the Savior,* probably composed around 800, came to have considerable influence. As in the portrayal of St. Anne and the Holy Kinship in the high Middle Ages, interest in the Virgin and Child more portrayed holy mothers and the sanctification of motherhood than the Holy Family.[149]

The Holy Family was nevertheless sometimes the subject of exegetical reflection, and Irish meditation on this subject had a small role in forming its future. An eighth-century Irish Gospel commentary went so far as to say that the *ecclesia primitiva,* the first or original church, was the Holy Family. Although the interest of such commentary was more in ecclesiology than in the human institution of the family per se, the symbolism of the Holy Family, a symbolism quite distinctive to Christianity, especially to Catholic Christianity, became widespread. Just as the idea that each bishop is married to his church was to have far-ranging juridical effects, the Holy Family presented a powerful image to society. The circle of commentators around St. Virgilius of Salzburg (d. 784), perhaps in recollection of patristic discussion of the family as a domestic church, went so far as to call the house of the Holy Family a church. Indeed the Irish laid special weight on the Holy Family in the history of salvation. One gloss on Luke 2:16 said of Mary, Joseph, and Jesus, "Through these three the world was healed."[150]

When we put prescriptive documents aside, the nature of the internal life of the family and of family relations in these centuries is very difficult to determine. Some have suggested that the early medieval laity had much of which to repent. At the end of our period, the great educational ideal, accessible only to a small minority of the population, was of the school master and of education as peace-bringing. In a still very brutal society, the hope was to be able to teach friendship, love, harmony, and manners.[151] In the early Middle Ages such aspiration was a hope against hope. Some have estimated that the average life expectancy, brought down by a high rate of infant mortality, was about thirty years, though members of the upper classes could expect to live considerably longer. Women of all classes had shorter lives than men, due presumably to frequent child-bearing, heavy fieldwork for most, and special susceptibility to certain endemic diseases, such as tuberculosis. Family size seems to have varied according to class, but an average of 2.6 children per marriage has been discovered in documents from Fulda. The strikingly high proportion of males in the total population revealed by more than one study has set scholars to wondering whether additional cause beyond the shorter lives of women must be sought for this disparity. The early penitential literature has many references to parents "overlaying" their children in their sleep, and this suffocating of children has led to suspicion of the presence of infanticide as a fairly common practice. Study of French evidence has revealed that the number of female peasant births varied inversely with the number of females already on a given holding. This suggests that the peasantry practiced especially female infanticide as a form of birth control. More generally, though the subject has not received systematic study, evidence exists of the practice of abortion and contraception. Indeed, it has been suggested that the 25 percent increase in European population from 1150 to 1200 was one result of greater knowledge of and obedience to Christian sexual teaching generally, resulting specifically in decline in infanticide.[152]

As we noted in the last chapter, the view that ancient and medieval marriage and family life were simply cold and loveless — no one denies that they must often have been so — has been shown to be quite misinformed. Indeed, a study of "kissing on the mouth" from the eleventh through fifteenth centuries has provocatively subtitled its chapter on kissing and familial love "When the family was a place of love (*Quand la famille était un lieu d'amour*)."[153] Such a title, which flies in the face of everything an earlier generation of social historians said about the Middle Ages, is part of a larger revolt in which medievalists have pushed the hunt for evidence of marriages built on free choice, sexual desire, and loving relationships back into the twelfth century.[154] At that time writers such as Pope Alexander III (1159–81) replaced a static notion of marital affection with "one implying the desirability of growth."[155] Here the road opened to Chaucer's late fourteenth-century portrayal of Griselda in "The Clerk's Tale." Griselda, we are told, not only loved her children "perfectly," but loved her husband so that "as she aged the love in her begun / Continued even truer, made addition, / If that could be, in love and true submission."[156]

Henry Ansgar Kelly, combating widespread views associated with C. S. Lewis, more generally has shown the existence, both in the ancient world and from the twelfth century, of belief in "the Compatibility of Love and Marriage."[157] Perhaps such was in evidence in a tale told of the taking of the castle of Weinsberg in Suabia. When Conrad III (1138–52) of Germany told the women of the defeated castle that they could leave with as much as they could carry on their backs, they carried out their husbands piggyback.[158] In any case, a number of twelfth-century writers such as the author of *Girart de Roussillon,* written sometime between 1136 and 1180, had a concept of conjugal love.[159] Many expected love and friendship of marriage. Some also appreciated the carnal aspects of sexual desire as appropriate to marriage. Such appreciation must have been present even in the remedies for impotence which bulk so large in the love magic used across the centuries to manipulate desire between spouses. Frequent (usually misogynous) comments about the strength of woman's sexual desire indicate that it was assumed that women enjoyed sexual relations, and if we have any doubt the eleventh-century *Life of Godelieve* tells us so.[160] The monk Constantine the African (d. 1087), writing at Monte Cassino and probably translating an Arabic medical text, opened his *On Coitus* by stating:

> The Creator, wishing the race of animals to remain firmly established ..., disposed that it would be renewed by coitus.... Therefore he shaped for the animals the natural members which are apt ... for this work, and provided them with such wonderful virtue and lovable pleasure that there is no animal that does not excessively delight in coitus.[161]

As we will see in the next chapter, in their analysis of friendship especially twelfth-century monastic writers developed ideas of intimacy, warmth, and love, which were increasingly expected of marriage. Thus Aelred of Rievaulx rewrote Augustine to say:

> woman was created expressly as an incentive for happiness and friend-ship.... It is beautiful that the second created being was taken from the side of the first, so that nature might teach that all are equals, as it were "collateral." In human affairs there is to be neither superior nor inferior; this is the appropriate mark of friendship.
>
> So from the very beginning nature impressed upon human minds the emotional desire for friendship and affection, a desire which mankind's inner sense of love increased with a certain taste of sweetness.[162]

We need not follow Aelred's account of how the Fall affected affection and friendship, narrowing its practice to those good people who continued to follow the natural law. The point is that he saw humans, specifically Adam and Eve, as equals constituted from the beginning for friendship and hap-piness. The idea that Eve was "collateral" with Adam, a pun on her being drawn from Adam's side, expressed the idea of "companionate marriage," that the marital couple was made for a life of companionship. Elsewhere, in a treatment something in the manner of St. Bernard's analysis in his *Sermons on the Song of Songs* of the kinds of kissing, spiritual and corporeal, Aelred noted that a kiss might be a sign of affection, as between husband and wife. Aelred's interest in marital friendship is evidence of continued Christian labor to present marriage as both theologically and emotionally attractive.[163]

In sum, one cannot doubt the frequent expectation and presence of love in twelfth-century marriage. The question many ask is whether this also existed earlier. For instance, what is one to make of the fact that love poetry largely disappeared from Latin literature in the period between 400 and 1000? Love poetry in those ancient forms, the kind known to C. S. Lewis, which centered on eroticism, passion, and extramarital relationships, is no indication of marital love. Quite the contrary, its decline might be taken as evidence of the advance of Christian influence, and its return toward 1100 as an attack on Christian discipline. Too much has been lost to stand on firm ground here. Where the evidence has been competently studied, such as for Ireland between 700 and 1100 by Lisa M. Bitel, we find marriage for many motives, lust, love, and reproduction; marriage praised and marriage blamed.[164]

The last chapter suggested that in specified ways love was found in early Christian marriage. Practices such as elopement, described in the present chapter, also presumably frequently involved "marrying for love."[165] We have noted the frequency of the language of love in the Church's liturgical books and other prescriptive documents. Anyone marrying under their influence in the early Middle Ages would have heard that marriage was about mutual love. For some times and places relevant documentation hardly exists. Only three love poems from Anglo-Saxon England survive, for instance, and only one of these is definitely about marital love. But this tenth-century example, "The Wife's Lament," clearly expressed both friendship and love of wife for a husband caught in feud:

> Then I found myself a most husbandly man,
> ... Very often we boasted that
> none but death alone would drive us apart — ...
> now it's as if it never had been,
> the loving friendship the both of us had.
> Far and near I must suffer the feud
> of my dearly loved man.
>
> (lines 18–26)[166]

In the Latin Middle Ages, *caritas,* which generically expressed the idea of a moral love, was probably the most commonly used word to speak of love, including that between man and wife. Thus Augustine's older contemporary, Ausonius, wrote of his wife with love and affection, and a late fifth-century Christian monument has been reconstructed to speak of *[coniu]GALI ADFECTV ET CARITA[te . . .],* "conjugal affection and love." *Caritas* did not necessarily carry an erotic charge, but it could. Sometimes, as when early medieval formulas of divorce spoke of the absence of *caritas,* this meant no more than that discord had replaced peaceableness. Unfortunately, although pagan and Christian epitaphs frequently spoke of marital love and affection, the medium of funerary commemoration does not lend itself to elaboration of the nature of this love. We cannot tell from such commemoration when in a marriage love had appeared. The monuments merely suggest that it was not uncommon for love to exist in marriage. The problems of interpretation here are similar to those concerning the many early medieval references to love potions and magic and dicing to ask love questions and increase desire.[167]

We learn a little more from the testimonies to marital love found in a number of early medieval saints' lives about spiritual marriage. These tell us of the deep love of couples who had renounced sexual intercourse. They were living witnesses to Augustine's idea that marriage could exist as a friendly union even where sexual intercourse had been foresworn. These couples saw their "sexless" earthly lives as anticipating heaven, where they would also be together. The use by Romans, pagan and Christian, of double sarcophagi for the burial of couples continued into the Merovingian period, and Gregory of Tours (c. 538–94) tells us of the bones of a "sweetest spouse" from a spiritual marriage moving in the tomb to make room for the body of her husband. In another burial the individual tombs of a departed couple moved together, thus giving the spot the name "the Two Lovers." Gregory also tells us of a couple who embraced celibacy later in marriage. When after death the wife was placed in the tomb, her already dead husband's arm embraced her. All realized "what love there was between them in the world, who embrace each other in the tomb." Such examples implicitly spoke to the populace of the preservation of the marriage bond in a "spiritual marriage" beyond the grave. Gregory also tells us of a beloved husband who returned from the dead in a dream to his wife to complain of the quality of the vinegar the priest had been substituting for the special wine she had given for masses to be offered for him.[168]

Emma, the wife of Charlemagne's biographer Einhard, was one of only two ninth-century women who have left us evidence of their Latin literacy. Through one of her letters we can glimpse the existence of love in a non-aristocratic marriage between a serf and a free woman. The two had fled for refuge to Emma and Einhard to ask aid in sustaining a marriage the serf's lord had forbidden. The legal situation was the following. Both civil and canon law recognized the capacity of serfs to marry, but the expectation was that a serf's master had to consent to a marriage. A number of early medieval sources expressed a deepening sense of the equality of all humans before God by insisting that such marriages could not be broken. But of course this was not necessarily the view of a given master. Apparently having heard of Emma's reputation for just dealing, this peasant couple had come to her monastery at Seligenstadt as a place of refuge where they might find a defender. If we remember that in Roman times lower-class unions often were formed more out of emotional attachment than property considerations, we should not be surprised to find love between a ninth-century couple well down in the social order.[169]

As precious as such testimony of love in marriage in the lower levels of society is, equally important is the exchange of letters Emma's death occasioned between the bereft Einhard and the monk Lupus of Ferrières. There emerges from this exchange a picture of their marriage as companionate in two senses. First, at an advanced age, with mutual consent, Einhard and Emma apparently decided on abstention from marital intercourse and took up spiritual marriage. As a lay abbot Einhard jointly with Emma administered the monastery to which they had retired after his years of service at the Carolingian court. But this marriage also was companionate in a second sense we have found above in some twelfth-century materials, and the origins of which we observed in the last chapter in writers such as Tertullian and Augustine. The letters used the word *socia* of Emma, thus designating her as Einhard's companion. They also presented her marriage as formed around companionship and growth in love. Emma had been an unequal equal, capable of the same virtue as a man. Her marriage must have expressed in a particularly clear way the Augustinian ideas that consent makes marriage, and that marital companionship is to grow in love. There is therefore no reason to disbelieve Lothair II when, a few years later in a series of events already described, he called Waldrada *amantissima coniux*, "beloved wife."[170]

The lamentation of Einhard and consolation of Lupus on the death of Emma witness the Christian obligation of a living spouse to pray for the other in death. Christians were enjoined in general to remember the dead. Study of these practices and of the ritualization of the moment of death also reveals something of the internal life of marriages. Although the acts of grief and remembrance varied across Europe, at least in Germany women seem to have had a special place in them, more generally in the preservation of family memory. Thus Bishop Thietmar of Merseburg (975–1018) portrayed Empress Adelaide of Germany (931–99) as praying "to the end of her days" for her deceased son and husband. There were of course important differences between Germany and France in Adelaide's day. While the French emphasis was increasingly on lineage formation, Germany retained more of its earlier clan structure. In some ways not unlike the Romans with their marriage *cum manu*, the French tended to view a woman who married into a family as an outsider, as not a part of her husband's — or children's — family. Especially at the upper levels of society, she was valuable as someone who might bring money or a desirable alliance to the family, but for all that might easily remain a foreigner. More a guest than a family member, the French wife could easily be portrayed as not suitable to be in charge of family memory. This was especially true if the assessment of suitability came from a Cluniac monk, himself anxious for the monies which came with supervision of prayers for the dead of a wealthy family. Germany was freer of this ancient Mediterranean way of looking at things. In Germany women were given the task not just of making donations to religious houses

to remember the dead, but of active intervention for them through their
own prayers, fasts, and penances. Thus Thietmar also tells us that Countess
Liudgard offered all these latter, including fasts in the cold, along with acts
of charity, for her dead husband Margrave Werner. Such practices expressed
a specific sense of social and family solidarity, a kind of division of labor
in which works were expected of the living female to aid the dead on their
way. Mutuality was not necessarily in evidence here, for, in spite of the evidence from Einhard and Emma, most commonly it was the wife who was
expected to pray for the husband, not the husband for the wife. This said, in
regions where women were prominent in the preservation of family memory, it is hard not to see in this the occasional expression of affective family
relations.[171]

We have noted above that the larger teaching, grounded in 1 Cor. 7:14
and 16, was that spouses were to exercise a pastoral role toward each other
as an expression of their mutual love. Though this idea on its face carried a
sense of equal obligation, beginning in the ancient Church some writers had
affirmed the primary responsibility of husbands for the spiritual instruction
and care of their families, while others saw the primary responsibility to lie
with mothers or grandmothers. John Chrysostom desired that the wife create in the household a sanctuary for her husband from the cares of public
life, giving him consolation, good counsel, and sweet love. The Merovingian and Carolingian tendency was to see women as primarily responsible
for the conversion of pagan husbands or the Christian education of children, but husbands, or parents together, could also have their place. The
wife's pastoral role in the family, preaching by love, was sometimes emphasized. This received its completion in the tenth and eleventh centuries, when
much of the work of initial conversion had been completed. Its essential
affirmations were that conjugal and divine love were compatible, that the
spouses were equal, and that the wife was central to the salvation of her
husband. Aristocratic wives were to be persuasive, urging their husbands
through sweet words especially to endowments on behalf of the Church.
Weak in many ways, wives were perceived to be strong in their power to se-
duce their husbands and insinuate ideas into their hearts. The ninth-century
Life of Rictrude portrayed the foundation of marital love on which such persuasion rested. Rictrude was "loved" (*diligitur*) by her husband-to-be, who
embodied hoped for qualities in a husband, including amorous affection (*ad
amoris affectum*). In Rictrude's case, love was not only said to precede marriage, but her hagiographer stressed the unanimity shared by husband and
wife. United by faith and charity, two in one flesh, determined to honor God
with one voice, they lived in concord. When Adalbaud was killed, Rictrude
grieved much.[172]

About the year 1000 the monk Syrus of Cluny composed a warm eulogy of the German imperial couple, the aforementioned Adelaide and Otto the Great (936–73). In it he complemented the nun Hrotsvitha of Gandersheim's ascription of a lively conjugal affection to Adelaide and Otto. Syrus wrote:

> If according to the Apostle (1 Cor. 7:14) the unbelieving husband will be saved by the faith of his Christian wife and the unbelieving wife by her Christian husband, how much more those who are united [*copulati*] in Christ, those who exercise justice through faith.... [They are] both hearers and doers of the Gospel.[173]

One of Syrus's goals was to praise the imperial couple for good works, including solicitude for monks, but more importantly he presented the married couple as a couple, each working for the salvation of the other, and together doing good and working for justice in the *saeculum*.

In a common "nuptial legend" told of a number of early medieval royal marriages, one of the lives of St. Matilda more specifically expressed the idea of marriage for love we have already met in the *Life* of Rictrude. Matilda's life tells us that when Henry the Fowler first saw his future queen Matilda as a charming young woman of about fourteen years, he was so enflamed by love that he decided immediately to marry her. The girl had been reared in a nunnery by the abbess, her grandmother. Henry, unable to abide a lengthy betrothal and having obtained the grandmother's consent, secretly gathered his men and stole Matilda away. He then led her in honor back to Saxony and Wallhausen and a nuptial meal. There they united in legitimate love (*licito perfruuntur amore*), and he gave to her the city and dependencies in dowry. Here in "fairy tale" fashion, love and desire, but also something close to *raptus*, preceded marriage. Both consummation and the granting of dowry seem to have followed the nuptial banquet. No more than in the later *Cid* did the stages of marrying, such as they were, follow a pattern set by any liturgical book. We gather that in the aristocratic circles to which this tenth-century fiction was addressed, the notion of a marriage having begun in such a manner expressed how desirable Matilda was. She was a heroine capable of awakening Henry's sentiments.[174]

The original form of the story was unacceptable to the Church, and in its subsequent use in Saxon pastoral ministry, it was transformed into a classic tale of (1) elaborate premarital negotiations in which the consent of the parents was central (no mention was made of the consent of the couple), (2) betrothal, and (3) wedding, the latter in the setting of a banquet (with no mention of a marriage liturgy) at which dowry was given. A conjugal love aimed at mutual salvation became the source of the couple's subsequent shared life, mutual respect, equality, and collaboration (*aequa coadunatio in bono...aequalis compassio in subjectos*). The compatibility of conjugal and divine love was pointedly affirmed. United in the flesh (*in carne coad-*

unati), Henry and Matilda were also of one heart and soul (*in animo uno et spiritu:* possibly an allusion to Acts 4:32), quick to good works, and of a single love for Christ and neighbor. Marital chastity, living in dignity and reserve within the Church's prescriptions regarding marriage and the periods of prohibited sexual intercourse, was a grace they possessed near virginity. Henry died first. Widowhood had traditionally been presented in monastic exposition as an opportunity to free oneself from the flesh and embrace celibacy. Matilda's long widowhood, however, was in turn portrayed as a prolongation of her marriage, not as something to be turned against it. That is, she viewed the death of her husband as neither the occasion for embracing a state of life higher than marriage, nor for remarriage. Matilda saw her marriage tie as indissoluble and remarriage after the death of her husband as almost inconceivable. Marriage defined her sanctity. As Matilda's death approached, she requested to be buried at her husband's side. Such was marriage in its most developed ecclesiastical representation around the year 1000. Similar if less fulsome views could be found elsewhere. In a tenth-century Italian "mirror," Bishop Rather of Verona told the king to "love his wife, avoid consorting with concubines," and explained that concubinage had been allowed when there was a scanty population, in Old Testament times, but not since "a New Man has given new commandments."[175] The teaching of the mirrors spread in the eleventh-century Ottonian empire not least because the Ottonian dynasty embraced them.

The foregoing examples show that love in marriage was an idea and experience found in every early medieval century. We generally do not know whether this love had preceded marriage or was seen in any sense as a pre-condition for marrying, though in some of the examples just given it clearly was. This was true also of the eleventh-century Spanish liturgy for second marriage after the death of a spouse. The Spanish *Liber ordinum* repeated an Augustinian distinction in saying that the remarrying individual, like Ruth, remarries not for lust but for love.[176] There also was some understanding and expectation that in any case love would develop after marriage. In treating the origins of courtly love, C. Stephen Jaeger has noted innovations which took place toward the end of the eleventh century. Although he does not consider the liturgical, hagiographical, and theological language of love and friendship adduced in the present chapter, and thus has only a partial view of the matter, that view is illuminating. Until the late 1000s, according to Jaeger's argument, literary discourse about love and friendship for the most part continued to take the Ciceronian form of a friendship between men which expressed equality or made them equals. Then women, previously overwhelmingly restricted to a private or domestic realm, were allowed into public discourse on the nature of love. They in turn became the educators in love. "Ovid supersedes Cicero as the ancient authority on love relationships."[177] Love between men and women had previously existed, says Jaeger, but it had been largely mute. Then a little before 1100 long-standing public discourse on the teaching and embodying of virtue and manners, previously centered in courts and schools and therefore on relations between men, became an appropriate language to treat love between men and women. "Women [are] admitted to the gentleman's club of discourse on virtuous love." The poet who wrote *Ruodlieb* around 1070 was the herald of this development. His hero sought a bride who would ornament his "nobility with her manners and with the inborn nobility of her conduct." Such a woman was found, Ruodlieb's "equal in probity of manners, virtue and nobility." Thus a formerly masculine cult of manners was imposed on courtship. At the end of the century, Baudri of Bourgueil showed courtship metamorphizing into courtly love in his portrayal of Countess Adela of Blois, beautiful and of pleasant conversation, courted by many but chaste and faithful.

The *Ruodlieb* seems as much to create expectations about the nature of courtship and love as a witness to current practice. By comparison *The Cid*, set in the later eleventh century but written about 1140, seems witness to notions of love in marriage achieved, as well as to how marriage remained caught between aristocratic and ecclesiastical conceptions. In the matter of love in marriage, Martin Aurell has observed for nearby Aragon and Catalonia that burying spouses in the same place, which he takes to express belief in a conjugal love which would survive death, only appeared about the middle of the eleventh century. Before that, in this area, an aristocrat was in good patrilineal fashion commonly buried with his father. Spouses could be buried in different cities. Then increasingly toward 1100 couples were buried, not in the double sarcophagi of Merovingian times, but in individual sarcophagi in the same location. Just as the growing emphasis on consent in marriage drew couples together and, relatively speaking, in that degree separated them from fathers and family, so in death a man no longer returned to his father but remained with his wife. Prayer of course was not simply for the dead, and in Spain we find wives giving alms for the safe return of husbands taken prisoner by the Moslems. Men, who often remarried after the death of a spouse, seem more easily to have forgotten and more rarely to have prayed for a departed wife. But the ideal was a conjugal love which in life persuaded one's spouse to proper action. These developments are a larger context in which to read the *Cid*.[178]

The *Cid* gives a portrayal of marrying and marriage which fits very well with the evidence we have already developed. Near the beginning of the work the Cid leaves his wife to make his fortune in the world and in parting tells her: "Doña Ximena, my noble wife, I love you as I love my soul!" Doña Ximena in turn prays to God to keep the Cid from harm, and that the two

might reunite still in this life. Then the authorial voice informs us in a typically vivid way: "They parted as the nail is parted from the flesh." One can
hardly doubt the love and pain of separation of this couple, as painful as the
tearing out of a fingernail. Marriage in a more conventional and calculating
sense, however, is always in the background. The Cid hopes to return to give
his daughters in marriage. The princes of Carrión, observing the growing
fame of the Cid, say, "It might be well for us to marry his daughters, for our
profit." They are very realistic in their expectations: " 'My Cid's affairs go
well!' they said. 'Let us beg of him his two daughters in marriage, and thus
we shall gain in honor and riches.' " This and what follows closely repeats
the stages of marrying articulated by Hincmar almost three centuries earlier.
The Cid, although disliking the princes and wishing to protect his daughters
from marriage to them, refuses to cross King Alfonso, who wills the marriages. Mother and daughters set off for Valencia, where the Cid has won
a name. The Cid and his wife are reunited and, apparently not completely
honestly, he tells his daughters he has found them good husbands. Both
daughters are delighted: "How rich we shall be when we are married." The
Cid makes it clear that it is the king, not himself, who has arranged these
marriages. The reader is thus led to understand the constraints within which
the Cid acts. We seem hardly to have left an ancient Roman world in which,
because no welfare system nor state would step in to take care of children if
parents failed, their life and death was in the father's hands. Parents' prime
responsibility was to provide for the financial future of their children, not
to make sure that no "emotional damage" was done in the process.[179]

Next we glimpse the wedding ceremonies. In the palace, the Cid gives his
daughters into the hands of a vassal, and in turn the Cid's chief lieutenant
gives them to the princes. This purely secular (no priest is involved) *traditio* or "handing over" accomplished, all move to church where the bishop
gives his blessing and mass is sung. Most interpreters understand the "handing over" of the daughters to be the point at which they were considered
married, and the subsequent blessing, mass, and banquet to be celebrations
of this marriage. At the most, the mass might have been understood to be
what sealed the marriage. The marriages apparently are consummated ("the
princes of Carrión . . . [held] their wives in their arms as if with love"), but
the princes subsequently prove themselves cowards and traitors. In revenge
for having been shamed, they abandon and dispossess their wives, robbing
them of their dowry, beating them senseless, and leaving them for dead.
The deed discovered, the Cid declares his daughters will still marry well.
Pedro Bermúdez, no more than anyone else even raising the question of
the legitimacy of such a second marriage, agrees: "You have lost a good
[i.e., "advantageous"] marriage, but you shall have a better!"[180] The Cid
acknowledges that he had allowed the original marriages rather than cross

King Alfonso and give up his own aspirations to legitimacy: "I it was who accepted your marriage, for I dared not do otherwise. But now, please God, I shall see you better wed!" The Cid asks the king to judge the wrongs done, "for he it was who gave my daughters in marriage, not I." The King gives justice, and the dowry is restored. In the process, the Cid notes the princes had never loved his daughters, and thus suggests that this was a normal expectation of marriage. In a storybook ending, ambassadors of the princes of Navarre and Aragón ask that the daughters become the queens of their respective kingdoms. Alfonso authorizes the marriages, and they take place. Clearly we are in a world which expects love of marriage, but in which lay authority and custom rule. The Church has only a very subsidiary place. From the same period there survives Spanish sculptural evidence of, apparently, marital love (it is not always clear whether the couples portrayed are married to each other or not). Couples are shown embracing and kissing, and some of these kisses seem distinctly tender, to manifest the affections of everyday life.[181]

There also is some evidence of love and appreciation of children. All through the Middle Ages, parents were encouraged to bring sick children to shrines for healing. St. Aegidius, the purported founder of St.-Gilles-du-Gard, who may have died in the eighth century and for whom a tenth-century *Life* exists, became not merely the patron of cripples and the indigent, but the protector of children, nursing mothers, and animals. His cult spread by the late Middle Ages throughout much of Europe as far north as Scandinavia and east into the Slavic regions, and was very popular in Great Britain. Especially royal and noble children who had died young were commemorated in epitaphs. If Einhard's portrayal of Charlemagne's deep love for his children and grief over the death of his adult sons is quite well known, no less significant is Paul the Deacon's epitaph on the death of Charlemagne's daughter:

> In this tomb a pretty little girl lies buried....
> She was born near the lofty walls of Pavia....
> But hastening towards the river Rhone she was taken from the
>   threshold of life
> and the heart of her mother is wounded with sorrow from afar.
> She died on the point of seeing her father's triumphs.
> Now she holds the blessed domains of the Eternal Father.[182]

Many other examples could be cited. The mid-ninth-century noblewoman Dhuoda was a most exceptional woman. Nevertheless, the strong love she expressed for her children in her *Manual* and her hope for their and her husband's salvation is further evidence of intrafamilial love among the aristocracy.[183] The tenth-century Lanalet Pontifical and prayers descendant from it prays specifically for joy in procreation of children.[184] We catch vignettes of childhood and family life in the early eleventh-century *Book of Sainte Foy*, which tells us of the female child martyr Foy, who liked to play jokes and could cause a pregnancy. The oldest *Life* of Ida of Boulogne tells us that Ida insisted on breast-feeding her own children to avoid bad influences on them (it was believed that the qualities of character of a wet nurse were passed on through her milk). And who, in the presence of the immensely sad twelfth-century portrayal of a father grieving for his dead child found in the chapter of Saint-Benoit at Vézelay, could doubt the existence of love for children?[185] Barbara Hanawalt, although mostly for a later period, has shown the widespread existence in England of affectionate peasant families.[186] In sum, Philippe Ariès was wrong to deny that interest in and love of children existed in this period.[187]

In conclusion, the reform movements of the late eleventh century spurred reflection on the needs of married people and on their place in the life and mission of the Church. By 1100 there was a gathering tendency, stemming from earlier Carolingian pastoral effort, to find positive and helpful things to say about marriage, and to see in it a specific form of unreserved love built on fidelity and service rather than domination. A long-standing theological language of marital love, earlier found in liturgy, sermon, and saint's life, increasingly insinuated itself, if imperfectly, throughout society. This was the positive face, the goal in mind, of so many centuries of attempting to teach a discipline built around the idea of indissolubility. Although struggle between Christian and pre-Christian views of marriage would continue until the present, during the early Middle Ages the Church had recast the shape of European life. By 1100 marriage increasingly stood forth not just as a God-given road to salvation, but as a mystery and sacrament participating in the bond between Christ and Church.[188]

Notes

1. Hugh Magennis, " 'Listen Now All and Understand': Adaptation of Hagiographical Material for Vernacular Audiences in the Old English Lives of St. Margaret," *Speculum* 71 (1996): 27–42, at 31–32, 38–40. In addition to Brian Brennan, "Deathless Marriage and Spiritual Fecundity in Venantius Fortunatus's *De Virginitate*," *Traditio* 51 (1996): 73–97, see Penelope D. Johnson, *Equal in Monastic Profession: Religious Women in Medieval France* (Chicago, 1991), esp. 13–34, 248ff. Giles Constable, *Three Studies in Medieval Religious and Social Thought: The Interpretation of Mary and Martha; The Ideal of Imitation of Christ; The Orders of Society* (New York, 1995), 249–360, and index under "marriage, married order," describes early medieval schemata of the orders of society/perfection.

2. Dyan Elliott, *Spiritual Marriage: Sexual Abstinence in Medieval Wedlock* (Princeton, N.J., 1993), 65–66, 73–79: I am both using and correcting 51–55.

3. Johannes Bernaldo, "Patronal Monasticism? About a Much Discussed Fea-

ture of Early Spanish Monasticism," *In Quest of the Kingdom,* ed. Alf Härdelin (Stockholm, 1991), 27–63, though unevenly informed, supersedes all earlier study of what Bernaldo suggests might be called patronal monasticism.

4. Manuel C. Díaz y Díaz, *Vie chrétienne et culture dans l'Espagne du VIIe au Xe siècles* (Brookfield, Vt., 1992), IX, 32–33, 38–39, and X, esp. 150.

5. Below n. 169, and Renée Nip, "Godelieve of Gistel and Ida of Boulogne," in *Sanctity and Motherhood: Essays on Holy Mothers in the Middle Ages,* ed. Anneke B. Mulder-Bakker (New York, 1995), 191–223 at 210, 214. Donald Hochstetler, *A Conflict of Traditions: Women in Religion in the Early Middle Ages 500–840* (Lanham, Md., 1992), gives general orientation.

6. André Vauchez, *The Laity in the Middle Ages: Religious Beliefs and Devotional Practices,* ed. and intro. by Daniel E. Bornstein, trans. Margery J. Schneider (Notre Dame, Ind., 1993), and Jean Chélini, *L'aube du moyen âge: La vie religieuse des laïcs dans l'Europe carolingienne (750–900),* preface by Pierre Riché, afterword by Georges Duby (Paris, 1991).

7. Peter Brown, *The Rise of Western Christendom: Triumph and Adversity, AD 200–1000* (Cambridge, Mass., 1996), 211–12, 227–28; and on Radegund, Marcelle Thiébaux, ed., *The Writings of Medieval Women: An Anthology,* 2d ed. (New York, 1994), 85–124; with note 16 below.

8. Brown, *Rise of Western Christendom,* 91–92, 205–7, 228, 314–15.

9. See André Vauchez, *The Spirituality of the Medieval West: From the Eighth to the Twelfth Century,* trans. Colette Friedlander (Kalamazoo, Mich., 1993), 13–16, 21, 116, noting the infrequency of lay communion; and notes 30–34 below. For orientation to the penitential literature, see Pierre J. Payer, *Sex and the Penitentials: The Development of a Sexual Code, 550–1150* (Toronto, 1984), with his review in *Catholic Historical Review* (hereafter *CHR*) 81 (1995): 640–42, and his "Confession and the Study of Sex in the Middle Ages," in *Handbook of Medieval Sexuality,* ed. Vern L. Bullough and James A. Brundage (New York, 1996), 3–31, a book with many valuable essays.

10. Oronzo Giordano, *Religiosidad popular en la Edad Media,* trans. Pilar García Mouton and Valentín García Yebra (Madrid, 1983), 75–96.

11. Judith Evans Grubbs, *Law and Family in Late Antiquity: The Emperor Constantine's Marriage Legislation* (Oxford, 1995), 222–23: penance for adultery could include lifelong abstention from marital sexual relations.

12. William E. Klingshirn, *Caesarius of Arles: The Making of a Christian Community in Late Antiquity* (Cambridge, 1994), as at 49–51, describes the religion of the countryside. See below notes 31 and 33.

13. James A. Brundage, *Law, Sex, and Christian Society in Medieval Europe* (Chicago, 1987), 52–61, with Brundage's *Sex, Law and Marriage in the Middle Ages* (Brookfield, Vt., 1993), III, and Elliott, *Spiritual Marriage,* 66–67, with n. 9 above.

14. John W. Baldwin, *The Language of Sex: Five Voices from Northern France around 1200* (Chicago, 1994), 226, reviewed in *CHR* 82 (1996): 79–81. Thomas F. X. Noble, "Morbidity and Vitality in the History of the Early Medieval Papacy," *CHR* 81 (1995): 505–40 at 520, makes a similar point in regard to the early medieval papacy.

15. Díaz y Díaz, *Vie chrétienne,* VIII, 371–73.

16. Michel Rouche, *Clovis* (Paris, 1996), 223–52, with his "Des mariages païens au mariage chrétien: Sacré et sacrement," in *Segni e riti nella Chiesa altomedievale occidentale,* 2 vols. (Spoleto, 1987), 2:835–80; Cordula Nolte, *Conversio und Christianitas: Frauen in der Christianisierung vom 5. bis 8. Jahrhundert* (Stuttgart, 1995), II, "Ehe und *conversio*"; Susanne Wittern, *Frauen, Heiligkeit und Macht: Latein-*

ische Frauenviten aus dem 4. bis 7. Jahrhundert (Stuttgart, 1994), esp. chap. 4; and Madeleine Anjubault Simons, *La force dans la faiblesse: A propos du rôle des femmes dans l'Eglise (IVe–XIIe siècles)* (Paris, 1995), 74–75.

17. *Historia ecclesiastica gentis anglorum*, II, 11, ed. B. Colgrave and R. A. B. Mynors (Oxford, 1969), 172–74. For orientation to the Anglo-Saxon period, see two articles in *Past and Present:* Pauline Stafford, "The King's Wife in Wessex," 91 (1981): 3–27, and Margaret Ross, "Concubinage in Anglo-Saxon England," 108 (1985): 3–34; Joel T. Rosenthal, "Anglo-Saxon Attitudes: Men's Sources, Women's History," in *Medieval Women and the Sources of Medieval History*, ed. Joel T. Rosenthal (Athens, Ga., 1990), 259–84; and Henrietta Leyser, *Medieval Women: A Social History of Women in England, 450–1500* (New York, 1995).

18. In addition to the following note, see Suzanne Fonay Wemple, *Women in Frankish Society: Marriage and the Cloister 500 to 900* (Philadelphia, 1981), a useful book in spite of anachronistic "status-measuring" of the type criticized in nn. 20–21 below, which, 12–13, discusses the historiography of Germanic marriage and, 59–61, 103, 125, the role of mothers in instruction; and Glenn W. Olsen, "One Heart and One Soul (Acts 4:32 and 34) in Dhuoda's 'Manual,' " *Church History* 61 (1992): 23–33.

19. For the phrase quoted, see Ineke van't Spijker, "Family Ties: Mothers and Virgins in the Ninth Century," in *Sanctity and Motherhood*, ed. Mulder-Bakker, 165–90, at 176, and also Anneke B. Mulder-Bakker's "Introduction" to this volume at 9; Clarissa W. Atkinson, *The Oldest Vocation: Christian Motherhood in the Middle Ages* (Ithaca, N.Y., 1991); the uneven translations in *Sainted Women of the Dark Ages*, ed. and trans. Jo Ann McNamara and John E. Halborg, with E. Gordon Whatley (Durham, N.C., 1992); and below n. 182.

20. See on the difficulty of measuring either status or "positive" and "negative" images of women the introduction by Carolyne Larrington, *Women and Writing in Medieval Europe: A Sourcebook* (London, 1995), 2, 9–10.

21. Francis Martin, *The Feminist Question: Feminist Theology in the Light of Christian Tradition* (Grand Rapids, Mich., 1994), 124–39, esp. 124–26, though himself offering generalizations with which I am uncomfortable, shrewdly calls attention to problems in measuring the status of women. Rodney Stark, *The Rise of Christianity: A Sociologist Reconsiders History* (Princeton, N.J., 1996), is one of the more convincing attempts to trace change in status in regard to a limited number of issues over a relatively short period. Stark argues that women had a higher status in Christian subculture than in pagan, and that the Christian prohibitions of abortion, infanticide, polygamy, divorce, and birth control contributed to women's well-being. In studying women's rights and the construction of gender, Guy Halsall, *Settlement and Social Organization: The Merovingian Region of Metz* (Cambridge, 1995), as at 61–72, stresses the great variations over time and geography found in Merovingian Europe alone.

22. The seminal study is Pierre Toubert, "La théorie du mariage chez les moralistes carolingiens," *Il matrimonio nella società altomedievale*, 2 vols., Settimane di Studio del Centro Italiano di Studi sull'Alto Medioevo 24 (Spoleto, 1977), 1:233–82 (with Discussione, 283–85). See also, in spite of its serious flaws, P. A. Maccioni, " 'It Is Allowed, neither to Husband nor Wife . . . ' The Ideas of Jonas of Orléans on Marriage," in *Vrouw, familie en macht: Bronnen over vrouwen in de Middeleeuwen*, ed. M. Mostert et al. (Hilversum, 1990), 99–125. Vauchez, *Spirituality*, 12–13, treats Charlemagne's "incarnationism"; 21–22, Jonas; and 35–74, esp. 44–52 and 54–58, the monastic age. David F. Appleby, "Sight and Church Reform in the Thought of Jonas of Orléans," *Viator* 27 (1996): 11–33, gives orientation to recent work on

Jonas and, 23–24, his ideas about marriage, and see Hans-Werner Goetz, *Frauen im frühen Mittelalter: Frauenbild und Frauenleben im Frankenreich* (Weimar, 1995), esp. 165–242.

23. Patrick Corbet, *Les Saints Ottoniens: Sainteté dynastique, sainteté royale et sainteté féminine autour de l'an Mil,* pref. Michel Bur (Sigmaringen, 1986), 5, 181–207 at 187–88; Carolyn Edwards, "Dynastic Sanctity in Two Early Medieval Women's *Lives,*" in *Medieval Family Roles: A Book of Essays,* ed. Cathy Jorgensen Itnyre (Hamden, Conn., 1995), 3–19; and the last section of the present chapter. For orientation to the Gregorian Reform, see my "The Investiture Controversy," *Religion in the Making of Western Man,* ed. Frank Coppa (New York, 1970), 79–93.

24. Trans. Vauchez, *Spirituality,* 55 n. 10.

25. Trans. Vauchez, *Spirituality,* 116.

26. *Woman Defamed and Woman Defended: An Anthology of Medieval Texts,* ed. and trans. Alcuin Blamires with Karen Pratt and C. W. Marx (Oxford, 1992), 228.

27. In addition to the last chapter, see Christopher N. L. Brooke, *The Medieval Idea of Marriage* (Oxford, 1989), 131–32; John T. Noonan Jr., *Contraception: A History of Its Treatment by the Catholic Theologians and Canonists* (Cambridge, Mass., 1965), 187–89, 241–43, 353–56; Henry Ansgar Kelly, *Love and Marriage in the Age of Chaucer* (Ithaca, N.Y., 1975), 249–54; and Christopher J. Renz, "Let the Body Speak: Domestic Rites of Blessing in Christian Marriage," a thesis presented to the Graduate Theological Union, Berkeley, Calif., 1997, which gives some consideration to the domestic rites described later in this chapter and describes Albert and Thomas.

28. Valerie I. J. Flint, *The Rise of Magic in Early Medieval Europe* (Princeton, N.J., 1991), 239, 299–300, considers the story of Lonoghyl and similar materials.

29. Trans. Vauchez, *Spirituality,* 116, revised, and Patrick J. Geary, *Phantoms of Remembrance: Memory and Oblivion at the End of the First Millennium* (Princeton, N.J., 1994), 120–23.

30. David Cressy, "Purification, Thanksgiving and the Churching of Women in Post-Reformation England," *Past and Present* 141 (November 1993): 106–46.

31. Peter Browe, *Beiträge zur Sexualethik des Mittelalters* (Breslau, 1932), 114–21, 130–35, treats Caesaraius and the nights of Tobias, as does Brian Bethune, *The Text of the Christian Rite of Marriage in Medieval Spain,* 201, a valuable unpublished 1987 dissertation, which the Library of the Pontifical Institute of Mediaeval Studies of the University of Toronto made available to me. Bethune makes it clear that though at the end of our period the nights of Tobias were asked of couples in Spain, in northern France the expectation was that the couple would proceed from wedding to feast and bed. Throughout he improves Jean-Baptiste Molin and Protais Mutembe, *Le rituel du mariage en France du XIIe au XVI siècle* (Paris, 1974). See Kelly, *Love,* 164–65, 276, for the ninth century.

32. My "The Idea of the *Ecclesia Primitiva* in the Writings of the Twelfth-Century Canonists," *Traditio* 25 (1969): 61–86 at 68–69, describes the debate over the authenticity of Gregory's answers. For menstruation, see Wemple, *Women in Frankish Society,* 22. Cyrille Vogel, *En rémission des péchés: Recherches sur les systèmes pénitentiels dans l'église latine,* ed. Alexandre Faivre (Aldershot, 1994), VI, 183, gives a seventh century example of the kind of views Gregory presumably was trying to combat: a woman wishing to take communion the morning after having had intercourse (*nocte pollutionis*) was refused because she had not done penance.

33. See notes 12 and 31 above; Flint, *Rise of Magic,* 296; John Boswell, *Same-Sex Unions in Premodern Europe* (New York, 1994), 168–69; Browe, *Beiträge,* 15–136;

Jean Devisse, *Hincmar Archevêque de Reims 845–882,* 3 vols. (Paris, 1975–76), 1:367–466 at 376–77, 379; David Brakke, "The Problematization of Nocturnal Emissions in Early Christian Syria, Egypt, and Gaul," *Journal of Early Christian Studies* (hereafter *JECS*) 3 (1995): 419–60; and Jean Verdon, *La nuit au Moyen Âge* (Paris, 1994), 58–59.

34. Trans. Maccioni, "'It Is Allowed,'" 115. See also for context Jane Bishop, "Bishops as Marital Advisors in the Ninth Century," in *Women of the Medieval World: Essays in Honor of John Mundy,* ed. Julius Kirshner and Suzanne F. Wemple (Oxford, 1985), 53–84

35. Maccioni, "'It Is Allowed,'" 108, and n. 22 above.

36. Trans. Maccioni, "'It Is Allowed,'" 112–13.

37. Ian Wood, *The Merovingian Kingdoms 450–751* (New York, 1994), 308, 312; Rudolf Weigand, *Liebe und Ehe im Mittelalter* (Goldbach, Germany, 1993), 77–91; Toubert, "Théorie."

38. Dorothy Africa, review, *Speculum* 71 (1996): 129–32 at 131; Lisa M. Bitel, *Land of Women: Tales of Sex and Gender from Early Ireland* (Ithaca, N.Y., 1996), 76–77 (valuable on all things Irish); John M. Riddle, *Eve's Herbs: A History of Contraception and Abortion in the West* (Cambridge, Mass., 1997), 26–28, 90, who notes the presence of a recipe for abortion in a Lorsch abbey manuscript from about 800; and below nn. 136, 152. In the first chapter of the present book, Fr. Martin speaks of "miscarriage" in terms of the practice described in Numbers 5:11–31. See also Luke Demaitre and Anthony Travill, "Human Embryology and Development in the Works of Albertus Magnus," in *Albertus Magnus and the Sciences: Commemorative Essays,* ed. James A. Weisheipl (Toronto, 1980), 405–40 at 407, 424; Jean Claude Bologne, *La naissance interdite: Stérilité, avortement, contraception au Moyen Âge* (Paris, 1988); Sylvie Laurent, *Naître au Moyen Âge: De la conception a la naissance: La grossesse et l'accouchement (XIIe–XVe siècle)* (Paris, 1989), chaps. 2, 9.

39. Of the articles on the Council in Trullo in *Greek Orthodox Theological Review* 40, 1–2 (1995), only that of John H. Erickson, "The Council in Trullo: Issues Relating to the Marriage of Clergy," 183–99, mentions the studies of C. Cochini and R. Cholij, listed in chapter three above, around which the controversy centers. Erickson, who makes valid criticisms of these authors, does not come to terms with their central argument (184 n. 1). He is substantially correct that "often the very texts which the authors adduce show how widespread — and widely accepted — clerical use of marriage was in Christian antiquity." But Cochini and Cholij know this, and the issue, rather, is the existence and precise nature of early norms and expectations that married clergy would give up intercourse upon ordination. Here Cochini and Cholij seem to me to "overclarify" the first centuries. However, the criticisms found in reviews such as that by Peter L'Huillier, *Sobernost* 12 (1990): 180–82, are not carefully worked out.

40. Peter Brown, "'A More Glorious House,'" *New York Review of Books* 44, no. 9 (May 28, 1997): 19–24 at 21; Eve Levin, *Sex and Society in the World of the Orthodox Slavs* (Ithaca, N.Y., 1989), of which chap. 2 on marriage is uneven.

41. Bart Jaski, "Marriage Laws in Ireland and on the Continent in the Early Middle Ages," in *"The Fragility of Her Sex"? Medieval Irishwomen in their European Context,* ed. Christine Meek and Katharine Simms (Dublin, 1996), 16–42, at 32, and see Bitel, *Land of Women,* 177–78.

42. In addition to the following notes, see David Herlihy, "Land, Family and Women in Continental Europe, 701–1200," *The Social History of Italy and Western Europe, 700–1200* (London, 1978), VI, 89–120 at 110. Gabriella Rossetti,

"Il matrimonio del clero nella società altomedievale," *Matrimonio,* 1:473–554, is fundamental, and see Brian Brennan, "'Episcopae': Bishops' Wives Viewed in Sixth-Century Gaul," *Church History* 54 (1985): 311–23.

43. R. I. Moore, "Family, Community and Cult on the Eve of the Gregorian Reform," *Transactions of the Royal Historical Society,* 5th ser., 30 (1980): 49–69. For the tenth century see Henrich Fichtenau, *Living in the Tenth Century: Mentalities and Social Orders,* trans. Patrick J. Geary (Chicago, 1991), 115–19.

44. On this and the following, see Georges Duby, *The Three Orders: Feudal Society Imagined,* trans. Arthur Goldhammer, with a foreword by Thomas N. Bisson (Chicago, 1978), 27, 29–30, with Georges Duby, *France in the Middle Ages 987–1460: From Hugh Capet to Joan of Arc,* trans. Juliet Vale (Oxford, 1991), 36. For appraisals of the former work, see Karl Leyser, *Communications and Power in Medieval Europe: The Gregorian Revolution and Beyond,* ed. Timothy Reuter (London, 1994), 200 n. 49.

45. See Geary, *Phantoms,* 4; Leyser, *Communications,* 1–3. For the Cluniac context of William's thought, see Dominique Iogna-Prat, "Continence et virginité dans la conception clunisienne de l'ordre du monde autour de l'an mil," *Académie des Inscriptions et Belles-Lettres, Comptes Rendus* (1985): 127–46. Cf. R. I. Moore, "Heresy, Repression, and Social Change in the Age of Gregorian Reform," in *Christendom and Its Discontents: Exclusion, Persecution, and Rebellion, 1000–1500,* ed. Scott L. Waugh and Peter D. Diehl (Cambridge, 1996), 19–46 at 31–41.

46. Vauchez, *Spirituality,* 36.

47. Duby, *Three Orders,* 36. Peter Biller and Anne Hudson, eds., *Heresy and Literacy, 1000–1530* (Cambridge, 1994), has several relevant studies.

48. In addition to the preceding and following notes, see Jo Ann McNamara, "Chaste Marriage and Clerical Celibacy," in *Sexual Practices and the Medieval Church,* ed. Vern L. Bullough and James Brundage (Buffalo, 1982), 22–33, 231–35, with Elliott, *Spiritual Marriage,* 13, 98–99; Horst Fuhrmann, *Germany in the High Middle Ages c. 1050–1200,* trans. Timothy Reuter (New York, 1986), 97–98; and Gerd Tellenbach, *The Church in Western Europe from the Tenth to the Early Twelfth Century,* trans. Timothy Reuter (New York, 1993), 80, 161–67, 175, 188, 193–94, 197–98, 208, 213, 220, 249, 335–36. Karen Louise Jolly, *Popular Religion in Late Saxon England: Elf Charms in Context* (Chapel Hill, N.C., 1996), 64–65, treats England.

49. Michael Frassetto, "Reaction and Reform: Reception of Heresy in Arras and Aquitaine in the Early Eleventh Century," *CHR* 83 (1997): 385–400 at 394.

50. Vauchez, *Spirituality,* 36, 53–54, 105; Georges Duby, *The Knight, the Lady and the Priest: The Making of Modern Marriage in Medieval France,* trans. Barbara Bray (New York, 1983), 57–74; and the following note. For orientation to Burchard, see my "Reference to the 'Ecclesia Primitiva' in the *Decretum* of Burchard of Worms," *Proceedings of the Sixth International Congress of Medieval Canon Law, School of Law, University of California, Berkeley, July 27–August 2, 1980,* Monumenta Iuris Canonici, series C, subsidia 7 (Vatican City, 1985), 289–307.

51. Trans. Duby, *Three Orders,* 32, and see also 40, 49–50, 59, 89, 165–66, 209, on this and the following. See also Yves Congar, "Les laïcs et l'ecclésiologie des *ordines* chez les théologiens des XIe et XIIe siècles," in *I Laici nella "Societas christiana" dei secoli XI e XII* (Milan, 1968), 83–117 (all the articles in this volume are relevant), and Constable, *Three Studies,* part 3. For clerical marriage in Germany from the late eleventh century, see *Die Traditionen des Kollegiatstifts St. Kastulus in Moosburg,* ed. Klaus Höflinger (Munich, 1994), nos. 27, 45, 100, 176, 181, 206. Innocent III in 1203 expressed a suspicion that the bishop of Norwich might

have knowingly granted benefices to married priests: *Die Register Innocenz' III*, ed. Othmar Hageneder et al. (Vienna, 1995), 6:168–69 (no. 103).

52. Thus Moore, "Family," at 56–57, with Elliott, *Spiritual Marriage*, 98; Amy G. Remensnyder, "Pollution, Purity, and Peace: An Aspect of Social Reform between the Late Tenth Century and 1076," in *The Peace of God: Social Violence and Religious Response in France around the Year 1000*, ed. Thomas Head and Richard Landes (Ithaca, N.Y., 1992), 280–307.

53. Duby, *Three Orders*, 208–12; Fuhrmann, *Germany*, 45–46, 71, for the un-believable figure for Constance; Elliott, *Spiritual Marriage*, 13–14, 86–91; Mark F. Williams, trans., *Aelred of Rievaulx's "Spiritual Friendship"* (Scranton, Pa., 1994), 9–10; and Bernhard Schimmelpfennig, *The Papacy*, trans. James Sievert (New York, 1992), 184–85, noting that in late thirteenth-century Scandinavia 10 percent of the clergy were priests' or celibates' sons, and that Innocent IV gave seven dispensations to priests' sons to be consecrated as bishops. For Innocent III's attempt to separate canons and clergy of the cathedral and province of Lund from their concubines, see *Register Innocenz' III*, vol. 6, ed. Hageneder et al., 333 (no. 196).

54. "Disce personae vitium esse, non sexus. Sexus enim sanctus est," and "Omnes laici et clerici, quicunque sunt filii ecclesiae, sacerdotes sunt," cited in Cesare Alzati, *Ambrosiana Ecclesia: Studi su la chiesa milanese e l'ecumene cristiana fra tarda antichità e medioevo* (Milan, 1993), 231 and 243; 189–96, 202–47 treat the entire early Middle Ages. For the limitations of Anne L. Barstow, *Married Priests and the Reforming Papacy: The Eleventh-Century Debates* (New York and Toronto, 1982), see my review in *The American Historical Review* 88 (1983): 660–61, and that of R. Schieffer in *Deutsches Archiv* 40 (1984): 688–89. See also Ernst Werner, "Pataria und virginitas," in *Religion und Gesellschaft im Mittelalter*, foreword Cinzio Violante, ed. Silio P. P. Scalfati (Spoleto, 1995), 139–50.

55. Trans. Duby, *Three Orders*, 89, and see Constable, *Three Studies*, part 3, and Fichtenau, *Living in the Tenth Century*, 1–77.

56. Duby, *Three Orders*, 178.

57. Ibid., 90–91, 95, 97–98; with Carl Erdmann, *The Origin of the Idea of Crusade*, trans. Marshall W. Baldwin and Walter Goffart (Princeton, N.J., 1977), 87–89, 142; Joseph-Claude Poulin, *L'idéal de sainteté dans l'Aquitaine carolingienne d'après les sources hagiographiques, 750–950* (Quebec City, 1975), 81–98, 127–28; S. Airlie, "The Anxiety of Sanctity: St. Gerald of Aurillac and his Maker," *Journal of Ecclesiastical History (hereafter JEH)* 43 (1992): 372–95; Leyser, *Communications*, 199; and Marcus Bull, *Knightly Piety and the Lay Response to the First Crusade: The Limousin and Gascony c. 970–c. 1130* (Oxford, 1993). Thomas F. X. Noble and Thomas Head, eds., *Soldiers of Christ: Saints and Saints' Lives from Late Antiquity and the Early Middle Ages* (University Park, Pa., 1995), give a translation of Odo's *Life*.

58. Duby, *Three Orders*, 89–90, and Duby, *France*, 8, 80–83.

59. *Spiritual Friendship*, I, 65, trans. Williams, 40–41.

60. Philip L. Reynolds, *Marriage in the Western Church: The Christianization of Marriage during the Patristic and Early Medieval Periods* (Leiden, 1994), 328–61, treats Germanic views of what constitutes marriage.

61. See Rouche, *Clovis*, 237; Bernard F. Reilly, *The Medieval Spains* (Cambridge, 1993), 35, 46; Jean Gaudemet, "Le lien matrimonial: les incertitudes du haut Moyen Âge," in *Le lien matrimonial*, ed. René Metz and Jean Schlick (Strasbourg, 1970), 81–105, at 90–91, for Benedictus Levita (the other conditions for a legitimate marriage are dowry, a priest's blessing "according to the custom," and the leading of the maid by groomsmen to her solemn reception at the groom's house. The priest's bless-

ing here seems to be of the bride, and it was common to the end of our period thus to refer to marriage ceremonies); Régine Le Jan, *Famille et pouvoir dans le monde franc (VIIe–Xe siècle)*: *Essai d'anthropologie sociale* (Paris, 1995), specifically 263–71, on *Muntehe;* and nn. 69, 74–76 below.

62. Le Jan, *Famille,* 429–34; Robert Jacob, *Les époux, le seigneur et la cité: Coutume et pratiques matrimoniales des bourgeois et paysans de France du nord au moyen âge* (Bruxelles, 1990); Alexander C. Murray, *Germanic Kinship Structure: Studies in Law and Society in Antiquity and the Early Middle Ages* (Toronto, 1983); and Steven A. Epstein, "The Medieval Family: A Place of Refuge and Sorrow," *Portraits of Medieval and Renaissance Living: Essays in Memory of David Herlihy,* ed. Samuel K. Cohn Jr. and Steven A. Epstein (Ann Arbor, Mich., 1996), 149–71 at 149–50. Jean-Marie Martin, *La Pouille du VIe au XIIe siècle* (Rome, 1993), 172, describes southern Italian slaves as married and living in conjugal families, and see 532–62 on marriage in southern Italy, and index under "mariage."

63. This idea arguably reappeared in many forms in the Middle Ages. Joaquín Yarza Luaces, *Formas artísticas de lo imaginario* (Barcelona, 1987), 232, cites a law of Sepúlveda treated by Heath Dillard, "Women in Reconquest Castille: The Fuero of Sepúlveda and Cuenca," *Women in Medieval Society,* ed. Susan Mosher Stuard (Philadelphia, 1976), 71–94, which punishes a man who grabs a woman's breast or vulva twice as much if she is married, that is, is "a man's," than if she is single.

64. In addition to the following note, see Evans Grubbs, *Law,* 183–93; Antti Arjava, *Women and Law in Late Antiquity* (Oxford, 1996), 37–41; Angeliki E. Laiou, ed., *Consent and Coercion to Sex and Marriage in Ancient and Medieval Societies* (Washington, D.C., 1993), esp. part 3; Rebecca Colman, "Abduction of Women in Barbaric Law," *Florilegium* 5 (1983): 62–75; Boswell, *Same-Sex Unions,* 34–35, 45–46, 92–94, 170; Devisse, *Hincmar,* 1:372; James A. Brundage, "Rape and Marriage in the Medieval Canon Law," in *Sex, Law and Marriage,* and *Law, Sex, and Society,* 188–89, with Elliott, *Spiritual Marriage,* 97 n. 10. Van't Spijker, "Family Ties," and Nip, "Godelieve of Gistel," 183, 201–2, see the Church's promotion of consent and indissolubility as working in the interest of women.

65. In addition to the last note and Jaski, "Marriage Laws," 26, see James A. Brundage, "The Paradox of Sexual Equality in the Early Middle Ages," in *Shifting Frontiers in Late Antiquity,* ed. Ralph M. Mathisen and Hagith S. Sivan (Brookfield, Vt., 1996), 256–64; and on Elvira, Judith Evans Grubbs, " 'Pagan and Christian' Marriage: The State of the Question," *JECS* 2 (1994): 361–412 at 399–402. Ricardo Córdoba de la Llave, "Criminalidad sexual en la Edad Media: Fuentes, estudios y perspectivas," *Historia a debate: Medieval,* ed. Carlos Barros (Santiago de Compostela, 1995), 49–61, treats rape as well as adultery. He reads the Church as increasingly tolerating the civil law idea that the "problem" caused by rape is to be solved, if possible, by a consenting marriage between violator and violated (52–57).

66. *Ravishing Maidens: Writing Rape in Medieval French Literature and Law* (Philadelphia, 1991), surveys the entire Middle Ages.

67. Giordano, *Religiosidad popular,* 60.

68. Jolly, *Popular Religion,* 42–45.

69. In addition to the preceding and following notes, see Devisse, *Hincmar,* 1:396–403; Gaudemet, *Le lien matrimonial,* ed. Metz and Schlick, 90–91; and Boswell, *Same-Sex Unions,* 174–75. *Pace* Duby, *Knight,* 32–35, at 34, Hincmar discusses consent, understood familially. The views Duby expressed in this book and his earlier *Medieval Marriage: Two Models from Twelfth-Century France,* trans. Elborg Forster (Baltimore, 1978) are largely repeated in his *Love and Marriage in the Middle Ages,* trans. Jane Dunnett (Chicago, 1994), and in *History Continues,* trans.

Arthur Goldhammer, foreword and notes by John W. Baldwin (Chicago, 1994), 35–39, 120–26. See the review by Michael Sheehan, *CHR* 66 (1980): 647–49. On intentionality see Flint, *Rise of Magic,* as at 301–2 (and see 293 n. 111), and my "One Heart," and "Christian Perfection and *transitus ad monasterium* in Lupus of Ferrières' Letter 29," *Proceedings of the Eighth International Congress of Medieval Canon Law, University of California, San Diego, August 20–27, 1988,* Monumenta Iuris Canonici, series C, subsidia 9 (Vatican City, 1991), 355–68.

70. Duby, *Three Orders,* 370 n. 11, with 16, 18, 78.

71. Jean Gaudemet, *La doctrine canonique médiévale* (Brookfield, Vt., 1994), 16:75–76, on this and the following.

72. Trans. Mark Searle and Kenneth W. Stevenson, *Documents of the Marriage Liturgy* (Collegeville, Minn., 1992), 48 (this collection is not always well informed), ed. Jean Deshusses, *Le Sacramentaire Grégorien, ses principales formes d'après les plus anciens manuscrits,* vol. 1 (Fribourg, 1971), "ORAT. AD SPONSAS VELANDAS," p. 310: "deus qui tam excellenti mysterio coniugalem copulam consecrasti, ut christi ecclesiae sacramentum praesignares in foedere nuptiarum." The preface of this prayer, p. 309, also speaks of "foedere nuptiarum blando concordiae iugo et insolubili pacis uinculo nexuisti." *Coniugalem copulam* should be understood as capable of bearing the meaning "conjugal union" as well as "bond of marriage" to understand the derivation of Hincmar's views. By the time of Cassiodorus (*Var.* 7.40.2), *copula* could mean copulation as well as the matrimonial bond.

73. See the following note. Joseph Decreaux, *Le sacramentaire de Marmoutier* (*Autun 19 bis*) *dans l'histoire des sacramentaires carolingiens du IXe siècle,* 2 vols. (Città del Vaticano, 1985), 2:443–46, gives a "Prayer for Blessing Brides" which speaks of marriage as indissoluble and as a bond of love (*dilectionis*) and peace, and associates *sacramentum* with both *coniugalem copulam* and *foedus nuptiarum* with the same prayer quoted in n. 72 above. The early eleventh-century Mass for Blessing Brides of the *The Missal of Robert of Jumièges,* ed. H. A. Wilson (1896; rpt. Woodbridge, Suffolk, 1994), 269–70, is almost identical. On this work see Kenneth Stevenson, *Nuptial Blessing: A Study of Christian Marriage Rites* (New York, 1983), 65–67. As noted below n. 110, the *Sacramentarium Fuldense Saeculi X,* ed. Gregor Richter and Albert Schönfelder, Henry Bradshaw Society, 101 (Fulda, 1912; rpt. Farnborough, Hampshire, n.d.), 323–27, uses similar language. Richard W. Pfaff, ed., *The Liturgical Books of Anglo-Saxon England* (Kalamazoo, Mich., 1995), 103, lists other missals in which similar prayers appear.

74. Boswell, *Same-Sex Unions,* 124, 166; Elliott, *Spiritual Marriage,* 78, 82–83; Gaudemet, "Lien matrimonial," with Michael M. Sheehan, "*Maritalis affectio* Revisited," in *The Olde Daunce: Love, Friendship, Sex, and Marriage in the Medieval World,* ed. Robert R. Edwards and Stephen Spector (Albany, N.Y., 1971), 32–43, 254–60 (notes) at 33; and Brundage, *Law, Sex, and Christian Society,* 136–37. For the history of consent into the early twelfth century, see John Noonan, "Power to Choose," *Viator* 4 (1974): 419–34. For the influence of Latin ideas in Byzantium, see Angeliki E. Laiou, "Consensus facit nuptias — et non: Pope Nicholas I's *Responsa* to the Bulgarians as a Source for Byzantine Marriage Customs," in *Gender, Society and Economic Life in Byzantium* (Brookfield, Vt., 1992), 4.

75. In addition to the following notes, see Devisse, *Hincmar,* 1:396–403; Jaski, "Marriage Laws," at 27–29; Vogel *En rémission,* II, 21; and Penny S. Gold, "The Marriage of Mary and Joseph in the Twelfth-Century Ideology of Marriage," in *Sexual Practices,* ed. Bullough and Brundage, 110–17, 249–51.

76. Evans Grubbs, " 'Pagan' and 'Christian' Marriage," 404; Jaski, "Marriage Laws," 29–30; Brent Shaw and Richard Saller, "Close-Kin Marriage in Roman So-

ciety?" *Man: The Journal of the Royal Anthropological Institute,* n. s. 19 (1984): 432–44 at 433; Bitel, *Land of Women,* 60–61; Wemple, *Women,* 2, 76–77, 79, 143; Fichtenau, *Living in the Tenth Century,* 94–96; and Michael M. Sheehan, *Marriage, Family, and Law in Medieval Europe: Collected Studies,* ed. James K. Farge, intro. Joel T. Rosenthal (Toronto, 1996), 253–56. Martin Aurell, *Les Noces du Comte: Mariage et pouvoir en Catalogne (785–1213)* (Paris, 1995), as at 41, 46–48, and the entries "computation" and "inceste" of his Glossary, is very clear on computation of degrees of relationship. Le Jan, *Famille,* 305–27, considers the question of the endogamous and exogamous features of Carolingian society, and see below nn. 82ff.

77. Jaski, "Marriage Laws," 34, and 35–41, on Irish polygyny; Le Jan, *Famille,* 274–77. On early Irish family and marriage customs, Nerys Thomas Patterson, *Cattle-Lords and Clansmen: The Social Structure of Early Ireland,* 2d ed. (Notre Dame, Ind., 1994), esp. chap. 11, should be read with the review of Lisa M. Bitel, *Speculum* 71 (1996): 188–90.

78. Trans. Janet L. Nelson, "Parents, Children, and the Church in the Earlier Middle Ages," in *The Church and Childhood,* ed. Diana Wood (Oxford, 1994), 81–114 at 98; and see Janet L. Nelson, *The Frankish World, 750–900* (London, 1996), 232–42. In addition to the preceding and following notes, see Anjubault Simons, *Force,* 75–76, 82, and Pierre Riché, "Columbanus, His Followers and the Merovingian Church," in *Education et culture dans l'Occident médiéval* (London, 1993), II.

79. Flint, *Rise of Magic* (see 7 n. 3 on the attempt to rationalize or secularize a pagan sacral category), with Conrad Leyser, "Arts and Rites," *Religious Studies Review* 20, no. 3 (July 1994): 202–4; Frederick S. Paxton, *Christianizing Death: The Creation of a Ritual Process in Early Medieval Europe* (Ithaca, N.Y., 1990); Patrick J. Geary, *Before France and Germany: The Creation and Transformation of the Merovingian World* (Oxford, 1988); and Richard E. Sullivan, *Christian Missionary Activity in the Early Middle Ages* (London, 1994). I consider the simultaneous process of secularization and sacralization present in all societies in "Cultural Dynamics: Secularization and Sacralization," *Christianity and Western Civilization* (San Francisco, 1995), 97–122.

80. "Discussione," in *Matrimonio,* 1:317–18 (Vogel's important contribution to these volumes is "Les rites de la célébration du mariage: Leur signification dans la formation du lien durant le haut Moyen Âge," 397–465), with Boswell, *Same-Sex Unions,* 108. For Theodulf see Angel del Olmo García and Basilio Varas Verano, *Románico erótico en Cantabria* (Palencia, 1988), 180, and J. M. Wallace-Hadrill, *The Frankish Church* (Oxford, 1983), 195, 217–25, 279.

81. Siegmund Hellman, "Die Heiraten der Karolinger," in *Ausgewählte Abhandlungen zur Historiographie und Geistesgeschichte des Mittelalters,* ed. Helmut Beumann (Weimar, 1961), 293–391; Egon Boshof, *Ludwig der Fromme* (Darmstadt, 1996).

82. Jean Gaudemet, " 'Separare': équivoque des mots et faiblesse du droit (IIe–XIIIe siècles)," in *Droit de l'église et vie sociale au moyen âge* (Aldershot, 1989); Sheehan, *Marriage, Family,* 253–56; and Jean Chélini, "Les laïcs dans la société ecclésiastique carolingienne," in *Laici,* 23–50 at 45–46. *Register Innocenz' III,* vol. 6, ed. Hageneder et al., 125–27 (no. 80), gives an example from 1203 of a royal marriage which was incestuous even by the restriction of relationship to the fourth degree the Fourth Lateran Council was to promulgate in 1215.

83. Duby, *France,* xii; and see *Three Orders,* viii, 13–16, 51, 58, 108, 165–66, 209, and *History Continues,* 120–26. For the tenth century see Fichtenau, *Living in the Tenth Century,* 81–132.

204 *Glenn W. Olsen*

84. Philippe Buc, *L'Ambiguïté du livre: prince, pouvoir, et peuple dans les commentaires de la Bible au Moyen Âge* (Paris, 1994), 314 n. 7; Duby, *Knight*, 3–21, and *France*, 105, 108–9, 114.
85. This is one of the themes for the eleventh century of Duby, *Knight*.
86. Duby, *Love and Marriage*, 7; Wendy Davies, "Celtic Women in the Early Middle Ages," in *Images of Women in Antiquity*, ed. Averil Cameron and Amélie Kuhrt, rev. ed. (Detroit, 1993), 145–66; Jaski, "Marriage Laws," 17–18.
87. Trans. Maccioni, " 'It Is Allowed,' " 116.
88. Trans. Helen M. Jewell, *Women in Medieval England* (Manchester, 1996), 28, and see index under "marriage."
89. Kelly, *Love*, 164–65; Stevenson, *Nuptial Blessing*.
90. Halsall, *Settlement*, 278–82, says sensible things about the limitations of both those who see 1000 marking a radical break from a relatively static earlier Middle Ages, and of "gradualists," those who see only slow evolution throughout our period.
91. Robert R. Edwards and Stephen Spector, "Introduction" to *Olde Daunce*, ed. Edwards and Spector, 3, and 6; Kelly, *Love*, who throughout gives a sense of the distance between the ideas about marriage of the canonists and theologians and actual practice.
92. Duby, *France*, xii, xiv–xv (where Duby, not wholly convincingly but in a fashion found in many of his books, contrasts the paternal familial model of married society with the egalitarian familial model of the groups at the margins of married society, brigand, shepherd, heretic, or monk), 88–89, and *Love and Marriage*, 6–7. Bull, *Knightly Piety*, convincingly argues for the great influence of the eleventh-century Church on lay society, but see the just criticisms of this book in a review by Richard Landes, *Speculum* 71 (1996): 135–38.
93. In a review of Dominique Barthélemy, *La société dans le comté de Vendôme: De l'an mil au XIV siècle* (Paris, 1993), Stephen D. White provides a useful guide to the controversy: *Speculum* 71 (1996): 116–20; and Le Jan, *Famille*, surveys the historiography in her Introduction and 331ff. Claude Duhamel-Amado and Guy Lobrichon, eds., *Georges Duby: L'écriture de l'Histoire*, preface by Jean Lacouture (Brussels, 1996), has a number of relevant articles, as does *Femmes, mariages — Lignages, XIIe–XIVe siècles: Mélanges offerts à Georges Duby*, ed. Jean Dufournet et al. (Brussels, 1992). Nip, "Godelieve of Gistel," 197, 206, criticizes Duby's analysis of good and bad eleventh-century marriages in *Knight*, 130–38. Kimberly A. Lo Prete's review in *Speculum* 70 (1995): 605–7 of Duby's *Love and Marriage* is a good guide to the flaws which mar all Duby's very influential books. See also the review by Edward Collins Vacek in *Theological Studies* 55 (1994): 786.
94. Halsall, *Settlement*, as at pp. 65, 67–68, shows that the equal partibility of early Frankish law was of movable goods, that landed property was not divided equally, and that women could inherit.
95. George Beech, "Prosopography," in *Mediaeval Studies: An Introduction*, ed. James M. Powell, 2d ed. (Syracuse, N.Y., 1992), 185–226, esp. 204; Karl Schmid, "The Structure of the Nobility in the Earlier Middle Ages," in *The Medieval Nobility: Studies on the Ruling Classes of France and Germany from the Sixth to the Twelfth Century*, ed. and trans. Timothy Reuter (Amsterdam, 1979), 37–59 (see also the article by Karl Hauck); Karl J. Leyser, *Medieval Germany and Its Neighbours, 800–1250* (London, 1982), 161–89; Moore, "Heresy," in *Christendom*, ed. Waugh and Diehl, 19–46, at 28–36, in which see also James Given, "Social Stress, Social Strain, and the Inquisitors of Medieval Languedoc," 67–85 at 72–73, on the persistence of patrilineal and matrilineal principles; Le Jan, *Famille*, which excellently treats the

Carolingian background; and Christine Meek, "Women, Dowries and the Family in Late Medieval Italian Cities," *"The Fragility of Her Sex"?* ed. Meek and Simms, 136–52.

96. Duby, *Love and Marriage*, 105–9, *France*, 60, 62–63, 67–69, 74–75, and *Medieval Marriage*, on courtly love.

97. Beech, "Prosopography," 204–5, referring to the studies in *Matrimonio*.

98. Aurell, *Noces:* the historical sketch in the following paragraphs rests on esp. 12–18, 35, 49–50, 52–53, 64–70, 73–74, 78, 80–81, 110, 128. This book is illustrated with a miniature from the *Libro de Feudos* of Alfonso II of Aragón (and see pp. 317, Figure 24, and 273, Figure 19).

99. In addition to nn. 72–73 above, see Marcel Metzger, *Les sacramentaires*, Typologie des Sources du Moyen Âge Occidentale 70 (Turnhout, 1994). Reynolds, *Marriage*, 315–419, gives a detailed exposition of "The Nuptial Process."

100. Stevenson, *Nuptial Blessing*, 51; Cyrille Vogel, *Medieval Liturgy: An Introduction to the Sources*, rev. and trans. by William G. Storey and Neils Krogh Rasmussen (Washington, D.C., 1986), esp. 190.

101. Cyrille Vogel, "La réforme liturgique sous Charlemagne," in *Karl der Grosse Lebenswerk und Nachleben*, 5 vols. (Düsseldorf, 1965–68), vol. 2: *Das geistige Leben*, 3d ed., 1967, ed. Bernhard Bischoff, 217–32, and Vogel, "Les échanges liturgiques entre Rome et les pays francs jusqu'à l'époque de Charlemagne," *Le chiese nei regni dell'Europa occidentale e i loro rapporti con Roma sino all'800*, 2 vols., Settimane di Studio del Centro Italiano di Studi sull'Alto Medioevo 7 (Spoleto, 1960), 1:185–295; Boswell, *Same-Sex Unions*, chap. 6, esp. 162–68, 289–90.

102. Devisse, *Hincmar*, 1:396–403; P. D. King, *Law and Society in the Visigothic Kingdom* (New York, 1972), 224–53; Elliott, *Spiritual Marriage*, 66–68, 77–82, 126–27; Halsall, *Settlement*, 62–66; Boswell, *Same-Sex Unions*, 164, 169–70; and Katherine Fischer Drew, *Law and Society in Early Medieval Europe: Studies in Legal History* (Aldershot, Hampshire, 1988), containing several studies of barbarian family law.

103. Stevenson, *Nuptial Blessing*, 29. Le Jan, *Famille*, chap. 8, is fundamental.

104. Aurell, *Noces*, 113–62, and the following note.

105. In addition to the following notes, see Reynolds, *Marriage*, index under "Germanic Law: dotation and dotal documents," and Jaski, "Marriage Laws," 22–27, 34, who is better informed than some of the contributors to *The New Cambridge Medieval History*, vol. 2, *c. 700–c. 800*, ed. Rosamond McKitterick (Cambridge, 1995), 383–430 at 422; 451–80 at 465–69; and 654–78 at 667 and 670.

106. For Norman, Danish, and English law, see Frederick Pollock and Frederic William Maitland, *The History of English Law before the Time of Edward I*, 2d ed. S. F. C. Milson, 2 vols. (Cambridge, 1968), 2:15–16, 292, 415, 420 n. 1.

107. In addition to the preceding notes, see Wemple, *Frankish Women*, 209 n. 44, and index under *"Friedelehe"* and the misleading term "Trial marriage." I am following Rouche, *Clovis*, 237–38, and Le Jan, *Famille*, 263–74.

108. In addition to n. 76 above, see Devisse, *Hincmar*, 1:380–83; Gaudemet, "Lien matrimonial," 88–95; Paul Mikat, *Die Inzestgesetzgebung der merowingisch-fränkischen Konzilien (511–626/27)* (Paderborn, 1994), and "Zu den merowingisch-fränkischen Bedingungen der Inzestgesetzgebung," *Vom mittelalterlichen Recht zur neuzeitlichen Rechtswissenschaft: Bedingungen, Wege und Probleme der europäischen Rechtsgeschichte*, ed. Norbert Brieskorn et al. (Paderborn, 1994), 3–30, with, in the same volume, Hans Hattenhauer, *"Observantia Christianitatis*. St. Dunstan und das Eherecht," 31–57; David Herlihy, "Making Sense of Incest: Women and the Marriage Rules of the Early Middle Ages," in *Women, Family and Society in*

Medieval Europe: Historical Essays, 1978–1991, ed. A. Molho (Providence, R.I., 1995), 96–109; Halsall, *Settlement,* 60–61, 254–56; Chélini, "Laïcs," 45.

109. Boswell, *Same-Sex Unions,* 13–14, 180, 185, 203, 206–9, 211, 214, with Chiara Frugoni, "L'iconografia del matrimonio e della coppia nel medioevo," in *Matrimonio,* 2:901–66, esp. 966; Stevenson, *Nuptial Blessing,* 44–45, 53–54; Raymund Kottje, "Kirchliches Recht und päpstlicher Autoritätsanspruch: Zu den Auseinandersetzungen über die Ehe Lothars II," in *Aus Kirche und Reich: Studien zu Theologie, Politik und Recht im Mittelalter: Festschrift für Friedrich Kempf,* ed. Hubert Mordek (Sigmaringen, 1983), 97–103; Sheehan, *Marriage, Family,* 278–91. For the liturgy of marriage, see above nn. 72–73, 99–101, and below nn. 110, 116, 121; Elliott, *Spiritual Marriage,* 57, 78; Vogel, "Rites"; and Sheehan, *"Maritalis Affectio,"* 41. For the use of two rings in Spain, see Heath Dillard, *Daughters of the Reconquest: Women in Castilian Society, 1100–1300* (Cambridge, 1984), 36–67 at 46–47, 59–63, 125, and Bethune, *Rite,* 31–35.

110. *Sacramentarium Fuldense,* ed. Richter and Schönfelder, 323–27. Stevenson, *Nuptial Blessing,* 35–58, 63–68, 91–94, gives a good idea of the language of mutual love which fills the Church's liturgical books: the Leonine sacramentary taught that marriage is not simply for children, but for "the exercise of fidelity, love, mutual support, and...*pudor* [modesty]" (37), and the *Liber ordinum* requested love, mutual support, and love and friendship for others (48–53). For further translations see Searle and Stevenson, eds., *Marriage Liturgy,* 40–147. The sentiments of the short sermons on marriage found in Castilian endowment charters from the ninth century complement the theology of the liturgy: Dillard, *Daughters,* 48.

111. Moore, "Heresy," 38.

112. Brooke, *Marriage,* 248–57; Santiago Sebastián, *Mensaje simbólico del arte medieval: Arquitectura, liturgia, e iconografía* (Madrid, 1994), 299–300.

113. Trans. Emilie Amt, ed., *Women's Lives in Medieval Europe: A Sourcebook* (New York, 1993), 83–89 at 83–84. R. W. Southern, *Scholastic Humanism and the Unification of Europe,* vol. 1: *Foundations* (Oxford, 1995), 147–52, notes the great uncertainty regarding marriage law in England following the Norman Conquest of 1066.

114. Michel Parisse, *Noblesse et chevalerie en Lorraine médiévale: Les familles nobles du XIe au XIIIe siècle* (Nancy, 1982), 193–234; Boswell, *Same-Sex Unions,* 212, 306–11 (trans. of a French twelfth-century ceremony); Pollock and Maitland, *History of English Law,* vol. 2, chap. 7 at 423; Searle and Stevenson, eds., *Marriage Liturgy,* 2, 5–8.

115. Henry Ansgar Kelly, "Joan of Arc's Last Trial: The Attack of the Devil's Advocates," in *Fresh Verdicts on Joan of Arc,* ed. Bonnie Wheeler and Charles T. Wood (New York, 1996), 205–35 at 205 and 228–29. *Register Innocenz' III,* vol. 6, 203–5, 290–91 (nos. 119, 175), describe two interesting cases from 1203 involving many of the problems listed here.

116. In addition to the following notes, see Larrington, *Women,* 10; Dillard, *Daughters,* 57; and A. J. Finch, "Sexual Relations and Marriage in Later Medieval Normandy," *JEH* 47 (1996): 236–56, esp. 254–56. Finch, p. 248, questionably, defines a stable relationship as one which lasts at least a year. Bethune, *Christian Rite of Marriage,* throughout compares the rites.

117. In addition to the last chapter, see Louis Reekmans, "La 'dextrarum junctio' dans l'iconographie romaine et paléochretienne," *Bulletin de l'Institut Historique Belge de Rome* 31 (1958): 24–95; Edwin Hall, *The Arnolfini Betrothal: Medieval Marriage and the Enigma of Van Eyck's Double Portrait* (Berkeley, Calif., 1994), figures 3 (fourteenth century), 9–10, and 14; and plate 4; and Marty Newman Williams

and Anne Echols, *Between Pit and Pedestal: Women in the Middle Ages* (Princeton, N.J., 1994), 64.

118. Sandra Shaul, "The Joey and Toby Tannenbaum Gallery of Byzantine Art," *Rotunda, the Magazine of the Royal Ontario Museum* 30/1 (Summer 1997): 28–33 at 33, pictures various wedding rings, one with a couple with a cross between them and OMONOIA ("concord") written below; and another with the head of Christ above a cross between the busts of the two spouses.

119. Ann Eljenholm Nichols, *Seeable Signs: The Iconography of the Seven Sacraments, 1350–1544* (Woodbridge, Suffolk, 1994), has many plates and a separate section on matrimony and its iconography, 274–86. The marriage of Christ to Church is frequently depicted: for introduction see Ernst Kantorowicz, "On the Golden Marriage Belt and the Marriage Rings of the Dumbarton Oaks Collection," *Dumbarton Oaks Papers* 14 (1960): 3–17.

120. MS Bodl. 264 fol. 105v, Figure 1 in Larrington, *Women*, 11.

121. Eric Palazzo, *Les sacramentaires de Fulda: Étude sur l'iconographie et la liturgie à l'époque ottonienne* (Münster, 1994), 45–48, 183–92, 206–10, with plates 4, 32 and 107; Bernard Botte, *Les Origines de la Noël et de l'Épiphanie* (Louvain, 1932), 13, 16, 34–37, 41–45, 48–49, with Flint, *Rise of Magic,* 366; Diane Apostolos-Cappadona, *Dictionary of Christian Art* (New York, 1994), 60, 228–29; and below n. 168.

122. Corbet, "Mariage," in *La Femme au Moyen-Âge,* ed. Michel Rouche and Jean Heuclin (Paris, 1990), 189 n. 10.

123. MS M. 492, fol. 83v, C. R. Dodwell, *The Pictorial Arts of the West 800–1200* (New Haven, Conn., 1993), 150, 171, 238.

124. Meyer Schapiro, *The Romanesque Sculpture of Moissac* (New York, 1985), 2 and 72–75 on dating, 23–56 on the cloister capitals (24, 26, 32, 37–38, 50–51, and 54 on the Cana capital), with figures 7, 30, and 52. See Gertrud Schiller, *Iconography of Christian Art,* trans. Janet Seligman, 2 vols. (Greenwich, Conn., 1971), index under "Marriage in Cana."

125. Edward G. Tasker, *Encyclopedia of Medieval Church Art* (London, 1993), 50–51.

126. Bradley Smith, *Spain: A History of Art* (New York, 1966), 71; Boswell, *Same-Sex Unions,* 9, 200, 203, 210–14, 217, and figures 14–15; and Vogel, "Rites," 457.

127. Smith, *Spain,* 71 and 290; Aurell, *Noces,* 316–19, 347, 477; and above n. 98. In addition to Yarza Luaces, *Formas,* 234–44, see throughout Justo Pérez de Urbel, *Historia del Condado de Castilla,* 3 vols. (Madrid, 1945), for Spanish royal couples.

128. Brundage, *Law, Sex,* 114–17, 134–37. The present chapter cannot write the history of marriage in the Eastern Churches, but see Korbinian Ritzer, *Formen, Riten und religiöses Brauchtum der Eheschliessung in den christlichen Kirchen des ersten Jahrtausends,* ed. Ulrich Hermann and Willibrord Heckenbach, 2d ed. (Münster, 1962), 70–151, and Angeliki E. Laiou, *Mariage, amour et parenté à Byzance aux XIe–XIIIe siècles* (Paris, 1992).

129. Córdoba de la Llave, "Criminalidad." As with many sins treated in the penitential literature, the gravity of the punishment for adultery varied with social standing, heaviest for bishops and lightest for laity: Raoul Manselli, "Il matrimonio nei Penitenziali," in *Matrimonio,* 1:285–315, and "Vie familiale et ethique sexuelle dans les Penitentiels," *Famille et parenté dans l'Occident Médiéval* (Rome, 1977), 363–78.

130. Noble, "Morbidity," 538–39; Gaudemet, *Droit,* XIII, 12–20; Jo Ann McNamara and Suzanne F. Wemple, "Marriage and Divorce in the Frankish Kingdom," in *Women in Medieval Society,* ed. Mosher Stuard, 95–124.

131. Le Jan, *Famille,* 277–85.

132. See on this and the following, Larrington, *Women*, 9; Jaski, "Marriage Laws," 22 and 30–41 (secular law also said that a man could divorce his wife if she had an abortion or committed infanticide), with the following notes.

133. In addition to the following note, see Stephanie Hollis, *Anglo-Saxon Women and the Church: Sharing a Common Fate* (Woodbridge, Suffolk, 1992), which, while devoting a chapter (2) to the *Penitential*'s treatment of marriage, is full of misleading perspectives and status-measuring.

134. Devisse, *Hincmar*, 1:368, 403ff.; Larrington, *Women*, 8–9; Gaudemet, "Lien matrimonial," 96–105.

135. Trans. Wemple, *Women in Frankish Society*, 8–10 at 9. This passage stands in a tradition of Christian description of the ideal wife which includes Isidore of Seville and Jonas of Orléans, and commonly mentions beauty and intelligence: see Le Jan, *Famille*, 288. Jonas could also warn about the superficiality of giving undue weight to some attributes on such lists. He wrote, "Let those who are married consider carefully that...external beauty and the carnal delight in one's wife are not at all to be preferred to the chaste love of her interior. Therefore, not so much riches and beauty, as rather shame and probity of morals are to be looked for in wives." Trans. Maccioni, " 'It Is allowed,' " 108.

136. In addition to nn. 69–74 above, see Flint, *Rise of Magic*, 64, 155–56, 231–39 (also on magic to prevent conception or cause abortion), 290–99 (misreading Devisse at points); Frances and Joseph Gies, *Marriage and the Family in the Middle Ages* (New York, 1987), 88–94; Janet L. Nelson, *Charles the Bald* (London, 1992), 198–201, 215–18; and McNamara and Wemple, "Marriage and Divorce," 108–13. Hincmar's view of women's weakness implied that they were less morally strong than men.

137. Gaudemet, "Lien matrimonial," 104–5. Leyser, *Communications and Power*, treats Thietmar throughout (see index), but see here 58.

138. Fuhrmann, *Germany*, 82; Aurell, *Noces*, 58, on "Danish conubinage"; and Karl Leyser, *Rule and Conflict in an Early Medieval Society: Ottonian Society* (Oxford, 1989), 49–62, and *Communications*, 197.

139. *L'Aube du moyen âge*, 206–17, 221–40.

140. Duby, *Three Orders*, 76.

141. Buc, *L'Ambiguïté*, 334 n. 62; Jean Gaudemet, "L'apport d'Augustin à la doctrine médiévale du mariage," in *Droit*.

142. Trans. Maccioni, " 'It Is Allowed,' " 99.

143. Toubert, "Théorie," as at 258–62; Le Jan, *Famille*, 344–51; Buc, *L'Ambiguïté*, 103–6.

144. Leyser, *Communications*, 101, 128–29; Halsall, *Settlement*, 72, 254–57; David Herlihy, *Medieval Households* (Cambridge, Mass., 1985), as at 73–78, 103–11.

145. Le Jan, *Famille*, esp. 333–79, arguing, 339, for simple conjugal family units at the level of the peasantry and more complexity at the level of the aristocracy.

146. Jaski, "Marriage Laws," 20, 23, for the phrases quoted, and see 28.

147. Trans. Maccioni, " 'It Is Allowed,' " 117–22 at 119; Duby, *France*, x–xiii, 38.

148. Jenny Jochens, *Women in Old Norse Society* (Ithaca, N.Y., 1996), esp. chap. 2, with the review of Ruth Mazo Karras in *Speculum* 72 (1997): 495–97, and Jochens, "Old Norse Motherhood," in *Medieval Mothering*, ed. John Carmi Parsons and Bonnie Wheeler (New York, 1996), 201–22; *Old Norse Images of Women* (Philadelphia, 1996); and "Marriage and Divorce," in *Medieval Scandinavia: An Encyclopedia*, ed. Phillip Pulsiano (New York, 1993), 408–10. Stephen N. Tranter, " 'Wed in Haste, Dissent at Leisure': The Marriage Feast as a Structural Component

in Icelandic Feud Narratives," in *Medialität und mittelalterliche insulare Literatur,* ed. Hildegard L. C. Tristram (Tübingen, 1992), 148–69, in spite of difficulties in dating the materials of the sagas, conveys a vivid sense of how far from a Golden Age pre-Christian Iceland was and of the degree to which the forms rather than content of Christianity were appropriated with conversion. See also Judith Jesch, *Women in the Viking Age* (Woodbridge, Suffolk, 1991), index under "marriage"; and above n. 41 for bibliography on the Irish comparison.

149. Mulder-Bakker, "Introduction," and Ton Brandenbarg, "Saint Anne: A Holy Grandmother and Her Children," in *Sanctity and Motherhood,* ed. Mulder-Bakker, 4–11, 31–65 at 39–41; Gilian Clark, "The Fathers and the Children," in *The Church and Childhood,* ed. Wood, 1–27 at 20; and Atkinson, *Oldest Vocation.*

150. Trans. Glenn W. Olsen, "Reference to the *Ecclesia Primitiva* in Eighth Century Irish Gospel Exegesis," *Thought* 54 (1979): 303–12 at 306.

151. C. Stephen Jaeger, *The Envy of Angels: Cathedral Schools and Social Ideals in Medieval Europe, 950–1200* (Philadelphia, 1994), esp. 134–60.

152. Halsall, *Settlement,* 71 n. 25, 256; Fuhrmann, *Germany,* 10–11; Angus McLaren, *A History of Contraception: From Antiquity to the Present Day* (Oxford, 1990), 101–40; Le Jan, *Famille,* 346–47; and Rob Meens, "Children and Confession in the Early Middle Ages," in *Church and Childhood,* ed. Wood, 53–65 at 56–59, with Nelson, "Parents," 92–93. See Brenda Bolton, *Innocent III: Studies on Papal Authority and Pastoral Care* (Brookfield, Vt., 1995), XIX, for the high Middle Ages.

153. Yannick Carré, *Le baiser sur la bouche au Moyen Âge: Rites, symboles, mentalités, à travers les textes et les images, XIe–XVe siècles* (Paris, 1992), 114–26: the love with which Carré concerns herself in this chapter is affectionate bonds between parents and children, and the evidence she gives is quite limited. Rüdiger Schnell, *Causa amoris: Liebeskonzeption und Liebesdarstellung in der mittelalterlichen Literatur* (Bern, 1985), esp. 115–26, treats love in marriage.

154. Flemming G. Andersen and Morten Nøjgaard, eds., *The Making of the Couple: The Social Function of Short-Form Medieval Narrative* (Odense, Denmark, 1991), 9–11, describes and pursues this project, but almost wholly for materials after 1100. Nelson, "Parents," is a convenient guide to the historiographical issues. Pierre J. Payer, *The Bridling of Desire: Views of Sex in the Later Middle Ages* (Toronto, 1993), as in its treatment of "pleasure," 30–34, although on a later period, is relevant.

155. Sheehan, *"Maritalis Affectio,"* in *Olde Daunce,* ed. Edwards and Spector, 37, with 4 of the Introduction to the same book; Finch, "Sexual Relations," 238–39.

156. *The Canterbury Tales,* trans. Nevill Coghill (Harmondsworth, Middlesex, 1960), 358–59.

157. Kelly, *Love,* 29–67 (the quotation is the subtitle of part 1 of Kelly's book); and see M. L. Stapleton, *Harmful Eloquence: Ovid's "Amores" from Antiquity to Shakespeare* (Ann Arbor, Mich.: 1996), 45, 66–69.

158. Fuhrmann, *Germany,* 27.

159. Keith Nickolaus, "Marriage Fictions in *Girart de Roussillon,"* a paper given at the 1996 annual conference of the Medieval Association of the Pacific at the University of San Diego.

160. Nip, "Godelieve of Gistel," 198–99; Vogel, *En rémission,* X, 755–56; and Richard Kieckhefer, "Erotic Magic in Medieval Europe," in Joyce E. Salisbury, ed., *Sex in the Middle Ages: A Book of Essays* (New York, 1991), 30–55.

161. Trans. Nancy G. Siraisi, *Medieval and Early Renaissance Medicine: An In-*

troduction to Knowledge and Practice (Chicago, 1990), 111–13, stressing that such ideas are common in the medical literature from the twelfth century.

162. *Spiritual Friendship*, I, 57–58, trans. Williams, 39, with 109 n. 30. See also III, 77–80, 74–75. Buc, *L'Ambiguïté*, 324, 334, discusses "egalitarian" themes. See Jean Leclercq, "The Development of a Topic in Medieval Studies in the Eighties: An Interdisciplinary Perspective on Love and Marriage," in *Literary and Historical Perspectives of the Middle Ages: Proceedings of the 1981 SEMA Meeting*, ed. Patricia W. Cummins, Patricia W. Conner, and Charles W. Connell (Morgantown, W.Va., 1982), 20–37; *Love in Marriage in Twelfth Century Europe*, University of Tasmania Occasional Papers 13 (Hobart, Tasmania, 1978); "L'amour et le mariage vus par des clercs et des religieux, spécialement au XIIe siècle," in *Love and Marriage in the Twelfth Century*, ed. Willy Van Hoecke and Andries Welkenhuysen (Leuven, 1981), 102–15; and *Monks on Marriage: A Twelfth-Century View* (New York, 1982).

163. *Spiritual Friendship*, II, 24, trans. Williams, 47; with Glenn W. Olsen, "Recovering the Homeland: Acts 4:32 and the *Ecclesia Primitiva* in St. Bernard's Sermons on the Song of Songs," *Word and Spirit* 12 (1990): 92–117.

164. "Reproduction and Production in Early Ireland," in *Portraits of Medieval and Renaissance Living*, ed. Cohn and Epstein, 71–89. Cf. Clancy, "Women Poets," 43–72; Boswell, *Same-Sex Unions*, 109–10; and see Eric Jager, "The Book of the Heart: Reading and Writing the Medieval Subject," *Speculum* 71 (1996): 1–26 at 12.

165. The thirteenth-century story of "The Lovers of Teruel," sculpted into sarcophagi in a chapel in Teruel, presumes that love should lead to marriage: see Conrado Guardiola Alcover, *La verdad actual sobre los Amantes de Teruel* (Teruel, 1988).

166. Trans. Thiébaux, *Writings of Medieval Women*, 135–49 at 147, and see Jan W. Dietrichson, "The Making of the Couple in Old and Middle English Literature," in *Making of the Couple*, ed. Andersen and Nøjgaard, 113–27 at 113–15. Thomas Owen Clancy, "Women Poets in Early Medieval Ireland: Stating the Case," *"The Fragility of Her Sex"?* ed. Meek and Simms, 43–72, makes a case for female authorship of certain anonymous Irish love poems.

167. Elliott, *Spiritual Marriage*, 61, 69–72, for this and the next paragraph; Marie-Hélène Soulet, "L'image de l'amour conjugal et de l'épouse dans l'épigraphie chrétienne lyonnaise aux VIe et VIIe siécles," in *La femme au moyen-âge*, ed. Michel Rouche and Jean Heuclin (Maubeuge, 1990), 139–45 (140–41, describes the Christian appropriation of the classical *lamentatio* on love broken by the physical separation of death); Boswell, *Same-Sex Unions*, 9, 39–40, 172, 202; Flint, *Rise of Magic*, 69–70, 155–56, 220–21, 228, 231–39, 241, for love magic; and n. 160 above.

168. Flint, *Rise of Magic*, 110, 282. Among the sarcophagi at Les Alyscamps in Arles are examples of double sarcophagi with partitions in the middle, for the use of married couples. *Naissance des arts chrétiens* (Paris, 1991), 277, portrays an early fourth-century Arles "couple's" tomb with gestures of affection between husband and wife and toward children and a scene of the Wedding of Cana (next to which is an Adoration of the Magi: see above n. 121). Halsall, *Settlement*, 90–91, treats Merovingian double burials. Peter Dronke, *Women Writers of the Middle Ages: A Critical Study of Texts from Perpetua (†203) to Marguerite Porete (†1310)* (Cambridge, 1984), 21–26, gives further evidence of marital love in the early Middle Ages.

169. I hope to tell the story summarized in this and the next paragraph in a study I am preparing, "On the Death of Emma: Love in Marriage in the Ninth Century." This article will present further evidence for love in marriage. For now see Goetz,

Frauen, 386–88; Erik Kooper, "Loving the Unequal Equal: Medieval Theologians and Marital Affection," in *Olde Daunce,* ed. Edwards and Spector, 44–56, 260–65 (notes), with the Introduction to the same book, 4; and Boswell, *Same-Sex Unions,* 35. On slavery and serfdom, see Halsall, *Settlement,* 41–45, 56–60, 258, 263, 266–67, 270, 274, 277; Martin, *Pouille,* 171–73; Gaudemet, "Lien matrimonial," 95–96, 99–100; and Brundage, *Law, Sex,* 196.

170. Nelson, *Charles the Bald,* 199.

171. Geary, *Phantoms,* 52–70; Boswell, *Same-Sex Unions,* 38. See also on Thietmar, Henri Platelle, "L'epouse: Gardienne aimante de la vie et de l'âme de son mari": quelques exemples du haut Moyen Âge," in *Femme,* ed. Rouche and Heuclin, 171–85 at 171, 173–75, with, 176–79, analysis and reproduction of an eleventh-century miniature portraying the *diligens custodia,* prayer for the soul of a dead husband.

172. Jean Leclercq, "Role et pouvoir des epouses au Moyen Âge," in *Femme,* ed. Rouche and Heuclin, 87–98, gives an overview. I am virtually translating his translation of *Vita S. Rictrudis,* 5–7. See above nn. 18–19, 162.

173. Trans. Corbet, *Saints Ottoniens,* 109, 112, 116, for further materials on conjugal love.

174. Corbet, *Saints Ottoniens,* 30–40, 120–54 at 129–31, for both this and the next paragraph. See 131–32, on Matilda as loving mother, with 164; 133–35, on her subsequent development; 181–91, 204–7, on the hagiographic ideal of marriage (in later telling, the Latin becomes "ibi perfruebantur connubiis et licito foedere amoris"); 191–200, on widowhood; and 258–60. See also Patrick Corbet, "Le mariage en Germanie ottonienne d'après Thietmar de Mersebourg," in *Femme,* ed. Rouche and Heuclin, 187–213; Pauline Stafford, *Queens, Concubines and Dowagers: The King's Wife in the Early Middle Ages* (London, 1983), here 32–34. It was unusual at this time to apply Acts 4:32, describing the life of the first Christians, to any but monks: Olsen, "One Heart."

175. Trans. Peter L. D. Reid, *The Complete Works of Rather of Verona* (Binghamton, N.Y., 1991), 154.

176. Dillard, *Daughters,* 65, 234 n. 91. The benedictions of the eleventh-century Bobbio Missal to which Dillard compares the *Liber ordinum* speak similarly: Ritzer, *Formen,* 353.

177. *Envy of Angels,* 316–17 at 317, for this and the following quotations, and 317–19, on Baudri. Cf. Gerald A. Bond, *The Loving Subject: Desire, Eloquence, and Power in Romanesque France* (Philadelphia, 1995), 42–69.

178. Aurell, *Noces,* 78–97, and see also 132–33 n. 5, 166–68, on conjugal love as a means of preaching and persuasion.

179. Clark, "Fathers and the Children," 2–11. The quotations in this and the next paragraph are taken from *The Poem of the Cid,* trans. Lesley Byrd Simpson (Berkeley, Calif., 1957), 16, 19, 56, 72, 83, 104, 109–11. For an annotated edition see Alberto Montaner, ed., *Cantar de Mio Cid* (Barcelona, 1993), index under "matrimonio," and see Michael Harney, *Kinship and Polity in the Poema de Mio Cid* (West Lafayette, Ind., 1993), 99–150.

180. Harney, *Kinship,* 100–110, and María Luzdivina Cuesta, "Notes on Family Relationships in Medieval Castilian Narrative," in *Medieval Family Roles,* ed. Itnyre, 197–224 at 198–99. Spanish liturgy for second marriages, nowhere evident in the *Cid,* is discussed throughout Bethune, *Christian Rite of Marriage.* Cf. Manuel Santana Molina, *Las segundas nupcias y la reserva de bienes en los furs de Valencia* (Alicante, 1992), for the secular law beginning in the ancient world.

181. Olmo García and Varas Verano, *Románico erótico,* 61 (with 123–24 for dating), 73 (with 125 for dating), and 75.

182. Trans. Guy Halsall in Nelson, "Parents," 91–92 at 91, and see 93–94, for Rictrude's grief on the death of her daughter (see above nn. 18–19), and 106; Richard B. Lyman Jr., "Barbarism and Religion: Late Roman and Early Medieval Childhood," in Lloyd deMause, ed., *The History of Childhood* (New York, 1974), 75–100, esp. 94–95 on Einhard's *Life of Charlemagne,* and in the same volume Mary Martin McLaughlin, "Survivors and Surrogates: Children and Parents from the Ninth to the Thirteenth Centuries," 101–81; and Pierre Riché, "L'enfant dans la société chrétienne aux XIe–XIIe siècles," in *Education et Culture* 15. Angela Giallongo, *Il bambino medievale: Educazione ed infanzia nel medioevo* (Bari, 1990), while somewhat scattershot in presentation and with only relatively few materials from our period, has many useful illustrations beginning in the twelfth century. See especially the tender portrayal of Adam, Eve, Cain, and Abel in a 1186 bas-relief of the Cathedral of Monreale, Figure 9.

183. Olsen, "One Heart." Dhuoda's *Manual* has received a new edition: *Manuel pour mon fils,* ed. Pierre Riché, Bernard de Vregille, and Claude Mondésert, Sources Chrétiennes 225 bis (Paris, 1991).

184. Stevenson, *Nuptial Blessing,* 64–66. Maria Giuseppina Muzzarelli, "Le donne e i bambini nei libri penitenziali: Regole di condotta per una società in formazione," in *Profili di donne: Mito, immagine, realtà fra medioevo ed età contemporanea,* ed. Benedetto Vetere and Paolo Renzi (Lecce, 1986), 143–92 at 180–89, gathers materials on the relations between mothers and children as revealed in the penitential literature, but is not fully in control of her sources.

185. For Foy see *The Book of Sainte Foy,* trans. Pamela Sheingorn (Philadelphia, 1995), and for Vézelay, François Vogade, *Vézelay* (Vézelay, 1992), plate 44, with "Répertoire des photographies." For Ida see above n. 5 and Nip, "Godelieve of Gistel," 210, 214.

186. *The Ties That Bound: Peasant Families in Medieval England* (New York, 1986), esp. viii, 3–15 and part 4, and *Growing up in Medieval London: The Experience of Childhood in History* (New York, 1993), esp. 5–13. Pierre Riché and Danièle Alexandre-Bidon, *L'enfance au Moyen Âge* (Paris, 1994), give an excellent overview with many later medieval illustrations.

187. *Centuries of Childhood: A Social History of Family Life* (New York, 1962). In addition to nn. 152–54, 182, and 186 above, guides to evaluation of this book are given by Lloyd deMause, "The Evolution of Childhood," in *History of Childhood,* ed. deMause, 1–73, esp. 5–6; David Herlihy, "Medieval Children," in his *Women, Family,* 215–43; and Shulamith Shahar, *Childhood in the Middle Ages* (New York, 1990), 1–7.

188. Elliott, *Spiritual Marriage,* 94–113, implausibly reads the Gregorian Reform as generally working to marriage's disadvantage. Michel Grandjean, *Laïcs dans l'Église: Regards de Pierre Damien, Anselme de Cantorbéry, Yves de Chartres,* Théologie Historique 97 (Paris, 1994), is a much more helpful attempt to assess the growing positive evaluation of the lay state. I wish to thank my wife, Suzanne, and my colleague, Isabel Moreira, for many helpful suggestions for the improvement of this and the last chapter.

Chapter Five

MARRIAGE, BODY, AND SACRAMENT IN THE AGE OF HUGH OF ST. VICTOR

Teresa Olsen Pierre

As the Church entered upon the reforms of the eleventh and twelfth centuries, it underwent great self-examination. Many questions were asked about the significance of the Christian life and how the Church could best foster it. A variety of economic and social changes prepared the way for reform.

Especially from the last quarter of the eleventh century onward, life became more peaceful, and the economy began to expand rapidly. The clearing of vast amounts of forest land and the draining of marshes put large amounts of new lands under cultivation. Urban society expanded similarly; the communes of Italy and Flanders emerged as the dominant powers in the new network of international trade made possible through the greater use of money.

Intellectual centers reflected this energy and vitality. Cathedral schools began to offer a level of instruction not seen since the classical period; a few schools, such as Paris, Bologna, and, in the thirteenth century, Oxford, blossomed into university centers. Though in many regions secular authority was strengthening, twelfth-century government was still relatively weak and local enterprises flourished. This contributed to a very creative and diverse intellectual environment. Study could be promoted by cities, monasteries, and cathedral schools in addition to kings. Local endeavors fed into regional and international developments, such as Church reform, which lent a growing coherence to Western society.[1]

Tendencies toward centralization were also beginning to emerge. The bureaucracies of both the monarchical states and the Church intensified their competition and became more efficient: an outgrowth was the parallel development of secular and ecclesiastical court systems. Marriage cases heard by these courts were a major impetus for the development of a rationalized body of law. Canon law represented the Church's attempt to legislate on a multitude of issues touching Christian life. To do this, it was necessary to sort through the accumulated opinions of the Church Fathers and popes.

This chapter will explore the Church's teachings on marriage as they evolved under the aegis of twelfth-century reform. Following a discussion of the key ideas comprising the Church's teachings on marriage in the twelfth century (for our purposes this term will encompass broadly the period from 1100 to the Fourth Lateran Council of 1215) I will explore how the Church disseminated its ideas.

In the twelfth century, monks increasingly explored the interior dynamics of human love. The notion that true love for the divine begins with self-knowledge (i.e., properly ordered human love) permeated the age, popular in both secular and monastic milieux. *Affectio maritalis,* or marital affection, became ever more celebrated over the course of the century and was promoted in scholastic and pastoral theology and law. In literature love between men and women was an extremely popular topic as well; according to the perspective of the author, marriage was portrayed as irredeemable, problematic, or sublime.

The Church exerted its influence aggressively at times in a society that still resisted notions such as the free consent of spouses, or resented confining sexual activity within the marital sphere. The line of demarcation between "ecclesiastical" and "aristocratic" views of marriage, however, frequently blurred as a result of a shared desire to promote the stability of marriage and a Christian vision of the conjugal union.[2]

Getting Married in the Twelfth Century

Church Teachings on Marriage

Free Consent

The last chapter showed that during the early Middle Ages, especially for the upper classes, marriage usually had the appearance of a transaction involving property. When noble parents contracted marriages for their children, they usually aimed to maintain or increase the family fortune; the family status and property of each suitor was weighed meticulously before an agreement was concluded. Roman and Germanic law had considered women the property of the father of the household to dispose of as he willed. The wishes of daughters or minor children did not have to be consulted.[3] Nevertheless, within the Church there had always been those who said that forcing children into marriages was not a good idea, since, as "Ambrosiaster" had said, "unwilling marriages usually have bad results."[4] The first canonist to systematize the Church's tradition that individuals should be free to determine their marriage partners was Gratian. Although Gratian, writing around

1140, clearly desired to advance the free choice of marriage partners, he seems to have been unclear about how this ought to be done, since he also assumed that parental consent was necessary for a valid marriage.[5]

In any century, of course, children could be wheedled or intimidated into giving their consent by persistent parents, such as those of Christina of Markyate (1096?–1155). Christina was a twelfth-century noblewoman, who vowed publicly to enter the life of consecrated virginity and refused to consent to the marriage that had been arranged for her by her parents.[6] Succumbing eventually to the threats of her parents, Christina was forced to participate in a ritual of betrothal. Believing that her prior vow constituted an impediment to this betrothal, Christina refused to consummate the marriage. Her parents brought her to Fredebert, the prior of the local college of canons, to decide the matter. The testimony of the parties reveals much about the contradictory views of marriage held by different segments of twelfth-century society. Her father is reported to have stripped Christina of her clothes, saying, "If you want to have Christ, follow him naked."[7] Playing on a twelfth-century image of the religious life, her father was implying that her decision would drastically alter her economic situation. He further declared that Christina was dishonoring not only her parents, but the whole of the noble class by her actions. Her father, however, was the model of civility in comparison to her mother, who declared that she would just as soon see her daughter raped, since any consummation would seal a marriage under current custom. These testimonies reveal a conflict between two sets of assumptions: Christina's Anglo-Saxon parents viewed marriage as a simple agreement between families that was ratified by sexual intercourse; on the other hand the prior held that marriage was more than just a social custom. It established a sacred bond, a sacrament. The prior's main concern was to determine at what point and to whom Christina's free consent had been given. Originally Fredebert had counseled her to accept the marriage, since the betrothal ceremony had been performed in a church.[8] Eventually he reversed his decision when it was proven to his satisfaction that her prior vow should have acted as an impediment to the betrothal.

Christina of Markyate's story highlights the challenge faced by the Church in its struggle to resist parental control of marriage. Parental control, however, was only one problem that faced theologians during the twelfth century. Another problem in the Anglo-Norman lands was the custom whereby a lord who controlled a fief inherited by a woman might marry her to a man of lesser nobility willing to pay for the match, since the woman could not herself perform the military service upon which the feudal relationship was based. Robert of Courçon denounced this type of marriage sale at about the same time that the English barons forced King John to guarantee marriage without disparagement to a woman's status in the provisions of *Magna Carta.*[9]

These problems represented a challenge that became ever more pressing for the Church because of its increasing involvement in the pastoral care of the laity. Gratian came of age in a period of reform in which many new religious orders began to reexamine what their relationship to the laity ought to be. Some of the reformed monastic orders tried to separate themselves from the world, and to inspire by example. But some monks, such as Bernard of Clairvaux (1090–1153), possessed such a heightened desire for Church unity that they were incessantly involved in the lives of lay friends and devoted a certain amount of thought to the responsibilities attached to the lay state.[10] Other orders, such as the orders of canons regular, consisted of priests who lived under a common rule; their day-to-day activities in a cathedral or an abbey or parish church involved them intimately with the laity.[11] The canons' ideal was a life of service "in, but not of, the world" to build up the body of Christ. They were quite conscious of their new mission to the laity: the canonical author of a book describing the many new religious orders of the twelfth century organized it according to the relative proximity of each order to the cities and towns.[12] In their preaching the canons took pains to assert that men and women in all secular occupations could embrace the Christian faith and live it out in a way appropriate to their own vocation.[13] As the canons began to sketch a positive image of the lay life, the polarity between clergy and laity began to recede in their writings.[14] One of the most influential houses of canons, the abbey of St. Victor in Paris, recorded that people of all stations were given the honorary title *canonicus noster* (our canon) at a special ceremony at chapter, as if the canons were seeking to bring lay people "into the family," so to speak.[15]

One record we have of the new involvement of religious orders with the laity is the great proliferation of *sententiae* (collections of Church teaching on different subjects used as teaching tools in the new cathedral schools and universities). In these collections, which are oriented to teaching the religious the doctrines they must in turn pass on to laymen, marriage is one of the subjects most commonly treated.[16] These *sententiae* were avidly copied in reforming monastic and canonical houses.

The spiritual climate of mutual lay-religious cooperation in the late eleventh and early twelfth centuries encouraged the settling of many questions surrounding the nature and meaning of marriage. Free consent was one such issue: by 1216 canon law made it explicit that the consent of the couple was all that was required for a valid marriage.[17] As the Church clarified its position, it sought avenues for popularizing its conclusion. Michael Sheehan has shown that by the end of the twelfth century local councils in England were enjoining the clergy to question couples about their consent prior to marriage.[18] Manuals called confessionals, composed to guide priests during confession, were still admonishing priests about the importance of free consent in the thirteenth century, and, in fact, free consent continued to be an issue during the whole of the later Middle Ages.

The Consent-Consummation Debate

In the Church's centuries-long struggle to understand the nature of marriage, two old views contended for supremacy in the twelfth century. One view, that of Germanic custom, had been held by earlier Churchmen such as Archbishop Hincmar of Rheims. It focused on the sexual element within marriage and proposed that marriage was complete only with sexual intercourse.[19] Another view, held by many reformers,[20] went back to the Romans,[21] and was articulated most clearly by Hugh of St. Victor (d. 1141). This was that sexual intercourse was secondary to consent, or the choice of the will. Twelfth-century scholasticism was fruitful both because the schools provided a suitable environment for sustained inquiry, and because they allowed interaction between theologians such as Hugh and the developing body of legal thought. Among theologians Peter Lombard (c. 1095–1160), who will be discussed later, is a good example of a theologian who borrowed from canon law; among canonists, Huguccio is an example of a canonist who was influenced by theology.[22] But to stay with Hugh, Hugh of St. Victor was one of the first scholars to treat marriage systematically. However, his work greatly depended on the collections of *sententiae* connected with the school of Laon, so it will be helpful to survey the ideas of one collection attributed to Anselm of Laon (d. 1117) before turning to Hugh himself.

Anselm is important in the history of marriage because he lent new breadth and depth to the term "sacrament." The word "sacrament" had been applied to marriage since the earliest times.[23] Ambrose and Augustine had both claimed that marriage as a sacrament was an image of Christ and the Church.[24] Augustine made a further distinction between the sacrament or sign, which he never identified precisely, and the product of the sacrament, the *res* or *bonum sacramenti*, which was the indissoluble covenant between the spouses.[25] Carolingian commentators on Ephesians 5:32 developed ideas about the way the marriage of the first parents, Adam and Eve, images the marriage between Christ and the Church. Paschasius Radbertus (c. 785–c. 860) and Rabanus Maurus (776/84–856) expounded on the Epistle's analogy that just as a man leaves his parents to cling to his bride, so Christ left his father and emptied himself to become a slave in order to cling to his wife, the Church.

In Anselm's hands the Ephesians passage yielded further ideas. In common with his predecessors, Anselm held that not only the Genesis marriage, but all marriages, are images of the Christ/Church relationship. In Augustinian and Pauline fashion, he emphasized that human marriage is indissoluble and reflects Christ's unwavering love for his Church. But Anselm distinguished between indissolubility (the *res* according to Augustine) and the *res*, or effect, of marriage. He argued that the *res* is to become members of Christ through the couple's service to God and the Church.[26] Anselm thus went to the heart of the Christ/Church image, to reflect on how the life of service within marriage images Christ's sacrifice for the Church.

Anselm further distinguished between the two institutions — Christian and non-Christian — of marriage. Anselm observed that marriage, unlike the other Christian sacraments, was practiced in pre-Christian societies. How is this to be understood? Is marriage merely different from the other sacraments or not really a sacrament at all? An ancient tradition in the Church, at least as old as Isidore, asserted that all marriages — even those of non-Christians or those dating before the time of Christ — are sacraments.[27] Anselm agreed that this was true in one sense, but he made a distinction between non-Christian and Christian marriage. He said that all marriages are *sacramenta,* or images of the Christ/Church relationship, but only Christian marriages involve spouses in the grace of a life in the Church. When God instituted marriage with Adam and Eve, it fulfilled the natural good of continuing the race by procreation. After Christ, marriage was reinstituted, taking on the additional purpose of acting as a remedy for the sin of sexual relations. Like Augustine, Anselm understood this sin to be a reminder of the sin of the first parents, not something intrinsic to intercourse.[28]

As Anselm began to probe the relatively unexamined human reality of marriage, he distinguished between the sign, the reality signified, and the effect of the sign. The sign, according to him, was sexual consummation. Here, though he strongly affirmed that the exchange of the words of consent is vital, he also insisted that marriage is not completed until consummation. Second, marriage *signifies* the indissolubility of the Christ/Church relationship. Finally, marriage is not only a sign of this reality, but a participation in the reality itself.

Hugh of St. Victor began to write about marriage some fifteen years after Anselm. He first approached this topic in considering the theological question of whether or not Mary was truly married to Joseph. The problem, discussed above in the third chapter, was whether an unconsummated marriage counted as a marriage. This question forced Hugh to sort through broader issues. With Augustine, he came to affirm that human marriage is primarily about human partnership, and that Mary and Joseph therefore had a true marriage. Considering what a couple consents to in marriage, Hugh strikingly concluded that each agrees to owe the entire self to the other. This "owing" may be understood in two ways: in one way, the spouses should reserve themselves to one another; in another way, they may not deny themselves to one another. Both meanings are contained in consenting to share a life of charity: the couple both reserve the depth of their love to each other and give it without denial.[29] Going back to Genesis 2:24, Hugh argued that the command to generate children rests on the prior fact that men and women were made for each other, and for this reason a man shall leave his family to cling to his wife.[30]

Although the couple is bound to exclude others from the sexual sphere, Hugh agrees with Augustine that they may also deny themselves access to the marriage bed by mutual agreement, may live a "spiritual marriage."[31] But Hugh does not manifest the overt hostility to the sexual relationship sometimes found among proponents of the ascetical life. He merely seems to have made the practical judgment that those who renounced intercourse (presumably to devote themselves more deeply to spiritual pursuits) suffered no loss in their marital relationship. These views on spiritual marriage did not remain unchallenged. In late twelfth-century illustrations of the sections on marriage in Gratian's *Decretum,* one finds miniatures apparently condemning spiritual marriage: they depict false lovers carrying symbols of purity, such as olive branches, luring women into sexless marriages.[32] Against Hugh's emphasis on the primacy of consent stood the long-dominant view, dependent on the social tradition that a marriage was not complete until it had been consummated. Among theologians, intercourse was a fitting symbol for Christ's union with his Body, the Church, in the Incarnation. Treatises associated with the school of Laon had gone so far as to say that an unconsummated marriage was not a sacrament.[33] In a show of great creativity, Hugh now found a way to preserve this tradition and still argue that the moment of consent took priority. He did so by inventing a second sacramental symbolism for marital consent. This has sometimes been referred to as his "two-sacraments" theory of marriage.

Both marital consent and sexual intercourse (his terms are "matrimony" and the "function" of matrimony) are sacramental for Hugh, or as he says, both are sacraments. The term "sacrament" had a looser meaning in Hugh's day than it would a hundred years later. For him as for others before him, the term "sacrament" was used not only of the great sacraments such as Baptism, but also of things of lesser symbolic value, such as priestly vestments. Each marital "sacrament" represents a different mystery. As he says:

> Matrimony was a sacrament of a certain spiritual society which existed between God and the soul through love.... The function [*officium*] of matrimony was a sacrament of a certain society which was to be between Christ and the Church through the assumption of flesh.[34]

Hugh's "two-sacraments" theory, which found spiritual significance in both consent and consummation, was popular in intellectual circles throughout the twelfth century. The double signification of marriage was used by later writers such as Rufinus, Huguccio, and Guy of Orchelles.[35] Perceiving the confusion caused by the "two-sacraments" terminology, Peter of Poitiers emphasized that there are not two sacraments in marriage, but one sacrament which has a double signification of the union of Christ and the Church.[36] This idea has continued to thrive even into the present, appearing in a recent encyclical letter of John Paul II.[37] Alongside Hugh's views developed another tradition that suggested that if marriage was established through consent, it was also oriented toward procreation. In his *Tractatus de sacramentis,* Master Simon (1145–60) wrote that marital consent is that by which marriage was concluded (*per quod fit*), while intercourse is that for which it was undertaken (*ad quod fit*).[38] This distinction found its full expression in the thought of later scholastics such as Bonaventure and St. Thomas.

Courts wanted to determine the place of consent and consummation in marriage because they needed to resolve the vexatious practical problem of when a marriage begins and how it is legally contracted. Over time the view first expressed by Hugh of St. Victor, which saw consent as the determinative cause of marriage, replaced the coital theory initially popular at the law school at Bologna. The consent theory became prominent in the schools especially through its endorsement by the Paris theologian Peter Lombard.[39] His book the *Sentences* became the standard textbook for theological study in the later Middle Ages and was enormously influential. He distinguished between *verba de futuro,* a promise regarding the future, and *verba de praesenti,* an explicit statement of a couple's wish to be married.

One of the earliest canonists to attempt to produce a coherent theory of marriage, Gratian took up the proposition that consummation was necessary for a marriage to exist.[40] He observed in the *Decretum* that marriage was a two-step process, initiated through consent but perfected in consummation.[41] He argued that consummation made the union into a sacrament and hence made it indissoluble. Gratian had the views of French theologians about the primacy of consent available to him, but he did not choose to use them. James Brundage suggests that Gratian may have been primarily occupied with the problem of determining proof of marriage in cases where there was no public record. Brundage notes that both oral agreements and claims about intercourse can be difficult to prove, but he observes that it might be easier to demonstrate an alleged act of consummation by circumstantial evidence than to demonstrate a contract for which there are no witnesses.[42]

Gratian's *Decretum* was adopted as a textbook by the law schools that were emerging in response to the expanding need for clergy trained in canon law to staff the Church's growing bureaucracy. The decretists (students of the *Decretum*) who succeeded Gratian sought to reconcile the old law gathered by him with the law that continued to be made, notably in papal decretals, or in decisions made by the popes in appellate court cases. The decretists followed diverse paths in their attempts to resolve the consent/consummation conflict, but few emulated their master.

The displacement of the coital theory among canonists was a gradual process. Its relative demise was probably related to the growing interest in defining and numbering the sacraments and placing marriage among them.[43] Because canonists were interested in proving that a marital union was different from a casual (dissoluble) sexual union, it was logical that they should emphasize consent over consummation. Some, such as Huguccio, seem to have rejected consummation as an unsuitable symbol for this sacrament out of a common belief that sex was sinful because it was pleasurable.[44] The drift was toward locating consent in both words of agreement and the act of intercourse. An uneasy alliance of the consent and consummation schools was manifested in the marriage decretals of Pope Alexander III (1159–84).[45]

Alexander III taught that both *verba de praesenti* (present consent) alone and also *verba de futuro* (future consent) followed by consummation were acceptable means of contracting a valid marriage.[46] His teachings, which we now refer to as the "Alexandrine rules," emphasized the role of consent in marriage and denied that sexual intercourse alone, without the presence of consent, could establish a marriage. Innocent III (1198–1216) attempted to implement the rules of his predecessor and consciously strove to replace the view that sexual union alone, even with other elements such as rings, marital portions, etc., is sufficient to establish a marriage without proof of consent.[47] Innocent noted that the practice in the city of Modena was that if a man promised to marry a woman, but later espoused a second woman and had intercourse with her, the second marriage would stand. Innocent decreed that the church in Modena must now observe his teaching that mutual consent *de praesenti* creates the marital bond and supersedes any later union. The "Alexandrine rules" guided his decisions in specific marriage cases that we know about. In one case, a woman in the diocese of Siponto married a man whom she subsequently discovered was impotent.[48] Thereafter she took a young lover whom she married. Innocent decreed that the second marriage was invalid because the woman had not sought to have the first marriage properly annulled on grounds of impotence before she took her lover. Sexual intercourse alone did not legitimate the second marriage, and Innocent called for the woman to return to her first husband. The canonist Huguccio, writing in the last quarter of the twelfth century, reiterated the Lombard's argument that marriage was indissoluble from the moment of present consent. With Huguccio and the papal decretals of the late twelfth-century popes, the victory of the consensual theory of marriage was all but assured in the schools.[49]

The popes of the late twelfth century, notably Alexander III and Innocent III,[50] created a definition of marriage which emphasized the importance
of the free consent of the couple.[51] These popes explicitly declared that any
marriage contracted under duress made the compact null and void.[52] Nevertheless, certain consequences were seen to follow from consummation. If
consummation followed a promise to marry, the couple were considered to
be married. If a conditional consent were followed by intercourse, even if
the condition had not yet been met at the time of intercourse, the union was
considered a marriage.[53] Alexander III further recognized that a marriage
contracted without parental consent was legitimate. He was thus forced by
the logic of his position to sanction secret or clandestine marriages.

The Problem of Clandestine Marriage

In 1100 the Church still did not require that marriages take place in a Church
ceremony. Though a marriage liturgy had been in development since the
early Middle Ages, throughout Europe it was common merely to bless the
union at or after a marriage celebration at the home of one of the couple's
families. During the eleventh and twelfth centuries we find a growing insistence that marriages should take place in the parish church.[54] The reasons
given included: (1) the church environment signified that the Church considered marriage to be a sacred matter, which ought to be regulated and
administered by the Church; (2) the public nature of the ceremony, with the
entire parish witnessing it, decreased the incidence of clandestine marriage.

Clandestine marriage posed innumerable problems both to pastors,[55] who
had to determine the justice of each situation, and to the courts, which had
to hear the contested marriage and inheritance cases. Clandestine marriages
seriously undermined the stability of marriage and family relationships, since
no husband or wife, even in a publicly solemnized union, could be sure that a
mate from a previous clandestine marriage might not someday appear on the
scene to claim his or her spouse. A long-standing solution that was adopted
in England and France during the twelfth century was the publication of
banns, an announcement of a couple's intention to marry made in the parish
several Sundays in succession prior to the marriage ceremony.[56] Clandestine
marriage remained a problem for ecclesiastical and secular courts throughout the high Middle Ages and beyond, as the secular laws and censures of
numerous local church councils throughout Europe attest.[57]

Though medieval popes were willing to confront the problem of secret
marriage, the inconsistency of a policy that both discouraged clandestine
marriage and tolerated it has been treated harshly by modern historians.[58]
In defense of the papal approach, Brundage has pointed out that it represents
an attempt to deal in realistic terms with the problem of parental coercion.[59]
Charles Donahue and others also have pleaded that papal policy played a

role in changing society's view of marriage.[60] Marriage came increasingly to be seen primarily in terms of the good of the couple.

Sacramental Theology

Hugh of St. Victor's works reflect two additional twelfth-century achievements in the understanding of marriage. The first is the recognition that marriage must have something in common with the other great sacraments in the Church, be part of a sacramental system. Hugh of St. Victor gave marriage a place within salvation history that had only been faintly foreshadowed by previous thinkers such as Anselm of Laon. Second was a focus on the affective nature of the bond. Both insights, especially the former, reflected great shifts in ecclesiastical views of marriage that would flower in the thought of later scholastics such as Albert the Great, Bonaventure, and Thomas Aquinas. In his meditations Hugh brought to bear knowledge from canon law, exegesis, theology, and his own mystical experience. St. Bonaventure later gave tribute to the rich texture of his thought: "Anselm excelled in reasoning, Bernard in preaching, and Richard in contemplation — Hugh in all of these."[61] Attuned to the major topics and modes of twelfth-century intellectual life, Hugh's thought embodies many of the new currents of the twelfth century.

His theology of marriage cannot be understood without reference to his sacramental view of reality. Like his successor St. Bonaventure, Hugh believed that creation was strewn with sacred symbols, or "sacraments," which God implanted to lead human beings to a fuller appreciation of himself. Hugh was one of a number of early scholastic theologians to attempt to develop a sacramental system. He and other contemporaries turned to the definition of the term "sacrament."[62] This first stage of reflection culminated in the diffusion of Peter Lombard's influential definition of marriage, to which we will turn below. The second stage developed a theology of grace in the marital sacrament, but this lies largely outside our period. In Hugh's attempt to define the term "sacrament," he distinguished the sacraments of the Old Law from the sacraments of the New Law, but he argued that there was a continuity between the two, with the former foreshadowing the latter, which completed them. Like many before him, Hugh further found marriage existed in the garden of Eden as well as after the Fall. He was therefore faced with the difficult task of constructing a notion of sacrament that made sense of two such radically different contexts.

Hugh's understanding of symbol was influenced by the late fifth-century Neoplatonic spiritual writer Pseudo-Dionysius the Areopagite. According to Pseudo-Dionysius, the relationship between a symbol and the transcendent reality it signified was a relationship of participation.[63] Thus not only does the symbolic object take its being from God, but lower things participate in the perfection of higher things. This is called participation by similitude. This ontological affinity of lower to higher orders the universe. Within the human mind, when the sense faculties participate in rationality their participation is realized in moral virtue. Man realizes the fullness of his rational nature when he achieves a supernatural union with God through grace, which is a participation in the life of God himself.

Human beings, situated between the world of created reality and God, can perceive the similitudes of created objects to their creator but, due to original sin, can do so only imperfectly. Hugh of St. Victor uses a metaphor of three "eyes" to describe the ravages of original sin: "The sensible eye remains fully functional, the eye of reason is bleared, and the eye of contemplation is blinded."[64] The human mind is now distracted by the forms of created things and cannot perceive the invisible goods of which they should remind us. Now humans need the help of grace to return the mind to its proper function. According to Hugh, the sacraments help cure the mind's blindness in three ways: they (1) instruct the mind about truth; (2) lead the mind toward internal order by the cultivation of virtue; and (3) confer grace.[65]

Hugh develops these three functions in the following way. The first function of the sacraments is the instruction of the mind through the signification of truth. That is, symbols act naturally on the mind by drawing human attention to the echo of God eternally made manifest within the symbol.[66] The nature of this intellectual process of understanding truth is not discursive or syllogistic; rather it is intuitive and mystical.[67]

The second function is to order the human mind by the cultivation of virtue. The term Hugh uses for this is "exercise." Through exercise virtues are cultivated within the mind while it is occupied exteriorly by various works. Hugh means that the sense faculties come to participate in rationality through the doing of good works.[68] The examples he gives of works include the singing of psalms, readings of lessons for the formation of character, and instruction in the good life: all of the things that were intended to give order to the daily life of regular canons like himself.[69] Remarkably, Hugh suggests that the activities of the lay life might function analogously to order and redirect the layman's passions. The full importance of this suggestion is tied to Hugh's view that the "exercise" proper to the lay life is intercourse.[70] He seems to have caught the significance of Augustine's belief that though postlapsarian marital intercourse is a remedy for concupiscence, it was originally created without sin. This is made clear in the following passage from *De sacramentis*, in which he states that after sin marriage has the three features presently possessed by the sacraments (instruction, exercise, and remedy), but before the Fall, marriage had not possessed the last: "the reason for the [second] institution was not at that time that there might be a remedy, but a function (*officium*), because there was no sickness in man to be cured but virtue to be exercised."[71] Hugh thus deepened the Augustinian idea that intercourse within the laws of faithful marriage restrains concupiscence. Furthermore there is an analogy between the canons' "exercise" of chanting the prayers of the Church, which fosters priestly virtue, and the married "exercise" of a disciplined marital intercourse, which fosters lay virtue. This is an extraordinary view, because it centers more on the opportunities for virtue the married life presents than on the stain of the Fall it carries.

The final component of restoration, the third function of the sacrament, is its efficacy. The sacrament's effect is wrought first and foremost by grace.[72] For Hugh, grace is like medicine held out to humankind in its sickened state.[73] In attributing saving grace to marriage, Hugh was probably influenced by the treatises associated with the school of Laon.[74] The majority of early scholastic writers disagreed with Hugh's view.[75] Peter Lombard argued that marriage only interceded for the concupiscence of sexual relations.[76] William of Auxerre and many of the canonists argued similarly that marriage was only a remedy for sin.[77] After the definition of marriage as one of the seven sacraments by the Fourth Lateran Council of 1215, Bonaventure and Thomas Aquinas helped to reverse this trend by arguing that the Christian sacrament of marriage confers a type of grace that helps couples to persevere in their charity, a type of grace that draws its source from Christ's self-giving love.[78] By the end of the thirteenth century there was general theological consensus on this point.[79]

Hugh proposed a view of the efficacy of sacraments that allowed for their existence in humankind's pre-fallen state. Two purposes of the sacraments, instruction and exercise, are common to the pre- and postlapsarian periods, while only the remedial dimension is proper to our fallen state. Hugh thus distinguished which activities proper to the unfallen human state are present in the fallen human condition, even if only in an analogous fashion. He pointed out that we can still perceive God in the corporeal things of the physical world and they can draw us to God in the way God always intended, once we concentrate our attention on them properly. Conversely, we may be infer that Hugh considered sacraments a normative part of human cognition and experience of God, at least during terrestrial life, a view not made explicit by his contemporaries. This opened the door to a reassessment of the importance of bodies and the physical world.

Hugh of St. Victor had a developed sense of the capacity of the physical world to show forth the goodness and the providential care of God. He shared Dionysius's sense of the close ties between the created and redemptive orders; both writers believed the world of creation was providentially fashioned by God precisely to enable humankind's restoration.[80] What was begun at the coming of Christ was the restoration of the cosmos from the ground up; what remains is getting humans to see this and to persevere in perfecting this work. Due to the ravages of original sin, human beings must begin to be re-educated through the faculties that remain most unimpaired, that is, the sensory faculties. Therefore the physical world not only shows forth the glory of restoration, but it also provokes and participates in its realization. This will be explored further below.

Hugh of St. Victor possessed a rather precise theological notion of how sacraments affected the human individual. He created a similarly precise definition of sacrament. In his day a sacrament was commonly described as a "sign of a sacred thing" (*sacrae rei signum*). This definition, with its emphasis on *sacra res,* was a reaction against Berengar of Tours, who had claimed that the Eucharist was a sign that effected what it signified. Berengar's opponents had responded that the Eucharist is more than a sign; it actually *is* the Body of Christ.[81] Hugh of St. Victor averred that the phrase *sacrae rei signum* was appropriate for common parlance, but was imprecise as a definition, because other things such as pictures can be signs of sacred things as well. Hugh's definition of a sacrament was "a corporeal or material element displayed to the senses, representing [something] by its likeness and signifying it by its institution [by Christ] and containing through sanctification an invisible and spiritual grace."[82]

The idea that the sacrament represented by similitude some sacred thing must be understood within the Neoplatonic context discussed above: The earthly object manifests its participation in some higher mystery by its similitude. This can help explain why Hugh felt it was important to invent a second symbolism for marriage.[83] The validity of a marriage was intimately connected with its sacramentality, which in turn was thought to signify something. As consent lacked a significative value, it was imperative to supply one.

Later twelfth-century thinkers were not entirely content with Hugh of St. Victor's solution. The language of two sacraments made for a cumbersome definition of sacrament. A figure such as Master Simon later viewed the two parts of marriage, consent and consummation, as symbolic of one and the same reality, the union of Christ and Church. Consent requires three things, according to Master Simon: "a union of wills, mutual love, and the protection of the wife by the husband."[84] Each of these conditions is also present in the union between Christ and his Church. A consummated union that gives birth to children corresponds to the birth of souls through the grace of Christ active in the Church he is united to.

The latter part of the twelfth century saw a return to a broader, yet increasingly more nuanced, definition of the term "sacrament." As Seamus Heaney has shown, the work of Peter Lombard aided greatly in the progress of definition. The Lombard was a schoolmaster at Notre Dame and then from 1159 bishop of Paris. Formerly a student at St. Victor and deeply influenced in many respects by Victorine ideas, he nevertheless rejected Hugh of St. Victor's notion of sacrament, returning to the classic Augustinian definition of sacrament as sacred sign: "For that is properly called a sacrament, which is in such a manner the sign of the grace of God, and the form of invisible grace, that it bears its image and is its cause."[85] The Lombard rejects Hugh's notion that a sacrament must be a corporeal object in favor of a definition that more obviously makes possible the inclusion of penance and marriage among the sacraments.

With regard to symbolism, Peter Lombard attached to sexual relations one sign of the union of Christ and the Church. His attempt to resolve the debate over the respective roles of consent and consummation in the creation of the marriage bond proposed that each symbolizes a different aspect of this union, and on this he clearly depended on Hugh. As in marriage a bride is united to her bridegroom spiritually and physically, or by love and by nature, so Christ is united to the Church by love and by nature. As the harmony of the husband and wife signifies the spiritual union of Christ and the Church, so the physical union symbolizes the joining of the Body of Christ to Christ, her Head, through the Incarnation. Quoting Augustine, the Lombard said that a consensual union lacking consummation is just as valid as a consummated one. It merely lacks the symbolism of the physical union of Christ and the Church. It does have, however, "a sign of the spiritual union and affection of souls, by which husbands and wives ought to be united."[86] A century later the scholastic definition of marriage in terms of the *sacramentum* (the consent), the *res et sacramentum* (the marriage bond, signified and effected by the exchange of consent),[87] and the *sacramentum tantum* (the conferral of grace) resolved the anomalies that remained after the Lombard's synthesis. Later scholastics would argue that marriage has two causes: efficient, which effects marriage (consent); and final, which determines the end of marriage (the procreation and education of children).

Betrothal and Nuptial Rites

In the twelfth century the Church possessed a nuptial rite and numerous ancillary rites. In the Anglo-Norman churches nuptial ceremonies began when the bride and groom, with their family and friends, met the priest at the church door. The priest then determined whether the conditions for a valid marriage had been met using an older Gallican betrothal rite adapted for this purpose.[88] He next blessed a ring or other token of the marriage contract, coins symbolizing the dowry, and the written record of endowment.[89] While these ceremonies sometimes took place in the home, a nuptial benediction would then take place at a church. This nuptial benediction involved the veiling of the bride, in traditional Roman fashion, while in northern European countries the rite was expanded to include both bride and groom.

According to Brian Bethune, the Spanish Church used numerous rites peculiar to it that tended more than other European rites to stress the participation of both the bride and the groom. For instance, the Spanish version of the *traditio puellae* underwent numerous unique permutations. In ancient Rome the ceremony had symbolized the giving of the bride to the groom and had been the prerogative of the bride's attendant. In the Gallican Church the father of the bride normally led her by the hand to her husband at the end of the betrothal ceremony. In the Spanish Church, in Catalonia, as part of the nuptial mass, the bride's father might take his daughter's hand and give it to the priest. This was the first stage of the *traditio puellae*.[90] After communion the priest would then give her to her husband. Elsewhere in Catalonia, the groom's family presented him to the priest, who then directed the bride to stand by the groom's right side for the blessing. Spanish nuptial benedictions prescribed the exchange of two rings, unlike their French counterparts, in which only the groom might give a ring to the bride.

Anglo-Norman marriage ceremonies might culminate in the blessing of the bed chamber. Both Roman and older Gallican custom had prescribed this *traductio*, whereby the couple were led to the home of the groom, where the couple were blessed in their bed, after which consummation would follow.[91] The Spanish Church once again pursued a different course of action, blessing the bedchamber (but without the couple) only and at least one night before the ceremony, thus enforcing the religious character of the ceremony rather than giving it the appearance of a fertility rite.[92]

A treatise by Innocent III, entitled *On the Fourfold Types of Marriage*,[93] reflects many of the customs surrounding medieval wedding celebrations. Probably just after he became pope in 1198,[94] Innocent III received a request from a priest named Benedict to help him understand how Psalm 44 describes the way human marriage could serve as a metaphor for other realities. The biblical commentary that he wrote in response, *On the Fourfold Types of Marriage*, proposed four meanings of marriage (also found in writings by Cistercians, such as Bernard of Clairvaux, Aelred of Rievaulx, and Isaac of Stella), each meaning corresponding to one of the levels of biblical interpretation.[95] The treatise discussed all the stages of a wedding, though not in a strictly chronological order. Innocent sought to show that parallels exist between the marriage of Christ and the Church and human marriage. His suggestion that Jesus came out of the best of families is a reminder of societal preoccupation with maintaining social status. He mentioned a donation on the part of the groom.[96] Describing the marriage ceremony, he emphasized the presence of witnesses[97] — he will later say that "sacramental marriage does not wish to be secret, but obvious to all."[98] Innocent's description of the marriage ceremony probably reflected Roman ceremonies. Although he does not explicitly mention benediction by a priest, Connie Munk thinks that Innocent would have assumed it.[99] He makes further reference to a best man; bridesmaids; an incantation against evil; the exchange of vows, rings, and kisses; and the crowning with crowns, understood as a symbol of victory over the passions.[100]

The final part of the treatise describes the *traductio,* the leading of the bride by the groom to their new home and the sexual consummation of the union. Next he depicts the busy scene of the wedding banquet: decorated tables loaded down with food and wine in gold and silver cups, waiters, and guests. Innocent then begins to comment on Psalm 44; the commentary is cast as the nuptial song provided for the entertainment of the guests. Another contemporary touch added to Innocent's story is the dialogue between the arriving singer and the doorkeeper, who presses him to promise that he is not one of those "jongleurs" who might provide the guests with unsuitable fare. Here, as Leclercq says, "we can guess the whole contemporary social context: the Catharist errors about marriage [the Cathars were dualists who stigmatized marriage along with all things material]; the battle of the Christians in the Holy Land; the influence of courtly literature; the reform of morals."[101] The singer, with the accompaniment of lute players, praises the beauty and the finery, as well as the chastity and wisdom, of the bride and groom. Wedding celebrations could last well into the evening with feasting, dancing, jousts, and games, and revellers could sometimes be expected to incur fines in the course of the event in medieval Catalonia.[102]

The Fourth Lateran Council of 1215

On the eve of the Fourth Lateran Council the Church had largely systematized its teachings on marriage. Its theologians had scrutinized all the things that had at one time or another been called sacraments, clarifying the status of each and forming an official list of sacraments. Marriage had been included in this list in conciliar decrees since the first half of the twelfth century; it appeared in a list of sacraments from the Council of Verona in 1184.[103] The canonical definition of marriage emphasized the primacy of consent, but acknowledged that consummation was in some sense proof of consent. The Fourth Lateran Council, convoked by Innocent III, also tried to reduce the number of clandestine marriages by decreeing that marriages should be both celebrated in public[104] and publicly pronounced by means of banns.

Another task attempted by the Council was to clarify the degrees of relationship within which it was acceptable to marry. The medieval Church recognized that people were related not only by blood (consanguinity), but also by marriage (affinity) and spiritual relationships, such as godparenthood (relationship through the sacraments). As the last chapter showed, the number of degrees of relationship within which marriage was prohibited had been a source of great confusion. The Church had legislated about these degrees since the fifth and sixth centuries, but its interest in this matter increased during the Gregorian reform of the eleventh century.[105] By the twelfth century it was common to find prohibitions of marriage to kin related to the seventh degree, but this was not universal.[106] The Fourth Lateran Council prescribed the reduced system of prohibitions of relationship to the fourth degree already being endorsed by the schoolmasters of Paris such as Peter the Chanter in their disputations and handbooks on penance.[107]

In sum, by the early thirteenth century a substantial agreement on marriage doctrine existed at the highest level of the Church and expressed itself in the decisions of the Fourth Lateran Council.

Being Married in the Twelfth Century

We have seen that in the twelfth century marriage was receiving new attention. It is difficult to discern all the reasons why marriage achieved this new prominence in the life of the Church, but central was the attempt to give a higher level of pastoral care. For the centuries covered by the earlier chapters of this book, the scarcity of historical evidence often makes it difficult to understand the process of becoming married. But even more obscure to our view is the state of being married, the daily experiences of marriage. This problem only slightly abates in the twelfth century.[108] Still, we know enough to conclude that the spirituality of marriage has developed from the Carolingian period.

A Spirituality of Marriage

First we will look at how the notion of marital love, either broadly or as the *affectio maritalis* of the lawyers, features in works intended largely for an ecclesiastical audience, such as Bernard of Clairvaux's sermons on the Song of Songs. The influence of a figure such as Bernard in the dispersal of what we would call a "spirituality" of marriage should not be discounted. As Jean Leclercq has noted, although monks in the twelfth century did not develop a spirituality of marriage, "they supposed that such a spirituality existed, and they indirectly spread it abroad in every milieu by exposing their own thought on the matter."[109] At virtually the same time that Bernard was preaching the same kinds of themes were being deployed in Hugh of St. Victor's great theoretical treatise on the sacraments, *De sacramentis*. This work was extremely influential: it was copied in over one hundred manuscripts in the twelfth and early thirteenth centuries[110] and it exercised further influence indirectly through the incorporation of key ideas into Peter Lombard's

Sentences. Among intellectuals Hugh and Bernard's ideas would undoubtedly have been well known, but it is difficult to know how widely their ideas penetrated outside of those circles. Speculation about how much of the theology of marriage reached the popular level will be offered later. The important point here is that by the twelfth century we do have the elements of a self-conscious spirituality of marriage.

Marital Love and Affectio Maritalis

The first topic to be explored will be themes related to the notion of *affectio maritalis,* understood as the idea that the marriage bond entails affection between the spouses. The idea of *affectio maritalis* goes back to the Romans, yet twelfth-century canonical collections undoubtedly register the amplification of the concept. Here marital affection includes not just sharing of life with perhaps some expectation of affection and love but, increasingly, growth in affection and love. Reflections on marital love multiplied among theologians in monastic and canonical orders, for whom marriage became a favorite metaphor for the nature of the love between God and humankind. Such reflections are a hallmark of the twelfth-century development of a collective inner life in the Church. One of the features of this movement was fascination with the great motions of the spirit, such as human love. The relative peace of this period allowed the courts and schools to meditate on the interior dimension of marriage.

The text most often used to explore the arena of human love was the biblical poem the Song of Songs, interpreted as God's courtship of his chosen people as well as the story of the development of each individual's relationship with God.[111] Twelfth-century commentators sometimes took the Bride to refer to the Virgin Mary as well.[112] Hugh of St. Victor specifically applied this imagery to marriage, as we have seen, but the great exegete of the Song of Songs from this period was Bernard of Clairvaux.

From 1135 to 1153, St. Bernard wrote a famous series of sermons on the Song of Songs,[113] which drew from previous commentaries on the poem by Origen, Ambrose, and Gregory the Great. We can discern two themes in Bernard's exegesis: the story of the Church's pilgrimage and the story of the individual's search for Christ.[114] The latter receives primary focus,[115] but it is completed only within the context of the Church's pilgrimage. According to Bernard, the Song of Songs tells the story of the soul's search for her Groom. Rashly seeking a full disclosure of her Groom's beauty, she learns that she must learn to "know herself," that is, to purify and humble herself. This can be done only by entering into the Church's sacramental economy, whereby she can recall the suffering and death of the Lord. Thus "each person flourishes to the extent that he or she becomes integrated into the supra-personal 'personality' of the Bride."[116]

Bernard portrayed the lovers of the scriptural poem as married because he considered this the highest form of heterosexual love. As Leclercq has shown, Bernard's embellishments of the text, such as his mention of the marriage contract, *inire foedus societatis,* show the *sponsa* of the poem to be a bride recognizable to the times.[117] Leclercq has also described how Bernard innovates by using physical language about love to evoke in a sublime manner the successive stages by which people fall in love with God.[118] There has been a good deal of speculation about why Bernard used realistic and naturalistic language taken from marriage in writing about theology. He develops marital imagery far beyond the Song of Songs text itself. Among scholastic writers one finds far less usage of such naturalistic language. This is not to detract, however, from the achievements of scholastic preachers in examining the human reality of marriage and especially the interior dimensions of the marital bond, but they expressed it differently.[119] Caroline Bynum has argued that monastic culture was less fearful of the potential for corruption associated with bodies and organic change; monks and canons were among the leading twelfth-century spokesmen for the view that the body is important in the composition of the human person.[120] One explanation for this is that their intellectual activities consisted largely of meditation upon Scripture, in which God's connection to the physical world (and marriages) is constantly stressed.

Bernard describes the lovers of the Song of Songs as pressing their lips together in a kiss. At one point the bride bursts in on the bridegroom in his chamber and, in Leclercq's description, "the bridegroom recognizes her and takes her to himself in loving embrace entailing warmth, pressure and friction, union, effusion, reception."[121] The kiss is evocative for Bernard, as it had been since at least the fifth century, of several great Christian mysteries.[122] It signifies the unity and equality of the love between the three Persons of the Trinity. In his eighth sermon on the Song of Songs, Bernard describes how, "in God, each Person embraces the Other in preferential love, hugs him to himself in affection, 'This exchange of knowledge and love between the Engendering and the Engendered, what is it if not a very sweet and very secret kiss?' "[123] He also depicts as a kiss the mystery of the Incarnation: "The lips of the Word press the human nature, and in this way God is united to man in whom henceforth he dwells as the fullness of the Godhead."[124] By this kiss man becomes divine: "this alliance of the two natures adapts the human to the divine."[125]

The union of bride and bridegroom, writes Bernard, gives us a glimpse of the soul's conversion to the Word through its conformation to him through love. Bernard uses the language of human love to express the penetration of the soul by God, an experience which is beyond words but occasionally suggests images of marital love: the kiss, the embrace, union. In the ecstasy of love, the soul, made to the image of the Word in her nature, shows herself like him in will, loving as she is loved.

Being only an image of God, the soul experiences not only conformation, but also dissimilarity and inferiority to God, and yet this difference is in a sense washed away by the overpowering unity of love: "Nor should it be believed that the inequality of persons makes the accord of wills incomplete, for love has no regard for such distinctions."[126]

Finally, the soul is able to taste something of the fullness of the interior, communal love of the Trinitarian processions, and to learn that the true essence of love is to be in ceaseless communion.[127] This deep union of the soul with God resides not only in contemplative repose within the love-nest but also in activity. The visitation with the bridegroom makes the soul fruitful, glowing, naturally attractive to others: "For so great is the potency of that holy kiss, that no sooner has the bride received it than she conceives and her breasts become swollen, bearing witness, as it were, with this milky abundance."[128]

Like a mother, she bears the truth within her and later brings it to birth. The milk that flows from her breasts can nourish her spiritual child; in other words, she can initiate other people into the secrets of love. The spiritual mother brings forth milk to nourish her child, and "the milk means either spiritual nourishment or compassion with those who are in crisis, and rejoicing with those who are progressing."[129]

Bernard constantly chooses images from the realm of human love and fertility to express spiritual growth. The common joy they inspire is written deeply into the nature of things, and a similar pattern repeats itself at the natural, psychological, and spiritual levels.

Hugh of St. Victor also favored the metaphor of marriage in his depiction of the delights of God's love for man, *The Soliloquy on the Bridal Gift of the Soul.*[130] He explores the topic of marital love in a purely human context in *De Beatae Mariae virginitate*, written probably after 1131.[131] In this treatise he uses Genesis 2:23–24, "For this cause shall a man leave father and mother, and shall cleave to his wife, and they two shall be in one flesh," to show that the marital community is founded on consent, after which the sexual consummation, the "two in one flesh," may follow. For Hugh consent is hardly merely a legal agreement. This is how he describes the marital contract:

> See now the contract by which they bind themselves willingly in marriage. Henceforth and forever, each shall be to the other as a second self in all sincere love, all careful solicitude, every feeling of affection, every compassionate exertion, unflagging consolation, and faithful devotion.... Thus they will remain in the peace of a holy society and

quiet communion so that it no longer be the one who lives, but the other.[132]

The attitude of the spouses is summed up in the second sentence: "each shall be to the other as a second self." This passage, no doubt an extension of the imagery of Ephesians 5:28, "Husbands must love their wives as they love their own bodies; for a man to love his wife is to love himself," simultaneously expresses the Platonic idea that love is unitive and the Christian idea of divine charity that becomes more perfect as it becomes more directed toward others.

Bernard of Clairvaux taught similarly that marital *affectio*, like the love of God, is an end in itself, so powerful that it overrides even the bonds between the separate spouses and their parents. Bernard emphasized this point in his sermons on the Song of Songs:

> What other bond or union would you have between spouses, except to love and to be loved? This bond prevails even over that by which nature binds most firmly: the tie between parents and their children. And hence it is said: This is why a man should leave his father and mother and cleave to his wife (Gen. 2:24).[133]

While emphasizing the functional character of much of canon law, Brundage notes that marriage for the decretists was more than just a contract, a bond between families, or a means of procreating children. Canonists viewed the bond of "marital affection" as a usual part of married life:

> This enlargement of the decretists' concept of marriage was part of a broader movement in the late twelfth century that has been called the discovery of the self. Along with poets and theologians among their contemporaries, the decretists believed that intimate relationships should be grounded in a sharing of personal identity and outlook.[134]

Gratian took steps to clarify the notion of *affectio maritalis* from a legal point of view.[135] He separated the two notions of willingness to take another person as a spouse and marital affection, which had been fused in Roman law in the idea that where marital affection ceased, marriage could be dissolved. Gratian argued that the presence of marital affection created the bond, but that nothing, not even death, could sever the relationship.

With Alexander III we find that spouses were expected to cultivate marital affection, as "an active disposition"[136] implying growth or progress in love. This understanding of marital affection may lie behind Innocent III's response to Peter II of Aragon's request for an annulment from his wife, Marie, daughter of William VII, Count of Montpellier.[137] Peter and Marie had been married in 1204, but one year later Peter tried to dissolve the marriage to marry the daughter of the king of Jerusalem. Innocent decided against the annulment, and decreed that Marie should be received by Peter as his wife and treated with marital affection, since she had borne his child and was a pious woman. It is difficult to know precisely what the pope had in mind. Innocent frequently seems to use the term "marital affection" as equivalent to marital intercourse: as in the case of a woman, B., who had taken a vow of continence. When her husband decided he no longer wished to be continent, B. sued for the restitution of the marital right. Innocent ordered that the husband should take her back and treat her with marital affection, which clearly refers to sexual intercourse. In cases where a vow of continence was not an issue, the equal right of the spouses to intercourse was taken very seriously, because the refusal to render the marital debt could result in fornication. Thus we can understand why the term *affectio maritalis* frequently has a sexual connotation in Innocent's writings. In the case of Peter and Marie it seems that conjugal relations were restored, for after a brief reconciliation with Peter in 1207, she gave birth to a son, James.

As Sheehan has commented, to a modern audience the forcible restitution of a spouse might not seem the most desirable way of dealing with marital problems, but judging from the number of requests that came through ecclesiastical courts, it was an end that was often voluntarily sought: "This fact needs to be underlined for it is an important indication of what some spouses expected of marriage, of what made it desirable and worth defending in court: a sexual partner though another was preferred, a place in society, shelter and sustenance, etc."[138] A second case from the pontificate of Innocent dramatizes this well. In 1198 Innocent ordered Philip Augustus of France to take back his wife, the Danish princess Ingeborg, whom he had repudiated the day after their marriage and imprisoned in a monastery.[139] Ingeborg had appealed to Rome for protection. Despite papal pressure, Philip did not take her back until 1213, and it seems unlikely that he restored her conjugal rights. The term *affectio maritalis* need not necessarily include the marital right, as is shown in a decision by Alexander III that the spouses of lepers ought to minister to their companions with conjugal affection.[140]

Medieval law never endowed the term "marital affection" with specific content that would make it possible for a court to determine its existence in a given marriage. It was often employed against certain abusive behaviors as an ideal, or alluded to in connection with more positive actions such as the provision of nourishment, dress, etc. Gratian's criteria for the presence of marital affection relied on external evidence: the agreed statement of the couple or the observance of visible formalities.[141]

Fruitfulness

While twelfth-century writers could be effusive about both the theological
and romantic dimensions of love, they did not lose sight of the active labors
that marriage entailed or of the sexual side of married love.

In one work Hugh of St. Victor echoes the common theme of the anxiety
attending the birth, nourishment, and education of children. Paraphrasing
Gregory the Great, he laments, "If those who are getting married would only
remember this, they would understand that in marriage there will be more
tears than laughter."[142] Elsewhere Hugh could write more sanguinely about
human sexuality. "Fruitfulness" for St. Bernard, as previously mentioned,
connoted goodness in action: it is attractive, compelling, and nourishing.
Bernard felt "fruitfulness" to be so imperative for the Christian life that he
instructed his monks to beware lingering in the embraces of contemplation.
Far better that the breasts should flow in the service of preaching, for in
service one begins to conquer selfishness. When in turn Hugh of St. Victor
speculates about the original purpose of sexual intercourse as instituted at
creation, he says only that procreation is "fruitful." He does not mention
service explicitly, but his notion of "exercise" (see above) and Bernard's
notions of "fruitfulness" applied to the married life have much in common
with Hugh's idea that marriage issues in virtue and progeny:

> Again, in order that the conjugal society of man and woman might not
> be idle, after the sacrament of matrimony there was added the function
> which was to have been fulfilled in the mingling of flesh, so that those
> joined in matrimony might be exercised through obedience unto virtue
> and might bear fruit through the generation of progeny.[143]

For Hugh of St. Victor, sexual intercourse was from the beginning a sacrament of the unity between Christ and his Church that is obtained through
the physical sharing of Christ in human nature.

> The function of matrimony was a sacrament of a certain society which
> was to be between Christ and the Church through the assumption of
> flesh, and in this society Christ was to be the bridegroom, and the
> Church the bride.[144]

Sexual intercourse is a sign of the Incarnational union of God and humankind.[145] While for Hugh the spiritual union lies at the center of the sharing
of two lives, the sexual bond also has a role in binding the couple together:

> Can you find anything else in marriage except conjugal society that
> makes it sacred and by which you can assert that it is holy? And is it
> not much more true when two become one in mind than when they
> become one flesh? If they make each other partner of their flesh and

are holy, then if they make each other partners in soul are they not holy? Far be it. They will be two in one flesh, this is a great sacrament; [but I speak] in Christ and in the Church (Eph. 5:31–32).[146]

Hugh wishes to emphasize the spiritual bond in marriage without detracting from the holiness of the physical bond of intercourse.

He shares the long-standing view that the married couple ought to channel the powerful force of intercourse moderately so as not to become inordinately passionate.[147] We saw above that Hugh took the idea of intercourse as a remedy for sin, and argued that intercourse obeying the laws of faithful marriage is a discipline which restrains concupiscence. Then he drew an analogy between the "exercise" of the regular canons and the "exercise" of the married state (a disciplined marital intercourse) in fostering virtue. Of course his contemporaries understood the delights of the marital bed, and Bernard of Clairvaux tried to enlist these delights to ameliorate marital discord. Thus in a letter to Adelaide of Lorraine he urged her to use the "chaste and dear embracings in which [she and her husband] took delight, so that in both of them the love of Christ might prevail," to resolve conflict between them.[148] But in calling intercourse holy Hugh went beyond Bernard's recognition of the positive role of intercourse within the marriage relationship. This also sets him apart from later scholastic theologians, who usually emphasize the remedial nature of marital chastity.

Domestic Violence

Hugh's works also register awareness of the violence that domestic society could potentially contain. In *On the Vanity of the World* he writes:

When that society itself which ought to generate concord has become tiresome, how quickly does it serve to kindle hatred and discord.... After this daily quarrels and disputes become frequent, and after harsh words follow furious blows. Neither can escape the other; they share one home, one table, one bed, but nothing is worse than the fact that they have neither a friendly companion nor a separated enemy. For just as those whose minds are united in charity can withstand being separated physically, the physical association is a great torment to those who disagree.[149]

Richard of St. Victor too noted the ease with which love can turn to hate, and the way that people who hate each other can continue to burn with lust. He drew a striking picture of the type of love that could easily afflict spouses locked in a diseased marriage:

Hence arises what we have often seen in some people, namely, that the more ardently they seem to love one another at first, the more they

persecute each other afterwards with passionate hatred. Indeed, and
this is even more astounding, at one and the same time they hate and
yet do not cease to burn with desire for each other, and love in such a
way that they do not desist from persecuting each other by hatred.[150]

This is another facet of increasing attention toward the ways in which the
physical and everyday manifest the kinds of love.

An Incarnational Theology

We have seen that the theologians' interest in marriage was part of the
twelfth-century discovery of the self and alluded to the idea that twelfth-
century authors chose naturalistic images to express their notion of the
marital union. It is important to place this new exploration of the human
side of marriage in context within the culture's growing emphasis on "incarnationalism" — on the implications of Christ becoming a man and on how
God shapes the drama of redemption from within human history.

The older Western view focused on Christ's redemptive act as God's restitution of justice. In the eleventh and twelfth centuries writers began to offer
new suggestions that humankind had a part to play in redemption through
Christ's participation in human nature. These writers began to offer new
views of Christ's reasons for choosing to become a human being. Gradually
a new perspective on human nature itself also began to form. Bernard of
Clairvaux's conception of the importance of the body changed dramatically
during the course of his life under the influence of his changing Christology.
Even in the early evolution of his anthropology, he balanced a tendency to
view the body negatively[151] with a positive attitude in which he viewed it
as possessing a pedagogical dimension.[152] He taught that Christ assumed
a body not only to give human beings a model to imitate but to inspire
them to follow it. Human beings are inspired through their perception of
the magnificent divine mercy which allows itself to be subjected to all the
misery of the fleshly human condition. Bernard suggests that human beings
will return this gift of charity by leading charitable lives themselves. Thus,
though the flesh stands for all that is weak and limited in humankind, it is
also the instrument through which God reveals his mercy. As Bernard ma-
tured he began to soften his view that embodiment spelled only misery for
humankind. He began to emphasize that the Incarnation had been eternally
designed to accomplish the perfect unity of God and human beings, the divinization of humanity. He developed a new devotion to the things God had
done "in the flesh" and argued that one had to worship Christ's humanity
before proceeding to his divinity.

At the same time, through reading the Greek fathers, Bernard also began
to develop a more optimistic view of persons' ability to co-operate with God

in their own divinization. He began to suggest that just as in the person of the Word, the lower is transformed by the higher, so in the human person, the human body will be transformed by the divine power reaching it through its soul. For Bernard, "the perfect union of 'clarity' between the individual and the Word will be manifested exteriorly as well as interiorly. If one's soul is pure and transparent before God, it will transform everything exterior into the splendor of God."[153]

Through varied theological routes, new attention came to be paid to the body and its role in salvation history. Bernard and the other writers that we have discussed possess a rigidly hierarchical view of the soul/body relationship and frequently caution their audiences to remember that the soul has greater dignity than the body.[154] Moreover, they tend to associate the negative aspects of earthly life with the body, using the adjective "carnal" frequently as a term of denigration.[155] This said, these authors began to develop the idea that the body has a role in revealing the destiny of the person and participating in salvation.[156]

An appreciation of the way human restoration is enacted by means of the flesh (a word on whose various meanings he plays) can be discerned in this letter from Adam of Perseigne:

> Thus the Word came through the flesh, and it chose this method of coming so that in the flesh which it receives through the Virgin, the flesh forgets the love of fleshly life; nor should the divinity of the Word offer itself to fleshly people without flesh, nor could the love of fleshly things better perish in men than if the presence of the incarnate Word were to teach them concerning heavenly things.[157]

In his theology of the sacraments, Hugh of St. Victor also hopes for the reconstruction of both dimensions of the human being, interior and exterior:

> For since the whole man had been corrupted, the whole that belonged to man outside had to be assumed for the sacrament, that the whole might be sanctified without in the sacrament and that in the whole the virtue of the sacrament might operate a remedy within. And so sacraments had to be sanctified in things that the matter of man might be sanctified, as works in deeds, as words in speech; in that way the whole indeed might be holy, both what is man and what is of man.[158]

Other monastic theologians of the twelfth century voice, in at least a halting way, a belief that the body reveals the inner transformation of the soul. William of St. Thierry longed to see the signs of this *renovatio* in the faces and bearing of his monks.[159] Not only does the body reveal the glory of the soul, but various figures claim that the body itself[160] contributes to salvation. The Virgin Mary received great devotion, since through her

Christ received his humanity. As Adolf Katzenellenbogen has shown, the late twelfth-century facades of Senlis, Laon, and Chartres show us Christ and Mary surrounded by scenes from the life of Mary.[161] This was a pictorial representation of the idea that Christ's marriage to the Church, and his assumption of her human nature, was made possible through his mother, through whom he received his humanity.[162] The French cathedrals show us Christ's marriage to humanity as a spiritual communion with the capacity for exalting human nature to the status of partner with divinity itself.

Especially among Cistercian writers, marriage became popular as a metaphor for the Incarnation, God's unity with the corporate Church and with each individual member.[163] Innocent III borrowed from a variety of Cistercian writers as well as Hugh of St. Victor in two important works on marriage. One, a treatise entitled *On the Fourfold Types of Marriage,* discussed in part above, treats four interpretations of marriage corresponding to the four levels of scriptural interpretation. The four unions are (1) union of the flesh, between a man and a woman (historical); (2) union of the body, between Christ and his Church (allegorical level); (3) union of the spirit, between God and the soul (tropological or moral level); and (4) the union of the Person of Christ, between the Word and human nature (anagogical level). The first twenty-four chapters describe the marriage between Christ and the Church. Innocent teaches that the cause of this marriage was the Incarnation, and its effect was the total restoration in body and soul of each of the faithful.

The second work he composed is a sermon written on the anniversary of his consecration as pope. It described his own relationship to the Church as a "spiritual marriage." The canonist Huguccio had proposed this image to explain why the pope could exercise powers of administration from the moment of election, even before his confirmation. The three traditional blessings of marriage (faith, offspring, and the sacrament) are given spiritual meanings (chastity, fertility, and stability). Innocent expresses thanks for being chosen to wed the Church. He says that the calling surpasses all his prior blessings because his love for the Church has been aroused anew.[164] Directing attention to the passionate element of spousal love, he then speaks of how this issues in a life poured out for her in daily activity. The carnal union of marriage is compared to the knowledge gained by the pope about the Church through his administration of it. Innocent symbolized the bride as various great female figures of the Scriptures: Sarah the mature, Rebecca the wise, Leah the fertile, etc. As a *sponsus,* standing in for the *Sponsus,* Christ, his celibacy found its meaning in relation to the fruitfulness of the Church. Innocent reveals a Bernardine appreciation of human fertility as a metaphor for spiritual fertility. His audience saw marriage presented as holy because the spouses' concern for their offspring mirrored a concern for the salvation of souls.

Innocent portrayed himself as "having it all" in the sense of having a life that was simultaneously celibate and fruitful. On a practical level, however, most people were required to choose one or the other. Innocent did reluctantly permit individuals to leave a vow of betrothal to pursue a life of celibacy. His conviction that consummated marriages could not be dissolved on these grounds marks a shift from earlier canon law.[165] His estimation of the importance of the active dimension of love may shed light on his changed perspective.

While these treatises certainly direct attention from the human institution of marriage to the higher realities of which they are a sacrament, they also show us the human institution gaining in esteem. As Hugh of St. Victor had stressed that sexual relations invest marriage with holiness, Innocent lent dignity to the marriage bed by celebrating the love and fruitfulness common to the physical union of marriage and the union of divine and human natures in Christ taught in Ephesians.

In summary, twelfth-century writers provide the beginnings of a rich spirituality of marriage. In general we find in this period a growing incarnationalism, a reassessment of the role played by humankind in the drama of redemption. In this context marriage began to be portrayed as a means to salvation. Anselm of Laon articulated the theme of self-sacrifice as the heart of the meaning of marriage. This insight had germinated in earlier Carolingian writers but flowered in the thought of Bonaventure and Aquinas. Figures[166] such as Master Simon and Innocent III suggested a parallel between the procreation of children and the fruitfulness of the relationship between Christ and his Church: both bring new Christians into the Church. Sexual intercourse was further rehabilitated by Hugh of St. Victor, who like Augustine suggested both that intercourse is natural to the human condition and that it is not merely an after-effect of the Fall. He also compared the discipline of faithful sexual expression among the laity with the spiritual discipline asked of monks and priests. Apart from elaborating on the value, joy, and responsibilities attached to parenthood and the married state, twelfth-century writers displayed an awareness of the pitfalls of married life — not only physical violence and the debilitation of love into a flammable combination of love and hate, but also the heartaches attached to raising children.

Literary Images of Marriage

Leclercq asserts that the developing spirituality of the Church's conception of marriage had considerable influence. Popular romances, often told in royal courts, were one means by which complicated theological ideas were popularized.[167] This literature reveals varied, complicated, and diverse authorial motives. Its presentation of marriage varied from profoundly Christian to overtly anti-Christian. A Christian vision of married love is displayed in the later works of Chrétien de Troyes.[168] Chrétien, a cleric and poet at the court of Champagne, at one time or another participated in most of the currents of twelfth-century love literature. Initially he suggested that passionate, erotic love inevitably leads a knight to clash with his social commitments and thus to tragedy. Later, he rejected the secular code of love in favor of a religious one, which Joan Ferrante has suggested "proved to be the future of the entire romance tradition."[169]

Chrétien's masterpiece, *Cligès,* conveys a strong sense of the mysterious coexistence of the human and the divine in love. From the courtly love tradition came the idea that love operates according to its own rules, and that the depths of passion are infinite. The character of Fénice, at first fearing to subject herself to love, ultimately realizes that her womanhood and stability consist in submission to love:

> Her devotion made articulate is laying a unifying foundation to her life and to the poem, a binding stone the more firm through the process of yielding to commitment and the humility which makes her ready for every sacrifice; the universal Christ, whose name is love, is lending of his spirit to the structure of her character.[170]

The purely passionate element of Fénice's love is burned away, as iron is tested in fire, and *amors* (human love or desire) yields to self-giving love. Here the preparatory role of *amors* echoes Marie de France's conception that one must first learn to love at a natural level before progressing further in love. The transmutation of *amors* into self-giving love is symbolized by *Amors*' opening of the door while the lovers are cloistered in an idyllic orchard cared for by the Unseen Gardener. At the end of the story the lovers are released from the orchard, the mystical tableau dissolves and is replaced by the marriage of the two lovers, presided over by Guinevere. The conversation between Guinevere, the hero, Cligès, and heroine, Fénice, after the marriage is an experience of "heaven on earth."[171]

In Chrétien's *Erec and Enide,* Erec passes through several stages of education in love: at the beginning of the story Erec falls in love with Enide, who resembles a divine image.[172] The couple are married, but then their love begins to interfere with Erec's chivalric duties. One day Enide awakens from sleep and begins to lament Erec's decline in status in the Arthurian community. The pair undergoes a series of trials. Chrétien evokes a heart-wrenching portrait of a woman torn by the passion of love and the dictates of reason; she has antecedents in the Ovidian tradition as well as in the person of Heloise. As her love is tested in the course of the romance, it repeatedly breaks out of restraints in order to save her husband. Eventually

Enide gains the ability to discipline her passions, and Erec in turn discovers his own physical vulnerability. Their newfound self-awareness enables them to withstand the final test of their love, at the point of death. Possessed of unsurpassed happiness, the couple desire to share their discovery of the rewards of selfless love with others. As the story closes, the couple are crowned king and queen. The quadrivium on Erec's robe signifies that the motions of his heart now harmonize with the laws that regulate the cosmos.

Originally the object of Erec's desire and quest, Enide at first plays the secondary, passive role typical of some of her predecessors in the romantic genre. The narrative voice changes at the couple's "awakening" in the marriage bed, and the focus shifts to her. Her awakening is an allusion to Bernard of Clairvaux's interpretation of the Bride's words in the Song of Songs: "I sleep and my heart keeps watch." Bernard interpreted it as a call to turn to the inner voice of the heart in contemplation, but here we find it used in a lay context.[173] The narrative recounts Enide's vigilance, intuitive vision, heroism, and refusal to keep silent. By listening to Enide, Erec learns to yield to her inner strength, thus restoring balance to their relationship and, ultimately, to the kingdom.

Enide recedes behind the figure of her husband at the end of the story, and this also reveals the medieval notion of marital partnership. The male figure traditionally wielded public authority, but this is not to say that feminine deference precluded action. This is dramatized in a medieval epic titled the *Song of William,* probably written about the middle of the twelfth century. The action moves between the home of William and his wife, Guiburc, and the field of battle where William is fighting the Saracens and preserving his family's honor. William repeatedly returns home for rest, and each time he consults with his wife on the progress of the battle. Repeatedly Guiburc urges him to return to the battle or even plans independently to send soldiers to his aid. Penny Schine Gold points out that Guiburc is able to influence the outcome of action on the battlefield even though she never leaves the sphere of the home.[174] Guiburc, in fact, so inevitably steps into the breach when her husband's nerve fails him that she emerges as the more forceful, even conniving, character. This may indicate the author's awareness of how much authority a female could wield in an age in which the Crusades could keep a man away from home for years. The problem of the integration of male and female achieves resolution, due to Guiburc and William's shared familial goals — the military success of the family. Guiburc sends her nephew Gui to William's aid just as he is about to be beaten by the Saracens in battle.

Wolfram von Eschenbach, a knight writing in the first decade of the thirteenth century, presents a vision of marriage shaped by notions of feudal loyalty.[175] In *Parzival,* Wolfram's hero, Parzival, searches for the Grail, which is his knightly destiny. At the beginning of the story, as Parzival begins to learn the rudiments of knightly behavior, he rescues and marries his wife, Condwiramurs. The author emphasizes that the marriage was not consummated for three days, perhaps echoing the biblical marriage of Tobias and Sara, but after the exchange of consent Condwiramurs nevertheless considered herself a matron, binding up her hair as was customary. Christopher Brooke avers that this shows the author's belief that consummation is secondary to the loyalty, or *triuwe*, of husband and wife. After Parzival's first trial to secure the Grail fails, he is sent on a five-year quest. In the course of his quest, it is his marriage vow that sustains him. As Brooke has written, "we are frequently reminded that while other folk were inspired by a variety of ladies, Parzival never ceased to recall his wife: his *triuwe*, his loyalty to her, is more constant than his loyalty to God."[176] Though Wolfram claimed to be without formal theological training, he weaves together the themes of knightly adventure with the purgation of his character's weaknesses through love. The development of *triuwe* to self, wife, and king go hand in hand. Wolfram's vision of marriage values the pleasure of husband and wife in each other and in their children above all other aspects of marriage.[177]

Courtly Love, Epic, and Satire

Authors of other genres of literature also explored the interior motions of the human heart in the twelfth century. Whether they dramatized their insights in fabulous, epic, or mocking language, their wit and imagination found an amiable subject in love and marriage.

Much twelfth-century literature shows the influence of "courtly love" or *fin' amors* (fine love). C. S. Lewis argued in the *Allegory of Love* that the creation of the notion of romantic love in the twelfth century was one of the most fundamental cultural shifts the West has ever known, with repercussions in literary taste, social customs, and ethical standards.[178] Lewis proposed three elements of courtly love: the worship of women; sublimation of the lover through the performance of chivalric deeds; and the purification of the lover through passionate love. Since Christian love had no place for such passion, according to Lewis, this passion had to be extramarital. Lewis's theories have been criticized on a number of counts, above all for his notion that courtly love is necessarily adulterous or necessarily anti-Christian:[179] Some have even said that "courtly love" is anachronistic when applied to the Middle Ages.[180] Roger Boase, however, shows that medieval authors did sometimes use the term "courtly love,"[181] and that courtly and chivalric ideals were not merely literary postures but informed the manners and conduct of the aristocracy.[182] Those who accept the validity of the term "courtly love" today understand it as the idealization of a lady and elevation of a lover through chivalrous deeds performed in her honor.

The first literary form taken by courtly love — the poems of the troubadours, or traveling songsters — flourished from about 1100 to 1300.[183] It has the appearance of an elaborate game, and in fact the poets frequently outlined its "rules." Their lyric poems sang of *fin' amors,* usually erotic, but subtly so. The troubadours flirted with the ladies to whom they addressed their poems, but rarely was the nature of their love or the lady in question identified; as William Paden says, "the songs make a spectacle of the speaker, not of his beloved."[184]

Myriad theories have been proposed to explain the nature and origins of courtly love. Boase has concluded that two theories command the greatest assent. The first is that courtly love was imported from Hispano-Arabic culture into southern France from Muslim Spain. European courtly love and Arabic poetry have structural similarities and a number of shared themes: the purification of the lover through his devotion; the potentially dangerous, even lethal, effects of love; and the idealization of women. The paradoxical language that typifies Arabic medical treatises on the destructive effects of love are important witnesses to the influences of this tradition.[185]

As Eastern ideas were transported into the Western medieval context, the Arabic notions were transformed. The idea of the lover's submission, for instance, became cloaked in the guise of the feudal oath. Some have suggested that the courtly genre evolved in response to certain sociological factors. This is the second theory favored by Boase: that the ideals of courtly love were formed by a petty nobility at a time of rapid social change. An increase in the wealth of the ruling classes in southern France provoked an increase in those employed in service to the nobility. At the same time, the growth of the bourgeoisie threatened noble power. Payments in kind were increasingly replaced by money payments, relaxing personal ties of dependence. Therefore:

> In an age when the feudal contract ceased to exercise the same moral compulsion over lords and vassals, and when rapid changes in the structure of society resulted in friction and insecurity, Courtly Love, itself a patron-client relationship, may have acted to some extent as a cohesive force between the ruling élite and those who were affiliated to them.[186]

As noted in chapter 4, Georges Duby has shown that medieval French families discouraged younger sons from marrying to prevent fragmentation of the patrimony, or familial lands.[187] The results were large bands of youths (*juvenes*), dependent on patrons who housed them at their courts. The *juvenes* roamed the countryside in search of adventures, or, better yet, a wealthy wife, presenting a constant challenge to the patron's authority. The troubadours' poems possibly allowed the *juvenes* to engage in fantasies of wife abduction, not infrequently directed toward the patron's own wife; from the patron's point of view, they functioned as an escape valve for the restless energies of these young men.

Boase argues that while some courtly poetry resembles Neoplatonic doctrines about love, the influence of Neoplatonism was marginal. The relationship of the troubadours to Catharism is slightly more complicated. Dualism was popular with aristocratic ladies, so it is conceivable that the poets played to Catharist beliefs, particularly Catharism's opposition to marriage. Anti-clericalism, by itself, does not distinguish Cathar sympathizers in southern France. Therefore, "although the troubadours and Cathar heretics both depended for their survival on the patronage of an aristocracy opposed to ecclesiastical interference, their coexistence was coincidental."[188]

Many scholars have observed that courtly love, as originally formulated, depicts the lady as a rather passive object, merely inspiring the deeds of men.[189] Sometime in the second half of the twelfth century a distinctive female voice began to write romances that emphasized personal relationships. Little is known about the woman called Marie de France other than her name and that she addressed her works to a certain Count Guillaume and a king, probably King Henry II.[190] In Robert Hanning's view, Marie exalts the power of imagination and love as an antidote to the ethic of violence and martial prowess;[191] at times she also seems to treat the escapist function of romance in the lives of unhappily married women with some irony. As the imprisoned wife in *Yonec* says:

> I've often heard that one could find in this land adventures that brought relief to the unhappy. Knights might find young girls to their desire noble and lovely; and ladies find lovers so handsome, courtly, brave and valiant that they could not be blamed and no one else would see them.[192]

Marie de France generally chooses adulterous loves for her stories. In *Yonec*, Marie suggests that an adulterous love may be truer, even more acceptable to God, than a loveless marriage, and help one to endure the latter, until the day when the love-child avenges the love which brought him forth.

Medieval notions of marital friendship assumed a measure of inequality between the sexes.[193] At times twelfth-century writers extended this belief into full-blown misogyny. John of Salisbury (1115–80) included a critique of matrimony and the immodesty of women in general in his *Policraticus,* as did the *De amore* of Andrew the Chaplain, an encyclopedic and idiosyncratic treatise on love in the Ovidian tradition dating from the end of the twelfth century.[194] Leclercq has argued that misogynistic medieval authors generally drew their inspiration from the rich vein of misogyny in the classical authors. By contrast the more favorable view of women and marriage found among the reforming monastic orders drew from the biblical and patristic traditions.[195] In any case, texts like Andrew's had a much more limited circulation than monastic texts such as those of Bernard of Clairvaux.[196] Only in the thirteenth century, when extracts from such misogynous texts began to be included in university compilations and in the *exempla* of the mendicant preachers, did they became more widely known.

When the vernacular sagas are examined, the depth of resistance in some places to the Christian moral code becomes obvious. Whole cultures, especially on the edges of Christendom, seem to have felt a profound antipathy toward the imposition of quite foreign values and ideas. Ecclesiastical beliefs about marriage and celibacy must indeed have looked strange to many twelfth-century cultures.[197]

A twelfth-century Icelandic saga records the deeds of a bishop who expended most of his energy ferreting out irregular marital situations and exhorting the offenders to mend their ways. Although this bishop was canonized, the author of the saga takes wry satisfaction in his eventual replacement in 1198 by his married nephew, the illegitimate son of the former bishop's sister.

In conclusion, the popularity of love and marriage as subjects in the literature of the twelfth century shows that love in all its forms had become an endlessly fascinating object of analysis. Love was seen as a "figment of the imagination," that is, something in which the imagination played a powerful role.

Dissemination of Ecclesiastical Teachings

The Church's ideas about marriage were also disseminated in other ways. Ideas developed at the highest level of the Church tended to appear in the legislation of regional councils within about a generation. Reforming ideas spread further down the ecclesiastical ladder through the injunction that the statutes of local synods be made available to the rector of each parish.[198]

Much still remains unclear about the education of twelfth-century pastors themselves, but current research indicates that from the later twelfth century, confessionals, the manuals designed to instruct priests in hearing confessions, were one means of transmitting new ideas to them. Confession was one way in which the complicated theology of marriage being developed in the schools could be transmitted to lay people. How many twelfth-century schoolmasters were hearing confessions is not known, but Hugh of St. Victor's treatise *De sacramentis* indicates that he may have been hearing confessions at the royal abbey of St. Victor in Paris.[199] This would not be surprising, since one of the first penitentials, Robert of Flamborough's *Liber penitentiale,* written between 1208 and 1213, originated at St. Victor,[200] even before the abbey shared jurisdiction with the bishop of Paris over the hearing of confessions of Parisian students.[201] Robert's treatise makes no references to academic life and so was presumably intended to advise those ministering to the lay public generally. Robert's main influence seems to have been not Hugh of St. Victor, but Peter the Chanter (d. 1197).

Peter the Chanter's contribution to the ministration of penance was two-fold. His method was to discuss specific cases for the guidance of confessors. He also sought to replace the rather mechanical dispensing of appropriate punishments for various sins with the more "medicinal" objective of heal-ing the penitent's soul.[202] Confessionals show that important regulations touching consent were transmitted to pastors as early as 1216. Thomas of Chobham, subdean and judge of Salisbury and rector of Chobham, Surrey, includes them in his *Summa Confessorum*, written at this time. It is not until the fourteenth century that we have certain evidence that numerous parishioners knew enough canon law to appreciate the necessity of consent. Then we find couples successfully defending their unions in the ecclesiastical courts against parental opposition.[203]

Thomas of Chobham's *Summa*, like that of Peter the Chanter, teaches through concrete examples, and thus gives a fascinating look at behaviors priests were told to promote among married couples. Medieval confessors might be instructed to treat the marriage bed as an opportune place for moral persuasion.[204] Women were encouraged to preach to their husbands:

> When they are alone and she is in her husband's arms she ought to speak to him soothingly, and if he is hard and merciless and an op-pressor of the poor she ought to invite him to mercy, if he is a plunderer to desist his plundering; if he is grasping, let her inspire generosity in him and let her secretly give alms from their common property.[205]

Chobham appeals to women to use their feminine wiles, while he appeals to the protective instincts of the male. Husbands are told to honor their wives, regarding them like a part of their own bodies:

> If she is dull, let him correct her moderately and discreetly, and, if necessary, punish her. For he ought to be more careful about the care of his wife than about any worldly possession, because nothing should be more dear to him than his wife.[206]

The Pauline idea of mutual submission is here expressed in the practical order. One senses that Chobham attributes a natural desire for peace, jus-tice, and charity to women; an anxiety to alert confessors to the possibility of domestic violence is similarly palpable. This gives a fascinating view of clerical perceptions of the daily lives of ordinary men and women.

Rural deans also enforced the marriage teachings on a very widespread scale in the countryside.[207] It has been said that the deans were motivated primarily by greed, profiting from the fines imposed on offenders, but much more remains to be learned about these courts before we conclude too much about motivation.[208] Rural deans undeniably helped to bring about conformity to Church teaching, so much so that by 1200 it was clearly the norm that a peasant girl from a family with any land at all participated in a formal marriage.[209]

Among the highest levels of the élites, either local or papal censure could usually achieve grudging obedience to Church teaching, though some battles went on for years. By the end of the twelfth century, the papacy played a central role in resolving disputes over the validity of given marriages.[210] This was the result of the restructured system of appeals during the time of Alexander III, and of Innocent III's determined policy to become the final arbiter of valid marriages. The relationship between the papacy and European nobility was consequently transformed. Huw Pryce has noted that the acceptance of the Church's complicated rules on prohibited degrees of marriage marks a change in Welsh aristocratic attitudes.[211] As societies came to be more Christianized, the desire for social respect undoubtedly played a part in changing aristocratic attitudes. Diane Hughes has shown in her study of medieval Genoa that the Church sometimes received a good measure of respect from the members of the bourgeoisie, who frequently named parishes as their residual heirs.[212]

Scholarly research on marriage sermons is as yet incomplete. Two main genres have thus far been identified: sermons for the celebration of the marriage at Cana and *ad status* marriage sermons, sermons on the topic of marriage directed at lay people. Preliminary work on *ad status* sermons reveals a good deal of uniformity. They emphasized traditional themes such as the evils of adultery.[213] They also transmitted the doctrine of the three Augustinian goods of marriage: faith, children, and sacrament. They gave moral and spiritual guidance, such as recommending periodic times of abstention from intercourse (during Lent, for example). *Ad status* sermons by Jacques de Vitry (d. 1240), a student of Peter the Chanter,[214] contain material of a canonical nature, explaining what a marriage is and the Pauline privilege.[215] More generally, thirteenth-century preaching often contained the "rib-topos" elaborated earlier by such writers as Hugh of St. Victor. The creation of Eve from Adam's rib shows that she was created for equality.[216]

It is difficult to know how much of the theology surrounding the notion of sacrament, including the affective and symbolic nature of the bond, was popularly diffused. The topic of marital affection does not seem to have been popular in the *ad status* collections. Honorius of Autun (c. 1080/89–c. 1156), one of the earliest authors in the genre, is something of an exception in calling upon husbands to love their wives and vice versa.[217] Very little study has been devoted to how the laity received the preaching of twelfth-century Victorines and Cistercians.[218] Outsiders were welcome to hear the abbot of St. Victor deliver his homilies; this would be one way that the lay public might hear the teachings carefully refined in the classrooms of school-masters such as Hugh of St. Victor.[219] The Victorine sermons have yet to be studied in their entirety.[220] The *ad status* sermons tell us that in every case, popular preachers used the term "sacrament," which suggests that people were familiar with the idea of marriage as a holy institution.[221] This would no doubt also have been a theme of the Cistercians, such as Fulk of Toulouse, appointed by Innocent III to preach the crusade against the Cathars through-out southern France.[222] Sermons commemorating the marriage at Cana have been examined by D. L. D'Avray in a cross-comparison of thirteenth and seventeenth-century sermons.[223] D'Avray cites a sermon by the Dominican Guillaume Peyraut, which enjoins husbands to love their wives.[224] D'Avray notes that the notion of love conveyed by medieval preachers (1) does not imply sexual attraction (while not excluding it); and (2) is "voluntaristic" rather than "romantic," in the sense that love is viewed as a choice rather than a passion.[225] Guillaume's sermon, which teaches men to long for their wives' salvation and to offer them an unlimited store of forgiveness, shows the moral emphasis in medieval preaching on marriage.

Other ways in which the Church disseminated its teaching include the liturgy and liturgical drama. The first and most obvious example was the marriage liturgy itself.[226] The liturgical drama and morality play were other ways to disseminate relatively sophisticated theological ideas. Contemporary redrawings of the Adam and Eve story in vernacular liturgical plays, for instance, depicted doctrines such as the moral equality of men and women, due to their creation in the image of God.[227]

Legal codes are a useful source of information about popular behav-ior. One historian, Brundage, has discovered in them a certain toleration for the practice of concubinage in canon law.[228] Difficult as it was to dis-tinguish concubinage from clandestine marriage, he says, medieval popes tended to exercise caution, preferring to leave questionable alliances alone, rather than separate legitimately united couples. Brundage gives evidence for the widespread practice of concubinage, citing studies of areas from Nor-mandy to Iceland.[229] In his study of native law in medieval Wales, Pryce shows that divorce, usually on grounds of adultery or infertility, was con-sidered legitimate during the first seven years of a couple's marriage.[230] Because children of adulterous unions could legally inherit, this combination of elements probably created a great deal of fluidity in Welsh familial rela-tionships. Concubinage was practiced among both rich and poor: among the rich, who wished to avoid marrying women of inferior social status, and among the poor, who often lacked the means or incentives to formalize their relationships.[231]

Lack of means could have a very specific meaning—lack of a dower, the gift given by the groom to the bride, or a dowry, bestowed on the bride by her family (neither the terminology nor type of arrangements were standard throughout Europe). Peasants were also expected to pay a *merchet,* or a marriage tax, to their lords. Even the unfree and poor seem to have considered endowment to be of importance, although the official Church teaching was that it was not essential.[232] Indeed, Pope Innocent seems to have been concerned that economic status not prevent people from entering into marriage. In one case, he intervened on behalf of a poor man, Hugo, whose father-in-law refused to transmit the dowry to the couple on grounds of Hugo's poverty. Innocent demanded that the dowry be provided, but compromised by giving it into the hands of a merchant who would then dispense the interest, if Hugo could not provide suitable security for it.[233]

In sum, we have considerable evidence of both dissemination of and resistance to Church teaching on marriage. The popes considered that local resistance to ecclesiastical injunctions arose because many people were accustomed to "regard marriage as a private matter and to ignore canonical rules that conflicted with personal preference or family interest."[234]

The Contribution of Social History

Social historians in recent decades have not just unearthed information about the ecclesiastical influence on marriage practices.[235] They have provided a window into the daily lives of medieval men and women and the ways that gender shaped behavior and experience. One rich source of information has been notarial collections — repositories of written documents such as marriage contracts and dowry pledges, wills, real estate transactions, commercial contracts, and the like. One of Europe's oldest and fullest collections of notarial records, which contains transactions from the mid-twelfth century onward, is preserved in Genoa. In one study of these records, Hughes compared the marriage practices of the Genoese merchant aristocracy and artisan classes.[236]

Genoese aristocrats normally lived in joint family compounds. Several branches of a family occupied adjacent houses, often along the perimeter of a small square, sharing common shops, baths, and church, and protected by the great towers that marked the cityscape. In these common areas the family would mix and share the latest gossip. Families were patriarchal and inheritances descended through the net of male kin, called the lineage, when no son stood to inherit. A single male leader often functioned in a political fashion as a spokesman for the entire lineage, as Nicolo Doria acted on behalf of his house in 1200.[237] The artisan family, by contrast, was usually a single-family household, although wealthier artisans sometimes created extended family households. For public activity, the artisan usually turned to the Church, but the majority of time was spent within the household, and the household was defined primarily by the conjugal bond.

Hughes underlined the importance of the conjugal bond to the artisan family by showing that twelfth-century wives were made heirs by artisan husbands in 23 percent of the extant wills, even if children were living. In defiance of the Genoese law that prohibited the size of the *antefactum,* or gift from groom to bride, from exceeding half the value of the dowry, over 70 percent of artisans contributed gifts above this amount. This compared to 44 percent in aristocratic marriages. Hughes believes that among the aristocracy, the size of a daughter's dowry conferred status, a consideration that had little meaning for working-class fathers, who were more concerned with giving their children as favorable a start in life as possible.

Hughes suggests that the bond between spouses in the Genoese artisan class may have been strengthened by employment at a common task. On the other hand, wife-beating among artisans was far higher than in the aristocratic families, where men more often directed their anger toward fathers or uncles. Artisans seem to have had somewhat more freedom in the selection of a mate; and "it is an artisan who first appears in the extant notarial records to exercise the marital choice that the church was coming to advocate by running to her priest to refuse her assigned partner."[238]

Genoa's social structure was not typical for all of Europe; in fact, no family arrangements typify the same classes even in one country.[239] Further to the west, in France, Toulousan aristocratic families might lodge additional family members in their houses, but they had nothing like the aristocratic Italian extended family, whose members worked in concert. A few economic trends among noblewomen do, however, appear throughout most of Europe. A general trend among the nobility toward patrilineal succession, or succession through the male line, existed, as we saw in the last chapter. At the same time, societal preoccupation with war decreased the number of men available for marriage. As competition between women on the marriage market rose, each woman commanded less of an advantage. The amount of money demanded from a woman's family as a dowry began to climb.[240] The economic and legal autonomy of noblewomen seems to have deteriorated throughout much of Europe.

An unforgettable view of how unstable the position of noblewomen in twelfth-century France was is provided by Dominique Barthélemy. During the twelfth century France underwent a transition from the feudal disorder especially of the early eleventh century to the social order achieved under the thirteenth-century monarchic state. In this milieu women suffered from the strain placed on familial bonds, a prime source of social order: "Alliances based on marriage, necessary for securing peace between lineages and factions, were no more secure than peace itself."[241] Women sometimes were torn between loyalty to their families and their husbands. One such woman was the wife of Gui de la Roche-Guyon, who, seeing her husband and children killed by her brother in front of her own eyes, cried "Were you not joined by indissoluble friendship? What is this madness?"[242]

Marriage's role in maintaining social stability is underlined by the not infrequent injunctions made by Genoese male testators that their wives should not inherit. If a woman did choose to remarry, she would inherit only her dowry and marriage gift. Steven Epstein has speculated that men sought to prevent their wives from remarrying primarily to protect their children: "men tried to preserve the integrity of the household in order to provide a safe nest for the young."[243]

The dowry, which formerly could be under a woman's jurisdiction after marriage, was increasingly administered by her husband in the twelfth century, and could even be alienated by him.[244] The only time that a woman normally administered land was in widowhood, when she controlled the portions assigned to her.[245] Married French noblewomen nevertheless seem to have possessed some economic power during the twelfth century. The limited number of letters that survive from twelfth-century women precludes the kind of study done by Barbara Hanawalt on the letters of a sixteenth-century female aristocrat, Lady Lisle, and the network of social connections she developed to achieve her own and her family's goals.[246] The work done by John Parsons on Eleanor of Castile, however, reveals similar networks created by thirteenth-century noblewomen.[247] One could make similar speculations about industrious twelfth-century women such as Marie de Champagne. Michelle Freeman's work on the household relationships described by Marie de France already points in this promising direction.[248] Another aspect of domestic power involved the responsibility that mothers had over the education of their children. This encompassed not only the commissioning of books and the consequent choice of suitable material, but also encouraging the translation of Latin works into the vernacular.[249] This research challenges the common view that a patriarchal society precludes significant forms of women's authority.

There is some truth in Duby's idea that two parallel "theories" of marriage, one ecclesiastical and one aristocratic, existed and often came into conflict in the twelfth century. Nevertheless Sheehan correctly argued that one should not polarize these two "camps" too completely, since the members of both groups came from the same families.[250] The obviously disparate ends of each group did not preclude a degree of cooperation. We see this in the aristocracy's growing acceptance of ecclesiastical jurisdiction over marriage law and ritual. The Church sought reconciliation among different parties or accommodated itself in some degree to the pragmatic mode of thought of the great dynasties.[251] Duby's concept of a clash between a lifeless, skeletal "Church" and the larger "society" should give way to a view of interpenetration and mutual encounter between the two.

Duby succeeds brilliantly, however, in evoking the lengths to which medieval rulers would go to preserve the royal succession, and less successfully, in distinguishing how churchmen chose to respond. Philip I of France, who dismissed his wife, Bertha, because she was too fat, and also because she had provided him with only one son, is a case in point. In the early 1090s Philip married a second wife, Bertrade. She had left her husband, Fulk of Anjou, who had repudiated his first two wives on charges of immoral behavior. Hugh of Die condemned Philip for bigamy and incest at a council at Autun. Despite papal censure from Urban II, Philip clung stubbornly to Bertrade, who produced two sons. Because Philip's first wife had died in 1094, by the first decade of the twelfth century his adultery was no longer the primary criticism of Ivo of Chartres, the churchman who sought to make Philip take responsibility for his scandalous behavior. Rather, Ivo focused on the consanguinity between Philip and Fulk of Anjou. The papacy received the occasional motion of obeisance from Philip as he became more involved in his war with William Rufus, but it was not until 1104 that there was "a reconciliation, largely encouraged by Ivo of Chartres, in which everyone gave ground to some extent."[252]

In 1152 Louis VII and Eleanor of Aquitaine, his wife of fifteen years and mother of his two daughters, decided to separate, claiming kinship to the fifth degree. They obtained conciliar approval of their separation through the intercession of the accommodating archbishop of Sens, despite Pope Eugenius III's efforts to reconcile the pair. With the dispensation of the pope,[253] Eleanor immediately took a new husband, Henry Plantagenet, while Louis remarried two years later. The chronicles differ as to who initiated the separation, but all record contempt for the royal scheme.

That there was confusion among Church authorities as to the proper way to deal with marital irregularities during the twelfth century is evident. Twelfth-century popes frequently employed the ruse of dissimulation, recognizing the irregularity of a given relationship but refusing to take action against it.[254] Local churches also received the authority to dispense marriage impediments.[255] Paris theologians such as Robert of Courçon decried the injustice and arbitrariness of the papal dispensation granted Eleanor of Aquitaine and Henry II.[256] The notoriety of such cases has led some to theorize that reducing the degrees of prohibited relationship was a response to the proliferation of such cases. It is still not known, however, precisely how widely the prohibitions to the seventh degree were enforced, or abused. Therefore, this explanation for reducing the degrees of prohibited relationship may be too simplistic.[257] Charles Donahue has suggested that annulment became rarer in the twelfth century as lay society came to depend on the ecclesiastical enforcement of indissolubility for the orderly regulation of the transfer of inheritance.[258] It is certain, however, that by the time of the Fourth Lateran Council a reduced system of prohibitions of relationship to the fourth degree was seen to be desirable.[259]

Duby consistently portrays key ecclesiastical figures, such as Ivo of Chartres, as heartless ideologues with little esteem for the married state and no capacity for tenderness toward women; the limitations of his account of Ivo of Chartres's behavior are shown by a comparison with the more generous treatment of the same events by Christopher Brooke.[260] Duby's depiction of women's prospects for marital happiness is equally negative and relies on the frequently misogynous courtly love literature. Barthélemy, too, argues that during the twelfth century, as women were relegated from more public matters to the confines of the household, their social role resembled their "sentimental sovereignty" in the world of the tournament, i.e., women were only pawns in the political games played by men. For Barthélemy, the romanticization of women provoked no real tenderness toward them; treatment of wives remained brutal. However, ample evidence argues that this unrelievedly bleak portrait must admit revision.

People in the twelfth century, like their predecessors and successors, knew what it was to give up heart and soul to another as well as to live as partners.[261] Though friendship between married couples might not exclude numerous extramarital affairs, as the story of Baldwin II, Count of Guines (d. 1169), shows, it could still include a permanent bond of affection and honor.[262] In Baldwin's case, his reverence for his late wife led him to take over the good works that had been part of her domestic duties before her death. William of Tyre describes the happy union of Ida of Lorraine (1040–1113) and Eustace, Count of Boulogne, thus: "she had the grace and the art of being loved by her husband."[263] Recounting that Ida had insisted on breast-feeding her three sons, William describes how she and her husband played upstairs in the castle with their young children. Ida also acted as advisor to her husband for administrative and financial affairs. Another witness to domestic harmony is the vernacular French lyric written by the poet Mouskès to celebrate the concordant union of Blanche of Castille (1180–1252) and Louis VIII:

> Never did a queen love
> her lord so well nor hold
> her children so strongly in her affection.
> And the king also loved them
> because they loved each other so deeply
> that they held everything in one accord.[264]

Conclusion

The twelfth century was a period of crisis and change in marriage and marriage law. The social changes of the twelfth century, the decline in the power of the seigneury, and the solidifying of patrilineal succession put new pressures on marriage relationships among the nobility. Women stood to lose husbands and children in these social conflicts; at the highest levels of noble society women could be repudiated rather easily if they failed to produce heirs for the continuance of the lineage. Though women may have lost authority in a legal and economic sense, at all levels of society they could play authoritative roles. The Church continued its clarification of the nature of marriage. The formula that was developed in canon law held that marriage was created by consent, *per verba de praesenti*, but consent *per verba de futuro* followed by consummation was also held to create a valid marriage.

As ecclesiastical thinkers of the twelfth century examined the human reality of marriage, they developed a new vision of it. Twelfth-century thinkers focused particularly intently on the fact that marriage had a spiritual meaning connected with the union of Christ and the Church. Attempts were made to connect this meaning with both consent and consummation; about midcentury, Peter Lombard proposed that both were equally sacramental. His definition became standard in the schools and lay behind the official listing of marriage among the seven sacraments by the Fourth Lateran Council in 1215. The Church's conception that marriage be marked by free consent and marital affection emphasized the good of the couple over the interests of their families.

The idea of "marital affection" received new emotional associations especially in the writings of monks and canons. This idea reverberated everywhere in the twelfth century, in theology, law, and literature. Particularly in monastic and canonical circles, a tentative exploration of the positive aspects of sexuality took place. As a feature of the growing awareness of the contribution of the body in the life of the person, both sexuality and marriage began to be explored for their capacity to reveal God's love.

Pastors transmitted their ideas to their parishioners in various ways; one of the most common was the liturgy itself. Thus a medieval Spanish marriage rite offered the following prayer, in which a blessing is invoked over the rings that the spouses exchange as a sign of their spiritual and companionate union:

> O God, who blessed the multiplication of children from the beginning of the world, look kindly on our petitions, and pour out the richness of your blessing on this, your servant, N., and this, your handmaiden, so that in conjugal society they may be joined as like companions in similarity of mind and mutual sanctity.[265]

Here we have the heart of the Church's teaching on marriage.

Notes

1. Colin Morris, "Christian Civilization (1050–1400)," in *The Oxford Illustrated History of Christianity*, ed. John McManners (Oxford, 1992), 196–232, esp. 199–200.

2. Georges Duby, *Medieval Marriage: Two Models from Twelfth-Century France*, trans. Elborg Forster (Baltimore, 1978).

3. Georges Duby and Dominique Barthélemy, "Aristocratic Households of Feudal France," in *A History of Private Life*, ed. Philippe Ariès and Georges Duby, vol. 2, *Revelations of the Medieval World*, ed. Georges Duby, trans. Arthur Goldhammer (Cambridge, Mass., 1988), 35–155, esp. 119–24.

4. On the theme of free consent see John Noonan Jr., "Power to Choose," *Viator* 4 (1973): 419–34. On the identity of "Ambrosiaster" see ibid., 419, n.1.

5. Michael Sheehan, "Choice of Marriage Partner in the Middle Ages: Development and Mode of Application of a Theory of Marriage," in *Studies in Medieval and Renaissance History*, n.s. 1 (1978), 1–33, esp. 12–13. This article has been republished in *Marriage, Family, and Law in Medieval Europe: Collected Studies*, ed. James K. Farge (Toronto, 1996), 87–117, esp. 96–97. Cf. Raymond Decker, "Institutional Authority versus Personal Responsibility in the Marriage Sections of Gratian's *A Concordance of Discordant Canons*," *The Jurist* 32 (1972): 51–65.

6. This discussion owes a great deal to the treatment of the *Life of Christina of Markyate* by Thomas Head, "The Marriages of Christina of Markyate," *Viator* 21 (1990): 75–101.

7. *The Life of Christina of Markyate, A Twelfth-Century Recluse*, ed. and trans. C. H. Talbot (Oxford, 1959), section 23, p. 72.

8. Ibid., 85, and n. 38.

9. John Baldwin, *Masters, Princes, and Merchants: The Social Views of Peter the Chanter and his Circle*, 2 vols. (Princeton, N.J., 1970), 1:249.

10. Jean Leclercq has examined the letters of Bernard of Clairvaux to lay women in the second chapter of his book *Women and Saint Bernard of Clairvaux*, Cistercian Studies Series 104 (Kalamazoo, Mich., 1989). He says that these letters show us a great deal about Bernard's conception of the role women should play in the Church and within society as a whole. Cf. Lois L. Honeycutt, "Female Succession and the Language of Power in the Writings of Twelfth-Century Churchmen," in *Medieval Queenship*, ed. John Carmi Parsons (New York, 1993), 189–201, nn. 220–21.

11. M.-D. Chenu, *Nature, Man, and Society in the Twelfth Century*, trans. Jerome Taylor and Lester K. Little (Chicago, 1968), 213–19.

12. Ibid., 218, n. 35.

13. Ibid., 222–24, and n. 40, mentions Gerhoh of Reichersberg. Honorius of Autun followed suit by creating sermons for various secular trades and professions.

14. Chenu has developed this point with reference to the writings of Pope Urban II and the famous preacher Jacques de Vitry. See ibid., 221–22, and n. 39.

15. Fourier Bonnard, *Histoire de l'Abbaye royale et de l'ordre des chanoines réguliers de St. Victor de Paris*, 2 vols. (Paris, 1904–8), 1:60.

16. Valerie Flint, "The 'School of Laon': A Reconsideration," *Recherches de Théologie Ancienne et Médiévale* 43 (1976): 89–110.

17. Sheehan, "Choice of Marriage Partner," 14–15; rpt. *Marriage, Family, and Law*, ed. Farge, 98–99.

18. Ibid. Cf. idem, "Marriage Theory and Practice in the Conciliar Legislation and Diocesan Statutes of Mediaeval England," *Mediaeval Studies* 40 (1978): 408–60; republished in *Marriage, Family, and Law*, ed. Farge, 118–76.

19. See above chap. 4 and Philip Lynden Reynolds, *Marriage in the Western Church: The Christianization of Marriage during the Patristic and Early Medieval Periods* (New York, 1994), 328–61.

20. James Brundage, *Law, Sex, and Christian Society in Medieval Europe* (Chicago, 1987), 187–88.

21. See above, chap. 3.

22. See Nicholas Häring, "The Interaction between Canon Law and Sacramental Theology in the Twelfth Century," in *Proceedings of the Fourth International Congress of Medieval Canon Law, Toronto, August 21–25, 1972*, ed. Stephan Kuttner, Monumenta Iuris Canonici, series C, subsidia 5 (Vatican City, 1976), 483–93, esp. 492–93.

23. On patristic usage of the term "sacrament," see above, chap. 3, and Seamus Heaney, *The Sacramentality of Marriage: From Anselm of Laon to Thomas Aquinas,* Studies in Sacred Theology, 2d ser., 134 (Washington, D.C., 1963), 4.

24. Theodore Mackin, *The Marital Sacrament* (Mahwah, N.J., 1989), 196–227. This work, though comprehensive, is not always reliable.

25. Ibid., 216.

26. F. Bleimetzrieder has edited the *Sententiae Anselmi* in "Anselms von Laon systematische Sentenzen," *Beiträge zur Geschichte der Philosophie und Theologie des Mittelalters* 18, h. 2–3 (Münster, 1919), 47–163. On indissolubility and its *res,* see 134–35.

27. This was also apparently assumed by Augustine in *De nuptiis et concupiscentia ad Valeriam comitem libri duo.* See Mackin, *Marital Sacrament,* 246.

28. See above, chap. 3.

29. Mackin, *Marital Sacrament,* 294.

30. Ibid., 296.

31. Cf. Dyan Elliott, *Spiritual Marriage in Medieval Wedlock* (Princeton, N.J., 1993), 138.

32. Jennifer Forbes kindly informed me that these images have been collected in Anthony Melnikas, *The Corpus of the Miniatures in the Manuscripts of Decretum Gratiani,* 3 vols., Studi Gratiani Series 16, 17, and 18 (Rome, 1975) 3:863–68.

33. Heaney, *Sacramentality of Marriage,* 6–8.

34. Hugh of St. Victor, *De sacramentis* 1.8.13. See *De sacramentis Christianae fidei,* in Patrologia cursus completus: series latina, ed. J. P. Migne, 221 vols. (Paris, 1841–64) (hereafter PL), vol. 176, cols. 173–618. There is a translation by Roy Deferrari, entitled *On the Sacraments of the Christian Faith (De sacramentis)* (Cambridge, Mass., 1951), but as this translation is not always reliable, I have provided my own translations.

35. Heaney, *Sacramentality of Marriage,* 18 and 22.

36. Ibid., 22.

37. *The Role of the Christian Family in the Modern World (Familiaris Consortio)* 3.1.20 (Boston, 1981), 35.

38. Heaney, *Sacramentality of Marriage,* 25–26.

39. Ibid., 264.

40. Brundage, *Law, Sex, and Christian Society,* 188.

41. Ibid., 235.

42. Ibid., 237–8.

43. Ibid., 270.

44. Ibid., 260.

45. See James Brundage, "Marriage and Sexuality in the Decretals of Pope Alexander III," in *Miscellanea Rolando Bandinelli Papa Alessandro III,* ed. Filippo

Liotta (Siena, 1986), 57–83; cf. Charles Donahue, "The Policy of Alexander the Third's Consent Theory of Marriage," in *Proceedings of Medieval Canon Law Held in Toronto, August 21–25, 1972*, ed. Stephan Kuttner (Vatican City, 1976), 251–81.

46. See Constance M. Rousseau, "The Spousal Relationship: Marital Society and Sexuality in the Letters of Pope Innocent III," *Mediaeval Studies* 56 (1994): 89–109, esp. 92–93.

47. Rousseau, "Spousal Relationship," 93.

48. Ibid., 104.

49. Brundage, *Law, Sex, and Christian Society*, 268.

50. Cf. on Innocent, Brenda Bolton, *Innocent III: Studies on Papal Authority and Pastoral Care* (Brookfield, Vt., 1995), vi, 167, 169; xvi, 102–3.

51. Donahue, "Policy."

52. Noonan has shown that force and fear constituted grounds for annulment from the twelfth century on, but that annulments on such grounds were rare ("Power to Choose," 433–34). Penalties were infrequently exacted upon parents in such cases.

53. Brundage, *Law, Sex, and Christian Society*, 335, 338–39.

54. Nevertheless, in the latter half of the century appear portrayals in art of marriage ceremonies with no ecclesiastical personages in sight, as in the commemoration of the marriage of the daughter of Bernart Ató discussed in the last chapter.

55. Hugh of St. Victor's discussion of the problem seems to reflect actual pastoral experience; see *De sacramentis* 2.11.6 PL 176, 488C–494A, esp. 491C.

56. See Sheehan, "Choice of Marriage Partner," 15; rpt. *Marriage, Family, and Law*, ed. Farge, 99.

57. G. H. Joyce, *Christian Marriage: An Historical and Doctrinal Study*, Heythrop Series 1 (New York, 1933) 111–15.

58. Ibid., 336. Cf. James Brundage, "Concubinage and Marriage in Medieval Canon Law," *Journal of Medieval History* 1 (1975): 1–17, esp. 6. This article has been republished in *Sex, Law, and Marriage in the Middle Ages* (Brookfield, Vt., 1993).

59. Brundage, *Law, Sex, and Christian Society*, 336.

60. Donahue, "Policy."

61. Bonaventure, *Opusculum de reductione artium ad theologiam* 5, in *Opera theologica selecta*, 5 vols. (Florence, 1964), 5:221.

62. Heaney, *Sacramentality of Marriage*, 4.

63. See Bernard McGinn, "Pseudo-Dionysius and the Early Cistercians," in *One Yet Two: Monastic Tradition East and West*, ed. M. Basil Pennington, Cistercian Studies Series 29 (Kalamazoo, Mich., 1976), 200–241. See esp. 211–12, n. 58, and 216–21. Gerhart Ladner has written a useful survey of medieval symbolism, "Medieval and Modern Understanding of Symbolism: A Comparison," *Speculum* 54 (1979): 223–56.

64. Hugh of St. Victor, *De sacramentis* 1.10.2 PL 176, 329C–330A.

65. This is my own synthesis of Hugh's discussion of the nature of the sacraments. His narrow definition of sacrament as sacred symbol appears in *De sacramentis* 1.9.2 PL 176, 317D and has been most ably discussed by Heinrich Weisweiler, "Sakrament als Symbol und Teilhabe: Der Einfluss des Ps. Dionysius auf die allgemeine Sakramentenlehre Hugos von St. Viktor," *Scholastik* 27 (1952): 321–43. In what follows I meld Hugh's strict definition of sacrament with the implications of his continued treatment of the term in *De sacramentis* 1.9.3, which I take as evidence of a new twelfth-century attitude toward body and the world. On this see Teresa Olsen, "Hugh of St. Victor's Theory of Marriage," a research report submit-

ted in partial fulfillment of the requirements for the degree of Licentiate of Mediaeval Studies, Pontifical Institute of Mediaeval Studies, Toronto (Toronto, 1993), 46–56.

66. Weisweiler, "Sakrament als Symbol," 332–34. Hugh's emphasis on the mystical and intellectual process which leads from the symbol to God has been almost entirely lost to modern theology. This happened through a series of theological shifts, beginning in the scholastic period, which are discussed in Olsen, "Hugh of St. Victor's Theory of Marriage," 54–56. Cf. Colman E. O'Neill, *Sacramental Realism: A General Theory of the Sacraments* (Wilmington, Del., 1983).

67. Chenu, *Nature, Man, and Society,* 140.

68. *De sacramentis* 1.9.3 PL 176, 320C.

69. Ibid., 1.9.3 PL 176, 320C–322A.

70. Ibid., 1.8.13 PL 176, 314CD.

71. Hugh continues: "On this account, of the three causes for the institution of the sacraments, we find here only two, namely, instruction and exercise." Ibid., 1.8.12 PL 176, 314B.

72. Hugh called by the name of "sacrament" many things besides the official list of seven sacraments of the Fourth Lateran Council of 1215, but he considered some sacraments, including marriage, to be preeminent because, in addition to being images, they bestowed saving grace: they healed the mind and heart of the wounds of original sin. Another twelfth-century treatise which argues that marriage bestows grace is the *Ysagoge in theologiam* (1148–52) of the school of Abelard, according to Heaney, *Sacramentality of Marriage,* 11.

73. Hugh, *De sacramentis* 1.9.4 PL 176, 323B. The idea of the sacrament as vessel of grace stems from Augustine: Heinrich Weisweiler, *Die Wirksamkeit der Sakramente nach Hugo von St. Viktor* (Freiburg, 1932) 11ff., 15ff., 44–45, 146ff.

74. See Weisweiler, "Sakrament als Symbol," 335.

75. For a survey of twelfth- and thirteenth-century writers' views on the efficacy of grace in marriage see chap. 2 of Heaney, *Sacramentality of Marriage.* Cf. Mackin, *Marital Sacrament,* 364–65.

76. Ibid., 309.

77. Ibid., 303–4.

78. Ibid., 366–71. D. L. D'Avray and M. Tausche's study of twelfth- and thirteenth-century marriage sermons, "Marriage Sermons in *Ad Status* Collections of the Central Middle Ages," *Archives d'histoire doctrinale et littéraire du Moyen Âge* 47 (1980): 71–119, shows that preachers did not commonly speak of grace as a feature of marriage.

79. Heaney, *Sacramentality of Marriage,* 136.

80. Weisweiler, "Sakrament als Symbol," 331.

81. Nicholas Häring, "Berengar's Definitions of *Sacramentum* and Their Influence on Mediaeval Sacramentology," *Mediaeval Studies* 10 (1948): 109–46.

82. *De sacramentis* 1.9.2 PL 176, 317D.

83. Cf. Heaney, *Sacramentality of Marriage,* 9–10.

84. Ibid., 25.

85. Peter Lombard, *Sententiae in IV libris distinctae* 4, Dist. 1, c. 2, ed. Colegii S. Bonaventurae ad Claras Aquas, 3d ed., 2 vols. (Rome, 1971–81), 2:232. See the translation of book 4's discussion of the sacraments in E. Rogers, *Peter Lombard and the Sacramental System* (Schenectady, N.Y., 1917; rpt. Merrick, N.Y., 1976), 80.

86. Peter Lombard, *Sententiae* 4, Dist. 26, c. 6, trans. Rogers, 246.

87. The crucial scholastic breakthrough here was to clarify that the marriage bond (as the middle term, in logical terminology) not only symbolized but also *effected* the conferral of grace. Of all the twelfth-century thinkers, Anselm

of Laon probably foreshadowed this development the most clearly. Cf. Heaney, *Sacramentality of Marriage,* 145–48.

88. Brian Bethune, "The Text of the Christian Rite of Marriage in Medieval Spain," Ph.D. dissertation, University of Toronto, 1986, 13.

89. Jean Baptiste Molin and Protais Mutembe, *Le rituel du mariage en France du XIIe au XVIe siècle,* Théologie historique 26 (Paris, 1974) 135–66, 179–88.

90. Bethune, "Christian Rite of Marriage," 181.

91. Ibid., 14.

92. Ibid.

93. Innocent III, *Innocent III, De quadripartita specie nuptiarum,* in *A Study of Pope Innocent's Treatise "De Quadripartita Specie Nuptiarum,"* ed. Connie M. Munk, 4 vols., Ph.D. dissertation, University of Kansas, 1975.

94. Munk, *De quad. spec. nuptiarum,* 1:4.

95. Ibid., 1:40–44.

96. Innocent III, *De quad. spec. nuptiarum* 2.9, ed. Munk, 2:9; cf. ibid., 2.54, ed. Munk, 2:39–40.

97. Ibid., 2.13, ed. Munk, 2:11.

98. Ibid., 2.64, ed. Munk, 2:50.

99. Munk, *Study,* 1:118–20.

100. Innocent III, *De quad. spec. nuptiarum* 2.16–21, ed. Munk, 2:12–14; cf. ibid. 2.61–2, ed. Munk, 2:56–57.

101. Jean Leclercq, *Monks on Marriage: A Twelfth-Century View* (New York, 1982), 38.

102. Heath Dillard, *Daughters of the Reconquest: Women in Castilian Town Society, 1100–1300* (Cambridge, 1984), 61–64.

103. See Mackin, *Marital Sacrament,* 318, and also the decrees of the Third Lateran Council (1179) in *Decrees of the Ecumenical Councils,* ed. Norman Tanner, vol. 1, *Nicaea I to Lateran V* (Washington, D.C., 1990), 215.

104. The Fourth Lateran Council did not legislate about the number of witnesses, but English legislation of this period decreed that three or four witnesses should be present. Cf. Jean Dauvillier, *Le mariage dans le droit classique de l'Eglise* (Paris, 1933), 105.

105. Contemporary observers tried to justify why the degrees should be observed, proposing in adopting an Augustinian idea that it was to extend the bonds of love in society beyond one's immediate family. See David Herlihy, "Making of the Medieval Family: Symmetry, Structure, and Sentiment," *Journal of Family History* 8 (1983): 116–30, esp. 122–23.

106. See Michael Sheehan, "The European Family and Canon Law," *Continuity and Change* 6 (1991): 347–60, esp. 351–53; republished in *Marriage, Family, and Law,* ed. Farge. 247–61, esp. 253–56.

107. Baldwin, *Masters, Princes,* 336.

108. Legal evidence of a sort that actually records reflections by couples about their unions is scanty even at the end of the twelfth century. Apart from papal decretals there are occasional records from the episcopal courts. See for examples Norma Adams and Charles Donahue Jr., eds., *Select Cases from the Ecclesiastical Courts of the Province of Canterbury c. 1200–1301,* Publications of the Selden Society 95 (London, 1981); cf. Christopher Brooke's discussion of the famous Anstey case, which reveals, among other things, popular confusion over whether consent or consummation makes a marriage, *The Medieval Idea of Marriage* (Oxford, 1989), 150–52.

109. Leclercq, *Monks on Marriage,* 70.

110. Rudolf Goy, *Die Überlieferung der Werke Hugos von St. Viktor* (Stuttgart, 1976), 133–72.

111. On the medieval Song of Songs commentaries as a genre, see E. Ann Matter's study, *The Voice of My Beloved: The Song of Songs in Western Medieval Christianity* (Philadelphia, 1990).

112. Penny Schine Gold, *The Lady and the Virgin: Image, Attitude, and Experience in Twelfth-Century France* (Chicago, 1985), 56–61.

113. Leclercq, introduction to Bernard of Clairvaux, *Sermones super Cantica Canticorum*, vols. 1 and 2 of *Sancti Bernardi Opera*, ed. J. Leclercq, C. H. Talbot, and H. M. Rochais, 8 vols. (Rome, 1957–77), 1:xv.

114. See Roch Kereszty, " 'Bride' and 'Mother' in the *Super Cantica* of St. Bernard: An Ecclesiology for our Time?" *Communio* 20 (1993): 415–36.

115. Étienne Gilson describes the mystical nature of the sermons in *The Mystical Theology of St. Bernard*, Cistercian Studies Series 120 (New York, 1940; rpt. Kalamazoo, Mich., 1990).

116. Kereszty, " 'Bride' and 'Mother,' " 423.

117. Leclercq, *Monks on Marriage*, 78.

118. Ibid., 73–76.

119. D. L. D'Avray, "The Gospel of the Marriage Feast of Cana and Marriage Preaching in France," in *The Bible in the Medieval World: Essays in Memory of Beryl Smalley*, ed. Katherine Walsh and Diana Wood, Studies in Church History, Subsidia 4 (Oxford, 1985), 207–24, and *The Preaching of the Friars: Sermons Diffused from Paris before 1300* (Oxford, 1985).

120. See chaps. 3, 4, and 5 of Bynum, *The Resurrection of the Body in Western Christianity, 200–1336* (New York, 1995).

121. *Monks on Marriage*, 75.

122. Augustine and St. Ambrose both associated the Holy Spirit with love; *Monks on Marriage*, 80. In the fifth century St. Fulgentius of Ruspe "applied to the Holy Spirit the image of the human breath exhaled when bride and bridegroom kiss.... It is from then onward that we can trace the avatars of the conjugal and family analogy in the history of the theology of the Trinity"; ibid.

123. Ibid., 80.

124. Ibid., 82.

125. Ibid.

126. Bernard of Clairvaux, *Serm. Cant.* 83.3, in *Sancti Bernardi Opera*, ed. Leclercq, 2:299–300.

127. Ibid., 83.4, 2:301.

128. Ibid., 9.5, 2:46. My attention was drawn to this passage of Bernard by Prof. Janine Langan.

129. Kereszty, " 'Bride' and 'Mother,' " 425.

130. *Soliloquium de arrha animae* PL 176, 951–97.

131. R. Baron, "Note sur la succession et la date des écrits de Hugues de Saint-Victor," *Revue d'Histoire Ecclésiastique* 57 (1962): 88–118, esp. 101.

132. Hugh of St. Victor, *De Beatae Mariae virginitate* 1 PL 176, 860CD.

133. Bernard of Clairvaux, *Serm. Cant.* 83.3, in *Sancti Bernardi Opera*, ed. Leclercq, 2:300.

134. Brundage, *Law, Sex, and Christian Society*, 274; cf. ibid. nn. 76, 77, which refer his readers to Caroline Bynum, *Jesus as Mother* (Berkeley, Calif., 1982) and Leclercq, *Monks on Marriage*.

135. The following depends in great part on Michael Sheehan, " 'Maritalis affectio' Revisited," in *The Olde Daunce: Love, Friendship, Sex, and Marriage in*

the Medieval World, ed. Robert R. Edwards and Stephen Spector (Albany, N.Y., 1991), 32–43, 254–60 (notes); republished in *Marriage, Family, and Law,* ed. Farge, 262–77.

136. John Noonan, "Marital Affection in the Canonists," *Studia Gratiana* 12 (1967): 479–509.

137. Rousseau, "Spousal Relationship," 94–95.

138. Sheehan, " 'Maritalis affectio' Revisited," 37.

139. See Rousseau, "Spousal Relationship," 95–96; Bolton, "Philip Augustus and John: Two Sons in Innocent III's Vineyard," in *The Church and Sovereignty c. 590–1918: Essays in Honour of Michael Wilks,* ed. D. Wood, Studies in Church History, Subsidia 9 (Oxford, 1991), 113–34, esp. 129; reprinted in *Innocent III.*

140. Sheehan, " 'Maritalis affectio' Revisited," 37; rpt. *Marriage, Family, and Law,* ed. Farge, 269.

141. Ibid., 37; rpt. *Marriage, Family, and Law,* ed. Farge, 268–69.

142. Hugh of St. Victor, *De vanitate mundi et rerum transeuntium usu* 1, PL 176, 709B; cf. Gregory the Great, *Dialogues* 4.13, ed. Adalbert de Vogüé, Sources Chrétiennes 251, 260, 265 (Paris, 1978–80), 3:56.

143. Hugh of St. Victor, *De sacramentis* 1.8.13 PL 176, 315BC.

144. Ibid., 1.8.13 PL 176, 314D.

145. Ibid., 1.6.13 PL 176, 315B.

146. Hugh of St. Victor, *De virginitate* 1 PL 176, 860C.

147. Michael Sheehan, "Theory and Practice: Marriage of the Unfree and the Poor in Mediaeval Society," *Mediaeval Studies* 50 (1985): 457–87, esp. 460; republished in *Marriage, Family, and Law,* ed. Farge, 211–46, esp. 214.

148. Leclercq, *Women and St. Bernard,* 37.

149. Hugh of St. Victor, *De vanitate* PL 176, 708CD.

150. *The Four Degrees of Violent Charity,* in *Richard of St. Victor: Selected Writings on Contemplation* (New York, 1957), 220.

151. See his Letter 144, written c. 1137, where the Pauline notion of flesh as sinful man seems to be associated with the physical body: "we are shut up in the horrible prison of a body stinking of muck, we are shackled by sin and death." *Epist.* 144.1, in *Sancti Bernardi Opera,* ed. Leclercq, 7:344.

152. The following is dependent on I Deug-Su, introduction to *Liber de gradibus humilitatis et superbiae,* in *Opere di Bernardo,* ed. F. Gastaldelli, 2 vols. (Milan, 1984–), 1:21–25.

153. Glenn Olsen, "Twelfth-Century Humanism Reconsidered: The Case of St. Bernard," *Studi Medievali,* 3d ser., 31.1 (1990): 27–53, esp. 52.

154. Innocent III, *De quad. spec. nuptiarum* 2:32, ed. Munk, 2:22: "Let him love more in himself that which is greater, that is, the soul; and less that which is lesser, that is, the body."

155. Hugh of St. Victor reminds us of the sin exhibited in the mind's lack of control over the body during sexual arousal, a theme we have already encountered in Augustine.

156. On Bernard and the body, see John Sommerfeldt, *The Spiritual Teachings of Bernard of Clairvaux: An Intellectual History of the Early Cistercian Order,* Cistercian Fathers Series 125 (Kalamazoo, Mich., 1991), 13–14, 31–38.

157. *Epistola* 51 PL 211, 46D–647A. Cf. Benincasa's *Life* of Rainerius of Pisa, *Vita s. Raynerii Pisani* 4.54, in the entry for June 17 in *Acta sanctorum...editio novissima,* eds. J. Carnandet et al., June, 4 vols. (Paris and Rome, 1867), 4:357D: "I have made you in my likeness; for just as I made myself the Son of my [Jewish] people for the salvation of humankind, assuming flesh from my handmaid, and I

carried that flesh into heaven where it remains with me, so now I have been made the Son of my Christian people for their salvation, taking on your flesh, and I shall make it remain on earth and be adored by all the races that are there."

158. *De sacramentis* 1.10.6 PL 176, 326C. The departure here from the Augustinian and Pauline contrast between the interior and exterior man cannot be emphasized enough.

159. *The Nature and Dignity of Love*, trans. Thomas X. Davis, Cistercian Fathers Series 30 (Kalamazoo, Mich., 1981), 84–85. I have considered William at length in " 'That We May Glorify Him in Our Bodies': William of St. Thierry's Views of the Human Body," Ph.D. dissertation, University of Toronto, 1997.

160. William of St. Thierry, *The Nature of the Body and Soul*, trans. Benjamin Clark, in *Three Treatises on Man: A Cistercian Anthropology*, ed. Bernard McGinn, Cistercian Fathers Series 24 (Kalamazoo, Mich., 1977), 151.

161. Adolf Katzenellenbogen, *The Structural Programs of Chartres Cathedral: Christ, Mary, Ecclesia* (Baltimore, 1959).

162. Twelfth-century exegetes of the Song of Songs stressed the interchangeability of Mary and the Church: ibid., 60.

163. Munk, *Study*, 1:40–44.

164. *Sermo III in consecratione pontificis de quatuor speciebus desponsationum*, in *De quad. spec. nuptiarum*, ed. Munk, 2:3.

165. Munk, *Study*, 1:148–50.

166. In general, before the twelfth century, marriage was thought to be symbolic of the unity of Christ and his Church. One exception to this was the treatise *In coniugio figura et vestigium Trinitatis*, affiliated loosely with the school of Laon, which treated the marriage of the first parents, and them alone, as being a figure of the Trinity in the sense that the two parents produced a third being in love. See Heinrich Reinhardt, *Die Ehelehre der Schule des Anselm von Laon*, Beiträge zur Geschichte der Philosophie und Theologie des Mittelalters, neue Folge, 14 (Münster, 1974), 36–37. Cf. Heaney, *Sacramentality of Marriage*, 5.

167. I am grateful to Prof. Ann Hutchison, Pontifical Institute of Mediaeval Studies, Toronto, for reading this section of this chapter and offering many suggestions.

168. See Leslie T. Topsfield, *"Fin' Amors* in Maracabru, Bernart de Ventadorn and the *Lancelot* of Chrétien de Troyes," in *Love and Marriage in the Twelfth Century*, ed. Willy Van Hoecke and Andries Welkenhuysen (Louvain, 1981), 236–49, esp. 247.

169. See p. 173 of Joan M. Ferrante, "The Conflict of Lyric Conventions and Romantic Form," in *In Pursuit of Perfection: Courtly Love in Medieval Literature*, ed. Joan M. Ferrante, George D. Economou, and Frederick Goldin (Port Washington, N.Y., 1975), 135–73, 174–87 (notes).

170. See Helen Laurie's *Two Studies in Chrétien de Troyes* (Geneva, 1972), 110.

171. Helen Laurie, "The Letters of Abelard and Heloise: A Source for Chrétien de Troyes?" *Studi Medievali*, 3d ser., 27, 1 (1986), 123–46, esp. 136–37. See also Laurie's *Two Studies in Chrétien de Troyes*, 94. Cf. John Baldwin, *The Language of Sex: Five Voices from Northern France around 1200* (Chicago, 1994) 32–33. The biblical reference is to Phil. 3:20.

172. The following is dependent on a paper given by Jeanne A. Nightingale on the impact of the Song of Songs commentary tradition on the development of secular love literature. The paper, which she kindly made available to me, "From Epithalamium to Conjointure: Bernard of Clairvaux's Reliteralization of the Song as Model for the Structuring of Courtly Romance," was delivered at the 28th International Congress

of Medieval Studies, May 6–9, 1993, at Western Michigan University, Kalamazoo, Michigan. Many of the same themes appear in her earlier article "De l'épitahalame au roman courtois: l'exégèse ad litteram du Cantique des Cantiques comme modèle heuristique pour la 'conjointure de Chrétien de Troyes," in *Erec, ou l'ouverture du monde Arthurien,* Actes du Colloque du Centre d'Études Mediévales de l'Université de Picardie-Jules Verne, Amiens, January 16–17, 1993 (Greifswald, 1993), 75–87.

173. Enide is a strong-willed individual and, like the wives in some of the twelfth-century epics, such as the *Song of William,* an active participant in the planning of her husband's military campaigns. Cf. Jean Hagstrum, *Esteem Enlivened by Desire: The Couple from Homer to Shakespeare* (Chicago, 1992), 230–33. Cf. Gold, *The Lady and the Virgin,* 1–42.

174. Gold, *Lady and the Virgin,* 10.

175. See Brooke, *Medieval Idea of Marriage,* 173–210.

176. Ibid., 191.

177. Ibid., 186–202.

178. Subtitle: *A Study in Medieval Tradition* (Oxford, 1936).

179. Ruth Harvey, *The Troubadour Marcabru and Love* (London, 1989) shows that the troubadour Marcabru's poems are, on the surface at least, moralistic in tone.

180. Cf. John Benton, "Clio and Venus: An Historical View of Medieval Love," in *The Meaning of Courtly Love,* ed. F. X. Newman (Albany, N.Y., 1968), 19–42.

181. *The Origin and Meaning of Courtly Love* (Manchester, 1977).

182. For a concise summary of the controversy over courtly love, see Velma Bourgeois Richmond, "Pacience in Adversitee: Chaucer's Presentation of Marriage," *Viator* 10 (1979): 323–54, esp. 327–32. Cf. Georges Duby, *Love and Marriage in the Middle Ages,* trans. Jane Dunnett (Chicago, 1994), 32–33, 56–63. At least one contemporary chronicler blamed the destruction of Eleanor of Aquitaine and Louis VII's marriage on courtly love.

183. See introduction to *The Voice of the Trobairitz: Perspectives on the Women Troubadours,* ed. William D. Paden (Philadelphia, 1989), 14.

184. Ibid., 6.

185. Cf. Helen Laurie, "Philosophy and Medicine in Early Courtly Romance," in *The Making of Romance: Three Studies* (Geneva, 1991), 11–71.

186. Boase, *Origin of Courtly Love,* 92.

187. Duby, *Love and Marriage,* 61–62.

188. Boase, *Origin of Courtly Love,* 126.

189. Ibid. Cf. Gold, *Lady and the Virgin;* Roberta Krueger, *Women Readers and the Ideology of Gender in Old French Romance* (New York, 1993).

190. Baldwin, *Language of Sex,* 29.

191. Robert W. Hanning, "Love and Power in the Twelfth Century, with Special Reference to Chrétien de Troyes and Marie de France," in *Olde Daunce,* ed. Edwards and Spector, 87–103, 267–68 (notes).

192. Marie de France, *Yonec,* in *The Lais of Marie de France,* trans. Robert Hanning and Joan Ferrante (Durham, N.C., 1978), 137–52. See vv. 91–100, p. 179.

193. See Erik Kooper, "Loving the Unequal Equal: Medieval Theologians and Marital Affection," in *Olde Daunce,* ed. Edwards and Spector, 44–56, 260–65 (notes).

194. Baldwin, *Language of Sex,* discusses Andrew the Chaplain and his *De amore,* whose tone is notoriously difficult to capture. On Andrew cf. J. F. Benton, "The Evidence for Andreas Capellanus Re-examined Again," *Studies in Philology* 59 (1962): 471–78.

195. Leclercq, *Women and Saint Bernard,* 157.

196. Ibid., 147.

197. As Roberta Frank has pointed out, the Icelandic language itself presented an obstacle to the recognition of the value of an ideal such as celibacy. The Old Norse word for "bachelor" and "unmarried woman" both tended to carry pejorative overtones. Frank, "Marriage in Twelfth- and Thirteenth-Century Iceland," *Viator* 4 (1973): 482.

198. Sheehan, "Choice of Marriage Partner," 17; rpt. *Marriage, Family, and Law,* ed. Farge, 102.

199. We find the following remark in a discussion of the problem of clandestine marriage in *De sacramentis* 2.11.6 PL 176, 491C: "The sinner comes to me and sets forth his conscience to me seeking counsel for salvation."

200. Baldwin, *Masters, Princes,* 1:32.

201. Ibid., 1:139–40.

202. Ibid., 1:55.

203. Sheehan, "Choice of Marriage Partner," 21; rpt. *Marriage, Family, and Law,* ed. Farge, 102.

204. See Michael Sheehan, " 'Maritalis affectio' Revisited," 39; rpt. *Marriage, Family, and Law,* ed. Farge, 272.

205. *Thomae de Chobham Summa Confessorum,* ed. F. Broomfield, Analecta Mediaevalia Namurcensia 25 (Louvain, 1968), 375.

206. Ibid.

207. Jean Scammell, "Freedom and Marriage in Medieval England," *The Economic History Review* 27 (1974): 523–36, esp. 535.

208. Fourteenth-century records give no indication that episcopal courts imposed any kind of penalties on couples in cases of adultery. Rather, they were released to their confessors for penance. See Marcia Stentz, "A Calendar of a Consistory Court Record from the Diocese of Ely, 1374–1382," Ph.D. dissertation, University of Toronto, 1989. See the case of Stephen Bernewelle and Isabell Tavern, sessions 5.14 and 24.15. Although one cannot presume that this later practice necessarily reflects twelfth-century customs, it gives one reason to pause in lieu of more definitive findings.

209. Scammell, "Freedom and Marriage," 535.

210. Adams and Donahue write that marriage cases at the beginning of the thirteenth century often involved property disputes subject to royal authority while the validity of marriage was a matter for spiritual authorities, *Select Cases,* 85. Ecclesiastical jurisdiction over cases involving the validity of marriage was assumed at the council of Lillebonne in Normandy in 1080, according to Frank Barlow, *The English Church 1066–1154* (London, 1979), 149, and also in the Anstey case in England in the middle of the twelfth century.

211. *Native Law and the Church in Medieval Wales* (New York, 1993), 185–86. Pryce notes that for the twelfth century we mainly have records of the behavior only of the very highest echelon of society, usually the royal family. The ecclesiastical courts were in the process of formation, and have left few records. He also notes that the evidence which is growing about the courts of twelfth-century rural deans may be a possible source of new information.

212. Diane Hughes, "Domestic Ideals and Social Behavior: Evidence from Medieval Genoa," in *The Family in History,* ed. Charles E. Rosenberg (Philadelphia, 1975), 115–43.

213. See D'Avray and Tausche, "Marriage Sermons."

214. Baldwin, *Masters, Princes,* 1:38.

215. D'Avray and Tausche, "Marriage Sermons," 86.

216. Ibid., 106, 108.

217. Ibid., 78–80.

218. Much of the Victorine material remains unstudied. From St. Victor itself, we have the sermons addressed to the brothers at St. Victor usually ascribed to Richard of St. Victor, *Sermones Centum* PL 177:899–1222. In addition there are unedited sermons by Hugh of St. Victor listed in "Repertorium der Lateinischen Sermones des Mittelalters," ed. J. Schneyer, *Beiträge zur Geschichte der Philosophie und Theologie des Mittelalters* 43, no. 2 (Aschendorff, 1970), 786–813.

219. Bonnard, *Histoire de l'Abbaye royale,* 1:74.

220. The only edited Victorine sermons are usually ascribed to Richard of St. Victor, *Sermones Centum* PL 177:899–1222.

221. See D'Avray and Tausche, "Marriage Sermons." They discuss the sermons of Alan of Lille and Honorius of Autun.

222. Brenda Bolton, "Fulk of Toulouse: The Escape That Failed," in *Studies in Church History* 12 (Oxford, 1975): 83–93; republished in *Innocent III.*

223. "Marriage Feast of Cana."

224. Ibid., 214–15.

225. Ibid., 216.

226. See Molin and Mutembe, *Rituel du mariage.*

227. See E. Jane Burns, *Bodytalk: When Women Speak in Old French Literature* (Philadelphia, 1993), 80, n. 23.

228. See Brundage, "Concubinage and Marriage in Medieval Canon Law."

229. Brundage, *Law, Sex, and Christian Society,* p. 297, n. 177.

230. Pryce, *Native Law,* 89–92. Cf. Frank, "Marriage in Twelfth- and Thirteenth-Century Iceland," 478.

231. Brundage, *Law, Sex, and Christian Society,* 297.

232. Sheehan, "Theory and Practice," 482; rpt. *Marriage, Family, and Law,* ed. Farge, 240.

233. Rousseau, "Spousal Relationship," 96–97.

234. Brundage, *Law, Sex, and Christian Society,* 340–41.

235. Many thanks to Prof. John Parsons for reading and commenting on the last section of this chapter.

236. See "Domestic Ideals and Social Behavior."

237. Ibid., 123.

238. Ibid., 136.

239. See John Hine Mundy, "Urban Society and Culture: Toulouse and Its Region," in *Renaissance and Renewal in the Twelfth Century,* ed. Robert L. Benson and Giles Constable (Toronto, 1991), 231–32.

240. David Herlihy, "The Medieval Marriage Market," *Medieval and Renaissance Studies, Proceedings of the Southeastern Institute of Medieval and Renaissance Studies, Summer, 1974,* ed. Dale B. Randall, vol. 6 (Durham, N.C., 1976), 3–27; reprinted as no. 14 in Herlihy, *The Social History of Italy and Western Europe,* Collected Studies (London, 1978).

241. Duby and Ariès, eds., *History of Private Life,* 2:137.

242. Ibid., 138.

243. *Wills and Wealth in Medieval Genoa: 1150–1250,* Harvard Historical Studies 103 (Cambridge, Mass., 1984).

244. Cf. Judith Weiss, "The Power and the Weakness of Women in Anglo-Norman Romance," in *Women and Literature in Britain, 1150–1500,* ed. Carol Meale, Cambridge Studies in Medieval Literature 17 (New York, 1993), 8.

245. See Janet Senderowitz Loengard, " 'Of the Gift of Her Husband': English Dower and Its Consequences in the Year 1200," in *Women of the Medieval World: Essays in Honor of John Mundy,* ed. Julius Kirshner and Suzanne F. Wemple (Oxford, 1985), 215–55, esp. 225. Cf. Lois L. Honeycutt, "Images of Queens in the High Middle Ages," *The Haskins Society Journal* 1 (1989): 61–71.

246. "Lady Honor Lisle's Networks of Influence," in *Women and Power in the Middle Ages,* ed. Mary Erler and Maryanne Kowaleski (Athens, Ga., 1988), 188–212.

247. John Carmi Parsons, "Mothers, Daughters, Marriage, Power: Some Plantagenet Evidence, 1150–1500," in *Medieval Queenship,* ed. Parsons, 63–78, and nn. 206–9; cf. chap. 2 of his *Eleanor of Castile* (New York, 1995), esp. 89, 90.

248. "Power of Sisterhood: Marie de France's 'Le Fresne,' " in *Women and Power,* ed. Erler and Kowaleski, 250–64.

249. Susan Groag Bell, "Medieval Women Book Owners: Arbiters of Lay Piety and Ambassadors of Culture," in *Women and Power in the Middle Ages,* 149–87. Cf. the illustration of Blanche of Castille overseeing the education of her son Louis IX, in *History of Private Life,* ed. Duby and Ariès, 2:152.

250. "Theory and Practice," 462 and n. 14; rpt. *Marriage, Family, and Law,* 217 and n. 14.

251. Thomas Bisson, review of *Medieval Marriage: Two Models from Twelfth-Century France,* in *Speculum* 54 (1979): 364–66.

252. Duby, *Medieval Marriage,* 40.

253. Ibid., 335.

254. Baldwin, *Masters, Princes,* 1:334.

255. Ibid., 1:333–34.

256. Ibid., 1:335.

257. Cf. Sheehan, "European Family and Canon Law," 352; rpt. *Marriage, Family, and Law,* ed. Farge, 254.

258. Charles Donahue, "Marriage in the Central Middle Ages," in *Marriage and Society: Studies in the Social History of Marriage,* ed. R. B. Outhwaite (London, 1981), 17–34, esp. 26.

259. Ibid., 336.

260. See *Medieval Idea of Marriage,* 119–25.

261. Leclercq, *Monks on Marriage,* 1–9, 43–52.

262. See *History of Private Life,* ed. Duby and Ariès, 2:145–46.

263. Ibid., 52.

264. See v. 27145ff. of Mouskès, *Chronique rimée,* ed. F. de Reiffenberg, 2 vols. (Bruxelles, 1836–38).

265. Prayer taken from Bethune, "Christian Rite of Marriage," 263.

Chapter Six

THE REFORMATIONS OF THE SIXTEENTH AND SEVENTEENTH CENTURIES

R. V. Young

Marriage has always been the object of a certain ambivalence. Patching together a number of classical authorities, after his usual fashion, Robert Burton (1577–1640) delivers himself of the following paean:

> ...there's something in a woman beyond all human delight; a magnetic virtue, a charming quality, an occult and powerful motive. The husband rules her as head, but she again commands his heart, he is her servant, she his only joy and content: no happiness is like unto it, no love so great as this of man and wife, no such comfort as *placens uxor,* a sweet wife.[1]

Burton, however, never married, and his celebration of wedded bliss is merely the ideal set against his account of the devastations of "love melancholy." His younger contemporary, Sir Thomas Browne (1605–82), is openly disdainful of marriage:

> The whole world was made for man, but the twelfth part of man for woman: man is the whole world and the breath of God, woman the rib and crooked piece of man. I could be content that we might procreate like trees, without conjunction, or that there were any way to perpetuate the world without this triviall and vulgar way of coition; It is the foolishest act a wise man commits in all his life, nor is there any thing that will more deject his cool imagination, when he shall consider what an odde and unworthy piece of folly he hath committed.[2]

This passage from *Religio Medici* was written in the mid-1630s, but, by the time the work was first published in 1642, Browne had been married for a year. As Dr. Johnson observes, the lady had "no reason to repent: for she lived happily with him one and forty years; and bore him ten children, of whom one son and three daughters outlived their parents: she survived him two years, and passed her widowhood in plenty, if not in opulence."[3]

Burton and Browne illustrate how a man's words about marriage, even when printed, may not correspond to his actions. Such inconsistency is, doubtless, perennial — inconstant creatures that we are. During the seventeenth-century, however, discrepancies between profession and practice, between system and sensibility, were deeper and more complex, if not more common than what might be expected from the mere frailty of the individual human disposition. The sixteenth and seventeenth centuries witnessed the unfolding of the Protestant Reformation and its Catholic counterpart, and marriage was not uninvolved in the Reformation. In addition to the part played in the English Reformation by Henry VIII's marital discontent, the doctrine and practice of marriage were radically altered as part of the general Reformation program. The most immediately and visibly practical change was a matter of discipline: not only were married men admitted to holy orders after more than four centuries of exclusion in the Western Church, but clergymen were even permitted to marry after ordination. Ultimately more significant, however, was the desacramentalization of marriage, which was part of the Protestant reduction of sacraments in number from seven to two, and a general deemphasis of the role of sacraments in Christian life and worship.

Luther and Calvin on Companionate Marriage

Modern historiography has tended to find in the Reformation the origins of "companionate marriage"; that is, marriage based on the individual inclinations and choice of the spouses and including increased freedom and equality for wives. Historians have frequently asserted, for example, that clerical marriage enhanced the importance of women and sexuality by elevating marriage's status, while removing sacramental status from marriage made it an individual, human concern of this world. Certainly the suppression of religious orders during the Reformation was a practical embodiment of the Protestant notion that the married state was equal, if not superior, to celibacy.[4] While the preceding chapter generally confirms that various constraints during the late Middle Ages continued the elevation of the social and familial over the individual interests in marriage, the Reformation's revolutionary role requires some qualification: As chapters 3, 4, and 5 have shown, companionate marriage, at least in limited circles, had been developing since ancient Christianity.

Although it is difficult to assess accurately Protestantism's role in this development, the Reformation coincides with a widespread growth in the perception that marriage was more a personal affair than a social institution. One effect of Protestant doctrine seems certain: to deprive marriage of sacramental status is to secularize it and, in effect, to add momentum to the overall secularization of society, since marriage is the fundamental social institution. A look at the English literature of love and marriage in the sixteenth and seventeenth centuries suggests a curious development: When marriage ceases to be regarded as a sacrament in Protestant England, and the focus shifts to the personal fulfillment of the spouses rather than the procreation and education of children, then marriage comes under a tremendous burden of expectation. Ironically, for some imaginative souls, nonsacramental marriage assumes the status of a virtual religion — or at least a source of nearly religious bliss and satisfaction. It is the disappointment of such expectations, along with the removal of religious sanctions from what is becoming a secular institution, that builds the growing pressure during the modern era for legal divorce.

Although many generations passed before substantial changes in marital practice took hold, the first Protestant Reformers held a very different conception of holy matrimony from the sacramental view that the medieval Church had worked laboriously to establish over the preceding centuries. No longer a sacrament, marriage was handled in a fashion parallel to the dominant Reformation theology of the Eucharist, which tied the reality and efficacy of the rite to the subjective disposition and actions of the individual participants. Even though Martin Luther retained a medieval Catholic belief in the Real Presence in the Eucharist, he furnishes a good example of the new approach to marriage: "There is no Scriptural warrant whatsoever for regarding marriage as a sacrament," he maintains and proceeds to suggest that the nature of marriage is determined by the spirit and conduct of the participants:

> The marriages of our ancestors were no less sacred than our own, nor less real among unbelievers than believers. Yet no one calls marriage of unbelievers a sacrament. Also, there are irreligious marriages even among believers, worse than among any pagans. Why then should it be called a sacrament in such a case, and yet not among pagans?[5]

There is a kind of individualistic logic at work here: if a couple is "irreligious," then the marriage cannot be a sacrament. Although Luther does not hold a radically Protestant conception of the Eucharist, his denial that marriage can be a sacrament rests on such a basis. According to most Protestant formulations, the sacramental presence is either nonexistent or depends upon the worthiness of the minister and the proper disposition of the recipient. Because not even the holiest spouses always live out their marriage "religiously," the subjective test of sacramentality cannot be met: Christian marriage is in essence no different from pagan marriage.

If marriage is not a rite of the Church, not an objective institution of Christ, then its substance and validity result largely from the spouses' experience of fulfillment. Luther asks us to imagine a woman married to an impotent man:

> [She] cannot, or perhaps will not, prove in court her husband's impotence, because of the numerous items of evidence, and the notoriety, which would be occasioned by a legal process. Still she wishes to have a child, and is unable to remain continent. In addition, suppose I had advised her to seek a divorce in order to marry another, as she was content, in her conscience, to do, and after ample experience on the part of herself and her husband, that he was impotent; if, then, however, her husband would not agree to her proposal, I myself would give the further advice, that, with her husband's consent (although now really he is not her husband, but only a man who lives in the same house) she should have coition with another man, say her husband's brother, but keeping this "marriage" secret, and ascribing the children to the putative father, as they call such a one. As to the question whether such a woman is "saved" or in a state of salvation, I would reply, Yes, because in this case a mistake due to ignorance of the man's impotence created a false situation which impedes the marriage proper; the harshness of the law does not allow divorce; yet by divine law the woman is free and so cannot be forced to remain continent.[6]

For the present purpose we do not need to sort out the tortuous reasoning here, by which the possibility of annulment on the objective grounds of non-consummation is simply discounted. It is sufficient to note that the substance of marriage is determined subjectively; that is, there is no "real" marriage unless the expectations of the spouses are satisfied.

Luther proceeds to assert that, should the husband refuse to assent to such an arrangement, "rather than let her burn or commit adultery, I would counsel her to contract matrimony with someone else, and flee to a distant and unknown region. What other counsel," he asks, "can be given to one constantly struggling with the dangers of her own natural emotions?" Having advised the avoidance of adultery by what surely appears to be bigamy, Luther offers the following comment: "In regard to divorce, it is still a subject for debate whether it should be allowed. For my part, I have such a hatred of divorce that I prefer bigamy to divorce, yet I do not venture an opinion whether bigamy should be allowed."[7] Here Luther asserts that he is *personally opposed* to divorce and does not positively recommend bigamy. But his reasoning would constrain him to accept both on occasion, since he understands the essence of matrimony to lie in the individual's judgment of his own well-being in a particular marriage.

While he is by no means so incautious a writer as Luther, John Calvin's view of marriage is fundamentally the same. His approach parallels his own treatment of the Eucharist; in each instance he reduces to a figure the literal substance of a scriptural passage with which the Catholic Church buttresses a doctrine. Calvin denies the dogma of the Real Presence by insisting that Christ's words of institution, "This is my body ... " (Matt. 26.26ff.), are to be taken not literally, but figuratively, as a metonymy; that is, as a trope that substitutes an associated item for the thing itself. For example, a reporter might ascribe a policy statement to the "White House," meaning thereby the president or a member of his staff; so Calvin argues, "This, as the sacrament of the body of Christ is, after a certain manner, the body of Christ."[8] Calvin's treatment of marriage works the same way. When St. Paul calls marriage "a great mystery," and adds, "but I speak concerning Christ and the Church" (Eph. 5.32), he is not calling marriage a sacrament (*sacramentum* in the Vulgate), Calvin maintains, but rather distinguishing between earthly, human marriage and the heavenly mystery of Christ's relation to the Church. Although *mysterion* is the standard Greek term for "sacrament," Calvin derides Catholic interpreters for taking "mystery" literally as the Latin *sacramentum* in the Pauline context. "To treat Scripture thus," he maintains, "is to confound heaven and earth."[9]

Of course in the Catholic perspective, the purpose of a sacrament is, in a sense, "to confound heaven and earth," or at least to make heavenly grace accessible to men and women by means of earthly signs. Depriving marriage of its sacramental element deprives it of its heavenly dimension and leaves it only a means of earthly fulfillment. Protestant polemicists claimed, however, that the secularization of marriage, in conjunction with the rejection of religious and clerical celibacy, amounted to an affirmation of marriage; and they pointed out what they perceived as a contradiction in the Catholic position. "Marriage being thus recommended by the title of a sacrament, can it be anything but vertiginous levity," scoffs Calvin, "afterwards to call it uncleanness, and pollution, and carnal defilement? How absurd is it to debar priests from a sacrament!"[10]

Despite the significant opposition in recent decades, most historians have accepted the proposition that the Reformation liberalized marital attitudes and practices and led to the rise of companionate marriage. As with all issues regarding human relationships, the evidence is complex and ambiguous. For instance, Patrick Collinson points out that the Reformation not only "riveted home patriarchy" but also finds that it "deepened the emotional quality of family life."[11] Taking up the same theme, Anthony Fletcher argues that the Puritan marital conduct books of the seventeenth century "portray a distinctive English version of the Protestant idea of marriage," which contrasts decisively with Catholic views of marriage.[12] Fletcher maintains that

the Old Testament patriarchal bias of Protestantism is diminished by a stress
on spousal affection, and by an affirmation of conjugal sexuality far more
unqualified than what appears in contemporaneous Catholic discussions of
marriage. Fletcher's evidence from sermons and marriage manuals seems
confirmed by the poetry of Anne Bradstreet (1612–72), who sailed to the
Massachusetts Bay Colony with her husband of two years in 1630. I am
acquainted with the work of no Catholic wife of this period that expresses
sexual desire as intensely as Bradstreet's "A Letter to Her Husband, Absent
upon Publick Employment":

> I like the earth this season, mourn in black,
> My Sun is gone so far in's Zodiack,
> Whom whilst I 'joy'd, nor storms, nor frosts I felt,
> His warmth such frigid colds did cause to melt.
> My chilled limbs now nummed lye forlorn;
> Return, return sweet *Sol* from *Capricorn;*
> In this dead time, alas, what can I more
> Then view those fruits which through thy heat I bore?[13]

Counter-Reformation sources, like their Protestant counterparts, similarly
stress the mutual obligations of spouses; but the Catholic commentators are
less enthusiastic about erotic ardor between husband and wife. It would
seem, then, that Protestantism enhanced marriage as a means of personal
companionship and individual, earthly happiness, but, in desacramentalizing
it, lowered its resistance to the pressures of the secular world.

Renaissance Humanism

Of course Protestantism was not the only new influence on marriage in the
sixteenth century. Renaissance humanism also encouraged the development
of companionate marriage, although it is not always easy to distinguish between humanist and Reformation attitudes. The *Colloquies* of Desiderius
Erasmus provide a suitably equivocal example. They may have been stimulated in part by Luther's newly emerging radical views, since the Dutch
humanist's most notable writings on marriage appear between 1523 and
1526. Erasmus plainly shares many of the views of the Reformers, especially
in his bias against monastic life and clerical celibacy and in his insistence that
marriage is spiritually equal, for most individuals perhaps superior, to the religious state. On the other hand, he does not openly attack the institution of
monasticism as such, only its abuses, and he seems to take very seriously the
relationship between human marriage and Christ's nuptial relation with the
Church.[14] In any case, Erasmus continues, with the Church, to regard mar-

riage as a sacrament, praising it as the first of all the sacraments, instituted by God himself.[15]

His amusing — almost Shakespearean — dialogue between "A Suitor and a Girl" (*Proci et Puellae*), strikes a balance between passion and prudence, between the wishes of young men and women and the rule of parents. It is also an excellent witness to the continuing tension between the Church's emphasis on a couple's mutual consent in establishing a marriage and society's bias in favor of parents and family. The young suitor, Pamphilus, has absorbed the ardent language and melancholy air of the desperate Petrarchan lover: his figures of speech are those of a man doomed to hopeless, introspective worship of a distant and inaccessible lady who scorns his ardor. His expectations, however, are less idealistic than a Petrarchan lover's, and he assails the maid, Maria, for not marrying him instantly and gratifying his passion: "But what will you say," he complains, "if I show with Achillean arguments both that I am dead and that you are the murderess?"[16] By the charm of her wit the prudent Maria readily subjects Pamphilus's precipitous expostulations to reason. If I have killed you, she points out, you can hardly expect me to marry a dead man; and she resists his exhortation that they enter into a clandestine marriage by plighting troth on the spot — still a valid and binding form of marriage at this time (though, as earlier chapters point out, discouraged by the Church). Maria promises to be tractable, and he replies, "But meanwhile utter three words" ("I am yours" — a binding promise). Maria almost seems to anticipate the concerns of the 1563 *Decree on Matrimony* (*Tametsi*) of the Council of Trent that, seeking to curb abuses, stipulated that a valid marriage must be contracted before "the parish priest and two or three witnesses."[17] "Nothing easier," she replies, "but words, once they have first flown out, do not fly back again. I shall give advice more suitable for us both. Get busy with your parents and mine, so that the affair is settled with the good will of both sides."[18]

If Maria constrains her suitor's urgency, she seems to concede, nonetheless, his main point: that it is better to be married than celibate, that chastity within marriage is a more suitable choice for her than a vow of virginity. After all, she gives him great encouragement to press his suit upon their parents, and she suggests that underneath her cool, prudent exterior lurks a passion as ardent as his: "It is your job to woo; it isn't fitting for us. For virginity rejoices in being carried off, even though we sometimes love more vehemently."[19] Without abandoning the notion of marriage as a sacrament, then, Erasmus seems to favor marriage over religious celibacy in a way that is commonly associated with Protestantism. As the preceding chapter makes clear, such a promotion of the personal and sexual aspects of marriage was already developing in the Italian humanism of the fourteenth and fifteenth centuries; it was an attitude that the Protestant

Reformers, along with Erasmus, were quick to seize upon for anti-monastic polemic.[20]

A conservative Counter-Reformation account of marriage is set forth, in the vernacular, by the Spanish Augustinian Fray Luis de León. Addressed to a recently married kinswoman, its very title — *The Perfect Wife* — evinces the Spanish friar's emphasis on the duties and subordinate position of a woman in marriage. A Scripture scholar, Fray Luis endeavors to show how a woman can approach the ideal standard of a wife held up in the thirty-first chapter of Proverbs. The points he emphasizes are modesty, frugality, industry, obedience, good temper, and diligent care of husband, children, and home. The friar's "perfect wife" is not, however, to be utterly submissive to a despotic husband: "although it is true that nature and status oblige a wife . . . to be concerned about her house and to comfort her husband and constantly to relieve him of cares, and that no fault of his removes this obligation, yet for all this husbands should not think that they have a license to be lions and make their wives slaves; rather, as in all the rest the man is the head; thus all this loving and honorable treatment must begin with him."[21]

Fray Luis, himself a humanist, emphasizes mutual love between husband and wife and, while maintaining the superiority of continence and virginity, observes that marriage is "very honored and privileged by the Holy Spirit in Sacred Letters."[22] He points out that Christ expressly raised the status of women in marriage, which had often been little better than that of a temporary maid. "Above all," Fray Luis continues, Christ "made of the marriage that men contract among themselves, a signification and most holy sacrament of the bond of love with which He joins himself to souls; and He wished that the matrimonial law of man with woman would be like a portrait and living image of the most sweet and intimate unity between Him and His Church, and thus He ennobled matrimony with the richest gifts of His grace and with other goods of heaven."[23] Unlike Erasmus, Fray Luis has nothing explicit to say about marital sexuality, but he does mention the intimate love of man and wife by way of insisting that mothers care for their children personally, and especially that they nurse them at their own breasts. In addition to demanding — as one would expect — absolute marital fidelity, Fray Luis also attacks excess in dress, cosmetics, and any preoccupation with seductive appearance on the part of a married woman.

Unlike thirteenth-century confessors' manuals, which acknowledged a woman's beauty as a valid secondary reason for seeking marriage, Fray Luis is suspicious of desire based on physical attractiveness. "Not only is this beauty dangerous because it calls attention to itself and inflames with desire the hearts of those who gaze upon it, but also because it awakens in those who possess it a pleasure in being desired." The prudent man will avoid such beauty in a wife, since "he who seeks a very beautiful woman travels with gold through a land of highwaymen, and with gold that he does not even consent to hide in his pocket." Besides, he continues, "Who does not know what this flower is worth and how long it lasts? How quickly it is finished? With what trivial occasions it withers?"[24] "The beauty of the good woman," Fray Luis maintains, "lies not in the features of her face, but in the secret virtues of the soul, which are all comprehended in Scripture under the phrase *fear of God.*"[25] Insofar as the virtuous wife is concerned with physical appearance it is a matter of what is within her own control: cleanliness and neatness, which transfigure her body as the light within illuminates a lantern. "Thus," Fray Luis asserts, "if bodily cleanliness and neatness are not virtues of the soul, they indicate a soul in harmony, pure, and well ordered."[26]

In Fray Luis de Leon's vision, marriage is a sacrament — an essentially religious institution, ordained for the procreation of children and the mutual strengthening of the spouses in the life of grace. The advice he gives to the aspiring "perfect wife" is in accord with this view: prudence, obedience, self-control, and charity are highlighted — not passion or romance. The advice offered married couples by a great Catholic devotional writer of the next generation, St. François de Sales, is similar, but he is considerably more explicit about the role of sexuality in marriage than his Spanish predecessor. At the heart of Christian marriage should be charity:

> O you who are married, it means nothing to say, "Love one another with a natural love" — two turtle doves make such love. Nor does it mean anything to say, "Love one another with a human love" — the pagans have duly practiced such love. With the great apostle I say to you, "Husbands, love your wives as Christ also loved the Church," and you wives, love your husbands as the Church loves her Saviour.[27]

The rule of charity in marriage entails what St. François calls "the sanctity of the marriage bed," with implications for practical moral life that should come as no surprise:

> In fact, marital intercourse, which is so holy, virtuous, and praiseworthy in itself and so profitable to society, is nevertheless in certain cases a source of danger to those who exercise it. Sometimes it causes their souls to become seriously ill with venial sins, as in cases of simple excess. Sometimes it effectively kills the soul by mortal sin, as when the order appointed for the procreation of children is violated and perverted.... Procreation of children is the first and principal end of marriage. Hence no one can ever lawfully depart from the due order that this end requires.

St. François takes the story of Onan in Genesis 38 as a scriptural basis for the condemnation of contraception, and, as his comments make clear, today's controversies often have roots in the past: "Certain heretics in our own times...have been pleased to say that merely the perverse intention of that wicked man [Onan] offended God. Scripture positively asserts the contrary and assures us that the act he committed was itself detestable and abominable in God's sight."[28]

The great spiritual director applies to marriage St. Augustine's distinction between use and enjoyment: "We should enjoy spiritual things but only use corporeal things," St. François says. "When their use is turned into enjoyment our rational soul is also changed into a brutish and beastly soul." Essentially he argues that sexuality should not be a constant preoccupation that distracts the mind from more important spiritual concerns: "[Spouses] should not keep their affections fixed on the sensual pleasures they have indulged in as part of their vocation in life. When they are over, they ought to wash their hearts and affections and purify themselves from them as soon as possible so that afterwards they can with calm minds practice purer and higher actions."[29]

To be sure, both St. François and Fray Luis set forth ideal standards for the conduct of married men and women. The conduct of actual sinners would rarely attain this ideal. Peter Paul Rubens, the Flemish painter, diplomat, and courtier, would seem to furnish a paradigm of the kind of serious, educated Catholic for whom *The Introduction to the Devout Life* was written. A cultivated intellectual who devoted his life and talents to the service of the Church and the Hapsburg monarchs, who were his chief worldly champions in the seventeenth century, Rubens manifests both the endeavor to realize the sanctity of matrimony and the human material in which the ideal must be achieved. His grief for the death of his first wife, Isabella Brant, expressed in a letter of 1626, reveals the mutual love and respect that St. François and Fray Luis regarded as crucial to the relationship of Christian spouses:

> Truly I have lost an excellent companion, whom one could love —
> indeed had to love, with good reason — as having none of the faults
> of her sex. She had no capricious moods, and no feminine weakness,
> but was all goodness and honesty. And because of her virtues she was
> loved during her lifetime, and mourned by all at her death.[30]

Four years later, however, Rubens, then fifty-two, married the sixteen-year-old Helena Fourment. A letter of 1634, explaining the marriage, reveals a more pragmatic and carnal side to the famous painter:

> I made up my mind to marry again, since I was not yet inclined to live
> the abstinent life of the celibate, thinking that, if we must give the first

place to continence, *fruimur licita voluptate cum gratiarum actione* [let us enjoy lawful pleasure with thanks]. I have taken a young wife of honest but middle-class family, although everyone tried to persuade me to make a court marriage. But I feared *commune illud nobilitatis malum superbiam praesertim in illo sexu* [the common evil of aristocrats, pride, especially in that sex], and that is why I chose one who would not blush to see me take my brushes in hand. And to tell the truth, it would have been hard for me to exchange the priceless treasure of liberty for the embraces of an old woman.[31]

It is important to bear in mind that the intentions that Rubens expresses here are not illicit. Availing himself of an analogy to eating in his discussion of conjugal relations, St. François de Sales observes, "To eat...merely to satisfy our appetite may be tolerated but not commended. Mere pleasure in satisfying a sensual appetite cannot be a sufficient reason to make an action praiseworthy but it is sufficient if the action is permissible."[32] What is disturbing to a twentieth-century reader, Catholic, Protestant, or indifferent, is, I suspect, the lack of fine sentiment — the want of any (dare I say it?) sense of romance. But of course Rubens's grieving tribute to his first wife was not romantic: he expresses deep personal affection for his lost spouse, as well as charity, but not the romantic passion that has been so frequently associated with erotic love for many centuries in the Western world. It is the attachment of such passion to marriage that I wish to take up presently, but first it is necessary to point out that, however disappointing the marital attitudes of a Rubens may seem to modern sensibilities, the Church had reason to prize them during the time of the Counter-Reformation.

The evidence of the historians suggests that the actual practice of most Europeans during the late Middle Ages showed little respect for the sacramental status of matrimony or even for ordinary Christian morality. As a result, in Catholic and Protestant countries alike, the period of the Reformation witnessed a determined effort by ecclesiastical authorities to regulate sexual activity and reinforce the public, institutional status of marriage. "The evidence from Spain," according to Henry Kamen, "suggests that there was no clearly established traditional Catholic morality, and that the Counter-Reformation was attempting to enter into new areas."[33] Since Kamen seems to mean by "traditional morality" the ordinary moral practice of the people as a whole, this is not so shocking a statement as it seems at first. For example, there is plentiful evidence that Catalonians had for many generations taken prostitution and fornication largely for granted. Brides were often pregnant when they married, and marriages were often private, even clandestine, affairs. A mutual promise followed by sexual intercourse constituted a valid marriage according to canon law inherited from the Middle

Ages. The denizens of northeastern Spain were not exceptional in their practices, and Protestant as well as Catholic authorities during the sixteenth and
seventeenth centuries labored to convince their flocks that sexual relations
should be confined to marriage, and that marriages should not be consummated until publicly witnessed in a church ceremony.[34] Thus the Church
often held up standards that remained largely unmet by the faithful.

It seems undeniable (although some recent historians disagree) that
people's attitudes toward marriage and their expectations of it began to
change during Reformation period, especially in Protestant England. Dom
Jean Leclercq professes dismay that scholars still say that "the Christian
Middle Ages were truly ignorant of desire and tenderness and considered
love an affair for extramarital relations," and that "C. S. Lewis and Denis
de Rougement are still being quoted as authorities on the matter."[35] But
there is a certain ambiguity in the term "love." C. S. Lewis was as aware as
Dom Leclercq that medieval husbands and wives felt tenderness and desire
for one another, and experienced deep and lasting affection in marriage —
in short, "loved" one another. Lewis was convinced, however, that what
he calls "courtly love" (admitting that the term is not unequivocal), arising about the end of the eleventh century in southern France, amounts to
a convergence of sexual desire and spiritual idealism that makes erotic love
virtually an end in itself and implies an idolatrous preoccupation with the
passionate relationship. This view of human love remained in the culture of
Western Europe down through the sixteenth century, when it began to be as-
similated into the concept of an intensely passionate marital love, especially
in England.[36]

Lewis's point is dramatized in the contrast between the love sonnet se-
quences of Sir Philip Sidney (1554–86) and Edmund Spenser (1552–99).
Although these two men were allies in politics, religion, and literature, loyal
to the same faction in Queen Elizabeth's court, their respective treatments of
the Petrarchan sonnet tradition are strikingly different. Sidney's posthumous
Astrophil and Stella (1591) insofar as it depicts unrequited love for an aloof,
unattainable, thoroughly idealized beauty, adheres to the original Petrarchan
schema of the *Rime Sparse*. Spenser's *Amoretti* (1591) is unique in celebrating a successful courtship, with the sequence culminating in an elaborate
wedding hymn.

Like Petrarch's persona, Sidney's Astrophil admits that his adoration for
his mistress amounts to a form of idolatry. Astrophil, or "Star Lover," is as
much preoccupied with the creature of his own imagination as he is with
the actual woman behind his "Star" (Stella):

> It is most true, what we call Cupid's dart,
> An image is, which for ourselves we carve;

> And, fools, adore in temple of our heart,
> Till that good god make Church and churchman starve.[37]

The ironic truth of this admission, that Astrophil worships the work of his own imagination (if not exactly of his own hands), becomes apparent when we consider the actual model for Stella — Penelope Devereux Rich. Sister of the earl of Essex, Robert Devereux, who would rise to be Queen Elizabeth's favorite, only to be subsequently executed for treason, Penelope Devereux was forced into marriage with Lord Robert Rich (son of the Richard Rich, who became very rich indeed by perjuring himself at the trial of St. Thomas More). Lady Rich was altogether lacking in Stella's aloof reserve and icy virtue. After Sidney's death in 1586, Lady Rich abandoned her husband and lived openly as the mistress of Charles Blount, Lord Mountjoy, who became earl of Devonshire. She bore him several children, and the earl attempted to marry her in 1605 after Rich divorced her for adultery. After Lord Mountjoy's death, however, the validity of the marriage was questioned.[38]

In the fiction of *Astrophil and Stella*, Astrophil remains despairingly possessed of unrequited desire for Stella, who is bitterly faithful to an unhappy marriage. The final lines of the poem find the persona a hopeless prisoner of a paradoxical and unedifying passion:

> So strangely, alas, thy works in me prevail,
> That in my woes for thee thou art my joy,
> And in my joys for thee my only annoy. (108.12–14)

Here Sidney's treatment of unsatisfied desire, with its defiant persistence, differs markedly from the Petrarchan model. The *Rime Sparse* concludes with a grand canzone in honor of the Virgin Mary in which Petrarch renounces the love of "a little frail mortal dust" ("poca mortal terra caduca") and begs the Blessed Mother to "accept [his] changed desires" ("prendi in grado i cangiati desiri").[39] Petrarch's love of Laura, although it must finally be renounced as "youthful error" (*Rime Sparse* 1:3: "giovenile errore"), has not been a total loss: it has refined his soul and opened him up to truly divine love. Astrophil achieves neither satisfaction nor transcendence. As Anthony Low points out, "Sidney finds, in *Astrophil and Stella*, that the courtly Petrarchan stance of endless desire without requital no longer works. But he is still too much immersed in an older, aristocratic culture to find a way out of this dead end."[40] Even more significant, as a militant English Protestant, Sidney, unlike Petrarch, could not turn to the Blessed Virgin for solace.[41] He could only leave Astrophil in erotic despair and, in one of his *Certain Sonnets,* recommend to himself a tight-lipped Stoic impassivity:

> For virtue hath this better lesson taught,
> Within myself to seek my only hire,
> Desiring naught but how to kill desire. (31:12–14)

The solution devised by Edmund Spenser is to channel desire into marriage. The *Amoretti* also bears the marks of a Petrarchan sonnet sequence, but it is unique as an account of courtship and marriage. The poetic persona seems at times to acquiesce in the standard hopeless frustration, but the tone of the sequence is consistently distinguished by a delicacy and a genial irony.[42] What is more, even when the persona seems to justify his idolatry of his mistress, the Petrarchan conceits that parody Christian devotion are pushed toward assimilation with a genuine Christian perspective:

> The glorious image of the makers beautie
> My souerayne saynt, the Idoll of my thought,
> dare not henceforth aboue the bounds of dewtie,
> t'accuse of pride, or rashly blame for ought.

The speaker of the sonnet thus upbraids himself for challenging the lady's reserve and self-possession, which are becoming to a Christian. She is his "souerayne saynt" in the courtly or Petrarchan sense, but she is also one of God's saints, and her dignity must therefore be respected:

> what reason is it then but she should scorne
> base things, that to her loue too bold aspire?
> Such heauenly formes ought rather worshipt be,
> then dare be lou'd by men of meane degree.[43]

Unlike the frustrated Astrophil, who chafes at the inexorable chastity of his Petrarchan mistress, Spenser's persona manifests the self-effacing ardor of the tradition at its most idealistic; but the pervasive Christian references tend to undercut the Gnostic implications of his most extreme conceits.

In fact, it is the lady herself who draws attention to the unreality, even impiety, of the Petrarchan ethos:

> One day I wrote her name vpon the strand,
> but came the waues and washed it away:
> agayne I wrote it with a second hand,
> but came the tyde, and made my paynes his pray.
> Vayne man, sayd she, that doest in vaine assay,
> amortall thing so to immortalize,
> for I my selue shall lyke to this decay,
> and eek my name bee wyped out lykewize.
>
> (*Amoretti* LXXV.1–8)

To be sure, the poet closes the sonnet by promising to immortalize his lady and their love in his verse, but the lesson of humility stands. Increasingly as the sequence proceeds, the lady's spiritual beauty is emphasized over her physical charms; and in the crucial "Easter" sonnet, the love of the man and woman is explicitly subordinated to the saving, sacrificial love of Christ: "So let vs loue, deare loue, lyke as we ought, / loue is the lesson which the Lord vs taught" (LXVIII.13–14).

Placed at the end of the *Amoretti*, occupying the same place in that sequence as Petrarch's great canzone to the Blessed Virgin Mary in the *Rime Sparse*, is Spenser's *Epithalamion*, or wedding hymn. Spenser's poem is unique among epithalamia in that he wrote it for his own wedding. While *Astrophil and Stella* lightly disguises Sidney and Penelope Rich under the names of the title characters, the *Amoretti* openly proclaims itself an account of the poet's courtship of Elizabeth Boyle during the year 1594 — there are references to specific dates in several of the sonnets. The *Epithalamion* likewise proclaims itself a wedding gift for the poet's bride.

The classical epithalamion, written by another man with the groom in focus, stresses marriage as a religious and social institution with procreation as its goal. The tone is usually mildly bawdy, and some seem suitable only for bachelor parties. Renaissance imitations generally are comparable to the classical models. Since Spenser writes his own wedding hymn, with his bride in view, there is not a hint of bawdiness in the tone. Moreover, his poem represents a convergence of ardent erotic idealism with the vision of matrimony as a religious and social institution.

If the *Epithalamion* is free of ribaldry, it cannot be said to lack passion. Spenser is explicit about the groom's delight in his bride's beauty and his desire for sexual consummation. He details her physical charms in an elaborate anatomical catalogue (171–80); and since the marriage takes place at midsummer, the longest day of the year, the poet bemoans with mock impatience the "ill ordained" time of the wedding ceremony: "Ah when will this long weary day haue end, / And lende me leaue to come vnto my loue?" (270, 278–79). His unblushing anticipation of the wedding night is expressed in the sensual terms of pagan mythology:

> Behold how goodly my faire loue does ly
> In proud humility;
> Like vnto Maia, when as Ioue her tooke,
> In Tempe, lying on the flowry gras,
> Twixt sleepe and wake, after she weary was,
> With bathing in the Acidalian brooke. (305–10)

As in the *Amoretti*, however, the erotic passion is constrained by other considerations. The tribute to the bride's bodily beauty is followed by a tribute to her virtue and "that which noe eyes can see, / The inward beauty of her liuely spright" (185–86ff.).

What is more, the eager desires of the groom fall within the framework of God's plan of procreation and the growth of the Church, as he calls upon the heavenly powers:

> Poure out your blessing on vs plentiously,
> And happy influence vpon vs raine,
> That we may raise a large posterity,
> Which from the earth, which they may long possesse,
> With lasting happinesse,
> Vp to your haughty pallaces may mount,
> And for the guerdon of theyr glorious merit
> May heauenly tabernacles there inherit,
> Of blessed Saints for to increase the count. (415–23)

In Spenser's poem, the most intense and individualistic passion — an idealized desire that elevates a woman to a virtually divine level — dovetails neatly with marriage conceived as a social and religious institution ordered to the procreation of citizens and the glorification of God in His saints. Spenser uses the same poetic form and fervid language to celebrate his bride as Sidney uses to express his illicit desire for another man's wife. The unattainable Penelope Devereux Rich is immortalized as Stella; Sidney's wife is remembered in no sonnets. In some respects, the difference may result from class differences. Sidney was a prominent aristocrat, Spenser unaffectedly bourgeois: the bridesmaids in the *Epithalamion* are "merchants daughters" (167). In any case, Spenser gives us a vision of the sacramental mystery of marriage becoming part of domestic wedded bliss in an immediate literal sense. This is especially curious because Article 25 of the Articles of Religion of the Church of England of 1563 specifically excludes matrimony (along with confirmation, penance, orders, and extreme unction) from the "evangelical sacraments…instituted by God."[44] Nevertheless, the poet imagines his wedding vows exchanged before a "high altar," a "sacred Altare," surrounded by angels and the music of "roring Organs." These are likewise appurtenances not customary in Tudor Protestant churches.

John Donne and the Privatization of Love

It would almost seem that the romanticization of marriage in Reformation England is a reaction to the loss of sacramental depth in official Protestant worship. The example of John Donne would seem to enhance this speculation. As Anthony Low points out, "Donne was a chief actor and influence in what may be called the 'reinvention of love,' from something essentially social and feudal to something essentially private and modern." What is invented is "an inner space, a magic circle of subjective immunity from outward political threat and from culturally induced anxiety."[45] From the very first Donne suffered a powerful source of anxiety. His mother was the niece of St. Thomas More, and, in Donne's own words, he was "derived from such a stocke and race, as, I beleeve, no family, (which is not of farre larger extent, and greater branches,) hath endured and suffered more in their persons and fortunes, for obeying the Teachers of Romane Doctrine, then it hath done."[46] During his youth and young manhood in the 1580s and 1590s, the persecution of Catholic recusants was at its most intense in Elizabethan England. One of Donne's Jesuit uncles, Jasper Heywood, was sentenced to death, although the sentence was never carried out; and his younger brother Henry, arrested for harboring a Catholic priest in his rooms at Oxford, died of the plague that was raging in Newgate prison.[47]

John, however, was evidently not cut out to be a martyr. What is more, he was a very ambitious young man, with a longing for "preferment" — a position at the royal court that his satirical poetry affected to despise. His religious affiliation during the 1590s is uncertain to historians and probably to Donne himself, and there are other signs of an anxiously divided mind in the young poet. It was during this decade that he probably wrote both his third satire, which broods anxiously over the difficulty of determining the identity of the one true Church, and a number of erotic elegies and lyrics that seem designed to outrage respectable sensibilities with paradoxical defenses of promiscuity, witty schemes of seduction and adultery, and occasional obscenity. Permeating the dominant aura of sexual libertinism in these poems, however, are strains of religious and political satire. The greed, self-righteousness, and obsessive spying of the society that persecuted his family are held up to ridicule in poems that outwardly deal only with illicit love; and the jaded, rakish persona betrays a fearful preoccupation with discovery by pursuivants (informers on Catholic recusants).[48] Naturally, these poems, which in all likelihood circulated in manuscript only among a small coterie of intellectual malcontents, were not published until after Donne's death.

By 1597 Donne must have been at least an outwardly conforming member of the Church of England, for he had secured a foothold on the slippery ascent to courtly preferment in the household of Sir Thomas Egerton, Lord Keeper of the Great Seal to Queen Elizabeth. How far Donne might have risen from this promising beginning cannot be known: late in 1601 he dashed his own prospects by eloping with the seventeen-year-old niece (by marriage) of his employer. Ann More was the daughter of Sir George More, and her wealthy and influential father had no difficulty furnishing her four

sisters with husbands of far greater prospects and higher standing than John
Donne; that is, they were not burdened with his debts, his suspicious recu-
sant background, and his reputation as a sexual libertine. When news of
the marriage reached Sir George, he became enraged. He prevailed upon
Egerton to dismiss his brilliant protégé, had Donne and all the witnesses to
the marriage jailed, and attempted to procure an annulment.

In due course Donne and his friends were released from jail, and the marriage to Ann, though illicit, was ruled valid. Sir George relented enough to
attempt to convince Sir Thomas Egerton to reinstate Donne, but Sir Thomas
thought it beneath his dignity to fire and rehire at the whim of others. Once
disgraced, Donne was unable to find another suitable position. For more
than a decade, with a young wife accustomed to better things and a growing family, the poet lived off the residue of his inheritance, the charity of
friends, and the sporadic patronage of aristocratic lords and (especially)
ladies, to whom he wrote flattering verse epistles. Finally, in 1615, Donne
was induced by James I to take holy orders in the Church of England and
went on to become one of the greatest preachers in an age of great sermons. Ann, regrettably, did not long enjoy her husband's success; she died
in 1617, aged thirty-three, shortly after the birth and death of the couple's
twelfth child.[49]

But all this is another story. What is germane to our present purposes is
the spectacle of a man with the reputation of a rake and dandy who not
only married for love, but sacrificed his worldly prospects and became a
virtual pariah for more than ten years. It is poignantly ironic that a man
who in witty verse had ridiculed chastity and fidelity and extolled a cynical
licentiousness should stake everything on the love of a teenage girl. The
extent to which Donne's poetic pose as blasé seducer was based on real
experience rather than on his reading of Ovid and other risqué classical
authors cannot be known, but there is no doubt that gossips took the poems
at face value. In one of his pleading letters to Sir George More, he attempts
to exonerate himself of the charge not only "of loving a corrupt religion,"
but also "of having deceived some gentlewomen before."[50]

Not all of Donne's love poems are bawdy celebrations of illicit sexuality
or sardonic debunkings of fidelity, but even his affirmations of constancy
and commitment are not simple romantic idealizations of love, neither of
unrequited passion for an unattainable Petrarchan icon, nor of marriage
as a religious and social institution in which the desires of individuals are
wholly subsumed, after the fashion of Edmund Spenser. Although there are
indications that some of Donne's love poems were written after his marriage
and reflect his experience as a husband, there is no hard evidence for dating
these poems; and the character of the love described is decidedly equivocal.
Consider, for example, "The Sunne Rising":

> Busie old foole, unruly Sunne,
>   Why dost thou thus,
> Through windowes, and through curtaines call on us?
> Must to thy motions lovers seasons run?
>   Sawcy pedantique wretch, goe chide
>   Late schoole boyes, and sowre prentices,
> Goe tell court huntsmen, that the King will ride,
> Call countrey ants to harvest offices;
> Love, all alike, no season knowes, nor clyme,
> Nor houres, dayes, moneths, which are the rags of time.[51]

                                                  (1–10)

The poem recalls Ovid's *Amores* I.13, where the poet humorously chides Aurora, goddess of the dawn, for awakening lovers too early. Such associations carry overtones of illicit love; however, at least one detail in the poem suggests that it was written after the accession of James I in 1603, hence several years after Donne's marriage: "Goe tell court huntsmen, that the King will ride." James's preoccupation with hunting was as much a part of the gossip of the early years of his reign as President Eisenhower's avid interest in golf was in the 1950s.[52] It would seem too much of a coincidence for Donne to hit upon just this characteristic of a hypothetical king. Besides, how could Donne have anticipated his own situation during the first decade of the seventeenth century when he would be just such a man as the speaker of "The Sunne Rising," with nothing to do but stay at home in bed with his young wife?

The second stanza combines Petrarchan motif with its antithesis; the lady possesses the dazzling eyes of a Laura or a Stella, but she is hardly aloof and unattainable. Unlike the frustrated Petrarchan poet, Donne's persona shares the bed of his lady; and he claims, in extravagant terms, that the experience is a sufficient compensation for missing the affairs of the royal court or the exploration and conquest of empires in the old and new world: "Aske for those Kings whom thou saw'st yesterday, / And thou shalt heare, All here in one bed lay" (19–20). In other words, in this poem love takes the place of all the opportunities that Donne lost as a result of his secret marriage.[53]

In the closing stanza the hyperbole reaches a pitch of rueful defiance as the persona claims that his beloved is "all States" and he "all Princes":

> Thine age askes ease, and since thy duties bee
> To warme the world, that's done in warming us.
> Shine here to us, and thou are every where;
> This bed thy center is, these walls, thy sphere. (27–30)

Here is certainly an idealization of erotic love: Donne spins out a witty cosmic conceit to identify the conjugal bed with the universe; to assert that the lovers "mean the world" to each other. Yet, although it is difficult not to associate this poem with the historical John Donne, out of work and in disgrace during the early years of the reign of James I, there is no mention of marriage as a grand social and religious institution. Marriage lies in the realm of the irate patriarch, Sir George More, and under the control of canon law. It is precisely such institutions that the lovers of "The Sunne Rising" seek to escape and defy.

This sense of love as a private erotic refuge from conventional respectability is even more pronounced in "The Canonization," where contempt for bourgeois morality is displayed in a burst of exasperation:

> For Godsake hold your tongue, and let me love,
>   Or chide my palsie, or my gout,
> My five gray haires, or ruin'd fortune flout,
>   With wealth your state, your minde with arts improve,
>   Take you a course, get you a place,
>   Observe his honour, or his grace,
>   Or the Kings reall, or his stamped face
>   Contemplate, what you will approve,
>   So you will let me love. (1–9)

It is pleasing to imagine that the speaker of this poem has just interrupted a private lecture, filled with good advice, by Francis Bacon or one of his disciples. "The stage is more beholding to love than the life of man," Bacon writes in his essay, "Of Love"; and, toward the close of the piece, he offers a recommendation that the speaker of "The Canonization" seems to have neglected as egregiously as the poet had done in real life: "They do best, who, if they cannot but admit love, yet make it keep quarter, and sever it wholly from their serious affairs and actions of life; for if it check once with business, it troubleth men's fortunes, and maketh men that they can no ways be true to their own ends."[54] In "The Canonization," as well as in "The Sunne Rising," Donne offers a dramatic expostulation that love is an end in itself, displacing "the serious affairs and actions of life." For more than a decade Donne himself had little recourse but to accept this poetic fancy as sober truth.

In the second stanza of "The Canonization," the poet ridicules Petrarchan conceits by ostentatiously declining to deploy them. Our love is not altogether out of control, the speaker wryly tells his interlocutor: my sighs have raised no storms at sea, my tears have caused no floods, my chills and fevers have not increased the death toll from the plague, and soldiers and lawyers have lost no business because our love has created a more peaceable atmosphere in the world. Having thus mocked the clichés of Elizabethan Petrarchanism, Donne produces conceits in his third stanza more outrageous than anything in the Petrarchan tradition, saying that the lovers at their "owne cost die":

> The Phoenix ridle hath more with
> By us, we two being one, are it.
> So to one neutral thing both sexes fit,
> Wee dye and rise the same, and prove
> Mysterious by this love. (23–27)

"Die" is, of course, familiar Elizabethan-Jacobean slang for sexual climax, here raised to the level of a theological "mystery," namely, the resurrection. In the world of the poem, however extravagantly or ironically expressed, mutual erotic fulfillment is depicted as a quasi-religious mystery: a "resurrection" into a new life.

By the end of the fourth stanza, the lovers have been "*Canoniz'd* for love" by popular acclamation, and in the fifth stanza they are held up for both emulation and intercession throughout the kingdom by "Countries, Townes, Courts" (44). In the fiction of the poem, the social and political realm that Donne lost by his clandestine marriage is both dismissed and reclaimed by the poetic persona. The lovers who have made a "hermitage" of each other have sworn off the world in a way that parodies the withdrawal of Catholic monks or nuns, but the speaker of the poem confidently predicts their vindication: busy, unhappy worldlings will admire and seek to imitate the "peace" of their love just as they admire the peaceful sanctity of religious life.

The erotic hagiography of "The Canonization" is only the most extreme example of Donne's Catholic upbringing slipping into his poems of profane love. "Aire and Angels" involves an elaborate conceit based on Thomist angelology; both "The Funerall" and "The Relique" fantasize about the remains of the poetic persona and his mistress furnishing objects of veneration for worshipers of an idealized Eros. In "A Valediction: forbidding mourning," the lovers must avoid vulgar Petrarchan displays of grief at parting, because they are conceived as members of a religious order of love: "T'were prophanation of our joyes / To tell the layetie our love" (7–8). If, as is probable, these lyrics were written in the aftermath of Donne's marriage, the question arises whether marriage has tamed the poet's erotic ardor, or whether Eros has subtly infiltrated, even corrupted, the Christian institution? "Although few have doubted Ann More's influence on the later *Songs and Sonets*," Anthony Low remarks, "Donne says nothing in them about marriage or its traditional functions. In short, he effectively anticipates Romantic and modern views of marriage as a retreat from, rather than an integrated aspect of, the daily interactions of people in society."[55] We may surmise that Donne's marriage marked the final decisive step in his apostasy from the Church of his family — the point of no return. It is hardly surprising that, for a lapsed Catholic, love itself, as distinct from the human and social institution that matrimony is in the Protestant conception, would assume a quasi-sacred role by expropriating in a profane, sometimes blasphemous manner the sacramental language of Catholicism. In his often anguished devotional poems, Donne sometimes, in typical baroque fashion, substitutes Christ for Cupid; but in his most "serious" poems of faithful, conjugal love Cupid seems to displace Christ as an object of worship.

It is of no small significance that Donne's wedding sermons as an Anglican cleric are not just rigorously orthodox in Protestant terms, but even rather dour. The earliest of these sermons to survive, preached less than three years after the death of Donne's wife, celebrates the marriage of the daughter of his old friend, Sir Henry Goodyer, to Sir Francis Nethersole. One hopes that the bride's expectations of her wifely status were not altogether dampened by this dash of cold water from the presiding clergyman:

> ... even the workes of God, are not equally excellent; this [the creation of woman] is but *faciam,* it is not *faciamus;* in the creation of man there is intimated a Consultation, a Deliberation of the whole *Trinity;* in the making of *women,* it is not expressed so; it is *faciam.* And then, that that is made here, is but *Adjutorium,* but an accessory, not principall; but a *Helper.* First the wife must be so *much,* she must *Helpe;* and then she must be *no more,* she must *not Governe.*[56]

Donne then reminds the groom, in the words of St. Jerome, "*Nihil foedius, quam uxorem amare tanquam adulteram,* that there is not a more uncomely, a poorer thing, then to love a Wife like a Mistresse."[57] A true enough observation, but not especially festive, given the occasion; and one can only wonder how it must have sounded to Donne's old crony, Henry Goodyer, coming from the author of "The Canonization" and "The Sunne Rising." In a wedding sermon preached about a year later, after a bit of obligatory denigration of Catholic marital practice, Donne admits to a preference for clerical celibacy:

> When men have made vowes to abstain from marriage, I would they would be content to try a little longer then they doe, whether they could keep that vow or noe: And when men have consecrated themselves to the service of God in his Church, I would they would be content to try a little farther then they doe, whether they could abstain or noe.[58]

Donne himself, somewhat atypically for an English Protestant clergyman of his day, remained a celibate widower after the death of his wife in 1617 until his own death in 1631 — a period comprising the greater part of his clerical career.

For present purposes Donne's most interesting marriage sermon comes in 1627 at the wedding of the granddaughter of Sir Thomas Egerton, the preacher's former employer, and the nephew of the poet George Herbert. Here, after averring that marriage is not "a *Sacrament, as Baptisme,* and the *Lords Supper* are Sacraments," and adding the gratuitous abuse of the Catholic Church usual in such contexts, Donne concedes that Christian marriage is different from pagan marriage because it is, well, sacramental:

> Mariage among Christians, is herein *Magnum mysterium,* A Sacrament in such a sense; a mysterious signification of the *union of the soule* with Christ; when both persons professe the Christian Religion, in *generall,* there arises some signification of that spirituall union: But when they both professe Christ in *one* forme, in one Church, in one Religion, and that, the right; then, as by the *Civill* Contract, there is an union of their *estates,* and *persons,* so, as that they two are made one, so by this *Sacramentall,* this mysterious union, these two, thus made one, between themselves, are also made one with Christ himself; by the *Civill* union, common to all people, they are made *Eadem caro,* The same flesh with one another; By this mysterious, this Sacramentall, this significative union, they are made *Idem Spiritus cum Domino;* The same Spirit with the Lord.[59]

Was ever any Jesuit such an equivocator? Note that Donne, unlike Calvin, does not reduce the Pauline term "mystery" to a mere figure; marriage is not simply a metaphor for the relation between Christ and the Church or Christ and the soul: it is a means of uniting this particular man and woman, by way of their marriage, with Christ. Marriage is, then, a sacrament. As is not infrequently the case, on the issue of marriage, the moderate position of the Church of England between Rome and Geneva turns out to be equivocal.

Donne the poet and Donne the preacher together embody the Protestant dilemma regarding marriage: the poet makes a private, personal sacrament of his own transfigured desire; the preacher tries to salvage something of the unique holiness of Christian marriage without embracing the full sacramental theology of the Catholic Church. Although the psychology of the situation is very understandable, its logic is untenable; and it remains for that most brilliant and portentous figure of seventeenth-century English poetry and theology, John Milton, to draw out the full implications of the Reformation treatment of the sacraments.

Milton is not only the greatest poet of his age; he is also one of the seminal thinkers of the early modern era, whose influence extends beyond the range of poetry. Milton is the first important proponent of modern notions of divorce in the Christian world; in fact, so radical was his proposal for what amounted to "no-fault" divorce that it would only become law three hundred years later in the middle of the twentieth century. Although he scandalized his contemporaries, his championing of divorce seems a logical consequence of the Reformation principle of private judgment. The ultimate implication of this principle is that good and evil are defined by subjective private experience. Conscience is, then, not the faculty that warns an individual that he has violated an objective norm of right and wrong; it is, rather, the individual's means of determining what right and wrong are *for him.*

Like Donne's intriguing love poetry, which turns a refined conception of Eros into the idol of a private quasi-religion, Milton's radical call for divorce develops against a background of personal marital crisis. In the late spring of 1642, Milton, then in his thirty-fourth year, set out for Oxfordshire, perhaps to confer about a debt owed his father by Richard Powell. In the words of Milton's nephew, Edward Phillips, "after a month's stay, home he returns a married man, that went out a bachelor";[60] and his bride was none other than Richard Powell's seventeen-year-old daughter, Mary. We do not know what was done about the debt, but the marriage was quickly in trouble. The bride, John Aubrey tells us:

> was brought up and lived where there was a great deal of company and merriment (dancing etc.). And when she came to live with her husband,... she found it very solitary: no company came to her; oftentimes heard his nephews beaten and cry. This life was irksome to her, and so she went to her parents.[61]

In addition to the evident personal incompatibility between the new spouses, there was political tension: the Powells were staunch royalists and adherents of the established church; Milton was a vociferous anti-prelatical pamphleteer and supporter of Parliament. By the time Mary was supposed to return to her husband in September of 1642, the nation was on the brink of open civil war. Mary, doubtless with the urging of her parents, declined to rejoin her husband in London — the center of Parliamentary resistance to the King — and Milton was enraged. (It should be added that three years later, in 1645, after he had composed his divorce pamphlets, Milton not only received Mary back into his house but also succored her parents and relations, who were left penniless and dispossessed in the wake of Parliamentary victories in Oxfordshire.)

The more proximate result of Milton's desertion by his young wife, however, was the composition of four pamphlets during the next two and a half years arguing for the legalization of divorce on the grounds of incompatibility with the right to subsequent remarriage. The first and most important of these tracts, *The Doctrine and Discipline of Divorce,* was published in

August 1643 and was regarded — at least among the respectable elements of society — with shock and outrage. The following year a Presbyterian divine, Herbert Palmer, preaching before Parliament and urging a restoration of strict control over the press, cited Milton's divorce pamphlet as an example of an opinion so manifestly absurd and immoral that it could not possibly be tolerated.[62] To be sure, there was an underground sentiment in favor of legal divorce and remarriage, especially among the more extreme sects that flourished among the lower classes and came out into the open during the social breakdown of the Civil War. The first edition of *Doctrine and Discipline* sold out very quickly, but it is apparent from a remark in the dedication of the second edition, published six months later, that the author was embarrassed by at least some of his readers:

> What though the brood of Belial, the draffe of men, to whom no liberty is pleasing, but unbridl'd and vagabond lust without pale or partition, will laugh broad perhaps, to see so great a strength of Scripture mustering up in favour, as they suppose, of their debausheries; they will know better, when they shall hence learne, that honest liberty is the greatest foe to dishonest license.[63]

It is, I think, crucially important to recognize Milton's sincerity: he is such a dangerous foe to Catholic teaching on the indissolubility of marriage because he is no mere libertine, but someone convinced that he is following the dictates of his conscience.

To be sure, Milton faces an extraordinarily difficult problem: the demonstration that one of the seemingly clearest dominical utterances in the New Testament means exactly the opposite of what it appears to say: "And I say to you that whosoever shall put away his wife, except it be for fornication, and shall marry another, committeth adultery; and he that shall marry her that is put away committeth adultery" (Matt. 19:9). For our purposes here we can ignore the fornication exception — divorce and remarriage for the unoffending party were permitted under English law in Milton's time — and consider how Milton handles the general prohibition. His basic strategy is to appropriate two features of Reformation doctrine to his own ends: (1) the Calvinist principle of private judgment by which Scripture is interpreted in accordance with the elect believer's inner awareness of his own regeneration by grace; and (2) the general Protestant denial that marriage is a sacrament.

Although Milton repudiates the notion of the bondage of the will, which is so important to Lutheran and Calvinist theology, he is still influenced by the Calvinist notion of the believer's inward assurance that he is saved by faith alone. Milton seizes on this idea of assurance in a way that seems to make the effects of original sin virtually negligible in the moral life of the elect. Hence *Doctrine and Discipline* describes the man who is unhappy in his marriage as "a blameless creature," "such as hath spent his youth unblamably," a "good and peaceable man," and yet again a "blameless creature" (II.244, 254, 306, 335). Since Moses had provided for divorce (Deut. 24:1), and Christ could not have intended the Gospel to be harsher and more restrictive than the Law, surely Christ's remarks about divorce were intended only to discomfit hard-hearted, hypocritical pharisees, not to thwart the happiness of a "blameless creature."

According to Milton's argument, the purpose of marriage is to make man happy by dispelling loneliness through agreeable companionship. An unhappy marriage is therefore no marriage at all. The aggrieved husband, since he is "peaceable" and "blameless," cannot be at fault; the only explanation is that he has married the wrong woman — one who is not "a help meet" for her husband. She does not fulfill the criteria for a wife set forth in Genesis 2:18, for it is plain, Milton asserts, "that in God's intention a meet and happy conversation is the chiefest and the noblest end of mariage." If this end is not attained, if the man's loneliness is not assuaged, then "such a mariage can be no mariage whereto the most honest end is wanting" (II.246, 247). In effect, Milton makes the validity of marriage depend upon the state of mind of the husband: his sense of discontent amounts to an annulment. He sounds quite contemporary in maintaining that a loveless marriage is no marriage at all, especially since "love" is so clearly a feeling rather than an act of will: "Love in mariage cannot live nor subsist, unlesse it be mutual; and where love cannot be, there can be left of wedlock nothing, but the empty husk of an outside matrimony; as undelightful and unpleasing to God, as any other kind of hypocrisie." The termination of an empty marriage thus becomes a moral duty, but the determination of the marriage's condition is altogether subjective and inaccessible to any external rule or observation: "to interpose a jurisdictive power upon the inward and irremediable disposition of man, to command love and *sympathy,* to forbid dislike against the guiltles instinct of nature, is not within the province of any law to reach, & were indeed an uncommodious rudenes, not a just power" (II.256, 346).

In works such as *Areopagitica* and *Paradise Lost,* Milton offers a bracing vision of free will, but, as Anthony Low observes, human freedom disappears along with virtue and grace from *Doctrine and Discipline:*

> Milton's natural incompatibility takes no account of Christian virtue, divine grace, or remediable free will. In short, it radically anticipates the Romantic and Modern habit of grounding ideal sexual love in a kind of mysterious "natural supernaturalism," which is beyond our ability to change or control.[64]

What Low here describes seems to be a naturalized version of Calvinist irresistible grace. Milton denies the obvious literal meaning of Christ's prohibition of divorce because he simply cannot accept it and retain his own sense of election and grace, that is, his sense of being a good Christian and a good man. Unhappiness in marriage, he says, is "a daily trouble and paine of losse in some degree like that which Reprobates feel" (II.247). If one's faith depends on an inner assurance of salvation, then whatever interferes with that assurance must be rejected; if Scripture's meaning is given by grace to the elect believer, then scriptural interpretations that fail to enhance the interpreter's sense of election will necessarily be repudiated. The intensely and defiantly passionate erotic bliss of Donne's *Songs & Sonets,* which may be in marriage but is not *of* it, becomes for Milton the measure of a marriage's validity. Thus marriage becomes a public official institution that is defined by the private, subjective experience of the spouses (or, for Milton, the husband).

Milton takes advantage of Reformation sacramental theology by pointing out its inconsistencies: Protestant divines "dare not affirm that marriage is either a Sacrament, or a mystery,... and yet they invest it with such an awful sanctity, and give it such adamantine chains to bind with, as if it were to be worship like some *Indian* deity, when it can conferre no blessing upon us, but works more and more to our misery" (II.277–78). Here the poet scores a point against the theologians: if marriage is not a sacramental channel of grace, if it is merely a human contract, then it is hard to see how a man can be expected "to grind in the mill of an undelighted and servil copulation... with such a yokefellow, from whom both love and peace, both nature and Religion mourns to be separated" (II.258).

Milton further observes that the literal way Reformation divines accept Christ's words about the indissolubility of marriage (which they do not regard as a sacrament) ill accords with their treatment of Christ's words instituting the undoubted sacrament of the Eucharist:

> I shall not much waver to affirm that those words which are made to intimate, as if they forbad all divorce but for adultery (though *Moses* have constituted it otherwise), those words taken circumscriptly, without regard to any precedent law of *Moses* or attestation of Christ himself, or without care to preserve those his fundamental and superior laws of nature and charitie, to which all other ordinances give up their seals, are as much against plain equity, and the mercy of religion, as those words of *Take, eat, this is my body,* elementally understood, are against nature and sense. (II.325)

Although the English Calvinist divines of Milton's day were scandalized by his argument for divorce, what he does with Christ's words regarding marriage is essentially what Calvin had done in the preceding century with Christ's words at the Last Supper by which the sacrament of the Eucharist was begun. Centuries before Jacques Derrida, both interpretations are acts of deconstruction, making Christ say exactly the opposite of what Christians had for centuries thought he said.

There is an ironic inconsistency in Milton's attitude toward marriage. He denies that it is indissoluble, arguing that it is not a sacrament or even a divine mystery. Still, a man can expect "his chiefest earthly comforts in the enjoyment of a contented mariage" and look for his wife "to be the copartner of a sweet and gladsome society." If these hopes are disappointed, "though he be almost the strongest Christian, he will be ready to dispair in vertue, and mutin against divine providence" (II.254). Such an idealization of marital love creates expectations so intense that any actual marriage is bound to fall short. The irony lies in the way that the demand for divorce arises precisely from the exalted ideal he raises of the possibilities of marriage. In *Paradise Lost* a key element of prelapsarian bliss is the exquisite personal and sexual harmony between Adam and Eve. The archangel Michael promises the fallen Adam that he and his postlapsarian descendants can recover, through God's grace, "A paradise within thee, happier farr."[65] An unhappy marriage would seem to indicate a lack of grace, a sign of God's disapproval.

Evidently, in Milton's mind the early Reformation notion of inner assurance of election had become identified with personal happiness and contentment, and personal experience thus became the measure of right and wrong. In our own day Milton's vision has triumphed. We see the results not only in no-fault divorce, but in an entire society which measures moral norms by subjective longings. Out of the Reformation concepts of salvation by faith alone and private judgment, Milton devised one of the central principles of the modern, secular world: We are saved not by faith in God, but by faithfulness to our own restless desires, to our own vaguely idealized inner self.

Conclusion

But the ascendancy of this view was three centuries in the future. At the end of the seventeenth century, divorce was rare and legally restricted in England and other Protestant countries — and of course still forbidden in Catholic countries. With the accelerating emergence of the middle class during this century, qualities that are still prized in marriage today — privacy and personal intimacy — were increasingly valued. In the words of John R. Gillis:

> The "middling sorts"...were now rejecting the notion of marriage as a public institution imposing obligations that extended beyond the

nuclear family. They also stressed the importance of the conjugal relationship but, instead of launching an all-out assault on patriarchy, they redefined it as a private matter, no longer subject to public control. The authority of priest and parish was reallocated to the father and husband.[66]

As we have seen in this and earlier chapters, a strengthening of "companionate" elements in marriage had already been encouraged in the late Middle Ages and early Renaissance. In Catholic France a number of Molière's comedies, for example, suggest that marriage was coming to be regarded as an intimate, personal affair in which both parental and ecclesiastical interference were frowned upon.[67] Nevertheless, it is probably safe to say that this tendency was swifter and more pronounced in England and other Protestant countries, because marriage was no longer considered a sacrament. If marriage is an essentially secular institution, rather than a mysterious channel of grace, then there is a clear rationale for allowing the spouses to determine its form and disposition. Ultimately, the loss of sacramental status is the most important development in marriage during the period of the Reformation; for it is most fraught with implications for the secularization of the modern world.

Notes

1. Robert Burton, *The Anatomy of Melancholy* III.2.1.2, ed. Holbrook Jackson (London, 1932), III, 53.

2. *Religio Medici* II, in *Sir Thomas Browne: The Major Works,* ed. C. A. Patrides (Harmondsworth, 1977), 148–49.

3. "Samuel Johnson's Life of Browne," ibid., 490. Actually, Lady Browne bore her husband twelve children, as Patrides points out in a footnote.

4. William and Malleville Haller, "The Puritan Art of Love," *Huntingdon Library Quarterly* 5 (1941): 235–72; Lawrence Stone, *The Family, Sex and Marriage in England 1500–1800* (New York, 1977), 135–42. But cf. Ralph A. Houlbrooke, *The English Family 1450–1700* (London and New York, 1984), 5–6, 30–32, 76, 96, 102–5; and Alan Macfarlane, *Marriage and Love in England: Modes of Reproduction 1300–1840* (Oxford, 1986), 44, 135–36, 151, 182. For a recent treatment of the way in which medieval Catholic theology stressed mutual love and equality between spouses, see Michael M. Sheehan "'Maritalis affectio' Revisited" and Erik Kooper, "Loving the Unequal Equal: Medieval Theologians and Marital Affection," both in *The Olde Daunce: Love, Friendship, Sex, and Marriage in the Medieval World,* ed. Robert R. Edwards and Stephen Spector (Albany, 1991), 32–43, 44–56. None of the sources cited by these scholars seems to me as sympathetic to, even enthusiastic about, marital sexuality as the Protestant authors cited by Anthony Fletcher. See below, n. 12.

5. *The Pagan Servitude of the Church* in *Martin Luther: Selections from his Writings,* ed. John Dillenberger (Garden City, N.Y., 1961), 326.

6. Ibid., 337.

7. Ibid., 337–38, 339.

8. *Institutes of the Christian Religion* IV.21, trans. Henry Beveridge (Grand Rapids, Mich., 1957), II.574.

9. Ibid., IV.19.34–36; II.646–48.

10. Ibid., IV.19.37; II, 648.

11. *The Birthpangs of Protestant England: Religious and Cultural Change in the Sixteenth and Seventeenth Centuries* (New York, 1988), 62–63.

12. "The Protestant Idea of Marriage in Early Modern England," in *Religion, Culture and Society in Early Modern Britain,* ed. Anthony Fletcher and Peter Roberts (Cambridge, 1994), 161–81, esp. 175–80.

13. *Seventeenth-Century American Poetry,* ed. Harrison T. Meserole (New York, 1968), 32–33.

14. See the brief introductions to "Courtship" (*Proci et Puellae*) and "The Girl with No Interest in Marriage" (*Virgo misogamos*) by Craig R. Thompson, trans., *The Colloquies of Erasmus* (Chicago and London, 1965), 86–87, 99–103. For an extremely negative critique of Erasmus's attitudes toward marriage and monasticism, cf. Émile V. Telle, *Érasme de Rotterdam et le Septième Sacrement* (Geneva, 1954), who argues that under a quasi-orthodox guise, Erasmus rejected traditional Catholic teaching: "Because he saw in monasticism the enemy of the *Philosophia Christi* and in Catholic theology of the seventh sacrament a means devised by the scholastics for the enslavement of the consciences of laymen, he was convinced that monasticism was the enemy of marriage" (p. 6).

15. *Encomium matrimonii,* ed. J.-C. Margolin, in *Opera Omnia Desiderii Erasmi Roterdami* (Amsterdam and Oxford, 1975), I-5.388: "Iam si caetera sacramenta, quibus Ecclesia Christi potissimum nititur, religiosa quadam veneratione coluntur, quis non videt huic plurimum religionis deberi, quod et a Deo, et primum omnium est institutum?"

16. "Proci et Puellae," *Colloquia,* ed. L.-E. Halkin, F. Bierlaire, R. Hoven, in *Opera Omnia Desiderii Erasmi Roterdami* (Amsterdam, 1972), I-3:278: "Sed quid dices, si argumentis Achilleis euincam et me esse mortuum et te esse homicidam?"

17. *Canones et Decreta Sacrosancti Oecumenici Concilii Tridenti* (Rome, 1862), 173–75. See also James A. Brundage, *Law, Sex, and Christian Society in Medieval Europe* (Chicago and London, 1987), 563–65.

18. Ibid., 287: "PAMPHILVS. Sed interim pronuncia tria verba. MARIA. Nihil facilius, sed verba, simul atque semel euolarint, non reuolant. Dabo consilium vtrique commodius. Ages cum tuis ac meis parentibus, vt vtrorumque voluntate res transigatur."

19. Ibid.: "Et vestrum est ambire, nobis decorum non est. Gaudet enim rapi virginitas, etiamsi nonnunquam vehementius amemus. See also *Coniugium: Uxor Mempsigamos,* ibid., 309–10, where Eulalia recommends that Xanthippe make special efforts to please her husband sexually in order to win his good will: "vxorem omnem curam adhibere oportere, vt in congressu connubiali iucunda sit marito, quo recalescat ac redintegretur amor ille maritalis, et discutiatur ex animo, si quid erat offensionis aut taedii" (p. 310).

20. Erasmus himself paints a wholly negative view of the consecrated virginity of the religious life in the paired colloquies, *Virgo Misogamos* ["A Girl Who Despises Marriage"] and *Virgo Poenitens* ["A Penitent Girl"], ibid., 289–300.

21. *Obras completas castellanas de Fray Luis de León,* ed. Félix García, 4th ed. (Madrid, 1957), 1:271: "aunque es verdad que la naturaleza y estado pone obligación en la casada...de mirar por su casa y de alegrar y descuidar continuamente a su marido, de la cual ninguna mala condición de él la desobliga, pero no por eso

han de pensar ellos que tienen licencia para serles leones y para hacerlas esclavas; antes, como en todo lo demás, es la cabeza el hombre; así todo este trato amoroso y honroso ha de tener principio del marido."

22. Ibid., 244: "Porque, a la verdad, aunque el estado del matrimonio, en grado y perfección, es menor que el de los continentes o vírgenes, pero por la necesidad que hay de él en el mundo para que se conserven los hombres y para que salgan de ellos los que nacen para ser hijos de Dios, y para honrar la tierra y alegrar el cielo con gloria, fue siempre muy honrado y privilegiado por el Espíritu Santo en las Letras Sagradas.

23. Ibid., 245–46: "Y, lo que sobre todo es, hizo del casamiento que tratan los hombres entre sí, significación y sacramento santísimo del lazo de amor con que Él se ayunta a las almas; y quiso que la ley matrimonial del hombre con la mujer fuese como retrato e imagen viva de la unidad dulcísima y estrechísima que hay entre Él y su Iglesia, y así ennobleció el matrimonio con riquísimos dones de su gracia y de otros bienes del cielo."

24. Ibid., 353–54: "Y no sólo esta belleza es peligrosa porque atrae a sí y enciende en su codicia los corazones de los que la miran, sino también porque despierta a las que la tienen a que gusten de ser codiciadas.... Así que quien busca mujer muy hermosa camina con oro por tierra de salteadores, y con oro que no se consiente encubrir en la bolsa.... Mas ¿quién no sabe lo que vale y lo que dura esta flor? ¿Cuán presto se acaba? ¿Con cuán ligeras ocasiones se marchita?"

25. Ibid., 351: "Pone la hermosura de la buena mujer, no en las figuras del rostro, sino en las virtudes secretas del alma, las cuales todas se comprenden en la Escritura debajo de esto que llamamos *temer a Dios*."

26. Ibid., 352: "Así que, si no es virtud del ánimo la limpieza y aseo del cuerpo, es señal de ánimo concertado y limpio y aseado."

27. *Introduction to the Devout Life*, trans. John K. Ryan (New York, 1972), 220.

28. Ibid., 227–28. See the references cited by John T. Noonan Jr., *Contraception: A History of Its Treatment by the Catholic Theologians and Canonists* (Cambridge, Mass., 1966), 34–36, for the typical twentieth-century interpretations of this scriptural passage. Noonan is of course aware of St. François; see 343–44, 372.

29. *Introduction to the Devout Life*, 229.

30. *The Letters of Peter Paul Rubens*, ed. and trans. Ruth Saunders Magurn (1955; rpt. Evanston, Ill., 1991), 136.

31. Ibid., 393.

32. *Introduction to the Devout Life*, 227.

33. *The Phoenix and the Flame: Catalonia and the Counter Reformation* (New Haven, Conn., and London, 1993), 275. See the entire chapter "The Reshaping of Marriage and Sexuality," 275–339.

34. In addition to Kamen, *The Phoenix and the Flame*, 281, see also John R. Gillis, *For Better, for Worse: British Marriages, 1600 to the Present* (New York and Oxford, 1985), 16–21; Jack Goody, *The Development of the Family and Marriage in Europe* (Cambridge, 1983), 174–75; Houlbrooke, *The English Family*, 80–83; Macfarlane, *Marriage and Love*, 304–5; Stone, *The Family, Sex and Marriage*, 30ff.; Brundage, *Law, Sex, and Christian Society*, 551–75.

35. *Monks on Marriage: A Twelfth-Century View* (New York, 1982), 107. See also Macfarlane, *Marriage and Love*, 332–33.

36. Such is the main thesis of *The Allegory of Love: A Study of Medieval Tradition* (London, 1936). Lewis's conception of courtly love is severely critiqued by Peter Dronke, *Medieval Latin and the Rise of European Love-Lyric* (Oxford, 1968), 1:2–9, 46–56. Since Dronke has nothing in particular to say about marriage, however,

this quarrel over the nature and influence of courtly love is not wholly germane to our subject.

37. *Astrophil and Stella* 5, in *Sir Philip Sidney*, ed. Katherine Duncan-Jones (New York and London, 1989). All quotations of Sidney's poems are from this edition.

38. *Dudley Carleton to John Chamberlain, 1603–1624: Jacobean Letters*, ed. Maurice Lee Jr. (New Brunswick, N.J., 1972), 77. See also Chamberlain's tart comment on the affair in a letter to Ralph Winwood, April 5, 1606, *The Letters of John Chamberlain*, ed. Norman Egbert McClure (1939; rpt. Westport, Conn., 1979), 1:226: "happy had he ben yf he had gon two or three yeares since, before the world was wearie of him, or that he had left that scandall behinde him."

39. *Rime Sparse* 366:121, 130, in *Petrarch's Lyric Poems*, ed. and trans. Robert M. Durling (Cambridge, Mass., and London, 1976).

40. *The Reinvention of Love: Poetry, Politics, and Culture from Sidney to Milton* (Cambridge, 1993), 14.

41. For the argument that Sidney was more attracted to Catholicism, especially as distinct from loyalty to the papacy, see Katherine Duncan-Jones, *Sir Philip Sidney: Courtier Poet* (New Haven, Conn., and London, 1993), 124–28. Such religious inclinations would, of course, only make his erotic passions more troubling and difficult to deal with.

42. For a discussion of the unusually light tone of the *Amoretti*, see Louis L. Martz, "Spenser's *Amoretti*: 'Most Goodly Temperature,'" in *From Renaissance to Baroque: Essays on Literature and Art* (Columbia, Mo., and London, 1991), 100–114.

43. *Spenser: Poetical Works*, ed. J. C. Smith and E. de Selincourt (London and New York, 1912). All quotations of Spenser's poems are taken from this edition.

44. See the official Latin version of the Articles of 1571 in Felix Makower, *The Constitutional History and Constitution of the Church of England* (London, 1895; rpt. New York, 1960), 485: "Quinque illa vulgo nominata sacramenta: scilicet, confirmatio, poenitentia, ordo, matrimonium, et extrema unctio, pro sacramentis evangelicis habenda non sunt, ut quae, partim, a prava Apostolorum imitatione profluxerunt, partim vitae status sunt in scripturis quidem probati: sed sacramentorum eandem cum baptismo, et coena Domini rationem non habentes, ut quae signum aliquod visibile seu caeremoniam a Deo institutam, non habeant."

45. *The Reinvention of Love*, 33, 51.

46. *Pseudo-Martyr*, ed. Anthony Raspa (Montreal and Buffalo, 1993), 8. See also R. C. Bald, *John Donne: A Life* (Oxford, 1970), 22.

47. Bald, *John Donne*, 58.

48. On the theological and political implications, see R. V. Young, "'O my America, my new-found-land': Pornography and Imperial Politics in Donne's *Elegies*," *South Central Review* 4, no. 2 (1987): 35–48. See also the first four chapters of John Carey, *John Donne: Life, Mind and Art* (New York, 1981), on the tension between Donne's residual Catholic loyalties and his ambition.

49. This account of Donne's marriage is largely based on Bald, *John Donne*, 109–54.

50. Edmund Gosse, *The Life and Letters of John Donne* (New York, 1899), 1:106.

51. Donne's poetry is quoted throughout from *Donne: Poetical Works*, ed. H. J. C. Grierson (1929; rpt. London, 1971).

52. See *The Letters of John Chamberlain* 1:201, 209, 240, 253, 282, 316, passim.

53. In real life the poet was not satisfied with love alone. For example, in a 1609 letter to Dudley Carleton, John Chamberlain, *Letters* I.209, writes curtly, "Newes

here is none at all but that John Dun seekes to be preferred to be secretarie of Virginia."

54. *Essays,* ed. Michael J. Hawkins (London, 1972), 29, 30.

55. *The Reinvention of Love,* 64.

56. *The Sermons of John Donne,* ed. George R. Potter and Evelyn M. Simpson (Berkeley, Calif., 1955), 2:337.

57. Ibid., 345.

58. Ibid., 3:243.

59. Ibid., 8:104.

60. *The Life of Mr. John Milton,* in *The Student's Milton,* ed. Frank Allen Patterson (rev. ed., New York, 1933), xxxvii.

61. *Minutes of the Life of Mr. John Milton,* in *The Student's Milton,* xxiii.

62. Ernest Sirluck, "Introduction," *Complete Prose Works of John Milton* (New Haven, Conn., 1959), 2:103.

63. *Complete Prose Works,* 2:225. Milton's pamphlet is quoted throughout from this edition, cited henceforth parenthetically in the text. See also Gillis, *For Better, for Worse,* 99.

64. *The Reinvention of Love,* 196.

65. *Paradise Lost* XII.587, in *The Poetical Works of John Milton,* ed. Helen Darbishire (London, 1958), 280.

66. *For Better, for Worse,* 82–83.

67. This is an issue in, for example, *The School for Husbands* (1661) and *Tartuffe* (1664).

Chapter Seven

THE EMERGENCE OF
THE MODERN FAMILY

James Hitchcock

At the beginning of the eighteenth century, marriage in the Western world was heavily determined by considerations of property and social status, as it had probably been almost everywhere throughout most of human history. Most prominent were the diplomatic marriages arranged among royalty to cement national alliances or create dynastic links. The negotiated marriage, however, prevailed at every level of the social hierarchy.[1]

Although the law did not forbid marriages across class lines, these were rare, especially among the aristocracy, and there was strong pressure against them. Both titled families and those with landed property took great care to preserve the male line if at all possible. For the most part the upper ranks of society practiced primogeniture, whereby the title and the bulk of the estate passed to the oldest male heir only, to prevent the family's assets from being divided and thereby steadily diminished.[2] A marriage seldom took place without a marital agreement arranged with the consent of the parents, only after negotiations which defined precisely what economic assets each party would bring to the union.[3]

Among royalty it was essential for a marriage to be arranged between countries which at least temporarily sought one another's support in international affairs, although afterward, if the countries became enemies, the wife was expected to remain loyal to her adopted nation.

Daughters and younger sons of the aristocracy were a perennial problem. Ideally daughters were themselves placed in advantageous marriages which enhanced their families' status, and the fulfillment of that ambition was usually determined by the size of the dowry a father was willing to bestow. Younger sons were given assets of various kinds, but they inherited only if an elder brother died. Otherwise they had to seek a place for themselves in the army, the Church, or the professions, or in marriage to an heiress.

Among the lower classes status and property were also important. The vast ranks of the rural laboring classes, which might look homogeneous to their social superiors, in fact contained numerous distinctions, and peasants also could marry above or beneath themselves in the eyes of the community. The poor too used marriage to enhance income, so that marriage negotiations might be protracted even if the absolute value of the property was relatively small. In agricultural areas young couples might have to wait for a "place" to open in the village community, through death or retirement, a farm becoming vacant in the tightly knit and intensely cultivated local economy.[4]

Courting customs varied but did not on the whole encourage, or even permit, young people to spend long periods alone with one another. Marriages were not uncommonly arranged by parents, so that the bride and groom might know each other only slightly before the wedding. Among the aristocracy, and especially among royalty, a marriage might actually be arranged without the two parties meeting at all. On lower social levels young people might meet one another at village dances, for example, but formal courting usually required permission from the girl's father, then seeing one another only under confined and supervised circumstances.[5]

Contrary to the Romeo and Juliet legend, couples in the Western world generally married only in their twenties, even though the canon law of the Catholic Church and, somewhat anomalously for a Protestant country, the common law of England permitted marriage at age fourteen for a boy and twelve for a girl.[6] If nothing else, the need to accumulate at least a minimum of property tended to forestall young marriages.[7]

All social rules are sometimes broken, and couples did occasionally elope to escape parental control and exercise their free choice. In fact, in England prior to the passage of the Marriage Act of 1753 (Lord Hardwicke's Act), it was sometimes difficult to judge who was legally married, since couples could present themselves to Anglican ministers of dubious canonical status and thereby become wed. The Marriage Act sought to put an end to this abuse by requiring publication of the banns in church, obtaining a license, and entry of a record of the marriage into the parish register. Clergy who ignored or thwarted these provisions were transported to the colonies, and one cleric in Dublin was actually hanged to show that the government was serious about the new law.[8]

Clandestine marriages had been fairly common and were probably entered into for a variety of reasons — because the couple were under legal age, because their parents were opposed to the match, because it was inconvenient to delay marriage for the duration of forbidden liturgical seasons such as Lent, to avoid publicity if the marriage might bring notoriety (a widow marrying an old friend), to avoid delay when the bride was already pregnant, even to avoid the expenses incurred in observing all the formalities of an official wedding.[9]

Common-law unions — involving a variety of practices which people ignorant of the law seem to have regarded as legally binding, such as having the couple jump over the handle of a broom together — may have increased as a result of the Marriage Act.[10] But the act did not apply in Scotland, and a place called Gretna Green, just across the border, for generations served as a favorite matrimonial refuge for couples eloping from England.[11]

On the whole the appropriate basis for marriage was thought to be something other than personal attraction. Moralists hoped that bride and groom would come to love and cherish one another as the marriage progressed, but this was not thought to be essential, so long as each fulfilled the appropriate social role. Above all marriage was considered a binding commitment that retained its power and authority independent of the feelings of the participants.[12]

It was of course patriarchal, deriving from ancient religious and philosophical principles. While cruelty by a husband to his wife might be censured by society and even occasionally punished by law, the role of the male as head of the house was to be honored. The "rough music," or *charivari*, by which village society punished the transgression of custom, was sometimes directed at despotic husbands but more commonly at husbands thought to be dominated by their wives, who thereby upset the natural order of the world.[13]

A husband's authority was recognized by law in various ways; in France he might even have his wife imprisoned by *lettres de cachet* obtained from the king, in order to punish her or restrain her from alleged transgressions. For the most part husbands were conceded the legal right to inflict some physical punishment on their wives if they deemed it appropriate. (Moralists were divided on the fittingness of this.)[14] Overall the husband's status as head of the household had legal ramifications which were enforced. The wife retained only partial control over whatever property she brought to the union, and in certain ways she was regarded as her husband's property in law, in that he could, for example, sue her seducer if she committed adultery.[15]

The husband's authority was almost unassailable given the fact that divorce did not exist in a good part of Europe in the eighteenth century. In most Protestant countries it was allowed for adultery and desertion, and permitted the former spouses to remarry.[16] Elsewhere the term "divorce" meant legal authorization to separate from one's spouse, with the right of a wife to expect financial support from her husband, but it did not include the right to remarry. Both Catholics and Protestants recognized the annulment of a marriage found to be no marriage at all, but such proceedings were not easily accessible to anyone outside the ranks of the aristocracy.[17] (In France a wife might also have her husband imprisoned by *lettres de cachet*, if she could produce credible testimony — from a parish priest, for example — that the husband was dangerously abusive.)[18]

In England — paradoxically, considering the matrimonial history of Henry VIII — the divorce laws were strict and did not permit remarriage, although aristocrats sometimes got divorced by special act of Parliament. The bizarre popular custom of "wife-selling," described in Thomas Hardy's novel *The Mayor of Casterbridge*, was practiced well into the nineteenth century, whereby a man brought his wife into the marketplace, often with a halter around her neck, and accepted bids for her. Usually the "buyer" seems to have been a man with whom the woman already had relations, and the "sale" was an illegal form of divorce which ignorant people thought was official.[19]

Patriarchal authority naturally extended to children; again, the most extreme example is the French law whereby fathers could obtain *lettres de cachet* from the king authorizing the imprisonment of recalcitrant older children at the king's pleasure.[20] Children had few legally recognized rights and could be subjected to almost unrestrained discipline at home, in school, and in places of employment or apprenticeship.[21]

Dead children were mourned, but in an age when infant mortality reached 50 percent in some places, and many of the children who survived infancy did not live to adulthood, there may have been a certain fatalistic callousness about the suffering of children. One indication is the custom of giving a child the name of an older sibling who had died, as though the deceased child had had no real identity.[22] (The last Stuart monarch of England, Anne, who died in 1714, had been pregnant seventeen times, but between miscarriages, stillbirths, and child deaths she survived all her offspring. Her ordeal was not rare.)[23]

Many infant deaths were preventable. Over the course of the eighteenth century thousands of infants were abandoned by their parents to institutions devoted to the care of foundlings, where the mortality rate was sometimes as high as 90 percent. While most of these foundlings were probably illegitimate, many were given up by married parents who either could not or would not support them. In rural areas of France and England parents might pay traveling peddlers to carry infants to the foundling hospitals of Paris and London, or lay them on wagons which went from village to village for that purpose, an ordeal which few of the infants survived and which all concerned must have known amounted to certain death. (In the event that a foundling did survive, the parents might reclaim it later, when it had become old enough to engage in productive work.)[24] Deliberate infanticide was also not unknown.[25]

Only somewhat less lethal was the widespread practice of wet-nursing, whereby infants were given to women other than their mothers to be nursed for the first year or more of their lives. Upper-class mothers did so because the physical tasks of motherhood were considered more appropriate to a servant than a lady, while poor women did it so that nursing did not interfere with their labors in field or workshop. Prosperous parents could hire a wet nurse's exclusive services (slaves often performed the function in America), so their children probably suffered no serious ill effects. The poor, however, often gave their infants to professional nurses who were already servicing several other babies and might not produce enough milk for all of them. In some places over a third of wet-nursed babies died, roughly twice the proportion of those nursed by their own mothers.[26]

Childbirth was for centuries also frequently lethal for mothers. Until the diagnosis of purpureal fever and improvements in obstetrical techniques in the nineteenth century, death in childbirth was probably the single major reason why women had shorter life expectancies than men, a pattern which reversed itself in the twentieth century.[27]

Contrary to popular belief, the premodern family was much more likely to be "nuclear," that is, composed of parents and children, than "extended," including other relatives.[28] As in other things, there were notable differences between North and South. In Mediterranean countries young couples were far more likely to live with the husband's family, for example.[29] However, even where the couple did not live with relatives, they were in some ways more a household than a single family. At the higher social levels each house included numerous servants — several hundred for royalty — all of whom were officially considered members of the family, subject to patriarchal authority in ways not greatly different from those of children and, like children, excluded from full participation in their parents' lives. (Aristocratic children, for example, did not usually eat at their parents' table.) Except for the very poor, people of humbler social status also had a few servants, often farm laborers who lived with the family. Before industrialization, household service was the major kind of employment open to the children of laboring-class families, and servants have been called merely "children who changed houses."[30] Apprentices lived with their masters as well as worked for them, and poor farmers sometimes even opened their houses to a different sort of servant — farm animals might be kept in the family cottage during the winter if no suitable barn was available.[31]

In a sense even the families of the upper classes were economic as well as social units, since family life was centered on the estates that were the basis of the family's wealth, and wives and children might to some degree be involved in administering those estates.

But those with the heaviest economic dependency on the family were the laboring classes, who made up the great majority of people. A farm would be viable only if the father tilled the fields alongside the older sons, younger sons performed lighter chores, and wives and daughters gathered food, cooked, processed cloth, and cared for the smaller animals. An urban craftsman usually plied his trade in his house, where his wife and children assisted him and where the wife under some circumstances might actually manage the business.[32] Apart from moral and legal restrictions, divorce was unthinkable for many people because it would have meant economic ruin. The success of a marriage was judged less by qualities of personal satisfaction than by how efficiently the family members discharged their allotted tasks.

Since relatively few people lived to advanced ages in premodern societies, the care of the elderly was not a major problem, and it was dealt with in a variety of ways. Upper-class fathers did not relinquish their titles or their estates until death, and an upper-class widow either received a "dower house" of her own or lived with her eldest son. Among farmers a son might find it impossible to marry until his father relinquished the farm, and this might be preceded by negotiations concerning the care the father would receive. Not uncommonly, elderly people seem to have been neglected by their children and forced onto the poverty rolls.[33] In Italy the parents or siblings of a deceased husband got legal control of his property and his children, with the widow entitled only to the dowry which she had brought to the marriage, unless he provided otherwise in his will.[34] At the other extreme, sometimes in the North a widow took over her husband's business and operated it successfully.[35]

At least in England, the proportion of people who never married (usually daughters or younger sons) seems to have increased during the eighteenth century among the upper classes, perhaps indicating that the marriage market was exacting larger and larger financial settlements, leaving little for younger children. The noble bachelor might live off an allowance from his older brother, but the lives of genteel spinsters could be bleak — living alone in a town on an allowance, or as half-welcome guests in a sibling's household. Working-class spinsters might secure a niche as life-long servants.[36]

A very high proportion of widows and widowers remarried, often within a few months of a spouse's death. This practice was probably dictated by economic considerations — a desire to extend an aristocratic estate still farther, or the need of a laboring man for a wife. Stepparents were thus common, and legends of the wicked stepmother probably reflected a reality in poor families where every child had to labor and the stepmother controlled the meagre food supply, naturally tending to favor her own offspring.[37]

Although individual households were likely to contain only the nuclear family and its servants, family life was nonetheless lived amid a large and intricate network of kin. Children were sometimes sent for periods of time to be virtual servants in the household of a relative, relatives might give a home to orphaned children, and relatives were expected to aid one another in times of need. Sometimes discussions concerning marriage alliances involved kin who also had some acknowledged interest in the future of the family. Although Church and State prohibited the marriage of close relatives, the limited opportunities of village society often dictated that people marry their mediate or distant relatives.[38]

Religion enjoined premarital chastity and marital fidelity, but both were widely flouted. The often loveless marriages of the aristocracy in particular seem to have encouraged the "double standard" whereby a husband might have one or more mistresses, but his wife, at least until she had borne an heir and several additional children as a margin of security, remained faithful to her husband.[39] George III of England and Louis XVI of France, both of whom reigned in the late eighteenth century, were unusual in being faithful to their wives.[40] At the other extreme was the appropriately dubbed Augustus the Strong, elector of Saxony and king of Poland, who acknowledged 354 illegitimate children.[41] In aristocratic circles illegitimate children were usually acknowledged and provided for in some way, sometimes even becoming part of their father's household.[42] (The double standard had a practical rationale in that an unfaithful wife introduced an alien bloodline into her family, whereas an unfaithful husband did the same to someone else's family.)

Sexual behavior became looser in the eighteenth century probably in part because of changes in belief. In England there was an anti-Puritan reaction after 1660, the aristocracy leading the way in flaunting their liberated sexuality,[43] and there was a flourishing trade in printed pornography in the eighteenth century, including salacious accounts of aristocratic adultery trials.[44]

John Wesley, the greatest English apostle of the devout Christian life in an age of skepticism, once exclaimed in exasperation that scarcely anyone in the kingdom seemed to live chastely.[45] Rare for a Protestant, he advocated celibacy as appropriate to all true Christians, treated marriage as merely a concession to weakness (he entered late, and probably unwillingly, into a disastrous marriage), and broke with his friends the German Pietists because their leader, Count Nicholaus Zinzendorf, preached that the Incarnation bestowed positive value on human sexuality.[46]

The *philosophes* of the Enlightenment had some effect in changing sexual attitudes among the educated all over Europe. While most of the Enlightened thinkers did not make a frontal assault on Christian sexual morality, they did swipe at it, sneering at most of its tenets as mere social custom dressed up in religious garb and, as in Denis Diderot's fictional account of a French merchant's visit to Tahiti, contrasting corrupt European customs with the naive innocence of unspoiled peoples. Some Enlightened thinkers exalted the sacredness of sincere emotions, which they argued should not be thwarted by mere convention.[47] A thriving underground pornography industry lampooned the clergy and the religious ideal of chastity.[48] For the Catholic Church, the eighteenth and early nineteenth centuries were intellectually barren, and few religious thinkers of stature rose to counter these attacks.[49] The illegitimacy records show that the lower classes, probably little influenced by radical ideas, also widely disregarded sexual prohibitions.[50]

In most places in Europe illegitimacy rates increased quite sharply during the century.[51] Premarital pregnancy was also common, with more than a third of brides giving birth less than nine months after marrying.[52] In America the premarital pregnancy rate was about 10 percent under Puritanism in the seventeenth century but had increased to more than a third by 1800 (half in one Rhode Island town). Then it began to decline to about 17 percent by 1880.[53] Both illegitimacy and premarital pregnancy were probably in part a result of economic forces. When a couple got betrothed, they might begin sexual relations in anticipation of marriage, but a sudden fall in wages could delay or cancel the marriage.[54]

Beginning about 1750 there emerged a paradoxical pattern of population development which has proven normative for the modern world—the simultaneous decline in both the mortality and the fertility rates, so that population continues to increase even as the birth rate decreases. A decline in infant mortality was probably the major cause of the population increase, although the reasons for this, before the era of modern medicine, are somewhat mysterious. Perhaps the major cause was that certain epidemic diseases such as bubonic plague had run their course by the early part of the century. By 1800, in a reversal of the previous pattern, the poor were on the average producing more children than the rich, because more of their children were surviving.[55]

Some of the fertility decline must have been due to deliberate acts of birth control, for which there can be little direct evidence. Various contraceptive methods existed, including condoms, but moralists judged that coitus interruptus was the most common method. The subject was rarely discussed in public and, when it was, such practices were usually condemned. But the decline of the pregnancy rate, especially among the aristocracy and the upper middle class, indicates that contraception of some kind was indeed being practiced, both in Europe and America.[56]

The history of family life is necessarily speculative, because there are so few windows into the intimate relationships of past times. Rarely can a historian penetrate to the real feelings of a husband for his wife, or a mother for her children. Certain family relationships do lend themselves to statistical study — age at marriage, life expectancy, fertility, infant mortality, illegitimacy, remarriage, and other things. However, only a small fraction of the thousands of communities of the Old Regime have been studied in this way, so that even these precise statistics can only be assumed as valid samples of the whole. However, as nearly as can be determined within those limitations, at some point after 1700, if not before, signs of the modern concept of the family began to show themselves.

The problem of elopement, which the Marriage Act of 1753 sought to rectify, shows that some young people had always sought to marry for love, and at least the upper and middle ranks of society increasingly began to see this as a condition for marriage, without abandoning the requirements of status and property (witness the contrasting attitudes of Squire Western and Squire Allworthy in Henry Fielding's novel *Tom Jones*). In England, if not in France, it had become almost obligatory to pay lip service to the wishes of the young couple, and most marriage settlements were coming to involve a balance between the desires of the couple and the requirements of the family.[57] Recognizing that the two need not be in opposition, the aristocracy in the eighteenth century developed a national network of social events, centered both in London and select provincial centers such as Bath (the world of Jane Austin), where eligible young people of good families could meet one another. In general, the higher individuals were in the social scale, the more likely they were to marry someone from outside their immediate circles, while the poorest people almost inevitably ended by marrying someone from the same village.[58] Among the American colonial aristocracy similar customs developed, with the great balls and house parties giving young people freer kinds of courting opportunities.[59] At the same time the Marriage Act of 1753 for the first time in England forbade children under age twenty-one to marry without parental consent, a measure opposed by some critics as giving parents undue authority over their children. But one of Lord Chancellor Hardwicke's stated purposes was precisely to prevent "fortune hunters" from eloping with aristocratic heiresses, which is probably how tradition-minded people saw the new freedom by which spouses asked to be allowed to choose one another.[60]

The Council of Trent (1545–63) had in a sense already aligned the Catholic Church with a more voluntaristic approach to marriage, when it decreed that marriages were valid even without parental consent, provided that the couple were of sufficient age. But, when the decrees of the council were at last promulgated in France in 1597, that provision was omitted at the behest of the aristocracy, who feared "fortune hunters" and did not want to risk losing parental control over family property. In 1776, Spain enacted a law in contradiction to the Tridentine decree, and in 1803 went so far as to raise the age of consent to twenty-five for men and twenty-three for women.[61] Thus Protestant countries tended to be more "progressive" on the matter than did Catholic countries, but "Catholic" practice was in fact in opposition to church law.

That the new attitudes were gaining acceptance even in ordinarily conservative circles is revealed in a defense of elopement (the groom had been imprisoned at the instigation of the bride's parents) by an Italian cardinal, Prospero Lambertini, in 1740, on the grounds that "the grace of the sacrament hallows the consent of both parties." It was an opinion given much weight because Lambertini would soon be elevated to the papal throne as Benedict XIV.[62]

Implied in the new "romantic" idea of marriage was the desire for personal and emotional satisfaction for the spouses. The "honeymoon," a private period of sexual and psychological exploration, came to be an aristocratic fixture during the eighteenth century.[63]

But, if husband and wife were to entertain a belief in the "companionate" marriage in which they were expected to be sensitive to each other's feelings, even to cultivate a friendship with each other, some diminution of patriarchal authority was required, and this too seems to have been occurring.

Secular Enlightenment thinkers tended to urge this emotional liberation, as they saw it, but the long-term influence of the Counter-Reformation also seems to have had an effect. Thus the influential monk-moralist Antoine Blanchard urged husbands to treat their wives with kindness and understanding, as befitting genuine Christians.[64] Jansenism had tended, in this as in everything else, to define marriage sternly, in terms of duty and the primary justification of the procreation of children. But some eighteenth-century Catholic thinkers, like the Italian moralist Alphonsus Liguori, instead emphasized the love between Jesus and his disciples, between Mary and her spiritual children, and hence among family members as well. Liguori, while reaffirming that the begetting of children was the primary end of marriage, also justified marriage for love among those incapable of having children.[65] Several Catholic theologians affirmed that romantic attraction was intended by God and urged young men to search for the one woman whom God had prepared for them alone.[66]

Despite the anti-Puritan reaction, Puritanism in England had left a legacy of introspection and moral seriousness which could be applied to personal relations,[67] and the novelist-journalist Daniel DeFoe, a Protestant Dissenter, scathingly attacked arranged marriages without love as equivalently a form of prostitution and urged the religious necessity of an affectionate relationship.[68]

Enlightenment thinkers almost routinely began to extol marital love and mutual respect between spouses as part of their general rebellion against what they considered dead and oppressive social forms and their campaign to liberate human feelings from artificial constraints. Whatever the sources, upper- and middle-class people of the eighteenth century increasingly embraced these same qualities, at least in principle, although more traditional patterns of behavior did not disappear.[69]

As always, ideal marital relationships extolled in books, pamphlets, sermons, and other forms of exhortation were often far from reality. However, by the end of the century it had become necessary, among people claiming to be truly civilized, at least to affirm that personal love, emotional fulfillment, and friendship ought to characterize spousal relations. (A telling index of change was the hesitant but growing practice of spouses actually addressing each other by their first names.) Some English critics, perhaps too chauvinistically, claimed that similar developments had not occurred in France and touted this as the reason almost all French husbands were unfaithful to their wives.[70] Colonial America, at least among the upper classes, seemed to follow the English pattern.[71]

The new sensitivity extended even to children. They were still subject to often strict discipline, but writers and moralists appealed to adults to treat them with kindness and with due regard for an "innocence" that earlier ages had not been sure they possessed.[72] Mothers from the privileged classes (if not yet fathers) began to take a new interest in the raising of their children, although the practical tasks were still left largely in the hands of servants.[73]

The modern "moderate" theory of child-raising was perhaps first formulated by John Locke, whose influence as a theorist of government was almost bound to extend to family matters as well, in an age when the family was still sometimes described as a "little commonwealth" and in which habits formed within the family were thought to determine people's general social and political behavior. As early as 1690 Locke identified a tendency toward overindulgence as parents' most common error in raising children, and he proposed a balance of punishment and encouragement. Children were to be taught to regard their parents as "their lords, their absolute governors," which would thereby render harsh punishments unnecessary. Locke regarded children as rational creatures responsive to rational methods, once their natural willfulness (crying to get what they wanted, for example) had been overcome.[74] Altogether his highly influential theories seemed to many people virtually self-evident in a new age of limited government resting on the consent of the governed.

But, as with the treatment of wives, the kindly treatment of children was also urged for religious motives by Catholic moralists like Blanchard[75] or the Scottish-American theologian John Witherspoon, who a century after Locke merely assumed the approach which Locke had advocated and feared that the pendulum of child-raising had swung too far toward indulgence.[76]

Wesley continued to speak for an older tradition. His mother, Susanna, described her own methods, highly successful in terms of her children's adult characters, in which children were subject to rigid restrictions — limited food, unquestioning obedience, little play, and beatings as early as age one — in order to "break the spirit" of inherently willful infants.[77] John Wesley preached his mother's practice, going so far as to forbid praising children, who should rather be taught that they were "fallen spirits." He was perhaps the first pedagogical theorist to identify the doting grandmother as a danger to the child's character, sentimentally undermining parental authority.[78]

In the eighteenth century, if not before, there occurred the "discovery of childhood," in the sense of the modern awareness of children as distinct beings and not simply as small adults. For the first time a kind of culture of childhood began to appear, as children started to wear distinctive clothes, adults devised separate games and stories for their amusement and instruction, and family portraits showed children playing instead of stiffly formal as in earlier pictures. At school they were now segregated according to age, and parents were warned not to allow their children to be corrupted by older persons, especially servants or schoolmates. The frequency of corporal punishment seems always to have varied widely, with some parents considering it essential while others eschewed it. In the eighteenth century it seems to have declined, with an alternative emphasis on exhortation and instruction instead of coercive discipline.[79] Distinctive events of childhood were created, such as the formal public ceremony of First Communion, to define the progress toward adulthood.[80] By the end of the century reformers were inveighing against wet-nursing and warning mothers of the catastrophes resulting from it.[81] As the infant mortality rate declined, open mourning for children became customary, and the practice of reusing the name of a dead child disappeared.[82]

Customs were inevitably inconsistent, however. For example, in the English public schools, which were in reality elite private schools, boys continued to live largely unsupervised until well after 1800, prey to bullying or seduction by older boys and subject to harsh physical discipline. Occasionally such schools erupted in open rioting, to the point where troops had to be called. Locke was among those condemning the schools' disorderly character and bullying violence, although others praised them as environments which effectively prepared boys for the realities of life. Under the leadership of the famous headmaster of Rugby, Thomas Arnold (see Thomas Hughes's novel *Tom Brown's School Days*), the public schools were transformed into nurseries of "muscular Christianity," emphasizing courage, honesty, loyalty, faith, and patriotism, although corporal punishment remained an important part of their system. There were no comparable schools on the European continent.[83]

Among the aristocracy the family remained an economic unit, with its material well-being lying in the family estates, but now the privileged (including the upper middle class) began to cultivate their feelings as assiduously as they cultivated their fortunes.

The gradual spread of the Counter-Reformation in Catholic countries also had its effect, as evangelizers attempted to reconcile the essentially juridical concept of marriage (which had probably governed most relationships previously) with ideals of love and personal commitment. The Counter-Reformation involved a systematic effort to instruct the Catholic laity in the official teachings of the Church and to bring conduct into conformity with doctrine. This program sometimes put clergy into conflict with long-established popular customs and attitudes, but did have some effect — as in reducing illegitimacy in certain regions.[84]

Inevitably the privileged classes led the way in social and moral changes, if only because the harsh lives of laboring people made the ideal of marriage based on refined sentiment both unattainable and irrelevant. However, by the end of the century, and amid the first stirrings of the Industrial Revolution, change was occurring also among the poor. More and more young men and women began to leave village and home to seek employment, not only as servants (where their behavior was still closely supervised) but as laborers in industrial workshops or as agricultural laborers now living apart from their employers. Especially in cities, young people could enjoy almost unrestricted courting, and traditional restraints on contact between the sexes started to erode in the villages as well. The newer kinds of employment gave working-class youth, including women, regular wages which could substitute for the laborious accumulation of capital necessary before preindustrial era marriage. Young people in the embryonic industrial economy did not have to wait for a place to open in the agricultural village community.[85] In the United States economic changes in the late eighteenth century also began to affect family life, as the institutions of apprenticeship and servanthood declined, industrialization spread, and traditional patterns of farming changed, in part because of westward migration.[86]

Under the old Regime, "youth" was a somewhat loosely understood category, and there were relatively few ways for young people to form bonds with one another. But with the double emancipation of the young toward the end of the eighteenth century — the loosening of patriarchal authority and expanding opportunities for economic self-sufficiency — the concept took on new meaning as a time of testing and exploration. Romanticism described it as a time of passionate, even anguished, searching, and in time the concept of adolescence was born.[87]

The rise of illegitimacy among working-class people in the late eighteenth century also reflected the decline of the various institutional restraints which had previously governed social life.

Probably the most effective of these had been village custom itself, which enforced its rules by the *charivari* and other means, directed at anyone who violated those rules, such as wives who dominated their husbands or girls who allowed themselves to be courted by boys from another village. Now more and more young people went out of the village for employment, often never returning.[88]

Civil and religious punishments for sexual transgressions had never been extremely harsh, for the most part consisting of penance performed in front of the congregation, although in Puritan New England they could be much more severe. However, these penalties began to fade in the eighteenth century, sometimes as a result of popular opposition. Some critics complained that church and community could no longer, as they once did, force young men to marry girls they had made pregnant, and the illegitimacy rate may have increased partly for that reason.[89]

The Enlightenment's war on religion had its effects, especially in France, where the Revolution beginning in 1789 all but destroyed Catholic life for a decade. Although the Church revived spectacularly in the early nineteenth century, a permanent layer of unbelief and antireligious hostility survived. While the disruption was far less severe in England, there too the social influence of religion seems to have declined, shored up mainly by Wesley's Methodists and other Dissenters.[90]

Just as Locke's theories of child-raising paralleled his theories of the state, the American Revolution had an inevitable effect on ideas of the family life. The radical pamphleteer Thomas Paine explicitly connected political independence with emancipation from loveless arranged marriages suitable only to a despotic political order. He did not oppose the institution of matrimony itself but favored freely chosen, affectionate unions, an opinion shared by, among others, Witherspoon and John Adams.[91]

By the time of the Revolution, New England was in full retreat from its Puritan heritage. The move toward Unitarianism was primarily a rejection of the stern, absolutely authoritarian Calvinist God[92] and, since patriarchal authority in human affairs was usually justified as a reflection of divine authority, such rebellion inevitably led to a weakening of the authority of human fathers as well. The post-revolutionary family was defined as a voluntary society held together by affection, charged with cultivating virtues appropriate for the free citizens of a republic.[93]

The Revolution stimulated a quest for women's rights as the natural extension of the principles on which the War of Independence had been fought. However, this incipient feminism did not finally result in political and economic equality but in the fashioning of a new concept of women as creatures of delicate feeling and strict morals, hence as uniquely suited to the crucial vocation of training future citizens, elevating the maternal calling to unprecedented exaltation.[94]

Thus by 1800 most of the elements characteristic of the modern idea of
the family had achieved social acceptance — the free choice of one's spouse,
a softening of patriarchal authority over both wives and children, and an
ideal of mutual love and respect among family members. Still far off was the
"child-centered" mode of family life. The highest aristocracy, notably royalty itself, did not adopt these new ideas, because considerations of dynasty
and fortune were still paramount. For the most part the new forms seem
to have developed, both in Europe and America, mainly among the growing urban middle class and the land-owning classes just below the highest
level.[95]

But while working-class youths were freeing themselves from parental
control over the choice of their spouses, the economic developments which
made this possible were also aborting the new model of family life among
the industrial lower classes. Wives and children increasingly went out of
the home to earn wages under conditions which were often degrading and
even brutal. In the burgeoning industrial towns laborers were crowded into
tenements where more than one family sometimes occupied a single room.
Under such conditions delicacy of feeling was scarcely thinkable, much less
possible, and reformers reported endemic marital violence and widespread
incest. The infant mortality rate among industrial workers rose even as it
declined elsewhere,[96] and conditions would not improve significantly for
decades.[97]

In the rural areas where illegitimacy rates were already high, conditions
did not change noticeably. In early nineteenth-century Bavaria, for example,
strenuous efforts both by Church and State to enforce premarital chastity
had little measurable impact. Priests sometimes found that very devout peasants approached their religion largely through its sacred rituals and did not
seem to connect it with sexual behavior.[98] However, prolonged efforts could
be successful. In France the institution of the parish mission, preached by
charismatic visiting clergy belonging to religious orders, does seem to have
affected sexual behavior.[99]

But it was in America, in the slave states of the South, that the social and
economic system presented the starkest contrast between two kinds of family life. On the one hand quasi-chivalric notions of honor, gentlemanliness,
respect for women, and refined feelings were extolled to a degree seldom
equalled in Europe, while on the other hand, for the most part, slave marriages were not legally recognized, so that members of slave families had
no rights toward one another and could be separated through sale or other
means. Polygamy and promiscuity were thus common among the slaves, and
masters easily demanded and obtained sexual favors from female slaves and
begat children by them. Parental authority over children, and the ability to
protect them, were undermined among slaves by the authority of the mas-

ters. This legacy of family pathology from the antebellum period wounded but did not destroy the black family for many decades to come.[100]

The claim that capitalism was responsible for the social and psychological revolution that produced the modern family[101] has some validity, because it was primarily among the middle class that the family ceased to be an economic unit. Increasingly in urban areas, family members daily went outside the home to earn their livings, separating work and living spaces in a way that had never been done before. While the laboring family remained an economic unit in the sense that it often could not survive unless each member earned money, there were scarcely any jobs for middle-class wives and children, and the father of the family became the "breadwinner."

The ideal of domesticity was in many ways the key to the new concept of family — the belief that home was a comfortable and loving environment where family members preferred to spend their time and invest their energies. Thus parents paid more attention to their children, wives and husbands shared each other's interests, recreation occurred in a family setting, and household chores were willingly undertaken. While the family remained basically patriarchal, it had in some ways become a community of equals, in contrast to the traditional, rigid domestic hierarchy which still prevailed among the aristocracy who maintained platoons of servants.[102]

But the rising incidence of "companionate marriage," with its concomitant sense of almost exaggerated respect for womanly virtue, did not signal the end of male authority but almost the opposite. There were now clearly separate spheres of male and female activity, and women were expected to be emotionally supportive of their husbands and thought to be in need of protection from the harshness of the larger world.[103]

It was also primarily among the middle class that the ideal of sexual restraint — chastity before marriage, fidelity during marriage — was enshrined. This development was due in part to the renewed religiosity of the nineteenth century, following the skepticism of the eighteenth; in part to the logic of romantic love, seeking fulfillment in only one soul mate; and in part to worldly prudence — it was economically wasteful, even disastrous, for a man to keep a mistress and to beget illegitimate children (which is not to say that middle-class husbands never did so).[104]

When marriages were arranged by parents, the desire to separate must have been strong among many spouses, although the desertion rate seems seldom to have been more than 5 percent.[105] Dissatisfaction was offset, however, by the fact that most spouses perhaps did not expect the union to be personally fulfilling. But with the new ideal of marriage there inevitably came a demand for easier divorce. If marriage was not simply a binding contract but a mating of souls, relief had to be available to those who chose badly.

The French Revolution first declared marriage to be a civil relationship only, then enacted by far the most permissive divorce law ever seen in Europe to that time. Divorce and remarriage were allowed for a range of causes. Most important, divorce could be obtained simply by mutual consent. In 1803, the government of Napoleon Bonaparte tightened the law considerably, but divorce by mutual consent was still permitted, and in 1809 the emperor persuaded his reluctant consort Josephine to agree to such a dissolution, so he could marry Marie-Louise of Austria in the hope of begetting an heir. In 1816, after the restoration of the monarchy, the Catholic political theorist Louis de Bonald argued against legal divorce as undermining every aspect of the social fabric, and it was repealed. Only in 1884 did France again permit divorce.[106]

Napoleon's armies brought divorce to Italy, where it seems to have been tacitly rejected by the people themselves and was quickly abolished following the emperor's defeat in 1815. In common with most Catholic countries, Italy had no legal divorce throughout the nineteenth century. Most Protestant countries allowed some divorce, and the Catholic Austrian empire permitted divorce to its non-Catholic subjects.[107] England got its first divorce law in 1857, after long debate.[108]

New England had been surprisingly tolerant of divorce, in part because of the Puritan rejection of matrimony as a sacrament, in part perhaps because the very intensity of the Puritan ideal of family life required an escape for those who found this intolerable. In New England divorce was permitted for adultery or desertion, but it was not authorized in the Southern colonies until after the Revolution. Many divorces were granted by special act of a colonial legislature, a practice which the British government sought to nullify, such nullification probably constituting one of the minor grievances contributing to the Revolution. (There were 800 divorces in Massachusetts and Connecticut between 1760 and 1800, as contrasted with 150 in England during the same period, although the population of England was many times that of these two colonies.)[109]

Although moralists attacked the new laxness, most states liberalized their divorce laws after the Revolution to include other grounds besides the traditional ones. New York was unusually stringent in this respect, and South Carolina was the sole exception in not permitting divorce at all.[110] During the second half of the nineteenth century California had already earned a reputation for instability in marriage, as the divorce rate increased about three times as fast as the population. Child custody contests were common, with almost all mothers asking for and obtaining custody, even though three quarters of divorcing fathers also requested it.[111]

One of the principal arguments against divorce was that it would cause the dissolution of many marriages and thus undermine the social and moral order. In 1880, Pope Leo XIII noted that Protestant countries had first allowed divorce for very limited reasons, then found it impossible to stem the tide.[112] Over twenty thousand divorces are known to have been granted in France between 1792 and 1816, an average of fewer than a thousand a year, and in England the numbers had risen to just under six hundred a year at the end of the century, numbers which, while troubling at the time, are almost insignificant by later standards.[113] By time of the Civil War there were 1.5 divorces for every thousand marriages in the United States, and this increased to four per thousand by the end of the century, giving the United States the highest divorce rate in the world.[114]

Religion helped fuel the movement toward companionate marriage, with a proliferation of sermons, pamphlets, and other literature extolling the holiness of matrimony and urging spouses to show Christian affection and respect for one another. Thus the influential German theologian Matthias Scheeben exalted marriage as an integral extension of the Mystical Body of Christ, modeled on the marriage of Christ and the Church and requiring that the couple love one another with a supernatural love. He strongly affirmed, in the teeth of criticism, that it was the nuptial couple, not the priest, who administered the sacrament to one another.[115] Leo XIII's *Arcanum divinae* ("The Hidden Plan of Divine Wisdom," 1880) in effect gave Catholic ratification to the view of family life that had emerged in the previous two centuries. The pope extolled marriage as a companionship in which the husband rules but the wife is not a servant. Both have equal rights, and Leo observed that the Church had always rejected the "double standard" of sexual behavior, even as it forbade husbands to violate their wives' persons. The Church had also eliminated the power which parents once had to dictate their children's choice of spouses.[116]

However, the new model of the family emerged in an age when marriage was for the first time in many centuries becoming a secular as well as a religious institution — a legal effect accomplished, after the false start of the French Revolution, by the Napoleonic *Civil Code* in France, for example, and an 1837 English law that for the first time allowed marriage before someone other than a clergyman.[117] While in the Anglo-Saxon countries this merely provided an alternative wedding ceremony for non-religious people, anticlerical governments in Europe sometimes moved to define marriage as the preserve of the state alone, denying its religious significance. This move was denounced by popes as early as Benedict XIV,[118] and the condemnation was repeated by Pius IX in his *Syllabus of Errors* (1864)[119] and by Leo XIII in *Arcanum*.[120] While denying the state the power to dissolve genuine sacramental marriages, the Church did recognize impediments to marriage placed by the civil government, such as minimum age or family ties.[121]

Crucial to the new concept of marriage was the status of women. The middle-class revolution of the nineteenth century in one sense further emancipated women from patriarchal control, by extending property rights and giving women greater recourse to the courts against mistreatment. Although divorce often left women financially and emotionally bereft, it was almost the only way they had of enforcing their rights against their spouses.[122]

Above all, the nineteenth-century middle-class ideal of the family exalted women as deserving of protection and a sometimes exaggerated respect, ideals which, as always, were not universally observed. The change in status of American women which followed the Revolution imperceptibly blended into this Victorian ideal. Women were routinely described as emotionally vulnerable and physically weak, thus in need of firm but loving guidance from their husbands or other males. A distinctively female sphere of life — essentially presiding over the management of the household, the raising of children, and charitable works in the community — was clearly defined, and the fact that most business was now transacted outside the home meant that wives seldom were involved in, or even particularly informed about, the sources of family income. They were expected to cultivate distinctively feminine virtues, which included delicacy of feeling, innocence of worldly realities, and a loving submission to their husbands. In return they were considered the true moral guardians of society, precisely because they were insulated from the harsher realities of the world and had the sacred obligation of forming the morals of their children.[123] The rising chorus of nineteenth-century feminism diagnosed precisely those attitudes as a new form of imprisonment,[124] responding to the almost complete separation of middle-class women from the world of remunerative labor, which for the first time created a wholly separate "domestic" sphere of life.[125]

For the first time the family might appear to be, and its members might take it to be, a refuge from the larger world, where bewildering changes threatened personal, familial, and social stability. Middle-class families moved as far as possible away from both the neighborhoods of the poor and from the centers of industry, attempting to create islands of tranquillity.[126] For those who could afford them, middle-class homes were designed for formality and solidity on the one hand and privacy and comfort on the other.[127] In the United States both Protestants and Catholics attempted to create a "domestic church" in their homes, with regular prayers and devotions and with Catholics erecting small shrines to their favorite saints.[128]

Although the new ideals of family life could perhaps only be fully realized by comfortable middle-class families, so powerful were the ideals themselves that they carried weight even on the American frontier. Amid the grim hardships of the prairie and the westward trek, the necessary sharing of oppressive labor was itself extolled as a bond of union between men and women.[129]

The French Revolution abolished the rule of primogeniture, and with this abolition came a new ideal that all children in a family be treated alike.[130] Along with the new emphasis on the tender treatment of women went a related sense of the innocence and vulnerability of children. This too was mainly confined to the well-to-do levels of society, and industrialization if anything made the lot of working-class children even grimmer than it had been before, until public outrage began to have its effect about mid-century.[131]

Just as, paradoxically, the romantic notion of marriage naturally led to more divorce, so the new attitude toward children seems to have led to the increasing practice of birth control. Since each child was to be cherished, their numbers should be limited within each family. Throughout the nineteenth century there was an underground contraceptive industry which became increasingly bolder, and fertility rates continued to fall.[132]

Most religious and medical authorities continued to denounce birth control, and as late as 1908 the Church of England condemned it in a strong statement.[133] Although John Henry Newman apparently said nothing on the subject, his militantly Protestant brother, Francis, strongly denounced the idea that men were incapable of sexual restraint, in a pamphlet titled *The Conception Now called Neo-Malthusianism.*[134]

The Anglican clergyman Thomas Malthus's famous book warning against population growth[135] came at a time when the practice of contraception was slowly spreading. Malthus himself opposed the practice and thought that disease, war, and a prudent sexual restraint (mainly through late marriages) would solve the problem. Although nineteenth-century families on the average produced many more children than do their modern descendants, the "new" ideal of the family can be characterized as "Malthusian." It combined the new romanticism with a prudent regard for the economic well-being of the household, including a conscious decision to limit family size to conserve economic resources and perhaps achieve what is today called "quality of life."[136] The gradual abolition of child labor and the prolonging of the period of middle-class education made children an economic liability rather than an asset for perhaps the first time in history. At the same time, large families seem to have helped children better cope with the complex world, avoiding the potential trap of the isolated, mainly inward-looking family circle.[137]

In the first half of the nineteenth century the Holy See began to receive inquiries from French bishops on how to deal with penitents (apparently mainly women) who confessed to deliberate acts designed to thwart pregnancy. Confessors found that many people did not realize that contraception was a sin and, among other considerations, the priests wondered how far they should go in dispelling this ignorance. The Holy See's consistent answer concerning coitus interruptus was that, if the woman was an unwilling accomplice who feared the wrath of her husband, she could be absolved, even though it was likely that the offense would be repeated. In 1853 the first inquiry concerning condoms was submitted, and the unequivocal answer was that no absolution could be given in such cases without complete repentance.[138]

Abortion had always been practiced in European society, but little is known about the practice. Laws against it were strengthened beginning about mid-century, mainly at the insistence of the medical profession, which had gained clearer understanding of the realities of fetal life.[139] It had likewise always been condemned by the Catholic Church, but about the middle of the nineteenth century it began to attract more notice from church officials, and the ecclesiastical penalties were stiffened.[140]

As the family lost its economic identity, and as emotional qualities became more important, households for the first time began to seek the kind of privacy that traditional families on all social levels seem to have ignored. By 1800, except among the well-to-do, it was no longer common to have servants and hired laborers living with the family. Although most agricultural families still lived in one-room cottages where family members could not escape one another, there was a decline in the ability of the village community to intervene in the internal affairs of married couples. The middle class in particular began to value the home as a refuge from a cruel world. The desire for privacy among the aristocracy was reflected in the invention of something whose advantages seem obvious to us now — the corridor by which individual rooms could be shut against outsiders, in contrast to earlier designs in great houses whereby one room led directly into another, and paraphernalia like screens and bed curtains were used to provide a minimal privacy from servants and others.[141] Late eighteenth-century weddings, even among the wealthy, were ceasing to be public ceremonies and were celebrated quietly. The church ceremony took place early in the morning and the wedding dinner was confined to a few intimates, a fashion which would prevail for the entire nineteenth century.[142]

Thus already by about 1825 the major contours of modern family life were discernible: spouses freely chosen according to romantic expectations (although middle-class courting was still highly supervised), an ideal of spousal friendship and mutual personal fulfillment, the separation of work from home, clearly separated spheres of activity for wives and husbands, tender solicitude for children and responsibility for their upbringing, a modified idea of patriarchal authority. Although some of the roots of this idea of marriage and family life lay in the antireligious forces of the previous century, Christianity also played a major role in its formation, as in Leo XIII's *Arcanum divinae*. This modern idea of marriage came to be seen as the one appropriately Christian way for families to live.[143]

As the coercive penalties once imposed on sexual transgressors by both Church and State rapidly disappeared, middle-class respectability became a more powerful weapon for enforcing the obligations of family life. Religion necessarily played a major role in the formation of the new model of the family precisely because there was now so little institutionalized social control, and people were urged to develop their interior spiritual discipline for a way of life which was rewarding but difficult. Respectability itself, the desire to be well regarded by society, was considered a distinctively middle-class phenomenon, or at least much stronger among the new middle class than among higher social groups. The bourgeoisie did not automatically have status, as did the aristocracy, but had to earn it.

Because it set such high standards of behavior, and because it longed for social respectability, the middle-class family also professed a way of life which invited charges of hypocrisy — the family which showed a happy face to the world but was inwardly wretched, the upright husband who kept a mistress or visited brothels, secret alcoholism, and other things. The unthreatened status that allowed aristocratic men scarcely to bother to conceal their sexual transgressions gave way to a sense of discretion which easily slipped into dishonesty. Even as the ideals of the middle-class family spread, sexual transgressions of various kinds also proliferated. The respectable home could itself become an occasion of vice, as in the seduction of female servants by their employers, which was recognized as a persistent problem.[144] And, while the new ideals of family relations gained wide theoretical acceptance, the stern Victorian father continued to be a familiar figure long after the Victorian age had passed.

While the sexual behavior of the lower classes continued to depart greatly from officially approved norms, religious influence, working-class desire for respectability, and the gradual amelioration of the harshest aspects of industrialism all permitted middle-class ideals of family life to begin permeating the working classes later in the century. (In Charles Dickens's *A Christmas Carol*, the life of the poor is bleak indeed, even hopeless, while the Cratchits, clinging to the lowest rung of middle-class life — Bob Cratchit is a clerk in a counting house — manifest the genuine spirit of family life. Ebenezer Scrooge is meanwhile contemptuous of his nephew who has committed the folly of marrying for love rather than money.)

To the extent that the new ideal of the family can be called middle-class, it represents one of the major triumphs by which that class replaced the aristocracy as the true leaders of society. Many in the upper classes still adhered to traditional patterns of behavior, especially the open "double standard" whereby husbands might be adulterous but wives, at least up to a point, were to be faithful. However, bourgeois attitudes were making themselves felt. In 1820, George IV of England brought charges of adultery against his wife, Caroline of Brunswick, at a time when adultery by the queen was still the crime of treason. Caroline was certainly guilty, and in a flagrant way — she had cruised the Mediterranean with a man of dubious reputation, an Italian at that. She was put on trial, but George's own philandering was so notorious that there was a popular outcry against him, the case was dropped, and Caroline was treated as a wronged woman.[145]

When George IV died he was succeeded by his brother William IV, who died without a legitimate heir in 1837. But William left ten children, all by the same mistress, with whom he had lived openly for years before finally marrying a German princess and failing to produce a legitimate offspring. William lived by the older aristocratic code in that he publicly acknowledged his bastards, who were given the family name of FitzClarence (after his ducal title) and whose careers he aided in every way possible, even assisting one to become a clergyman. His children did not always return the affection that his wife, Adelaide of Saxe-Meiningen, showed toward them.[146]

Thus the failure of the direct male line of the house of Hanover brought the throne to a nineteen-year-old princess, niece of George and William, who determined to put an end to the sexual scandals that had marred the image of the court for almost thirty years. She chose to adopt what many of the aristocracy contemptuously dismissed as middle-class standards of respectability — premarital chastity, absolute fidelity to her husband, passionate love between them though theirs was an arranged marriage, a doting attitude toward children, and concern for a respectable image.[147] In adopting these standards Victoria gave her name not only to a historical era but to the new familial morality that, backed by unimpeachable royal authority, soon came to be regarded as normative by most of society.

Notes

1. Jean-Louis Flandrin, *Families in Former Times: Kinship, Household, and Sexuality in Early Modern France*, trans. Richard Southern (Cambridge, England, 1979), 1–50; Alan Macfarlane, *Marriage and Love in England: Modes of Reproduction 1300–1840* (Oxford, 1986), 263–90.

2. Flandrin, *Families*, 76, 91.

3. Macfarlane, *Marriage*, 263–87; Bridget Hill, *Women, Work, and Sexual Politics in Eighteenth-Century England* (New York, 1989), 174–95; Olwen Hufton, *The Prospect before Her: the History of Women in Western Europe* (New York, 1996), 1:107–29.

4. Flandrin, *Families* 46–60; David Levine, *Family Formation in an Age of Nascent Capitalism* (New York, 1977), 45; Kevin O'Neill, *Family and Farm in Pre-Famine Ireland* (Madison, Wisc., 1984); Gerard DeLille, *Famille et proprieté dans le Royaume de Naples, XV–XIX siècles* (Rome, 1985); James C. Davis, *A Venetian Family and Its Fortune, 1500–1900: The Dora and the Consumption of Their Wealth* (Philadelphia, 1975).

5. Richard Adair, *Courtship, Illegitimacy, and Marriage in Early Modern England* (Manchester, 1996); Hufton, *Prospect*, 130–36.

6. J. Hajnal, "European Marriage Patterns in Perspective," *Population in History: Essays in Historical Demography,* ed. D. V. Glass and D. E. C. Eversley (London, 1965), 101–43; David I. Kertzer and Richard P. Saller, eds., *The Family in Italy from Antiquity to the Present* (New Haven, Conn., 1991), 253–55, 276.

7. Peter Laslett, *Family Life and Illicit Love in Earlier Generations* (Cambridge, England, 1977), 40; Lawrence Stone, *The Family, Sex, and Marriage in England, 1500–1800* (New York, 1977), 46–48; Kertzer and Saller, *Family in Italy*, 253–54, 276.

8. R. B. Outhwaite, *Clandestine Marriages in England, 1500–1850* (London, 1995); Randolph Trumbach, *The Rise of the Egalitarian Family: Aristocratic Kinship and Domestic Relations in Eighteenth-Century England* (New York, 1978), 98–106; John R. Gillis, *For Better, for Worse: British Marriages, 1600 to the Present* (Oxford, 1985), 140; Lawrence Stone, *Road to Divorce: England 1530–1987* (Oxford, 1990), 96–128.

9. Outhwaite, *Clandestine*, 55–61.

10. Gillis, *Better or Worse*, 200–210.

11. Stone, *Road*, 130–31.

12. For accounts of particular marriages see Stone, *Uncertain Unions: Marriage in England, 1660–1987* (Oxford, 1992); Edward Shorter, *The Making of the Modern Family* (New York, 1975), 54–65.

13. Gillis, *Better or Worse*, 131–34; Flandrin, *Families*, 125.

14. Roderick Phillips, *Putting Asunder: A History of Divorce in Western Society* (Cambridge, England, 1988), 302–44; Hufton, *Prospect*, 289–96.

15. Flandrin, *Families*, 112–14; Trumbach, *Rise*, 150–57.

16. Trumbach, *Rise*, 199–202.

17. Phillips, *Putting Asunder;* Stone, *Road*, and *Broken Lives: Separation and Divorce in England, 1660–1857* (Oxford, 1993).

18. Hufton, *Prospect*, 288.

19. Samuel Dyeatt Menefee, *Wives for Sale: An Ethnographic Study of British Popular Divorce* (New York, 1981); Gillis, *Better or Worse*, 211–19.

20. Flandrin, *Families*, 154.

21. Ivy Pinchbeck and Margaret Hewitt, *Children in English Society* (London, 1973), IV; Shorter, *Making*, 168–86, 203, 348–51; Hufton, *Prospect*, 211.

22. Philippe Aries, *Centuries of Childhood*, trans. Robert Baldick (New York, 1962 [original French edition 1960]), 40–41; Hufton, *Prospect*, 194–96. The pioneering work in the field, Aries's book suffers from the somewhat random and fragmentary nature of his evidence.

23. David Green, *Queen Anne* (New York, 1970), 335–38.

24. Flandrin, *Families*, 186, 204; Stone, *Family*, 475–76, Hufton, *Prospect*, 210.

25. Peter C. Hoffer and N. E. H. Hull, *Murdering Mothers: Infanticide in England and New England, 1558–1603* (New York, 1984); Hufton, *Prospect*, 274–80.

26. Flandrin, *Families*, 203–8; Daniel Blake Smith, *Inside the Great House: Planter Family Life in Eighteenth-Century Chesapeake Society* (Ithaca, 1980), 37.

27. Irving Loudon, *Death in Childbirth: An International Study of Maternal Care and Maternal Mortality 1800–1950* (Oxford, England, 1992); Hufton, *Prospect*, 177–220.

28. Flandrin, *Families*, 68–86; Laslett, *Family Life*, 13, and *Household and Family in Past Time* (Cambridge, 1972); Kertzer and Saller, *Family*, 291.

29. Hufton, *Prospect*, 143.

30. Laslett, *Household*, 147; Hill, *Women, Work*, 103–47.

31. Flandrin, *Families*, 4–10, 104; Shorter, *Making*, 22–39; Laslett, *Household*, 74–85, 130–31, 138.

32. Flandrin, *Families*, 113–14; Hill, *Women, Work*.

33. David G. Troyansky, *Old Age in the Old Regime: Image and Experience in Eighteenth-Century France* (Ithaca, N.Y., 1989); David I. Kertzer and Peter Laslett, eds., *Aging in the Past: Demography, Society, and Old Age* (Berkeley, Calif., 1994); Hill, *Women, Work*, 240–58; Hufton, *Prospect*, 221–26.

34. Hufton, *Prospect*, 229.

35. Ibid., 244–54.

36. Stone, *Family*, 380–83; Hill, *Women, Work*, 221–39; Hufton, *Prospect*, 257.

37. Flandrin, *Families*, 40–42, 115; J. Dupaquier, E. Helin, P. Laslett, M. Livi-Bacci, and S. Sogner, eds., *Marriage and Remarriage in Populations of the Past* (New York, 1981).

38. Flandrin, *Families*, 4–39.

39. Stone, *Family*, 388.

40. John Brooke, *King George III* (New York, 1972), 262–64; Saul K. Padover, *Louis XVI* (New York, 1939), 96–104.

41. Stone, *Family*, 532–33.

42. Trumbach, *Rise*, 162–63.

43. Stone, *Family*, 546–99; Anthony Fletcher, *Gender, Sex, and Subordination in England, 1500–1800* (New Haven, Conn., 1995), 342; Arnold P. Harvey, *Sex in Georgian England* (Manchester, 1996).

44. Paul-Gabriel Bouce, ed., *Sexuality in Eighteenth-Century England* (Manchester, 1982), 120–40.

45. Ibid., 10. Conditions against which Wesley struggled are described by R. F. Wearmouth, *Methodism and the Common People of England* (London, 1945).

46. Henry Abelove, *The Evangelist of Desire: John Wesley and the Methodists* (Stanford, Calif., 1990), 49–73.

47. Peter Gay, *The Enlightenment: An Interpretation* (New York, 1969), 2:194–201. Diderot's celebration of primitive "innocence" was *Supplement au Voyage de Bougainville* (Geneva, 1955 [original text probably 1773]).

48. Robert Darnton, "Sex for Thought," *New York Review of Books*, December 22, 1994, 65–74. Darnton reviews the series *L'Enfer de la Bibliothèque Nationale* (Paris, 1994), a modern edition of the eighteenth-century pornography kept in the library's special collections.

49. Robert R. Palmer, *Catholics and Unbelievers in Eighteenth-Century France* (Princeton, N.J., 1939).

50. Outhwaite, *Clandestine*, 143; Adair, *Courtship*, 8; Stone, *Family*, 612.

51. Jeffrey R. Watt, *The Making of Modern Marriage: Matrimonial Control and the Rise of Sentiment in Neuchatel, 1550–1800* (Ithaca, N.Y., 1992), 179; Rosalind Mitchison and Leah Leneman, *Sexuality and Social Control: Scotland 1660–1780* (Oxford, 1989), 134–64; John Knodel, *Demographic Behavior in the Past: A Study of Fourteen German Villages in the Eighteenth and Nineteenth Centuries* (Cambridge, England, 1988), 450–51; Bouce, *Sexuality*; Stone, *Marriage*; Adair, *Courtship*, 8–43; P. Laslett, K. Oosterven, and R. Smith, eds., *Bastardy and Its Comparative History* (London, 1980); G. J. Barker-Beinfield, *The Culture of Sensibility: Sex and Society in Eighteenth-Century Britain* (Chicago, 1992). The claim that there occurred a kind of "sexual revolution" in eighteenth-century England seems based on rather slight and impressionistic evidence.

52. Knodel, *Demographic Behavior*, 209–46; Macfarlane, *Marriage*, 305; Adair, *Courtship*, 100–119.

53. Michael Gordon, ed., *The American Family in Social-Historical Perspective* (New York, 1973), 323; Helena M. Wall, *Fierce Communion: Family and Community in Early America* (Cambridge, Mass., 1990), 134; Smith, *Inside*, 139.

54. Levine, *Family*, 132–39.

55. Ashley J. Coale and Susan Cotts Watkins, eds., *The Decline of Fertility in Europe* (Princeton, N.J., 1986); Wally Seecombe, *A Millennium of Family Change: Feudalism to Capitalism in Northwestern Europe* (New York, 1992), 197–201, 208–11; Michael W. Flinn, *The European Demographic System, 1500–1820* (Baltimore, 1981), 76–102; Massimo Livi-Bacci, *History of Italian Fertility during the Last Two Centuries* (Princeton, N.J., 1977), 45–47; Knodel, *Demographic Behavior*, 35–101; Ron J. Lesthaeghe, *The Decline of Belgian Fertility 1800–1970* (Princeton, N.J., 1977); Flandrin, *Families*, 191–98, 213–14; Stone, *Family*, 66–73, 421, 479.

56. Orest and Patricia Ranum, eds., *Popular Attitudes towards Birth Control in Pre-Industrial England* (New York, 1972); Stone, *Family*, 417–24; Trumbach, *Rise*, 170–76; Richard Sennett, *Families against the City: Middle-Class Homes of Industrial Chicago 1872–1890* (Cambridge, Mass., 1970), 111; Janet Farrell Brodie, *Contraception and Abortion in Nineteenth-Century America* (Ithaca, N.Y., 1994).

57. Flandrin, *Families*, 169–73; Jeffrey R. Watt, *Making*, 210–14; Trumbach, *Rise*, 98–119; Gillis, *Better or Worse*, 109; Macfarlane, *Marriage*, 132–40.

58. Stone, *Family*, 288–315.

59. Smith, *Inside*, 130–37; Ellen K. Rothman, *Hands and Hearts: A History of Courtship in America* (New York, 1984); Brenda E. Stevenson, *Life in Black and White: Family and Community in the Slave South* (New York, 1996), 54–58.

60. Gillis, *Better or Worse*, 140–41; Stone, *Family*, 34–35.

61. Hufton, *Prospect*, 193–96.

62. Renee Haynes, *Philosopher-King: The Humanist Pope Benedict XIV* (London, 1970), 151–52.

63. Stone, *Family*, 334–36.

64. Flandrin, *Families*, 127–29. Blanchard's principal work was *Essai d'exhortation pour les états differents des malades* (Paris, 1713).

65. Flandrin, *Families*, 237; Pierre Pourrat, *Christian Spirituality*, trans. Donald Attwater (Westminster, Md., 1955), 4:363–95; John T. Noonan Jr., *Contraception: A History of Its Treatment by Catholic Theologians and Canonists* (Cambridge, Mass., 1986 [original edition 1965]), 348–49, 370–79. Liguori discussed marriage in his *Theologia moralis* (Rome, 1905 [original edition 1748]).

66. Joseph E. Kerns, S.J., *The Theology of Marriage: The Historical Development of Christian Attitudes towards Sex and Sanctity in Marriage* (New York, 1964), 227. The theologians were Paolo Segneri and Jean Grou. Segneri was expressing such ideas already in the late seventeenth century (*La felicità introdatta nelle famiglia* [later edition Rome, 1755]), Grou about a hundred years later (*Le livre du jeune homme* [later edition Paris 1874]).

67. Macfarlane, *Marriage*, 225.

68. *Conjugal Lewdness, or Matrimonial Whoredom: A Treatise concerning the Use and Abuse of the Marriage Bed* (Gainesville, Fla., 1967 [original edition 1727]).

69. Flandrin, *Families*, 127–68; Flinn, *European System*, 47–78; Trumbach, *Rise*, 119–23; Bouce, *Sexuality*, 20; Macfarlane, *Marriage*, 125–26; Stone, *Family*, 221–33, 266–67; Gay, *Enlightenment*, 2:194.

70. Flandrin, *Families*, 169–73; Trumbach, *Rise*, 112–18; Macfarlane, *Marriage*,

154–56; Stone, *Family,* 283–87, 329–30, 388. For detailed accounts of romantic marriages in the period see Stone, *Uncertain Unions,* 360–74.

71. Stephanie Coontz, *The Social Origins of Private Life: A History of American Families, 1600–1900* (London, 1980), 106–7; Jan Lewis, *The Pursuit of Happiness: Family and Values in Jefferson's Virginia* (New York, 1983), 171–72, 184, 188, 191–95; Smith, *Inside,* 130–37, 140–49, 153–59; Steven Mintz and Susan Kellogg, *Domestic Revolutions: A Social History of American Family Life* (New York, 1988), 19.

72. Aries, *Centuries,* 262–67, 398–403; Flandrin, *Families,* 127–41, 169–73; Shorter, *Making,* 227; Watt, *Making,* 210–14; James F. Traer, *Marriage and the Family in Eighteenth-Century France* (Ithaca, N.Y., 1980); François Lebrun, *La vie conjugale sous l'Ancien Regime* (Paris, 1975); Stone, *Family,* 325–28, 408, 452–63; Trumbach, *Rise,* 243–48; Smith, *Inside,* 44–45, 48, 50–53, 83; Mintz and Kellogg, *Domestic Revolutions,* 20; Bernard Wishy, *The Child and the Republic: The Dawn of Modern American Child Nurture* (Philadelphia, 1968).

73. Trumbach, *Rise,* 224–29, 237–42; Jonathan Gathorne-Hardy, *The Unnatural History of the Nanny* (London, 1973).

74. "Some Thoughts concerning Education," *Child-Rearing Concepts, 1628–1861,* ed. Philip J. Greven Jr. (Itaska, Ill., 1973), 20–40.

75. Flandrin, *Families,* 138–56.

76. "Letters on Education" (1797), in Greven, *Child-Raising,* 89–91.

77. "On the Education of Her Children" (1783), in ibid., 46–49; Maldwyn Edwards, *Family Circle: A Study of the Epworth Household in Relation to John and Charles Wesley* (London, 1949).

78. "Sermon on the Education of Children" (1783), in Greven, *Child-Rearing,* 53–65; Abelove, *Evangelist,* 101–3.

79. Linda A. Pollock, *Forgotten Children: Parent-Child Relations from 1500 to 1900* (Cambridge, England, 1983), 199–200, 266; Fletcher, *Gender, Sex,* 302; Hufton, *Prospect,* 211.

80. Aries, *Centuries,* 30–249; Flandrin, *Families,* 206–8; Pinchbeck and Hewitt, *Children,* 2:371–86; Trumbach, *Rise,* 187–229; Stone, *Family,* 246, 408–12, 433; Francelia Butler, ed., *Masterworks of Children's Literature* (New York, 1994). Volumes 2 and 3 contain material from the early modern period.

81. Flandrin, *Families,* 206; Hufton, *Prospect,* 200.

82. Trumbach, *Rise,* 188–90.

83. Gathorne-Hardy, *The Old School Tie: The Phenomenon of the English Public School* (New York, 1978); Aries, *Centuries,* 265, 313; Fletcher, *Gender, Sex,* 305–8.

84. J. Michael Phayer, *Sexual Liberation and Religion in Eighteenth and Nineteenth-Century Europe* (London, 1977), 57–58, 67–77, 94–154.

85. Shorter, *Making,* 256–63; Phayer, *Sexual Liberation,* 53–54, 60–62; Elinor Accampo, *Industrialization, Family Life, and Class Relations: Saint Chamord 1815–1914* (Berkeley, Calif., 1989).

86. Wall, *Fierce Communion,* 128–33; Coontz, *Social Origins,* 106–7, 116–28, 161–80; Tamara Hareven and Maris A. Virovskis, eds., *Family and Population in Nineteenth-Century America* (Princeton, N.J., 1978); Bernard Forbes, *Guardians of Virtue: Salem Families in 1800* (New York, 1972); Mintz and Kellogg, *Domestic Revolutions,* 500–502; Mary Ryan, *Cradle of the Middle Class: The Family in Oneida County, New York, 1790–1865* (New York, 1981), 231–32.

87. John R. Gillis, *Youth and History: Tradition and Change in European Age*

Relations, 1770 to the Present (New York, 1974); Joseph F. Kett, *Rite of Passage: Adolescence in America, 1790 to the Present* (New York, 1977).

88. Flandrin, *Families*, 125–26; Shorter, *Making*, 256; Gillis, *Better or Worse*, 121–22.

89. Shorter, *Making*, 10–13; Richard J. Evans and W. R. Lee, eds., *The German Family: Essays on the Social History of the Family in the Nineteenth and Twentieth Centuries* (Totowa, N.J., 1981), 84–87; Gillis, *Better or Worse*, 115; Mitchison and Leneman, *Sexuality*, 180–210; Bouce, *Sexuality*, 2–21, 47–58; Macfarlane, *Marriage*, 210–14; Stone, *Family*, 633–35, 639; Wall, *Fierce Communion*, 1–29, 128, 135.

90. Flandrin, *Families*, 230–31, 238–39; Watt, *Making*, 182–84, 266–75; Gillis, *Better or Worse*, 191; Stone, *Family*, 232–33, 677; Wearmouth, *Methodism and Common People*.

91. Jay Fliegelman, *Prodigals and Pilgrims: The American Revolution against Patriarchal Authority* (New York, 1982), 123–26, 133.

92. Ibid., 155–94.

93. Wall, *Fierce Communion*, 128, 138, 141.

94. Ibid., 139; Coontz, *Social Origins*, 154–80, 194; Nancy F. Cott, *The Bonds of Womanhood: "Woman's Sphere" in New England, 1780–1835* (New Haven, Conn., 1977), 197–206; Mary B. Norton, *Liberty's Daughters: The Revolutionary Experience of American Women, 1750–1800* (Boston, 1980); Linda K. Kerber, *Women of the Republic: Intellect and Ideology in Revolutionary America* (Chapel Hill, N.C., 1980).

95. Stone, *Family*, 260–61, 392; Leonore Davidoff and Catherine Hall, *Family and Fortune: Men and Women of the English Middle Class, 1780–1850* (Chicago, 1987), 193–316; Evans and Lee, *German Family*, 51–83; Coontz, *Social Origins*, 190–92, 196, 210–18.

96. Accampo, *Industrialization*, 111–15, 123–35; Macfarlane, *Marriage*, 76–86; Evans and Lee, *German Family*, 95–101; Anthony S. Wohl, ed., *The Victorian Family: Structure and Stresses* (New York, 1978), 197–216; Stone, *Family*, 469–74; Levine, *Family Formation*, 78–80; Pinchbeck and Hewitt, *Children*, 2:387–610; Katherine A. Lynch, *Family, Class, and Ideology in Early Industrial France* (Madison, Wisc., 1988); Mintz and Kellogg, *Domestic Revolutions*, 83–95; Coontz, *Social Origins*, 287–312.

97. Pirckbeck and Hewitt, *Children*, 2:611–37; George K. Behlmer, *Child Abuse and Moral Reform in England, 1870–1908* (Stanford, Calif., 1982).

98. Evans and Lee, *German Family*, 85–92; Phayer, *Sexual Liberation*, 67–93; Flandrin, *Families*, 79–83, 261–62; Seecombe, *Millennium*, 225–35.

99. Phayer, *Sexual Liberation*, 113–26.

100. Stevenson, *Life in Black and White*; Herbert G. Gutman, *The Black Family in Slavery and Freedom, 1750–1925* (New York, 1976); Coontz, *Social Origins*, 312–16; Jane Turner Censer, *North Carolina Planters and Their Children, 1800–1860* (Baton Rouge, La., 1984), 135–40; Mintz and Kellogg, *Domestic Revolutions*, 67–80; Carl N. Degler, *At Odds: Women and the Family in America from the Revolution to the Present* (New York, 1980), 111–43.

101. Shorter, *Making*, 255; Stevenson, *Life in Black and White*.

102. Shorter, *Making*, 148–61, 265–67; Wohl, *Victorian Family*; Coontz, *Social Origins*, 224–36.

103. Fletcher, *Gender, Sex*, 394–96.

104. Flandrin, *Families*, 261, 263–65. For deviations from the Victorian ideal see Françoise Barret-Ducrocq, *Love in the Time of Victoria: Sexuality, Class, and*

Gender in Nineteenth-Century London, trans. John Howe (London, 1991); Coontz, *Social Origins,* 187, 190–92, 196; Michael Mason, *The Making of Victorian Sexual Attitudes* (London, 1994) and *The Making of Victorian Sexuality* (London, 1996); Patricia Anderson, *When Passion Reigned: Sex and the Victorians* (New York, 1995).

105. Phillips, *Putting Asunder,* 46–58, 246–65, 285–89, 370–72.

106. Ibid., 422–28; Bonald, *On Divorce,* trans. Nicholas Davidson (New Brunswick, N.J., 1994 [original edition 1816]).

107. Phillips, *Putting Asunder,* 538–49.

108. Ibid., 412–21; Stone, *Road.*

109. Phillips, *Putting Asunder,* 134–58, 246–51.

110. Ibid., 439–63; Glenda Riley, *Divorce: An American Tradition* (New York, 1991); Richard H. Chused, *Private Acts in Public Places: A Social History of Divorce in the Formative Years of American Family Law* (Philadelphia, 1994).

111. Robert L. Griswold, *Family and Divorce in California, 1850–1890: Victorian Illusions and Everyday Realities* (Albany, N.Y., 1982), 1, 125–31, 153–63.

112. *Arcanum divinae sapientiae* ("The Hidden Purpose of Divine Wisdom," 1880), in Claudia Carlen, I.H.M., ed., *The Papal Encyclicals, 1878–1903* (Wilmington, N.C., 1981), 2:29–40.

113. Phillips, *Putting Asunder,* 543–44, 565.

114. Ibid., 439–63.

115. *The Mysteries of Christianity,* trans. Cyril Vollert, S.J. (St. Louis, 1947 [original edition 1865]), 599–609.

116. Carlen, *Encyclicals,* 2:29–40.

117. Olivier Orban, *L'enfant, la famille, et la Revolution Française* (Paris, 1990), 351–414.

118. Ramon Garcia de Haro, *Matrimonio et famiglia nei documenti de Magistero* (Milan, 1989), 44–49.

119. *Pii IX Pontificis Maximis Acta,* Pars Prima, II (Graz, Austria, 1971), 714–16. English translations of this document are not readily accessible.

120. Carlen, *Encyclicals,* 2:32–33.

121. Charles A. Schleck, C.S.C., *The Sacrament of Matrimony: A Dogmatic Study* (Milwaukee, 1964), 234–36.

122. Phillips, *Putting Asunder,* 260–62.

123. Pat Jalland, *Women, Marriage, and Politics, 1660–1914* (Oxford, 1986); Trumbach, *Rise,* 150–57; Joan Perkin, *Women and Marriage in Nineteenth-Century England* (London, 1989); Griswold, *Family and Divorce,* 10–15, 39–48, 173–74; Anne Firor Scott, *The Southern Lady from Pedestal to Politics, 1830–1930* (Chicago, 1970); Patricia Branca, *Silent Sisterhood: Middle-Class Women in the Victorian Home* (Pittsburgh, 1975); Coontz, *Social Origins,* 218–36; Cott, *Bonds.*

124. Jalland, *Women;* Susan Staves, *Married Women's Separate Property in England, 1660–1833* (Cambridge, Mass., 1990); A. James Hammerton, *Cruelty and Companionship: Conflict in Nineteenth-Century Married Life* (London, 1992); Davidoff and Hall, *Family Fortunes,* 321–415; Wohl, *Victorian Family,* 59–81.

125. Davidoff and Hall, *Family Fortunes,* 193–316; Stone, *Family,* 244.

126. Sennett, *Families;* Steven Mintz, *A Prison of Expectations: The Family in Victorian Culture* (Ithaca, N.Y., 1980).

127. Donald Handlin, *The American Home: Architecture and Society 1815–1915* (Boston, 1979).

128. Colleen McDonnell, *The Christian Home in Victorian America* (Bloomington, Ind., 1986).

129. Scott G. and Sally Allen McNall, *Plains Families: Exploring Society through Social History* (New York, 1983); John Mack Farragher, *Women and Men on the Overland Trail* (New Haven, Conn., 1979); Mintz and Kellogg, *Domestic Revolutions,* 95–105.

130. Aries, *Centuries,* 493; Orban, *Enfant,* 107–42; Flandrin, *Families,* 232.

131. Colin Heywood, *Children in Nineteenth-Century France* (Cambridge, England, 1988); Barret-Ducrocq, *Love,* 39–44; Pirckbeck and Hewitt, *Children,* 2:354–637; Lynch, *Family;* Clark Nardinelli, *Child Labor and the Industrial Revolution* (Bloomington, Ind., 1996).

132. Flandrin, *Families,* 215–32; Robert Wheaton and Tamara K. Hareven, eds., *Family and Sexuality in French History* (Philadelphia, 1980), 135–71; J. A. and Olive Banks, *Feminism and Family Planning in Victorian England* (New York, 1972 [original edition 1964]); J. A. Banks, *Victorian Values: Secularism and the Size of Families* (London, 1981), and *Prosperity and Parenthood: A Study of Family Planning among the Victorian Middle Class* (London, 1954); Levine, *Family Formation,* 66–67; Angus Maclaren, *Birth Control in Nineteenth-Century England* (New York, 1978); Knodel, *Demographic Behavior,* 287–317; Sennett, *Families,* 111; Degler, *At Odds,* 210–26; Brodie, *Contraception.*

133. Maclaren, *Birth Control,* 43–55.

134. Ibid., 131–32.

135. *An Essay on the Principle of Population* and *A Summary View of the Principle of Population,* ed. Anthony Flew (Harmondsworth, England, 1970 [original editions 1798, 1803]).

136. Macfarlane, *Marriage,* 8–20, 33–52, 59–64.

137. Sennett, *Families,* 77, 122.

138. Noonan, *Contraception,* 397–404.

139. Macfarlane, *Marriage,* 31–55, 322–42; Maclaren, *Birth Control,* 31–55, 124, 232–45; Degler, *At Odds,* 227–48; James L. Mohr, *Abortion in America: The Origins and Evolution of National Policy, 1800–1900* (New York, 1978). Mohr shows that better medical knowledge directly led to the prohibition of abortion, but he disregards his own evidence in reaching a different conclusion.

140. John R. Connery, S.J., *Abortion: The Development of the Roman Catholic Perspective* (Chicago, 1977).

141. Aries, *Centuries,* 398–99; Flandrin, *Families,* 61, 94–98; Stone, *Family,* 253–55; Jennie Calder, *The Victorian Home* (London, 1977); Jessica Gerard, *Country House Life: Family and Servants, 1815–1914* (London, 1981).

142. Gillis, *Better or Worse,* 137–38.

143. Davidoff and Hall, *Family Fortunes,* 76–148; Stone, *Family,* 673–78.

144. Trumbach, *Rise,* 147–50; Barret-Ducrocq, *Love,* 45–72; Wendel Stacy Johnson, *Living in Sin: The Victorian Sexual Revolution* (Chicago, 1979).

145. Roger Fulford, *The Trial of Queen Caroline* (London, 1967); Davidoff and Hall, *Family Fortunes,* 150–52; Phillips, *Putting Asunder,* 414–16.

146. Philip Ziegler, *King William IV* (London, 1970), 83–84, 99–100, 157–58, 269–70; Clare Tomalin, *Mrs. Jordan's Profession* (New York, 1994) is the biography of the future king's long-time mistress.

147. Stanley Weintraub, *Victoria: An Intimate Biography* (New York, 1987), 139–98.

Chapter 8

THE CONTEMPORARY WORLD

John M. Haas

The contemporary world has seen many paradoxes when it comes to the subject of marriage. Almost never before in the West has there been such praise of marital love and yet seldom has the institution of marriage and family been perceived as so under siege.

The present period has seen a radical and precipitous decline in the health of the institution of marriage and family in what are known as the First World nations. Marriage is delayed or forsaken altogether. The birthrate has plummeted. Eastern Europe is experiencing radical population decline. In the 1980s the German state of Brandenburg experienced the sharpest drop in births ever recorded in Europe in a period not marked by famine or plague. In addition to covering prenatal and delivery costs, the government of Brandenburg established a policy of paying couples a flat sum of almost $700 for every child they bore.

Population decline is becoming an increasingly alarming problem in many formerly Christian nations. In the encyclical *Sollicitudo rei socialis* Pope John Paul II wrote that in the northern hemisphere,

> the cause for concern is the drop in the birthrate, with repercussions on the aging of the population, unable to renew itself biologically.... It is very alarming to see governments in many countries launching systematic campaigns against birth, contrary not only to the cultural and religious identity of the countries themselves but also contrary to the nature of true development.[1]

A brief look at the United States will suffice to gain some appreciation of the malaise in marriage and the family which has generally spread throughout the West. In the *Journal of Marriage and Family,* David Popenoe, a professor of sociology at Rutgers University, noted in 1993 that the period from roughly 1960 to 1990 "witnessed an unprecedented decline of the family as a social institution" in the United States.[2]

In June of 2000 the National Marriage Project based at Rutgers issued its report "The State of Our Unions 2000: The Health of Marriage in America," authored by Professor Popenoe and Barbara Dafoe Whitehead, which demonstrated that the decline had not abated.[3] Americans continued to be less likely to marry. It reported a decline of more than one third, from 1970 to 1996, in the annual number of marriages per one thousand unmarried women. Some of this decline might be attributed to women marrying later, from twenty years of age in 1960 to twenty-three in 1996. Other factors were the increase of unmarried cohabitation and a decrease in the tendency of divorced people to remarry. But what was clear was that fewer in the population were marrying.

The declining birthrate about which John Paul II expressed concern is also evident in the United States. According to the report of Popenoe and Whitehead, the decline of births had a significant impact on the makeup of households in the United States. It is estimated that in the middle of the 1800s more than 75 percent of all households in America contained children under the age of eighteen. One hundred years later, in 1960, this number had dropped to slightly less than half of all households. In 2000, just four decades later, only 34 percent of households included children under the age of eighteen.

The report also referred to studies which had determined that in 1960 the proportion of one's life spent living with a spouse and children was 62 percent, the highest in U.S. history. This was the result of a declining death rate and preceded the tremendous increase in the divorce rate which was to come in succeeding decades. By 1985, just twenty-five years later, the proportion of one's life spent with spouse and children dropped to 43 percent — the lowest in U.S. history. This remarkable reversal was caused mainly by a drop in the birthrate and the weakening of marriage through divorce and unwed births.

There has been a sharp decrease in families in which the father is the principal wage earner and the mother stays home with the children. Popenoe pointed out in an earlier study that in 1960, 42 percent of all families had a father and husband who was the sole wage earner; by 1988 this figure had dropped to 15 percent. By the 1990s as many mothers were in the job market as women who were not mothers. The fastest growing group entering the work force are the mothers of young children. In 1960 only 19 percent of married mothers with children under the age of six worked outside the home. By 1990 59 percent of married mothers with children under the age of six worked outside the home.

Increased sexual activity among unmarried people and a diminished respect for the family has led to an explosion of children not living in a family setting with both parents. In 1960 only 9 percent of U.S. children under eighteen lived with a lone parent. By 1990 that figure had risen to 24 percent.

There have also been fewer children born per capita in the United States. In the late 1950s an American mother had an average of 3.7 children over the course of her life. By 1990, the average had dropped to 1.9 children which is below the figure of 2.1 needed for population replacement.

With a decline in the social recognition of the institution of marriage there has come a considerable increase in men and women living together without being married. In 1960 there were 439,000 such arrangements in the U.S.; in 1990 there were 2,856,000, a sixfold increase! Some have tried to justify such arrangements by presenting them as trial marriages undertaken to test compatibility. However, cohabitation does not seem to have served that end well. Studies have shown that divorce is far more likely among couples who have cohabited prior to marriage.

"The State of Our Unions 2000" showed that between 1960 and 1998 the number of unmarried couples in America increased by close to 1000 percent. Unmarried cohabitation, i.e., the status of couples who are sexual partners, not married to each other, and sharing a household, is particularly common among the young. The report estimated that "about a quarter of unmarried women age 25–39 are currently living with a partner and an additional quarter have lived with a partner at some time in the past. Over half of all first marriages are now preceded by living together, compared to virtually none earlier in the century."

Government policies and court decisions have also had the effect of weakening marriage in those Western countries dominated by Enlightenment ideology and its tendency to deny any reality to things that cannot be empirically measured. In the United States, for example, recent Supreme Court decisions have tended to weaken the institution of marriage by viewing it increasingly as an arbitrary contractual arrangement that can be dissolved by either virtually at will.

In a decision known as *Eisenstadt v. Baird*[4] the Supreme Court struck down a state law forbidding the sale and distribution of contraceptives to couples who were *not* married. The Court held that such a law impinged unjustifiably on individual constitutional rights. What is interesting for our purposes is the understanding of marriage expressed in the Court's rationale for striking down the law. The Justices pointed out that seven years previously the Court had struck down as unconstitutional a law which had made it a criminal act for a husband and wife to have contraceptive intercourse in their own bedroom. That of course was the famous case of *Griswold v. Connecticut*, which found a "zone of privacy" which the state simply could not violate.[5] In *Griswold* this right to sexual acts in private without government intrusion was ascribed only to spouses. By *Eisenstadt v. Baird* the Court was ready to ascribe such a right to people who were not married and to claim that they could not be prevented from obtaining contraceptives for this purpose.

In *Eisenstadt* the Court referred to married couples being able to obtain and use contraceptives because of the *Griswold* decision and went on to argue that if married couples were constitutionally protected to engage in contraceptive intercourse, so could single individuals be so protected since "the marital couple is not an independent entity with a mind and heart of its own, but an association of two individuals each with a separate intellectual and emotional make-up."

There is some truth to what was stated in *Eisenstadt*. The marital couple always retain their own individual personalities and attendant rights. But in the past, marriage jurisprudence had recognized that two individuals acquired a new status with attendant, inescapable rights and obligations upon entering into matrimony. It understood that married couples, for example, gave to one another exclusive rights over those bodily acts which of their nature were apt for the generation of children. Sex acts had long been licensed by the state, as it were, since the acts had such profound consequences, good or ill, for society at large. The state had an obligation to regulate the sexual acts of its citizens which it did through marriage licenses. Today such regulation is increasingly becoming honored in the breach.

In another case the U.S. Supreme Court struck down a city ordinance which had defined "family" as an institution based on marriage and comprised of husband, wife, and children. The Court wrote that "The Constitution prevents [the government] from standardizing its children — and its adults — by forcing all to live in certain narrowly defined family patterns."[6] The Court went so far as to say that the definition of a family as comprised of husband, wife, and children was "senseless and arbitrary...eccentric... [and reflecting] cultural myopia."

The understanding of marriage as a union of man and woman for the purpose of creating a family was struck another blow by the Supreme Court in *Roe v. Wade*,[7] which of course voided state laws which would interfere with a woman's supposed right to destroy, with the assistance of a physician, her child. In the past children had been seen as the primary purpose for marriage and an inviolable good to be protected. When the state of Missouri attempted legislation to afford as much protection for the unborn child as it thought might be possible under *Roe v. Wade* by requiring parental and spousal consent before an abortion could be obtained, it had its new law challenged by Planned Parenthood. In the decision *Planned Parenthood v. Danforth* the Court struck down the provision for spousal consent, saying that "the state cannot delegate to a spouse a veto power which the state itself is absolutely and totally prohibited from exercising."[8]

In this Supreme Court decision the radical changes in societal understanding of marriage and the family can easily be seen. Formerly society understood that the mother and father of a child have not only a right but an obligation to do everything in their power to protect the life and well-being of their child. *Roe v. Wade* presumed to release a mother from that obligation. In the case just cited, *Planned Parenthood v. Danforth*, the Court held that the father of the child, who was previously understood to have a natural obligation to do everything in his power to protect his child, is prevented by the state from acting on that obligation. The Court went so far as to say that the father of the child cannot have such a right to intervene since the *state* does not have such a right. Increasingly, husband and wife are no longer seen as bound together for the benefit of society in the common enterprise of building a family with shared rights and obligations. Marriage is seen more and more as a tenuous and temporary arrangement between two individuals largely for self-gratification, personal fulfillment, or economic gain.

Today marriage is increasingly held to be merely an arbitrary construct of society. Homosexual organizations have exerted tremendous pressure to have same-sex relationships acknowledged as marriage or at least afforded the same benefits as marriage. More and more companies and political jurisdictions are responding to pressure to implement so-called "domestic partnership" laws so that the homosexual partner of the employee can receive health and other benefits that would normally go to a spouse. The state of Vermont now provides virtually all the benefits of marriage to individuals in homosexual relationships.

Another sign of decline in the status of marriage can be seen in its being treated increasingly as a commercial venture. In some ways this returns marriage to its status in the ancient or early medieval world when, before the permeation of a Christian view of the matter, marriage was largely perceived as an institution built around property. The no-fault divorce laws first introduced into California in 1969 now apply in every state in the Union. (South Dakota was the last state to capitulate in 1985.) These laws attempt to avoid assessing blame and hence imposing penalties for the disintegration of marriages. When the relationship is no longer profitable or satisfying, either partner can dissolve it at will. In most states property is to be divided evenly between the husband and the wife in a supposedly equitable arrangement.

The problem is that the husband usually receives half the property and an average of three persons (mother and two children) receive the other half. Also, the only thing that is divided is the tangible property. However, over the years the husband has usually accumulated a non-tangible type of property, often with the help of the wife: a law degree, a medical license, business contacts, etc. Commonly those who suffer most from divorce are the wife and children. There seems to be no empirical evidence that no-fault divorce has done anything to strengthen marriage and family. In 1970 there were 708,000 divorces; in 1993 1,187,000. The divorce rate now seems to have reached a plateau, but a high one with between 50 percent and 60 percent of all marriages ending in divorce.

The increased commercialization of marriage is also reflected in such child-bearing arrangements as surrogate mothering. Under these commercial contracts, a woman who is not the wife of the husband is artificially inseminated by him, bears his child, and relinquishes her rights to the child for the consideration of a certain sum of money. According to traditional definitions such an act could be seen as a species of adultery since it shares the reproductive capacities of the man (the use of which had been given exclusively to his wife at marriage) with a woman who is not his wife and has no right to those reproductive powers. The practice is also a kind of trafficking in human flesh since the mother of the child is actually selling her "interests" in her offspring for an agreed upon sum of money.

All this data, and much more, indicate that marriage and the family in the West generally are in deep decline. One family sociologist, Mary Jo Bane, who was formerly very optimistic about the health of the family, had to change her assessment. In an article published in 1988 she wrote: "Family situations of children have changed dramatically since 1970.... The change is astonishing both for its size and for the speed with which it has happened."[9] "The real force behind family change," she wrote, "has been a profound change in people's attitudes about marriage and children."[10]

Professor Popenoe points out in his studies that the family in the United States had undergone various transformations over the last two hundred years. The most significant had been the change from the extended family of parents, grandparents, aunts, uncles, brothers, sisters, and cousins to the nuclear family of parents and children. The nuclear family then became a highly specialized institution providing only two key social functions: the rearing of children and providing an atmosphere of affection and companionship for its members. Popenoe points out in his studies that by the 1990s even the nuclear family was disintegrating. It was no longer a matter of the transformation, but of the dissolution, of the nuclear family. And there were no social institutions capable of taking over the specialized functions which have been performed by the nuclear family.

It is impossible to discuss marriage in the contemporary world without acknowledging its precipitous decline. Other ages grappled with what it meant for marriage to be a sacrament, what actually brought it into being, consent or consummation, the relationship between the contract and the sacrament, who were the proper ministers of the sacrament, what were property rights within marriage, and so forth. It was left to the twentieth century, however, to grapple with the most fundamental question of what marriage itself is. Today one looks at what has been a universal human phenomenon — marriage — and the question is asked if Western society currently even knows what it is. This confusion could perhaps be seen in a very striking way in the presidential inaugural parade of Bill Clinton. In the parade was a family float which featured a lesbian couple, one member of which had a child by artificial insemination, a "gay" couple with an adopted child, and a husband and wife with their own biological child.

The Catholic Church has been keenly aware of these social developments. It perceived throughout the twentieth century these growing threats to what it considers to be the divine institution of marriage and has tried in a number of ways to clarify the issues at stake and to strengthen marriage both within the Church and society at large.

It is interesting to note that at the very beginning of the twentieth century the Church's concern with threats to marriage led it to seek a precise definition of marriage to incorporate into the *Code of Canon Law* which would be promulgated on Pentecost Sunday in 1917. Pietro Cardinal Gasparri, a canonist specializing in marriage law, oversaw the writing of the new Code. He had occupied a chair in canon law at the Insitut Catholique in Paris and had published a major work on marriage in 1892, *Tractatus Canonicus de Matrimonio.* This work served as the major source for Title VII of the Code, which dealt with marriage. In 1932 Cardinal Gasparri published the second edition of the *Tractatus,* which he had revised *ad mentem Codicis Iuris Canonici* (that is, "according to the mind of the Code of Canon Law"). In it he incorporated the rulings on marriage which had resulted from fifteen years of the use of the Code.

Certain elements were included in Cardinal Gasparri's definition of marriage which were drawn from the Catholic tradition and stated in the lapidary and precise style of legal statutes. The first of these to be considered here is that of "contract." Canon 1012, paragraphs 1 and 2, of the 1917 Code read:

1. Christ our Lord elevated the contract itself of marriage between baptized persons to the dignity of a sacrament.

2. Therefore it is impossible for a valid contract of marriage between baptized persons to exist without being by that very fact a sacrament.[11]

The fact that marriage is immediately presented not only as a sacrament but also as a contract reflects a struggle which the Church had been waging with civil governments for a good four hundred years. With the rise of the nation states and the growing secularization of society, governments increasingly wanted to claim for themselves the right to determine the conditions for bringing marriages into being and for judging their validity. The claim was often put forward that since marriage was a "natural" institution as well as a sacramental one, the state should be able to determine the validity of its natural quality, that is, marriage as a contract, with the Church free to determine its sacramental quality.

The Church responded that for Christians the reality of marriage as contract could not be separated from its reality as sacrament. That is, if two baptized persons entered into a valid marital contract, it was also, by definition, a sacrament. The sacramental and contractual character of marriage were both essential to it and inseparable.

In 1817, one hundred years before the new Code, there had been a strong pronouncement of the Sacred Congregation of the Holy Office with respect to the question of the inseparability of contract and sacrament in marriage.

> It is heresy ... to separate absolutely by means of a law the sacrament of matrimony from the contract of matrimony, just as if the contract did not enter into the essence and substance of the sacrament by the force of divine institution, and the sacrament of marriage would be discovered to be nothing other than a quality floating over the contract or a frame decorating a painting to which it is foreign.... Matrimony ... is on that account a sacrament because the contract also pertains to the sacrament and enters into the definition of the sacrament. There can be a contract of marriage which may not be a sacrament; nevertheless, there cannot be a sacrament of marriage, in which the contract itself is not a sacrament.[12]

Pius IX reiterated in his allocution *Acerbissimum* that sacrament and contract arise together in Christian marriages.[13] Leo XIII in *Arcanum divinae sapientiae,* issued February 10, 1880, wrote at length of the inseparability of sacrament and contract which constitute the one reality of marriage. He wrote "For Christ the Lord has enriched [*auxit*] matrimony with the dignity of a sacrament; matrimony, however, is the contract itself, provided that it is done according to the law [*si modo sit factus iure*]."[14]

Some attention is here given to the contractual nature of marriage because there are theologians who have written in the aftermath of the Second Vatican Council claiming that the Council Fathers had repudiated the notion of contract in Christian marriage and had substituted the idea of covenant. It is true that the conciliar *Pastoral Constitution on the Church in the Modern World, Gaudium et Spes,* never refers to marriage as a contract. But there is no evidence that the Council rejected the contractual character of marriage. Indeed, from a theological point of view this would be impossible to do since the magisterium has taught that it is essential to marriage, and it has been included in the revised *Code of Canon Law.*

The Second Vatican Council was arguably the most important development in the life of the Church in the twentieth century. There has been an unfortunate tendency since the Council, however, for theologians to write as though there had been a radical break in the life and teaching of the Church which occurred with the Council. Because *Gaudium et Spes* uses the more biblical language of covenant rather than contract to speak of marriage does not mean the two are incompatible. Indeed, a covenant is itself a kind of contract.[15] And the preconciliar magisterium spoke of marriage as covenant as well as contract.

The preparatory commissions for what came to be known as the First Vatican Council treated at length the question of the inseparability of sacrament and contract. The final version of the *Schema de Rebus Theologica Dogmaticis* dealt in its first chapter with marriage and described it with both categories as a "conjugal covenant [*coniugale foedus*] entered into by a legitimate contract."[16] The Catholic understanding of marriage until the mid-twentieth century tended to incorporate and order all the essential ends and properties of marriage. This easy inclusion of the concepts of both covenant and contract in the *Schema*'s discussion of marriage is certainly more characteristic of previous Catholic tradition than many theological tendencies of the post–Vatican II period. The *Schema* to the First Vatican Council insisted that the sacrament could not be distinguished and separated from the marital contract: "Whence among Christians matrimony cannot be entered into without it being in one and the same act a sacrament."[17]

Any contract carries rights and obligations for the contracting parties. This is no less true for baptized husbands and wives who commit themselves exclusively and permanently to one another and who give to one another rights to those bodily actions which of their nature are apt for the generation of children and which express their mutual gift of self.

Since one cannot enter into a contract without knowing what one is binding oneself to, it was important that the 1917 *Code* explain succinctly and clearly what marriage is. This was done in Canon 1013 which stated: "The primary end of marriage is the procreation and education of children; the secondary end is mutual help and a remedy for concupiscence."[18] This particular formula was the guiding one in marital jurisprudence until the *Code* was revised in 1983. This formulation by Cardinal Gasparri engendered a vast literature about the precise meaning of these ends and their relationship to one another.

It would be impossible in a short space even to begin to cover the literature, but attention should be drawn to the works of two men who seemed to call into question the hierarchical ordering of the ends of marriage: Dietrich von Hildebrand and Heribert Doms. Many Catholic scholars feared that the concise, Spartan definition of marriage found in the *Code* neglected the elements of warmth, love, and a shared life which all understand to play significant roles in married life.

Von Hildebrand wrote as a faithful Catholic but not from within the

Thomistic tradition. In fact, he was more Bonaventurian in his approach. He attempted to be more descriptive, psychological, indeed phenomenological in his treatment of his subjects. In 1929 von Hildebrand published his essay *Die Ehe,* which was published in English in 1942 as *Marriage.* His treatment of marriage contributed to the debate surrounding the ends of marriage simply by virtue of the language he chose to use. Although the debate became quite heated prior to the Second Vatican Council, it has in reality continued to the present.[19]

Rather than dealing in the metaphysical terms used in the canonical definition, von Hildebrand reflected on the meaning of marriage as understood by those who were married. Here it is obvious, he wrote, that love serves as the fundamental meaning of marriage; love is the reason people marry and bind themselves to one another for life. Marriage is fundamentally a community of love, and sexual intercourse is not simply an instrumental means to procreation but is the most complete expression of a couple's love for one another. His psychology of marital love sees the husband and wife giving of themselves totally to one another. It is this mutual surrender which truly brings the community of love into being. As he puts it in *Marriage:* "The act of voluntary surrender of one's own person to another, with the intention of forming a permanent and intimate union of love, creates an objective bond, which once established is withdrawn from the sphere of arbitrary decision of the persons concerned."[20]

Von Hildebrand preferred speaking of the meaning of marriage rather than its ends. His approach of "Christian personalism" has been tremendously influential among Catholic scholars, and there is no doubt that his writings helped shape the passages on marriage found in the Second Vatican Council and in the writings on marriage of Pope Paul VI and Pope John Paul II, which are clearly more personal and psychological than they are juridical.

Heribert Doms was not so faithful to the tradition as was von Hildebrand as he tried to find new ways of expressing the nature of marriage. Doms did not so much deny that procreation and nurture were the primary end of marriage as to say that marriage ought not to be understood principally in terms of ends but rather it should be understood in terms of its meaning for those who entered into it. However, the ambiguities found in his *The Meaning of Marriage* caused it to be withdrawn from publication in the early 1940s by order of the Sacred Congregation of the Holy Office.[21]

The early twentieth century saw a papal intervention into the heated public debates about the nature of marriage in the encyclical *Casti Connubii* by Pope Pius XI. The pope was dismayed by the assaults which seemed to be launched against marriage from every side. The evils threatening marriage which he mentioned in the encyclical sound remarkably contemporary:

contraception, abortion, sterilization, adultery, trial marriages, cohabitation, religiously mixed marriages, and divorce. He wrote the bishops of the world:

> We observe — and you, Venerable Brethren, cannot but share Our sorrow as you also observe — that there are many unmindful of this divine work of renewal, who are totally ignorant of the sanctity of marriage, who imprudently deny, who even allow themselves to be led by principles of a modern and perverse ethical doctrine to repudiate it with scorn.... These pernicious errors and degraded morals have begun to spread even among the faithful.[22]

All these evils derived in one way or another from the profound modern error which holds that marriage is not a divine institution but rather a human institution established by the arbitrary wills of human beings. Over against this error Pius XI insisted, "Not men but God, the Author of nature, and Christ our Lord, the restorer of nature, provided marriage with its laws, confirmed and elevated it; and consequently those laws can in no way be subject to human wills."[23]

If marriage was an objective reality created by God it should be able to be defined. Pius did this by turning to St. Augustine, who spoke of "the blessings which make matrimony itself a blessing: offspring, fidelity, sacrament."[24] The pope then goes on to say that "among the blessings of marriage offspring holds the first place."[25] Later he quotes Canon 1013 of the *Code*: "The primary end of marriage is the procreation and education of children."[26] There can be no doubt that Pius XI considers the procreation and education of children to be hierarchically ordered above the other ends.

In fact it was an event within Christianity itself which Pius XI saw as a disturbing and grave threat to the primary end of marriage which led him to issue this encyclical in 1930. In that year, after lengthy debate and with a close vote, the Lambeth Conference of Anglican bishops issued a resolution which stated that Christian couples might, in difficult situations, practice contraception if they found the more Christian approach of abstention impossible. Even this tentative approval of contraception struck the sensitive soul of Pius XI as an abomination and was the direct occasion of his issuing the encyclical *Casti Connubii, Of Chaste Marriage*. He spoke out emphatically against contraception as a direct and dangerous threat to the very integrity of marriage since it was directed against its primary end:

> Wherefore, since there are some who, openly departing from the Christian teaching which has been handed down uninterruptedly from the beginning, have in recent times thought fit solemnly to preach another doctrine concerning this practice, the Catholic Church, to whom God has committed the task of teaching and preserving morals and right

conduct in their integrity, standing erect amidst this moral devastation, raises her voice in sign of her divine mission to keep the chastity of the marriage contract unsullied by this ugly stain, and through Our mouth proclaims anew: that any use of matrimony whatsoever in the exercise of which the act is deprived, by human interference, of its natural power to procreate life, is an offense against the law of God...and that those who commit it are guilty of a grave sin.[27]

It is difficult to stress too much the importance which the papal magisterium of the first half of the twentieth century placed on a sound understanding of the hierarchical ordering of the ends of marriage. From a survey of the pertinent literature it would appear that a majority of Catholic authors writing on marriage today see this as a dead issue. Most believe that the Second Vatican Council actually changed the teaching on the hierarchy of ends contained in the 1917 *Code* and *Casti Connubii*. But the Council Fathers were not ignorant of the significance of this teaching.

Despite the clear teaching of the *Code of Canon Law* and the encyclical *Casti Connubii* there were Catholic authors who called into question the teaching on the hierarchy of ends in the name of Christian personalism. In response to these authors the Holy Roman Rota issued a sentence in January of 1944 which stated emphatically, "Matrimony has a primary and a secondary end. This is evident from the Constitutions and the numerous Encyclicals of the Supreme Pontiffs, from the common doctrine of theologians, canonists and moralists, and from the explicit words of Canon Law."[28] Without denying the importance of the other ends of marriage, the sentence teaches that "the primary and principal, one and indivisible *finis operis* of matrimony which *uniquely specifies* its nature is the procreation and education of the offspring."

Jurisprudence, however, did not seem sufficient to settle the controversies surrounding this point. Such confusion seemed to be developing on the question that the Sacred Congregation of the Holy Office itself issued a decree in the same year. It spoke of those writings which "take the terms used commonly in Church documents, such as 'end,' 'primary,' 'secondary,' and give them meanings discordant with the meanings commonly attributed to them by theologians." The Holy Office went on:

This novel way of thinking and writing is prone to breed error and uncertainty. In view of this the Most Excellent and Reverend Fathers of this Supreme Congregation, charged with the defense of faith and morals, met on Wednesday, March 29, 1944, to consider the following question: "Whether the opinion of some current authors is admissible which either denies that the primary end of marriage is the generation and nurture of offspring, or teaches that the secondary ends are not essentially subordinate to the primary, but are independent of it and equally primary." Our response to this in decree: negative.[29]

The Fathers of the Second Vatican Council knew of this decree of the Holy Office and certainly were intimately familiar with the address of Pius XII to the Union of Italian Catholic Obstetricians on October 29, 1951. Pius warned of misunderstandings arising from certain writings on the nature of marriage:

> "Personal values," and the need to respect such are a theme which, over the last twenty years or so, has been considered more and more by some writers.... Now the truth is that matrimony, as an institution of nature, in virtue of the Creator's will, has not as a primary end the intimate and personal perfection of the married couple but the procreation and upbringing of new life. The other ends, inasmuch as they are intended by nature, are not equally primary, much less superior to the primary end, but are essentially subordinated to it.[30]

When the Fathers at the Second Vatican Council were debating the texts on marriage and the family which would eventually be incorporated into the *Pastoral Constitution on the Church in the Modern World, Gaudium et Spes,* there was considerable discussion as to the nature of the text and the language which would be used in it. The scholarly controversy surrounding the hierarchical ordering of the ends of marriage was very much in the background of the discussion.

After Pope John XXIII issued his call for an ecumenical council the Sacred Congregation for the Discipline of the Sacraments and the Sacred Congregation of the Holy Office both asked that the Council deal with the question of marriage. Alfredo Cardinal Ottaviani was not only prefect of the Holy Office but also the president of the Theological Commission which was established to prepare the agenda for the Council. The Preparatory Commission for the Council received the recommendations of Ottaviani's Theological Commission, which called for a clear description of the nature and objective ends of marriage making use of the standard philosophical/theological language of the day.

Most of the cardinals on the Preparatory Commission found no problem with the draft on marriage submitted by Ottaviani's Theological Commission, but there were four who found it unsatisfactory. They were Julius Cardinal Döpfner of Munich, Emile Cardinal Léger of Montreal, Bernhard Jan Cardinal Alfrink of Utrecht, and Leo Joseph Cardinal Suenens of Malines-Bruges. The principal concern of all of them was that the draft did not sufficiently take into account the psychological, personalist dimension of marriage, particularly the notion of marital love.

Cardinal Döpfner wrote: "What the [draft] constitution says about the ends of marriage...is in general true. But it will bring little light to the contemporary discussion of the subject." The reason for this, the cardinal maintained, was that so many different languages were using the same words but with different meanings: the language of jurisprudence, of psychology, of theology, of Scripture. He argued that greater use be made of the concept of marital love. After all, he said, this is why a man and a woman marry. "This constitution ought," he wrote, "to free itself from the merely juridical and traditional way of thinking and treat more profoundly the role of marital love itself in marriage. Perhaps it could include something on the subject from Pope Pius XI's encyclical, *Casti Connubii*, which contains a number of beautiful statements on marital love. It seems certain that many of the Catholic faithful await urgently some statement of this kind from the council."[31]

Those critical of the Theological Commission's document finally won the day. Of the sixty members of the Central Preparatory Commission, thirty-five concurred with the criticism expressed by Cardinal Döpfner and the others. Cardinal Bea summed up the criticism of the draft by saying: "The text ought to be less juridical — more positive and constructive. Let it use Sacred Scripture more fully and let its language be less technical."[32]

In the final analysis this is exactly what happened in the marriage text finally accepted by the Fathers of the Council. It was less technical and was more cognizant of modern sensibilities about the role of love in marriage. Chapter one of the Second Part of *Gaudium et Spes*, 47 through 51, is a presentation of the Church's teaching on marriage and the family which incorporates the personalist developments in Catholic thought even while it does not forsake any of the essential insights of the more ancient tradition. In its very first paragraph it speaks of the "community of love" which is brought into being by marriage. But it also speaks of the primary end of marriage without using that technical language. In section 50, for example, one reads: "Marriage and conjugal love are by their nature ordained toward the begetting and educating of children. Children are really the supreme gift of marriage and contribute very substantially to the welfare of their parents."

There can be little doubt that the magisterium of the Church in the Council and afterward opted for a less technically philosophical, theological, and juridical vocabulary in teaching about and regulating marriage. When Pope Paul VI issued his encyclical on the moral regulation of births in 1968, just three years after the close of the Council, he no longer used traditional scholastic language to describe the institution of marriage. He notes the changes that have taken place in the societal understanding of marriage. "A change," he writes in *Humanae Vitae*, "is...seen in the manner of consid-

ering the person of woman and her place in society, and in the value to
be attributed to conjugal love in marriage, and also in the appreciation to
be made of the meaning of conjugal acts in relation to love."[33] And when
Paul VI speaks of the conjugal act he no longer does so in terms of its ends,
as had been common in previous papal teaching, but of its meanings.

The Church's disapproval of contraception, Pope Paul wrote, "is founded
upon the inseparable connection, willed by God and unable to be broken
by man on his own initiative, between the two meanings of the conjugal
act: the unitive meaning and the procreative meaning."[34] Here it would appear that the debate between the "classicists" and the "personalists" with
regard to the best language to use to speak to the men and women of the
twentieth century about marriage was won by the personalists. In just these
two quotations from *Humanae Vitae* one can see the influence of the ax-
iological or "value" approach to morality developed by Max Scheler and
Nicolai Hartmann in the early part of the century as well as the influence
of phenomenologists such as Merleau Ponty, Edmund Husserl, or Dietrich
von Hildebrand.

In the preface to his book *Marriage,* which appeared in English in 1942,
von Hildebrand had written: "In stressing the primary *end* of marriage —
procreation — certain theological treatises have overlooked the primary
meaning of marriage, which is love."[35] But in trying to correct what was
perceived as an impersonal, classical definition of marriage, von Hildebrand
in no way repudiated the traditional teaching. He wrote later in the book:
"Love is the primary *meaning* of marriage just as the birth of new human
beings is its primary *end.*"[36] In his *Man and Woman,* which first appeared
in 1966, von Hildebrand maintained the distinction. "Stress on the *meaning*
and value of marriage as the most intimate indissoluble union of love," he
wrote, "does not contradict the doctrine that procreation is the primary *end*
of marriage."[37]

The language of ends to describe marriage was finally dropped from official Church documents altogether with the promulgation of the new *Code
of Canon Law* in 1983. The first Canon in Title VII of the *Code* reads: "The
matrimonial covenant, by which a man and a woman establish between
themselves a partnership of the whole of life, is by its nature ordered toward
the good of the spouses and the procreation and education of offspring."[38]
Although the language of ends has disappeared, the reality to which those
technical terms had always referred remains and is now simply expressed in
the more personalist language of partnership, community of life and love,
and marital goods.

However, in the years since the Council, the fears which the more conservative prelates at the Council expressed about the consequences of dropping
the strictly technical language have proven to have been justified. Virtu-

ally every Catholic author since the Council who has written on marriage and sexual morality and who has departed from magisterial teaching has made the claim that the magisterium has repudiated the traditional teaching on the hierarchy of the ends of marriage. In fact, even some orthodox authors have claimed that the Church has changed its teaching on the subject. For example, an article appeared in the *Homiletical and Pastoral Review* which claimed that in the thought of Paul VI in conjugal relations "the unitive function is central and is equal to the procreative function."[39] At a conference on morality another orthodox theologian maintained that the unitive meaning of marriage was now to be considered primary because in *Humanae Vitae*, section 12, it appears first in the sentence! Such an observation hardly constitutes a theological or philosophical analysis of the matter.

Among authors dissenting from magisterial teaching on marriage, the claim is almost universally made. Two examples are illustrative of many others. In 1979 the Catholic Theological Society of America issued a book entitled *Human Sexuality*. In it the authors presented arguments on behalf of a large number of deviant sexual practices, from masturbation to homosexual acts to contraception. Numerous passages from the book show the authors' desire to separate sexuality from procreation. To achieve their end, they believed it necessary to show that sexuality is not "primarily" ordered to procreation. They made the claim that this precisely is the teaching of the Second Vatican Council since it no longer uses the language of primary and secondary ends.

They write: "Vatican II took a major step forward when it deliberately rejected [the] priority of the procreative over the unitive end of marriage."[40] Again: "Vatican II, however, officially and explicitly rejected such a view [that the purpose of sexuality is primarily procreative] as incomplete, and with good reason."[41] Or again: "The Council's deliberate rejection of the centuries-long tradition that regarded the procreative end as supreme necessitates a thorough rewriting of the theology of marital sexuality found in the moral manuals."[42]

Elsewhere, they write: "In rejecting this hierarchical ordering of the ends of marriage, Vatican II...."[43] And again: "The deliberate refusal of the Council Fathers at Vatican II to retain the traditional hierarchy of primary and secondary ends of marriage...."[44]

In fact, one can simply look to the section on marriage in *Gaudium et Spes*, without referring to the pages of conciliar debate which produced it, to see that the Council did not intend to reject the received teaching.[45]

Section 48 of *Gaudium et Spes* speaks of the benefits and purposes of matrimony and directs the reader to a footnote for a clarification of what the Council Fathers understand those purposes to be. The first text referred to is St. Augustine's *De bono coniugii,* which speaks of the marital goods of the child, fidelity, and sacramentality. The reader is next referred to the *Summa Theologica* of St. Thomas Aquinas, question 49, article 3 ad 1 in the Supplement in which he points out that "the end as regards the intention stands first in a thing, but as regards the attainment it stands last. It is the same with offspring among the marriage goods; wherefore it is the principal end in one way and not in another"[46] Next to be cited is the *Decretum pro Armeniis* of the Council of Florence which refers to children as the first good of marriage.[47] Finally reference is made to Pius XI's *Casti Connubii,* which, of course, speaks explicitly of the hierarchical ordering of the ends of marriage. The texts in the footnote to section 48 are clearly meant to elucidate what the Council Fathers meant when they referred to the purposes of matrimony.

The same section of *Gaudium et Spes* also states that "by their very nature, the institution of matrimony itself and conjugal love are ordained for the procreation and education of children, and find in them their ultimate crown." The footnotes to the conciliar texts are most useful but an unprejudiced reading of the conciliar texts themselves would lead one to no other conclusion than that the Fathers never intended to repudiate the classical teaching on the ordering of the ends of marriage.

Prior to the final vote on the marriage section of *Gaudium et Spes,* a group of Council Fathers appealed once again for the inclusion of the language of the hierarchy of ends. The conciliar Commission on Emendations did not accept their recommendations. However, it reassured the Fathers that there was no need to incorporate such language since their concerns were already addressed in the body of the text. The Commission stated: "In a text that is to be pastoral in character and aims at fostering a dialogue with the world, there is no need of introducing juridical elements. . . . In any case, the primordial importance of procreation and education is pointed out at least 10 times in the text."[48]

However, certain theologians wasted no time in interpreting the marriage texts in *Gaudium et Spes* in a way which deviated from the received teaching. The book *Human Sexuality* by the Catholic Theological Society of America (CTSA) was simply one of the more obvious attempts at reinterpretation. Shortly after its publication the American bishops said the CTSA Study could not be used for catechesis or pastoral practice. Then in July 1979, the Sacred Congregation for the Doctrine of the Faith issued its own ruling on the book. One of the errors of the book which the Congregation most explicitly repudiated was the claim that the Second Vatican Council had rejected the former magisterial teaching on matrimony, particularly with regard to question of the ends of marriage. The Congregation wrote:

Furthermore, we must point out another mistaken notion regarding the teaching of Vatican II. The book repeatedly asserts that the council deliberately refuses to maintain the traditional hierarchy of the primary and secondary ends of marriage, and is teaching the Church a new and deeper understanding of the meaning of conjugal love.[49]

This is presented as clearly erroneous.

One of the greatest difficulties surrounding this debate has been the various ways in which the terms "primary end" and "secondary end" are used. Because Cardinal Gasparri had incorporated the language of primary and secondary ends into the *Code of Canon Law,* the terms came to be referred to as juridical categories. In fact, this is even the way in which the conciliar Commission on Emendations referred to the terms, as did many of the Council Fathers in the course of the debate. But "primary and secondary ends" are not taken principally from jurisprudence but from metaphysics. Cardinal Gasparri wanted to be able to define the reality as precisely as possible in order to assist the Church in its legal judgments regarding marriage. The discipline of metaphysics was employed to develop the clearest, lapidary description of what the reality of marriage was, the *matrimonio in facto esse.*

Gasparri merely drew on a tradition stretching back as far as St. Augustine himself to understand marriage in terms of its ends. As a scholar he understood the metaphysical principle that the nature or essence of a thing is known in its ends. He understood the teleology of a thing as grounded in its very being. A pair of eyeglasses is understood to be a pair of eyeglasses by virtue of the fact that it was created to assist a person in the act of seeing.

According to this manner of metaphysical analysis one understands what a thing *is* by virtue of what it *does,* by virtue of the end toward which it is ordered. In most of the magisterial documents up until the middle of the twentieth century one encounters the use of classical scholastic metaphysics with a teleology grounded in ontology. The principle that *"agere sequitur esse"* is never questioned. Action follows on being.

Since, by scholastic analysis, any given thing may have more than one end, it is important to identify which end most adequately defines a thing. The end which most completely clarifies what a thing is in terms of what it does is what is called the primary end. It was important for Cardinal Gasparri to identify which end of marriage most adequately explained marriage, for this would belong to its very essence.

If one looks at the ends of marriage in terms of the child, mutual support, and a remedy for concupiscence, it is not too difficult to identify the one which most adequately explains the institution of marriage. It cannot simply be mutual support since two individuals of the same sex could forge a community of love and support and look after one another. Of the three ends, the one which is completely unique to marriage is the procreation and education of children. This is precisely what St. Thomas means when he says in his commentary on Peter Lombard's *Sentences:* "The child is the most essential good of marriage, second is faith and third the sacrament."[50]

There is clearly no more excellent good than that of the sacrament, the life of grace. Obviously St. Thomas does not mean that the "sacrament" of marriage is only third in importance after the other goods. He merely affirms that what is most essential to marriage among its goods is the child. It most adequately, in the final analysis, explains why people get married and what is unique about the institution of marriage.

Today people tend to think of marriage merely as the legal context in which sexual activity can take place. But the Catholic philosophical and theological tradition teaches that sexual activity is hardly an end in itself. It is ordered toward an end beyond itself which is still intrinsic to it and ultimately makes sense of it.

As Bernard Lonergan puts it cogently and concisely: "Marriage is more an incorporation of the finality [end] of sex than of sex itself. Of course, it is just the opposite that seems true to phenomenologist scrutiny, for that ignores the metaphysical principle that what is prior *quoad se* [in itself] is posterior *quoad nos* [to us], and that the more ultimate final cause enters more intimately into the nature of a thing than the more proximate."[51]

Lonergan goes on to say that, in metaphysical terms, "the more ultimate final cause enters more intimately into the nature of a thing than the more proximate." He then adds in a footnote: "What is first in the ontological constitution of a thing is not the experiential datum but, on the contrary, what is known in the last and most general act of understanding with regard to it." And the last and most general act of understanding with regard to sexual intercourse is that it engenders a child, not the experiential data that the conjugal act here and now is sensuously pleasurable and is an act of surrender to one's spouse.

Since a metaphysical analysis of marriage merely *describes* what is, it does not *prescribe* anything. That, according to the Catholic and other traditions, is for the natural moral law to do. Metaphysical analysis does not even make "value judgments" about the ends. It simply states what they are and how they are ordered to one another in terms of clarifying the reality under scrutiny. It is necessary to understand the reality upon which the law will bear before making ordinances directive of human behavior with respect to that reality. There is vast confusion on this point in the majority of the literature dealing with the question of the ends of marriage.

Some authors have argued that there is a difference between the ends and the meanings of marriage. However, if, in a metaphysical analysis, a thing is understood by virtue of its ends, then its meaning coincides with its ends. Second, as has been pointed out, in a metaphysical analysis, "primary" does not refer to that which has greater "value." This is a mistake most twentieth-century critics of the teaching on ends made.

For example, Theodore Mackin speaks of a parity of "value" which the Council and postconciliar magisterial teaching has ascribed to the unitive and procreative ends. He writes of those Council Fathers who feared the elimination of the language of primary and secondary ends of marriage:

> For if the plural ends to be attained are equal in value, no compelling reason for having one rather than the other rule the moral choice could be found within the ends themselves. The choice could and would then have to be made according to the real needs of the spouses as persons trying to sustain a love relationship. It is not exaggeration to say that the challenge to the morality of inherent ends of the physical act of intercourse was a challenge to an entire moral system.[52]

Of course if the discussion of ends is really of parity of value, there would be a grave problem with the new magisterial formulae. But if the traditional teaching on the ends of marriage is a matter of description of what is, then the whole issue of parity of value versus hierarchy of ends does not even arise. When Paul VI spoke of the unitive and procreative meanings of the marital act being inseparable, he was saying that if a person suppresses or acts against one of those meanings, it is no longer the marital act. There will be a human act of some sort, but not the marital act since that act of its nature is ordered toward procreation and the uniting of the spouses. If the language of hierarchy is reintroduced, it simply helps one understand the reality by the way in which the ends are ordered to one another. It is not at odds with the new formulations used after the Council.

According to Catholic tradition, the bodily pleasures of the marriage bed are good and wholesome and will remain so if one sees their relation to the other goods of mutual support and procreation. As St. Thomas said, "The end which [God] intends in copulation is offspring to be procreated and educated and that this good might be sought [He] has put delight in copulation."[53] This is not to say the delight of conjugal copulation can be sought only when one is seeking to procreate, but it does mean that even this delight serves a more essential end, the child who is begotten and educated, for the good of the spouses and society. One cannot pursue this delight at the expense of the end which makes sense of it.

Again, the language of primary and secondary ends belongs fundamentally not to jurisprudence but to metaphysics. Even some of the cardinals involved in the debates of Vatican II fell into calling it juridical language when they called for its exclusion from a "pastoral" constitution. Michael

Cardinal Browne of England, however, who argued strongly for its inclusion in the Constitution, noted:

> ...this teaching, which is Catholic doctrine, namely that procreation and nurture are the primary end of marriage, is not a juridical teaching. It is an expression of the law of nature, the philosophy of nature (i.e., metaphysics)....
>
> It is truly necessary that we hold to this teaching most strictly and rigorously. I would never admit that this is said according to a merely juridical concept, for then we would be seeking something less than a philosophical or theological statement. But in itself it is an application of the philosophy of nature.[54]

Cardinal Gasparri had tried to locate what was most essential to marriage so that if a couple had given themselves to that essential end, which could be understood as subsuming the other ends, they would be considered married. However, if "marital love" came to be seen somehow as an end of marriage which was necessary to bring it into effect, what would happen to those arranged marriages common in many countries which are not predicated on affection as much as on providing both the young woman and the man with a stable home, with mutual support, and with children for their own good and that of their respective families and society at large? Did not royalty truly marry when they married for dynastic purposes rather than out of sentiments of love? The Church taught that these were indeed truly marriages if the couples freely and knowingly entered into them by surrendering to one another perpetual rights to those bodily acts which were apt for the generation of children for the establishment of a family.

One of the principal reasons for the grave disorder in which marriage finds itself at the present is simply that society no longer knows what marriage is or what purposes it principally serves. This has been illustrated graphically in the confrontation of Pope John Paul II with the strongest nations on earth and with the world's most powerful international organizations over the very meaning of marriage and the family.

Civilization passes by way of the family, the pope has said. If the family is placed in jeopardy, so is civilization. And without marriage there is no family. Pope John Paul II had happily joined the United Nations in 1994 in its observance of the International Year of the Family. But his initial enthusiasm turned to profound dismay as he learned of the preparations being made for the United Nations Conference on Development and Population to take place in Cairo, Egypt.

The United Nations and several international organizations had developed a draft which redefined marriage and the family and which would initiate programs worldwide which through abortion and contraception would be directed against "the supreme gift of marriage," that is, "the primary end of marriage," children. In many respects the Cairo Conference was a defining moment for the *world's* understanding of marriage, and Pope John Paul II used all the resources and moral prestige of his papacy to combat what he saw as profound threats to civilization itself.

But it must be admitted that the condition of marriage in the Church is almost as grave as it is in society. Some have suggested that this has resulted from a lack of clarity in Church documents resulting from an unwillingness to use careful philosophical language in discussing marriage. The Second Vatican Council and its unwillingness to use the classical descriptive language of metaphysics when speaking of marriage are hardly to blame for the current disorder seen in civil society and even in the Church. The blame rests more with those who presumed to interpret the Council and subsequent magisterial teaching in ways which were not consistent with their expressed intentions. But even this was tied to something more basic, the acceptance of understandings and marriage practices coming from the secular world. That being said, the responsibility now rests with those who can provide sound, accurate analyses of marriage and especially those who are entrusted with the regulation of marriage canonically within the Church.

The condition of the institution of Christian marriage is probably as grave as it has ever been in the history of the Church. And no other pope in history ever wrote as extensively as Pope John Paul II on marriage and the family. It is difficult in a historical survey to assess at this point the impact of his papacy on the institution of marriage. But John Paul II, with his remarkable and unique combination of personal experiences, theological training, and philosophical schools of thought out of which he wrote seems to have met the needs of contemporary society for understanding marriage in our day.

It would seem essential that the positivism and subjectivism of the late twentieth century be overcome if marriage is to be truly restored and renewed. The Jesuit Theodore Mackin, in his book on marriage, argued that it is impossible to have a description of marriage which transcends cultures and that it must be left to the Christian people themselves who experience marriage to come up with "prescriptive definitions" of it, which, presumably, will simply differ from one culture to another. The task of metaphysics, however, is to confront such relativism and to find those enduring attributes in a thing which can be identified despite the change and flux which comprise human experience. This Cardinal Gasparri had earlier attempted in his distillation from centuries of Catholic experience and reflection on the essence of marriage in terms of ends, contractual consent, and sacrament.

At the beginning of the twenty-first century the same kind of clarity must be sought again. Such a search will have to confront the fact that the language of metaphysics is simply no longer used or understood in many quarters. It has become increasingly difficult to find even within the Church itself scholars who are still trained in this discipline. The confusion in so much of the literature on marriage at present is ample evidence of this.

The mind-set of the educated population today is principally that of psychologism, subjectivism, sensuality, materialism, and personalism. In John Paul the Church received a pope trained in and conversant with the language of phenomenology but who refused to forsake the approach to reality provided by the moderate realism of Thomism. He helped give rise to what has come to be known as Lublin-Thomism, which seeks to find ways to bring enduring truths to a world which often no longer believes in objective truth. He was a student of St. Thomas as well as Merleau Ponty, Edmund Husserl, Nicolai Hartmann, and Max Scheler. While a professor of philosophy he wrote a book about sex and marriage entitled *Love and Responsibility*,[55] which explored with daring and boldness the relationship between a husband and wife.

John Paul developed a "theology of the body" which takes modern materialist attitudes with full seriousness. In fact, he showed in his sexuality catechesis that modern man does not take the body as seriously as does the Church. He drew on the Bonaventurian tradition to explain marriage in terms of the divine *imago Dei* being seen not only in human reason and will but also in human maleness and femaleness. In other words, the natural complementarity of man and woman, according to John Paul II, reflects the nature of the triune God himself as the spouses surrender themselves to one another in such a way that a third person is engendered. John Paul spoke of the communion of husband and wife becoming the community of father, mother, child.

Consequently, according to this school of thought, the bodies of all men and women have a "nuptial meaning" which reflects not only their own make-up but reflects the nature of the triune God. The "nuptial" character of the Godhead can be seen also in the way in which God relates to the Church. Jesus is the Bridegroom, the Church his Bride. In the first years in his pontificate he offered weekly meditations on marriage and human sexuality, the full impact of which will probably not be realized until generations to come.[56]

John Paul had been influenced by the writings of theologians such as M. J. Scheeben, who treated of marriage in a less legalistic manner than was customary in the late nineteenth and early twentieth centuries when he wrote. Scheeben emphasized the mystical, sacramental character of Christian marriage over its legal character. He stressed the fact that the nuptials of husband and wife actually shared in the nuptials between the Bridegroom, Jesus Christ, and his Bride the Church. He even saw marriage as an analogy of the relation between reason and faith.[57]

Another theologian who influenced John Paul's understanding of marriage was the Swiss priest Hans Urs von Balthasar. Although von Balthasar did not write extensively on marriage as such, he did explore in a most profoundly theological manner the relationship between man and woman as reflecting God's creative design.[58] Von Balthasar was himself strongly influenced by Scheeben and in one of his books summarized his understanding of Scheeben's views on the nuptial meaning of the universe: "Grace and faith are ... but forms of expression of God's central *connubium* with mankind (and, through it, with the whole world) in the incarnation, which has among its conditions the mystery of Mary's maternal womb."[59]

Von Balthasar's theological reflections further contributed to a renewed and deepened appreciation of the mystical quality of the relationship between husband and wife. Indeed, the male/female complementarity seen in God's creation of humanity can be seen throughout all creation. This insight was in a peculiar way concretely manifested in his own life. Balthasar had forged a deep friendship with a Swiss mystic, Adrienne von Speyr, whose writings he always insisted complemented his own and should be read with his. The pope's appreciation of Balthasar's work can be seen in his having chosen him to be a cardinal at the end of his life, an honor he was unable to receive because of his untimely death.

The theologian John Saward calls attention to these influences on John Paul II: "First in his ethical and dramatic work and then in his official teaching, Pope John Paul II has done what M. J. Scheeben in the nineteenth century and Balthasar in the twentieth have tried to do in their theological syntheses: he has restored the nuptial mystery to its proper centrality in the understanding of faith."[60]

The pope's personal experiences, pastoral duties, and philosophical reflections led him to an understanding of the complementarity of the sexes constituting not simply the instrumental means by which God chose to perpetuate the species but rather a reflection of God himself. Some observers were surprised that the very first topic the pope chose to address in a systematic and extensive way in his pontificate was marriage and human sexuality. The reason for this would appear obvious. There was clearly in the West in the twentieth century a lack of consensus regarding the nature of the human. A common understanding of human nature and human rights had been lost. As a consequence persons fell victim to the most degrading assaults as can be seen in their enslavement in totalitarian regimes, in programs of genocide, in abortion and euthanasia. The pope was convinced that it was necessary for the state, for the molders of public opinion, and for those who shape cultural institutions to understand the true nature of the human person. An inescapable aspect of personhood is sexuality, and the meaning of that sexuality is essentially nuptial, in the pope's mind. No other pontiff ever wrote so extensively on human sexuality, marriage, and the family. Indeed, his Wednesday audiences, the sexuality catechesis delivered there, the teaching of the pontifical institutes on marriage and family will have an impact on the whole Church for many decades to come.[61]

Early in his papacy John Paul convoked a Synod of Bishops to deal with the subject of marriage and the family and issued his Apostolic Exhortation *Familiaris Consortio*,[62] in which he used the analytic and descriptive tools of phenomenology but insisted that the reality of marriage could be known. His call, "Families become what you are," was predicated on the belief that we could know what a family was and that it was the duty of the Christian to conform to that divinely established institution. He launched the bold initiative at the Lateran University in Rome of establishing the John Paul II Institute for Studies in Marriage and the Family to help implement the recommendations of the synod on the family and to provide assistance to the Church in its ministry to families. This had grown to four campuses of the Institute worldwide by the year 2000. In his annual addresses to the Rotal judges and auditors he insisted upon the true nature of marriage, its orientation to children, and its indissoluble bond. He cautioned particularly against too broad an application of the impediment of psychic incapacity and in 1983 eliminated the special procedural norms for marriage tribunals in the United States so that any granting of nullity in an ecclesiastical court of instance in the United States had to be appealed in favor of the bond to a court of second instance.

As has been said, it is difficult to assess what impact on marriage John Paul II's pontificate will have in the new millennium, but there is reason to hope that in his thought and his bold ecclesiastical initiatives the unwholesome division of the last century into what might be called a juridical half and a personalist half will be overcome with sound doctrine and sound jurisprudence leading to a flourishing of marriage and family life within the Church.

Notes

1. John Paul II, *Sollicitudo rei socialis*, December 30, 1987, §25.

2. "American Family Decline, 1960–1990: A Review and Appraisal," *Journal of Marriage and the Family* 55 (August 1993): 527–42, at 528.

3. "The State of Our Unions 2000" can be obtained through The Marriage Project at Rutgers University in New Jersey and can be accessed on the internet at http://marriage.rutgers.edu.

4. 405 U.S. 438 (1972).

5. 381 U.S. 479, 85 S. Ct. 1678, 14 L. Ed. 2d 510 (1965).

6. *Moore v. City of East Cleveland*.

7. 410 U.S. 113 (1973).

8. 428 U.S. 52 (1976).

9. M. J. Bane, and P. A. Jargowsky, "The Links between Government Policy and Family Structure: What Matters and What Doesn't," in *The Changing American Family and Public Policy*, ed. A. Cherlin (Washington, D.C., 1988), 222.

10. Ibid., 246.

11. *Codex Iuris Canonici* (New York, 1918).

12. *Codicis Iuris Canonici Fontes*, ed. Petrus Gasparri and György Justinianus Serédi (Rome, 1926), 4:137–38; this work is hereafter cited as *Fontes*.

13. Henricus Denziger, *Enchiridion symbolorum definitionum et declarationum de rebus fidei et morum*, ed. Adolfus Schönmetzer, 33d ed. (Barcelona, 1965), 2996; hereafter cited as DS.

14. *Fontes*, 3:160.

15. Cf., e.g., Edward Bagby Pollard, "Covenant," *The International Standard Bible Encyclopedia*, 727ff.

16. "Coniugale foedus per legitimum contractum ineatur." *Sacrorum conciliorum nova et amplissima collectio*, ed. Ioannes Dominicus Mansi, L. Petit, and J. Martin (Arnheim, 1927), 53:719.

17. "Unde inter Christianos matrimonium iniri non potest, quin uno eodemque actu sit sacramentum." Ibid.

18. "Matrimonii finis primarius est procreatio atque educatio prolis; secundarius mutuum adiutorium et remedium concupiscentiae." *Finis* can properly be translated as "end," "goal," or "purpose." I believe "end" to be the best translation because it connotes a teleology which is inherent to the reality itself.

19. For a bibliography, see J. C. Ford, S.J., "Marriage: Its Meaning and Purposes," *Theological Studies* 3 (1942): 333f.

20. Dietrich von Hildebrand, *Marriage* (Manchester, N.H., 1991), 23.

21. Doms's work was first published in 1935 while he was a *Privat-Dozent* at the University of Breslau under the title *Vom Sinn und Zweck der Ehe*. It was first published in French in 1937 as *Du sens et de la fin du mariage* and in English as *The Meaning of Marriage* (New York, 1939).

22. *Casti Connubii*, December 31, 1930, §3.

23. Ibid., §5.

24. Ibid., §13.

25. Ibid., §14.

26. Ibid., §19.

27. Ibid., §61.

28. *Acta apostolicae sedis* 36 (1944): 179–200.

29. Ibid., 103.

30. *Papal Teachings: Matrimony*, trans. Michael J. Byrnes (Boston, 1963), 422, 424.

31. *Acta et documenta Concilio Oecumenico Vaticano II apparando*, series II, vol. 2, 1960, *Pars* 3:960–62.

32. Ibid., 978.

33. *Humanae Vitae*, July 25, 1968, §2.

34. Ibid., §12.

35. Dietrich von Hildebrand, *Marriage*, vi.

36. Ibid., 4.

37. Dietrich von Hildebrand, *Man and Woman: Love and the Meaning of Intimacy* (Manchester, N.H.: Sophia Institute Press, 1992), 67. *Man and Woman* was first published in 1966 by Franciscan Herald Press. Henry Regnery Company issued a paperback edition in 1967. The Sophia Institute Press edition has made changes

in subheadings and has a completely new order of topics. It was published with the permission of the widow of Dietrich von Hildebrand, Alice von Hildebrand.

38. "Matrimoniale foedus, quo vir et mulier inter se totius vitae consortium constituunt, indole sua naturali ad bonum coniugum atque ad prolis generationem et educationem ordinatum." *Code of Canon Law* (Washington, D.C., 1983), Canon 1055, §1.

39. George Kendall, "Love or Death: Our Choice," *Homiletical and Pastoral Review* (October 1991): 59–63, at 60.

40. Anthony Kosnik et al., *Human Sexuality* (Washington, D.C., 1979), 85.

41. Ibid., 100.

42. Ibid., 107.

43. Ibid., 112.

44. Ibid., 125.

45. A thorough study of the conciliar discussion over the use of the classical language of ends can be found in Marcelino Zalba, S.J.'s article "Num Concilium Vaticanum II hierarchiam finium matrimonii ignoraverit, immo et transmutaverit," in *Periodica de Re Morali, Canonica, Liturgica* 68, no. 4 (1979): 613–35.

46. "Finis secundum intentionem est primum in re, sed secundum consecutionem est ultimum. Et similiter proles se habet inter matrimonii bona. Et ideo quodammodo est principalius, et quodammodo non."

47. "Assignatur autem triplex bonum matrimonii. Primum est proles suscipienda et educanda ad cultum Dei. Secundum est fides, quam unus coniugum alteri servare debet. Tertium indivisibilitas matrimonii, propter hoc quod significat indivisibilem coniunctionem Christi et Ecclesiae." DS 1327.

48. "In textu pastorali qui dialogum cum mundo instituere intendit elementa illa iuridica non requiruntur." *Relatio super Schema de Ecclesia in mundo huius temporis* (Rome, 1964). *Textus revisus. Expensio modorum ad* n. 52 (*nunc* 48), 15, c, *pag.*, 12.

49. "Morality in Sexual Matters: Observations of the Sacred Congregation for the Doctrine of the Faith on the Book 'Human Sexuality.' " This can be found in *The Pope Speaks* 25 (1980): 97–102.

50. "Proles est essentialissimum in matrimonio, et secundo fides, et tertio sacramentum," *In IV Sent.*, d. 31, q. 1, a. 3.

51. Bernard Lonergan, "Finality, Love, Marriage," in *Collection*, ed. F. E. Crowe (New York, 1967), 46–47.

52. Theodore Mackin, *The Marital Sacrament* (Mahwah, N.J., 1989), 237.

53. *Sentences IV,* 33.1.3.

54. *Acta et documenta,* 962.

55. Karol Wojtyla, *Love and Responsibility,* trans. H. T. Willetts (New York, 1981). The book was first published in Krakow in 1960.

56. Cf. John Paul II, *Original Unity of Man and Woman* (Boston, 1981), *Blessed Are the Pure of Heart* (Boston, 1983). *Reflections on Humanae Vitae* (Boston, 1984). *The Theology of Marriage and Celibacy* (Boston, 1986).

57. Matthias Joseph Scheeben, *The Mysteries of Christianity,* trans. Cyril Vollert (St. Louis, 1951). See "Christian Matrimony," 59ff. Cf. 78f. regarding marriage as an analogy between faith and reason.

58. Hans Urs von Balthasar, *Explorations in Theology The Word Made Flesh,* trans. A. V. Littledale with Alexander Dru (San Francisco 1989), 1:202ff.

59. *The Glory of the Lord: A Theological Aesthetic,* vol. 1 (Edinburgh, 1982), 114.

60. *Christ Is the Answer: The Christ-Centered Teaching of Pope John Paul II* (Staten Island, 1995), 65.

61. See, for example: John Paul II, *Original Unity of Man and Woman, Blessed Are the Pure of Heart, Reflections on Humanae Vitae,* and *The Theology of Marriage and Celibacy.*

62. *The Apostolic Exhortation on the Family,* November 22, 1981, *Origins* 2, nos. 28 and 29 (December 24, 1981).

INDEX OF
SELECTED SCRIPTURAL TEXTS

GENERAL INDEX